Y0-BDA-605

Understanding Exceptional Children and Youth

Understanding Exceptional Children and Youth

Peter Knoblock

Editor

Syracuse University

Little, Brown and Company

Boston   Toronto

Library of Congress Cataloging-in-Publication Data

Understanding exceptional children and youth.

Bibliography: p.
Includes indexes.
Contents: The disabled in America / Steven J. Taylor
and Stanford J. Searl, Jr. — Medical conditions that
affect learning / Mary Coleman and Deborah Olson — [etc.]
    1. Handicapped children—Education—United States.
2. Developmental disabilities. 3. Cognition in children.
4. Community and school—United States. 5. Exceptional
children—Education—United States. I. Knoblock, Peter,
1934–
LC4031.U44 1987   371.9   86–21449
ISBN 0–316–49952–8

Copyright © 1987 by Peter Knoblock

Library of Congress Catalog Card No. 86–21449

ISBN 0–316–49952–8

9 8 7 6 5 4 3 2 1

Don/H

Published simultaneously in Canada
by Little, Brown & Company (Canada) Limited

Printed in the United States of America

Cover photo by Frank Siteman/The Picture Cube

Credits

The editor wishes to thank the following authors and publishers for permission to reprint
their material in this text.

    p. 20, Table 1: Adaptation of Tables 5 and 8 in Lakin, K. C. (n.d.). *Demographic studies
of residential facilities for the mentally retarded.* Minneapolis: University of Minnesota,
Department of Psychoeducational Studies. Reprinted by permission.
    pp. 26–27: Excerpts from Blatt, B., & Kaplan, F. (1966). *Christmas in purgatory.* Boston:
Allyn & Bacon. Reprinted by permission of the Center on Human Policy.
    p. 58: Excerpt from Center on Human Policy (1979). *The community imperative.* Syr-
acuse: Center on Human Policy. Reprinted by permission.

(Continued on page 503)

To Todd, Craig, and Gary

Preface

Hopefully we are reaching a time in our understanding of children with special needs when we can view them as individuals first and not merely as categories and labels. This book is written with that intention.

You will notice that chapters are not designated by disability labels—mentally retarded, emotionally disturbed, physically disabled, learning disabled, and so on. We join the growing number of special educators, regular educators, and parents who no longer believe in narrowly defining and categorizing children for educational purposes. Labels of this kind have not proved to be educationally relevant. The children so labeled—indeed, all children—are complicated persons, and persistent efforts to fit them into predetermined categories and to teach them according to what we know about those categories have not proved to be instructionally sound. Thus we have tried to be judicious in our descriptions of special education labels. While we recognize their prevalent use as a kind of shorthand approach to understanding children, our decision was to offer an alternative approach—that of a noncategorical orientation to understanding disabled children. It is our belief that one's effectiveness may be enhanced by utilizing diverse information to study each child.

In writing this book, we did not attempt to convey an overburdening amount of detail on the various handicapping conditions and programs for exceptional children. Instead, we offer information, frames of reference, and descriptions of promising practices that can assist us in understanding children and designing school and community responses.

We decided to construct a text that reflects the major areas of functioning in a child's life: socioemotional development, communication and language development, and intellectual and cognitive development. In discussions of these areas attention was also paid to children's biological and physical development. These are important areas of development for all children, and our task has been to delineate what is involved in each of these and to indicate the particular needs and problems experienced by disabled children as they grow and develop in each area.

This approach reflects what nonspecialists as well as specialists know about children. For example, all children, regardless of their label, experience and show emotions. It is a mistake to focus only on a child's limited intellectual capacity as we tend to do with children labeled retarded. By doing so we ignore the child's feelings. It is inconceivable that these children—and all children regardless of their disability—are not experiencing emotions and processing them on some level. Because category designations are so imprecise, special educators often seek to determine a child's major liability. Again, in the case of those labeled retarded, the dimension of intellectual ability tends to be the primary focus. Even when other prominent skills or assets are present, they are perceived to be the exception, an oddity, not a central variable to be factored into educational placement and teaching programs. For example, educators and parents consistently report on the warmth and responsiveness of children with Down's syndrome (formerly referred to as "mongoloid"). However, it is only recently, as the children have been placed in mainstreamed classrooms, that this quality so long observed and documented has been turned to the children's advantage.

Organization

Part I, "History, Issues, and Advocacy," provides background information to help us understand how special education practices such as labeling have led an increasing number of professionals, parents, and legislators to seek innovative solutions to perplexing issues. For those readers new to special education, it may be helpful to realize that decisions about what is best for children have traditionally been made in the context of society's concerns and needs. Certainly, the persons responsible for those decisions believed they responded with the best of intentions. Yet on a number of issues, such as the benefits of placing disabled children in large institutions, thinking has changed dramatically over the years. Part I also points out that our current solutions to long-standing problems and issues in our field face problems of their own. The deinstitutionalization movement—or the removal of children and adults from institutions by placing them back into the community—is currently facing increasing criticism from the public and from policy makers who must contend with public attitudes and the lack of community facilities.

Part II, "Understanding and Teaching Disabled Students," provides descriptions of children and their needs and strengths that can help us understand why some of the issues and controversies described in Part I have remained so resistant to solutions, even though many changes have occurred. The chapters in this part describe essential areas of development for disabled children: socioemotional development, language and communication, intellectual and cognitive development, and physical development. Despite the fact that each of these areas is described in a separate chapter, we hope that you will keep in mind their interrelated nature. For teachers, it is important to look at the whole child and to recognize the contributions each area of functioning makes to a child's development.

Part II concludes with two chapters on instructional approaches, including detailed descriptions of teaching procedures that respond to children's needs. Again, while there are specific references to "types" of disability, the emphasis is on developing an instructional problem-solving orientation that will allow you as a teacher to assess disabled children's learning and social needs and to design instructional approaches responsive to those needs.

Part III, "Understanding Disabled Students in Context," contains three chapters: one on parents and professionals, and two on adolescents in the community. They serve to underscore the importance of viewing disability in a broader context, one that helps us recognize the pivotal role that parents play in a child's development and the importance of designing programs in the community that respond to the individual's needs for increasing independence. These chapters also underscore the importance of teachers actively involving themselves with parents, as support for both the child and the family. Moreover, the point is forcefully made that parents have much to contribute to the educational process and that teachers would do well to remain open to parent input. The chapters on adolescents in the community reflect the growing recognition of the need to design transitional services and programs for students as they move into adolescence and young adulthood and prepare for independent lives. The notion of independence is central throughout this book. All of the contributing authors believe that the goal of teaching is to foster independent and competent behavior in disabled children. It is fitting that the final chapter focuses on ways that educators and the public can structure community living arrangements and vocational and recreational opportunities to maximize a disabled person's functioning in the community.

Acknowledgments

I am grateful to the contributing authors, each of whom responded with enthusiasm and skill to the task of writing for a noncategorical textbook. They share my belief in the potential of all students to change, and they recognize that by studying the whole child we can learn to respond thoughtfully and systematically to children's needs. Others shared this vision: Mylan Jaixen, College Editor at Little, Brown and Company, responded to the challenge of publishing an innovative introductory textbook with thoughtful technical assistance and expertise. Deborah Olson and Connie Salvetti provided editorial and typing assistance throughout the preparation of this book.

Throughout the task of writing various drafts of the manuscript, we were given much help by our reviewers. I wish to thank Earl E. Davis, The University of Tennessee at Chattanooga; Richard I. Fisher, Colorado State University; Lois N. Hodgson, The University of Toledo; C. Julius Meisel, University of Delaware; Maurice Miller, Indiana State University; Stanley F. Vasa, University of Nebraska–Lincoln; and Sharon R. Vaughn, University of Miami.

I am particularly indebted to Steven Apter and Burton Blatt, colleagues and friends, whose works and lives have influenced me in profound ways. Their untimely deaths are felt deeply by many in our field, but they are remembered for their vision of a field in which all persons with disabilities are treated with dignity and respect.

P.K.

Brief Contents

Contents

Understanding Exceptional Children and Youth

Part I

History, Issues, and Advocacy

The inclusion of a chapter on the history of special education in an introductory textbook is predictable. Your reading of textbooks in other introductory courses may have conditioned you to bear with those authors who were convinced that a thorough approach to the field requires the inclusion of such material. You, on the other hand, were eager to get to the content of the field that lay beyond "ancient" history. Taylor and Searl, the authors of the following chapter on history, issues, and advocacy present a convincing argument of the relevance of this material for the present and everyday functioning of teachers. Their thesis is that current issues and practices can be best understood if one has some historical perspective. Also, an appreciation of the current political and social climate will help you analyze existing programs and public policies as they affect disabled children. Most important of all, this chapter stresses the impact that history and current practices have on you as a teacher in your efforts to respond to children, their families, and community agencies.

Your tasks, therefore, are to become an informed citizen, to utilize your understanding of the current climate to advocate for children's services and programs, and perhaps to seek political and social changes in our schools and in society. Before you cast yourself as an advocate, however, you should become familiar with a few of the current practices, policies, and issues that impinge on teachers, parents, and policy makers.

Deinstitutionalization, or the movement of persons from institutions into communities, is a current and rather dramatic example of an issue that has been with us for a long time. Our response to the question of whether or not to place children in institutions is influenced by the tenor of the times. In support of deinstitutionalization is litigation such as the consent decree between the Pennsylvania Association for Retarded Children and the Commonwealth of Pennsylvania guaranteeing a free public education for retarded children, as well as placing community emphasis in the wording of Public Law 94-142 (Education for All Handicapped Children Act of 1975), which calls for handicapped children to be educated with their nondisabled peers to an appropriate extent. Litigation and legislation, which are described in the following chapter, in the 1970s made powerful inroads into how we thought about separating disabled persons from the mainstream of school and community life. By the mid-1980s the populations of institutions for those who are retarded, mentally ill, deaf, and so on have been greatly reduced; thus what first appeared to some as a solution has become a problem. Communities and the public are growing increasingly alarmed with what they perceive to be the "dumping" of mentally ill and other disabled adults into the community without adequate planning. This trend is in marked contrast to the prevailing thought in the mid-1800s, when placement of children and adults into institutions was considered a desirable antidote to inadequate community practices.

As both a teacher and an informed citizen, you should recognize that the reintegration of disabled persons into regular school programs and into the community is indeed dependent upon the existence of responsive programs and the availability of supportive services. Currently, the deinstitutionalization movement is in difficulty because (1) communities never readied themselves for accepting disabled citizens, and (2) the federal government did not systematically follow through with its mandate of the 1960s to develop and fund community mental health centers. As a teacher you can contribute to more positive attitudes toward disabled children by creating programs that are effective and that include other teachers and school personnel as well as parents and other community members. It is the existence of negative attitudes toward the disabled, as well as the lack of community programs, that is contributing to the current controversy. The climate of the community, including the attitudes of its citizens, will directly affect you and your children in school. These factors are translated into the level of psychological and financial support that special and regular education programs receive. You can contribute to greater understanding and also provide technical assistance in your community and school.

Prevention of disability is another broad area of concern that has historical roots and immediate consequences for children and their families and implications for action on your part. Again, solutions are dependent upon the existence of an informed citizenry, and while answers remain elusive questions abound:

· Why do we still have over 600,000 children with lead levels in their blood over the safety levels set by the U.S. Centers for Disease Control in Atlanta? The informed segments of society now recognize that small doses of lead can harm children and that un detected and untreated lead poisoning can cause brain damage and retardation. This is just one example of how society creates disability.

· Why do we still have malnourished and hungry children in a society as affluent as ours? Malnutrition is another condition that contributes to diminished functioning and even disability—mental, physical, and emotional. The Children's Defense Fund (1984b)—a child advocacy organization—reported an increase of three million new children in poverty since 1979. In providing a portrait of child poverty, the organization states:

> The poor children in America are not just black children in shacks in a Southern town, towheaded white children in Appalachian hollows, or children in displaced rural families living in the mean streets of a barrio or ghetto. They are children nearby—in your town, your neighborhood, your street. They are the children of an unemployed steel worker or auto worker and his wife for whom the only available jobs are part time and low wage. They are the children of the single parent who gets little or no child support and who works at a minimum wage retail sales job. They are the children whose family broke up in divorce and who are now living with grandma and making it on social security checks. They are immigrants to this free land from wars in Asia and Central America. They are all races, sizes, ages, and descriptions. (p. 21)

And, of course, they can be found in special education programs and classrooms.

· Are children suffering unduly from the recession of the 1980s and the federal budget cuts that ensued? The authors of the Children's Defense Fund 1984 study believe they are, and a recent summary of the government's efforts to reduce access to social welfare programs by Robert Pear (1984) of the *New York Times* confirms this conclusion.

· Is the lack of permanency planning for children placed in foster care contributing to children's emotional instability and their inability to direct their energy to learning and positive interpersonal relationships? According to Dorcas Hardy (1984), Assistant Secretary for Human Development Services, Department of Health and Human Services in Washington, D.C., the situation of having more than 500,000 children in foster care by the late 1970s and the growing recognition of the actual and potential damage to such children mobilized policy makers at the state and federal levels to act. One outcome has been legislative reform to encourage the permanent placement or adoption of children in foster care. Special-needs children constitute a significant number of these: 36,000 special-needs children are legally free for adoption as well as thousands of others for whom adoption is the plan of choice. There is a national special-needs adoption initiative comprised of efforts to design legislation encouraging adoptions of hard-to-place children and adolescents and informing the public about the needs of children in foster homes, group homes, and institutions.

· Are the current critiques of American education relevant for us as special educators (Boyer, 1983; Ravitch, 1983; Sizer, 1984)? Because of the growing commitment to include disabled students in the mainstream of school and community life, special educators are increasingly aware of the impact that regular education has on them and their students. The range of concerns raised in the books cited above is diverse and it should be noted that some of the impetus for concern has been generated by the federal government, culminating in the creation, by the president, of the National Commission on Excellence in Education and its report, "A Nation at Risk: The Imperative for Educational Reform." Despite the fact that these statements by scholars and concerned citizens do not focus on the needs of disabled students, they do refer to the importance of curriculum innovation, maintaining high expectation levels for students, involvement of parents, and recognition of teachers, to cite just a few. All of these can be translated into our work with disabled students.

This first chapter, then, attempts to illustrate the rich and somewhat troubled history of special education and to highlight many of the current issues confronting teachers and schools, and parents and policy makers. The assumption is that your effectiveness as a teacher can be enhanced by understanding these issues.

Chapter 1

Steven J. Taylor

Stanford J. Searl, Jr.

Steven J. Taylor is Director of the Center on Human Policy and Associate Professor of Special Education at Syracuse University. He teaches courses in social policy and disability at Syracuse University and is involved in a range of research, advocacy, training, and technical assistance projects. His current interests include community integration for people with severe disabilities and the impact of federal and state policy on the local level. He has published numerous books and articles, has presented invited testimony at U.S. Senate hearings on deinstitutionalization, and has served as an expert witness in several court cases involving the rights of people with disabilities.

Stanford J. Searl, Jr., is Executive Director of East End Community Services, a home health care demonstration project in Cutchoque, New York. His interests include alternatives to total institutions, and community integration for people with severe disabilities.

The Disabled in America: History, Policy, and Trends

After reading this chapter, you should be able to:

1
Recall the new trends and controversies in special education.

2
Critique the practice of sterilization for persons with mental retardation.

3
Compare the earlier emphasis on institutional placement with the present trend toward deinstitutionalization and critique this trend.

4
Discuss the implications of the judicial ruling in the Rowley case for classroom teachers of students with disabilities.

Special education must be understood in the context of broad social forces. What, where, how, and whom teachers teach is determined by social, historical, political, legal, and economic forces. Thus, if we are to understand special education, we must understand these forces.

If you are reading this book, you are likely to be preparing for a career in special education or a related field. You are going to hear a lot about new trends, philosophies, and controversies, and you might have heard something about them already.

Institutions and deinstitutionalization. You probably know something about institutions. Chances are that you have read about bad conditions at institutions. Just the same, you probably think that some people with severe disabilities will always have to live in institutions. You probably also know something about group homes. Do you know *why* institutions were developed? Have you always assumed that our society developed institutions for the benefit of people with disabilities? Have you ever thought that maybe we developed institutions because we did not want certain people around? Are you aware that many people today believe that *all* people with disabilities should be integrated into the community?

Schools, mainstreaming, and integration. Did you know that as recently as ten years ago thousands of children with disabilities were excluded from America's schools? Do you know how that changed? Today, most children with disabilities receive some kind of an education. Where do you think these children should go to school? Have you considered that maybe children with disabilities should be educated alongside their nondisabled peers? What would you say if you were told that this is happening at an increasing number of schools across the country?

Charity and rights. You may be drawn to this field because you want to help other people. The field needs you—but be aware that people with disabilities and their families do not want charity or pity. They want their rights, just like anyone else. Did you ever hear about the disability rights movement? What do organizations of people with disabilities and their parents want? How has the government responded? What do you think the courts have said about the civil rights of people with disabilities?

These and other issues are described in the pages that follow.

The field of special education today is characterized by new and controversial ideas that emerged during the 1960s and 1970s. Indeed, this period can be characterized as nothing less than a revolution in our thinking about people with disabilities and our treatment of them. Yet each of these ideas has deep historical roots. Thus, we start with a look at the history of the disabled in America.

A Look at History: Institutions and Education

The history of special education in eighteenth- and nineteenth-century America is the history of institutions. It is only in the past eighty years or so that public schools had anything to do with students with significant disabilities. In fact, public school systems across the nation did not begin to accommodate students with a full range of disabilities until the mid-1970s.

The Origins of the Asylum

The segregation of disabled children and adults in special institutions is a relatively modern phenomenon. It was not until after 1820 that states began to develop separate institutions for a diverse range of deviant or dependent members of the population: insane asylums, orphanages and reformatories, penitentiaries, and asylums and schools for the so-called feebleminded.

The existence of large public state institutions is so taken for granted that it is difficult to imagine what happened to people with mental and physical disabilities in colonial America. Where were the physically disabled, the mentally retarded, and the emotionally disturbed? First of all, many people with severe disabilities simply did not survive. Indeed, it is only in recent years that medical advances have made possible life-saving treatment for many infants born with serious disabilities.

Second, Americans in the colonial period cared for elderly, dependent, and disabled family members at home. As historian David Rothman (1971) has pointed out, the colonists left poor and dependent people in the care of relatives and neighbors. There were no orphan asylums, nursing homes, mental hospitals, or institutions for the retarded.

Third, many people whom we would label mentally retarded or otherwise disabled today blended into the community because participation in society did not require sophisticated technical or intellectual skills, such as the ability to read and write. Practically everyone could perform some useful social role in society. Many people who might not blend into today's society could have been easily accommodated in eighteenth-century America. They were not regarded as a problem and, for all practical purposes, were not mentally retarded.

Beginning in the eighteenth century and extending into the early nineteenth century, larger towns and cities began to build workhouses, poorhouses, or almshouses for the destitute and dependent (Rothman, 1971). These were repositories for people who could not support themselves, including orphans, widows, the elderly, and paupers as well as people labeled idiotic, insane, crippled, and epileptic. As we shall see, conditions in almshouses were wretched.

The Development of State Institutions

The development of separate institutions for discrete populations of disabled and deviant people often has been characterized as progress in society's treatment of the so-called mentally retarded, mentally ill, and others. Yet, as Rothman (1971, p. xv) poignantly has asked, "Was an organization that would eventually turn into a snake pit a necessary step forward for mankind?" Rothman's question suggests the answer. The irony is that the first institutions were founded by social reformers who subscribed to humanitarian ideals.

Throughout the 1800s, and indeed extending into the 1960s, institutions were developed at a rapid pace. Almshouses for poor people proliferated. Rothman (1971) has reported that in Massachusetts sixty towns constructed new almshouses between 1820 and 1840; the number of people in New York almshouses grew from 4,500 in 1830 to roughly 10,000 in 1850; other states soon followed suit.

As almshouses flourished, states began to develop specialized institutions for other populations. New York and Pennsylvania led the way with the development of the first state penitentiaries for criminals. The Auburn system in New York, devised in 1819, stressed congregate activities and "the liberal use of the whip" (Erikson, 1966). The Pennsylvania system, developed in the 1820s and founded on Quaker ideals, stressed solitude and separate confinement (Erikson, 1966).

The nation's first public mental hospital for the "insane" and "idiotic" was established in Williamsburg, Virginia, in 1773 (Szasz, 1970). For fifty years, however, no other state established a mental hospital until Kentucky did so in 1824 (Scheerenberger, 1983). In the next several decades, practically every state opened public asylums for the insane. "A cult of asylum," wrote Rothman (1971, p. 130), "swept the country." By 1860 twenty-eight of the thirty-three states had established public insane asylums.

The development of separate institutions for the mentally retarded gradually followed the establishment of insane asylums. In 1848 Massachusetts opened the nation's first institution specifically for the mentally retarded. At Albany in 1851 New York established the second such institution, which was moved to Syracuse in 1854. Davies (1959, p. 22) has stated that by 1890 fourteen states had opened separate public institutions for the "mentally defective."

The institutional movement gripped other populations. Orphan asylums and reformatories for juvenile offenders flourished in the 1830s, 1840s, and 1850s. Similarly, institutions for the blind, such as Perkins Institute and Massachusetts School for the Blind, both opened in the 1830s, and the deaf, such as the American Institute for the Deaf and Dumb in Hartford, Connecticut, founded in 1818, were developed during the first half of the eighteenth century. Eventually, states and communities turned to asylums to care for the elderly, people with tuberculosis, and, in some places, people with epilepsy. By the end of the nineteenth century, some states had even established separate institutions for different categories of people labeled mentally retarded, including "feebleminded women" and "unteachable idiots."

The founders and early proponents of the asylum may be characterized as what sociologist Howard Becker (1963) has called "moral entrepreneurs." They were social reformers who succeeded in gaining public acceptance of their definitions of social problems and their proposed solutions to those problems. It is interesting to note that many reformers advocated for diverse populations; Dorothea Dix crusaded for the poor, "idiotic," and "epileptic," as well as for the "insane"; Samuel Gridley Howe was instrumental in the establishment of institutions for the blind and the mentally retarded; Benjamin Rush, regarded as the founder of American psychiatry, promoted asylums for the so-called mentally ill and mentally retarded in addition to a Quaker version of solitary confinement for criminals (Erikson, 1966, p. 199).

These moral entrepreneurs advocated for humane, if strict, treatment of the mentally retarded, mentally ill, and other populations. Dorothea Dix crusaded against the squalid conditions under which people were forced to live in the public almshouses. According to Scheerenberger (1983, pp. 105–106), Dix traveled over 10,000 miles in 1850, visiting jails, almshouses, and mental hospitals. She addressed the U.S. Congress and the legislatures of Massachusetts, New York, New Jersey, Pennsylvania, Kentucky, Tennessee, North Carolina, Mississippi, and Maryland, telling them what she had seen. In a famous address before the Legislature of Massachusetts, Dix (1843/1970) made a plea for humane care:

> I come to present the strong claims of suffering humanity. I come to place before the Legislature of Massachusetts the condition of the miserable, the desolate, the outcast. I come as the advocate of helpless, forgotten, insane, and idiotic men and women; of beings shrunk to a condition from which the most unconcerned would start with real horror; of beings wretched in our prisons, and even more wretched in our almshouses. And I cannot suppose it needful to employ earnest persuasion, or stubborn argument, in order to arrest and fix attention upon a subject only the strongly pressing in its claims because it is revolting and disgusting in its details. . . .
>
> I proceed, gentlemen, briefly to call your attention to the *present* state of insane persons confined within this Commonwealth, in *cages, closets, cellars, stalls, pens! Chained, naked, beaten with rods,* and *lashed* into obedience.

As Scheerenberger (1983) and Rothman (1971) have pointed out, Dix was joined by other reformers in exposing the institutions of her day. In 1857 a legislative committee in New York reported, "Common domestic animals are usually more humanely provided for than the paupers in some of these institutions" (Rothman, 1971, p. 198).

Dix exposed the asylums and pleaded for mental hospitals founded on humane principles for the insane and idiotic. Others advocated treatment based on scientific and educational grounds. Benjamin Rush's distinctive contribution to psychiatry was his claim that there was no difference between physical and mental illness. In a thought-provoking book on the history of mental illness, psychiatrist Thomas Szasz (1970) has attributed to Rush an ideological conversion from theology to science. What had been considered "sin" now had become "illness." The medical doctor replaced the priest, psychiatric treatment replaced religious ritual, and the asylum replaced the cathedral.

Rush offered the hope of curing mental illness. By placing the insane in mental institutions and subjecting them to various forms of treatment, including bloodletting, work, strict discipline, and a strange contraption known as a tranquilizing chair, the insane could be cured. "It will be necessary," wrote Rush, "to mention the means of establishing a complete government over patients afflicted with it [madness], and thus, by securing their obedience, respect, and affections, to enable a physician to apply his remedies with ease, certainty, and success" (Szasz, 1970, pp. 146–147).

In mental retardation, Edouard Seguin, Hervey B. Wilbur, and Samuel Gridley Howe played prominent roles in the establishment of the first institutions in America. Born in France, Seguin immigrated to the United States in 1848 and worked with Howe and Wilbur in developing institutions in Massachusetts and New York. He was a strong supporter of educationally oriented asylums for "idiots."

Like Seguin, Howe and Wilbur advocated for the education of the idiotic or feebleminded. As superintendents of the Massachusetts and New York asylums respectively, they envisioned their institutions as small boarding schools where higher-functioning retarded people would receive the training necessary to perform useful roles in society.

The founders of the first institutions believed, however, that not all people labeled mentally retarded could be educated. They advocated for the exclusion of people with severe disabilities. Thus, in 1852, Howe wrote, "The institution is not intended for epileptic or insane children, nor for those who are incurably hydrocephalic or paralytic, and any such shall not be retained, to the exclusion of more improvable subjects" (Wolfensberger, 1975, p. 25).

Seguin, Howe, and Wilbur shared a deep distrust of large segregated institutions. In 1866, in an address at the opening of a state institution for the blind in Batavia, New York, Howe seriously questioned the institution:

> As much as may be, surround insane and excitable persons with sane people, and ordinary influences; vicious children with virtuous people and virtuous influences; blind children with those who see; mute children with those who speak; and the like.
>
> People run counter to this principle for the sake of economy, and of some other good end, which they suppose cannot be had in any other way; as when they congregate the insane in hospitals, vicious children in reformatories, criminals in prisons, paupers in almshouses, orphans in asylums, blind children and mute children in boarding schools. Hence I begin to consider such establishments as evils which must be borne with, for the time, in order to obviate greater evils. I would take heed, however, against multiplying them unnecessarily. I would keep them as small as I could. I would take the most stringent measurements for guarding against those undesirable effects which lessen their usefulness; and for dispensing with as many of them as may be possible (quoted in Wolfensberger, 1975, p. 65).

The ideals of these reformers were never realized. In fact, many of their worst fears came true. Conditions at new asylums soon deteriorated to the level of those at the almshouses and sometimes were worse. Large isolated institutions replaced smaller ones. Once asylums were firmly in place, society turned to them to deal with the casualties of the emerging social and economic order. The reformers of the early years of the asylum were replaced by a new generation of leaders whose ideals were not nearly as humane or progressive.

The Era of Institutional Expansion

The turn of the twentieth century was a period of rapid institutional expansion in American society. The number of prisons, mental hospitals, asylums for the feebleminded, and reformatories increased at a rapid pace during this period. In an exhaustive review of historical trends in institutions for the so-called mentally retarded, Lakin (n.d.) reported that the number of facilities increased from ten in 1880 to twenty in 1890, twenty-eight in 1904, thirty-five in 1910, forty in 1916, sixty-six in 1923, and seventy-seven in 1926.

What were supposed to be small homelike facilities became large, overcrowded warehouses. Platt (1969) has noted that by 1899 an Elmira, New York, juvenile reformatory, then considered a model institution, housed as many as 1,500 juveniles though it had been built with only 500 cells. Asylums for the feebleminded swelled in size. The number of people in these institutions grew from 2,429 in 1880 to 55,466 in 1926; the average size of the asylums expanded from 243 to 720 in that time (Lakin, n.d.). Further, while the number of almshouses stabilized around the turn of the century and the percentage of the population in almshouses actually decreased dramatically, the number of feebleminded in these institutions jumped from 7,811 in 1890 to 16,551 in 1904 (Lakin, n.d.). Not only did institutional populations soar during that period, but also they greatly outpaced the growth of the general population, which itself increased dramatically throughout the nineteenth and into the twentieth centuries. According to Lakin (n.d.), the number of residents of public institutions for the mentally retarded alone per 100,000 of the general population grew from 4.8 in 1880 to 47.8 in 1926.

During that period there also was a retreat from the optimism and idealism of the asylum's earlier proponents (Rothman, 1971; Wolfensberger, 1975). In the 1870s Pliny Earle wrote a widely accepted article entitled "The Curability of Insanity," in which he disputed the claims of successful treatment of the founders of mental hospitals (Rothman, 1971). In the field of "feeble-mindedness," leaders too had their doubts about whether the lot of the feebleminded could be markedly improved. "Give them an asylum, with good and kind treatment," stated Governor Butler of Massachusetts, "but not a school" (Wolfensberger, 1975, p. 28).

As we shall see, the era of institutional expansion was marked not by a concern for deviant and disabled people, but by a conscious attempt to protect society by removing them altogether. In order to fully understand this era, we must look at what was happening in our society at the time.

The Social Context

The nineteenth and early twentieth centuries were a time of major social changes and disruptions in American society. What seemed to be a simple and stable society underwent tremendous social upheaval; yet, the changes that shook the nineteenth century did not occur overnight. They seemed, nevertheless, to have caught the attention of the social and political leaders of the time all at once and to have roused them to action.

Three major social trends confronted American society in the nineteenth century. The first was the growth of cities: urbanization. Throughout the century and extending well into the twentieth century, the American population moved out of rural communities and into cities and towns. During the latter half of the 1800s, the rural population doubled while the urban population increased by almost seven times (Platt, 1969). The percentage of the American population living in urban areas stood at 6.1 percent in 1800 (Stockwell, 1968). By 1870 the percentage had increased to 25.7 percent and by 1920 to 51.2 percent (Stockwell, 1968).

The second major trend, related to the first, was industrialization. It was the prospect of work in the industrial factory that lured people to urban areas. Not everyone could fit into the economic order, however. In an agricultural society, practically everyone can perform some useful social role; the elderly, the young, and the disabled—all can contribute to the household. In an urban industrialized society, one's social role, both job and social worth, is dependent upon the value of one's work in the competitive labor market. In the dog-eat-dog world of the marketplace, some people cannot compete on an equal footing.

The final trend, also related to the previous ones, was immigration. In the 1800s and early 1900s, millions of foreign-born persons migrated to American shores. Of course, America had always been a nation of immigrants. Toward the latter half of the eighteenth century, though, the annual number of immigrants increased at an incredible pace. In the 1820s a mere 151,000 people immigrated to the United States. In the next 100 years, over 38 million foreign-born persons came to America, reaching a peak of over 8 million in the period from 1900 to 1909, an average of over 800,000 per year (Stockwell, 1968). Just as significant as the number of immigrants was where they had come from. Those who arrived in the late eighteenth and early nineteenth centuries did not share the cultural and ethnic ancestry of the established class, and they were greeted by suspicion, resentment, and hostility.

It is not a coincidence that by the mid-1800s mental hospitals and almshouses were filled with immigrants. According to Rothman (1971, p. 283), at the mental institution in Worcester, Massachusetts, over 40 percent of the inmates in the 1850s were foreign born; at Ohio's Longview asylum 67 percent of the inmates in 1861 were immigrants; at the state asylum in Wisconsin the figure reached 60 percent in 1872. In Massachusetts state officials expressed grave concern over the number of poor immigrants filling the almshouses in 1857:

> Why has Massachusetts so many paupers? Because we have a larger pro-
> portion of foreigners from which they are made. . . . Our almshouses pau-
> pers are nearly all foreigners. . . . Aliens who have landed in this State and
> their children . . . embrace five-sixths of all those who become charge-
> able.

The combined effects of urbanization, industrialization, and immigration resulted in the rise of the first large-scale social problems in American society: slums, unemployment, homeless children and adults, culture conflict, crime, delinquency, and, according to many, vice and immorality. The asylum became the solution to these problems, providing a way to deal with homeless and idle populations and a way to remove from society those presumed responsible for causing the social problems. The political, social, and intellectual leaders of the time traced the roots of social problems to the victims of the emerging social and economic order: the poor, the deviant, and the disabled.

The Indictment: The Eugenics Movement

A new breed of moral entrepreneurs emerged in the latter part of the nineteenth century. Citing an equal concern for the preservation of society and the well-being of the feebleminded and other disabled, they sought to prevent the spread of degeneracy and immorality throughout society. Included in their ranks were institutional superintendents like Fernald and Kerlin, leaders of charitable organizations like Lowell, researchers like Dugdale and Goddard, and intellectuals like Spencer and Sumner.

In attempting to understand and explain the social problems of their times, social theorists, beginning with Spencer (1851) and Galton (1869), began to apply evolutionary theory to the development of society. The cause of the spread of poverty, crime, immorality, and other social evils throughout society, they reasoned, was the proliferation of people with defective genes. The feebleminded gradually came to be singled out as especially dangerous carriers of social disease. These theories were translated into a program of social action known as the eugenics movement.

By the 1870s and 1880s politicians, institutional officials, and leaders of charitable organizations were sounding the eugenics alarm. Feeblemindedness, they warned, was a major peril to society; it was the cause of most of society's problems, crime, delinquency, pauperism, prostitution, and immorality.

For almost the next fifty years, these moral entrepreneurs carried on their crusade against the evils of feeblemindedness with fanatic zeal. In 1907 Butler wrote: "While there are many anti-social forces, I believe none demands more earnest thought, more immediate action than this. Feeblemindedness produces more pauperism, degeneracy and crime than any one other force" (Wolfensberger, 1975, p. 34). Several years later, Walter Fernald, recognized as an early leader in the field, expressed the same sentiments more strongly:

> Feebleminded women are almost invariably immoral, and if at large usually become carriers of venereal disease or give birth to children who are as defective as themselves. The feebleminded woman who marries is twice as prolific as the normal woman. . . . Every feebleminded person, especially the high-grade imbecile, is a potential criminal, needing expression of his criminal tendencies. The unrecognized imbecile is a most danderous element in the community. . . . It has been truly said that feeblemindedness is the mother of crime, pauperism and degeneracy. It is certain that the feebleminded constitute one of the great social and economic burdens of modern times (Wolfensberger, 1975, pp. 35–36).

Supporting these outrageous claims was a series of studies of family histories that attempted to link crime, vice, insanity, and feeblemindedness, including *The Jukes* by Dugdale (1910), and *The Kallikak Family* by Goddard (1912). Goddard's study was especially well received in the "field" of feeblemindedness. In an attempt to prove the hereditary link between feeblemindedness and social evils, Goddard set out to study lines of descendants from a soldier in the Revolutionary War. One line descended from Martin Kallikak's illegitimate son from a sexual liaison with a feebleminded woman; the other came from Kallikak's marriage to a respectable woman from a good family after the war. Based on his fieldworker Elizabeth Kite's observations, interviews with family members, and whatever documents she could find, Goddard concluded that Martin Kallikak's illegitimate son yielded 480 descendants, of whom 143 were feebleminded, 36 were illegitimate, 133 were sexually immoral, 24 were alcoholic, 3 were epileptic, 3 were criminals, 8 kept houses of ill-repute, and 82 died in infancy (Sarason & Doris, 1959). On the "good" side of the family, there were 496 descendants, all of whom were reportedly doctors, lawyers, educators, landholders, and other good citizens. Of that group, only 15 children died in infancy; only 2 were alcoholics, 1 was insane, and 1 was a promiscuous male.

From this and other "research," which has been thoroughly discredited (see Gould, 1981; Sarason & Doris, 1959), Goddard concluded that "feeblemindedness" was a hereditary condition that caused such social problems as crime, prostitution, poverty, and intemperance. In 1915 Goddard wrote:

> For many generations we have recognized and pitied the idiot. Of late we have recognized a higher type of defective, the moron, and have discovered that he is a burden; that he is a menace of society and civilization; that he is responsible to a large degree for many, if not all, of our social problems (Wolfensberger, 1975, p. 34).

As Wolfensberger (1975) and other commentators have noted, the indictment of the feebleminded and other groups waned toward the end of the 1920s. In fact, many of the leaders of the eugenics movement later recanted their earlier alarmist statements. Yet, the eugenics movement played a major role in shaping public policy toward people with disabilities for decades to come and so pervaded public and professional thinking that many of the views expressed during the period persist today.

Social Control.   The leaders of the eugenics movement advocated a set of social policies designed to rid society of the alleged carriers of "defective genes" responsible for the spread of crime, vice, and degeneracy. In 1913 the American Breeders Association wrote:

> The following classes must generally be considered as socially unfit and their supply should if possible be eliminated from the human stock if we would maintain and raise the level of quality essential to the progress of the nation and our race: (1) the feebleminded, (2) paupers, (3) criminaloids, (4) epileptics, (5) the insane, (6) the constitutionally weak, (7) those predisposed to specific diseases, (8) the congenitally deformed, and (9) those having defective sense organs (Scheerenberger, 1983, p. 154).

The eugenics cause was soon taken up by charitable organizations, the U.S. Congress and state legislatures, and a range of public figures.

Beginning in the 1800s and extending well into the 1900s, the federal and state governments adopted a series of social control measures directed against people labeled mentally retarded, insane, epileptic, and otherwise stigmatized: segregation, sterilization, prevention of marriage and sexual relations, and restrictive immigration. Some leaders also considered a more drastic measure: euthanasia.

Segregation.   By the 1870s, leaders in the field of feeblemindedness were promoting the asylum as an effective means of segregation. In stark contrast to earlier times, the purpose of the asylum was not to train the feebleminded to perform useful roles in society, but to remove them from society altogether. Johnson wrote in 1908 that "the only just and humane and civilized way of stopping the transmission of defectiveness is by segregation" (Wolfensberger, 1975, p. 43). Murdoch and Johnstone called for the quarantine of mental defectives, while Barr proposed the establishment of one or more national reservations (Wolfensberger, 1975).

The history of the establishment of an institution in Newark, New York, lends insight into the tenor of the times. In 1878 New York created an experimental "Custodial Asylum for Feebleminded Women" of childbearing age at Newark as a colony of the Syracuse asylum. According to the state legislature, the purpose of the experiment "was to determine whether there are in county poorhouses or elsewhere feeble-minded women who need care and protection to prevent them from multiplying their kind and so increasing the number of dependent classes in the State; also, could they be maintained without undue cost" (quoted in New York State Custodial Asylum for Feebleminded Women, 1893). By the 1880s the experiment was declared a success and the legislature established a permanent location at Newark in 1885.

It was not until 1890 that the Newark Custodial, as it was called, was officially dedicated. The proceedings of the dedication contain several speeches by members of the board of trustees, one a state legislator, one a member of women's charities, and one a member of the clergy. Each speech, while testifying to the humaneness of the asylum, points out the need to control the spread of "feeblemindedness" and immorality. The dedicatory address by the Reverend M. S. Hard, cloaked in humanitarian concern, carried an underlying theme of social control:

> And here let me say, *that it is the duty of the State to be humane.* It is not possible that all who make a commonwealth should be equal in brain-force, in power to construct wealth, or in purity of purpose. The encouragement offered every boy to strive for the presidency is a sophistry. Inequality in mind creates grades in morals. When morals come to minds of low grade, there comes promptly the need of security to society. . . . For those who cannot elect success; who are not responsible for their infirmities; who enter the census-count because they have the form of beings that are human, who are the impersonation of social wrongs, and carry in face and speech and form the tenderest pleadings for protection; toward these, we maintain, the State should exercise the most pronounced humanity (New York State Custodial Asylum for Feebleminded Women, 1893, p. 24).

The establishment of the Newark asylum, and similar ones in New Jersey and Pennsylvania, was a blatant effort to prevent so-called feebleminded women from having children by segregating them during their childbearing years. While most institutions were designed to serve both sexes, men and women were separated within the institutions. Cornell warned in 1915, "The institution that places . . . boys and girls anywhere near each other will never do its part in the work of preventing feeblemindedness in the community" (Wolfensberger, 1975, p. 43). It is common practice even today for men and women to be segregated on different units or wards at institutions.

Sterilization.   Sterilization was viewed by some political and social leaders as an effective means of preventing the transmission of "defectiveness." By the early 1900s officials of leading charitable organizations were actively advocating sterilization or "asexualization" for the so-called feebleminded, epileptic, and insane. Barr wrote in 1902:

> Knowing the certain transmission of such taint, how can one fail to appreciate the advantage of prevention over penalty, or to recognize as the most beneficient instrument of law the surgeon's knife preventing increase. And why not? We guard against all epidemics, are quick to quarantine small-pox, and we exclude the Chinese; but we take no steps to eliminate this evil from the body social (Wolfensberger, 1975, p. 40).

Indiana was the first state to enact a sterilization law directed at disabled and deviant populations (Sarason & Doris, 1959, p. 287). By 1912 eight states had passed laws that required sterilization or made sterilization a condition for institutional release for disparate groups such as the "feebleminded," "insane," "epileptic," "confirmed criminals," "syphilitics," and others (Scheerenberger, 1983, p. 155). Other states soon followed suit, and by 1926 similar laws existed in 23 states (Scheerenberger, 1983, p. 191).

Courts gradually began to hear cases involving the constitutionality of the sterilization laws. In several states, including Nevada, Indiana, New Jersey, and New York, courts overturned sterilization statutes; courts in other states upheld these laws. In 1927 a famous case, *Buck v. Bell,* wound its way to the U.S. Supreme Court. This case involved a Virginia statute that applied to inmates of the state's institutions for the so-called feebleminded, insane, and epileptic and, in contrast to some of the laws overturned by courts, provided appeal procedures for people who were to be sterilized. The case was generated on behalf of Carrie Buck, an eighteen-year-old woman committed to the State Colony for Epileptic and Feebleminded of Virginia; she was the daughter of another inmate at the institution and the mother of an allegedly illegitimate, feebleminded child (Scheerenberger, 1983, pp. 191–192). In a resounding victory for the proponents of social control, the Supreme Court upheld the practice of forced sterilization. Writing on behalf of the Supreme Court, Justice Holmes commented:

> We have seen more than once that the public welfare may call upon the best citizens for their lives. It would be strange if it could not call upon those who already sap the strength of the State for these lesser sacrifices, often not felt to be such by those concerned, in order to prevent our being swamped with incompetents. It is better for all the world, if instead of waiting to execute degenerative offspring for crime, or let them starve for their imbecility, society can prevent those who are manifestly unfit from continuing their kind. The principle that sustains compulsory vaccination is broad enough to cover the cutting of the Fallopian tubes . . . three generations of imbeciles are enough! (Scheerenberger, 1983, p. 192).

With the endorsement of the nation's highest court of law, sterilization of the feebleminded and other groups continued on a broad scale up until at least the 1950s and 1960s. Davies (1959) reported that by 1958 twenty-eight states had enacted sterilization laws and 31,038 mentally retarded persons had been sterilized nationally.

It is interesting to point out that some of the leaders in the field of feeblemindedness questioned the practice of sterilization early on. Fernald (1912, pp. 95–96) warned:

> The presence of these sterile people in the community, with unimpaired sexual desire and capacity would be direct encouragement of vice and a prolific source of venereal disease. Sterilization would not be a safe and effective substitute for permanent segregation and control.

Prevention of Marriage and Sexual Relations. In line with the practice of forced sterilization, professional and political leaders around the turn of the century advocated restrictions on the rights of people labeled feebleminded, insane, epileptic, and so on to marry and have sexual relations. Speaking at a convention of what is now the American Association on Mental Deficiency in 1911, Diller stated:

> There is a very widespread notion that the marriage between two persons is a matter of their affair and their affair only and that the next door neighbor should not in any way meddle in the matter. I believe none of us here would subscribe to this doctrine. We have a right not only to take an interest in the subject of marriage, but I believe it is our duty to do so (Scheerenberger, 1983, p. 154).

According to Scheerenberger, 39 states eventually outlawed marriage among people with mental retardation or established mental retardation as a ground for annulment.

States also enacted laws imposing stiff penalties for anyone having sexual relations with an epileptic, insane, or feebleminded person. Wolfensberger (1975, p. 40) reported that Connecticut passed a law containing the following language around 1895:

> Every man who shall carnally know any female under the age of forty-five years who is epileptic, imbecile, feebleminded, or a pauper, shall be imprisoned in the State prison not less than three years. Every man who is epileptic who shall carnally know any female under the age of forty-five years, and every female under the age of forty-five years who shall consent to be carnally known by any man who is epileptic, imbecile, or feeble-minded, shall be imprisoned in the State prison not less than three years.

These laws are strikingly reminiscent of the Nuremberg Laws of 1933 that outlawed sexual relations between Jews and Gentiles and marked the beginning of the Nazi era in Germany. As we shall see, parallels between the eugenics movement in America and the Nazi reign of terror do not end here.

Restrictive Immigration. In United States immigration policies around the turn of the century, we find the clearest expression of what Sarason and Doris (1959, p. 289) called "the alliance of racism with eugenics." As noted earlier, the majority of immigrants during the latter half of the eighteenth and early part of the twentieth centuries did not share the Anglo-Saxon heritage of their forebears. They came to America with different customs, religions, and languages.

The professional and political establishment at that time viewed the new waves of immigrants as a severe threat to the purity of the American people. One after the other, political, civil, and professional leaders stood up to denounce the many "defective" among the "immigrant stock." In a study reported in 1917, Goddard reported that between 40 and 80 percent of the immigrants were feebleminded based on intelligence tests (Sarason & Doris, 1959, p. 293).

As early as 1891, the U.S. Congress amended the immigration law to exclude "idiots," "insane persons," and "paupers," among other groups. As the eugenics movement gathered steam, immigration laws became more strict and were more rigorously enforced. In the Immigration Act of 1917, Congress added provisions to exclude Orientals from admission into the United States, established Ellis Island as a clearinghouse for Europeans, and enacted a literacy test to ban illiterates from entering the country (Stockwell, 1968, p. 140). In 1924 Congress expanded the definition of undesirable groups and set firm quotas for immigrants from different nations.

According to Scheerenberger (1983), immigrants passing through Ellis Island were examined by two physicians, one to examine their physical condition and the other to test their mentality. Based on these examinations, "undesirables" were prevented from entering this country. In 1904 one immigrant out of every 5,300 was deported because of mental retardation. By 1927 the number had increased to one out of every 234.

Elimination.   The policies of the eugenics era stopped short of turning to elimination—mass murder—of people with mental retardation and other disabilities. Yet the eugenics movement came dangerously close to this. In 1901 Johnson, who had been president of the National Conference of Charities and Correction and what is now the American Association on Mental Deficiency, wrote: "I do not think that, to prevent the propagation of this class it is necessary to kill them off or to resort to the knife; but, if it is necessary, it should be done" (Wolfensberger, 1975, p. 37).

The sentiments that spawned segregation, asexualization, restrictive marriage, and selective immigration in America reached their logical extension in the so-called euthanasia program in Nazi Germany. The mass murder of millions of Jews, gypsies, and intellectuals in Nazi Germany is widely known. What is less known is that the Nazis first practiced their mass murder techniques on the inmates of Germany's institutions for the mentally ill and mentally retarded (Werthman, 1978). Cloaked in euphemisms such as "mercy deaths" and "destruction of life devoid of value," the Nazi "euthanasia program" resulted in the deaths of as many as 275,000 inmates of institutions through starvation, poisoning, and gassing beginning in 1939. In fact, the Nazis perfected the mass murder techniques associated with Auschwitz and Buchenwald in Germany's mental institutions. In a haunting book on the subject, Werthman (1978) has made a convincing case that Germany's physicians and professionals played a central role in legitimating and carrying out the mass murders. He provided a chilling account of how psychiatrists developed questionnaires to distinguish between those "not worthy to live" and those "worthy to be helped." The Nazi experience serves as a grim reminder of what can happen when any group of people is singled out as lacking basic human rights.

Institutional Momentum

The 1920s saw the waning of the eugenics movement, although it has resurged on occasion even until today. Intellectuals such as Walter Lippman and G. K. Chesterton first stood up to denounce the outrageous claims of the eugenics movement, and in 1922 the latter published a book entitled *Eugenics and Other Evils*. Gradually, leaders in the field of mental retardation, such as

Table 1

Public Institutions for the Mentally Retarded

Year	Number of institutions	Total population	Population per 100,000 of the general population
1880	10	2,429	4.8
1890	20	5,103	8.4
1904	28	13,884	17.5
1910	35	19,499	22.5
1916	40	27,665	30.0
1923	66	47,963	39.3
1930	77	68,035	56.4
1940	87	106,944	76.7
1950	96	124,304	81.6
1960	108	163,730	91.9
1970	190	186,743	92.1
1978	236	139,432	64.9

Source: Adapted from *Demographic Studies of Residential Facilities for the Mentally Retarded* by K. C. Lakin, n.d. Minneapolis: University of Minnesota, Dept. of Psychoeducational Studies.

Goddard and Fernald, began to recant their earlier views. By 1924 Fernald was forced to admit, "We have begun to recognize the fact that there are good morons and bad morons" (Wolfensberger, 1975, p. 54).

Wolfensberger (1975) has described the period from around 1920 to the 1950s as an era of institutional "momentum without rationales." That is to say, institutions continued to expand from the 1920s through the 1950s and into the 1960s in the absence of clear-cut rationales such as those provided in earlier periods. The belief that certain people belong in institutions came to be taken for granted. Of course, this view is held by many even today. Between 1930 and 1970, the number of public institutions for the mentally retarded increased from 77 to 190, while their populations grew from 68,035 to 186,743 (Lakin, n.d.). The populations of public institutions for the mentally retarded peaked in 1967 with 194,650 and have continued downward ever since (see Table 1). These figures do not include the number of people labeled mentally retarded in other kinds of institutions, including poorhouses, mental hospitals, jails, and nursing homes. Scheerenberger (1983, p. 199) indicated that many people with mental retardation were in almshouses as late as 1936. Lakin (n.d., p. 62) has reported that the number of people labeled mentally retarded in institutions for the so-called mentally ill peaked at 41,823 in 1961.

The populations of public institutions for other categories of dependent and deviant people similarly grew from the late 1920s into the 1950s and

1960s. Mental hospitals, nursing homes, detention centers, and institutions for the physically disabled experienced significant expansion. The populations of state mental hospitals reached their peak in 1955 at 558,922.

While the populations of public institutions steadily increased during the first half of the twentieth century, that period also was marked by efforts to develop community alternatives to institutionalization. In the late 1920s and 1930s especially, progressive leaders in mental health and mental retardation, equally cost conscious and disillusioned with institutions, explored a series of arrangements to care for and supervise former inmates in the community. Alternatives included parole, colony care, and family care.

The history of mental retardation in the United States has been described as a pendulum swinging back and forth between institutions and the community. The period of the 1920s and 1930s is often described as a swing toward the community. Colonies, family care, and the parole system are cited as evidence of that trend.

The sad truth, however, is that the community was never really given a fair chance. David Rothman (1980) has argued that in the field of mental health, community programs never received wholehearted acceptance and support. In the field of mental retardation, the ideas that guided the colony and family care programs were never broadly endorsed. Scheerenberger (1983, p. 196) has reported that a survey conducted by the Committee on Research of the American Association on Mental Deficiency in 1937 revealed that over 50 percent of the responding institutions had less than 10 percent of their residents on parole, 87 percent had not placed any residents in a boarding home, 84 percent had no residents in a colony, and only 23 percent had residents in training for community placement. Similarly, the statistics of Lakin (n.d., p. 87) show that the percentage of people on the books of public institutions (presumably those in family care and parole) living outside the institution did not change significantly from 1927 to the 1950s and mid-1960s (between 13 and 14 percent).

From the late 1840s to the late 1960s, institutions for the so-called mentally retarded and developmentally disabled developed and flourished. The institutional model essentially went unchallenged for over 100 years. But the 1950s through the 1970s ushered in a new day, and the institution struggled for its very existence.

The Emergence of Special Education in the Public Schools

In the early history of America, education was the privilege of the upper classes. It was not until the nineteenth century that states began to pass and enforce compulsory education laws.

Of course, the rise of compulsory education in America can be attributed to many of the same social forces that led to the widespread development of institutions. Like institutions, the schools were a response to the changes occurring in American society at the time. In the context of the social dislocations brought about by urbanization, industrialization, and immigration, the schools were to perform an important social function: what Michael Katz (1983, p. 373) has called "cultural standardization."

From the perspective of early proponents of compulsory education such as Horace Mann, the schools were to provide a way to socialize the young and train them to be better, more productive workers. Katz and others have argued that schools were designed not only to teach students the skills necessary to function in the workplace, but also to inculcate the values and beliefs necessary for the maintenance of an urban working class. Further, according to Katz and others, schools have played a more insidious role in teaching students to blame themselves for failure.

The spread of compulsory education meant that schools had to begin to deal with students with disabilities. Prior to the latter part of the nineteenth century, of course, the only places at which mentally retarded, blind, or deaf children could receive an education were institutions. As we have seen, the first institutions established in the mid-eighteenth century were designed to be small boarding schools.

Toward the end of the nineteenth century, the public schools were first confronted with a large number of "backward" students. Many educators at the time expressed alarm at the disruptive influence of children who were disruptive, slow in learning, or otherwise disabled. In 1908 the superintendent of the Baltimore public schools, James Van Sickle, stated:

> The presence in a class of one or two mentally or morally defective children so absorbs the energies of the teacher and makes so imperative a claim upon her attention that she cannot under these circumstances properly instruct the number commonly enrolled in a class. School authorities must therefore, greatly reduce this number, employ many more teachers, and build many more school rooms to accommodate a given number of pupils, or else they must withdraw into small classes these unfortunates who impede the regular progress of normal children. The plan of segregation is now fairly well established in large cities, and superintendents and teachers are working on the problem of classification, so that they may make the best of this imperfect material (Sarason & Doris, 1979, p. 263).

As Van Sickle's remarks make clear, school systems began to segregate disabled and otherwise "deviant" students who were forced on them through compulsory education (Sarason & Doris, 1979, p. 267). Separate schools and special classes were soon established throughout the country. According to LaVor (1976), Boston established the first public day school for the deaf in 1869; New York City first initiated special education classes in 1874. Most commentators argue that the Providence, Rhode Island, schools were the first to establish special classes for mentally retarded students in 1896. Scheerenberger (1983, pp. 129–130), however, has stated that there is evidence that Cleveland initiated a special class for mentally retarded students in 1875, although this class was disbanded at the end of the school year. In any case, many large cities had started special education classes for the mentally re-

Early intervention programs can provide opportunities for cognitive, physical, and social development. (Photograph by Mima Cataldo.)

tarded by the turn of the century: Chicago in 1898, Boston in 1899, Philadelphia in 1899, and New York in 1899 (Scheerenberger, 1983, p. 130).

Many of the first special education classes served as dumping grounds for a broad range of students who did not fit into typical school classes. Sarason and Doris (1979, p. 267) have written that these classes might include "slow learners, the mentally subnormal, epileptics, learning disabilities, chronic truants, behavior problem children, physically handicapped or immigrant children suffering from language or cultural handicaps." Sarason and Doris (1979, p. 266) have quoted Johnstone, then superintendent of an institution for the feebleminded in Vineland, New Jersey: "The special class must become a clearing-house. To it will not only be sent the slightly blind and partially deaf, but also the incorrigibles, the mentally deficients, and cripples." Similarly, Scheerenberger (1983, p. 130) has quoted Elizabeth Farrell, then inspector with the New York City schools who later was elected the first president of the Council for Exceptional Children:

> The first class was made up of the odds and ends of a large school. There were over-age children, so-called naughty children, and the dull and stupid children. The ages ranged from eight to sixteen years. They were the children who could not get along in school.

Throughout the twentieth century, special education grew at a steady pace. Scheerenberger (1983, p. 166) has written that by 1922, 133 cities in

23 states had enrollments of 23,252 pupils in special education classes of all types. States began to enact special education laws. New Jersey passed a law mandating special education for mentally retarded students in 1911 (Sarason & Doris, 1979, p. 309; Scheerenberger, 1983, p. 166). Withn the next ten to fifteen years, a large number of states passed laws mandating special education, providing state aid for special education, and requiring local school districts to identify students with handicaps.

Despite the gradual expansion of special education programs, students with severe disabilities were largely excluded from public education up until the 1970s. Sarason and Doris (1979, p. 312) have stated that a national survey found that there were no children labeled "trainable mentally retarded" in public schools in 1940, although they also cite other evidence indicating that at least some programs were in operation by that time. Scheerenberger (1983) has quoted a number of leading educators in the 1920s who advocated the exclusion of "low grade" cases from public programs. Finally, Lakin (n.d., p. 67) has reported that it was not until the mid-1950s that special education programs were serving more mentally retarded persons than were public institutions.

The period from around 1920 to 1950 was a relatively quiet one in special education. To be sure, the populations of public institutions as well as public special education programs gradually expanded. Further, the federal government initiated a number of programs designed to benefit the disabled during that period. In the aftermath of World Wars I and II, federal vocational programs directed at disabled veterans were initiated. As part of President Roosevelt's New Deal, the Social Security Act, which has become a basic income maintenance program for people with disabilities, was passed in 1935. Yet, compared to the decades either before or after, the 1920s through the 1940s were marked by a maintenance of the status quo and the absence of major controversies about what the disabled are like and how they should be treated. The forces for change grew steadily throughout the 1950s and exploded in the field in the 1960s and 1970s.

A Time of Change

The 1950s and 1960s marked a new era in the history of society's treatment of people with disabilities. Tentatively at first, and then with increased conviction, professionals, parents, and people with disabilities began to question the legitimacy of traditional and school practices. The era started with pleas for modest reforms. By the late 1960s and 1970s, however, parent and professional leaders and disability rights advocates demanded fundamental changes in educational and social service systems.

New philosophies emerged during that period, but the seeds of those philosophies had been planted in earlier times. As we have seen, leaders like Seguin and Howe in the mid-nineteenth century expressed distrust of "abnormal environments" such as large institutions. Beginning in the 1950s, a new generation of leaders, allied with parent groups, directly challenged prevailing practices and attitudes toward the disabled. They waged their battles in public forums, courts, and legislatures.

The Consumer Movement

In the 1950s parents began uniting to form strong local, state, and national organizations. The first national organization for retarded persons, what is now the National Association for Retarded Citizens, was founded in 1950. Gradually, parents of children with other kinds of disabilities organized to form organizations such as the National Society for Children with Autism, the Spina Bifida Association, and the Association for Children with Learning Disabilities.

Over time, parent groups have grown increasingly aggressive in advocating for their children's rights. Initially, parents came together to provide each other mutual support, to share information, to sponsor fund-raising events, and even to operate schools and day programs. In the 1960s and 1970s, however, parent groups started to demand quality services from school districts and other service providers. Parent groups took their demands to the nation's courts and legislatures.

The development of organizations composed of people with disabilities occurred during the 1970s. Just as blacks, Hispanics, and women organized to confront societal prejudice and discrimination, disabled adults joined together to form groups like Disabled in Action and the American Coalition of Citizens with Disabilities. Like other groups, national organizations of disabled persons challenged those who presumed to speak and act on their behalf. "You gave us your dimes," said many people with disabilities, "now we want our rights."

In recent years, national and international organizations of people labeled mentally retarded formed to speak on their own behalf. One of the most notable of these is People First, which, as the name implies, has demanded that people with mental retardation be afforded the same rights and privileges enjoyed by other members of society. In the early 1980s, a group of mentally retarded adults from Austria presented a moving and forceful statement at the United Nations:

> We are people first and only secondly handicapped.
> We wish to speak for our rights and let other people know we exist.
> We want to explain to our fellow human beings that we can live and work in a community.
> We want to show that we have rights and responsibilities like other people.
> Our voice is new.
> We must first learn to speak.
> And we ask everyone to learn to understand our voices.
> We need people who teach us to speak. People who believe in us.

Mentally retarded persons do not want to live in terrible institutions.
We want to live in the community.

Exposés

The 1960s ushered in an era of exposés of society's shameful treatment of
people with disabilities. Of course, scandals and exposés were not new to
the field of services for the disabled. Throughout the nineteenth and twentieth
centuries, reformers like Beers (1908) had occasionally exposed deplorable
conditions at institutions. Yet not since Dorothea Dix's crusades against the
wretched conditions in almshouses did exposés so stir America's conscience
as those that started in the 1960s.

"There is hell on earth, and in America, there is a special inferno," wrote
Burton Blatt (Blatt & Kaplan, 1966, p. v). "We were visitors there during
Christmas, 1965." A respected educator and researcher in the field of mental
retardation, Blatt closely followed the reactions of professionals and politicians to Robert Kennedy's unannounced tours of institutions in New York
State in 1965. After visits to Willowbrook and Rome state schools, Kennedy
had commented to the *New York Times:* "I was shocked and saddened by
what I saw there. . . . There were children slipping into blankness and lifelong
dependence." Blatt knew the truth of what Kennedy had reported. He, too,
had been to institutions and had found the same filth and deprivation that
Kennedy had decried. As Blatt listened to Governor Rockefeller, state legislators, and institutional administrators severely criticize Kennedy's "whirl-
wind" tours, he decided to follow through on what he termed a "seemingly
bizarre venture." That Christmas, Blatt, together with a photographer named
Fred Kaplan, secretly photographed the "back wards" at five institutions in
the eastern United States. Their book, *Christmas in Purgatory,* and a subsequent article in *Look* magazine, shocked America and fueled the growing
disenchantment with the institutional model.

It is difficult to put into words the conditions that Blatt and Kaplan found.
Indeed, pictures do not fully capture the horror. They found locked wards,
isolation cells, broken toilets, and incredible overcrowding:

> Beds are so arranged—side by side and head to head—that *it is impossi-
> ble, in some dormitories, to cross parts of the room without actually walk-
> ing over beds.* Often the beds are without pillows. We have seen mat-
> tresses so sagged by the weight of bodies that they were scraping the
> floor (Blatt and Kaplan, 1966, p. 1).

Blatt and Kaplan went on to describe the areas where people spent their
waking hours:

> In each of the dormitories for severely retarded residents, there is what is
> euphemistically called a day room or recreation room. The odor in each
> of these rooms is overpowering. . . . Most day rooms have a series of
> benches on which sit unclad residents, jammed together, without purpose-
> ful activity, communication, or any interaction. In each day room is an at-

tendant or two, whose main function seems to be to "stand around" and, on occasion, hose down the floor "driving" excretions into a sewer conveniently located in the center of the room (p. 22).

It was the infant wards, however, that Blatt and Kaplan found most distressing:

> The infant dormitories depressed us the most. Here, cribs were placed— as in the other dormitories—side by side and head to head. Very young children, one and two years of age, were lying in cribs, without any interaction with any adult, without playthings, without any apparent stimulation. In one dormitory, that had over 100 infants and was connected to 9 other dormitories that totalled 1,000 infants, we experienced a heartbreaking encounter. As we entered, we heard a muffled sound emanating from the "blind" side of a doorway. A young child seemed to be calling, "Come. Come play with me. Touch me." We walked to the door. On the other side were forty or more unkempt infants crawling around a bare floor (p. 34).

The Kennedy and Blatt discoveries were merely the first of a long set of exposés that received widespread public attention. Reporter Geraldo Rivera's exposé of Willowbrook in Staten Island, New York, in the early 1970s documented the same conditions found by Blatt and Kaplan five years earlier (Rivera, 1972). The artful documentary of Frederick Wiseman (1969), *Titticut Follies,* filmed at Bridgewater State Hospital in Massachusetts, and the book by Kenneth Wooden (1974), *Weeping in the Playtime of Others,* focused attention on mental hospitals and juvenile institutions, respectively.

In the late 1970s, Blatt, McNally, and Ozolins (1979) returned to the institutions depicted in *Christmas in Purgatory.* Institutional populations had declined; the budgets had soared—yet Blatt and his colleagues concluded that little else had changed:

> A decade or so ago we went to five state institutions for the mentally retarded. . . . Then, we found little to give us hope but we were reluctant to admit that the concept of "institution" is hopeless. Today we find much to give us hope, but we are now unable to see a way to save the institutions. . . . We must evacuate the institutions for the mentally retarded. The quicker we accomplish that goal the quicker we will be able to repair the damage done to generations of innocent inmates (Blatt, McNally, & Ozolins, 1979, p. 143).

The exposés of institutions go on today. In 1982 the Gannett newspapers undertook a major investigation of Oklahoma's institutions for juveniles and the mentally retarded. Hardly an institution in the nation has gone unscathed over the past two decades.

As professionals, reporters, and politicians exposed the shameful conditions in America's institutions, child advocacy groups began to focus public attention on the exclusion of disabled and minority children from public schools. In 1970 the Task Force on Children Out of School published a scathing indictment of school exclusion in Boston entitled *The Way We Go to School.* "At a time when the public schools must take giant strides to prepare children for today's world," the report's introduction read, "Some children are being excluded from school, others discouraged from attending, and still others placed in special classes designed for the 'inferior.' " The task force concluded that large numbers of culturally, physically, and mentally and behaviorally different children were denied the right to equal educational opportunity. Other task forces and reports documented school exclusion throughout the nation. A report issued by the Children's Defense Fund in 1973 estimated that as many as two million children with disabilities were denied the right to a public education.

Social Science Perspectives

Traditionally, the fields of special education and disabilities have been dominated by medical and psychological perspectives that focus on the defects or deficiencies of people with disabilities. In the 1950s and 1960s, however, social science perspectives began to play an important role. In contrast to traditional medical and psychological perspectives, these perspectives have directed attention to how society treats the disabled.

Sociologist Erving Goffman, in the classic study *Asylums,* was one of the first researchers to document the devastating effects on the identity and self-esteem of inmates of a broad range of institutions, including mental hospitals, nursing homes, tuberculosis sanatoriums, prisons, and concentration camps. Goffman (1961, p. xiii) coined the phrase "total institution" to refer generally to these facilities: "A total institution is a place of residence and work where a large number of like-situated persons, cut off from the wider society for an appreciable period of time, together lead an enclosed, formally administered round of life." Following in Goffman's footsteps, Vail (1966), Braginsky and Braginsky (1971), Morris (1969), Perrucci (1974) and others have studied the dehumanizing effects of institutions.

Social scientists also have focused attention on the social stigma that accompanies disabilities (Edgerton, 1967; Bogdan & Taylor, 1982; Scott, 1969; Hobbs, 1975; Mercer, 1973). Mental retardation, mental illness, and other such terms are labels or social constructs that demean those to whom they are attached. As Hobbs (1975, p. 24) has written:

> The categorization of exceptional children involves much negatively
> loaded terminology: crippled, handicapped, limited, impaired, disturbed,
> disabled. Each of these labels also has pejorative, slang, or colloquial
> counterparts used casually by children's peers . . . it is widely accepted
> that such negative labels create a unique atmosphere around the children,
> complicating their lives in significant though unmeasured ways. A very im-
> portant consequence of labeling is the tendency to stereotype.

If we abandon labels—that is, if we focus on people's humanity rather than their deficits—then we must abandon a whole set of discriminatory actions against those we call disabled.

In a wonderfully entertaining article written in 1959, Louis Dexter illustrated the relative nature of labels such as mental retardation. Dexter described a mythical society in which people value grace the way people in our society value intelligence. He pointed out that everything in this society would be designed in such a way as to require grace for the performance of everyday tasks, just like our society requires intelligence.

Dexter explained that clumsy people, whom he calls the "gawkies," would be a major target of societal discrimination in this society. He speculated on what would happen to the gawkies. All school children would be ranked by grace quotient (GQ). Some clumsy people would present an embarrassment to those around them and would be sent to special schools and institutions. Professional organizations like the National Association on Clumsiness would be formed. Dexter even went as far as to suggest that professionals would be engaged in major debates over whether all clumsy people should live in the community.

Out of social science perspectives such as these has come the principle of normalization. First developed in Scandinavia, the principle of normalization is an alternative philosophy to social exclusion and segregation of people with disabilities. As Perske (1980) has pointed out, the principle of normalization has had many definitions. Two Swedish leaders, Karl Grunewald and Bengt Nirje, defined normalization as follows: "Making available to all mentally retarded people patterns of life and conditions of everyday living which are as close as possible to the regular circumstances and ways of life of their society." Gunnar and Rosemary Dybwad and Wolf Wolfensberger first popularized the concept in the United States. *Normalization,* by Wolfensberger (1972), provides the most comprehensive statement of this important concept.

The concept of normalization has been subject to misunderstandings and misinterpretations. Some critics charge that normalization means that people's individual clinical or instructional needs should be ignored. Nothing in the concept implies this. Normalization simply means that we should stop treating people in abnormal ways; in the words of Perske (1980, p. 21): "Although the normalization principle is extremely positive, its strongest function lies in its power to uncover conditions and practices which for centuries had *denormalized* people with handicaps, and to which little attention had been paid."

Litigation

Toward the end of the 1960s, public interest and civil rights attorneys began to direct their attention to the plight of adults and children with disabilities. Their efforts resulted in a long series of smashing victories throughout the 1970s.

When the Supreme Court issued its landmark decision outlawing racial segregation in schools in the 1954 case, *Brown v. Board of Education* ("Separate but equal is inherently unequal"), few could have predicted that the logic underlying this decision would be incorporated by federal judges ruling on the educational rights of students with disabilities. Yet this is precisely what happened in a series of major class action law suits on behalf of children with disabilities in the early 1970s. In the *PARC (Pennsylvania Association for Retarded Children, Nancy Beth Bowman, et al. v. Commonwealth of Pennsylvania)* and *Mills (Mills v. Board of Education of the District of Columbia)* cases, federal judges upheld the constitutional rights of children with disabilities to a free public education in the "least restrictive" (most normalized) setting possible.

Filed on behalf of all school-aged mentally retarded children in Pennsylvania, the *PARC* case challenged traditional school practices such as exclusion and segregation. In October 1971, the plaintiffs (PARC) and defendants (the Commonwealth of Pennsylvania) settled the case through what is called a consent agreement (a court-approved and implemented settlement). The *PARC* consent agreement supported the right to education in clear and unequivocal terms:

> It is the Commonwealth's obligation to place each mentally retarded child in a free, public program of education and training appropriate to the child's capacity, within the context of the presumption that, among the alternative programs of education and training required by statute to be available, placement in a regular public school class is preferable to placement in a special public school class and placement in a special public school class is preferable to placement in any other type of program of education and training.

Less than one year after the signing of the consent agreement in the *PARC* case, a federal judge in the *Mills* case challenged the exclusion of children identified as "mentally retarded, emotionally disturbed, learning disabled, hearing or speech-impaired, visually impaired or physically handicapped" from Washington, D.C., schools. Rejecting the Board of Education's excuses for failing to provide an appropriate education for all children with disabilities, federal Judge Joseph Waddy issued a far-reaching set of orders upholding the rights of children to a "free and suitable publicly-supported education regardless of the degree of the child's mental, physical or emotional disability or impairment."

Both the *Mills* and the *PARC* cases had repercussions throughout the nation. By 1973 thirty-one similar cases had been filed throughout the nation (Weintraub & Ballard, 1982, p. 3). Also, as we shall see, the orders in these cases served as a model for Public Law 94-142, the Education for All Handicapped Children's Act, passed by Congress in 1975.

Just as parents turned to federal courts to enforce their children's educational rights, they, together with inmates themselves, began to challenge institutional abuse and neglect in lawsuits brought against state institutions across the country. From the 1960s to the 1980s, federal and state courts ruled on a broad range of institutional practices, including institutional peonage or forced labor (*Souder v. Brennan*), commitment procedures for adults (*Addington v. Texas*) and children (*Parham v. Institutionalized Juveniles*), involuntary administration of drugs and other "treatments" (*Rogers v. Okin*), the due process rights of juveniles in delinquency proceedings (*In re Gault*), and a host of other issues. In a major decision handed down in 1975, the U.S. Supreme Court ruled on the constitutional rights of "nondangerous mental patients" in *O'Connor v. Donaldson.*

In a unanimous decision in this case the Supreme Court ruled that Kenneth Donaldson, a "nondangerous" mental patient, had a constitutional right to liberty. Writing for the Supreme Court, Justice Stewart stated:

> A finding of "mental illness" alone cannot justify a State's locking up a person against his will and keeping him indefinitely in simple custodial confinement. Assuming that that term can be given a reasonably precise content and that the "mentally ill" can be identified with reasonable accuracy, there is still no constitutional basis for confining such persons involuntarily if they are dangerous to no one and can live safely in freedom.

Stewart went on to write: "In short, a State cannot constitutionally confine *without more* a nondangerous individual who is capable of surviving safely in freedom by himself or with the help of willing and responsible family members or friends [emphasis added]."

The *Donaldson* case resulted in the release of thousands of inmates from the nation's institutions. No longer could states warehouse people who harmed no one else and could live very well on their own. Clearly, this was an important case. Yet it was a series of class action lawsuits directed at institutional conditions and the very nature of institutions that had the most profound effects on services for people labeled mentally retarded, mentally ill, and developmentally disabled. Instead, these suits sent shock waves through institutions across the country.

In less than a fifteen-year span of time, major lawsuits were filed against (and in most cases won) mental retardation and mental health institutions in Alabama, Connecticut, Vermont, New Hampshire, North Dakota, New York, Massachusetts, Florida, Nebraska, New Jersey, Pennsylvania, Tennessee, Kentucky, Texas, Louisiana, Virginia, West Virginia, Michigan, Washington, the District of Columbia, and other states. Three cases during this period received special notoriety and set forth the legal principles on which other cases were based: *Wyatt v. Stickney* in Alabama (the *Wyatt* case), *New York State Association for Retarded Children v. Rockefeller* in New York (the *Willowbrook* case), and *Halderman v. Pennhurst State School and Hospital* in Pennsylvania (the *Pennhurst* case).

Filed initially on behalf of inmates of Bryce Hospital for the mentally ill in 1970 and expanded to include Searcy Hospital and Partlow State School and Hospital for the mentally retarded in 1971, *Wyatt* was the first case to receive widespread public and professional attention. Conditions at Alabama's institutions were atrocious, although certainly not unique at the time. Based on evidence presented regarding the Partlow institution, federal District Judge Frank Johnson was later to find:

> The evidence . . . has vividly and undisputedly portrayed Partlow State
> School and Hospital as a warehousing institution which, because of its at-
> mosphere of psychological and physical deprivation, is wholly incapable
> of furnishing (habilitation) to the mentally retarded and is conducive only
> to the deterioration and the debilitation of the residents.

Johnson also commented on "atrocities" that "occur daily":

> A few of the atrocious incidents cited at the hearing in this case include
> the following: (a) a resident was scalded to death by hydrant water; (b) a
> resident was restrained in a strait jacket for nine years in order to prevent
> hand and finger sucking; (c) a resident was inappropriately confined in se-
> clusion for a period of years; and (d) a resident died from the insertion
> by another resident of a running water hose into his rectum.

Judge Johnson was not a timid judge. Well-respected for his legal opinions, he had taken on controversial civil rights cases before. It was Judge
Johnson who had ordered Governor George Wallace to integrate the University of Alabama in the 1960s and who had employed federal marshals to
make sure his orders were followed.

In rulings handed down in 1971 and 1972, Judge Johnson had ruled that
mentally ill and mentally retarded persons committed to institutions had a
right to treatment (in the case of mental illness) and *habilitation* (in the case
of mental retardation). Basing his decision on a ruling handed down in *Rouse
v. Cameron* in the District of Columbia in 1966 and similar decisions, Johnson
reasoned that the only possible justification for committing a mentally ill or
mentally retarded person to an institution, which represents a significant
curtailment of one's civil liberties, is treatment or habilitation and, once committed, that person has an "inviolable constitutional right" to treatment or
habilitation.

Johnson also ruled that people committed to Alabama's institutions had
a right to treatment or habilitation under the *least restrictive circumstances*.
Over time, this principle has come to be equated with normalization.

In his decisions, Judge Johnson made it clear that Alabama and other
states were not under any obligation to maintain institutions for the mentally
ill and mentally retarded; however, once they had decided to do so, they
were obliged to operate the institutions in a "constitutionally permissible"
fashion.

Based on these legal principles, Johnson ordered far-sweeping changes
in Alabama's mental health and mental retardation system. He ordered the
institutions to comply with what he termed "Minimum Constitutional Standards," with separate standards for the mentally ill and the mentally retarded.
The standards were incredibly specific and covered almost every aspect of
inmates' lives at the institutions. The forty-nine standards for the habilitation
of the mentally retarded included the following:

> Each resident has a right to a habilitation program which will maximize
> his human abilities and enhance his ability to cope with his environment.
> The institution shall recognize that each resident, regardless of ability or

status, is entitled to develop and realize his fullest potential. The institution shall implement the principles of normalization so that each resident may live as normally as possible.

In the *Willowbrook* case, Judge Judd was faced with a similar situation as that which confronted Judge Johnson (for a history of the case, see Rothman and Rothman, 1984). Certainly, Willowbrook was not better than Partlow or the other Alabama institutions; it simply was larger. In fact, several years prior to the filing of the suit, in 1969, Willowbrook, with 6,200 inmates, was the largest institution for the mentally retarded in the world. By the time the suit was filed, it had 5,700; by the time Judd issued his initial ruling in December 1972, Willowbrook's population stood at 4,727.

Presumably, Willowbrook had undergone reform. The population had declined and the state of New York assured the judge that major improvements were under way. Yet Judge Judd found the same deplorable and dehumanizing conditions and the same atrocities as Judge Johnson found at Partlow:

> Testimony of ten parents, plus affidavits of others, showed failure to protect the physical safety of their children and deterioration rather than improvement after they were placed in Willowbrook School. The loss of an eye, the breaking of teeth, the loss of part of an ear bitten off by another resident, and frequent bruises and scalp wounds were typical of the testimony. During eight months of 1972 there were over 1,300 reported incidents of injury, patient assaults, or patient fights.

In contrast to Johnson, Judd argued that the failure of the state to accomplish its purpose in institutionalizing residents—to provide care and treatment—would only give them and their families the right to demand release from the institution. Judd thus rejected the constitutional right to treatment or habilitation for Willowbrook residents.

Judd ruled, however, that Willowbrook residents had another constitutional right: *the right to protection from harm.* Noting that federal courts had ruled that criminals in prisons had a right to be free from cruel and unusual punishment based on the Eighth Amendment of the Constitution, Judd reasoned that mentally retarded people confined to Willowbrook must be entitled to at least the same rights.

For Judd, the right to protection from harm entitled residents to safety, a tolerable living environment, medical care, "civilized standards of human decency," and freedom from conditions that "shock the conscience." He ordered New York to implement nine immediate steps to rectify some of Willowbrook's more blatant abuses, including a prohibition against seclusion and the hiring of additional ward attendants, nurses, physical therapy personnel, and fifteen physicians.

After his initial ruling, Judd encouraged the two sides in the case, the plaintiffs and the defendants, to negotiate a final resolution to the problems of Willowbrook. From 1973, when the decision was handed down, until 1975, the plaintiffs and the defendants were involved in protracted negotiations.

In 1975, soon after Governor Carey, who had made Willowbrook an issue in his election campaign, had taken office, the state and the plaintiffs entered into a binding consent agreement with Judge Judd's approval.

Ironically, the *Willowbrook* consent agreement contained many of the same provisions incorporated by Judge Johnson in his 1972 standards for the Partlow institution in Alabama. The consent agreement endorsed both the right to treatment and the principle of the least restrictive alternative. It also went much further than Johnson's order in mandating deinstitutionalization of Willowbrook. The consent agreement provided for Willowbrook to be reduced to a population of no more than 250 residents by 1981 and contained numerous standards for the operation of community programs.

Both the *Wyatt* and the *Willowbrook* cases were brought as institutional reform cases. In both cases, the plaintiffs argued on the basis of the need for massive improvements in institutional conditions. While both cases resulted in significant deinstitutionalization, it was not until the *Pennhurst* case, filed in 1974, that the institution itself was placed on trial. In the words of one of the attorneys who brought the case, *Pennhurst* represented a shift from institutional reform with deinstitutionalization to "anti-institutionalization" (Ferleger & Boyd, 1979).

In writing his opinion in the case in 1977, federal District Judge Raymond Broderick, who happened to have been one of three federal judges in the *PARC* education case, noted some of the same conditions and atrocities found by his legal predecessors. Broderick, however, paid closer attention to the nature of institutional life. Broderick wrote:

> At its best, Pennhurst is typical of large residential state institutions for the retarded. These institutions are the most isolated and restrictive settings in which to treat the retarded. . . . Pennhurst is almost totally impersonal. . . . Its residents have no privacy . . . they sleep in large, overcrowded wards . . . spend their waking hours together in large day rooms and eat in a large group setting.

Broderick proceeded to speak forcefully about the importance of the principle of normalization:

> Since the early 1960s there has been a distinct humanistic renaissance, replete with the acceptance of the theory of normalization for the habilitation of the retarded. . . . The environment at Pennhurst is not conducive to normalization. It does not reflect society. It is separate and isolated from society and represents group rather than family living.

Broderick could have been describing any institution in the nation.

Judge Broderick next turned to a consideration of the legal issues at stake. He ruled that the residents of Pennhurst had the same rights as those found by Johnson in Alabama and Judd in *Willowbrook*, and more. Citing Johnson's decision, among others, he ruled that Pennhurst residents had a constitutional right to minimally adequate habilitation. He cited Judd and others to uphold a constitutional right to be free from harm. And he cited a

Pennsylvania state judge to support a right to minimally adequate habilitation based on state law.

The judge then considered other rights based on the Constitution and Section 504 of the Rehabilitation Act of 1973, which prohibits discrimination against the handicapped. Broderick ruled that both the equal protection clause of the Fourteenth Amendment of the Constitution and Section 504 provided for a *right to nondiscriminatory habilitation.* "In this record," wrote Broderick, ". . . we find that the confinement and isolation of the retarded in the institution called Pennhurst is segregation in a facility that clearly is separate and not equal" (*Halderman et al. v. Pennhurst,* 1977, p. 203). Broderick was using the Supreme Court's language in *Brown v. Board of Education* to suggest that the segregation of the mentally retarded in institutions, like racial segregation in schools, is illegal and unconscionable.

In a memorandum of March 1978, Judge Broderick issued the farthest-reaching orders ever handed down in a case involving the disabled. He ordered Pennsylvania to provide "suitable community living arrangements for the retarded residents of Pennhurst" and, in essence, to close the Pennhurst institution.

Broderick's decision, it seemed, sounded the death knell for institutions. Calling Pennhurst, and by implication all such institutions, a "monumental example of unconstitutionality," his orders for the evacuation of Pennhurst were clear and unequivocal. Yet Broderick was only a district-level judge. His orders could be appealed to the Circuit Court of Appeals and then to the Supreme Court—and they were. As we shall see, in rulings on the *Pennhurst* case and on another case known as *Romeo,* the U.S. Supreme Court severely limited the role of federal courts redressing injustices at the nation's institutions.

The *Wyatt, Willowbrook,* and *Pennhurst* cases had profound effects, some real and some symbolic, far beyond the institutions named in the suits. For a time, at least, these lawsuits put state officials on notice that institutional abuse and dehumanization would no longer be tolerated and thus moved entrenched bureaucracies to develop community programs. They received widespread publicity, especially in the case of Willowbrook in New York City, and educated parents, the public, politicians, and even professionals on the evil of institutions. They also spurred Congress and state legislatures to enact laws to protect the rights of people with disabilities.

The Federal Response: Legislation

It was not until the 1960s that the federal government began to define a national policy toward the disabled. Starting with President Kennedy, whose sister happened to have been mentally retarded, five successive presidents endorsed the policy of deinstitutionalization of the mentally retarded and mentally ill (Herr, 1979). "We as a Nation," spoke Kennedy in an address to Congress in 1963, "have long neglected the mentally ill and mentally retarded." Kennedy went on to say: "We must act now . . . to reduce, over a number of years, and by hundreds of thousands, the persons confined to these institutions." Years later, in 1971, President Nixon announced a national goal to enable "one third of the more than 200,000 retarded persons in institutions to return to useful lives."

Throughout the 1960s, Congress expanded grant programs for the disabled in the areas of education, rehabilitation, research, housing, and social services. In 1963 Congress passed the Mental Retardation Facilities and Community Mental Health Centers Act, a grant program that was increased again in 1967.

In the 1970s federal involvement in services for the disabled increased dramatically. Spurred by exposés of institutional life and countless lawsuits filed on behalf of children and adults with disabilities, Congress passed a series of laws designed both to protect the rights of the disabled and to provide federal financial support for a broad range of services.

In 1971 Congress amended Title XIX of the Social Security Act, Medicaid, to create the Intermediate Care Facility for the Mentally Retarded (ICF/MR), which, ironically, has become one of the major obstacles to deinstitutionalization nationally. Under the ICF/MR program, a state is eligible to receive 50 to 78 percent reimbursement for the costs of services in facilities that have as the primary purpose the provision of health and rehabilitation services, provide Medicaid-eligible clients with "active treatment," and meet the standards developed by the secretary of Health, Education and Welfare (now Health and Human Services).

The federal government issued regulations for the ICF/MR program in January 1974. The regulations included detailed standards for facilities, which were in many ways similar to Judge Johnson's "minimum constitutional standards" for Partlow in the *Wyatt* case.

States seized the opportunity to pass on the costs for expensive institutional reforms to the ICF/MR programs in the 1970s. By 1978 forty-one states received federal funds for institutions under the ICF/MR program. In 1978 the ICF/MR program cost a total of $1,337,846,369 nationally, almost all of which went to support institutions. New York State's ICF/MR program alone cost $214,148,442.

The ICF/MR program represented a mixed blessing. The influx of federal dollars to institutions certainly contributed to improved conditions at ICF/MR-certified facilities. However, in order to continue to receive federal funds, states invested heavily in institutional staffing and capital construction. In the period 1977 to 1980 alone, states spent $821,456,000 in the construction or renovation of institutional facilities (National Association of State Mental Retardation Program Directors, 1980). This not only drained funds from community programs, but also, once states had invested massive sums in institutional buildings, served as a strong disincentive for deinstitutionalization in future years. Despite vast expenditures for staff and facilities, programming and conditions at ICF/MR-certified institutions remained woefully inadequate. In a review of federally mandated survey reports at forty-four institutions nationally (Taylor et al., 1981), major violations of the standards were found at each of the institutions, ranging from a lack of programming and activities to seclusion, unsanitary conditions, lack of privacy, and inappropriate use of restraints and drugs.

Toward the middle part of the 1970s, some states began to develop small community settings with ICF/MR funds. By 1978 seventeen states had established ICFs/MR for fifteen or fewer persons. At Michigan's Macomb-Oakland Regional Center, nationally known as a model community-based service system, officials developed small settings for six or fewer persons, including the so-called severely and profoundly retarded, using ICF/MR funds. In other states, however, officials established ICF/MR-certified "mini-institutions" containing as many as 100 or more people.

By the late 1970s, the ICF/MR program, like Medicaid, generally had generated strong criticism for encouraging costly, inappropriate, and restrictive institutional care. In 1981, as part of the "Omnibus Reconciliation Act of 1981," Congress passed the "Medicaid waiver" program. The thrust of the program was to encourage states to serve people in their natural families and home communities as opposed to placing them in institutions. Under the Medicaid waiver, states were allowed to receive federal reimbursement for a broad array of community services, including, among others, home health aid services, respite care, case management, homemaker services, day programs, and medical care. As of early 1984, some states were just beginning to offer community services under the Medicaid waiver.

Two years after the passage of the 1971 Medicaid amendments, Congress totally revamped federal rehabilitation legislation that had originally been passed in 1920 and amended on over a dozen occasions. The Rehabilitation Act of 1973 expanded the scope of vocational rehabilitation services, provided additional federal funds for rehabilitation, and included additional provisions to assure the appropriateness of rehabilitation services. This act also contained the much-heralded Section 504, the civil rights bill for the disabled:

> Section 504. No otherwise qualified handicapped individual in the United States . . . shall, solely by reason of his handicap, be excluded from the participation in, be denied the benefits of, or be subjected to discrimination under any program or activity receiving federal financial assistance or under any program or activity conducted by any Executive agency or by the United States Postal Service.

Section 504 called for the end of discrimination and the participation of people with disabilities into American life.

The federal government dragged its heels in developing regulations to implement Section 504. Without regulations, it was difficult to interpret 504 and, hence, end discrimination. It took a lawsuit and finally a sit-in by disabled people in the offices of then Secretary of Health, Education and Welfare Joseph Califano for the federal government to issue regulations for Section 504. In May 1977 the Department of Health, Education and Welfare published broad regulations that prohibited discrimination against the handicapped in employment, program accessibility, preschool, elementary, and secondary education, postsecondary education, and health, welfare, and social services.

As explained in the regulations, discrimination is a complex issue. In order to ensure equal opportunity, it is not enough simply to forbid exclusion of people with disabilities. The preface to the regulations states that "it is meaningless to 'admit' a handicapped person in a wheelchair to a program if the program is offered only on the third floor of a walk-up building." Recipients of federal funds thus are required to make "reasonable accommodations" for people with disabilities, including special aids, modified job or school requirements, and accessible facilities. While the regulations stop short of requiring accommodations that would result in an "undue hardship" on recipients of federal funds, they make it clear that ending discrimination may impose some costs and burdens:

> These problems have been compounded by the fact that ending discriminatory practices and providing equal access to program may involve major burdens on some recipients. Those burdens and costs, to be sure, provide no basis for exemption from Section 504 of this regulation: Congress's mandate to end discrimination is clear. But it is also clear that factors of burden and cost had to be taken into account in the regulation in prescribing the actions necessary to end discrimination and to bring handicapped persons into full participation in federally financed programs and activities.

In the 1978 amendments to the Rehabilitation Act, Congress authorized federal funds for "Centers for Independent Living." Modeled on the Berkeley Center for Independent Living established in 1972 as a self-help and self-advocacy organization, independent living centers provide a broad range of consumer-oriented services to enable people with disabilities to live as independently as possible, including advocacy, referral, housing assistance, peer counseling, community group living arrangements, attendant care, and others. Central to the concept of independent living centers is consumer self-determination. The 1978 amendments to the Rehabilitation Act mandate that "handicapped individuals will be substantially involved in policy direction and management . . . and will be employed." For the most part, independent living centers have been oriented toward people with physical disabilities, although several have begun to involve people with mental disabilities.

The year 1975 ranks with 1973 as the most important in the history of the disabled in America. In that year, both the Education for All Handicapped Children Act, popularly known as Public Law 94-142, and the Developmentally Disabled Assistance and Bill of Rights Act, the DD Act, were passed.

An amendment to the Mental Retardation Facilities and Community Mental Health Centers Act of 1963, the DD Act provided modest funds for grants for research and services for people with developmental disabilities. States accepting funds under the act were required to put into place a "protection and advocacy" system to protect the rights of the developmentally disabled.

The DD Act also contained a "bill of rights" (which the Supreme Court

This child is learning to grasp a pencil. Note the teacher's delight with his independence. (Photograph by Mima Cataldo.)

subsequently ruled in the *Pennhurst* case represented "national policy" but did not impose any obligations on the states):

> SEC. III. Congress makes the following findings respecting the rights of persons with developmental disabilities:
>
> (1) Persons with developmental disabilities have a right to appropriate treatment, services, and habilitation for such disabilities.
>
> (2) The treatment, services, and habilitation for a person with developmental disabilities should be designed to maximize the developmental potential of the person and should be provided in the setting that is least restrictive of the person's personal liberty.

The DD Act goes on to state that "The Federal Government and the States both have an obligation to assure that public funds are not provided to any institution or other residential program for persons with developmental disabilities that . . . does not provide treatment, services, and habilitation which is appropriate to the needs of such persons."

On November 29, 1975, President Gerald Ford signed into law Public Law 94-142, the Education for All Handicapped Children Act, approved some months earlier by a vast majority of both the U.S. Senate and House of Representatives. Public Law 94-142 guaranteed the right to education for all school-aged children with handicapping conditions, including those with the most severe disabilities.

As Zettel and Ballard (1982) have indicated, Public Law 94-142 was not a revolutionary piece of legislation. For some years previously, the federal government had enacted laws designed to encourage the education of children with disabilities. Federal courts, too, had begun to mandate that children with disabilities be provided with "equal protection" under the law based on the U.S. Constitution. Yet Public Law 94-142 was the first law to define the educational rights of children with disabilities in clear and specific terms.

"It is the purpose of this Act," reads Public Law 94-142, "to assure that all handicapped children have available to them . . . a free appropriate public education which emphasizes special education and related services designed to meet their unique needs, to assure that the rights of handicapped children and their parents and guardians are protected, to assist States and localities to provide for the education of all handicapped children, and to assess and assure the effectiveness of efforts to educate handicapped children." The law itself and regulations issued by the Department of Health, Education and Welfare (now Department of Education) in 1977 define the meaning of "free appropriate public education":

- "Zero-reject." *All* disabled children are entitled to a public education under Public Law 94-142. The law specifically provides for the education of children ages five through eighteen, or the ages at which typical children are educated in a state.
- Least restrictive environment. Public Law 94-142 endorses the principle of "least restrictive environment" as outlined in prior court cases. The federal regulations elaborate on the meaning of "least restrictive environment": "That to the maximum extent appropriate, handicapped children, including children in public or private institutions or other child care facilities, are educated with children who are not handicapped." The regulations further state that removal of a handicapped child from the regular educational environment occurs only when the child's handicap precludes education in regular classes with the use of supplementary services.
- Individualized education program. Each handicapped child must have an individualized written educational program, which must be reviewed at least annually.
- Due process procedures. Children with disabilities and their parents are guaranteed "due process" in educational classification and placement. This includes notification prior to changes in a child's classification or placement and procedures whereby educational decisions can be challenged through an impartial hearing.
- Protection in evaluation. The law and regulations contain provisions to ensure that educational tests and procedures used to evaluate children are free of racial and cultural bias and that educators do not rely on a single procedure to determine the appropriate educational program for the child.

In enacting Public Law 94-142, Congress also appropriated funds to assist states in educating children with disabilities and authorized increased levels of funding over the next seven years. Public Law 94-142 is what is termed a "funding statute." That is to say, states are mandated to meet the requirements of Public Law 94-142 only if they accept funds under the act. The federal government thus adopted a "carrot on a stick" approach to the education of children with handicaps. It was not until 1984 that the last state, New Mexico, finally applied for funds under Public Law 94-142, and hence became obligated to meet its provisions. Although funding under Public Law 94-142 has gradually increased since 1975, the federal government has never provided the level of funding authorized when the act was passed.

With the passage of Public Law 94-142, thousands of children with disabilities entered public school programs for the first time. Many thousands more began to have their educational needs met. Yet it would be naive to assume that this law has resolved the many problems confronting children with disabilities and their families; it has not.

It is safe to say that most students with disabilities receive some form of education, although some, especially those in institutions, clearly do not (see Lakin, Hill, Hauber, & Bruininks, 1983). Once disabled children have gotten through the school door, however, attention has turned to the quality and appropriateness of the education they receive. What does "appropriate" really mean? What is the meaning of "least restrictive environment" in practice? These are controversial issues, ones on which parents and educators often disagree. Many parents lack the stamina and resources to tackle them, and those who are willing to tackle them have found courts and other bodies increasingly reluctant to take a stand on them.

By the mid-1980s the federal government had enacted a diverse and often confusing range of laws directed at people with disabilities. Scheerenberger (1983, p. 250) reports that between 1963 and 1983, Congress passed 166 acts or amendments that provided support to the mentally retarded and their families.

The activities of the federal government in the 1970s and 1980s at times seemed contradictory. The government's posture on deinstitutionalization illustrates this. Section 504 and the DD Act call for participation in community life. Yet the ICF/MR program, the largest single source of funding for programs for the developmentally disabled, encourages institutionalization.

In 1977 the U.S. General Accounting Office, Congress's "watchdog" over the Executive branch, issued a critical report on the federal government's role in deinstitutionalization entitled *Returning the Mentally Disabled to the Community: Government Needs to Do More.* That report documented the failure of the federal government to adopt a coordinated and consistent approach to deinstitutionalization. Yet, government not only has to do more, but also must do things differently.

Controversy, Debate, and Backlash

Throughout the 1960s and 1970s, all trends in the field of disabilities seemed to move in one direction—toward expanded rights, increased social acceptance, fuller integration, and increased funds for programs and services. Yet, beginning in the latter part of the 1970s and extending into the 1980s, people with disabilities and their families began to experience serious challenges to the progress they had made in the preceding years. Deinstitutionalization, mainstreaming, integration, and civil rights became topics of bitter debate and controversy among parents, professionals, human service workers, politicians, and even members of the general public.

The Federal Mood

It is important to understand the social, economic, and political climate of the late 1970s and the 1980s. The previous decades had witnessed an expansion of civil rights and social programs designed to benefit poor people, members of racial minority groups, women, the elderly, and, of course, the disabled. Toward the end of the 1970s, political sentiments seemed to turn against minorities of all kinds.

In the early 1980s, a newly elected administration in Washington proposed major cutbacks in social programs and repeals of civil rights laws and regulations. Public Law 94-142 and Section 504 were among the laws targeted for repeal or "deregulation," although this was unsuccessful.

Just as attempts were made to weaken the rights protections contained in federal laws and regulations, the federal government proposed major cuts in funding for programs benefiting people with disabilities in the early 1980s. Thus the Department of Education proposed a 25 percent cut in state Public Law 94-142 monies for 1982, a figure amounting to $230.5 million. These budget cuts, too, were rejected by Congress.

Repeated attempts to change federal protections and funds for people with disabilities failed in the early 1980s. Yet the 1980s represented a new era in the federal government's relationship to citizens with disabilities. No new major federal rights laws or programs were established. Further, the federal government withdrew from aggressive enforcement of laws such as Section 504 and Public Law 94-142 (with the exception of federal involvement in the so-called Baby Doe case, as described later in this chapter). More than anything else, the federal government's posture helped create a political climate in which the rights of the disabled, and other groups, were pitted against the presumed general welfare of the society. It became acceptable to question the cost effectiveness of social justice.

The Judicial Retreat

Since 1954, when the *Brown v. Board of Education* racial desegregation case was handed down, the Supreme Court had been a strong supporter of civil rights. In the 1970s, however, justices appointed for "strict constructionism" and "judicial restraint" came into the majority on the Supreme Court. The Supreme Court pulled back from handing down far-reaching rulings on civil rights. Just as the disability rights movement had ridden on the waves of the civil rights movement, it was dragged down by a judicial backlash to civil rights.

In the late 1970s and early 1980s, major court cases filed on behalf of people with disabilities gradually wound their way up to the U.S. Supreme Court. Not all these cases resulted in unfavorable decisions for people with disabilities. Yet, in ruling on these cases, the Supreme Court issued a warning to lower federal courts to refrain from ordering major reforms in the areas of institutions and deinstitutionalization, nondiscrimination, and special education.

Nondiscrimination: Section 504 and the Davis Case.   Frances Davis was a licensed practical nurse with a hearing impairment who desired to become a registered nurse. When she applied for admission into a nursing program operated by Southeastern Community College in North Carolina, however, she was turned down based solely on her disability. Southeastern Community College argued that it would be impossible for Davis to participate safely in its nurses training program. Davis subsequently filed suit in federal court alleging a violation of Section 504, which prohibits discrimination based on handicap. While a federal district court sided with the community college, the Court of Appeals for the Fourth Circuit overturned the district court ruling. The Court of Appeals ruled that Section 504 required Southeastern Community College to make modifications in its program to accommodate Davis. Southeastern Community College petitioned the Supreme Court to hear the case. In June 1979 the Supreme Court issued a unanimous decision siding with Southeastern.

The Supreme Court's ruling in *Southeastern Community College v. Davis* centered on the meanings of the concepts of "otherwise qualified handicapped individual" and "reasonable accommodation." Davis argued that she was "otherwise qualified" to participate in the nursing program. An accomplished lip-reader, she maintained that she met the academic and technical qualifications for admission into the training program. She further argued that Section 504 required "reasonable accommodations" for her handicap. These might include modifications in program requirements (for example, waiving certain clinical requirements), the provision of a sign language interpreter, or individual clinical supervision. The Supreme Court was unpersuaded.

According to the Supreme Court, a "qualified handicapped" person is one who meets all the requirements for participation in a program *in spite of* his or her handicap. Southeastern required nursing students to participate in clinical situations in which medical personnel wore surgical masks. Because Davis obviously would not be able to read lips in these situations, according to the Supreme Court she was not able to meet all program requirements.

The Supreme Court also rejected Davis's arguments that Southeastern was required to make accommodations in its training program to enable

Davis to participate. According to the court, Section 504 did not require a program to undertake "affirmative action" or make "substantial modifications" to accommodate people with disabilities.

In analyzing the *Davis* case, it is important to point out that it involved admission to a training program and not employment for a specific nursing job. There are many nursing functions that an individual with a severe hearing impairment could easily perform—for example, private duty nursing or school nursing. Further, as the Appeals Court had noted, Davis would have been superbly qualified to serve as a nurse for other persons with hearing impairments. Indeed, many hearing-impaired persons currently function as nurses or physicians. Yet one obviously cannot practice nursing unless one has received the appropriate training. Would admission of Davis into Southeastern's program have required a lowering of standards, substantial accommodations, or undue financial burdens? Probably not.

Disability rights groups greeted the *Davis* case with dismay and anger. Many saw the Supreme Court's ruling as reflective of long-standing prejudice against the disabled. Like all cases, the *Davis* case merely applied to the specific facts in the case (a hearing-impaired individual's admission to a nursing program). However, the case signaled to other recipients of federal funds, such as universities, public transportation agencies, and employers, that Section 504 was not the powerful civil rights law that disability groups had hoped and claimed.

Institutions and Deinstitutionalization: Pennhurst and Romeo.   As we have seen, in the early 1970s federal courts started handing down far-reaching orders in cases involving the rights of developmentally disabled and mentally retarded people in institutions. The *Willowbrook, Wyatt,* and *Pennhurst* cases called for major reforms. In its 1975 *Donaldson* decision, the Supreme Court ruled that states could not simply warehouse "nondangerous" mental patients who could live safely on their own.

In a series of cases decided in the 1980s, the Supreme Court took an extremely narrow view of the rights of people with mental retardation confined to institutions. The court first considered the *Pennhurst* case. Judge Broderick's original decision in the case ordered the placement of all Pennhurst residents into community living arrangements. On appeal, the Third Circuit upheld the general thrust of Broderick's ruling. While Broderick had based his decision largely on Section 504 and the U.S. Constitution, the Court of Appeals looked to the Developmentally Disabled Assistance and Bill of Rights Act (the DD Act) to uphold Broderick. The state of Pennsylvania petitioned the Supreme Court to hear the case. In April 1981 the Supreme Court handed down its decision.

In a six-to-three decision, the Supreme Court overturned the Third Circuit's decision on *Pennhurst*. The decision focused narrowly on the DD Act and thus left unresolved the constitutional and statutory (specifically, Section 504) issues initially raised by Judge Broderick. Delivering the majority's opinion, Justice Rehnquist, known for his reluctance to impose obligations on the states, concluded that the DD Act, which includes a specific bill of rights, did not impose a mandate on states to provide treatment or habilitation in the least restrictive environment. According to Rehnquist, the DD Act's Bill of Rights was not a statement of rights at all. It merely expressed a congressional preference for certain kinds of treatment.

The Supreme Court sent the case back to the Third Circuit Court of Appeals for consideration of the constitutional and statutory issues initially raised by Judge Broderick in light of its opinion on the DD Act. In 1982 the Third Circuit ruled that it could affirm Broderick's decision on the basis of Pennsylvania state law alone. Once more, the state petitioned the Supreme Court to hear the case and, in 1983 the court accepted it for review. In yet another narrow decision, the Supreme Court ruled that a federal judge cannot order a state to take any action on the basis of state law; in other words, federal courts cannot enforce state law. Once more, the Supreme Court sent the case back to the Third Circuit for further consideration.

Shortly after the Supreme Court issued its original *Pennhurst* decision, another institutional case reached the court. This case, too, concerned the Pennhurst institution. In contrast to the preceding case, however, this one, *Youngberg v. Romeo,* involved a damages action filed by the mother of Nicholas Romeo, a Pennhurst resident, against the Pennhurst superintendent and other officials. Romeo's mother claimed that her son had been repeatedly injured, restrained, and denied treatment while at Pennhurst and requested a federal district court to award damages from Pennhurst officials.

In June 1982 the Supreme Court issued another cautious decision. Justice Powell wrote the opinion for an eight-member majority of the court. After noting that Romeo had a right to "adequate food, shelter, and medical care," which the state conceded, Powell considered whether Romeo had constitutional rights to safety, freedom from undue restraints, and treatment, which the state contested. Powell dispensed quickly with the rights to safety and freedom from restraint. Citing prison cases, Powell concluded that Romeo had rights to safe conditions and freedom from restraint based on his right to liberty under the Fourteenth Amendment of the Constitution.

Powell next turned to the right to treatment, which he described as more troubling. Treading cautiously, Powell ruled that Romeo at least had a right to that training or habilitation that would be necessary to avoid "unconstitutional infringement" of his other rights. Romeo's "liberty interests," Powell wrote, "require the State to provide minimally adequate or reasonable training to ensure safety and freedom from undue restraint" (*Youngberg v. Romeo,* 1982, p. 4684). Thus the majority left unresolved the issue of whether Romeo had an absolute right to treatment, although concurring decisions addressed this.

The Supreme Court thus ruled in the *Romeo* case that mentally retarded people committed to institutions have constitutional rights to safety, freedom from undue restraint, and treatment related to the preceding two rights. The court next considered the legal standard for determining whether these rights had been violated. Here the justices made it clear that courts should show deference to professional decisions. Powell wrote:

> Courts must show deference to the judgment exercised by a qualified professional. By so limiting judicial review of challenges to conditions in state institutions, interference by the federal judiciary with the internal operations of these institutions should be minimized (*Youngberg v. Romeo*, 1982, p. 4684).

In other words, according to the Supreme Court, federal courts should stay out of cases unless there is evidence that professional decisions represent a "substantial departure" from accepted professional judgment.

By the mid-1980s the legal challenge to institutions had lost much of its momentum. After a series of smashing victories against institutions in the early and mid-1970s, civil rights attorneys and the people they represented found federal courts increasingly reluctant to order sweeping changes in state mental health and mental retardation institutions. While the Supreme Court in the *Romeo* case ruled that mentally retarded people committed to institutions have certain constitutional rights, it showed tremendous deference to institutional officials and professionals, many of whom still subscribed to dehumanizing attitudes and had resisted the changes of the past two decades.

It is interesting to point out that the *Wyatt, Willowbrook,* and *Pennhurst* cases continue in litigation to this day. In the *Wyatt* case, the state of Alabama never complied with all Judge Johnson's standards for institutions and has attempted to have the case dismissed on many occasions. In 1978 Alabama brought in its own experts to testify that many residents of Partlow could neither benefit from training nor be placed successfully in community settings. The *Willowbrook* case has been subject to recurring battles between the plaintiffs, defendants, and an appointed review panel to oversee the consent agreement, which was subsequently disbanded by the state of New York (Rothman & Rothman, 1984). Most recently, the state successfully modified the *Willowbrook* consent agreement to waive some of the standards regarding the size of community settings. While Willowbrook has experienced significant deinstitutionalization, it never reached the projection of 250 residents by 1981. As late as 1983, over 1,000 people remained confined at Willowbrook in substandard, even squalid conditions.

An interesting footnote to the *Willowbrook* and *Pennhurst* cases is that both institutions are scheduled to be closed. In 1984 the governor of New York announced his decision to close the Willowbrook institution, while the state of Pennsylvania signed a consent agreement in which it agreed to close Pennhurst. It is indeed ironic that at a time at which the courts had retreated from ordering broad-scale reforms, states agreed to what the plaintiffs in these suits had wanted all along. This underscores the fact that lawsuits sometimes have profound effects far beyond judicial orders.

The Meaning of a Free Appropriate Public Education: Rowley and Tatro.   It took until 1982 for Public Law 94-142 to be interpreted by the Supreme Court. The case, known as *Board of Education of the Henrick Hudson Central School District v. Rowley,* involved a bright young girl named Amy Rowley who happened to be deaf. Mainstreamed into a regular elementary school class, Amy was doing quite well in school. She was performing better than the average child in her class and was advancing easily from grade to grade, but her parents thought she could be doing much better. While an excellent lip reader, she could understand much less of what went on in the class than the other children. Amy's parents, who were also deaf, asked the school district to provide a sign language interpreter so that she would have the same opportunity as other children. The school district refused, and a hearing officer and the state commissioner of education upheld this decision. Amy's parents filed suit in federal court. Both the district court and Court of Appeals for the Second Circuit sided with the Rowleys. Petitioned by the school district, the Supreme Court agreed to hear the case.

The *Rowley* case hinged on the meaning of "free appropriate public education" guaranteed to handicapped children under Public Law 94-142. Does this not mean that children with disabilities have a right to equal opportunity? Isn't that what Congress intended when it referred to "full educational opportunity" to all handicapped children? A majority of the Supreme Court said no.

Writing for the majority, Justice Rehnquist reasoned that Public Law 94-142 merely required that states provide disabled students with "access" to a public education program. The meaning of "free appropriate public education," according to the majority, is the requirement that "the education to which access is provided be sufficient to confer some educational benefit upon the handicapped child." Since Amy Rowley was advancing from grade to grade, she was receiving "some educational benefit." It was irrelevant that Amy would probably achieve much higher if she were provided with a sign language interpreter.

The majority went on to consider the role of the courts in deciding educational cases. The courts, wrote Rehnquist, should limit their involvement to reviewing whether states have complied with the procedures set forth in Public Law 94-142 (for example, due process procedures) and whether the individualized educational program is "reasonably calculated to enable the child to receive educational benefits." Consistent with the deference shown to professional decision making in the *Romeo* case, Rehnquist added, "Courts must be careful to avoid imposing their view of preferable educational methods upon the States."

Of course, the *Rowley* decision left many important questions unanswered. For example, would Amy have been entitled to a sign language interpreter had she been failing in school? What does "some educational benefit" mean for students with severe mental retardation? Further, some areas covered in Public Law 94-142 were not addressed in the *Rowley* case.

Many parents and disability rights groups were understandably concerned when the Supreme Court decided to hear a case filed under Public Law 94-142 and Section 504 known as *Irving Independent School District v. Tatro.* This case focused on school districts' obligation to provide related services to enable children with disabilities to participate in special education programs. Public Law 94-142 specifically mandates the provision of special education and related services for handicapped children. Related services are defined as:

> Transportation, and such developmental, corrective, and other supportive services (including speech pathology and audiology, psychological services, physical and occupational therapy, recreation, and medical and counseling services, except that such medical services shall be for diagnostic and evaluation purposes only) as may be required to assist a handicapped child to benefit from special education, and includes the early identification and assessment of handicapping conditions in children.

A young child with spina bifida, Amber Tatro required a health-related procedure known as clean intermittent catheterization (CIC) to avoid injury to her kidneys. CIC is a fairly simple procedure that can be performed by any nonmedical person with minimal training. Amber's parents, babysitter, and teenage brother performed the CIC procedure for her.

When Amber was first admitted to school, the school district refused to include the provision of CIC in her individualized education program. CIC, the school district argued, was a medical service (other than for diagnostic purposes) and did not fall under the definition of related services in Public Law 94-142. Amber's parents argued that CIC was a necessary supportive service and should be provided as a related service. A failure to provide CIC to Amber was tantamount to excluding her from school. The case eventually wound its way to the Supreme Court.

In the first clear-cut Supreme Court victory for the disabled and their families in years, the Supreme Court ruled that CIC is a related service under Public Law 94-142. The court distinguished between medical services provided by a licensed physician, which schools are not required to provide, and health-related services provided by a school nurse or other qualified person, which were mandated by Public Law 94-142. Chief Justice Berger wrote: "Services like CIC that permit a child to remain at school during the day are no less related to the effort to educate than are services that enable the child to reach, enter, or exit the school."

The Tatro family did not get everything they had requested. Amber's parents had also asked the court to award attorneys' fees under Section 504 based on their costs in upholding their child's rights. A majority ruled that Section 504 did not apply when plaintiffs could obtain what they wanted under Public Law 94-142; thus they were not entitled to attorneys' fees, which are not provided for under Public Law 94-142. What this means is that parents must be prepared to bear the costs of challenging violations of their children's rights.

By the mid-1980s, several clear trends had emerged in Supreme Court decisions on the rights of people with disabilities. The first is that the court was willing to grant only narrow rights to adults and children with disabilities. The era of far-reaching court orders on behalf of the disabled was over. The court seemed to be going out of the way to ignore even clear-cut mandates from Congress. The second trend is that the court was loath to let judges act as intermediaries in controversies among professionals and experts. The message was clear: show deference to institutional administrators, state policy makers, and school officials. The final trend relates to the costs of nondiscrimination. If it might require "undue" or significant financial resources, the Supreme Court seemed to be saying, then judges should not require it.

Unions

Many unions have a long history of supporting causes of civil rights and social justice. Indeed, early in their history, unions waged hard-fought battles for workers' basic rights. Yet, beginning in the 1970s, some public employee unions started to feel threatened by the changes that were occurring in the field of disabilities. Teacher unions, for example, sometimes express misgivings about educating students with disabilities in regular public school programs. In regard to deinstitutionalization, public employee unions have been among the most vocal opponents. Of course, the policy of deinstitutionalization does not have to result in the loss of jobs. However, deinstitutionalization poses the threat that jobs will be shifted from publicly operated institutions to privately operated community programs, resulting in a loss of public employee positions.

In 1975 the American Federation of State, County, and Municipal Employees (AFSCME), a public employee union representing 250,000 mental health workers nationally, released a scathing report that blasted the policy of deinstitutionalization. The report, entitled *Out of Their Beds and into the Streets,* presented deinstitutionalization as a sinister plot to relieve state governments of the responsibility for caring for the mentally ill, the elderly, and other groups and to put money in the pockets of private profiteers (Santiestevan, 1979). Jerry Wurf, then president of AFSCME, wrote in the introduction of the report:

> It seems to us that "de-institutionalization," a lofty idea, has become something very ugly—a cold methodology by which government washes its hands of direct responsibility for the well-being of its most dependent citizens. . . .
>
> Institutional reform need not be disruptive, discomforting or deadly to the thousands who look to the state to guarantee their survival. . . . It's time we came together, to build a constituency that supports the right of every American to proper institutional care, and takes the responsibility for that care out of the hands of private profiteers.

Several years after AFSCME expressed opposition to deinstitutionalization, the Civil Service Employees Association (CSEA), New York State's public employee union, took up the cause. In 1978 CSEA sponsored a major public relations campaign to convince politicians and the public that deinstitution- alization meant "dumping." "The State Calls It Deinstitutionalization," read one advertisement, "We Call It Cruel." As part of its campaign, CSEA prepared a series of sixty-second radio advertisements that painted deinstitutionali- zation as a cruel ripoff:

> It's bad enough that we New Yorkers pay one of the highest per-capita tax rates in the nation. But it becomes scandalous when the State of New York squanders our tax money by filling the pockets of private profiteers as part of a plan called deinstitutionalization. . . .
>
> State employees with many years service are being put on unemploy- ment and welfare roles instead of being allowed to provide services that are desperately needed. That's not what deinstitutionalization was sup- posed to be. It was supposed to give patients a better life. It's just not working.

It is difficult to gauge the impact of public employee union opposition to deinstitutionalization. Certainly, the public relations campaigns waged by AFSCME, CSEA, and other groups have fed public cynicism over the motives of state governments (some of which is undoubtedly warranted) and en- couraged community opposition to group homes and other community living arrangements. Their lobbying efforts probably have also scared away potential supporters of deinstitutionalization, including some politicians who depend on public employee union endorsements and campaign contributions.

The Public: Bad Neighbors

The general public seems supportive of the disabled as long as they are content to be on the receiving end of charity drives and annual telethons. But let them demand their share of the American dream and the mood of the public can change drastically. The hard-fought gains of the past two dec- ades often came at the cost of public support.

"Sometimes equality just costs too much," wrote Roger Starr, a member of the *New York Times* editorial board, in an article published in *Harper's* in 1982. According to Starr, laws like Section 504 and Public Law 94-142 demand too much too fast. It's a matter of dollars: "No matter how savage it sounds, spending money on the handicapped must be measured against the wealth produced by the nation's economy, and against other demands for help that similarly return a smaller amount of money to the national treasury than they cost (Starr, 1982, p. 14). Even if one could accept Starr's values and sense of national priorities, his position could be countered on factual grounds. The programs Starr would presumably cut are enabling millions of people with disabilities to be productive and contributing members of society.

Many educational officials and school board members have joined the backlash against disability rights. "Special Education Carried Too Far" read the headline on an article written by Max Rafferty in 1981. Rafferty's complaints against the disabled range from exorbitant costs to a decline in educational standards to a breakdown in school discipline.

> I don't believe it. Today's courts are holding that handicapped students, despite disruptive or even dangerously violent behavior, cannot be expelled from school. And yes, that's what I said: if a kid is classified as handicapped, he can get away with—almost—murder (Rafferty, 1981, p. A4).

Perhaps the most vicious attacks on people with disabilities have come from community opposition to deinstitutionalization. One need only pick up a local newspaper to see this. The myths and stereotypes promulgated during the eugenics movement have never totally disappeared.

Community resistance to deinstitutionalization takes many forms. It is not uncommon to find local editorial writers, politicians, and civic leaders decrying the release of "dangerous" people from institutions. *The Catholic Sun,* a central New York paper, reported a bizarre story in July 1976. Alarmed by the number of former residents of local mental health and mental retardation institutions wandering around the city, Mayor Edward Hanna of Utica banned all former residents from entering a city park without supervision. The mayor charged that there had been instances of panhandling, disrobing, and assaults by former residents. Two local priests and two nuns protested the action. Mocking the mayor's decree, they set up an "IQ booth" at the entrance to the park and asked visitors: "Do you have all of your mental faculties?" The mayor's decree was withdrawn.

Group homes have encountered stiff opposition in many communities across the country. The prospect of having so-called mentally retarded or mentally ill people next door seems to bring out all the stereotypes and prejudices. In Washington, D.C., and Staten Island, New York, prospective group homes were actually fire-bombed by fearful neighbors. Robert Keating, a free-lance writer, wrote an excellent article entitled "The War Against the Mentally Retarded," which appeared in *New York* in 1979. Keating wrote that "bomb threats, vandalism, violence, and phone threats have become our newest method of treatment for the mentally retarded." Quoting one prospective neighbor of a group home, he wrote, "We don't want them. Put them back in Willowbrook." Keating reported how local politicians and others stir up hostility at local public hearings on proposed group homes:

> Even though the politicians are doing an excellent job of stoking the fire of discontent, they could take a lesson in inflammatory rhetoric from a man not in their field per se. . . .
> "My name is Felton King," he begins in a slow, powerful voice. "I'm the president of local 429 at the Staten Island Developmental Center (Willowbrook). I'd like to give you some facts. . . . Approximately 88 percent of the clients being placed out in the community . . . have a severely bad behavior problem. . . . It is a fact that these kids have communicable diseases." The audience reacts with ahs and scattered whispers. King pauses after each fact.

"They say they're not going to harm your kids. . . . That's a bunch of crap. . . . " King leaves the microphone while the audience extends the enjoyment of its own disorder. It is clear that one of Felton King's primary concerns is the threat of losing union jobs when Willowbrook closes.

It is not necessary to go to New York City to find backward attitudes expressed toward the so-called retarded or mentally ill and strong opposition to proposed group homes. In Syracuse a 1981 article in the *Herald-American* quoted one prospective neighbor of a group home planned for an upper-middle-class neighborhood:

Mentally retarded people are impaired, they don't have the conscience we do to control our actions. They don't know right from wrong. . . . It's unfortunate. But they could start a fire. They could be sexually deviate.

Prospective neighbors often cloak their prejudice with fears about neighborhood deterioration, additional traffic, and a decline in property values. Studies have shown, however, that group homes have no adverse effects on residential neighborhoods or local property values (Wolpert, 1978). Further, Perske (1980) has reported that despite initial fears of resistance, most neighbors come to accept group homes and their residents over time.

Parents: Jet Lag

Like their children, parents have been victims of societal prejudice and discrimination. Prior to the 1970s, parents were often faced with two choices as to what to do with children with disabilities: keep them twenty-four hours a day with no supports or institutionalize them. Many made the painful decision to place their children in institutions, often on the advice of physicians and other professionals. In many communities, parents banded together to advocate special education programs. Their efforts often resulted in the establishment of special schools for the disabled.

It should not be surprising that many parents regard current trends like mainstreaming and deinstitutionalization with suspicion and distrust. These trends threaten their security in knowing their children will always have a program to attend or a place to live.

Parent groups at some institutions have become strong opponents of deinstitutionalization. Indeed, one of the saddest legacies of institutions has been to pit parent groups against one another, with one group supporting institutions and the other deinstitutionalization. In some states, deinstitutionalization lawsuits have fractured the parent movement. For example, the Connecticut Association for Retarded Citizens' courageous decision to file suit to close the Mansfield Training School and have its residents placed into the community eventually led several of its chapters to withdraw from the association.

Institutional parent groups in some states have been active in litigation involving institutions and legislative hearings regarding institutions and deinstitutionalization. The decision by the Supreme Court to hear the *Pennhurst* case brought forth a brief from a number of parent groups across the country urging the court to mandate institutional reforms, but not community placement. In 1981 the U.S. Senate Subcommittee on the Handicapped held hearings on deinstitutionalization in Hartford, Connecticut (U.S. Government Printing Office, 1982). The list of witnesses included many of the nation's foremost experts on services for people with developmental disabilities, in addition to various state officials and representatives of parent groups. The testimony of the parents was divided between those who spoke in favor of deinstitutionalization and those who spoke against it. One parent's testimony seemed to capture the feelings of those parents who oppose deinstitutionalization:

> The national policy of deinstitutionalization has affected the mental health services by stopping improvements and/or growth in institutions, stopped hiring very badly needed personnel for the care and education of the retarded, stopped instituting new programs and thousands of dollars spent on lawsuits.
>
> The severely and profoundly retarded need constant attention, care and direction. Their best care is in an institution where they have around-the-clock care and continuity of care.
>
> All facilities are provided for them on the grounds; medical, educational and recreational. Their surroundings are always the same so that they do not have to make any adjustments. They are not frightened or frustrated. It is a safe and happy environment for them. . . .
>
> Their needs and wants are not like the normal. If they could have remained in the community not one parent would have experienced the pain and agony of placing their child in an institution. They will never be adults, even though they get to be 100 years old.
>
> Mainstreaming is wishful thinking and to place the severely and profoundly retarded in the community is cruel. Anyone who has a severely and profoundly retarded child suffers the accompanying agony of knowing that that child is a misfit in society geared for normal people.

Parental opposition to integration and deinstitutionalization is probably a temporary phenomenon. There is a new generation of parents today. With the passage of Public Law 94-142, parents are growing accustomed to having their children attend regular public schools and having them live in the community. With few exceptions, these parents will never accept institutionalization.

Good integrated programs create a demand among parents for more integrated programs. In a follow-up study of people placed in the community from the Pennhurst institutions, Conroy and Bradley (1985) have reported that the vast majority of parents support their children's placement in the community, despite initial opposition.

In 1977 the Albuquerque public schools closed their only segregated facility for children with severe disabilities (Taylor, 1982). Over 100 children and youth attended regular public schools for the first time. While some parents supported the move, others opposed it fiercely. Many feared that their children would not be safe in regular schools or would receive a substandard education. A parent group formed to fight the closing of the segregated school and organized a legal defense fund. By the end of the 1977–78 school year, however, parents originally opposed to the integration program had become strong supporters. They donated thousands of dollars collected through the defense fund to support integration at the high school.

The Professional Backlash

Early in the 1970s, there seemed to be professional consensus on the dramatic need to correct injustices against the disabled. America's institutions were overcrowded and understaffed, abusive and dehumanizing. Public schools excluded large numbers of students with disabilities. Yet professional consensus on issues confronting the field was nothing more than an illusion. Professionals, researchers, and educators always have and always will disagree on key policy issues. It is simply that it took a while for the lines of controversy to be drawn.

As the disability rights movement gained momentum, a number of noted professionals and researchers began to speak out against community placement, normalization, mainstreaming, and other trends. In articles published in professional journals and papers presented at conventions, professionals claimed that the pendulum had swung too far. Not all disabled people could be trained, they asserted, and not all could benefit from community living. Many of these professionals eventually joined forces with states embroiled in litigation to attempt to reverse the tide of reform and change.

Defending itself against the plaintiffs' claims that it had not implemented Judge Johnson's 1972 minimum constitutional standards for mental health and mental retardation institutions, the state of Alabama turned to outside help in the *Wyatt* case in 1978. It enlisted ten professionals, called the Partlow Review Committee, to testify on its behalf. In a notorious memorandum introduced into court, the committee reached some startling conclusions:

1. Only a small number of the present Partlow residents can reasonably be expected to adjust to community living.
2. The potential for behavioral improvement in a substantial number of Partlow residents is very low and training programs seem inappropriate for them.
3. The 1972 court standards set unrealistic goals and are so restrictive that professional judgment is often precluded in the treatment of individual residents.

In short, according to the Partlow Review Committee, the severely and profoundly retarded cannot learn and certainly cannot live in the community; the mildly retarded may be dangerous; one mildly retarded resident, in fact, molested a child. As we have seen, these were not new ideas. They were first set forth nearly 100 years earlier.

The Partlow Review Committee proposed a program of "enriched living" for Partlow residents: "The new emphasis will, for example, increase the need for staff to provide snacks at prescribed times, to take residents on field trips (movies, to town, fishing, sporting events, etc.), to insure quiet, restful music rooms, or TV viewing areas, or to insure that an older resident is comfortably seated and monitored outside." What they were recommending was a return to custodial care.

After the introduction of the Partlow Committee Report in the *Wyatt* case, other professionals lined up to testify in other major court cases or to express similar views in published articles (Thorne, 1979; Ellis el al., 1981). Most stopped short of endorsing the Partlow Committee's bald assertions. It was much more common for professionals and researchers to demand more "research" on the issue of institutions and deinstitutionalization (see Landesman-Dwyer, 1981). However, research seldom, if ever, answers major policy issues and dilemmas. Rather, deinstitutionalization is first and foremost a moral and ideological issue.

Some professionals have even gone as far as to question the value of Public Law 94-142. The "least restrictive environment" provisions of the law, more generally, the principle of mainstreaming, have been a favorite target. One article published by Vernon in the *Peabody Journal of Education* in 1981 refers to Public Law 94-142 as education's "three mile island." Vernon (1981, p. 24) has written:

> In reality, P.L. 94-142 is an ill-conceived law embodying a "Pollyanna-Horatio Alger-like euphoria contrary to fact perception of reality." It threatens the education of an entire generation of handicapped youth and squanders the limited educational funds available for both disabled and regular children.

Later in the article, Vernon elaborates on this theme:

> Under P.L. 42-142, we as a country will be making by far our heaviest per capita financial investments in those youths least able to contribute to society. In fact, large sums of education money normally spent on gifted or average children, most all of whom will return a dividend to society, we must invest now in children with little or no probability of ever being other than wards of the state.

The backlash to disability rights was to be expected. Every social movement generates a counter movement. That is to say, periods of social change are marked by controversy, resistance, and attempts to restore the status quo. There was no Ku Klux Klan until *after* the slaves were freed; there was no antiwomen's movement until there was a strong women's movement; and there was no backlash to disability rights until there was a strong disability rights movement.

Current trends in the field of disabilities—deinstitutionalization, integration, mainstreaming, normalization—challenge traditional practices and policies and deeply held beliefs. If there were no backlash, there would have been no progress.

The Current Scene

For the disabled, the 1980s have lacked the dramatic breakthroughs that characterized the preceding decades. It would be misleading, however, to describe the latter part of the twentieth century as merely an era of retrenchment and backlash. The momentum has slowed, but progress has not come to a halt.

The late 1970s and 1980s have witnessed the steady development of integrated educational and community service systems across the country. The populations of public institutions for the mentally retarded continue to decline. As of 1982 the number of people living in public residential institutions for the mentally retarded had declined to slightly more than 110,000 (Hauber et al., 1984).

To be sure, in some states deinstitutionalization has meant "transinstitutionalization" and "dumping" (see Scull, 1981; Warren, 1981). That is to say, people have been transferred from large public institutions to somewhat smaller but equally restrictive private ones (for example, nursing homes, private residential facilities) or left to fend for themselves in urban slums. In a study of boardinghouses and similar facilities around Los Angeles, Bercovici (1983) found that many mentally retarded people were just as isolated and segregated as they were in institutions.

As early as 1977, Blatt, Bogdan, Biklen, and Taylor warned that unless deinstitutionalization were reconceptualized, it would fail, either by inertia or backlash.

> Too often, deinstitutionalization has simply meant releasing people from state facilities by moving traditionally institutionalized people into community institutions. These have usually been nursing homes, and boarding homes that sometimes provide little more than bed and board. However, the goal of deinstitutionalization should not be simply to move people from one building to another, from one location to another, from a total-care institution to a partial-care one, or from a custodial care facility to a non-care facility. The goal should be to transform a dehumanizing, segregated institutional model of services into a humanizing, integrated community model (Blatt et al., 1977, p. 40).

Deinstitutionalization does not, or rather should not, mean simply opening up the doors to the institution. It means putting into place a system of humane and responsive support services in the community.

In a growing number of places across the country, people labeled mentally retarded and mentally ill are living and thriving in small community settings and participating in community life. In the 1970s two prominent community-based service systems for the mentally retarded emerged in eastern Nebraska (ENCOR) and the Macomb-Oakland region of Michigan (see Perske, 1979). These service systems serve a large number of people with severe and multiple disabilities in small homes dispersed throughout the community. On a more modest scale, model community programs have been

At times it is appropriate for students with disabilities to receive individual attention. Teachers can structure academic tasks to allow children to work together, thus encouraging peer support and social interaction. (Photograph by Mima Cataldo.)

developed in Rhode Island, Pennsylvania, New York, Vermont, Kentucky, and a host of other states.

These models provide tangible evidence that mentally retarded and otherwise disabled people not only *can* live in community settings, but also *are* living successfully in the community throughout the nation. For every institutionalized person, no matter how retarded or physically disabled or behaviorally challenging, there is someone with the same level of disability thriving in a community environment.

The demands for total deinstitutionalization have grown louder and stronger. In 1979 the Center on Human Policy at Syracuse University issued The Community Imperative declaration, which was subsequently endorsed by hundreds of leaders and organizations across the country.

In the domain of Human Rights:
All people have fundamental moral and constitutional rights.
These rights must not be abrogated merely because a person has a mental or physical disability.
Among these fundamental rights is the right to community living.

In the domain of Educational Programming and Human Service:
All people, as human beings, are inherently valuable.
All people can grow and develop.
All people are entitled to conditions which foster their development.
Such conditions are optimally provided in community settings.

Therefore:
In fulfillment of fundamental human rights and
In securing optimum developmental opportunities,
All people, regardless of the severity of their disabilities, are entitled to community living.

Similar positions have been adopted by the Association for Retarded Citizens of the United States, the National Society for Autistic Children and Adults, and the Association for Persons with Severe Handicaps.

How we view people structures how we treat them. If we regard the disabled as a separate category of humanity, we will treat them in ways in which we would not like to be treated. We see this in history and in our contemporary institutions. If, however, we view the disabled as people more or less like ourselves, with potentialities as well as limitations, then we are obliged to open up our communities to them and encourage their participation in social life.

> The issue of institutionalization, like the issues of slavery and apartheid, strikes at the very core, the very essence of our common humanity. Just as the emergence of Jim Crowism, the Ku Klux Klan, and racist theories of black inferiority do not and cannot justify the conclusion that black Americans were better off under slavery, neither can neighborhood resistance, exclusionary zoning codes, expert claims that some people cannot learn or even firebombing of prospective homes be combined to justify the conclusion that mentally retarded people are better off in institutions. What is at issue here is fundamental human rights and the quality of the lives of human beings. To claim that some people cannot learn, to place those same people in isolated institutions, and then to suppose that the dignity and well being of those people can be protected, let alone enhanced, is to deny history. And to suggest that some people cannot and should not live amongst their fellow human beings is to deny our shared humanness (Center on Human Policy, 1979).

Despite some setbacks, an increasing number of children with disabilities and their families have found America's schools receptive to their needs during the 1980s. By 1984 the number of handicapped children benefiting under Public Law 94-142 had risen to 4,094,108 (Education of the Handicapped, 1984). Table 2 contains a breakdown of the number of handicapped children served in each state.

Table 2
1984 Handicapped Child Count

State	Children served	State	Children served
Alabama	83,339	New Mexico	26,651
Alaska	8,312	New York	244,965
Arizona	50,499	North Carolina	117,845
Arkansas	45,305	North Dakota	11,049
California	360,588	Ohio	191,695
Colorado	41,664	Oklahoma	63,739
Connecticut	62,310	Oregon	41,480
Delaware	11,487	Pennsylvania	178,319
Florida	149,691	Rhode Island	17,945
Georgia	106,073	South Carolina	71,200
Hawaii	12,086	South Dakota	11,270
Idaho	17,578	Tennessee	102,385
Illinois	223,478	Texas	280,092
Indiana	95,430	Utah	39,548
Iowa	55,854	Vermont	7,488
Kansas	41,049	Virginia	99,609
Kentucky	71,353	Washington	63,221
Louisiana	80,582	West Virginia	41,351
Maine	25,582	Wisconsin	71,201
Maryland	88,164	Wyoming	10,161
Massachusetts	124,786	District of Columbia	2,803
Michigan	146,932	American Samoa	229
Minnesota	78,338	Bureau of Indian Affairs	5,225
Mississippi	50,450	Guam	1,649
Missouri	96,252	Northern Marianas	—
Montana	15,059	Puerto Rico	34,038
Nebraska	29,993	Trust Territories	—
Nevada	12,932	Virgin Islands	—
New Hampshire	13,438	Total	4,094,108
New Jersey	160,346		

Source: U.S. Department of Education, 1985.

The issue of mainstreaming or integration looms as a major one in special education today. Like deinstitutionalization, mainstreaming has often meant "dumping"; that is, the placement of children with disabilities in regular classes without special aids and supports. That is why many teachers, principals, and school district officials oppose the concept of mainstreaming. Just as deinstitutionalization does not have to result in dumping, neither does mainstreaming. Here again, there are many successful integration models in schools across the country (Taylor, 1982; Biklen, Bogdan, Ferguson, Searl, & Taylor, 1985).

Current trends in special education today support the integration of students with even severe disabilities (severe and profound mental retardation, severe multiple disabilities, autism, and others) in normal educational settings. States (Vermont, Hawaii, and, for autistic students, North Carolina); school districts (Madison, Wisconsin; Albuquerque, New Mexico; Tacoma, Washington; Portland and Bangor, Maine; Birmingham, Alabama; Urbana and DeKalb, Illinois); and individual schools in many states are engaged in major integration efforts for students with severe and multiple disabilities (Taylor, 1982; Thomason & Arkell, 1980). Separate schools for the handicapped are slowly closing.

For students with severe disabilities, integration does not usually mean placement in classes with nondisabled students, although this also is happening (McCollum School in Albuquerque, New Mexico; Ed Smith School in Syracuse, New York). However, it does mean involvement in a broad range of extracurricular and nonacademic activities (cafeteria, assemblies, graduate exercises, field trips, music, art, physical education classes, and joint play sessions). In addition, a number of schools have developed elaborate buddy and tutoring systems for disabled and nondisabled students.

Integrating students with severe disabilities, and perhaps all disabled students, in regular school programs requires careful planning and preparation, the creation of specialized support positions, and development of facilitative policies and other carefully planned strategies. Yet it would be inaccurate to portray integration as simply a technical matter. What distinguishes successfully integrated programs is a strong commitment to the principle of integration.

The critical issue facing educators, administrators, and parents is not whether integration can work, but how to make it work. As Wilcox and Sailor (1980, p. 282) have stated:

> In light of the professional consensus and the various legal and programmatic arguments supporting it, the appropriate question is not, "Should we do it?" Now that the basic criterion has been articulated, it is time to focus, not on further consensus, but on implementation.

Deinstitutionalization (community integration) and mainstreaming (educational integration) are not the only issues that dominate the current scene in the field of disabilities. The promise of Section 504 has yet to be fulfilled. For a time it seemed that the much heralded Section 504 would bring an end to discrimination against disabled people in employment, education, and accessibility to public facilities such as transportation. As we have seen, Section 504 has lost much of its legal clout. How far must employers, educational institutions, and public facilities go to accommodate people with disabilities? Should people with disabilities be excluded from participation in normal life simply because the society is designed around the needs of the nondisabled? The federal government and the courts are providing conservative answers to these questions. Meanwhile, disability rights groups continue to press for the same rights and privileges enjoyed by other citizens.

The area of vocational rehabilitation is just now undergoing the revolution in thinking that occurred in residential services and education a decade or so ago. For the past twenty or more years, sheltered workshops have served as the primary site for vocational training for people with disabilities. In recent years, segregated day treatment and training programs have been established for people deemed too disabled to function even in sheltered workshops.

Just as integration is becoming a guiding principle in residential services and education, so, too, is it emerging as a principle in vocational rehabilitation. The shortcomings of sheltered workshops and other segregated day programs (low or no pay, meaningless activities, low expectations, little advancement or placement) are gradually being exposed (Bellamy, Sheehan, Horner, & Boles, 1980; Greenleigh Associates, 1975). An increasing number of leaders in vocational rehabilitation are advocating integrated work stations and job sites in industry and competitive employment (with vocational supports) even for people with severe disabilities (Brown et al., 1983; Wehman, 1981).

Perhaps no disability issue so grabbed the public spotlight in the mid-1980s as the situation of a young infant in New York referred to as "Baby Jane Doe." Born in October 1983, Baby Doe came into the world with spina bifida (an incompletely closed spine) and other disabilities. Baby Doe's parents were confronted with a confusing and painful decision. Without surgery, the infant would probably die within two years. With surgery, doctors told her parents, she might live to be twenty but would be severely retarded, paralyzed, and bedridden. Acting on their doctors' advice, Baby Doe's parents decided against the life-prolonging surgery. Their decision set into motion a flurry of lawsuits filed by a right-to-life attorney and then the U.S. Department of Health and Human Services based on Section 504 (discrimination on the basis of handicap). The courts eventually struck down outside intervention in the case, siding with the parents' decision and upholding their right to privacy.

The Baby Doe issue, as it has come to be called, is not new to the medical profession. In a recent article in *Pediatrics*, a group of medical professionals in Oklahoma described a decision-making process for determining which children with myelomeningocele should live and which should die. Of twenty-four infants who received no treatment, all died, with an average life of thirty-seven days (Gross, Cox, Tatyrek, Pollay, & Barnes, 1983). The physician, Raymond Duff of the Yale–New Haven Hospital has been one of the principal advocates of withholding medical treatment from handicapped infants. Duff (1981, p. 315) has decried what he refers to as an oppressive "medical Vietnam": "costly, sometimes abusive, use of technology to ensure biologic existence with little regard for quality of child and family life and competing interests."

The Baby Doe issue is surrounded with tremendous emotion, political controversy, and misinformation. Many individuals and groups, some of which have been supporters of the rights of the disabled in schools and institutions, view the federal government's intervention in the Baby Doe issue as a thinly veiled effort to impose a right-wing right-to-life agenda on prospective and actual parents. As evidence for this view, they point out that the Baby Doe case is the only one in which the federal government has attempted to enforce Section 504 aggressively. In such personal life and death decisions, they reason, why not let the parents decide?

Yet many disability rights activists and organizations, including the Association for Retarded Citizens and the Association for Persons with Severe Handicaps, strongly support federal intervention in Baby Doe cases and condemn the practice of withholding medical treatment from anyone based on handicapping conditions. Some express extreme discomfort at the involvement of the "right-to-life" movement in this issue. "The Right," wrote Mary Johnson (1984, p. 11), "is the wrong group to plead our rights."

In discussing the Baby Doe issue, it is important to point out that no disability rights group argues that extraordinary or heroic treatments should be employed to prolong the life of a *dying* infant, child, or adult. The question is *not* whether society or the government should intervene when parents decide to decline medical treatments that have little likelihood of saving their infant's life. The question raised by the Baby Doe issue is quite different: Should society or the government intervene when medical treatment is withheld solely because of an infant's disability and presumed future quality of life? The issue thus boils down to one of discrimination on the basis of handicap, which is what Section 504 was intended to end.

When stripped to its essentials, then, the Baby Doe controversy has to do with the value we place on the lives of people with disabilities. While sometimes cloaked in terms of *hopeless medical cases*, the arguments in favor of withholding medical treatment from disabled infants reflect deeply ingrained beliefs and values about the humanity and worth of the disabled.

> The surviving child's life at home might have such a detrimental effect on the family that the child, too, would suffer excessively. Deprived of a loving home, the severely handicapped child's life in a series of foster homes or an institution would be too miserable. Choosing death sometimes is viewed as an act of love because some life can only be wrongful (Duff, 1981, p. 316).

One theologian, Joseph Fletcher (1972), has even attempted to define "humanhood" based on IQ: "Any individual of the species homo sapiens who falls below the I.Q. 40-mark in a standard Stanford Binet test, amplified, if you like, by other tests, is questionably a person, below the 20-mark, not a person." Of course, this was the same view put forth by the Nazis in their "euthanasia program": "the destruction of life devoid of value."

What about the parents of these infants? From our point of view, no one has the right to judge parents who, shocked by the unexpected birth of a disabled child, might wish to let their infant die. Yet, as a matter of public policy in our society, parents do not have absolute rights to decide the fate of their children. We have mandatory education and child abuse and neglect laws. It is also not uncommon for courts to order medical treatment for "normal" children even though their parents object to such care on religious grounds.

Do people with disabilities have the right to live in normal communities? Do they have the right to be educated alongside their nondisabled peers? Do they have the right to equal opportunities in employment, transportation, and the use of public facilities? Do they have the right to lead meaningful and productive lives? Do they have a right to equal medical care? These seem like simple questions, but they are controversial ones. As we have seen, they have been answered differently by different people at different times. As uncomfortable as these questions may make us, they cannot be wished away.

Summary

This chapter has provided an overview of the various social contexts within which to understand the development of the field of special education, broadly defined. We argued that education, and in particular, special education, should be understood within the framework of broad social forces and developments in American society. The opening sections of the chapter thus traced the connections between social and economic forces such as urbanization, industrialization and immigration, and institutions and schools. The remainder of the chapter offered a critical review of the changes and challenges in social policy that have occurred since World War II. The chapter concluded with an analysis of some of the recent controversies in social policy and the disabled.

The opening sections of the chapter developed the idea that after an initial period of reform and idealism, specialized institutions for people with disabilities became settings in which to remove and segregate disabled people (the so-called feebleminded) from society. Thus, in part, the chapter argued that in the nineteenth and early twentieth centuries, the victims of social changes—the poor, deviant, and disabled—were blamed for these same problems and removed from society.

The next section of the chapter provided a number of perspectives about the various challenges to the earlier view of the feebleminded as the root of social evils. In addition to summarizing developments and changes in social policy connected to people with disabilities, that section did the following:

· Reviewed the growth of the parent and consumer movement.
· Reported on the exposés of institutional abuse and school exclusion in the 1960s and 1970s.
· Summarized the revolution of social science perspectives about the disabled, including the work of Goffman and others.
· Provided an analysis of key legal and constitutional challenges to segregation and exclusion of disabled people, including cases such as *PARC, Mills, Wyatt, Pennhurst, Willowbrook*, and others.
· Offered an overview of the federal initiatives during the 1970s on behalf of disabled people, including Public Law 94-142, Section 504 of the Rehabilitation Act of 1973, and other legislation.

The final section of the chapter brought the issues connected to social policy and the disabled up to date. It presented a review of the changes and limitations articulated by the Supreme Court in cases such as *Youngberg v. Romeo,* as well as the *Rowley* and *Tatro* cases. Finally, there was a brief analysis of the key issues in the current social policy scene, including the controversies about the Baby Doe issues.

Part II

Understanding and Teaching Disabled Students

This section includes chapters describing disabled children's socioemotional, intellectual and cognitive, communication, and biological development. The authors recognize that each of these aspects is important in all children's development—regardless of their diagnosis. Further, a solid understanding of each aspect can contribute to effective curricula and program designs. The section thus ends with a chapter on the instructional process that is applicable to all disabled students. Granted, there are highly specialized skills that a teacher needs to have when teaching disabled children. An example is knowing how to position a child with cerebral palsy at a table so the child feels safe and can attend to the activity. The chapter by Raymond Glass includes teaching specific skills, but it focuses primarily on the basic teaching skills that should be part of all teachers' repertoires. To be an effective teacher one must integrate diverse information about each child's current status and development and structure a learning program and an environment that respond to the student's immediate needs and long-term instructional, social, and vocational goals. This is a formidable task, but one worthy of serious effort. The chapters in this section are designed to provide a range of information and perspectives in major areas of children's functioning. This book emphasizes the view that each disabled child has more than one area of functioning affected, thus understanding each of the areas described in this section is crucial to an understanding of the whole child.

This move toward an integration of information about disabled children is relatively new and is captured in the concept of developmental disabilities. In the early 1960s President Kennedy provided leadership for the formation of the President's Panel on Mental Retardation to study the broad needs of persons with mental retardation, including treatment and prevention approaches. By its recognition of the multiple needs of each disabled child, this panel provided an impetus

for defining disability in a more generic, less categorical fashion. For example, recognizing that some physically handicapped children are also mentally retarded, they requested additional funds for the crippled children's program. This type of thinking led to the passage in 1975 of Public Law 94-103, the Developmentally Disabled Assistance and Bill of Rights Act. One of the requirements of the DD Act was the creation of a national task force on the Definition of Developmental Disabilities. The consensus of the task force was to recommend a generic or functional definition, thereby avoiding the use of specified categories and conditions.

Under this act a developmental disability is a severe, chronic disability of a person that:

1. Is attributable to a mental or physical impairment or combination of mental and physical impairments.
2. Is manifest before age twenty-two.
3. Is likely to continue indefinitely.
4. Results in substantial functional limitations in three or more of the following areas of major life activity:
   a. Self-care
   b. Receptive and expressive language
   c. Learning
   d. Mobility
   e. Self-direction
   f. Capacity for independent living
   g. Economic self-sufficiency
5. Reflects the need for a combination and sequence of special, interdisciplinary, or generic care, treatment, or other services that are:
   a. Of lifelong extended duration
   b. Individually planned and coordinated

Note that there is no mention of specific disabilities; instead, the functional limitations of persons with chronic disabilities are outlined. It is also one of the few definitions that contains a statement related to a lifelong need for services and treatment.

Thompson and O'Quinn (1979) devised a

schematic for visualizing the "multiple interactions of the many factors that affect the human organism at various periods of its development and that manifest themselves in various systems of functioning" (p. 16). Their developmental disabilities cube is depicted in Figure 1.

They summarize the potential benefits of the model:

> The conceptual schema of the Developmental Disabilities Cube provides not only a method for considering the etiology and manifestations of various developmental disabilities but also a method for integrating these components with treatment and prevention. Both treatment and prevention involve environmental manipulations of some kind designed to affect manifestations. Knowledge of the possible multiple causative factors of a recent or remote occurrence for patterns of manifestations can lead, however, to a specificity of intervention. In the case of manifestations attributable to genetic chromosomal causes, prevention by genetic counseling before

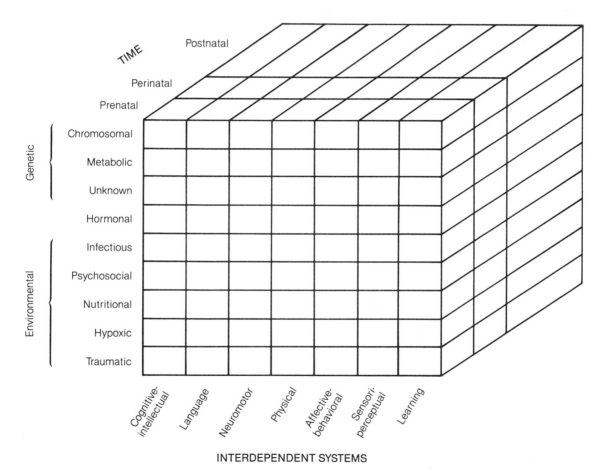

Figure 1. *Evolution of the concept of developmental disabilities. Cube depicts the interaction of etiologic factors occurring during a time period of development resulting in manifestations in various systems. (From Thompson & O'Quinn, 1979, p. 17.)*

subsequent concepts or treatment in the
form of hormone replacement can be used
for some syndromes. In the case of a genetic inborn error of metabolism, dietary
procedures after birth can actually be used
to prevent disability. Our ability to integrate
knowledge about etiology, manifestations,
and specificity of intervention needs to be
enhanced through research; it is hoped that
this schema will foster such integration (p.
18).

The chapters in this section describe ways
to integrate diverse sources of information
about children that will assist teachers in their
planning efforts. Rather than focusing exclusively on disabled children's deficits, an effort
is made to describe their competencies as
well. A more complete understanding of disabilities requires building on children's
strengths and incorporating such information
into programs that minimize children's
deficits.

Chapter 2

Mary Coleman

Deborah Olson

Mary Coleman, M.D., is a pediatric neurologist. She is particularly interested in the new-born diagnosis and later care of children with developmental handicaps. She edits the newsletters Down's Syndrome Papers and Abstracts for Professionals *and* Infant Screening *and has just completed the first medical textbook on autism,* The Biology of the Autistic Syndromes *(New York: Praeger Scientific, 1985).*

Deborah Olson is a doctoral candidate in special education at Syracuse University. She is the director of the Parent Training Project of the Parent's Information Group for Exceptional Children in Syracuse. She is also an advisor to Self-Advocates of Central New York, a self-advocacy group of people with developmental disabilities.

Medical Conditions That Affect Learning

After reading this chapter, you should be able to:

1
List the stages of early physical development and describe errors of development that may occur during each stage.

2
Recognize environmental conditions that can contribute to adverse physical development and discuss preventive efforts to reduce their potentially harmful effects.

3
Describe medical symptoms that affect learning and discuss classroom teaching practices that facilitate student learning.

At one time children with disabilities were totally excluded from school programs. Through the advocacy efforts of parents and educators, more and more disabled children found their way into the educational system, although often to segregated, self-contained classrooms and special schools. With the advent of Public Law 94-142, the Education for All Handicapped Children Act, children with disabilities could participate in school programs with varying degrees of integration into the mainstream of regular education. Today, teachers of both special and regular education see in their classrooms children with a variety of disabilities, many of them severe. This chapter attempts to describe the medical aspects of some of the disabilities commonly seen among children in school programs. It is not our aim to present teachers with an in-depth medical knowledge of these disabling conditions. Rather, we wish to acquaint teachers with some of the causes and symptoms of disabilities that affect a child's ability to participate fully in the educational environment. An understanding of the medical aspects of disabilities will enable teachers to deal more capably with the disabled child as a total person, the medical aspect being only one of the many factors teachers must consider to better serve children.

This chapter begins by describing some of the basic principles that underlie human development. Understanding the structure, growth, and development of the fetal nervous system can help us comprehend how and why disruptions that occur in the fetus result in a child born with various medical conditions. Next, the fragile nature of the fetus during the in utero period will be highlighted by a look at some toxic external agents that can interrupt or altar the delicate process of brain development. After reviewing fetal neuroanatomy, we will look at the chemical functioning of the basic unit of the nervous system, the neuron or nerve cell. An explantation of this neurochemistry will lead to a discussion of the errors that disrupt it, resulting in a variety of disorders, such as phenylketonuria. Then we will look at some of the genetic factors that contribute to specific conditions, such as Down's syndrome.

The last section of the chapter discusses specific medical symptoms that can interfere with the learning process. We will briefly review the causes and symptoms of auditory and visual impairments, learning disabilities, the autism syndromes, motor handicaps such as cerebral palsy and muscular dystrophy, and seizure disorders. A teacher may work very hard indeed, with very little result, if a child cannot adequately process in the brain what he or she is being taught. All the preceding disabilities can markedly alter the ability of a child to assimilate material. The importance of identifying medically limiting factors and building a teaching program to compensate for these limitations is one of the most challenging aspects of special education.

Brain Development and Developmental Disabilities

An understanding of the development of the nervous system in the fetus, the embryo, and the young infant gives a good foundation for understanding the brain dysfunctions that lead children to require specialized teaching strategies or materials. The processing difficulties are best understood by a look at embryology and fetal anatomy.

Early Development

Fetal neuroanatomy may be of value in understanding the causes of some of the most common malformations, such as spina bifida and hydrocephalus. The third and fourth weeks of gestation are the time when the embryological predecessor of the central nervous system can first be identified. The nervous system begins as tissue on the dorsal or upper aspect of the embryo differentiates into an elongated, shoe-shaped body called the *neural plate*. This plate is formed at approximately eighteen days of gestation. The lateral or side margins of the neural plate fold and close to form the *neural tube*. The first fusion, or closure, of the neural tube occurs at approximately twenty-three days of age (Figure 1). The process is completed approximately four days later at the posterior or bottom end of the neural tube. At this stage, the central nervous system resembles a closed tubelike structure, which will later differentiate into a brain and spinal cord.

Errors in the closure of the neural tube result in a variety of conditions commonly called spina bifida. Technically, the term *spina bifida* refers to a defect in the bony arch of the vertebrate protecting the spinal cord (Mitchell, Fiewell, & Davy, 1983). Occasionally, the covering of the spinal cord protrudes through the vertebrae in a meningocele, or membrane sac (see Figure 2). Although they require surgical correction, neither spina bifida nor meningocele necessarily impairs any motor or neurological functioning in the child.

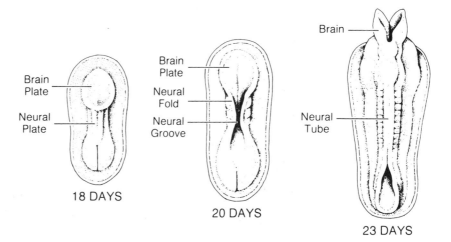

Figure 1. *Neural tube development. (From Batshaw & Perret, 1981, p. 154.)*

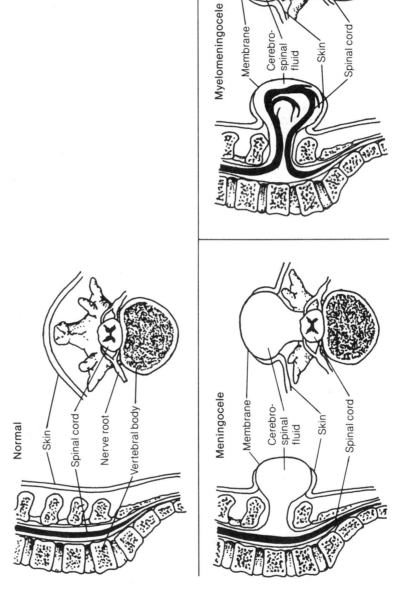

Figure 2. *Normal, spina bifida, and myelomeningocele development.*
(From Mitchell, Fiewell, & Davy, 1983, p. 118.)

Sometimes, however, the spinal cord is contained in the sac, a malformation called a *myelomeningocele.* This sac must be promptly treated surgically in order to close the opening and prevent infection. Even then, serious neurological impairments can occur. The condition of myelomeningocele is also often referred to as spina bifida because of the latter's more prevalent use and easier pronunciation; thus the practice will be continued in this chapter.

It is most likely that spina bifida occurs no later than the twenty-sixth day of gestation, the period in the fourth week, which is the time for normal neural tube closure (Volpe, 1981). An alternative explanation for the origin of this problem proposes that the neural tube closes, but is then reopened by an abnormal increase in pressure resulting from a hydrocephalic condition (Gardner, 1973).

Spina bifida comprises the single most common group of malformations, called the neural tube defects, which includes other syndromes occurring during this early stage of development. Examples are anencephaly (absence of most or all of the cranial portion of the brain) and encephalocele (a portion of the brain protruding outside the skull, probably a defect of neural tube closure in its anterior, or frontal, end).

Hydrocephalus is a serious complication of about 70 percent of the patients with spina bifida. The brain and the spinal cord are protected and cushioned by cerebrospinal fluid produced in four cavities, or ventricles, in the brain. This fluid, circulated over the base of the brain and the spinal cord, is reabsorbed over the surface of the brain. If this flow of fluid is blocked at any point, it backs up, causing the ventricles to swell and producing pressure on the brain. If untreated, this pressure affects the base of the brain, the respiration and cardiac control centers, and leads to death. Fortunately, surgical treatment exists. A bypass, called a shunt, is inserted into one of the ventricles, draining the fluid through a long plastic tube into the abdominal cavity (see Figure 3).

Hydrocephalus also is associated with the Arnold-Chiari malformation, in which there is displacement of the brain stem into the upper spinal canal, resulting in elongation and thinning of the brain stem. Also, another section of the brain, the cerebellum, may be displaced downward into the upper spinal canal area. Malformation in the lower portion of the cranium probably blocks the flow of fluid, causing increased fluid build-up inside the brain.

The incidence of these neural tube defects varies markedly between geographic areas. Like most disease entities, they appear to be due to a combination of both genetic and environmental factors. In a study conducted in Boston (Naggan & MacMahon, 1967), ethnic differences were found between the Irish (4.9/thousand) and the Jews (0.77/thousand). It has been noted, however, that the incidence in Ireland was 8.7/thousand and there is a decrease to 4.9/thousand in children whose mothers lived in the United States but were born in Ireland. There is a greater decrease to 3.1/thousand in children whose parents were second- or third-generation Irish.

A generation ago, children born with spina bifida were usually left to

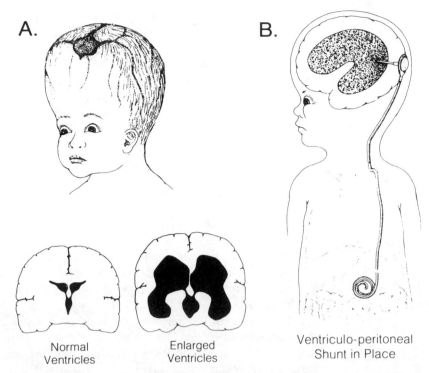

Normal Ventricles

Enlarged Ventricles

Ventriculo-peritoneal Shunt in Place

Figure 3.   *Hydrocephalus. A. The head is enlarged as is the "soft spot." A cross-section of the brain shows markedly enlarged lateral ventricles. B. A ventriculo-peritoneal shunt has been placed. A tube is inserted into the lateral ventricle and is attached to a pumping mechanism on the surface of the skull. A second tube runs from the pump under the skin and is inserted into the abdominal cavity. Enough extra tubing is left in the abdomen to uncoil as the child grows. The block is bypassed, and cerebrospinal fluid can then flow directly from the ventricles to the abdominal cavity. (From Batshaw & Perret, 1981, p. 167.)*

die. In the late 1950s, however, early closure of the spinal defect and intensive therapy for the problems associated with it became possible. In the modern era of medicine, immediate surgical closure of the opening as soon as possible after birth is recommended. Modern medicine thus has made it feasible to save the lives of many afflicted children and to improve their functional levels. Spina bifida, however, presents a complicated medical condition that may be related to a variety of other disabilities: paralysis, orthopedic problems, hydrocephalus, incontinence, mental retardation, and other congenital difficulties. The severity of these associated disabilities often varies, depending on the individual child and on early treatment. For example, the extent of paralysis depends on the location of the lesion, or opening, on the spinal cord. Some children may have other orthopedic problems associated with the paralysis, such as scoliosis, or curvature of the spine, and poor or delayed fine and gross motor development.

Spina bifida has often been associated with mental retardation. In reality the incidence of mental retardation has decreased, predominantly because of prompt and aggressive medical care, particularly in the treatment of hydrocephalus. Some children may have learning disabilities, poor motor-visual coordination and perception, and difficulty with attention span. Teachers of children with spina bifida should be aware that often they have undergone long hospital stays for multiple operations. They may also have poor self-care skills and low self-esteem. Thus, as with any child, teachers must look at the total socioemotional and physical well-being of the child with spina bifida.

The Next Stages of Development in the Fifth and Sixth Weeks

In the fifth and sixth weeks of gestation, growth occurs at the rostral or top end of the embryo, affecting the formation of much of the face as well as the forebrain. Disorders of brain development at this time can thus cause facial anomalies.

Examples of patients in whom errors may have occurred during this period are children whose eyes are spaced quite widely apart—or who have malformations of the nose, mouth, and palate, such as cleft lip and cleft palate and a flattening of the nose. The most extreme example of an error in this period is the facial anomaly that results in a single median eye (the so-called cyclops) or even no eye at all. In the group of patients with the more severe of these syndromes, often a chromosomal disorder (usually involving the thirteenth or the eighteenth chromosome) has been found. Only infants with the more mild form of these anomalies survive to reach childhood.

After the Seventh Week of Gestation

Starting with the seventh week of age and continuing through early infancy, the brain then starts developing its cells (neurons). During the third to fifth months of gestation, neurons are migrating to specific sites throughout the central nervous system. Errors that occur during this migration period may include the results of fetal alcohol syndrome; tuberous sclerosis, a disease often associated with seizures and brain tumors; and neurofibromatosis, a disorder in which tumors appear along the central nervous system.

The Last Developmental Stage

The last stage of brain formation occurs with the development of neuronal axons and dendrites. Each neuron contains dendrites, which receive information from other neurons. The information travels the length of armlike structures, called axons, to the body of the neuron (see Figure 4). This stage of development includes the perinatal or birth process. Difficulties in the birth process can alter the development of these neuronal axons and dendrites.

The neuronal connecting structures are wrapped in a special lipid coating of myelin. The time period of myelinization in a human being is quite long, beginning as early as the second trimester of pregnancy and actually continuing into early adult life. Myelinization progresses rapidly shortly after birth, and diseases that affect the brain in young infants can seriously damage this important process.

Toxicity and Fetal Development

During the entire gestational period, the brain of the fetus may be harmed both by the absence of certain nutrients and the presence of injurious agents. In the case of spina bifida, evidence suggests that adequate nutrition, especially adequate amounts of folate and vitamin B_6, may be necessary to prevent the expression of this malformation (Smithels et al., 1980). On the other hand, it has been established that certain environmental substances, such as lead, mercury, organic solvents, carbon monoxide, and ionizing radiation, can poison the brain of a young fetus. Another factor is extreme alcohol intake by the expectant mother.

With accumulation of data regarding the various adverse effects on the fetus by numerous agents, many pregnant women are immersed in guilt if they have a glass of wine occasionally or smoke a cigarette, much less take any kind of drug for a headache or a stomach pain. There is also evidence that a pregnant woman may harm the fetus by taking a sauna bath, for example,

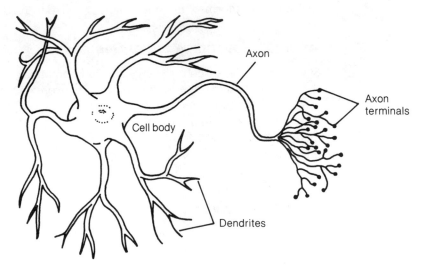

Figure 4. *A nerve cell. (From Lefton & Valvatne, 1983, p. 55.)*

since sharp temperature rises may cause brain defects in the fetus. Most fetuses, however, are not affected by an expectant woman's moderate indulgence.

At the present time, rapidly accumulating evidence indicates that the major teratogen in the United States appears to be alcohol. From a neurological point of view, microcephaly and mental retardation are known to be principal features of the fetal alcohol syndrome. The neuropathological findings suggest that many of the malformations in the brain come from errors of migration of the neuronal elements after the seventh week of gestation. Most women who have had these children seem to be in the older childbearing age group, suggesting either that the consumption of alcohol increases with age or that the effect of protection by the placenta decreases with age. The cases reported so far have all been associated with consumption of large amounts of alcohol during gestation; thus it is difficult to decide whether to advise pregnant women that *any* alcohol would have an adverse effect on developing fetuses.

In summary, fetal neuroanatomical development can be quite revealing about the etiology of some of the syndromes seen in living children. Starting with the early formation of the neural tube, moving through the period of neuronal growth and migration, and ending in the organization and myelinization periods of the brain, the sensitivity of the young brain to insults and the resultant type of disease process can be more fully understood.

The next section of this chapter presents the basic unit of the nervous system, the neuron, or nerve cell. Disruptions in the functioning of the chemical process in the neuron lead to a number of diseases, including phenylketonuria.

Neurons and Their Neurochemistry

The brain, along with the spinal cord of which it is an extension, comprises the *central nervous system*. The rest of the nervous system consists of the peripheral nervous system, which extends through the rest of the body. The peripheral nervous system consists of the somatic nervous system and the autonomic nervous system. The somatic nervous system controls muscle movement. The autonomic nervous system, in turn, consists of the sympathetic nervous system and the parasympathetic nervous system. The parasympathetic system regulates normal human functioning, such as digestion, heart rate, and blood pressure. The sympathetic nervous system is activated in emergencies. It prepares the body for the fight-or-flight reaction by increasing the heart rate and blood pressure and by decreasing the secretion of digestive fluids.

The smallest functional unit of the nervous system is the neuron, or nerve cell. Neurons come in different shapes and sizes, but one feature common to most neurons is that the branches of the axons, or dendrites, are separated by a very small space, called a synapse, from the dendrites of the next neuron

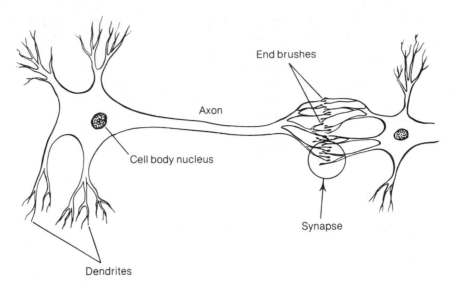

Figure 5. *A nerve cell synapse. (From Edwards, 1968, p. 33.)*

(see Figure 5). Neurons have the ability to produce an electrical current that travels down the axon until it reaches the synapse separating it from the next neuron.

Neurotransmitters are the chemicals that continue the effect of the electrical current by carrying the impulse across the synapse. Chemically formed in the nerve cell body, they are transmitted down the axon to the dendrites. When the electrical impulse goes down the axon and arrives at the end of the neuron, it causes the discharge of the neurotransmitters, which are then released across the synapse. The neurotransmitters cause a change in the permeability of the next neuron, which, if large enough, will allow the electrical impulse to travel on its course through the next neuron. Improper functioning of the neurotransmitters causes disruptions in the flow of impulses throughout the central nervous system.

There are metabolic diseases that cause improper functioning of the brain by affecting the creation or release of neurotransmitters. An example of a metabolic disease that interferes with neurotransmission is phenylketonuria (PKU). In the case of PKU, the beginning of an important pathway in the making of neurotransmitters is blocked. This block occurs because the enzyme phenylalanine hydroxylase is not working properly, either because it is too deficient or because of deficient cofactors involved in its working.

The result of this single enzyme defect is devastating to the child. Not only is a major pathway that makes important neurotransmitters such as dopamine and norepinephrine blocked, but also the minor metabolites that accumulate in the body because of the blocked pathway have toxic effects on the brain, including the neuronal elements and the myelin sheath covering them.

Phenylketonuric infants appear normal at birth. If the patients are not treated during the first two months of life, however, they begin to become irritable and to have unexplained vomiting. By four to nine months of age, the delayed intellectual impairment becomes apparent. The mental retardation may be quite severe, and untreated patients usually have IQs below fifty (Menkes, 1980). Seizures can start before eighteen months of age. The children are usually blonder than the members of their family (the enzyme phenylalanine is also the precursor of one of the major pigmenting pathways in the body). Their skin may be rough and dry, and sometimes they have eczema. As the children get older they become hyperactive and restless, and eventually they begin self-injurious behavior.

The only successful treatment is prevention of further damage from the blocking of phenylalanine by placing the child on a special diet that is very low in the amino acid phenylalanine. The disease, since it cannot be detected by clinical means, is part of a newborn screening program in which the blood of infants is tested in the first week of life. Phenylketonuria is a genetic disease because it is inherited.

Genetic Factors in Developmental Disabilities

In 1840 the Swiss botanist Nägeli looked in the nuclei of plants and described threadlike structures. In 1888 Waldemeyer coined the term *chromosome,* but it was beyond the scope of research in the nineteenth century to understand the role of these structures in the nuclei of all living cells.

At the beginning of the twentieth century, Mendel's laws of inheritance were reexamined, and the concept of assortment and independent segregation of hereditary traits became generally accepted. In the first decade of the century, it was finally understood that the hereditary traits were carried on the chromosomes. The term *gene,* to describe these hereditary traits, was coined in 1909 by Johannsen (Zellweger & Simpson, 1977).

Today we understand that defects in whole chromosomes or defects in single genes carried on them can cause developmental disability syndromes in a child. A single gene, which has mutated, can thus result in an abnormal single enzyme, such as the enzyme defects that affect neurotransmission in phenylketonuria.

In addition to single mutant genes, there also can be abnormalities of entire chromosomes. The actual loss of a chromosome is usually fatal to the fetus, but many people survive errors in the development of chromosomes that result in an extra chromosome.

The number of human chromosomes in most cells is 46, consisting of 23 pairs. Thus 23 (half of 46) is the number found in the reproductive cells (sperm and ova). If an error causes either the ovum or the sperm to have

24 chromosomes, then the resulting individual will end up with 47, rather than 46 chromosomes.

In the spring of 1959, Lejeune et al. (1959), in France, and Jacob et al. (1959), in England, discovered an extra chromosome in patients with Down's syndrome, or mongolism as it was then called. In the same year, two other well-defined clinical entities, Turner's (missing an X chromosome) syndrome and Klinefelter's (having an extra X chromosome) syndrome, were identified. This discovery, that chromosomal aberrations can cause disability in children, came as a revelation and led to a veritable explosion of cytogenetic research. Today it has been estimated that one in every 142 newborn infants has a chromosomal anomaly (Cohen & Nadler, 1983).

When a child is born with 47 chromosomes, the child is said to have trisomy because one of the 23 pairs has 3 chromosomes instead of having 2 chromosomes (bisomy). Trisomy is believed to occur during the stage of cell division called meiosis, in which a cell with 46 chromosomes divides in half to make an ovum or a sperm. During meiosis the cells line up and neatly separate into 2 new cells containing 23 chromosomes. Failure to line up and separate properly is called nondisjunction. It is believed to be the cause of the resulting trisomic individual when the cell with 24 chromosomes unites with a normal cell with 23 chromosomes, resulting in 47 chromosomes. A more thorough description of genetics and heridity is not possible in this brief review, but is available elsewhere to the interested reader (Singer, 1978; Thompson, 1979).

Down's Syndrome

Individuals with Down's syndrome have a trisomy of the 21st out of the 23 pairs. They thus have 3 chromosomes of the 21st type.

In order to have the Down's syndrome phenotype or physical characteristics, it is now known that there must be trisomy or extra material. It is this small segment of extra material that is responsible for the clinical characteristics associated with Down's syndrome. Down's syndrome children are born in approximately 1 of every 800 births in the United States.

It has been well understood for a long time that Down's syndrome children are more likely to be born to older mothers. If one looks at the rates compared to the age of the mother, there is a strikingly significant change in rate that occurs about the age of 30 and continues to rise every year as the mother becomes older (Pueschel & Rynders, 1982). At the maternal age of 40, Down's syndrome children occur at about 1 in every 100 births.

Because Down's syndrome is associated with increased maternal age, it has always been assumed that the ovum of the mother contained the abnormal cell bearing the extra chromosome. With modern techniques of studying nondisjunction, however, it has been found that in 20 percent of the cases it was the father, rather than the mother, that contributed the extra chromosome (Mikkelsen, 1982).

Physical Characteristics. Children with Down's syndrome have a number of physical characteristics that are apparent to a trained observer. One of their most striking characteristics is their oblique palpebral fissures, or slanted eyes, which led to the original erroneous name "mongolism" given them in 1855 by John Langdon Down, who was influenced by the Darwinian concepts of his age. Dr. Down is given credit for identifying the syndrome, although we now know that there is evidence indicating that these children have existed for centuries. There is even evidence that in the Olmec culture of 3,000 years ago, Down's syndrome individuals were revered, perhaps even idolized, because they were believed to be the offspring of the mating between a male jaguar and an Olmec woman. Jaguars were worshiped by many ancient peoples because of their great strength and cunning (Milton & Gonzalo, 1974).

Other facial characteristics include Brushfield spots in the iris ("stars in the eyes"), a flat nasal bridge, a dysplastic or small ear, and a protruding, sometimes furrowed tongue. The shape of the head of Down's syndrome children is called brachycephaly, meaning "round head." (This, of course, is also seen in many normal individuals, as is true of almost any of the signs seen in the developmentally delayed child.) The children also have anomalies of the hand, such as a transverse palmar crease, a short fifth finger with

This child can profit from physical support to function at a table with his peers. His teacher has placed him on her lap and guides his hand as he draws. (Photograph by Mima Cataldo.)

underdevelopment of the middle segment of it, as well as distinctive feet with a gap between the first and second toes.

Young infants have prominent hypotonia, or poor muscle tone characterized by floppiness. Also, between 30 and 40 percent of these children have clinically significant cardiac disease. Down's syndrome children, because of their hypotonia, are usually late with their motor milestones. The average age of walking is twenty-two months in most Down's syndrome clinics in the United States. Because most of them walk, run, and play, these milestones have relatively little significance.

Language Delay.   A more serious problem is the acquisition of language, which is often markedly delayed. For generations, this delay was assumed to have resulted from cognitive defects. In the last ten years, however, it has become clear that structural abnormalities and infections of the ear may be one important factor in speech delays and mispronunciations made by Down's syndrome children (Northern, 1980). There are up to eleven problem areas in the ear (Coleman & Balkany, 1983). One major problem is the increased acute and chronic middle ear infections that prevent them from attending school and can chronically interfere with their hearing, even when they are not apparently ill. In the modern understanding of Down's syndrome, these hearing problems are corrected by medical treatments and have enhanced the rate of language acquisition in many children. It is hard to overstate the importance of ear problems, which significantly increase their handicap in the language area. The problem begins early, as up to 15 percent of very young Down's syndrome infants have developed an ear infection before leaving the hospital nursery.

Thyroid Disease.   Another medical area of concern in Down's syndrome children is thyroid disease. Although less than 1 percent of Down's syndrome infants are hypothyroid at birth, by the time they are adults, 46 percent will have developed one or more abnormal tests of thyroid function (Murdoch, Ratcliffe, McLarty, Rodger, & Ratcliffe, 1976). If hypothyroidism develops early, it seriously impairs mental function, and in later childhood it is associated with obesity and behavior disorders in this group of children.

Potential and Brain Development.   What is the mental potential of Down's syndrome children? This question is difficult to answer. In 1954, for example, a paper entitled "Two Mongols of Unusually High Mental Status" described patients with Stanford-Binet IQs of 42 and 44 (Strickland, 1954). Today, patients of such levels tend to be in the *lowest* quarter of the population of a Down's syndrome clinic.

If one looks at Down's syndrome brains in pathological studies, one finds that they are smaller on the average because many of the patients are microcephalic. Quantitative analysis of the cerebral cortex, however, has shown very little hard evidence of other abnormalities. Biochemical studies in Down's syndrome contradict each other, but the majority seem to indicate normal levels of most metabolites studied. Detailed pathological studies have shown increased, normal, or decreased levels of neurons and their dendrites and the tiny spines that protrude from each dendrite.

Although pathological studies do not consistently reveal gross abnormalities in Down's syndrome brains, neurophysiological studies have indicated that the rate of glucose utilization in the brain is increased (Schwartz et al., 1983). This increased rate is consistent with the numerous studies that have demonstrated increased enzyme functions in many important enzyme systems in Down's syndrome. It is not surprising to see that the effect of extra genetic information is to increase rates of metabolism.

Thus, we return to the question of why Down's syndrome children today are functioning at such a significantly higher level than children thirty years ago, even though they continue to have the same extra chromosome and presumably the same biochemical, physiological, and pathological findings. The answer lies with improved educational and medical support. Probably the single most significant factor has been the development of infant stimulation and infant learning programs. The plasticity and potential of the very young human brain is only beginning to be understood. In animals there is evidence that enhanced sensory experiences affect neural structure, physiology, behavior, weight of the cortex, and DNA/RNA ratios (Lund, 1978; Mistretta & Bradley, 1978; Rosenzweig and Bennett, 1978). Morgan and Winnick (1979) have shown that environmental stimulation increases levels of ganglioside N-acetyl-neuraminic acid (NANA), which is thought to be a measure of the broadening of dendrites. Broader dendrites may facilitate passage of the electrical impulse through the neuron. One of the most interesting articles in the field shows that enriched maternal care and loving may actually induce enzymes (Butler, 1978).

Evidence for the long-term benefits from infant stimulation programs for Down's syndrome children is still being collected, but there is no longer any doubt that some significant benefit is occurring (Rynders, Spiker, & Horrobin, 1978; Bricker, Carlson, & Schwarz, 1981; Aronson & Falklstrom, 1977).

Down's syndrome patients do not usually live a full lifespan. There is considerable evidence for decline in mental functioning and a sharply increasing mortality rate in the fifth decade. Often there are signs of dementia, with mood changes and physical signs of premature aging (Wisniewski & Kozlowski, 1982). These changes have been compared to changes that are seen in presenile dementia, or Alzheimer's disease.

Other Chromosomal Syndromes

In addition to Down's syndrome, there are three other major chromosomal syndromes that are relatively common among live-born infants, each being roughly one in 1,000 live births. These three syndromes are all errors involving the 23rd pair of chromosomes, the two chromosomes that determine the sex of the infant. These three syndromes are the XXY syndrome in males, the XYY karyotype in males, and the XXX syndrome in females.

In the case of Klinefelter's (XXY) syndrome, mental retardation, if present, is usually mild and may not be much more frequent than in the general population. Aside from infertility, most affected males lead normal lives.

The XYY karyotype is not called a syndrome because there appears to be little clinical effect of the extra Y chromosome. A stigma originally was attached to the XYY males because the original studies carried out in a prison population reported an association with aggressive antisocial behavior. A recent Danish/American study did find that these individuals are slightly more likely to have an elevated crime rate, but found it was not related to aggression, but rather to other handicaps such as learning disabilities.

The XXX females (sometimes called super females) have no characteristic phenotype; they are usually identified by chance, as in a screening program. Recent studies, however, have suggested that there may be an increased frequency of some delay of both motor and speech development, some mild intellectual and cognitive problems, and an increased incidence of disturbed interpersonal relationships. Among females, sometimes four or five X's have been found, and mental retardation increases with increasing numbers of the X chromosome.

Other Medical Symptoms That Affect Learning

We usually think of the learning process in a rather typical fashion: for a child to be intact enough for learning, an elaborate system of neurological functioning must be in optimal condition. For the receptive part of learning, the child's visual and auditory systems must be intact at the eye and ear level and then the visual and auditory systems in the brain must also be functional. Also, at the brain (cortical) level the child must be able to focus on the problem, that is, have a long enough attention span to deal with the material coming in. Then on the expressive side of learning, the child must be able to express either through verbal language or through sign language the answers sought. In addition, the child's motor system must be intact so the child can have use of his or her hands for drawing and handwriting, and the motor system should be intact enough for the child to run around the classroom and play on the playground.

As teachers of children with special needs, however, we see a variety of children for whom this description does not fit. In the last section of this chapter, therefore, we will look at disabilities affecting auditory and visual processing, the learning disabilities, the autistic syndromes, motor handicaps, and seizure disorders. All these conditions affect the child's ability to function in the classroom and challenge the creative teacher to use techniques and strategies designed to facilitate optimal learning in the least restrictive environment.

Auditory Processing

The ability to process sound and language through an intact peripheral ear system into the thinking portions of the brain is critical for learning. There are three types of hearing loss that will affect this process: conductive, sensorineural, and mixed (Ballantyne, 1977). Conductive hearing loss occurs with damage to the external or middle part of the ear. Damage to the inner ear or the auditory nerve that transmits impulse to the brain results in sensorineural hearing loss. Mixed hearing loss occurs with both conductive and sensorineural hearing loss.

For half of all children with hearing impairments, no known cause exists. For the remaining half, loss may be caused by middle ear infections, genetic factors, and intrauterine infections (Batshaw & Perret, 1981).

The most common type of hearing loss, mild to moderate conductive hearing loss, results from middle ear infections. It is estimated that each year in the United States there are a million operations in which tympanostomy tubes are inserted for persistent middle ear effusions. This tube equalizes pressure between the ear canal and the middle ear, allowing fluid to drain. After a middle ear infection, fluid retention or middle ear infusions sometimes persist relentlessly. There is even some evidence that otherwise normal children can have their future learning slightly impaired by these persistent middle ear infections. The effects of these infections in very young normal children may, in some cases, result in substantial delay in speech and language, disturbances in auditory and visual integration, and impaired ability to read and spell (Zinkus, Gottlieb, & Schapiro, 1978; Paradise, 1981).

Genetic factors cause over half of the more severe sensorineural hearing losses (Konigsmark & Gorlin, 1976). More than seventy types of hereditary deafness have been identified. Intrauterine infections such as rubella and other viruses are also likely to cause severe hearing loss.

If children with hearing impairments are to benefit from educational opportunities, they must have aids for hearing and communication. Hearing aids improve the hearing of most children by raising the level of sound to one they can hear. Communication assistance, whether oral, manual, or a combination of the two, is usually necessary to enable a child to participate in the learning environment. Many children with severe or profound hearing loss have successfully learned to use a communication board or a specialized computer for learning.

Visual Perceptual Problems

The peripheral organ for vision, of course, is the eye. It is currently estimated that there are 500,000 legally blind persons in the United States, which results in a prevalence of 225 per 100,000 persons (National Society for the Prevention of Blindness, 1977). Causes of blindness in children are many. Intrauterine viral infections and malformations in the development of the visual apparatus of the fetus are the most common causes of visual impairments. Other causes can be infections, tumors, or trauma after birth. Retrolental fibroplasia (RLF) was once a frequent cause of damaged vision in premature infants in the 1940s and the early 1950s. Premature infants with respiratory difficulties were treated with 100 percent oxygen until it was discovered that this high concentration of oxygen destroyed blood vessels in the eye. Premature infants are now treated with lower levels of oxygen.

The effect of blindness on the brain is related to a number of factors, particularly the age at which it occurs. It has been known for some time that removal of congenital cataracts of adults does not restore vision to normal. Normal vision requires learning at an early age and results from the inner action of visual experience with genetically determined complex, anatomical organizations in both the retina and the brain.

Much work has been done on the anatomic and physiological changes occurring in blinded or visually deprived animals. If chimpanzees are reared in darkness, there are alterations of the retinal ganglia cells. Visual blinding in infancy results in degeneration in neuronal pathways of the visual system.

Information about anatomic changes in the brain of a child resulting from early loss of vision is less documented, of course, than that which has been recorded from studies of animals. If children have strabismus of a marked variety and it is not corrected, visual acuity will be permanently impaired, a fact that is now well documented. Input from the nonfixating eye is thought to be suppressed, thus avoiding double vision. Astigmatic children for whom corrective lenses were prescribed after age six have a permanent vision impairment, a situation that will not develop in a child for whom glasses are prescribed by age three.

The development of blind infants is somewhat different than that of sighted infants. The blind infants' lack of eye contact, their relative lack of facial expression, and the fact that they do not turn toward a voice for several months, cause distress in parents because they may seem apathetic or unresponsive (Fraiberg, 1977). Children blind from birth may be developmentally delayed in muscle tone and motor skills during the first few years. Many blind children do not walk until after 2½ years of age (Adelson & Fraiberg, 1974). Blind babies tend to smile later and less often than sighted babies. Even vocalization tends to be sparse in the first year of life. The blind infant has difficulty in constructing a mental image in space; this child thus needs special help in spatial orientation. Also, the blind child's sensitivity may be impaired. Sight appears to play a major role in building body image. Facilitating a child's body image can be achieved in specially designed classroom strategies. Children with visual impairments need specially adapted learning aids in the classroom such as large print materials or tape-recorded books. Children with no sight may learn braille and require special tutoring assistance. Mobility training is of crucial importance, beginning at an early age, if a child is to learn self-confidence and become as independent as possible.

Learning Disabilities

A learning-disabled child is one who appears typical but has trouble learning in school. In Public Law 94-142, learning disability is defined as "a disorder in one or more of the basic psychological processes involved in understanding or in using language, spoken or written, which may manifest itself in an imperfect ability to listen, speak, read, write, spell or do mathematical calculations" (U.S. Office of Education, 1977). While this definition appears to be a catch-all category, the majority of children labeled learning disabled exhibit reading problems (Batshaw & Perret, 1981).

Dyslexia. Reading disabilities, often called dyslexia, may range from the inability to recognize patterns of letters (e.g., "threw" for "through") to the more serious inability to associate symbols with sounds (e.g., "thruee" for "threw"). The essential feature of dyslexia is a significant impairment of development of reading skills that is not accounted for by chronological age, mental age, or inadequate schooling. If tests of intellectual capacity have been done, the child's performance often is significantly below his or her potential. Dyslexic children have a chronic condition, the correction of which requires special education skills. In their history, they sometimes have manifested delayed motor milestones, minor neurological findings, and problems with attention span.

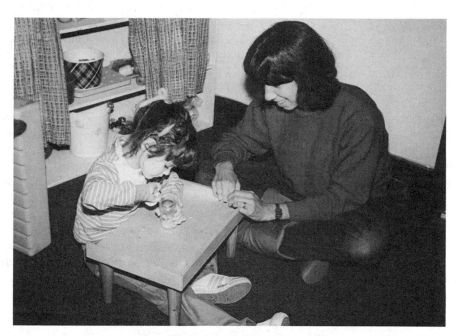

Students need to function independently. This teacher remains close to the child, offering support and guidance, but allowing the child the opportunity to complete the task. (Photograph by Mima Cataldo.)

Mathematics and Writing Disorders.   Two other types of learning disorders involve mathematics and writing. Disorders of calculation, or dyscalculia, are the failure to acquire basic mathematical skills at the expected rate, despite generally normal intelligence, educational opportunity, and emotional stability. As is the case with other specific learning disorders, the diagnosis of dyscalculia is more secure if the child is achieving satisfactorily in other basic skills.

Disorders of writing or dysgraphia are a more complicated syndrome, relating both to cognitive and motor skills. This group of disorders of written language is characterized by difficulty in one or more of the following: fluency, legibility, spelling, and written grammar. Many of these children also have a reading disability, although some children have dysgraphia.

Regardless of the type of learning disability, early identification of the problem is critical. Left unchecked, the child falls further and further behind in school. Psychological or behavioral problems may follow, as the child is unable to effectively cope with his or her environment.

Causation and Treatment.   The etiology of learning disability is unclear. A family history may reveal other family members with similar problems, indicating that genetic factors may be involved. A thorough medical history may also reveal episodes of chronic middle ear infections. Persistent middle ear infections can be treated successfully by myringotomy tubes, antibiotics, and decongestant medicines. Therefore, this particular cause of learning disability in otherwise normal children, as well as increased difficulty with learning in developmentally handicapped children, is a potentially preventable medical problem.

Once the problem is identified, two major courses of treatment for learning disabilities may be undertaken (Batshaw & Perret, 1981). One course is to attempt to alleviate the perceptual deficit. Treatments may include special diet and exercise, visual training exercises, megavitamin therapy, or alpha-wave conditioning. There are, however, insufficient studies to prove the effectiveness of any of these treatment claims. The second major and most professionally acceptable approach employs educational strategies to compensate for perceptual difficulties. No single education technique, however, appears to work best with all children. Each program must be individually tailored to meet the child's particular disability and learning style. Educational approaches may range from a multisensory, synthetic alphabet method (Orton, 1937) to a language experience approach (Benton & Pearl, 1978) to coding letters with colors. The creative, inventive teacher may have to use many methods before finding one that fits a particular child.

The Autistic Syndromes

Autism is a complex syndrome that is not easily defined or treated, either medically or educationally. Leo Kanner in 1943 originally described a child with early infantile autism as one with the following characteristics:

- Profound withdrawal from contact with people.
- Obsessive desire for the preservation of sameness.
- Skillful and even affectionate relationships to objects.
- Retention of an intelligent and pensive physiognomy and good cognitive potential manifested, in those who could speak, in feats of memory, and revealed in mute children by their facility with performance tests, especially the Seguin form board.
- Mutism, or the kind of language that does not seem intended to serve interpersonal communication (Everard, 1976, p. 2).

This description, however, neither adequately described many children labeled autistic nor provided useful guidelines or prescriptions for treatment or education. The National Society for Autistic Children thus responded with a more comprehensive definition that attempts to take into account the many diagnostic questions about autism and questions of etiology and treatment (Ritvo & Freeman, 1978). The shorter, working version of this definition not only describes the common characteristics of autism, but also refers to the syndrome's incidence: it occurs in approximately five out of every 10,000 births and is four times more common in boys than in girls. It includes reference to intellectual functioning; 20 percent have IQ scores greater than 70, 20 percent fall between 70 and 50, while 60 percent have IQ scores below 50. This definition contains implications for teachers by stating that specific, individually designed behavioral programs have been the most effective education programs (Ritvo & Freeman, 1978).

One of the interesting features of autism, the languuage pattern or lack of language, has long intrigued professionals. Children with autism appear to be more impaired in the receptive language area than do aphasic patients, and they seem to have a more global delay of language development than do retarded children of comparable mental age. Their failure of auditory competence in the receptive component of language can be demonstrated by their lack of ability to extract the details of structured auditory input.

In addition to difficulty with perceiving language, autistic children have problems with other auditory and, in fact, most perceptual responses to sensory stimuli. One explanation of the underlying mechanisms causing these symptoms is a failure of consistent processing of many sensory pathways or "perceptual inconstancy" (Ornitz & Ritvo, 1968). The identical sensory input from the environment may not be experienced in the same way each time by the autistic child. This variance may result from an imbalance in the regulation of the resting state of excitation of the brain, which could then produce inappropriate amplification, decreased amplification, or major distortion of apparently innocuous stimuli. Except for olfactory processing or smelling, all the other sensory modalities may be involved in perceptual inconstancy. Autistic children may smell a toy rather than feel, look at, or listen to it. They may have inconstant responses to a variety of sounds other than language, and deafness is usually suspected when an autistic child is young. Yet, they may hold their hands over their ears to diminish sounds in the presence of emotional talking or loud sounds. Their perceptual problems also relate to the tactile area, as exemplified by a child stiffening in the mother's arms, and to the optical area, in which gaze aversion has been documented.

Autistic children can be ritualistic and compulsive, but both habits can be used by a skilled teacher to reinforce learning. For example, a daily routine and well-organized, planned activities will help a child feel more comfortable in the classroom environment. Children often have an obsessive desire for sameness and have difficulty changing their schedule or moving from one classroom to another.

Kanner (1943) and Bettelheim (1967) attributed autism to parent, particularly maternal, ineffectiveness. Many parents, in fact, are still traumatized by contact with psychoanalytically oriented physicians. Professionals now know, however, that the autism syndromes may have many organic etiologies (Coleman & Gillberg, 1985). Much recent research has focused on brain dysfunctioning. Rimland (1964) and DesLauriers and Carlson (1969), for example, both proposed a theory of a neurophysiological disorder in the arousal system of the brain, which would account for the unresponsiveness of many autistic children. Other research has focused on autism as an auditory deficit. In autistic children, peripheral hearing may be totally intact, but when sounds or language reach the auditory cortex, they may not be processed normally, as measured by EEG auditory evoked potential studies. Thus, these children have a profound difficulty with language and some of them never attain meaningful speech.

Children with autism present a tremendous challenge to school systems. At one time, these children were totally excluded from educational opportunities, but Public Law 94-142 has afforded them the right to an education appropriate for their needs. Early educators felt that the severity of autism required intensive one-to-one programming in segregated classrooms. Now, professionals recognize that intensive programming that meets individual needs can occur in integrated school programs (Knoblock, 1982), and a variety of teaching techniques and strategies are available to develop the learning potential of children with autism.

Motor Handicaps

Children in classrooms may present various degrees of motor handicaps, ranging from very mild, such as the previously discussed dysgraphia, all the way to the severely motor handicapped child who cannot walk or stand, such as those children with the congenital brain syndromes (cerebral palsy) and advanced cases of muscular dystrophy.

Congenital Brain Syndromes: Cerebral Palsy.   Cerebral palsy has many different causes. Many occur prior to birth, for example, maternal infections such as the rubella syndrome, which causes fetal encephalitis. Other conditions affecting the mother, such as maternal diabetes, radiation, or intoxication, can cause a mental retardation syndrome that sometimes combines with cerebral palsy. There are a few rare genetic forms of a nonprogressive motor problem also labeled cerebral palsy. Another cause of cerebral palsy is brain injury arising around the period of birth. There can be lack of oxygen during the birth process, bleeding into the brain (particularly prevalent in premature newborn infants), jaundice damaging the brain, and infections (usually meningitis or infections of the coverings of the brain). After birth, any brain injury or meningitis or encephalitis infections can cause the syndrome.

Regardless of the cause, it is rare that only one part of the brain undergoes damage. Usually affected parts include the cortex (voluntary control of muscles), the cerebellum (muscle coordination and balance), and the basal ganglia (control and coordination of gross movement).

Children with cerebral palsy are usually classified into one of six categories.

1. Spastic. The spastic child is characterized by a loss of voluntary motor control. Without this control, the extensor muscles, which are used to extend the arm, and the flexor muscles, which are used to pull the arm toward the body, contract at the same time. This causes movements to be tense, jerky, and poorly coordinated. The spastic person may be easily startled by sudden noises or movements, which can cause rigid extension or flexion of the muscles. As a result, the spastic child may become fixed in a rigid position, which gradually relaxes as the child regains composure. As the child grows, the spastic muscles become shorter, which can cause limb deformities. For this and other reasons, it is important that the spastic child receive physical therapy. Spastic characteristics are found in about 50 percent of the cerebral palsied population.

2. Athetosis. Athetoid cerebral palsy is characterized by involuntary, purposeless movements of the limbs, especially at the extremities. Fluctuating muscle tone affects deliberate muscle exertions, which results in uncontrolled writhing and irregular movements. The throat and diaphragm muscles are also affected, which causes drooling and labored speech. The hands are affected most frequently, followed by the lips and tongue and then the feet. Excitement and concentrated efforts to control movement generally result in increased tension and spasticity; by contrast, athetoid movement stops during relaxation or sleep. There are at least two major types of athetosis, tension and nontension. The tension athetoid person's muscles are always tense, which tends to reduce the contorted movement of the limb. The nontension athetoid person has contorted movements without muscle tightness. Athetosis affects 15 to 20 percent of the cerebral palsied population. It is not uncommon for spasticity and athetosis to be found in the same individual.

3. Ataxia. Ataxia is caused by damage to the cerebellum, which results in balance problems. Individuals with ataxia have poor fine and gross motor movements, poor depth perception, slurred speech, and a staggering gait, and they frequently fall. About 25 percent of the cerebral palsied population is ataxic.

4. Rigidity.   Rigidity cerebral palsy has been described as a severe form of spasticity. It is characterized by continual, diffuse tension of the flexor and extensor muscles. This "equal pull" of the two muscles renders the limb rigid and hard to bend; once a limb is bent, it tends to stay in that position like a lead pipe. The words "lead pipe" are frequently used to describe this type of cerebral palsy.

5. Tremor.   Tremor cerebral palsy is characterized by the shakiness of a limb, which may be evident only when one is attempting a specific movement. This is called intentional tremor. The shakiness of the limb is caused by alternating contractions of the flexor and extensor muscles. Tremor cerebral palsy is differentiated from athetoid by the extent of the limb movement: athetoid motor movements are large and changeable, whereas tremor movements are small and rhythmic.

6. Mixed.   Most cerebral palsied individuals have more than one type of palsy; they are labeled according to the predominant type. A typical combination involves spasticity and athetosis.

In the education of a child with cerebral palsy, one must take several factors into consideration. First, what is the nature of the child's motor difficulties and how will they affect the learning process? Second, what resources are available—including adaptive devices such as positioning aids and braces, and physical therapy—to allow the child to take full advantage of the edu-

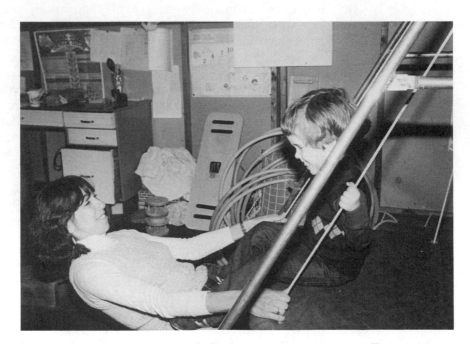

This child is swinging as part of his physical therapy program. The teacher positions herself to direct the swing and encourages eye contact and verbal communication. (Photograph by Mima Cataldo.)

cational environment? Third, how can these adaptive devices and therapies be integrated into the classroom routine? Many educators have come to believe that the integration of therapies into the classroom promotes a better learning environment, allowing teachers and children to make optimal use of their time. The creative use of therapies requires close cooperation between teachers and physical therapists. Last, the teacher and parents of a child with cerebral palsy must work together to find ways of integrating the child into the mainstream of school and neighborhood activities.

Duchenne Muscular Dystrophy.   Muscular dystrophy is a general term that includes those muscle diseases that are genetically determined and characterized by a progressive degeneration of the body's muscle fibers. Common to all these disease entities are the progressive course, a lack of effective treatment, and the deleterious effect of prolonged rest in bed.

The most common type in childhood is called Duchenne muscular dystrophy. First described in 1868 by Duchenne (1883), it is seen only in boys because it is the result of a sex-linked recessive gene. Early motor development is normal, and children learn to walk as early as or a few months later than the majority of healthy children. Sometime between two to four years of age, the parents become concerned because the children walk unsteadily, have frequent falls, and have difficulty getting up. Examination at the time will reveal weakness of the hip and thigh muscles and those of the pelvic girdle. Children may already, at that age, have begun to have a tendency to walk on their toes and develop a swayback.

All symptoms show a slow and steady progress. By four or five years of age, the child displays difficulty in walking; at some point before the teenage years, most patients become confined to a wheelchair. Eventually they are unable to wheel themselves because of increasing weakness in the arms. In the middle or late teens, most patients become confined to bed, and this is the age when these children often die. The cause of death usually is degeneration of the heart muscle, since complicating infections can now be treated. A program of physical therapy is important to maintain optimal functioning. A child in good physical condition may be able to forestall the use of a wheelchair and the deleterious effects of early prolonged bedrest.

Although children with Duchenne muscular dystrophy generally have normal intelligence, there is a slightly greater incidence of learning problems and mild mental retardation. They should be taught commensurately with their intellectual capacities. Although they should avoid overly strenuous school activities, these children should participate in a modified program to the greatest extent possible. Despite the terminal nature of this condition, the quality of the child's life may be much improved by as close to normal school participation as possible.

Seizure Disorders.   Another problem that may interfere with classroom performance of developmentally delayed children is the presence of apparent or not so apparent seizure disorders. Epilepsy was known to the ancient

Babylonians and was well described by Hippocrates, who understood that it was a disease of the brain. Epilepsy, or convulsive disorder, is not a single disease, but a symptom of many diseases. In most children, no obvious cause for the convulsions can be determined, and the term *idiopathic epilepsy* is then applicable.

Seizures are basically a short circuit in the electrical current passing from nerve cell to nerve cell throughout the body. The manifestation of the seizure depends on the location, severity, and type of short circuit coming from the brain (Nealis, 1983).

Young children are prone to seizures. Up to 9 percent of children can have one or more seizures under four years of age associated with a rapid rise or rapid decline of fever. These febrile convulsions are benign, age limited, and are therefore not considered an actual seizure disorder. A true epileptic seizure disorder occurs in about one in every 300 individuals (Kurland, 1959).

There are many types of seizure, and anyone may experience one or more types. Note the following simplified classification of seizure disorders:

1. Generalized seizures
   a. Absence (petit mal) seizures
   b. Myoclonic seizures
   c. Tonic-clonic (grand mal) seizures
   d. Atonic (includes infantile spasms) seizures
2. Partial seizures
   a. Simple
   b. Complex
3. Unclassified

Most seizures have motor components, thus they are obvious to the observer. When a grand mal or major motor seizure occurs in the classroom, the child should be helped into a resting position on the floor, and a washcloth or some other soft material should be inserted in the mouth, between the upper and lower teeth, so that the child does not bite his or her tongue. Epilepsy means loss of consciousness, so one must be very careful with the handling and care of children who are having a seizure.

A grand mal seizure may occur by itself or after a warning called an *aura*. Occasionally the child may be irritable or may manifest unusual behavior for several hours prior to the seizure. In the classic form, the child rolls up the eyes and loses consciousness. There is generalized tonic, or rigid, contraction of the entire body musculature, and the child may utter a piercing, peculiar cry, after which the child becomes short of breath and bluish in skin color. Next, the clonic phase of the convulsion begins, and the trunk and extremities undergo rhythmic contractions and relaxation. As the attack ends, the rate of movement slows, and finally the movements cease. The duration of the seizure during this time may vary from a few seconds to as long as a half hour or more. Occasionally, a child has a series of grand mal attacks at intervals too brief to allow the child to regain consciousness from one attack to the next. This is called *status epilepticus* and is one of the few neurological conditions requiring emergency treatment.

Following a seizure, the child may remain semiconscious and confused for several hours. When examined after the attack, the child is usually poorly coordinated, with mild impairment of fine movements. The child may vomit, complain of a severe headache, or wish to sleep.

Petit mal seizures generally begin between the ages of five and nine years of age and are slightly more common in girls than in boys. The child usually has an estimated twenty or more daily attacks. A characteristic attack is a brief arrest of consciousness, usually lasting five to ten seconds, appearing without warning. There can be a very slight loss of body tone, causing the child to drop objects from the hands, but this is rarely serious enough to induce a fall. There also can be minor movements, such as twitching of the eyelids or face, of which the child is usually unaware. When attacks are frequent, the child's intellectual processes are slowed, and sometimes the first indication is a deterioration of schoolwork and behavior. Sometimes a child can have many of these in the classroom without the teacher or anyone else being aware of them. During the period of the seizure the child is not learning the material being presented, so diagnosis of this type of seizure is very important because it is one of the hidden causes for failure to learn. Petit mal seizures are accompanied by classical changes in the EEG, often of a 3/second spike and wave pattern.

Psychomotor seizures have been defined as periods of altered behavior for which patients are amnesiac and during which they are able to respond in a limited fashion to their environment. Seizures are most characteristically associated with lesions of the temporal lobe of the brain and, therefore, are also termed *temporal lobe seizures*. These seizures may have many different manifestations, such as altered consciousness, change of position of body or limbs, confused activity, a dazed expression, nausea, vomiting, drooling, muttering, mumbling, wandering, pallor or flushing, fumbling, rubbing, incoherent or irrelevant speech, and inappropriate emotional disturbances. Hallucinatory experiences are reported by some children with psychomotor seizures.

Focal seizures are characterized with the development of very local motor or sensory symptoms. In many children, these spread to other parts of the body, ultimately becoming generalized with loss of consciousness. Sometimes there is an orderly sequential progression, a phenomenon known as the jacksonian seizure or jacksonian march.

Minor motor seizures, often called Lennox-Gastaug seizures, have a common electrographic picture characterized by spike and wave forms other than the regular three per second seen in petit mal. These seizures can be akinetic, meaning they are characterized by a sudden momentary loss of postural tone. They can be myoclonic, which consists of single repetitive contractures of muscle or a group of muscles, or they can be atypical petit mal, characterized by absence, which tends to occur in cycles and may disappear for periods of several days. The prognosis in minor motor seizures, in terms of both seizure control and intellectual development, is not as good as in most other seizure types.

Infantile spasms are a form of seizure commonly starting between two to eight months of age, and they are seen twice as frequently in boys as in girls. Because these seizures occur in young children, they are encountered by teachers in infant stimulation or infant learning classes or the early nursery school population. Attacks are characterized by a series of sudden muscular contractions in which the head is flexed, the arms are extended, and the legs are drawn up. Infantile spasms have a distinctive EEG, which includes sudden suppression of electrical activity, beginning with an attack and persisting for a brief time after its completion.

The objective in treatment of seizure patients is a complete stoppage of the seizures, and this is achieved in more than 90 percent of the patients under modern medical care today. In addition to a large range of anticonvulsants, new techniques of monitoring the levels of the drugs in the serum are enabling more specific and exact treatment.

Unfortunately, all anticonvulsants have at least some minor effect on learning, memory, or attention span. Thus, although there is no choice but to use these drugs in most individuals with seizure disorders, the effect on learning is an unfortunate price that must be paid for seizure control. In children with normal intelligence, the effects are not very limiting, but in a child with a developmental delay, the effects can have a measurable depression on learning.

It is important that the teacher be aware of drug side effects: drowsiness in the classroom, sudden increase of frequency of seizures, a change in the child's rate of learning and test scores, and the development of mental symptoms not formerly seen. If they occur, the teacher should alert the parents or the child's doctor. Because uncontrolled epileptic attacks may cause mental and emotional deterioration, it is important that children receive their medication regularly and not miss doses while at school.

Conclusion

When a special education teacher faces a classroom of students, it is necessary to see each child as an individual. Although this is true of all successful teaching programs, it is particularly important in special education. An understanding of the intellectual, perceptual, motor, and social difficulties of the students as related to their diagnoses can help prepare the teacher to compensate in advance and prevent problems. It is of primary importance that a teacher understand if a child is having difficulty perceptually comprehending the lesson, blocking out the lesson because of a seizure, or having a behavior problem that interferes with the ability to cooperate with the teacher. Handling the problem of failure to learn is different in each case and thus must be tailored to the individual child.

Many children formerly considered unteachable have begun to enter special education and regular classrooms, particularly because of the effect of infant learning programs. Children with disabling conditions formerly associated almost entirely with severe mental retardation are now able to learn at moderate, mild, and sometimes even higher levels. In the past, medical diagnosis often led to an immediate decreased expectation of the child's academic performance. This, then, became a self-fulfilling prophesy. Today, we do not look at the child in the light of the older literature that propounded limitations of the mental abilities. Instead, we try to look at each disabled child as an individual, to determine the reason for the learning problems, and to assist the child in overcoming these problems as intelligently and as consistently as possible. Today, teachers of children with special needs can take great pride in what their students have learned and can share the delight of the family and the community when the child exceeds the assumed level of achievement for disabled persons.

The plasticity of the brain of the infant and the young child applies to all children, no matter what their medical condition. The challenge of the future is to overcome these handicaps with accurate understanding and intelligent teaching methods directed specifically toward the problems of the individual young child. Among all the age groups of human beings, children have the capacity to reward us most greatly for our efforts.

Chapter 3

Harold R. Keller

Harold R. Keller is Associate Professor of Psychology and Education and Director of the School Psychology Program at Syracuse University. He is a member of Syracuse University's Center for Research on Aggression and serves as a part-time school psychologist in local schools where he concurrently conducts research with referred and nonreferred children. His interests are in studying alternative assessment strategies with socioculturally different and handicapped children and in children's interactions with peers and adults (teachers, parents). In addition to journal articles on these topics, he has written book chapters on behavioral assessment, consultation, observation, and child abuse. With Arnold P. Goldstein and Diane Erne, he has written the book Changing the Abusive Parent *(Champaign, Ill.: Research Press, 1985).*

Intellectual and Cognitive Development

After reading this chapter, you should be able to:

1
Distinguish between testing and assessment.

2
Recall several definitions of intelligence and discuss their implications for educational planning.

3
List assessment models and describe how you might apply one as a classroom teacher.

4
Critique the use of intelligence tests and contrast them with psychometric alternatives.

The nature and severity of a person's disabilities depend on the interaction of the strengths and weaknesses of personal characteristics (such as cognitive and intellectual abilities, personality, motivation, social-emotional maturity, previous knowledge), the characteristics of required tasks (e.g., the match of tasks to personal characteristics), and the settings in which the individual lives, studies, and plays (past and present home and school opportunities and learning experiences). Therefore, determining how the strengths of child/learner, task, and setting components can best be matched is critical in working with disabled individuals. This chapter will focus upon one pervasive set of personal characteristics, cognitive and intellectual abilities. For all people, cognitive and intellectual abilities both influence and are affected by other personal characteristics. Further, changes in cognitive and intellectual abilities with the development of the individual both influence and are affected by task and setting opportunities. This reciprocity of influence (or bidirectional influence) among aspects of the person and the environment is important to keep in mind when trying to understand and work with disabled individuals.

This chapter will begin with definitions of intelligence and cognition, along with a consideration of some of the myths surrounding the concept of intelligence. The pervasive role of intelligence tests in understanding intellectual functioning and in defining various exceptionalities will be discussed. Major influences (genetics, prenatal factors, environmental conditions, physical stigmata) on intellectual and cognitive development will be examined next. Our attempts at understanding and programming with exceptional children and youth are aided by assessment strategies. Assessment approaches are related to the different ways we try to understand human behavior in general. There is no one way of understanding human behavior that has all the answers, so we will examine different orientations that can influence our selection of assessment strategies and our interpretations of assessment results. The discussion of assessment is placed in this chapter because intellectual and cognitive assessment typically are important components of an assessment of exceptional individuals. Finally, we will discuss specific conceptual orientations to our understanding of intellectual and cognitive development and the kinds of measurement approaches that are derived from those orientations. In each case we will illustrate the assessment strategies, their strengths and limitations, and their educational implications.

Intelligence and Cognition—General Considerations

Definitions

Intelligence has been defined in many different ways (Sattler, 1982; Snow, 1978). One general means of defining intelligence refers to intelligence as the innate capacity of individuals. This meaning reflects a genotypic definition in that it refers to the genetic makeup of individuals. A second type of meaning refers to what individuals do, their behaviors involved in learning, thinking, and problem solving. Within this definition, intelligence results from an interaction of genes with the prenatal and postnatal environment, reflecting a phenotypic (or observable) form of definition. A third type of meaning refers to the results obtained on intelligence tests that sample specific abilities such as verbal, nonverbal, and/or mechanical.

Considering intelligence to be an innately determined capacity has often led to the assumption that intelligence is immutable or unchangeable. That is, as a genetically determined capacity, intelligence is considered fixed for the life of the individual. Such an assumption represents not only a misunderstanding of genetics, but also is not supported by data on intellectual abilities. The fact that a given characteristic is influenced by (a statement quite different from fully determined by) genetic factors does not mean that characteristic will not or cannot be influenced by environmental manipulations (Buss & Poley, 1976). Even if behavior in a certain environment is 100 percent heritable in a given population, it may still be manipulable by appropriate environmental manipulations (e.g., phenylketonuria—PKU—and its modification through dietary change). Longitudinal studies of intellectual functioning show dramatic shifts in test scores (e.g., Dearborn & Rothney, 1963; Shepard, 1970) and in specific intellectual abilities (e.g., McCall, Eichorn, & Hogarty, 1977) across age as individuals develop.

Binet (Binet & Simon, 1905), one of the originators of modern intelligence testing (see late section on psychometric tests), considered intelligence to be a collection of specific faculties or abilities, such as judgment, practical sense, initiative, and the ability to adapt to diverse environmental settings. His selection of subtests, however, was based upon empirical criteria (i.e., how well they predicted school success) and deciding what abilities the subtests were measuring was based upon his subjective opinion. Current approaches that focus upon the specific behaviors or abilities include the cognitive training and cognitive information processing approaches of Feuerstein and Sternberg, respectively (to be discussed in detail later). This focus on thinking, problem solving, and memory processes serves to differentiate cognition from general intelligence. However, the distinction between intellectual and cognitive development is somewhat arbitrary.

Regarding an understanding of intelligence based upon the results obtained on intelligence tests, Terman (1921) defined intelligence as the ability to conduct abstract thinking. He warned, however, about the danger of placing too much emphasis on the results of any one test. That warning against reliance upon a single test is stated explicitly in the current federal public law on education of handicapped children (Public Law 94-142). Wechsler (1958) also used a test-based definition of intelligence when he indicated that intelligence is composed of different elements or abilities that could be independently measured on a test. He clearly stated, however, that intelligence is not the mere sum of abilities on the separate subtests. Rather, intelligent behavior is influenced also by the way the abilities are integrated and by the individual's motivation. Like Binet, Wechsler emphasized the importance of adaptation to the environment (Wechsler's test will be discussed later in greater detail).

There are many different ways of defining intellectual abilities, each with their own set of implications for measuring cognitive skills and for educational planning. These implications will be examined more fully later in this chapter. Part of the confusion concerning definitions of intelligence and methods of measuring intelligence is due to the failure to understand that intelligence is an attribute, not an entity in the brain. Further, it is important to recognize that intelligence represents the accumulation of an individual's learning experiences (Wesman, 1968). Tests with different names (e.g., intelligence, achievement, or aptitude) are basically measuring similar abilities. In fact, in some of the group measures the same items are present in all such ability tests. The name merely reflects different emphases in test usage. Intelligence and aptitude tests are used when our concern is with prediction of future learning. Achievement tests are used to measure prior learning directly. All such ability tests measure what the individual has learned. In spite of these varying definitions, intelligence tests play a pervasive role in our society with regard to defining handicapping conditions.

Role of Intelligence Tests in Defining Exceptionalities

Three categories of exceptionality are defined specifically in terms of intelligence test performance. These categories comprise the mentally retarded, the learning disabled, and those who are gifted. The proportion of school-age children in the United States participating in special education programs for these three categories is as follows: mentally retarded, 1.7 percent; learning disabled, 2.3 percent; and gifted, 1.9 percent; (U.S. Department of Education, 1980; U.S. Office of Civil Rights, 1980). This intelligence-test-based definition of exceptional children represents two thirds of all children participating in special education programs. In addition, the category *emotional disturbance* is based upon, in part, the exclusion of intellectual deficits.

The actual proportions in these categories vary tremendously across locales and districts because the formal definitions and cutoff scores vary. Within the area of learning disabilities, formal categorical definitions generally refer to a severe discrepancy between intellectual ability and achievement in one or more specific areas (such as oral expression, listening comprehension, written expression, mathematics reasoning). The degree of discrepancy allowed as well as the minimal level of intellectual functioning (as measured by an intelligence test) required for a child to be considered in need of services for learning disabilities varies across states and across districts within states. Smith (1983) and Senf (1981) have described the many problems in defining and identifying learning-disabled individuals. Similarly, the cutoffs for identification of gifted children have varied, as has the inclusion of non-intellective variables within the definition (Rosenfield, 1983).

Mental retardation is a particularly confusing category. The American Association of Mental Deficiency (AAMD) defines this exceptionality in terms of performance on a test of intelligence (at least two standard deviation units below the mean) and performance on some measure of adaptive behavior (Grossman, 1973). Earlier (and, to some extent, still today because of the lack of adequate measures of adaptive behavior) practice labeled children retarded on the basis of only their performance on an intelligence test, a unidimensional definition, in spite of adequate adaptive functioning outside the school setting (Mercer, 1973). Because intelligence test performance correlates well with school achievement, use of this unidimensional definition resulted in the term "six-hour retarded child," that is, a child who is judged to be retarded within a single setting (the school) during school hours only. Even with a two-dimensional definition (based upon intelligence test and adaptive behavior), there is considerable variation because of inconsistency in cutoff points on intelligence tests. Some states use the AAMD two standard deviation cutoff, while others use a one-and-one-half standard deviation cutoff. So a child with low adaptive functioning and an IQ score of 77 may be classified mentally retarded in one district but considered nonhandicapped in another district. See Figure 1 for distribution of intelligence tests scores.

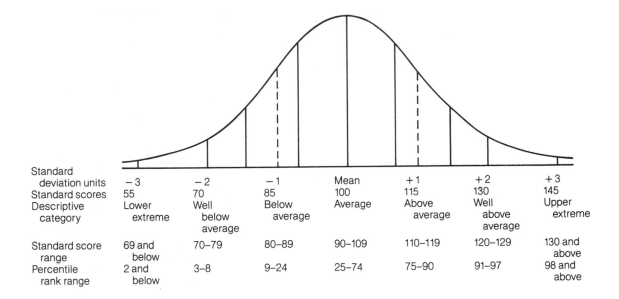

Standard deviation units	−3	−2	−1	Mean	+1	+2	+3
Standard scores	55	70	85	100	115	130	145
Descriptive category	Lower extreme	Well below average	Below average	Average	Above average	Well above average	Upper extreme
Standard score range	69 and below	70–79	80–89	90–109	110–119	120–129	130 and above
Percentile rank range	2 and below	3–8	9–24	25–74	75–90	91–97	98 and above

AAMD levels of mental retardation (must be accompanied by low performance on a measure of adaptive behavior):
    Mild, 55–69
    Moderate, 40–54
    Severe, 25–39
    Profound, 24 and below

Figure 1.   *Descriptive categories and corresponding standard scores and percentiles.*

The two-dimensional definition of mental retardation requires low performance on both measures of intelligence and of adaptive behavior. Such an individual is quite different from one who scores low on just a test of intelligence but performs at a typical level in terms of adaptive behavior. Mercer (1973) has referred to these latter individuals as "quasi-retarded" people; minority and culturally different children tend to fall disproportionately into this category. The case studies described in Box 1 differentiate retarded and quasi-retarded individuals. There are numerous issues and problems in using multiple criteria (such as intelligence and adaptive behavior tests) for defining handicapping conditions (see Reschly, 1982, for a discussion of these concerns). When faced with the provision of special educational services based upon people fitting into categories, as opposed to

---

Box 1
A Two-Dimensional Definition of Mental Retardation and Case Studies

The AAMD has proposed defining mental retardation in terms of low performance on an individual test of intelligence and on a measure of adaptive behavior (Grossman, 1973). Using these two dimensions, Mercer (1973) has described four general categories of functioning as follows:

		Intellectual abilities	
		Low	Average or higher
Adaptive behavior	Low	Comprehensively retarded individual	Socially maladjusted individual
	Average or higher	Quasi-retarded or educationally retarded individual	Typical individual

Quasi-Retarded Child
Bill, a ten-year-old boy, was given the Adaptive Behavior Inventory for Children (ABIC, described later) through a parent interview with his mother. His adaptive behavior scores were all in the average range. Bill was reported to get along well with other members of his family, to be helpful in teaching his younger brother to do chores at home, to assist in preparing food, to be helpful in cleaning the house, and to

(continued)

Box 1
(continued)

perform minor household repairs. He gets along well with children in school and in the neighborhood, usually approaching other children rather than waiting for them to approach him. He rarely gets teased, and he plays with children his own age and is not overly rough. While he is not a leader, he does not go off by himself and is accepted by others. Bill moves about the neighborhood freely and participates in neighborhood activities. He never skips school and is rarely tardy. His performance on an individual test of intelligence is in the lowest 2.5 percent on the standard norms, scoring well below the cutoff for classification into a class for mentally retarded children. He has been retained once and is having considerable trouble in all academic subjects. Bill is a minority child who has nine brothers and sisters. His mother is the head of the household, and the family is supported entirely by welfare. His mother had a tenth grade education and was raised in an inner-city environment. Socioculturally, Bill is very different from the dominant core society represented in his school. Bill is not classified as retarded, is in a regular fourth-grade class, and is receiving supplementary services to help him in reading, writing, and arithmetic.

Comprehensively Retarded Child

Sam's social role performance on the ABIC is so low that he scored off the low end of the scale on all six subtests (family, neighborhood, peers, school, earner/consumer roles, and self-maintenance skills). A nine-year-old boy, he had scores suggesting that his adaptive behavior was comparable to that of a five-year-old child. He gets along well with his family and with children in the neighborhood and in school, but he is teased by others and is somewhat more active than other children. He finishes projects and tasks less than half the time, and he is fairly easy to distract. Other children sometimes avoid him; he never plays games in the neighborhood, does not bring friends home from school, and is not permitted to go to a neighborhood store by himself or with peers. His parents are quite protective in that someone must always watch when he crosses an intersection with a traffic light; he is never left alone, even in the daytime, for just a short time; someone orders food for him at a restaurant; and he is not allowed to play with children across the street. He is not allowed to handle sharp objects and does not prepare even simple food like hot dogs. Someone else picks out his clothes. His performance on an individual test of intelligence is in the bottom 1 percentile, and he cannot deal with basic academic tasks beyond a readiness level. Sam's family background does not differ from the dominant core society. He is classified as mentally retarded and is receiving special education services in a self-contained class.

identified needs, professionals are confronted with the difficult task of setting cutoff points so that those who need services will be included within the category. At the same time, there is a concern that those who do not need the services provided for a given category do not get labeled and placed in more restrictive educational settings. The task is also made difficult by a consideration of the many factors that can influence intellectual functioning.

Influences on Intellectual and Cognitive Development

Both hereditary and environmental factors influence intellectual abilities. This chapter is not designed to review all the possible influences, but rather to highlight some of the important influences and to discuss issues relevant to those influences. (See also Chapter 2 for genetic influence on exceptional children in general; there the emphasis is upon the role of genetics on intelligence.)

Role of Heredity

An estimate of heritability of a given attribute (such as intelligence) describes the proportion of the variation of a characteristic in a given population that is attributable to genetic differences in that population. The degree of heritability can range from 0 to 100 percent. If we say that heritability of the IQ is .40 in a given population, we mean that 40 percent of the variation in IQs in that population is attributable to genetic differences among the members of the population and that 60 percent of the observed variation is attributable to other sources. An important point to recall is that a heritability estimate refers only to population variance in an attribute; it is not applicable to individuals.

Heritability estimates for human intelligence are based on a polygenic model that assumes that intelligence is the result of the combined influence of many genes. The estimates are obtained using the correlations between groups of individuals of different degrees of kinship, such as between monozygotic (identical) and dizygotic (fraternal) twins. Studies of European and North American white populations suggest that the heritability of intelligence varies from .40 to .80 (Sattler, 1982). Generally, as individuals become more similar genetically, their IQs also become more similar (see Table 1). It is important to note that even if genetic differences contribute more than environmental differences to the variation in IQs, that does not mean that intellectual abilities cannot be changed (Scarr-Salapatek, 1975).

In addition to polygenic combinations, other genetic factors that contribute to mental retardation include deleterious single gene pairs and gross abnormalities in the chromosomal complement. The majority of genetically determined syndromes associated with mental retardation are caused by pair-

Table 1
Correlations for Intellectual Ability

Correlations between	Number of studies	Obtained median
Unrelated Persons		
Children reared apart	4	−.01
Foster parent and child	3	+.20
Children reared together	5	+.24
Collaterals		
Second cousins	1	+.16
First cousins	3	+.26
Uncle (or aunt) and nephew (or niece)	1	+.34
Siblings reared apart	3	+.47
Siblings reared together	36	+.55
Dizygotic twins, different sex	9	+.49
Dizygotic twins, same sex	11	+.56
Monozygotic twins reared apart	4	+.75
Monozygotic twins reared together	14	+.87
Direct Line		
Grandparent and grandchild	3	+.27
Parent (as adult) and child	13	+.50
Parent (as child) and child	1	+.56

Source: Adapted from Scarr-Salapatek (1975).

ing of recessive genes. Such a recessive gene pair produces a faulty patterning for the formation of an enzyme necessary for an important metabolic process. Among the more common recessive disorders are galactosemia, phenylketonuria (PKU), a group of related disorders know as amaurotic familial idiocy, cretinism, and a number of anomalies of cranial formation (Robinson & Robinson, 1970). Dietary or hormonal treatment can prevent or reduce the degree of mental retardation for some of these disorders, including PKU and cretinism. The most common chromosomal anomaly is Down's syndrome in which there is an extra chromosome in the pair typically designated as number 21 (hence, the disorder is also called trisomy 21). With increasing age of the mother, the risk of having a Down's syndrome child increases. For example, the risk is less than 1 in 1,500 births for maternal ages between 15 and 24, but as high as 1 in 38 for mothers older than 45 (Knobloch & Pasamanick, 1974). Of course, genetic mutation and chromosomal anomalies can be produced before conception by environmental factors such as radiation, viral infections, and chemicals (Robinson & Robinson, 1970). Recent research has shown that various sex chromosome anomalies and children treated for PKU (thus sparing them from mental retardation) are strongly associated with different kinds of learning disabilities and speech and language disorders (Pennington & Smith, 1983).

Role of Environment

There are a wide variety of environmental influences on intellectual abilities as well. Perinatal factors including prenatal variables (e.g., abnormal fetus, prenatal accident), general birth process variables (e.g., abnormal delivery, delivery difficulties), and neonatal variables (e.g., brain damage, hemorrhage, and other physical malfunctions to the neonate) have received considerable research attention, but generally have been found to be only minimally associated with intellectual functioning and actual school performance (Rubin & Balow, 1977). There is some evidence of greater variability of intellectual performance for children born with poor physical condition (e.g., Shipe, Vandenberg, & Williams, 1968; Yacorzynski & Tucker, 1960). That is, children with a poorer physical condition at birth have a larger proportion with either high IQs or low IQs than children with typical physical conditions. Low birth weight and malnutrition have both been shown to be related to intellectual and cognitive functioning. Both of these conditions obviously can be influenced by improved care (Francis-Williams & Davies, 1974).

Family Factors. Other more general environmental influences have been shown to be related to intellectual abilities. These include socioeconomic status of the family (Buss & Poley, 1976) and family configuration variables (Zajonc, 1976) such as birth order, family size, and sibling birth intervals, plus father absence (Shinn, 1978) and divorce (Guidubaldi, Cleminshaw, Perry, & McLoughlin, 1983). Members of high socioeconomic groups tend to have higher IQs than those of low socioeconomic groups. While less clear-cut, the family configuration research suggests that children from larger families, who are born later into large families, and/or who are reared in father-absent homes, on average tend to score lower on tests of intelligence. Reduced cognitive stimulation may be the contributing variable in these findings, though anxiety and/or financial hardship may also be important contributing factors in the father-absent homes. In addition, Marjoribanks (1979) has shown that various home environmental variables (such as presses for achievement, activeness, intellectuality, and independence) are related to cognitive abilities to an even greater extent than global socioeconomic indices. McCall, Appelbaum, and Hogarty (1973), examining interaction patterns in the home more closely, found that children who showed decreases in IQ in the preschool years tended to come from homes that had minimal stimulation and that used punishment strategies that were either very severe or very mild and often irrelevant. In contrast, children who showed IQ increases through the early elementary years came from families that fostered cognitive stimulation and provided structure and consistent moderate discipline. Severity of punishment for misbehavior was particularly important in that children with the most depressed IQ patterns had parents who delivered the most severe penalties.

Early Intervention. The most intensely researched environmental variables showing dramatic effects upon intellectual functioning include those involved in the early intervention programs. Lazar and Darlington (1982) analyzed the long-term effects of eleven major preschool education projects. They conducted a follow-up of the original children who were nine to nineteen years of age at the time. All of these projects were conducted with children from low-income families. Children who attended early childhood programs surpassed control group children on individual tests of intelligence for several years after the programs ended. Raised IQs occurred regardless of initial abilities and regardless of variation in family background characteristics. In other words, intellectual improvement occurred even for children with very limited intellectual abilities at the start of the programs and even for children from families living under very poor conditions (in terms of financial resources and cognitive stimulation). Further, children who attended programs were more likely to meet basic school requirements. That is, they were less likely to be assigned to special education classes and less likely to be retained than were control children. Other school-related benefits of these programs were higher achievement motivation and more positive maternal attitudes toward school and vocational aspirations. While all these programs emphasized strategies for enhancing children's cognitive development, they varied considerably on many dimensions. The curriculum models and theoretical bases from which the models were derived were quite divergent. Both home-based and center-based programs were effective. Likewise, programs using paraprofessionals or professionals and those for infants as well as those for older children were successful. These successful programs also varied in the extent to which parents were involved, though some data suggest that greater parental involvement leads to greater maintenance of positive effects (Zigler & Valentine, 1979). The varying nature of these successful programs is positive in that program developers can be flexible and responsive to local needs and parental input in designing programs that build on the strengths of the families to be served.

It should also be noted that emotional and social characteristics as well as physical appearance might relate to intellectual functioning. For example, individuals with Down's syndrome often have readily observable physical characteristics that serve to identify them. Feuerstein (personal communication) conducted intensive interventions (with his Instrumental Enrichment curriculum, to be described later) with Down's syndrome individuals and found positive changes in cognitive skills. Because of their physical stigmata, however, few opportunities were provided these individuals. Feuerstein has now obtained plastic surgery for a number of them and observed dramatic changes in behaviors of the affected individuals as well as those in their social environments. These individuals were shown to be capable of much more than imagined and than allowed.

Assessment as Aid to Understanding

Before examining specific models and methods for understanding intellectual and cognitive functioning, it is important to look at assessment in general.

Assessment is the process of gathering data for the purpose of making decisions about or for individuals (Ysseldyke, 1979). Assessment is not the same as testing; testing may be just one part of the assessment process. Assessment includes many other means of data collection such as examination of cumulative records; interviews with the individual and significant others in that individual's life; observations of and by parent, teacher, and child; developmental and medical histories; check lists; evaluating curriculum requirements and options; trial teaching; task analysis; teacher and parent attitude ratings; and classroom climate measures. The primary task in assessment is to develop programs that allow the individual to grow educationally and psychologically. In order to make an appropriate assessment it is important to be aware of the different purposes, models, and methods of assessment, and to obtain sufficient educational background to evaluate and plan within the many domains of assessment (i.e., the variety of personal characteristics, tasks, and settings that are of concern to us).

Assessment Purposes

Assessment aids different kinds of decisions, and each decision often requires different sets of information. Ysseldyke (1979; Salvia & Ysseldyke, 1978) identified five basic purposes of assessment: screening identification, classification placement, psychological and educational planning, pupil evaluation, and program evaluation. Another reason for assessment is to evaluate and develop new assessment and intervention strategies, as well as to conduct research that might lead to a better understanding of disabled individuals. Our assessment purposes influence which assessment techniques are used.

Screening Identification. One purpose of assessment is to identify children who are significantly discrepant or significantly behind their peers in one or more areas of functioning so that additional programming or assessment can be provided. Typically in the educational domain, group norm-referenced tests are administered for screening purposes so that an individual is compared with others having similar sociocultural (experiential) backgrounds and ages. For example, standardized achievement tests might identify Michael as having learned less than expected, given his cognitive abilities, age, grade, years of schooling, and quality of home and school background. Further assessment is then indicated to determine the specific factors that might be involved and to aid in the development of different instructional strategies for Michael. (See Chapter 6 for discussion of specific assessment approaches for planning instruction.) Teachers might fill out behavior check lists to identify children whose social skills are discrepant from others of the same age, grade, and background and from the expectancies of the teacher for appropriate classroom behavior. Further assessment might identify specific skills that are lacking in the identified children, inappropriate teacher expectancies, and/or a mismatch in task or setting demands and child abilities. Intervention might then focus upon helping the child develop new social

Teachers can assist students to organize their work and they can provide useful feedback. (Photograph by Mima Cataldo.)

skills, changing expectancies, and/or trying to bring about a better match between environmental demands and child characteristics. Individual vision and hearing screening are conducted routinely in schools to identify children with visual and auditory acuity problems.

Classification Placement.   Current state and federal laws and regulations dictate that schools assess children for administrative purposes. Such assessment supports the classification of children under various handicapping conditions and their placement in appropriate (least restrictive) educational environments. Haphazard and capricious placement decisions based on subjective impressions can be avoided through the appropriate integration of assessment data on personal child characteristics with the appraisal of task and setting characteristics.

Psychoeducational Planning.   Assessment data are collected to assist educational personnel and other helping professionals in planning and implementing programs for disabled children that enhance their psychological adjustment and educational achievement. Within this assessment goal, emphasis is placed on determining specifically what skills children have and have not mastered, and how they approach learning and daily living tasks. The results help teachers design what and how to teach these individuals (more details are provided in Chapter 6).

Pupil Evaluation. Another purpose for collecting assessment data is to help professionals, parents, and children themselves to evaluate the degree to which disabled students are making progress in their programs. Grades derived from teacher-constructed measures, scores on standardized tests, and behavior check lists are frequent indicators of academic and social progress.

Program Evaluation. Assessment data are also gathered to evaluate programs for disabled individuals. Here the focus is on the program rather than the student. The school, for example, might evaluate specific reading programs or the effectiveness of specific interventions such as helping a child maintain attention during school instruction. Such evaluations compare students' progress relative to stated objectives or assess the progress of students in one program relative to progress in another program.

Our primary concern is with psychological and educational planning based upon needs of the individual within the context of the task demands and settings with which the individual is confronted. Assessment practices that merely lead to identification or classification-placement are not sufficient for designing appropriate instructional or intervention programs (Cromwell, Blashfield, & Strauss, 1975). Whether the programming occurs in the home, the regular classroom, or other more appropriate environments, professionals and helpers in those settings must assess the child's specific learning and socioemotional needs and how to help the individual to progress. The assessment process must be linked to intervention in ways that are continuous and that focus on behaviors (thoughts, feelings, and actions) relevant to the identified problems. It must emphasize behaviors that can be changed and improved, recognize the need for a child-parent-teacher partnership, and attempt to provide specific and useful information to this partnership (Oakland, 1977).

Once psychoeducational programs are implemented, pupil progress and program success must be evaluated systematically. Such evaluation determines whether the disabled individual is ready to move on to a less restrictive educational setting, and whether the intervention program might be used with similar individuals and problems in the future.

Assessment Methods

It is important to note that we cannot make program planning decisions based upon single tests or upon single assessment methods. Assessment can involve tests conducted with students or evaluation strategies focusing on child interactions with a variety of tasks and settings.

Tests used in assessment have been classified as norm-referenced or criterion-referenced measures. Tests that have been standardized on a normative group, in order to compare an individual's general performance to that of his peers, are called standardized or norm-referenced tests. Criterion-referenced tests may also be normed, but they are intended to measure whether or not a person has mastered very specific skills. Norm-referenced tests indicate an individual's standing relative to others' skill development (measuring *between* individual differences). Criterion-referenced tests, on the other hand, indicate whether or not the individual actually has mastered a particular skill (measuring *within*-individual skill attainment).

A test that shows Mary has performed a set of math computation problems better than 12 percent of children at her grade level nationally is norm-based. A test that indicates that she can add two-digit numbers with regrouping, but cannot multiply, is criterion-referenced. A norm-referenced test might measure Jim's knowledge of letter sounds by sampling ten letters and comparing his percentage correct with that of a standardization sample. A criterion-referenced test concerned with the same skill might ask Jim to give all twenty-six letter sounds and note his degree of mastery.

All tests, to some extent, reflect both between-individual differences and within-individual growth. However, because of the way they were developed, most tests do a better job along one dimension than the other. Norm-referenced tests are most useful for screening and classification, while criterion-referenced measures help identify what to teach. How to teach or intervene is best determined by informal evaluation strategies particularly adapted to the questions asked about the individual's interactions with tasks and settings.

Norm-Referenced Measures.   Characteristics necessary for norm-referenced tests to be useful in the decision-making process include (1) reliability—stability or consistency of scores, (2) validity—extent to which a test measures what it is supposed to measure, (3) standardized administration, and (4) norms based on standardization with a relevant comparison group. Reliability and standardized administration are probably self-evident, but the concepts of validity and norms are somewhat more complex. The issue with validity is whether or not a particular test does what it purports to do. For example, based upon court evidence presented in the *Larry P.* case (on discriminatory testing), Judge Peckham in the Northern District of California (*Larry P.*, Opinion, 1979) suggested that there was not sufficient evidence to support the validity of the intelligence tests used at that time. That is, the tests were used to identify and place children in classes for mentally handicapped children so that they might receive appropriate educational programs and return to mainstream society. The judge felt that while there was evidence indicating the tests measured what is commonly agreed to be intelligence, there was not sufficient validity evidence, with those tests, for the specific purpose of placing and educating handicapped children. In other words, for a test to be valid, we must ask "valid for what purpose?" There must be evidence not only that a test measures a particular theoretical construct (like intelligence or anxiety), but also that there is evidence to support its use in particular ways (e.g., as a predictor of school success, as a predictor that certain kinds of interventions will be effective in returning someone to mainstream society). Incidentally, that judge's ruling could be interpreted as questioning not only the validity of the intelligence tests used, but also the validity of self-contained special educational programming the children received.

Regarding norms, a critical point is that the comparison group be comparable to those individuals with whom the test is subsequently used. That is, in using standardized tests, it is typically assumed that the individual taking the test is similar to those in the comparison group on at least the following characteristics: (1) similar socialization and educational opportunities, (2) similar motivation to perform, (3) equal experience in test taking and with the test materials, (4) equally free of anxiety or emotional problems that might interfere with their performance, and (5) equally free of physical disabilities that might interfere with performance (Newland, 1971). When those assumptions are not met, which is often the case with culturally different and disabled individuals, the reliability and validity of the tests for those discrepant individuals can be affected (Cleary, Humphreys, Kendrick, & Wesman, 1975).

An important function of norm-based measures is in screening children who might be at risk for subsequent psychological and educational problems. Their global screening function provides a rapid guide to further assessment questions and methods. Norm-referenced tests thus represent only the beginning of the assessment process. Based upon these test results professionals can generate hypotheses regarding the potential problem areas and how the student might be learning or adapting to the environment. These hypotheses can be evaluated with additional assessment strategies, including criterion-referenced and nonstandardized measures (Keller, 1983; Mowder, 1980; Smith, 1980). This further assessment is necessary because norm-referenced tests sample too few behaviors within a specific skill area to be of much help in planning interventions.

Interdisciplinary teams engaging in the assessment process cannot limit themselves to the use solely of norm-referenced tests because the tests do not specify *what* and *how* to teach disabled children. Norm-referenced instruments gain value when, after standard administration, the examiner applies informal evaluation methods to the items on which the child erred so that the examiner can discover more precisely what components of the task the student has mastered. Further, the examiner can find out which aspects of the task are difficult and why, and how rapidly the student could learn the task and generalize this knowledge to new items given different instructional strategies (Smith, 1980).

Criterion-Referenced Measures. Criterion-referenced tests provide information on what to teach. While norms are not necessary for these measures, knowledge of the sample of individuals with whom the test was developed is important. Evaluators may not be interested in comparing a particular child with a normative sample, but information on the sample will help them judge the appropriateness of the test's mastery criteria for a particular child. It is possible that individuals with certain personal characteristics or instructional or experiential backgrounds would be expected to perform differently on particular criterion tasks. Items on criterion-referenced tests are often associated directly with specific instructional objectives and thus can help in the writing of individual educational plans and in evaluating pupil progress. It is important to note that users of commercially available criterion-referenced tests (e.g., achievement tests) must scrutinize test content to determine how well it matches the school's curriculum. The less it matches, the less valid it is. When students are instructed in new math, for example, but tested in traditional math, they may perform poorly on the tests. These scores do not validly reflect their math skills. Although criterion-referenced tests do not provide information on how to teach, application of informal evaluation strategies to the items on which the student was unsuccessful can serve this purpose.

Informal Evaluation Strategies.   A variety of nonstandardized assessment strategies can provide information about both what and how to teach. *Task analysis* procedures, for example, break down complex instructional goals into component skills and assess mastery of these subskills (Bijou, 1970; Gagne, 1977; Gold, 1972; Junkala, 1972, 1973; Resnick, Wang, & Kaplan, 1973; Smith, 1980, 1983). In this way, a child can be located on a hierarchy of component skills for a given task, and the next skill to be taught is identified.

Direct systematic *observation* of the child in the classroom can also provide information about what and how to teach, whether the evaluator's goals are academic or social in nature (Alessi, 1980; Keller, 1980a, 1980b, 1981). Classroom observation has the advantage of assessing the problem in the setting where it occurs. This contrasts with traditional testing, in which a child is typically assessed in a strange room, with a strange adult, and with a strange and perhaps irrelevant set of questions and tasks (Bronfenbrenner, 1976).

Trial Teaching.   This is an assessment strategy that gets most directly at the how-to-teach question (Salvia & Ysseldyke, 1978; Smith, 1980, 1983). Diverse instructional techniques are systematically tried and evaluated, including varying materials, methods of presentation, and methods of feedback. This approach can be used with an individual child in an office or in the classroom.

All these informal assessment procedures are related directly to the how-to-teach question. While time consuming, they are important aspects of an assessment system designed to develop individual educational plans. All are appropriate for assessing individual pupil progress.

Models of Assessment

Selection of specific assessment strategies is related to the different ways we conceptualize human behavior in general. There are nine basic models of assessment (Keller, 1983; Mercer & Ysseldyke, 1977). While some focus primarily upon the individual child, others focus on the child's interactions with tasks, the child's interactions with settings, or the individual in relation to broader sociocultural contexts. Overlapping all those focuses is a developmental model.

Each model has its own set of assumptions, measures, and relationship to interventions. Each model, viewed separately, provides only a partial view of the individual and his or her strengths and weaknesses. In working with disabled children and youth, professionals need to use an approach that views the child from multiple perspectives, including the developing child's interactions with tasks, settings, and broader sociocultural contexts. Public Law 94-142 requires that an interdisciplinary team participate in decision making and planning with disabled children, which, in turn, ensures that multiple perspectives are considered.

Focus on the Individual Child.   When the focus is on the child, the basic assumption is that problems exist within the individual. The primary concern is with deficits. The medical, process-deficit, and trait models all emphasize within-child problems. In the *medical* model a problem is defined in terms of biological symptoms of pathology. In other words, biological causes underlie the current problem. Interventions involve treatment of the biological conditions or deficits, such as prescriptions for glasses or hearing devices, outlining a balanced diet, or medications.

In a manner analogous to the medical model, the *process-deficit* model defines problems in terms of information-processing or ability deficits related to cognitive, motor, visual perceptual, language, or attention weaknesses; while a *trait* model assumes that behavior is determined primarily by generalized traits, or basic qualities (such as general intelligence, introversion, anxiety), within the person that express themselves in many contexts. The process-deficit model, then, tends to focus more upon cognitive or sensory component functions, while the trait model emphasizes general enduring personal characteristics. Within these models intervention might consist of remediation (building up deficits) and compensation (working around deficits by teaching to strengths). Assessment measures then try to identify both strengths and weaknesses. The measures assess hypothetical internal (within the child) determinants of behavior.

All three of these within-child models (medical, process, trait) suggest that problems can go unrecognized, so that assessment serves an important screening function. A child may be viewed as stupid rather than as having a hearing impairment, or a specific learning disability, or being severely withdrawn (as in elective mutism). In general these models consider settings (or environmental conditions) and sociocultural background variables relatively unimportant to assessment and intervention processes because the biological symptoms, process deficits, or traits are assumed to be carried by the person across all settings.

Assumptions within the process-deficit and trait models, in particular, have been challenged within the past two decades. Mann and Phillips (1967) question whether a child's behavior actually can be broken down into separate information-processing components that can be independently assessed and remediated. On most tasks each process is involved to varying degrees. Similarly, Mischel (1968) presented evidence that questioned our ability to identify separate traits commonly held to exist and influence behavior. The reliability of measures within these models also is often poor (Mischel, 1968; Salvia & Ysseldyke, 1978; Ysseldyke, 1973, 1979; Ysseldyke & Salvia, 1974).

In addition to the measures, some authors criticize the deficit orientation within these models (Keogh, 1972; Mischel, 1968, 1969, 1973, 1979; Tarnopol, 1969). They question the assumption that hypothesized deficits exists within the child alone and suggest that assessment focusing only on the child is too narrow. It should be noted that the lack of support for the basic assumptions of these models is based on currently used tests and remediation procedures. As we improve our methods of identifying precisely how process deficits or personal characteristics impair performance on actual educational and daily living tasks, support for incorporating these assumptions in intervention planning may increase. Further research will no doubt indicate how these within-child deficits and characteristics interact with outside-the-child variables (tasks, settings, and sociocultural context) to influence performance and development.

Focus on the Child's Interactions with Tasks.   The *task analysis* model is concerned with how the child relates to academic tasks as well as tasks of daily living. Task analysis methods help educators discover what task attributes best match a child's abilities and learning styles. It is basically a test-teach-test approach, geared toward the precise academic, job, or social skill criteria on which the individual experiences difficulty. Therefore, the relationship between assessment and intervention is much closer than in the process deficit and trait models.

The task analysis model evaluates a child's general level of skill development on different aspects of a task (e.g., recognizing sight words in and out of context), or the degree of mastery of a particular skill (e.g., sounds of letters). The task is broken into its component parts while task demands and modes of presentation are altered.

Smith (1980, 1983) describes how the educator, while observing a child's performance on various assessment tasks, formulates hypotheses about possible task characteristics that might get in the way of a child demonstrating knowledge. Smith suggests that the child try the task again, but with one or more task modifications suggested by the hypotheses. Instead of giving letter sounds, for example, the child could point to letters as the examiner gives their sounds. In addition to analyzing tasks into their component parts to determine at what point the child is successful, Smith suggests trying task modifications that might better match the student's learning style: directed instruction, increased time to solve the task, guided attention, self-verbalization of instructions, and motivational techniques. Success with such task modifications suggests discrepancies between the child's way of knowing and the way tasks are customarily presented in the classroom or on tests.

Focus on the Child's Interactions with Settings.   Another way of assessing the disabled child is by broadening the interactional focus to include the various settings with which the child relates. Here the basic assumption is that problems relate to the child's interactions with settings. Three assessment models place primary emphasis on child-setting interactions: the social systems, ecological assessment, and the behavioral assessment models.

The primary focus of the *social systems model* (Mercer, 1979) is on social expectations for a specific role in a given setting. The disabled child interacts with a variety of social systems (families, classrooms, stores, etc.) and assumes a variety of social roles, such as both student and playmate in a school social system. Each social role in each social system carries different expectations for behavior, so there are multiple definitions of typical and problem behaviors. The most powerful people in a given setting determine what is acceptable and what is not acceptable within various roles in the setting. For example, the school principal and teachers define standards for acceptable behavior and academic progress within a school. Within a classroom, a teacher's expectations about appropriate age-related behavior, coupled with the teacher's tolerance level, might determine whether or not a child is considered hyperactive. Thus, a person's behavior may be considered typical in one setting but judged atypical in another setting. A learning disabled child might be considered typical in reading classes but atypical in math classes. Another child might be considered retarded in the school setting, but quite adaptive in the home and neighborhood settings. This latter child (sometimes referred to as a "six-hour retarded child") is the center of considerable controversy in the area of intellectual assessment—a topic addressed more thoroughly later.

The basic task within the social systems model is to assess role behaviors and role expectations for the diversity of settings with which the child is likely to interact. Functioning well within any social system involves developing and maintaining interpersonal ties with individuals in the system, and attaining the skills necessary for functioning in particular roles in those settings. Intervention within this model helps the child develop the relevant interpersonal ties (with teachers and peers) and role skills (academics) necessary for success.

The *ecological model* is concerned primarily with the structural, affective, organizational, and opportunity components of settings. One basic premise is that people adapt and act selectively toward their environment to achieve a harmonious working relationship with it. Specific environments influence individual behavior and have dependable enduring effects on all individuals. To illustrate, the participants in a third grade reading group generally behave in consistent ways when in that group, even though the actual participants change throughout the morning. These consistent ways of behaving (reading silently, reading aloud when asked by the teacher, answering questions about the material) are different from the ways the same children act in other segments of the environment (such as the cafeteria). A lack of adaptive fit between an individual's behavior and a particular environmental setting is cause for concern.

The ecological model leads educators to examine an individual's natu-

rally occurring behavior, the environment immediately surrounding that behavior, and the ways the individual and the immediate environment are
linked. Assessment (Hiltonsmith & Keller, 1983) focuses on: (1) setting appearance and contents (such as design, contents—books, computers, curricular materials, and ambient features—noise, lighting), (2) setting operation
(such as organizational style, affective climate, reinforcement properties,
communication patterns, and usage patterns), and (3) setting opportunities
(for nurturance and sustenance and for cognitive and socioemotional stimulation). Educators might also assess a whole organization, its interlocking
systems (a school district and its buildings, support staff, interrelationships
among administration and teachers), and how it influences a child's behavior
within a given setting. Conoley (1980) illustrates the effect on a child's learning and social adjustment when the child moves from self-contained to resource to regular classroom within the same building. Intervention within
this model focuses on changes in the structural, affective, organizational, and
opportunity components of settings.

A *behavioral assessment model* relies heavily on direct measurement and
observation to assess difficulties in their natural settings (Keller, 1980a, 1980b;
Kratochwill, 1982). It is used to develop psychoeducational interventions and
to evaluate their effectiveness. Broadly based behavioral assessment incorporates both the social systems and ecological assessment models. Each child
is considered individually, and assessment takes place in many settings. Systematic observation, for example, might take place in the classroom, school
halls, cafeteria, playground, home, neighborhood, and in structured environments that might include role playing or trial teaching. This strategy of
direct measurement of behaviors in settings of concern to the child and the
person referring the child results in fewer inferences made from the assessment setting to the intervention setting, since the settings typically are
identical. In contrast, traditional assessment with standardized tests can be
characterized as testing a child by a strange adult in a strange room with a
strange set of questions and tasks (Bronfenbrenner, 1976). Because the child
may interact differently with a strange adult in an unfamiliar room (such as
the psychologist's office), on irrelevant tests, inappropriate inferences about
the child's classroom or home functioning might be made. Assessment within
this model is not limited to behavioral actions that can be observed. It also
focuses on cognitive (thoughts, images), affective (feelings, subjective meanings), physiological (increased heart rate prior to a test), and structural components (arrangement of desks) of the interaction between learner and settings. Interventions may address the individual (at action, cognitive, affective,
and/or physiological levels) and/or the settings. Such interventions are based
on a broad social learning approach that includes diverse streams of psychological and social science research and theory (Keller, 1981; Krasner,
1971).

Focus on the Child in Broader Sociocultural Contexts.   This focus
includes a diverse set of approaches designed to be more responsive to the

cultural pluralism that exists in this country and others. It attempts to make assessments less tied to the dominant culture (in America, the middle class and Anglo-American traditions). This relatively recent focus resulted from problems with test discrimination and over-representation of minorities in special education classes (Mercer, 1979; Oakland & Laosa, 1977).

The *pluralistic model* defines a psychoeducational problem as poor performance when sociocultural bias is controlled. The pluralistic model assumes that the potential for learning is similarly distributed in all racial, ethnic, and cultural groups. Individual differences in learning potential *within* each of these groups are acknowledged, but differences in test performance *between* cultural groups are assumed to be due to biases in tests and testing procedures. It is assumed that all tests are culturally biased because all tests assess what the child has learned about the cultural heritage represented in the tests' construction. Individuals socialized in the same cultural heritage as the test's norm sample will tend to perform better on the test than those not reared in that cultural tradition. The latter perform poorly because of differences in their socialization, not because of differences in learning potential. For example, knowing four presidents of the United States since 1900 (a question on an intelligence test) depends on a particular cultural heritage. Assessment in the pluralistic model attempts to control for such cultural biases in testing instruments and in testing procedures.

Several assessment strategies have been proposed to deal with the broad focus suggested by the pluralistic model. Reschly (1979, 1982) has suggested comprehensive multidimensional assessment that includes all the various domains (language, achievement, intellectual, perceptual-motor, medical-developmental, neuropsychological, adaptive behavior, socioemotional, settings). He has emphasized viewing nonbiased assessment as a process rather than as a set of instruments. The nonbiased assessment process must be oriented toward ensuring fairness and effectiveness of assessment and intervention decisions for all children. Complementing this strategy in pluralistic assessment are Mercer's (1979; Mercer & Lewis, 1978) System of Multicultural Pluralistic Assessment (SOMPA), Kaufman's (1983) Assessment Battery for Children (K-ABC), and Feuerstein's (1979, 1980) Learning Potential Assessment Device (LPAD). These strategies are viewed by their respective authors not as total assessment systems but as parts of a total assessment with culturally diverse children. These approaches (to be dealt with in greater depth later) are perhaps the most far-reaching attempts to deal with the issues of pluralistic assessment and nondiscriminatory testing.

Focus on the Developing Individual. A comprehensive *developmental model* encompasses all the previously discussed models. That is, with aging the biological structures of the individual change, as do the underlying cognitive processes and personal characteristics. The tasks with which the individual is confronted and expected to engage change, as do the modes by which the individual operates on those changing tasks. With growing independence the individual relates to changing and diverse settings in and outside the immediate home and community, and, because of our pluralistic society, is confronted with individuals who developed within different sociocultural contexts. Because of the tremendous importance of understanding the changing individual within changing contexts, the professional who works with disabled individuals needs to have a solid foundation in human development, of both typical and atypical individuals.

As stated previously, each model provides only a partial view of the individual. The issue is not which model is best, but rather a need to understand the individual from multiple perspectives. Comprehensive planning with disabled individuals requires consideration of multiple perspectives, applying those perspectives that address the individual's current needs, and recognizing that those needs may change with development and intervention.

Multidimensional Assessment.   In order to develop effective intervention programs that help the individual develop educationally and personally (the primary goal of assessment), evaluators need as much information about the child in as many domains as possible: a picture of the total child. Learning and development do not occur in isolation. This process necessitates a team approach to assessment and to decision making. Comprehensive assessment and intervention involve teachers, administrators, special educators, school social workers, school nurses, speech and hearing personnel, reading specialists, language specialists, school psychologists, parents, and children. The parents and, to whatever extent possible, the child are important components of the team process.

Multidimensional assessment is conducted through an examination of many aspects or domains of the child and of the child's interaction with tasks and settings (Reschly, 1979; Tucker, 1977). Although the identification procedures in Public Law 94-142 require that "no single procedure is used as the sole criterion for determining an appropriate educational program for a child" (*Federal Register*, 1977, p. 65082), a thorough assessment of and plan for a disabled student's daily learning program necessitates more than two measures. Possible assessment domains include language skills; sociocultural background; general and specific academic skills; intelligence; sensorimotor skills; medical, developmental, and neuropsychological information; adaptive behavior; and socioemotional characteristics (Keller, 1983). Assessment should also include consideration of the curriculum and settings to which the child relates, the child's interactions with those tasks and settings, and the child's and significant others' subjective impressions concerning all these aspects. In line with these perspectives, Public Law 94-142 requires that the student's academic performance be observed in his or her regular classroom by a team member other than the child's regular classroom teacher. If a child is less than school age or out of school, then the observation occurs in an environment appropriate for an individual of that age. Public Law 94-142 also requires that the testing materials not be racially or culturally discriminatory and that "tests and other evaluation materials are provided and administered in the child's native language or other mode of communication" (*Federal Register*, 1977, p. 65082).

While this chapter focuses primarily on cognitive and intellectual functioning of the disabled individual, it should be recognized that all these domains (cognitive, affective, social, motoric, physical, settings, etc.) are interrelated. The domains are not totally independent of one another. How people function cognitively can affect how they feel about themselves and how they interact socially. At the same time their social skills may influence the availability of opportunities for cognitive growth, and their current feelings may influence their performance on a particular measure of intellectual functioning. It is important to keep this interrelationship among domains in mind as we examine the measurement of and intervention with cognitive and intellectual functioning.

Measurement of Cognitive and Intellectual Functioning

Just as there were various definitions of intelligence, there are many ways of measuring cognitive functioning of individuals. As indicated earlier, perhaps the most pervasive approach to measuring intelligence is the psychometric one through the use of norm-referenced tests. We will first examine the most frequently used individual tests of intelligence, their strengths and their limitations, problems with intelligence tests, and recent psychometric alternatives. Then we will look at nonpsychometric approaches to assessing cognitive functioning.

Psychometric Approach

A psychometric approach is a test-based approach, specifically with norm-referenced tests. Such tests present a standard set of tasks that elicit a sample of behavior under highly standardized sets of conditions (materials, instructions, response format, etc.). Assuming the test is reliable (a necessary condition for a norm-referenced test), we can then compare a particular individual's performance on the tasks with those of a norm sample (a standardized reference group that is representative of those with whom the test is subsequently used). Knowing the validity of the particular test, we can make some inferences about how the individual might do in related situations.

Traditional Psychometric Tests of Intelligence. Intelligence testing as we know it today began in Paris, France, when in 1904 the minister of public instruction in Paris commissioned Alfred Binet to develop a measure to determine which children were capable of benefiting from public school instruction. Binet, along with Theodore Simon, constructed the first systematic and successful test of intelligence in 1905—which, oddly enough, was called the Simon-Binet Intelligence Scale. Because of the directive from the minister of public instruction, Binet selected tasks that were demonstrated to have predictive validity for school success. That is, tasks had to predict scholastic performance in order to be included as part of the scale.

There have been numerous revisions of the Binet scale. Lewis Terman at Stanford University standardized the Binet scale in this country in 1916, calling it the Stanford-Binet Intelligence Scale, and made major revisions in 1937 and 1960. The Stanford-Binet was again revised in 1972. This scale is the standard against which later tests of intelligence were compared. As such, intelligence tests in general are found to have excellent predictive validity for success in schoolwork. They do *not* predict well an individual's ability to survive interpersonally or occupationally (Mercer, 1979; Oakland, 1980). Given their predictive validity to the student role in a school setting, Mercer (1979) has argued that intelligence test measures are used most appropriately as indices of adaptive fit to that role and setting. Thus, intelligence tests are best viewed as standardized measures of school learning (Cleary, Humphreys, Kendrick, & Wesman, 1975; Wesman, 1968). Let us now examine some of these standardized measures of intelligence, or school learning.

Table 2 lists the major individual intelligence tests. Infant and preschool measures of intelligence do not predict well to academic performance. The three most popular individual tests of intelligence at the preschool level (indicated in the table) have the above limitation of poor predictive validity to school performance.

One measure yielded by the McCarthy scale is the General Cognitive Index score (GCI). The GCI includes common everyday skill attainments and

Table 2
Individual Measures of Intelligence

Preschool Measures

Stanford-Binet Intelligence Scale (2 yrs. to adult)
Wechsler Preschool and Primary Scale of Intelligence (WPPSI)
   (4–0 to 6–6 yrs.)
McCarthy Scales of Children's Abilities (2–6 to 8–6 yrs.)

School-Age Measures

Stanford-Binet Intelligence Scale (2 yrs. to adult)
Wechsler Intelligence Scale for Children—Revised (WISC-R)
   (6–0 to 16–11 yrs.)
Wechsler Adult Intelligence Scale—Revised (WAIS-R) (16–0 yrs. to adult)

Adult Measures

Stanford-Binet Intelligence Scale (2 yrs. to adult)
Wechsler Adult Intelligence Scale—Revised (WAIS-R) (16–0 yrs. to adult)

Recent Psychometric Alternatives

System of Multicultural Pluralistic Assessment (SOMPA) (5–0 to 11–11 yrs.)
Kaufman Assessment Battery for Children (K-ABC) (2–6 to 12–5 yrs.)

therefore could be compared to an IQ in an achievement-intelligence discrepancy formula for learning disabilities. While some studies appear to indicate that a GCI-IQ difference (i.e., GCI lower than Binet or WPPSI IQ) is indicative of learning disabled children (e.g., Kaufman & Kaufman, 1974, 1977), others suggest that the difference varies with age and may occur just as well with typical children (e.g., Gerken, Hancock, & Wade, 1978; Nagle, 1979; Phillips, Pasework, & Tindall, 1978).

The Binet and the Wechsler Intelligence Scale for Children—Revised (WISC-R) are the tests most frequently used with school-aged children. Kaufman (1979a, 1979b) has provided the most thorough set of guidelines for interpreting the WISC-R, along with other assessment measures, as a measure of learning potential. The WISC-R is composed of subtests that tap verbal comprehension and perceptual organization abilities, matching closely the Verbal and Performance scales of the WISC-R (see Table 3). When interpreted with other evidence, subtests that rely on focused attention (mental manipulations, remembering dictated digits, and rapidly copying a code) offer useful information about the child's "freedom from distractibility" (Kaufman, 1979a, 1979b), generalized or test anxiety (Lutey, 1977), sequencing ability (Bannatyne, 1971, 1974), and symbolic skills (Meeker, 1969, 1975).

Large discrepancies in subtest scores (subtest scatter) frequently have been considered an index of neurological impairment and learning disabilities. Kaufman (1979a, 1979b) has cautioned that this scatter must be compared to that of typical children. He has pointed out that the average verbal-performance discrepancy for typical children is 9.7 IQ points. Kaufman has suggested that discrepancies and subtest profile patterns may have educational significance (in that they may provide hypotheses for further assessment leading to educational planning), but they do not have diagnostic significance unless the same fluctuations occur infrequently in the normal population.

Research has shown that various WISC-R subtest profiles are related to cognitive style (Keogh and Hall, 1974), spatial relations in learning disabled children (Rugel, 1974; Smith, Coleman, Dokecki, & Davis, 1977a, 1977b), and cognitive processing in reading and learning disabled children (Das, 1973; Das, Kirby, & Jarman, 1975; Kirby & Das, 1977). While statistically significant for research groups, these patterns are not valid for making diagnostic statements about individuals.

Problems with Intelligence Tests

There has been a variety of criticisms of intelligence tests. One concern is that the items represent too small a sample of behavior from which to make inferences about a person. For example, at the school-age levels, the Binet appears to tap primarily verbal abilities, particularly verbal fluency and verbal reasoning. This restricted range of abilities assessed by the Binet is illustrated by the fact that Guilford (1967) has proposed a Structure of Intellect Model that postulates at least 120 possible intellectual abilities or factors.

Table 3
*Representative Items of Wechsler Intelligence Scale for Children—
Revised (WISC-R)*

Verbal Scale

1. Information
   Child answers questions of fact, such as "Name four presidents since 1900."

2. Similarities
   Child indicates how two things or concepts are alike; for example, "How are an apple and an orange alike?"

3. Arithmetic
   Oral questions that assess simple computational skills.

4. Vocabulary
   Child defines each of a list of words.

5. Comprehension
   Child answers questions concerned with what he or she would do in certain situations; for example, "What would you do if you lost a ball that belonged to someone else?"

6. Digits Span (supplementary subtest)
   Child repeats series of digits, presented by examiner, in same order and in reverse order.

Performance Scale

1. Picture Completion
   Child identifies important features missing in pictures.

2. Picture Arrangement
   Child arranges series of pictures in sequence that tells a story.

3. Block Design
   Child arranges colored blocks to match a design made by examiner or printed in booklet.

4. Object Assembly
   Child puts together small puzzles (e.g., child, face, truck).

5. Coding
   Child draws figures with numbers in random order as rapidly as possible with paper and pencil.

6. Mazes (supplementary subtest)
   Child draws line on mazes to get child from home to school.

In addition, the verbal skills assessed by our commonly used intelligence tests appear to tap those verbal skills acquired through education and socialization in the dominant cultural group of our society (middle-class Anglo-American). Therefore, individuals whose sociocultural backgrounds differ from the dominant core society tend to score more poorly on these tests.

The more similar a particular group's sociocultural characteristics are to the dominant group represented in the test items, the more similar are the intelligence test scores. Mercer's (1973) Riverside Study with black, Hispanic, and white children of varying sociocultural characteristics illustrates this fact (see Figures 2 and 3).

One consequence of this limited range of verbal skills represented on tests of intelligence is that various cultural groups are disproportionately represented in those exceptionalities defined, at least in part, by their performance on intelligence tests. Minority and lower social class white children are over-represented (given their proportions in society) in classes for mentally retarded individuals, while they are under-represented in learning disabilities and gifted categories. Precisely the opposite is typically found for middle social class white children. This disproportionate representation, particularly in the mentally retarded category, is compounded by the fact that historically classification of mental retardation has been based solely upon intelligence test performance. Such reliance upon the intelligence test has resulted in what Mercer (1973) has called the "six-hour retarded child," an individual who is judged to be retarded in one social setting (the school), on the basis of a single test (the intelligence test), but who is functioning

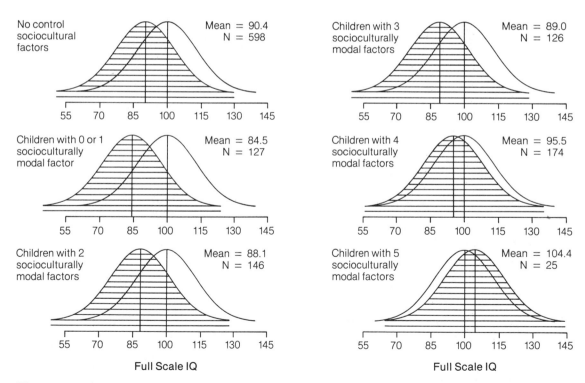

Figure 2. *Convergence of average full scale WISC with standard norms for Hispanic children with sociocultural factors held increasingly constant.*

adaptively in other social settings (home, neighborhood, community). This reliance upon a unidimensional definition of mental retardation remains prevalent in spite of Public Law 94-142, which clearly indicates the need for measures of both adaptive behavior and intelligence. Indeed, the American Association of Mental Deficiency (AAMD) has defined mental retardation in terms of performance on a test of intelligence *and* a measure of adaptive behavior (Grossman, 1973).

This problem of limited range of items and sociocultural bias in our intelligence tests is not new. A group of sociologists at the University of Chicago (Eells, Davis, Havighurst, Herrick, & Tyler, 1951) demonstrated the bias in the then current tests and in school curricula. They attempted to develop culture-free tests. The measures failed because they did not predict school performance (the school's goals being determined by the dominant culture) and because sociocultural differences were not eliminated from the measures (Cronbach, 1975). The finding of sociocultural differences on so-called culture-free tests is not surprising. There are no culture-free tests, and such a goal is unattainable. All tests' questions and materials must be developed within some cultural context. A test cannot be developed within a cultural vacuum.

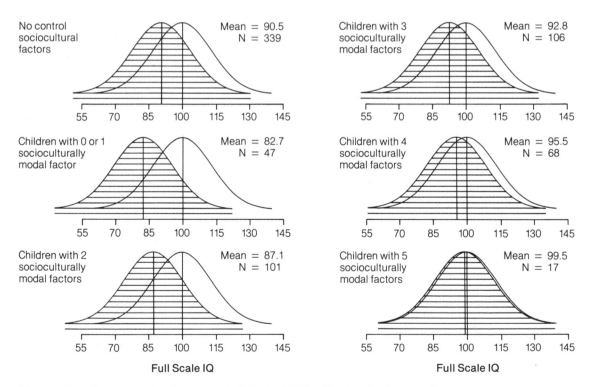

Figure 3. *Convergence of average full scale WISC with standard norms for black children with sociocultural factors held increasingly constant.*

The issues raised by Eells and his colleagues were criticized and soon ignored. The times (early 1950s) were just not right for addressing those disturbing issues. Since then the social climate has changed dramatically. The considerable litigation and legislation that were introduced challenged various assessment practices, particularly tests purporting to assess intellectual abilities, and practices resulting in the disproportionate representation of socioculturally different individuals in classes for mentally handicapped children. The civil rights movement gained momentum in that period. Concern for the education of handicapped children increased as well. All of these actions culminated in the passage of Public Law 94-142, which, among other things, very clearly mandates assessment that takes into account the language and sociocultural background of the individual being tested. Taylor and Searl (Chapter 1, this book), as well as Bersoff (1982a, 1982b) and Oakland and Laosa (1977), have reviewed legal, legislative, and advocacy issues leading up to Public Law 94-142 and beyond. These challenges and concerns have led to changes in psychometric measures of cognitive and intellectual assessment.

Recent Psychometric Alternatives

Part of the problem in implementing a two-dimensional definition of mental retardation (including both intelligence and adaptive behavior) has been the lack of adequate measures of adaptive behavior. From a social systems model perspective, adaptive behavior refers to how well a child fits the many roles he or she assumes in diverse settings. In a comprehensive assessment, evaluators are concerned with a child's adaptive fit not only to the student role, but also to nonacademic roles in and outside the school setting. In fact, Public Law 94-142 requires that assessment of adaptive behavior include nonschool settings. Adaptive behavior is defined as the degree to which the individual meets the standards of personal independence and social responsibility expected of his or her age and cultural group (Coulter & Morrow, 1978). As such it involves interpersonal and task-specific skills. Since these expectations vary across ages and cultures, so does the nature of adaptive behavior deficits (Grossman, 1973).

Norms, item distributions, reliabilities, and validities of older adaptive behavior scales such as the Vineland Social Maturity Scale and the AAMD Adaptive Behavior Scale–Public School Version (items are drawn from institutionalized populations) are being revised and studied. The Adaptive Behavior Inventory for Children (ABIC), part of the SOMPA, has broadened evaluators' focus by assessing some nonschool role functioning. Other formal and informal measures of adaptive behavior, including measures for specific populations (such as the Cain-Levine Social Competence Scale for trainable mentally retarded individuals), have been developed in recent years (Coulter, 1980; Walls, Werner, Bacon, & Zane, 1977), but they need to be examined carefully to make certain they meet quality standards and address children's needs.

Other sources of information can provide useful information about an individual's adaptive behavior. For example, direct observation across many settings can be very useful. Peer sociometric scales (that get at a child's popularity) can provide clues about a child's adaptation to a specific peer group through questions such as "Name three children that you would most and least like to do a project with or invite to a party." Various behavior rating scales (Wilson, 1980) can also provide useful information. For example, Brown and Hammill's (1979) Behavior Rating Profile uses ratings obtained from teachers, parents, peers, and the child. The whole area of adaptive behavior, its assessment and intervention, requires considerable research.

Two alternatives to the culture-free tests might be to develop culture-fair tests and many culture-specific tests. A culture-fair test would balance items across cultural groups. To some extent this strategy was employed by Mercer in the development of her adaptive behavior scale (the ABIC). As part of a measure of intelligence, this approach, however, would not predict performance in our predominantly middle-class, white American schools. Culture-specific tests would have the same problem—low predictability to school performance. In addition, a separate black or Hispanic test does not recognize the considerable heterogeneity that exists within each of these groups. Many culture-specific tests for each ethnic group would have to be developed. Two very recently developed psychometric attempts to consider background characteristics while measuring intellectual functioning are Mercer's (1979; Mercer & Lewis, 1978) System of Multicultural Pluralistic Assessment (SOMPA) and Kaufman's (1983) Assessment Battery for Children (K-ABC).

SOMPA.   Jane Mercer (1979) developed the *SOMPA* as a norm-based measurement system specifically designed to address issues of nonbiased assessment. Consistent with the mandates of Public Law 94-142, she has cautioned against the use of the SOMPA as the only measure within a comprehensive assessment. To ensure the use of multiple perspectives when examining a child, the SOMPA includes three assessment models, each with its own set of measures: medical, social systems, and pluralistic (see Table 4). These assessment models; their theoretical foundations; and Mercer's philosophical orientation to our pluralistic society, to education within that pluralistic context, and to issues of nonbiased assessment are described thoroughly in her technical manual (Mercer, 1979). The explicitness with which she provides this background information is an important contribution because the philosophical and value orientation (however implicit) of the person constructing a test has a profound impact on strategy, items selected, and so forth (see Box 2). While the test user does not have to agree with the test author's philosophical orientation, knowing the impact of that philosophy on the test itself will influence how we interpret a child's performance on that measure.

Children between five and eleven years of age (the elementary school years) were included in the normative sample because those are the years

Table 4
Mercer's System of Multicultural Pluralistic Assessment (SOMPA)

Model—Purpose	Measures	Description	Data source
Medical—Screen for potential biological and neurological problems	Health history inventories	Measures past and current health conditions	Parent
	Physical dexterity tasks	Measures fine and gross motor coordination and balance	Child
	Bender Gestalt	Copying test that assesses perceptual-motor maturity and screens neurological functioning	Child
	Visual acuity	—	Child
	Auditory acuity	—	Child
	Height by weight index	—	Child
Social systems—Assess the child's adaptive fit to school and nonschool roles and systems	Adaptive Behavior Inventory for Children (ABIC)	Assesses child's adaptive fit to family, community, peers, nonacademic school roles, earner consumer roles, and self-maintenance skills	Parent
	School Functioning Level (SFL)	Based on scores on the Wechsler Intelligence Scale for Children—Revised (WISC-R) and used as a measure of adaptive fit to the student role in the school social system	Child
Pluralistic—Estimate the child's intellectual potential	Sociocultural Scale	Assesses family's urban acculturation, socioeconomic status, family structure and size	Parent
	Estimated Learning Potential (ELP)	Measures intellectual potential, based on WISC-R score corrected by the family's ethnic and sociocultural characteristics	Child & Parent

Box 2
Personal Philosophy, Social Context, and Test Construction

All tests reflect the basic assumptions of those constructing them, however implicit those assumptions might be. Science is often presented as value free, and objective measures appear to be value free, but they are not.

When Terman (1916) developed the American version of the Binet (the Stanford-Binet Intelligence Scale) he piloted various subtests and test items with various groups. On some items he obtained gender differences favoring females. However, he commented that of course women were not more intelligent than men, and he presented a long discussion about the cultural factors involved in the discrepancy between IQ scores and the lack of eminence in the profession for women. Knowing (assuming) there were no gender differences, he threw out those items that showed sex differences on the preliminary research. The pilot research also found large ethnic and socioeconomic differences in IQ scores. Terman assumed these differences were real differences and did not modify the items of subtests to eliminate the group differences. Since the Binet is the standard against which other later tests were compared, it is not surprising that reviews of research on intelligence test performance consistently find no gender differences but considerable ethnic and sociocultural group differences.

The importance of social context in test construction is illustrated in the lack of public (and to some extent professional) reaction to the commentary by Eells, Davis, Havighurst, Herrick, and Tyler (1951) on tests and public school instruction and to the development of their "culture-free tests." The social context of the 1950s was not supportive of such efforts, but since then we have experienced the civil rights movement and considerable litigation and advocacy for individual rights in general. Such social action resulted in the passage of Public Law 94-142, which, among other issues, mandates the use of assessment strategies that take into account the cultural background of the individual being tested. In addition, this social action (including groups such as the National Educational Association and Black Psychological Association calling for a moratorium on testing) resulted in the revision of old tests and the development of new tests. One of the major changes in these revisions and new tests was the inclusion of minority group members in the standardization samples. Previously, the norm sample for most major nationally standardized tests of intelligence and achievement included only American-born, white individuals.

(continued)

Box 2
(continued)

As indicated, Mercer (1979) very clearly stated her philosophical orientation to our pluralistic society, to education within that pluralistic context, and to issues of nonbiased assessment in the development of the SOMPA. The maintenance of the WISC-R within the social systems model as a measure of adaptive fit to the student role in our middle-class, white-dominated schools reflects her assumption that the dominant core culture will continue to be perpetuated through the public schools and that *all* children must learn to master the language, skills, knowledge, and behavior styles of the core culture in order to participate fully in the economic and political life of American society. She also assumes that our society is a pluralistic one, that many ethnic groups in our society will remain structurally identifiable and culturally distinct, and that these sociocultural differences should be valued. Given this assumption and considerable research on access to educational opportunities when traditional tests are used, she developed her pluralistic norms and the Estimated Learning Potential (ELP) score that takes into account the ethnic group and sociocultural characteristics of the individual child. These assumptions and the SOMPA are not noncontroversial. The SOMPA has been the object of much, often acrimonious, debate. A special issue with follow-up articles in the immediately subsequent issue of the *School Psychology Digest* (vol. 8, nos. 1–2; now *School Psychology Review*) presented commentary of extreme positive and negative reactions to the SOMPA and to the assumptions of its author, with little or no research data to support any of the critiques. Just as tests cannot be developed in a cultural vacuum, neither are professional debates conducted in a value-free manner.

The K-ABC represents another shift in intellectual assessment based upon the authors' assumptions. Ethnic group differences are reduced considerably on the K-ABC because of the removal of highly verbal achievement-based items from the mental processing composite score and the inclusion of tasks that reflect cognitive processing styles different from those typically employed in tests of intelligence. The Kaufmans' designation of a "mental processing composite" score rather than an IQ score reflects their concern that the term "intelligence quotient" carries extra and inappropriate connotations for the public and professionals.

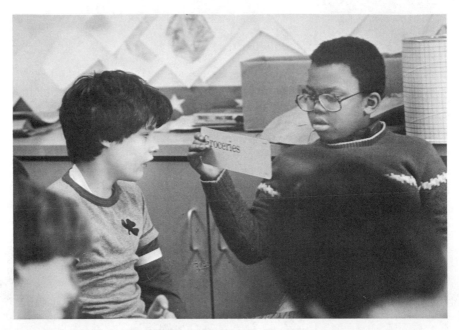

Peer tutoring may be beneficial as a way to facilitate learning and social interaction. Here a nondisabled student assists his friend with special needs. (Photograph by Mima Cataldo.)

when a child is most likely to be labeled mentally retarded (Mercer, 1973). Both the child and parents are sources of information for the SOMPA. The parent measures, consistent with the mandates of Public Law 94-142, ensure parental involvement beyond a cursory level of permission granting.

The SOMPA is a new assessment system, and much research is needed. One of its most serious limitations is the fact that it was standardized on California children only. How well the norms hold up across our culturally diverse country has yet to be demonstrated. Some studies suggest that we cannot readily generalize from the California sample (Oakland, 1977, 1980; Reschly, 1978, 1982). The potential need for pluralistic norms (which take into account ethnic background and sociocultural characteristics) for the ABIC has also been suggested in recent studies (Oakland, 1980; Reschly, 1982). The Educational Testing Service and other test publishers have long advocated the development and use of local norms. The need for local norms is illustrated by examination of the problems of a child in an inner city who scores in the average range on some standardized test, then moves to a suburban school where the average performance of all children is in the very high average range. Where previously that child may have been at the higher reading groups relative to his or her local peers, the same child is now in the lowest groups and possibly viewed as having an achievement problem relative to his or her new local peers. Mercer's system highlights again the need to use local norms.

The SOMPA has been criticized for not providing information directly relevant to educational and psychological programming. But this criticism is unwarranted, since Mercer developed the system to ensure fair and unbiased identification, screening, and classroom placement decisions (recall the preceding discussion of the relationship between assessment purposes and assessment measures). Basically, Mercer states that, as long as educators continue to ask how bright students are and place them on the basis of the answer to that question, the question should be answered in as fair and unbiased a manner as possible.

The Estimated Learning Potential (ELP) may be useful in identifying minority and socioculturally different children as gifted and learning disabled because the estimate of intellectual ability is adjusted upward. With respect to learning disabilities, educators using the ELP rather than the standard IQ are more likely to find a potential-achievement discrepancy for these children (Reschly, 1979). Mercer (1979) has argued that both sets of scores are useful because it is important and necessary to determine how well the child adapts to the dominant core society as well as to the child's own sociocultural settings. In this way intervention can focus on helping the child adapt to and maintain skills in the dominant society as well as in his or her own sociocultural context.

It should be noted that there are serious value and practical implications to the use of the SOMPA and the ELP score in placement decision making. Because the scores for minority and culturally different children are adjusted upward (with the pluralistic norms as opposed to the standard norms), children currently receiving services for mental retardation might be declassified. Indeed Fisher (1978) and Talley (1979) have shown that 40 to 75 percent of the children currently classified as educable mentally retarded (EMR) would be declassified if the ELP were used rather than the standard IQ score. While some of these children might be eligible for other special education classification (e.g., learning disabilities), others would be ineligible for existing special education services under current categorical funding arrangements, even though their standard intellectual and academic performances were well below average. In addition, new referrals of minority and culturally different children would result in less classification of mental retardation when using the SOMPA. Simply returning declassified students to regular classrooms, or avoiding special education classification with new referrals, does nothing about the academic problems of these children. Special transitional programs have been implemented for declassified children, but these are often temporary and do not address the problems presented in new referrals (Meyers, MacMillan, & Yoshida, 1978; Yoshida, MacMillan, & Meyers, 1976). The educator is placed in the dilemma of either using a standard IQ score and getting special education services for a child (though typical services for a comprehensively retarded child—i.e., low intellectual functioning relative to others of similar background characteristics and low adaptive behavior—

might not be appropriate for such a child) or using an ELP score (IQ adjusted for sociocultural background, though with little research justification yet) and getting no special education services for the child.

Certainly, another alternative could be resource rooms designed to deal with the specific academic needs of these children, with most of their time being spent in the regular classroom. Such an alternative would require a system whereby special services are provided on the basis of need rather than category. Or, if categorical funding is not removed, another possibility might be to designate another category with a more descriptive label, such as Reschly's (1982) suggested "educationally handicapped." It is apparent that children who score low on in-class and standard achievement measures and on standard intellectual measures (like the WISC-R) but in the typical range on adaptive behavior scale and/or on measures that specifically take into account sociocultural background and ethnic group membership are *not* retarded. It is also clear that such individuals need help with regard to social and/or academic skills. A major task for professionals working in this area is to develop more effective means of identifying the specific needs of these individuals and to develop effective intervention strategies for meeting those needs.

Kaufman Assessment Battery.   The Kaufman Assessment Battery for Children (*K-ABC*; Kaufman & Kaufman, 1983) represents another recent and dramatic shift in psychometric assessment of intellectual functioning. Kaufman (1979a) has argued that the development of intelligence tests has been directed by a pragmatic and empirical focus in that the primary concern from Binet to the present has been with the prediction of school success. Intelligence test construction has not been influenced by recent theory and research on cognitive information processing (e.g., Detterman & Sternberg, 1982; Sternberg & Detterman, 1979), on complex learning process (e.g., Gagne, 1977), or on neuropsychological processes (e.g., Bogen, 1975; Gazzaniga, 1975; Ornstein, 1972, 1973, 1978).

In developing the K-ABC the Kaufmans had a number of purposes, including: (1) to measure intelligence from a strong theoretical and research base; (2) to differentiate acquired factual knowlege from the ability to solve unfamiliar problems; (3) to bring about a closer relationship between intelligence test performance and educational interventions; and (4) to be sensitive to the needs of preschool, minority, and exceptional children. The standardization sample included the following variables: age (2½ to 12½ years), gender, geographic region, socioeconomic status (based upon parental education only), ethnic group, community size, and educational placement. Exceptional children, those individuals about whom we are most concerned when administering intelligence tests, typically have been excluded from standardization samples of individual intelligence tests. Based upon an additional sample of black and white children with parents of varying parental educational background, supplemental sociocultural norms were also developed.

Diverse research within the fields of cognitive psychology and neuropsychology have suggested a dichotomy of two basic types of information processing style (e.g., Bogen, 1969; Das, Kirby, & Jarman, 1975; Luria, 1966; Neisser, 1967; Paivio, 1975, 1976; Schneider & Shiffrin, 1977; Shiffrin & Schneider, 1977). One processing style is characterized as *sequential*, involving serial, time-based analysis of stimuli and tasks in terms of details and features. The contrasting processing style is *simultaneous*, involving holistic, unitary, time-independent processing of global properties of stimuli and tasks. These dichotomous processing styles have been linked to brain anatomy in cerebral specialization studies (e.g., Bogen, 1969; Gazzaniga, 1975; Luria, 1966; Nebes, 1974). Inclusion of simultaneous processing tasks is minimal in intelligence tests. Such under-representation of simultaneous processing style may penalize children from cultural groups that place primary emphasis upon such processing. There is growing evidence that this is particularly disadvantageous for blacks who are characterized as having right-hemisphere simultaneous processing preferences and strengths (e.g., Abrahams, 1973; Carter, 1977; Pines, 1973; Weems, 1975). The K-ABC, contrary to the Wechsler scales, which differentiate tasks according to their content (verbal or performance), presents tasks that are process oriented. That is, the scales are concerned with whether the stimuli are cognitively manipulated one at a time (sequentially) or simultaneously, regardless of content.

The K-ABC has a sequential processing scale, in which problems must be solved by arranging the input in sequential or serial order, and a simultaneous processing scale, in which problems are spatial, analogic, or organizational and input must be integrated and synthesized simultaneously in order to solve them (see Table 5). Together these scales yield a mental processing composite (MPC) score. This score label (just as with Mercer's ELP) is used instead of the IQ because of the extra inaccurate connotations that IQ has acquired in our culture. Mental processing tasks are novel (some totally new and some adapted from earlier cognitive laboratory research) and minimize the need for language, verbal skills, and acquired knowledge that are dependent upon educational opportunities, environmental background, motivation, and generally nonintellectual variables. As already indicated, other intelligence tests are heavily weighted with verbal and acquired knowledge tasks, and show considerable performance differences between core culture and culturally different children. The K-ABC, additionally, has an achievement scale that assesses acquired knowledge and school-related skills in areas such as reading, arithmetic, general information, early language development, and language concepts. This scale is separate from the mental processing scales and is explicitly *not* used to infer a child's intellectual potential. With this distinction, ethnic and sociocultural group differences appear to be considerably reduced on the K-ABC (Kaufman & Kaufman, 1983), relative to other individual intelligence tests.

The inclusion of separate mental processing and achievement scales within the same battery is particularly important for the identification of learning disabled children. As indicated earlier, many definitions of learning disability are based upon a discrepancy between intelligence and achievement. With other tests (not including both kinds of measures) comparison between intelligence and achievement test scores is difficult because the scores are based upon different normative samples. Therefore, it is not possible to determine the significance of the discrepancy (which is crucial for the definition of learning disabilities). This problem is minimized in the K-ABC because both kinds of measures are included, thus allowing direct comparison of mental processing and achievement scores based upon a single normative sample.

Table 5
Representative Items of the Kaufman Assessment Battery for Children (K-ABC)

Mental Processing Subtests

Magic Window (simultaneous processing scale, ages 2–6 through 4–11)
Child identifies and names an object whose picture is rotated behind a narrow slit, allowing only partial exposure of the picture at any point in time.

Face Recognition (simultaneous processing scale, ages 2–6 through 4–11; nonverbal scale, ages 4–0 through 4–11)
Child must attend to one or two faces whose photographs are exposed briefly, then selects the correct face(s), shown in a different pose, from a group photograph.

Hand Movements (sequential processing scale, ages 2–6 through 12–5; nonverbal scale, ages 4–0 through 12–5)
Child imitates the precise sequence of taps on the table with the fist, palm, or side of the hand performed by the examiner.

Gestalt Closure (simultaneous processing scale, ages 2–6 through 12–5)
Child names or describes a partially completed inkblot drawing by mentally filling the gaps.

Number Recall (sequential processing scale, ages 2–6 through 12–5)
Child repeats in sequence a series of numbers spoken by the examiner.

Triangles (simultaneous processing and nonverbal scales, ages 4–10 through 12–5)
Child assembles identical rubber triangles to match pictures of abstract designs.

Word Order (sequential processing scale, ages 4–0 through 12–15)
Child points to silhouettes of common objects in the same order as these objects were named by the examiner. For school-age children, recall is done both with and without an interference (color-naming) task.

Matrix Analogies (simultaneous processing and nonverbal scales, ages 5–0 through 12–15)
Child must select the picture or design that best completes a 2-by-2 visual analogy.

(continued)

Table 5
(continued)

Mental Processing Subtests (continued)

Spatial Memory (simultaneous processing and nonverbal scales, ages 5–0 through 12–5)
Child must recall the locations of pictures arranged randomly on a page.

Photo Series (simultaneous processing and nonverbal scales, ages 6–0 through 12–5)
Child must organize a randomly placed array of photographs illustrating an event and then order them in their proper time sequence.

Achievement Scale Subtest

Expressive Vocabulary (ages 2–6 through 4–11)
Child must state the correct name for objects pictured in photographs.

Faces and Places (ages 2–6 through 12–5)
Child must name the fictional character, famous person, or well-known place pictured.

Arithmetic (ages 3–0 through 12–5)
Child must identify numbers, count, compute, and demonstrate understanding of mathematical concepts.

Riddles (ages 3–0 through 12–5)
Child must infer the name of a concrete or abstract verbal concept when given several of its characteristics.

Reading/Decoding (ages 5–0 through 12–5)
Child must identify letters and read and pronounce words.

Reading/Understanding (ages 7–0 through 12–5)
Child must demonstrate reading comprehension by acting out commands that are given in sentences.

Finally, a subset of tasks from both the simultaneous and sequential scales makes up a nonverbal scale of mental processing. This scale, which can be administered in pantomime and responded to motorically, is helpful for assessing hearing-impaired, speech- and language-disordered, and non-English-speaking children. The novel nature of the tasks and the reduced language requirement also appears to make this test particularly useful at the preschool level. Preschoolers, as well as older children, find the tasks quite enjoyable (a fact likely to increase their motivation for performing on this measure). Other preschool intelligence tests involve several concepts (e.g., middle, few, same) in the directions to tasks that make it difficult to communicate what the child must do to solve a particular problem.

While the K-ABC is relatively new, it has substantially more research to support its use than other measures at the same level of development. Numerous reliability and validity studies were conducted prior to the publication of the test and were included in an interpretation manual (Kaufman & Kaufman, 1983). The reliabilities appear to be very high. The sequential-simultaneous dichotomy in processing style seems to be supported, and the measures show strong relationships to school functioning. Gunnison, Kaufman, and Kaufman (1983) have described educational implications of the sequential-simultaneous processing dichotomy. They have suggested that reading, spelling, and mathematics can be remediated through instructional strategies that are matched to a given child's relative strengths in processing style (see Box 3 for illustrations of this possible matching). This question of matching instructional strategy to cognitive processing style requires considerable research, as does the K-ABC in general, but there appears to be considerable promise in this approach.

Cognitive Training or Test-Teach-Test Approach

Feuerstein (1979) has argued that the traditional and recent psychometric tests of intellectual functioning are static measures. Such measures provide scores representing the products of prior learning. They support the tendency to infer within-individual abilities, characteristics that are relatively fixed or stable. Consistent with a more interactional view of intellectual and cognitive development, Feuerstein has called for dynamic assessment that addresses the processes of change in intellectual and cognitive development. His approach represents a rejection of standard psychometric tests. He suggests that what we are interested in when assessing an individual is not some sort of quantitative index of what the individual has, but rather an assessment of how changeable or modifiable the individual is and what conditions bring about change. Because dynamic or process assessment is so radically different from psychometric or static assessment, let us first examine why this approach is being increasingly considered as an alternative or important supplement to traditional assessment.

Rationale.   Meyers, Pfeffer, and Erlbaum (1985) have presented a number of reasons why we need to use dynamic process assessment rather than (or in addition to) static assessment. First, as specified in Public Law 94-142, assessment in schools must have clear implications for instructional decisions. Norm-referenced tests only indirectly address that purpose. They were designed to compare an individual with a normative standardization sample. Assessment that describes cognitive processes, how they change, and the conditions that bring about change will bring about a closer linkage between assessment and intervention.

A second reason relates to nondiscriminatory assessment. Meyers, Pfeffer, and Erlbaum (1985) argued that as long as we base educational decisions only on standardized norm-referenced instruments (that fail to identify in any precise manner the particular conditions that contribute to a given child's performance and thus lead to appropriate interventions), we are discriminating against *any* child (not just culturally different children, but any child) who deviates significantly from the norms. Such an argument takes the issues

Box 3
Possible Teaching Strategies Based upon Sequential-Simultaneous Processing Dichotomy (from Kaufman & Kaufman, 1983, pp. 253–254, 281–282)

Text Organization

Task: Sentence Combining
Content: Sentences from appropriate reading material, preferably from reading selections that will follow instruction.
Skill: Using sequence (syntax) to form a complete image and verbal concept.

Sequential Emphasis	*Method, Examples*
Arranging scrambled phrases into a logical sequence.	Read each phrase. Decide which phrase should go first, which one should go second, and so on. Write the first one here next to the number 1. Then write the second next to the number 2, and so on. 1) *The big horse* 2) *snorted with pleasure* 3) *and quickly galloped* 4) *toward the river* 5) *to get a drink of water*
Identifying specific details (who, what, why, when, where, and how) conveyed by individual phrases.	Now look over all the phrases again. Which phrase tells *who* did the action? Write *who* next to that phrase. Which phrase tells us *what*? Good. Is there another one that tells us *what*? How about *where*? *Why*? 1) *The big horse—who* 2) *snorted with pleasure—what* 3) *and quickly galloped—what* 4) *toward the river—where* 5) *to get a drink of water—why*
Copying the phrases on paper to form a complete sentence.	Now copy the whole sentence down. Remember to put it in the order that we decided. Think about each phrase as you copy it. Remember, each phrase tells us *who* or *what* or *where* or *why*.

(continued)

Box 3
(continued)

Simultaneous Emphasis
Forming a mental picture of the action portrayed in the phrases.

Method, Examples
Close your eyes. As I read each phrase, picture what is happening in your mind. Pretend that you are seeing a movie of the action in your head. Ready? *The big horse* (Do you see the big horse?) *snorted with pleasure* (See him lift his head and snort?) *and quickly galloped* (See the dust he left behind?) *toward the river* (See the river in the distance?) *to get a drink of water.* (What do you picture now?)

Sequential and Simultaneous Emphasis
Reading phrases one at a time and then arranging them to form a complete thought or action.

Method, Examples

Read each phrase to yourself, one at a time. Picture the action as you read each phrase.

Retelling the story and writing it down.

Remember what you just read. Write down as many things as you can remember.

Identifying the details by marking who, what, why, when, where, and how.

Read over the things you just wrote down. Which words tell us *who*? *Where*? *Why*? *What*?

Drawing a picture that shows the action and supporting details.

Now draw a picture or cartoon that shows the action that you just read. Put in as many details as you can.

Task: Understanding Place Value
Content: Numbers that represent differing place values.
Skill: Recognizing relationships between spatial placement and numerical value.

Sequential Emphasis
Verbalizing the place value of different numbers.

Method, Examples
Look at this number: *2123.* How do we read this number? *two thousands, one hundred, twenty (two tens), and three (ones)*

Writing the place value of different numbers.

Can you write two ones? *2* When you add one zero after the 2, how many ones will you have? *20.* We can write 20 ones in another way. We

(continued)

Box 3
(continued)

can write 20 ones as 2 tens. What number is *10 + 10? 20, or 2 tens.*

$$\boxed{1} + \boxed{1} = 2$$
one   one   ones

$$20 = 20 = 2 = \boxed{\begin{matrix}10\\10\end{matrix}}$$
ones   tens

Simultaneous Emphasis
Picturing numbers in different place values.

Method, Examples
Close your eyes. Picture three numbers side by side. Remember those three numbers. Now open your eyes and write the three numbers in the boxes.

☐ ☐ ☐
hundreds tens ones

Sequential and Simultaneous Emphasis
Recognizing the place value of different numbers.

Method, Examples

Look at this diagram:

	thousands	hundreds	tens	ones
1				
2				

In Row 1 put these numbers:
6 thousands
3 hundreds
5 tens or fifty
3 ones or 3
Close your eyes. Picture a number with 4 numerals. Open your eyes and put that number in Row 2. Then fill in the chart below:
_____ *thousands*
_____ *hundreds*
_____ *tens*
_____ *ones*
Now read the number to me.

of nondiscriminatory assessment beyond that of discrimination toward culturally different individuals. Reschly (1979) and Sewell (1981) have stated that nonbiased assessment results in needed services, effective interventions, and expanded opportunities for the individual.

A third concern relates to the issue of validity, that is, validity with respect to the purpose for which an assessment strategy is used. Assessment for purposes of developing instructional and psychological programs must be valid for those purposes. This issue was a major concern addressed by the judge in the previously cited *Larry P.* case about the constitutionality of intelligence tests (static measures). The judge ruled that there was no evidence to suggest that the static intelligence measures were valid for placing a child in an educational program designed to get a child back to mainstream society.

Fourth, in addition to knowing the products of previous learning, it is important to understand the individual child's cognitive functioning, learning strategies, and adaptive responses. A system is needed that allows direct description of those strategies and adaptive behaviors. Static measurement tells us *what* was learned, not *how* learning has taken place.

Fifth, consistent with Public Law 94-142, assessment must be individualized, dependent upon the child, the referred problem, and the settings in which the child thinks and acts. A standardized assessment package alone reduces the likelihood of an individualized approach.

As indicated earlier, assessment must be tied to the settings in which the child acts, learns, and develops. A major setting of concern is the instructional setting. Dynamic process assessment employs an intensive teaching relationship to bring about change and to determine the conditions for change. Such a teaching relationship is consistent with the view that a major form of learning is what Feuerstein (1979) has termed *mediated learning.*

Mediated learning is learning based upon intentional interventions in the environment, planned by an adult who helps to influence the child's perception of the environment, to structure appropriate learning situations and to frame questions that facilitate learning. Such mediated learning is considered prerequisite to learning that occurs more or less by chance through mere exposure to environmental stimuli. Because this planned interaction with the environment is essential to adaptive change, Feuerstein has argued that mediated learning should be a focus of the assessment process. So, in dynamic process assessment the relationship between examiner and examinee is dramatically different from that in traditional static assessment. In order to assess the learning process the examiner assumes an active role as teacher and mediator. Rather than being a neutral objective observer, the examiner becomes an active participant in the assessment process. The examiner becomes a teacher-observer and the examinee becomes a learner-performer in a two-way interactional process directed toward the goal of mutual problem solving.

This active interactional process leads to the last rationale for dynamic process assessment. Assessment can be described as a process of systematically generating and testing hypotheses about the child's behavior and possible interventions that might work. Advocates of static assessment strategies do emphasize the hypothesis generation function. Dynamic assessment involves the important and necessary additional step of testing the efficacy of those hypotheses. In other words, the assessor is not only asking what the person has acquired, but also trying to answer why the individual is performing in a particular way (i.e., how they are functioning cognitively) and what the mediator can do about the performance.

Learning Potential Assessment Device. Feuerstein's (1979) Learning Potential Assessment Device (LPAD) represents perhaps the most comprehensive dynamic process assessment strategy. It is related to other somewhat more limited learning potential approaches. These other approaches will be described briefly first. Haywood, Filler, Shifman, and Chatelanat (1975) have studied the ability of retarded individuals to form verbal abstractions. They have found that when retarded individuals were provided with enriched amounts of verbal information (i.e., increased number of examples of a given concept) during assessment, their ability to form verbal abstractions improved. Haywood and his associates concluded that retarded individuals may not necessarily be deficient in their ability to form abstractions (as might be inferred from a static measure score), but do have an information-input deficit that can be overcome by enriching the amount of information available to the individual.

Budoff (1968; Budoff & Hamilton, 1976) developed his learning potential assessment strategies out of a concern with differentiating between mentally retarded and educationally retarded children. He defined intelligence as the ability to profit from experience. He felt that many children labeled mentally retarded on the basis of IQ and school performance may actually be competent problem solvers who are able to profit from experience and thus, from his definition, not be retarded. Budoff suggested that prior experiences of culturally different children may not have provided them with the skills, strategies, and motivation necessary to succeed on IQ tests and in school, though they could effectively solve problems in their nonschool environments. Budoff presented an assessment method whereby a child's initial level of functioning on a nonverbal reasoning task is measured, then the child is provided with task-specific teaching in which each complex item is analyzed into simple components, and the child is retested again. Performance gains, following the opportunity to learn specific strategies for solving cognitive reasoning problems, provided an index of the individual's ability to profit from experience.

Similarly, in the Soviet Union, Vygotsky's (1978) theory of a "zone of proximal development" leads to an assessment strategy that provides a measure of learning potential. He has defined the zone of proximal development as the distance between the actual developmental level (measured by individual problem-solving performance) and the level of potential development (measured through problem solving under adult guidance or through interactions with more capable peers). In assessment, if a child cannot solve a particular problem, the child is given progressive cues and information until solution is attained, and the examiner measures the amount of additional information (e.g., number of cues) required. Then another version of the same task is provided and again the amount of cues needed for the child to transfer or generalize the earlier problem solution to the new task is counted. The measure of proximal or potential development is the amount of help needed by the child to solve an original problem and transfer the problem solution to a related but new task.

It should be noted that this dynamic process assessment has been proposed by others concerned with the application of cognitive skills to academic functioning. Such assessment strategies are represented in the work of the previously cited task analysis approach (Gold, 1972; Smith, 1983), Bijou's (1970, 1971) functional analysis approach, behavioral assessment generally (Keller, 1980a) and specifically with academic tasks (e.g., Elliott & Piersel, 1982; Sewell, 1979), and Bersoff and Grieger's (1971) psychosituational assessment.

Feuerstein's (1979) LPAD is derived from the above work (of Haywood, Budoff, and Vygotsky), from his work with Piaget (whose developmental model will be described later), and from his own clinical work in Israel with culturally diverse adolescent and adult immigrants. It is interesting to note (in relation to the earlier discussion on philosophical orientations and the construction of tests—Box 2) the differences between static and dynamic assessment systems and the cultural contexts out of which they developed. While static measures of intellectual functioning are predominant in Western society, the LPAD has thrived in a cultural system that could not afford to place people in segregated settings with little opportunity to return to mainstream society.

Feuerstein (1979, p. 76) has defined intelligence as "the capacity of an individual to use *previously acquired experiences* to adjust to new situations." Two important aspects to this definition are the individual's ability to be modified by learning and to use changes in cognitive functioning for future adjustments. Feuerstein has asserted that the cause of retarded intellectual development for nonorganically retarded individuals is insufficient mediated learning. Insufficient mediated learning experiences result in cognitive deficits that inhibit the individual's ability to profit from direct experience. These deficits can occur at the level at which the individual receives information (e.g., lack of attention to relevant aspects of task), at the elaborational level at which the individual mentally operates on information received, and/or at the performance level (e.g., impulsive responding, lack of verbal labels for task components).

The assessment strategy within the LPAD is to test to identify cognitive strengths and deficits on a variety of tasks, then to teach the child through a wide variety of alternative approaches, and finally to post-test the child again on similar and progressively different tasks to determine the amount of change or gain the child makes as a result of the teaching. While Budoff's teaching strategy is task specific, Feuerstein's training attempts to improve the child's ability to use a variety of cognitive operations so that transfer to new tasks should be greater. Training is designed to improve the specific cognitive deficits, not the specific task performance. The LPAD approach results in extensive information about the child's ability to grasp principles and cognitive skills underlying the initial tasks, the amount and nature of investment required to teach the child, the extent to which newly acquired principles and cognitive skills are successfully applied to the solution of problems that become increasingly different from the initial tasks, the child's preference for specific modalities in which tasks and teaching are presented, and the differential effects of different training strategies.

The tasks presented in the LPAD are novel, difficult, and not obviously academic in nature. The nonacademic nature of the assessment-teaching tasks is designed to combat the fact that referred children have been confronted with numerous previous experiences of failure on academic tasks. With such a previous history of failure, children view academic tasks as merely additional situations that they will again fail. So the nonacademic tasks are designed to enhance motivation of those being assessed. The very high difficulty level of the tasks is designed to enhance the child's sense of accomplishment at having solved the training problems, a condition that is likely to result in greater motivation on future tasks as opposed to a situation in which the child has merely solved easy problems. The tasks involve complex abstract reasoning skills in order to counter the frequently held assumption that mentally retarded individuals cannot engage in abstract reasoning and can only learn with concrete manipulatives. Feuerstein has argued that such an assumption leads to teaching, and subsequently the learners' cognitive functioning, at only concrete levels. The LPAD teaching actively prevents the learner from using concrete aids and forces the child to use imagery and abstract reasoning. Doing so, we find that children considered retarded on the basis of our standard static measures of intelligence can in fact engage in abstract reasoning (Feuerstein, 1979, 1980).

Curricular Materials.   Feuerstein (1980) has also developed curricular materials based upon his mediated learning model. The instrumental enrichment (IE) curriculum has been used as part of the curriculum within self-contained settings as well as in mainstreamed classrooms, with typical, gifted, and illiterate children, adolescents, and adults as well as individuals with different handicapping conditions (e.g., mentally retarded, learning disabled, emotionally disturbed). Rand, Tannenbaum, and Feuerstein (1979) have shown that the IE curriculum improved low-functioning adolescents' performance on standard cognitive and achievement measures. As in the LPAD the curriculum is noncontent based, but rather teaches complex thinking strategies that can be applied to a variety of learning contexts (social as well as academic). The application of these approaches to adolescents and adults is consistent with Feuerstein's assertion that it is never too late to intervene and bring about significant changes. (See Box 4 for an illustration of teacher-pupil interaction within one unit.)

Box 4
Illustration of Teacher-Pupil Interaction within Instrumental Enrichment Unit (from Feuerstein, 1980)

The following transcript illustrates the development of a lesson in the dynamic classroom situation. The teacher's objective was to teach transformation and the strategy of detour; however, the needs and comments of the students determined the course of what actually transpired. It should be noted that the subgoals of the program, especially the correction of deficient cognitive functions, are evident. The class is of seventh-grade culturally deprived slow learners.

T: I'll give you a few minutes to look at the page [the illustration shown on the next page] and then we'll discuss it. . . . All right. Who would like to start?

S1: In the first picture, the rat is looking at the thing on the table; he wants it so bad, he's crying.

S2: He's not crying. He's drooling.

T: Why do you say "crying," S1?

S1: I looked at it too fast. I can see now that he's drooling.

T: S1 said that the rat wanted the thing on the table so badly that he was drooling. Does one usually drool when one wants something? I saw a new book I wanted very badly. . . .

S3: (interrupting) No. Your mouth waters when you see something delicious that you want to eat.

T: Only when you see it?

S3: No. Sometimes when you smell it cooking and you're hungry.

T: All right. When you smell it. Anything else? (No answer.) Sometimes when I hear somebody describe a good dinner, my mouth starts to water. I begin to salivate. We'll discuss the reasons for this in our next general science lesson. But now, what is it that makes the rat drool, or salivate?

S4: The cake.   S5: The cheese.

T: Which shall it be?

S4: It looks like a piece of fruit cake.

S5: The only reason it looks like a piece of cake to him is because it's shaped like a piece of cake. But I never heard of a rat liking cake. I know mice and rats like cheese because that's how you catch them. My father puts cheese on a trap and. . .

T: Let's not wander too far from our subject. (To S4) Has S5 persuaded you? If so, what are those little things that you thought were fruit?

S4: Holes. Like in Swiss cheese.

(continued)

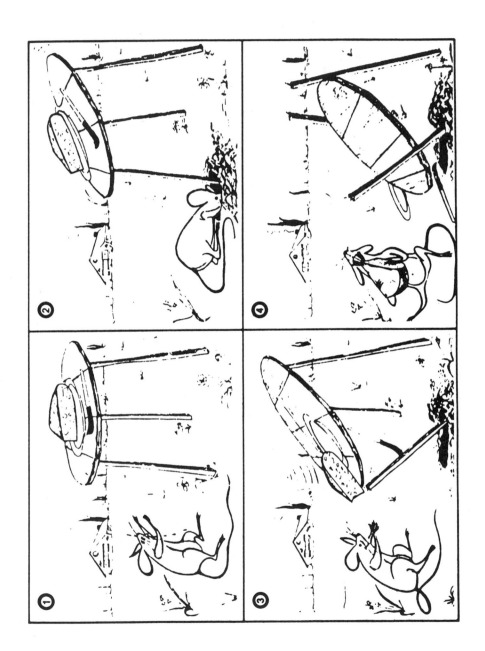

Box 4
(continued)

T: Yes, I think so. I'm not an expert on rats and don't know if they like cake or not. And in this case it isn't really important whether it is cake or cheese, but we want to learn to be precise and gather all the available information. So let's see how we arrive at a conclusion. There were two possibilities. Because of its shape and size, the object could be either a piece of cake or a piece of cheese. In order to decide, we have to put together what we see and what we know. We do know that rats really like cheese, and we see the rat's mouth watering. Is there anything else that shows us that the rat really wants the object?

S6:   The way his hands are lifted up.

T: Right. So we have additional evidence that he wants the object. Now, we must decide, on the basis of what we know, which of the two, the cake or the cheese, would cause the rat to act the way he does. Our conclusion?

All: Cheese.

T: What is the problem?

S7:   It's too high up for him to reach.

T: When something is too high to reach, what do we usually do?

S8:   Get a chair and climb up.

T: All right. We stand on something that will bring us up to the height of the object.

S: My mother uses a ladder in the kitchen because she can't reach the dishes on the top shelf.

T: Are there any other alternatives?

S9:   Get a stick.

T: Yes?

S9:   Get a stick. You know. Like the grocer. He can't reach the toilet paper on the top shelf so he gets a stick and knocks it down.

S10:   The janitor closes the transom with a pole.

S11:   When I can't reach the fruit on a tree, I get a stick and hit the branch.

S12:   No, it's better to throw something at the fruit and knock it down. That way you don't break the branches.

T: Let's see what you have been saying. When something is too high, we have two alternatives. (Writes on the board.) The first is to raise oneself up. (Writes: *Up: ladder, chair.*) The second?

(continued)

Box 4
(continued)

S13: To bring the thing down. (T writes on board: *Down: stick, rock.*)

T: Are there any other possibilities?

S14: You can try to jump up and reach it, or stand on tiptoes.

T: In which of the two categories would you place that? Or is it a new category? (S14 writes *jump* under *chair.*)

T: Right. Now let's see which of these strategies the rat used to solve his problem. Let's look at the next picture.

S15: He's digging a hole.

T: Just a hole any place?

S15: No, he's digging a hole around the table leg.

T: What do you think that will do?

S16: It will bring the front part of the table down so that the cheese will slide off.

T: You've thought of a good cause and effect relationship. Do you think the rat expects the cheese to slide off?

S17: Yes, in the third picture, he's standing there with his hands stretched out to catch it.

S1:   The rat thought about it beforehand. "Just a minute. Let me think."

T: Let's be a bit more specific. He thought about what?

S1:   His plan.

T: What did we call such a plan in *Organization of Dots*?

S18: A strategy. He planned his strategy.

T: Good. Do you all remember what a strategy is?

S15: A strategy is the steps I take to solve a problem. Like in checkers, when I make the other guy jump me so I can jump two of his men.

T: That's right. A strategy is a plan, method, or series of steps for reaching a specific goal or result. Did you know what the rat's strategy was when you looked at picture 2?

S3:   No, I only thought of it when I saw the third picture.

S14: That's some smart rat!

T: Do you all agree? Let's look at the board and see the alternatives we offered.

S19: He couldn't use any of them because they weren't around.

T: How could we classify the strategy he did use?

S20: Under the heading, "to bring the object down."

T: Because he couldn't get to the cheese directly, he used a detour strategy. Do you know what "detour" means?

(continued)

Box 4
(continued)

S: Yes, when you close the road, you can't get directly to where you want to go, so you have to go off on a side road and go around to get there.

S14: (interrupting) He used his imagination.

T: What do you mean?

S14: Well, he thought of all the possibilities in his head and saw that he couldn't use them and that he would have to come up with something new.

T: In other words, if we explore the various possibilities in our head before we start, we can save time, effort, and make fewer mistakes. The rat was certainly ingenious. Have you heard the word before? (On board, writes *ingenious.*) Look it up.

S: "Characterized by cleverness or originality of invention or construction. Cleverly inventive or resourceful."

T: S14 said that the rat was *clever* and thought of a *new strategy.* So we can agree that the rat was ingenious. Do you remember any other pages with an ingenious solution?

S: Yes, the mother dog and her puppies.

T: I'd like you to compare the two pages, in both of which there were ingenious solutions to the problems. How did the mother dog get her puppies across the stream?

S: She was a dachshund kind of dog. So she just lay across the water and the puppies walked across her back.

T: Is there any difference between that kind of solution and the one the rat used? I know it's a hard question, so I'm going to start and then let you carry on. The dog used a direct solution. She had a goal and her solution led directly to it, while the rat . . . ?

S: The rat had to do something first. He had to dig a hole first.

T: You're right. The rat had to use a detour, to reach the goal only by stages. It requires a plan. You know animals are quite clever. A rat who wants to steal eggs lies on his back and holds the egg with his four legs. Another rat pulls him along by his tail until they get back to the nest. Can you think of something where you reach the goal indirectly, and must do something else first to achieve your goal?

S: Do you mean something like this: If I want to make potato salad, first I have to peel my potatoes, then boil them, and then wait until they're cool before I cut them up.

(continued)

Box 4
(continued)

T: Very good, although in your example you are working on different steps of the process.

S: If I want to add fractions, first I have to find the least common denominator and change them all into the same thing.

T: Excellent. OK. Then the rat's ingenious solution was an indirect way of reaching the goal. It was a strategy of detour. S20, something is troubling you. Don't you agree the solution was ingenious?

S20:   I guess so.

T: Then what is bothering you?

S20:   I don't know how to say it. But look at the table!

T: What about the table?

S20:   The leg is broken . . .

T: Yes?

S20:   The table belongs to somebody else and so does the cheese. The rat stole the cheese . . .

S1:   He did not! He worked hard to get it.

T: Let's let S20 finish.

S20:   Well, even if he worked hard, the cheese didn't belong to him and to get it he broke somebody else's property.

T: S20 is saying something very important. Until now, we've been seeing the situation only from the rat's point of view. It seems there is another point of view in the situation. S20 is . . .

S4:   Putting herself in the shoes of the person who owns the house.

T: Yes. Is it reasonable for us to infer that it is the property of someone?

S4:   Yes, there's a house in the background of the first picture.

T: Yes, it's likely, though we can't be positive. All right. Let's return to what S1 said. The "rat worked hard to get it." Does anybody want to comment on this?

S: Wait, I want to say something else. It's his own fault! He shouldn't have left the stuff laying around.

T: I'm going to write *worked hard* on the board, so we won't forget it, because S1 has brought up another point that is worthy of discussion. What do you mean, S1?

S1:   I mean that anybody who leaves something lying around takes the chance of having it stolen! I remember when last year somebody stole my money off my desk. The other teacher said I should have put it away.

(continued)

Box 4
(continued)

T: Did you agree?

S1:   Not really. It was on *my* desk. Whoever took it just stole it.

T: It seems to me that what the other teacher was saying is that by leaving your money out you put temptation in the path of somebody who was unable to resist it. But let's separate the two instances: the rat who stole the cheese and the "rat" who stole S1's money. Are they the same or is there a difference?

S18: Animals don't know any better.

T: You're right. I remember once before Thanksgiving I put a turkey out to defrost. A cat ate a whole drumstick before I discovered her!

S21: My mother got mad at my puppy because he chewed her good shoe. He didn't know the difference between a new shoe and an old shoe.

T: So what you are saying is that the difference in the two instances is whether you could expect the thief to exercise judgment and to know right from wrong.

S1:   The kid who stole my money knew right from wrong. He just didn't care.

T: I stand corrected. The difference is whether you could expect the thief to know right from wrong or care about it . . .

S18: The rat doesn't know right from wrong. He doesn't think of it as stealing. He sees something good to eat and he wants it.

T: Let's take what you are saying one step further. Is an animal capable of saying this is right and this is wrong? No. That is what separates man from other animals. Our problem here is that we are using man's standards of property ownership and good and bad, and expecting the rat to know them too. . . . Now what is similar in the two instances of the rat who stole the cheese and the "rat" who stole the money?

S: Taking something that doesn't belong to you.

S: Stealing.   S: Temptation.

T: Can we arrive at a general rule based on these examples?

S: Well, if what you have is tempting to those who don't know or don't care about who it belongs to, then it is better to put it away or protect it somehow.

T: Very good. S1, do you understand now what the other teacher was trying to tell you? (S1 nods.)

T: We only have a short time, and I want to get back to S1's

(continued)

Box 4
(continued)

earlier statement. "He worked hard to get it." Do you want to explain it, S1?

S1: Well, the rat saw something he really wanted and he was willing to work hard to get it. He didn't give up. He kept digging even though it was hard work.

S20: Oh, teacher, that's stupid. On TV last night, I saw police digging up counterfeit money. The crooks that made it had to work hard to make it, and then work some more to bury it, but that didn't mean that what they were doing was right!

T: It seems we have a dilemma (writes *dilemma* on the blackboard), a difficult and perplexing problem, because what S1 says is true and what S20 says is true. Let's think for a moment and see if we can resolve it.

S: I think that what S1 means is that "God helps those who help themselves."

T: Yes?

S: Well, if you really want something you shouldn't sit around and wait for somebody to hand it to you. You should go out and work hard to get it.

S20: I still say that hard work alone isn't the important thing. It's what you're working hard at doing.

T: Let's see if this is the answer. S1 means that being willing to work hard to get something you want is a good trait, but S20 says merely working hard is not the main criterion on which to judge an act. Sometimes it is not even relevant. I'll talk to your English teacher about our discussion this morning and perhaps there will be further opportunity to explore the dilemma. But now, it's nearly time for the bell. Who would like to summarize this page?

S: A rat wanted some cheese that was out of his reach. In order to get it, he came up with (looks at the board) an ingenious solution that was a detour strategy.

T: Well done.

One of the major concerns about the LPAD is the lack of accessibility of the materials in this country. The procedures are highly flexible and require extensive supervised experience before they can be used. This flexibility represents both an advantage and a disadvantage. The flexibility results in a very individualistic approach to assessment and produces a wealth of instruc-

An art activity can facilitate motor and concept development. This student is gaining confidence in expressing his ideas by painting. (Photograph by Mima Cataldo.)

tion-relevant information about the individual. At the same time, because it is so flexible, it is highly dependent upon the clinical skills of the person doing the assessment and teaching. Further, considerably more research is needed to demonstrate the relationship between the cognitive operations that are the focus of the assessment and training and actual social and academic functioning. The LPAD does provide a fascinating and potentially useful model for assessing individuals and developing intervention programs. The model is one that can be used not only with LPAD materials but also with more directly academically relevant tasks.

Ethological Observation

At many points throughout this chapter the interaction between the person and the environment has been emphasized. Most of the intellectual testing discussed thus far has focused upon the individual, with Feuerstein's LPAD being the exception. Even the LPAD limits the interaction basically to instructional processes. Clearly, there are other interactions between the individual and the environment that would show the individual's ability to solve problems and adapt through the use of cognitive and intellectual skills. Charlesworth (1978; Charlesworth & Spiker, 1975) has described ethological observational approaches that can be used to assess cognitive and problem-solving behaviors as a primary means of adaptation.

Ethological observation originated in research investigating animal behavior, and it is tied to an evolutionary perspective by examining behavior reflecting the species' adaptation for survival. Adaptation within this model refers to the relationship between a living organism and an environment that requires something of the organism. The relational or interactional aspect of this definition is critical for ethologists. Using this basic notion of adaptation, Charlesworth (1978) has described detailed observational approaches, particularly for understanding how individuals solve social, physical, and cognitive problems with which they are confronted in their daily living environments. The individual's problem-solving behaviors are viewed as mediators between the individual and the environment. The child's behavior, as well as what precedes and what follows the behavior, is observed intensively as it occurs spontaneously in the natural environment. Observation occurs in a variety of natural settings, including the home and the classroom. Highly specific and descriptive behavioral definitions of adaptation and problem solving are used, rather than global categories. Therefore, such observations used during process assessment focus on naturally occurring, adaptive behavior and its interactive function in the settings of concern. The data obtained are both quantitative (frequency counts) and qualitative (descriptive). Charlesworth has used this strategy primarily within a research program, but has demonstrated its usefulness in understanding mentally retarded individuals. Whether one used Charlesworth's particular model and definitions of cognitive problem-solving behaviors, the strategy of observing adaptive functioning directly in the settings of concern is important and can be done by professionals in the field. A colleague (Renee Tapasak, personal communication, April, 1984), while working in a developmental center for retarded adults, described a technique of systematically observing retarded adults while accompanying them about the community and being confronted with various problems, including transportation, work, physical barriers, and knowledge demands. Information obtained from such an approach is much more useful for planning interventions than what would be obtained through the use of standardized measures of cognitive problem solving. Keller (1980b) has described alternative means of obtaining observational data through the use of important others (e.g., parents, peers) participating in the same settings, as well as through self-observation and recording. Certainly, questions of reliability and of representative sampling of settings and behaviors are no less important in this kind of assessment than in psychometric assessment.

Piaget's Developmental Approach

The work of Jean Piaget and assessment strategies derived from Piaget's theory also make extensive use of direct observation, though under structured conditions. The intent here is not to provide a thorough description of Piaget's model of cognitive development, since numerous texts and books provide good summaries of the theory (e.g., Ginsburg & Opper, 1979; Phillips, 1969; Piaget & Inhelder, 1969). Rather, following a brief outline of the theoretical model, assessment strategies that might be used will be described.

Piaget suggested that cognitive development consists of progressive organization and adaptation through a sequence of phrases or periods, each of which is characterized by distinct patterns of behavior and thinking (schemata). Each of the four major periods (sensorimotor, preoperational, concrete operational, and formal operational) involves a new level of cognitive organization that develops out of the preceding one.

Piaget distinguished six types of adaptive behavior patterns in the sensorimotor period, the first being that of reflexive actions. The next four are described in terms of the concept of circular reaction, an action that by chance produces or precedes an event the child sees or hears, and the action is then repeated. Initially, during the primary circular reactions substage, the objects of the child's actions are parts of the child's own body, such as the hand. External objects are involved in the next substage, secondary circular reactions (e.g., the child shakes a rattle). In the next substage, two behavior patterns from the previous level are coordinated so that one action serves as a means to carry out another (e.g., a screen is knocked over so that a toy behind it may be grasped). The fifth substage, referred to as that of tertiary circular reactions, involves the child engaging in more varied actions with objects in the environment to produce more varied and novel effects from the actions. For example, a rattle might be shaken, but also banged successively on different surfaces, thus producing different sounds. The last substage of the sensorimotor period involves trying out new means to solve common problems.

One of the major concepts investigated in this sensorimotor period is that of the development of object concept, which is concerned with children's reactions to the displacement and disappearance of objects from their perceptual field. Initially, when an object with which the infant had been playing is hidden, the baby in the second substage does not engage in any searching for the disappeared object. Subsequently, the infant's searching activity is limited to a brief duration of time and to the kind of action used by the infant with the object just before it was hidden. In the fourth substage the infant's searching is longer and more varied and active. At this point Piaget infers that the object has a reality that is differentiated from actions with that object. However, if an infant has found the object at a particular location, the child then searches at this location even when the object is observed to disappear at a new location. So the object concept is still quite primitive in that the infant's conceptualization of the object is apparently tied to action at a particular location. Subsequently, the infant no longer makes this location error as the child's object concept becomes based upon further coordination of action patterns and a cognitive network of spatial relations among objects whereby the relation of one object to another in space is no longer dependent upon the perspective of the viewer. At that point the infant is able to take into account several displacements of the hidden object. This concept of object permanence is important because of the extensive amount of research on its typical development and because its measurement forms the basis for the assessment of severely and profoundly retarded individuals when standardized tests of intellectual functioning are not helpful (Uzgiris & Lucas, 1978; Woodward, 1970).

When the child has internalized conceptualizations of objects and of actions in relation to those objects, cognitive organization moves into the symbolic phase of the preoperational period. Matching the placement of a row of beads in the same order as a model would represent this symbolic intuitive thinking. Class inclusion is beginning in this phase. For example, blue triangles and yellow triangles can be placed in two separate groups or they can be combined into one class of triangles, but they cannot be both at the same time. When the child can think in terms of both subclasses and the general class and can move easily from considering one to considering the other, the child has moved into concrete operational thought. Development of the concept of conservation (i.e., the awareness that a given object remains the same despite irrelevant changes in that object) is a much researched topic and a major accomplishment of this period. For example, the lack of a conservation concept in the preoperational child is shown when the child believes that the quantity of juice changes when we pour the juice from one glass into a taller and narrower glass. The concrete operational child would recognize that it is the same juice that has merely been poured into a different size container (an irrelevant change in shape of the container). Putting things in order of magnitude (serializing) and classifying (at least to two levels) are also main concrete operations. Finally, the formal operational period is characterized by hypothetical, logical thought (if, then thinking).

What is important in a Piagetian sense is the sequence of development of cognitive thought patterns, not the age at which various concepts are acquired. Thus, assessment within this model is applicable to all children no matter how slowly or how rapidly they develop. The focus of assessment is to determine through intensive clinical interactions with the child how far the child has progressed through the sequence and to design ways to enhance the child's cognitive development. From Piaget's theory, development is aided through a child's actions with the environment and active construction of internalized thought patterns for dealing with environment. There are few formal measures of Piagetian cognitive development that are readily available, but individuals well grounded in the theory could develop materials and tasks specific to the individuals with whom they work. Woodward (1970) has described assessment strategies within this framework for working with handicapped children in particular. Uzgiris and Hunt (1975) have described a wide variety of tasks for assessing an individual at the sensorimeter level, an assessment system often used with severely and profoundly retarded individuals.

Cognitive Information-Processing Approaches

You may have noticed that as you progressed through this chapter assessment strategies became less formal and more theoretically and/or research based. Actual assessment packages for implementing assessment strategies beyond the psychometric measures are not readily available. The tremendous and growing concern with the fairness and with the limitations of standardized tests has led to the development of alternatives and to the consideration of other bodies of knowledge as sources of direction. Recently, professionals concerned with assessment and planning in the area of cognitive and intellectual functioning have begun to examine the area of cognitive psychology. Interestingly, this area, which has traditionally been concerned with the laboratory study of cognitive processes, has only recently turned to practical questions of assessment and change in intellectual skills (Detterman & Sternberg, 1982; Sternberg, 1981; Sternberg & Detterman, 1979). Kaufman's psychometric measure (the K-ABC) and Feuerstein's LPAD are based heavily in this cognitive psychology tradition.

Sternberg (1981) has described a number of developments within the field of cognitive psychology on basic information-processing abilities that have important implications for the measurement of intelligence. One level of cognitive functioning that has a long history of research is that concerned with basic information-processing abilities or components, including perceptual processes, memory, and complex problem solving. Another level of cognitive functioning that recently has received attention refers to higher-order "executive processes" that serve to organize, plan, and monitor performance. These executive processes are sometimes referred to as metacomponents. This last section will briefly and selectively examine research on these two levels of cognitive functioning as it relates to disabled individuals. Most of the work relating to handicapped conditions involves learning disabled and mentally retarded children, though the research is applicable to typical children as well as to children with other handicapping conditions.

Cognitive Components.   Much of the early research at the level of basic cognitive processes focused upon visual and auditory perceptual processes, attention, and memory. As one might expect, much of that early work showed that handicapped individuals (mentally retarded and learning disabled children) did more poorly or less efficiently than nonhandicapped people (Haywood, Meyer, & Switzky, 1982). While memory and basic learning tasks were used with mentally retarded individuals, the perceptual and attentional tasks have been used with learning disabled children. Good and poor readers have been shown to differ on a variety of visual-perceptual factors, including discriminating visual forms (e.g., Benton, 1962; Colarusso, Martin, & Hartung, 1975), figure-ground perception (e.g., Strauss & Lehtinen, 1947), spatial orientation and disorientation (de Hirsch, 1952), visual memory (Samuels & Anderson, 1973), memory for sequence, form, and direction (Guthrie & Goldberg, 1972), reversals and rotations of figures when copying from short-term memory (e.g., Tjossem, Hansen, & Ripley, 1962), poor copying of designs (Keogh, 1969; Koppitz, 1970), reversal of letter order in reading and writing (Orton, 1937), auditory-visual and visual-auditory integration (Birch & Belmont, 1964; Samuels & Anderson, 1973), visual-sequential memory for letters (Amoriell, 1979), and simultaneous visual-auditory recall (Senf & Freundl, 1971). Because many of the tasks involved in this research require language and motor components as well as visual and auditory processes, many apparent weaknesses in visual and auditory perception actually may be due to poor language, motor, attention and/or memory skills. Visual perceptual weaknesses generally are found to have lower correlations with actual reading performance (Kavale, 1982; Keogh & Smith, 1967). These and other basic cognitive components are less correlated than the higher level executive processes to performance on academic tasks and in daily living, and training on these basic cognitive process deficits has not aided the performance of handicapped individuals appreciably (Morrison & Manis, 1982; Sternberg, 1981; Vellutino, 1979).

Attention is also viewed as a major problem with learning disabled children because, when information is attended to sufficiently to be learned, forgetting usually occurs no faster for learning disabled than typical learners (Shuell & Keppel, 1970). A basic contributor to learning problems, in both learning disabled and mentally retarded individuals, is poor or immature attending ability (Fisher & Zeaman, 1973; Keogh & Margolis, 1976; Tarver & Hallahan, 1974). This attentional ability includes the ability to be alert to material about to be presented, to be ready to respond, to focus on the appropriate stimuli (and ignore irrelevant and/or distracting stimuli), to sustain attention for adequate time periods, and then to decide on an answer or action. While some of these attentional deficits appear to be physiologically based (Kinsbourne & Caplan, 1979), there is growing evidence of the importance of language and the higher-order executive processes, metacomponents, of cognitive functioning (Smith, 1983).

Executive (Metacomponent) Processes.   Flavell (1976, 1978, 1981; Flavell & Wellman, 1977) has done a great deal of work on these executive processes, which he calls the area of metacognition. He has described various categories of knowledge about one's own cognition, including sensitivity, knowing what situations call for intentional cognitive activity; person variables, knowledge of those attributes that influence learning and memory; a task category, referring to characteristics of the tasks that influence performance; and strategies, or procedures for solution. These metacognitive processes make possible cognitive monitoring that can influence both the course and outcome of cognitive activities such as learning and memory (Brown, 1978). Experienced learners regularly seem to engage in cognitive monitoring and in the use of these higher-order executive processes. Young children and children with learning problems can be trained to use these strategies (Belmont & Butterfield, 1977; Campione & Brown, 1977; Markman, 1977).

In the area of attention and memory, Fisher and Zeaman (1973) have proposed what they call control processes, or strategies that can control memory and that can be trained. Mildly and moderately retarded research participants are inefficient in the spontaneous use of mnemonic strategies, but they can be taught to use these strategies when explicitly trained to do so (Paris & Haywood, 1973). It is the case, however, that training effects are typically limited to the training context (Belmont & Butterfield, 1977; Campione & Brown, 1977). Retarded people are especially inefficient at mnemonic strategies that require rehearsal, organization, and elaboration. Competent memorizers are able to evaluate task demands and then to select appropriate strategies for solution, and to revise strategies if necessary. These skills are either not used or done poorly by retarded persons (Brown, 1974). Retarded people can be taught to use appropriate strategies to improve performance, including rehearsal (Belmont & Butterfield, 1971; Turnbull, 1974), organization (Ashcraft & Kellas, 1974; Luszcz & Bacharach, 1975), and elaboration (Turnure & Thurlow, 1975; Wanschura & Borkowski, 1974).

While mnemonic strategies can be maintained up to one year (Brown, Campione, & Murphy, 1974; Kellas, Ashcraft, & Johnson, 1973), evidence for generalization of strategies across tasks is rare (Belmont, Butterfield, & Borkowski, 1978; Brown, Campione, & Barclay, 1979). Retarded people are found to be deficient in a number of executive processes that should aid generalization, including evaluating their recall readiness (Brown & Barclay, 1976), estimating memory span (Brown & Campione, 1977), and judging their feelings of knowing experience (Brown & Lawton, 1977).

In the area of attention, Meichenbaum (1977) has suggested that immature verbal mediation may underlie many children's poor attention. He has developed a self-instructional training procedure that has been demonstrated to aid learning disabled and hyperactive children with their attentional processes. When a child does not use verbal labeling and rehearsal to focus attention on relevant stimuli, the information that caught the child's attention is not likely to be organized for storage, thus reducing recall (Drew & Altman, 1970). Torgesen and Goldman (1977) demonstrated these skill differences between good and poor readers, but instruction on verbal mediation eliminated memory differences between the two groups. General language skills and verbal mediation strategies also have been shown to influence visual perception deficits (Vellutino, Smith, Steger, & Kaman, 1975; Vellutino, Steger, & Kandel, 1972) and auditory-visual integration abilities among reading disabled children (Vellutino, Steger, & Pruzek, 1973).

Cognitive rule learning skills are another executive process that differentiates good and poor readers. For example, Morrison and Manis (1982) have suggested that poor readers may fail to acquire rules that govern the relationship between English orthography and the speech sounds of language.

Das (1983) and his associates (Das, Kirby, & Jarman, 1979; Das, Snart, & Mulcahy, 1982) have shown the utility of assessment and educational intervention with handicapped individuals based upon a thorough understanding of cognitive functioning at both levels, that is, at the level of specific cognitive components and at the metacomponent level. Feuerstein's (1979, 1980) LPAD and IE curriculums, while directed primarily at the higher-level executive processes, address both levels. While packaged measures of the levels do not exist, a thorough knowledge of the literature on cognitive psychology will aid greatly in the measurement and intervention of cognitive and intellectual skills, potentially taking us far beyond what might have been imagined with just the use of standardized psychometric tests.

Summary

This chapter has dealt with intellectual and cognitive development. It began with a consideration of some of the many definitions of intelligence and with a consideration of some of the myths surrounding the concept of intelligence. The concept of intelligence and a consideration of various ways of measuring intelligence is important because intelligence test performance is crucial for the definition of various exceptionalities, including mental retardation, learning disabilities, and gifted children.

Intellectual development and performance on measures of intelligence are influenced by many factors. The chapter discussed the role of genetics, prenatal factors, environmental conditions, and physical stigmata.

Our attempts at understanding and programming with exceptional children and youth are aided by assessment strategies. Assessment is a process of gathering data for the purpose of making decisions about or for individuals. It can have many different purposes, including screening identification, classification placement, psychoeducational planning, pupil evaluation, and program evaluation. A variety of assessment methods were discussed from formal tests to observation and trial teaching. Assessment of intelligence was placed within the context of general assessment models because intellectual and cognitive abilities can influence, as well as be influenced by, other characteristics of a child. Assessment can focus upon the individual child, on the child's interactions with tasks, the child's interactions with settings (home, school, etc.), and the child within broader sociocultural contexts. It was pointed out that there is no one way of understanding human behavior that has all the answers. People in assessment and planning need to use a variety of different orientations and strategies to understand the handicapped child. Finally, different approaches to measuring intellectual and cognitive development were presented. These ranged from traditional psychometric approaches to more current testing systems that try to address some of the limitations of traditional intelligence tests (e.g., bias and the need to understand the child's different cognitive styles.) Then measurement approaches that reject standard testing and that engage in cognitive training were described. Feuerstein's LPAD represents a test-teach-test format that provides us with information about a child's strengths and weaknesses and information about teaching techniques that help the child perform better on the cognitive tasks. His assessment system is accompanied by a curricular package that shows promise with handicapped children. Observational approaches and Piaget's developmental approach were presented as alternative ways of understanding a child's intellectual and cognitive development. Finally, the literature on cognitive information processing was briefly reviewed as it related to handicapped children and to change in intellectual skills. Work on higher-order cognitive skills, referred to as executive processes (such as planning, organization, and monitoring), appears to offer tremendous potential for aiding handicapped children who have cognitive and learning problems.

Chapter 4

Judith Felson Duchan

Judith Felson Duchan is an associate professor at the State University of New York at Buffalo and the director of a diagnostic clinic for evaluating the communication of autistic children. Her interests include pragmatics, or the influence of different contexts on communication, and the ways language gets organized in conversations, stories, and classroom lessons. She is currently doing research on how arguments get organized between retarded adolescents and adults in group homes and between retarded children and different family members.

Perspectives for Understanding Children with Communicative Disorders

After reading this chapter, you should be able to:

1
Describe the influence that labels have on our interactions with students with communication difficulties.

2
Discuss the advantages and disadvantages of control and negotiation when interacting with students with disabilities.

3
List the frameworks for identifying and treating students with communicative disorders.

This chapter will elaborate some of the modern views of handicapped children. In particular, the emphasis is on children who are communicatively handicapped. The goal of the chapter is to examine current views of children with communication problems and to ask how these views affect the way these children are treated. The eventual purpose is to arrive at new ways to understand and interact with those who are communicatively handicapped. While the point of departure will be to examine interactions with children who are communicatively handicapped, the ideas in many cases apply to any groups of people who are judged abnormal.

Understanding Communication Handicaps

Interacting with Communicatively Handicapped People

The term *communicatively handicapped* can affect people in the same ways as terms such as fat and ugly. Judgments of which people deserve those labels and what the labels mean will depend upon one's cultural values, one's

---

Box 1
From "Children of a Lesser God" (Medoff, 1980)

For all my life I have been the creation of other people. The first thing I was ever able to understand was that everyone was supposed to hear but I couldn't and that was bad. Then they told me everyone was supposed to be smart but I was dumb. They said, oh no, I wasn't permanently dumb, only temporarily, but to be smart I had to become an imitation of the people who had from birth everything a person has to have to be good: ears that hear, mouth that speaks, eyes that read, brain that understands. Well, my brain understands a lot; and my eyes are my ears; and my hands are my voice; and my language, my speech, my ability to communicate is as great as yours. Greater, maybe, because I can communicate to you in one image an idea more complex than you can speak to each other in fifty words. For example, the sign "to connect," a simple sign—but it means so much more when it is moved between us like this. Now it means to be joined in a shared relationship, to be individual yet as one. A whole concept just like that. Well, I want to be joined to other people, but for all my life people have spoken for me: *She* says; *she* means; *she* wants. As if there were no I. As if there were no one in here who *could* understand. Until you let me be an individual, an *I*, just as you are, you will never truly be able to come inside my silence and know me. And until you can do that, I will never let myself know you. Until that time, we cannot be joined. We cannot share a relationship (p. 84).

---

experiences in the culture, and what is known about the person in question. Today, children are classified as learning disabled and therefore handicapped; twenty-five years ago, those same children would not have been considered handicapped (Carrier, 1983). Today, deaf people in deaf communities do not accept the designation handicapped, whereas normal-hearing people still regard the deaf as deviant, less competent, and communicatively handicapped (Medoff, 1980). (See Box 1.)

Labeling.   Once labeled handicapped, a child is subject to stereotyping, which accompanies any sort of cultural categorizing (Goffman, 1963; Wolfensberger, 1972). In fact, just being called handicapped has negative connotations (Combs & Harper, 1967). It is assumed that a communicatively handicapped person will have problems in many areas of learning, or that deaf people will be "dumb" (Ross & Calvert, 1974). A stereotype associated with the communicatively disordered is that people who are inarticulate are retarded (see Box 2). Some stereotypes are warranted—inarticulate people sometimes are retarded. But what might be the impact of being presumed retarded on those diagnosed language impaired? There is evidence that people, once categorized, develop the characteristics of their category stereotype (Becker, 1963; Rosenthal & Jakobson, 1968). Labeling someone communicatively handicapped, then, is not simply calling a spade a spade, but it can create an everyday context that pushes people into developing negatively

---

Box 2
From "The Elephant Man" (Montagu, 1979)

I supposed that Merrick was an imbecile and had been imbecile from birth. The fact that his face was incapable of expression, that his speech was a mere spluttering and his attitude that of one whose mind was void of all emotions and concerns gave grounds for this belief. The conviction was no doubt encouraged by the hope that his intellect was the blank I imagined it to be. That he could appreciate his position was unthinkable. Here was a man in the heyday of youth who was so vilely deformed that everyone he met confronted him with a look of horror and disgust. He was taken about the country to be exhibited as a monstrosity and an object of loathing. He was shunned like a leper, housed like a wild beast, and got his only view of the world from a peephole in a showman's cart. He was, moreover, lame, had but one available arm, and could hardly make his utterances understood. It was not until I came to know that Merrick was highly intelligent, that he possessed an acute sensibility and—worse than all—a romantic imagination that I realized the overwhelming tragedy of his life (pp. 17–18).

valued traits. Labeling someone handicapped is more like calling that person a spade and then putting him in environments that expect and encourage him to be like a spade.

Ascribing Causes.   Handicapped is not the only word used to describe communicatively handicapped children. They also are classified as having a particular type of handicap—a speech disorder, a cleft palate, a language disorder, a stuttering problem. Unlike descriptive epithets such as fat and ugly, these subcategories of handicap are often seen as "conditions" or "disorders" in the child. Once people name the difference and regard it as a disorder that the children have, they are compelled to ask what causes the disorder. The need to identify conditions and to find their causes is so strong in our culture that when there is no apparent identifiable condition or cause people may resort to taking the description of the deviance as its own condition and as its own causal explanation. Thus, one might hear people saying things such as: "he jumps all over the place because he is hyperactive"; "she doesn't communicate because she is autistic"; "he can't learn because he is learning disabled"; "they have trouble communicating because they are language disordered."

Besides *description-based* causes for handicapping conditions, there are *physically based* causes (brain damage causes language disorders—hearing losses cause speech problems), *emotionally based* causes (emotional stress can cause voice disorders—emotional trauma can lead to autistic-like social withdrawal), and *environmentally based* causes (modeling the speech and language of others can cause speech or language problems—institutionalization creates sterile environments that result in cognitive and language problems).

Nature of Handicap.   The type of cause assigned to a condition contributes to the conception of the condition and eventually to how people interact with those who display that condition. Causes considered irreversible, such as physical or mental handicaps, lead to thinking that there is nothing to be done to alter the condition. So, just as for incurable diseases, the symptoms of irreversible conditions are regarded as chronic and the disease is expected to have its effect throughout the bearer's lifetime. Retarded people are regarded as "eternal children" (Wolfensberger, 1972; Blatt, Biklen, & Bogdan, 1977), and cerebral palsied people are seen as having a life doomed to being communicatively handicapped.

The type of handicap also can carry with it a prescription for educational services and programming. Once a child is labeled communicatively handicapped, he or she is entitled by law to receive speech therapy by a certified speech-language pathologist. If that same child is labeled retarded, these services are no longer legally mandated. Autistic children are usually placed in small classes (one adult to every five children) and receive speech-language therapy five times weekly; emotionally disturbed children get the advantage of small classes, but not the speech-language therapy.

Different educational materials and curricula are designed for different handicaps, and communicatively handicapped children are often placed in special classes in which they receive this specialized instruction. There are classes for educable retarded children, and they are taught by teachers whose specialty is to teach the educable mentally retarded child. The teachers have been trained to design and carry out curricula that fit their ideas about the needs of children identified as educably retarded. There are also special classes with special teachers and curricula for children with behavior disorders, physical handicaps, learning disabilities, autism, and severe (trainable) or profound retardation, and in some places there are special classes made up of children with language disorders.

Similarly, speech-language pathologists provide different services depending upon how the communicative disorder is labeled. A child who speaks nonfluently may be classified a stutterer, and if so will be likely to receive therapy to smooth out the speech. Instruction will be given for how to begin to speak with easy physical contact between the articulators, how to bounce through stuttering blocks, and how to disregard minor nonfluencies. That same child, when labeled language impaired, will be helped to formulate his or her ideas, to build vocabulary, or to increase the complexity of his or her sentence structure. In this case the nonfluencies are seen as a symptom of the language problem.

In short, education and therapy for the communicatively handicapped children in our society stems from a set of ideas: handicaps are in the children; there are different types of handicaps with different causes; and there are special teachers, curricula, and therapies for the various categories of communicatively handicapped children. These *ideas* about handicapped children can influence the way a person interacts with them as much or more than that person's objective observations of the children.

Interpreting the Behaviors of Handicapped People

Imagine a child staring out a window at blinking lights while her five-year-old peers sit around her talking about going to MacDonald's to get a Big Mac. Noninteractive? Imaginative? Obsessed with lights? Tuned out? Vegetarian preferences? The explanation for why this child does something different will depend upon what else is known about her competencies, interests, and relationships with people. Some of those explanations will brand her deviant or communicatively handicapped, others will extol her as exotic or eccentric, and still others will not single her out as different but will regard her as being susceptible to the same cognitive meanderings that we all engage in. However one decides to interpret the child's tuning out, there seems to be agreement that such behavior is cause for concern. Adult onlookers become concerned when they see children not interacting or not participating in the ongoing event. Attention becomes focused on those nonparticipating members in order to determine the reason for their lack of participation.

Perhaps because of this cultural expectation that people should participate in the ongoing event, a particular child's frequent detours from the main interactive event are likely to get that child singled out, especially if the detours interfere with what the adult wants to have happen (Mercer, 1973). It is when things go wrong at the level of face to face interaction that adults first become concerned about children. Parents refer young preschool children to specialists for being inattentive, noninteractive, not responsive. Teachers refer school aged children for special testing when the children are noncooperative, acting out, or do not respond with the right answers (Mercer, 1973). Behavioral check lists designed by professionals to identify children as handicapped are heavily laden with items such as noncooperative and nonattentive (Krug, Arick, & Almond, 1980). In other words, children become labeled deviant when they noticeably violate adults' expectations for them, and this tends to occur when the children fail to interact in conventional ways.

Once children are categorized as deviant (i.e., handicapped) their noncompliant behavior is less likely to be regarded as exotic or normal meanderings. Instead, the child's noncompliance is seen as a manifestation of the handicap (see Box 3). When children are regarded as being noninteractive, adults try to involve them by calling them or having them look at what is going on. Or, when they are not participating, adults may ostracize them by putting them in a special "time out" chair or sending them to their rooms. Sometimes children might be allowed to continue the inappropriate behavior because "they don't know any better" and therefore "can't help it."

Noncompliance in handicapped children, when seen as part of their handicap, can become negatively valued (e.g., as inappropriate or wrong or "understandable given the handicap"). Mercer has referred to this potential

---

Box 3
From "On Being Sane in Insane Places" (Rosenhan, 1973)

It is not known why powerful impressions of personality traits, such as "crazy" or "insane," arise. Conceivably, when the origins of and stimuli that give rise to a behavior are remote or unknown, or when the behavior strikes us as immutable, trait labels regarding the behavior arise. When, on the other hand, the origins and stimuli are known and available, discourse is limited to the behavior itself. Thus, I may hallucinate because I am sleeping, or I may hallucinate because I have ingested a peculiar drug. These are termed sleep-induced hallucinations, or dreams, and drug-induced hallucinations, respectively. But when the stimuli to my hallucinations are unknown, that is called craziness, or schizophrenia—as if that inference were somehow as illuminating as the others (p. 254).

for negative evaluation of handicapped children's behavior as "negative sanctions" (Mercer, 1973, p. 23). When the child looks away or gets out of his or her seat, the behavior may be regarded as "being off task" rather than in a more positive light, such as being interested in something else or being bored. Categorizing noncompliant behaviors reveals the adults' preference for their own agenda. It also can indicate to the children that the adults are not interested in the meanings behind their actions. Adults may thereby unintentionally violate the children's right to be treated as intentional and thoughtful people. The effect may be to teach the children to be passive as interactants, a condition that has come to be known as *learned helplessness* (Seligman, 1975).

To summarize, adults dealing with handicapped children are concerned about children who are noncompliant, regarding their lack of participation as a lack of communication on the child's part. Adults are less likely to view their own inattention to the child's interests and intents as perhaps contributing to communication breakdowns with the child. Adults tend to view the noninteractive or communicatively different child in terms of their own ideas about handicapping conditions, rather than from the child's point of view.

The Process of Control and Negotiation

How is it that people know what to do when they are together? One way is for one partner to take the lead and to have the other partner follow. Another way is for both partners to engage in a prescribed sequence of things to do as if following the script of a play. A third way is for the partners to negotiate for who does what, with each taking the lead at times and following at other times.

These three interaction modes are characteristic of interactions between adults and children, and the particular mode engaged in depends upon a number of things, such as the history between the two, the adult's appraisal of the child's competence, the adult's usual style of interaction, and how both partners make sense of what is happening.

Adult Control.   When the adult controls the interaction, especially if the adult is a teacher, the event often takes the form of a lesson, in which the adult presents directives the child is expected to carry out. The directives may be instructions or questions to be answered. Once the directive is issued, the child responds, and the adult then evaluates the quality of that response. These three-part exchange units offer a basic organizational format to classroom lessons and curricula (Mehan, 1979; Tough, 1979). Once a unit is completed, the lesson progresses to the next round, and another directive is issued.

A second way adults conduct lessons is through demonstration. For example, they may present a sequence of actions, such as "peek-a-boo" or "patty cake," and then coax the child into participating in unison or taking an assigned part in the sequence (Ratner & Bruner, 1978; Cazden, 1979).

Child Initiative.   When children lead the interaction, the adult assumes a responsive role by commenting on what the child is thinking or doing, or by imitating or elaborating on what the child did. Children also may ask questions and issue commands and requests to which the adult responds. Unlike adult-controlled exchanges, when children issue directives the event seldom takes on the aura of lessons, since the children are not doing it to teach the adult something.

Negotiated Interactions.   For the more negotiated interactions, the partners respond to one another and both people direct the course of events. In negotiated interactions the adult's objective is neither to teach nor to respond to what the child is doing, but, rather, to do whatever the moment dictates. If the interaction is based on getting the child dressed, for example, the adult may direct the child or may comment or respond to what the child says or does, with the primary goal being to get the job done.

Communication between Handicapped Children and Adults.   The literature suggests that adults tend to be more directive with handicapped children than with normal children (Newhoff, Silverman, & Millet, 1980; Duchan, 1983). Adults who see children as poor learners would naturally resort to spending more time teaching them things. The cost of the increased time spent teaching is that children spend unnecessary time figuring out ways to please the adult, without fully understanding the lesson's import for their everyday life. Some autistic children, for example, respond to directives by repeating them, or by giving rote answers, or by focusing on peripheral aspects of answers such as intonation patterns (Duchan, 1983) or movement sequences (Frankel, 1982).

Other literature on interaction with the handicapped suggests that they are ignored and treated as if they are not there when they are not being told what to do. Helm (1981) has called this "cutting out" and describes it as "someone systematically kept out of the ongoing conversation." This cutting out is apparent when (1) adults talk about what is wrong with children in their presence without including them in the conversation; (2) adults answer questions put to children (e.g., What's your name? His name is Johnny); or (3) adults do things in front of handicapped people that they would only do in private (e.g., adjust an undergarment as described in Rosenhan, 1973).

Interactions do not always go smoothly, and sometimes partners must adjust or repair an interaction sequence. For the adult-controlled lessons, the breakdowns may occur becuse the adult is either overestimating or underestimating the child's competence, and as a result the child cannot or will not complete the directive.

An overestimate of children's competence may involve the adult's use of language that is too difficult for the child, or it may involve task intricacies that are too complicated for the child to follow. In either case, the adult must make adjustments to better approximate the child's comprehension. These adjustments have been called "fine tuning" (Cross, 1978); in the case of over-

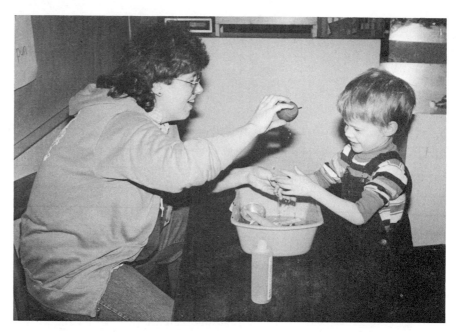

Learning to communicate takes place in the context of relationships. This language therapist actively participates in a pleasurable activity with the child. (Photograph by Mima Cataldo.)

estimated competence, fine tuning must be done to scale down the difficulty level. Fine tuning can adjust in the upward direction as well, and it is needed when the interaction breaks down because the adult underestimates the child's language or cognitive competence. In upward scaling the adult asks the child to say or do more difficult things.

The ideal interactions for enhancing children's learning have been identified by Vygotsky (in Cole, John-Steiner, Scribner, & Souberman, 1978) as those involving ideas that are just beyond the child's competence yet within the child's reach. These ideas reside in what Vygotsky has called the child's "zone of proximal development." Tuning to fit this zone represents the finest tuning of all in that the adult presents lessons that require new insights and the child attains those insights as he or she responds.

Breakdowns in child-directed interactions will occur when the adult fails to respond to a child's initiations or when the adult misinterprets what the child means or wants. Children may repair such breakdowns by repeating the act, by altering it in some way (Gallagher, 1981; Garvey, 1979), or by ignoring it and moving on.

Handicapped children, especially those who have problems communicating their wants and meanings, experience more than their share of breakdowns. The child whose speech is unintelligible lives a life of breakdowns, in which those with whom he or she interacts fail to respond to what he or she says. The means of repair and the willingness of peers and adults to crack the code of the child's mispronunciations are crucial factors that influence how well the interactions proceed.

Similarly, intelligible children who communicate their needs in unusual ways may or may not be understood by attending adults. If, for example, the adults understand that echoes for autistic children can be treated as coded messages (Prizant & Duchan, 1981), then the adults are likely to be much more responsive to how and when the children echo. Further, once they figure out the code, the adults can respond to the children accordingly, thereby changing the degree to which the child is communicatively handicapped.

It is the sensitivity of those in the child's environment that allows the interaction to move on, and it is in this sense that one can regard the communication disorder as being in the interaction rather than just in the child.

Quality and Success of Everyday Interaction

The communication problems of children labeled retarded, emotionally disturbed, or physically handicapped have been viewed as problems that are secondary to the main disorder. However, the negative effects of labeling can be so powerful that the secondary effects of the handicap can become a major source of current debilitation. That is to say, the children's current incompetencies may derive more from how they are treated in everyday contexts than from the so-called primary or original condition.

Social Interaction Perspective

The strongest evidence for this social interaction view of handicapped children's disabilities comes from studies of people who were mislabeled, who subsequently developed the symptoms ascribed to them. Rosenthal and Jacobson (1968) have demonstrated this self-fulfilling prophesy in their study of children they labeled "late bloomers." Teachers were told which of their children would be expected to develop extra rapidly. The prophesy was indeed fulfilled. The children labeled late bloomers did better on standardized achievement tests than their less favored classmates. It was only after the year was over that the researchers informed the teachers that those labeled late bloomers were selected randomly and were not different from the regular bloomers. The high expectations of the teachers were somehow communicated to the selected children, and they proceeded to bloom accordingly.

A second source of evidence for the strong role that face-to-face interactions play in determining the degree of handicap is the research that describes differences among people with the same handicap. There is general agreement that children who are institutionalized or otherwise isolated end up the most handicapped (Edgerton, 1967; Windle, 1962; Braginsky & Braginsky, 1971). (See Box 4.) In contrast to the debilitating effects of isolation is the positive role offered by strong support systems. Edgerton (1967) has described the importance of "benefactors" in assisting retarded adults to adjust their lives from being institutionalized to being in a community among nonretarded people.

A third source of evidence about the influence of interactions on the degree of handicap is the research that shows the same children varying from one context to another. Normal children will speak differently to different listeners (Shatz & Gelman, 1973) and to the same listener in different situations (Labov, 1970). Abnormal speakers also differ in the degree to which

---

Box 4
From "Hansels and Gretels" (Braginsky & Braginsky, 1971)

Once upon a time there dwelt on the outskirts of a large forest a poor woodcutter and his wife and two children; the boy was called Hansel and the girl Gretel. They had always little enough to live on, and once, when there was a great famine in the land, the woodcutter could not even provide them with daily bread.

One night, as he was tossing about in bed, full of cares and worry, he sighed and said to his wife, "What is to become of us? How are we to support our poor children, now that we have nothing more left even for ourselves?"

"Early in the morning," answered the woman, who was the children's stepmother, "we will take Hansel and Gretel out into the thickest part of the woods. There we shall light a fire for them, give them each a piece of bread and go on to our work, leaving them alone. They will not be able to find their way home, and we shall thus be rid of them."

"No, wife," said her husband, "that I won't do. How could I find it in my heart to leave my children alone in the woods? The wild beasts would come and tear them to pieces."

"Oh," said she, "then we must all four die of hunger, and you may just as well go and prepare the boards for our coffins." And she left him no peace till he had consented. (From *Hansel and Gretel*)

Were we to test Hansel and Gretel today, they would no doubt be diagnosed as mentally retarded. Their lack of formal education, their rejecting parents, and their general impoverishment would ensure poor performance on intelligence tests. Yet Hansel and Gretel were resourceful, clever, manipulative children, capable of controlling the hostile environment into which they were cast. The parallels between this folktale and the case histories of our subjects are distressingly similar (p. 159).

they have communication problems from one context to another. Stutterers, for example, are fluent under certain speaking situations (Andrews, Howie, Dosza, & Guitar, 1982).

Labels and Symptoms.   Knowing that wrong labels can lead to symptoms and that supportive people and contexts can minimize undesirable behavior leads to the question of what goes on in those everyday contexts that either inhibit or enhance the child's progression toward being more normal. Inhibitory interactions are those in which the child is treated as inept, deficient, and in terms of the handicap. The dehumanizing context regards ordinary behaviors as symptomatic of the disease and nonordinary behaviors as undesirable. For example, a wrong answer is seen as a sign of retardation, of a language problem, of hearing loss, or of a learning disability, depending upon the child's label. For normal children a wrong answer is simply a mistake. Even a right answer for handicapped children can be regarded in light of the handicap, such as when it is seen as compensation. A blind person identifying a smell, for example, might be seen as compensating for a lack of vision.

Behavioral Check Lists.   Negative sanctions placed on handicapped children can also be seen in some of the behavioral check lists designed to determine what handicapped children can and cannot do. One frequently finds items of such lists skewed toward viewing children in terms of their deficits. For example Krug, Arick, and Almond (1979) have developed a check list with items characteristic of autism. The negative value that such lists place on certain behaviors is apparent from the occurrence of negatively loaded words (e.g., does not, resists, avoids, has not developed); from the lack of concern for when, how much, and why the child does those things; and from the implication that normal people would not do such things. Box 5 provides an example of a behavioral check list for autism.

In contrast to the negative approach to interacting with handicapped children is what Helm (1981) has called "strategic contextualization," that is, adults give the children the benefit of not doubting their competence. Helm has described an incident in which a mother interprets her child's "wrong" answer as appropriate by casting it in a context that accounts for why the child may have said what he said (see Box 6). Legitimizing wrong answers casts children in terms of their competencies and allows the interaction to continue in a positive vein.

Using descriptors that commonly occur in autism behavioral check lists, one can easily construe contexts in which such behaviors would be appropriate. For example, if one were to provide a context for some of the behaviors listed, such as playing basketball, the power of strategic contextualization over the negative sanctions approach would be revealed. Within their negative-sanctions frame the behaviors would be interpreted in terms of the handicap (basketball players jump around because there is something wrong

Box 5
Some Behaviors Characteristic of Autistic Children

_____ 1. Engages in spinning.

_____ 2. Rocks back and forth.

_____ 3. Has difficulty with social interaction.

_____ 4. Has problem with intonation.

_____ 5. Gaze aversion.

_____ 6. Jumps around and walks on toes.

_____ 7. Has tactile defensiveness, resists being touched.

_____ 8. Reverses pronouns.

_____ 9. Flicks fingers in front of eyes.

_____10. Spins and bangs objects frequently.

_____11. Has trouble making friends.

_____12. Gets fixated on certain activities such as placing objects in exact places.

_____13. Is bothered by loud and unusual sounds.

_____14. Does not look directly into people's eyes.

_____15. Echoes what others say.

_____16. Stares into space.

_____17. Prefers objects to people.

Box 6
Strategic Contextualization (Helm, 1981)

Mother: Ted, look at me. The belt goes in the what?

Child: What is it?

Mother: Goes in the loo . . . (eliciting the answer "loops")

Child: Living room. What is it?

Mother: Where's the belt go, Ted?

Child: In the living room.

Mother: In fact, we were in the living room when I put his belt on.

with them; they seldom talk with others because they are noninteractive, etc.). Strategic contextualization legitimizes those same behaviors as part of playing basketball (they jump to get the ball, and they lunge and dart about to keep others from getting it). Basketball playing provides a context for those same behaviors that gives them normal status. By strategically contextualizing behaviors, one can legitimize them; in doing so one legitimizes the person who performs the behaviors.

There are possible problems for the strategic contextualization approach. There is always the possibility of a gap between the interpretation offered and the actual reason the child performed the act. For example, Helm (1982) has described a family whose members overestimated the competence of their retarded child, setting up the possibility for miscommunication and unrealistic expectations. Similarly, underestimates of children's competencies create miscommunication for the opposite reason, when event sequences are too easy and an affront to the child. Besides unrealistic expectations, there can be miscommunication that results from sheer misinterpretation. Richer and Richards (1975) have described the failure of adults to get autistic children to respond when the adults have pretended to ignore them. When the adults repeat louder, or lean closer, the autistic children shy away even more. The children become more attentive and responsive, however, when adults keep their physical and psychological distance.

This issue of how to strategically contextualize so that it places the adult in correct touch with what is going on with the child is the same problem as that of determining how the adult can fine tune the language spoken to the child so that it is in keeping with what the child is thinking and can understand. It is the core problem for developing successful interactions with handicapped children.

Frameworks for Identifying and Treating Children with Communicative Disorders

Typical figures on handicapped populations list the communicatively handicapped as comprising anywhere from 1.5 to 8.4 percent of the total population (Leske, 1981). As with any population statistics, these percentages depend upon the way the criteria are established to identify people as handicapped; the classification systems depend, in turn, on the frameworks of those doing the classifying. There are at least five frameworks that the various professional groups subscribe to: medical, psychological, linguistic, educational, and sociological. Each framework views the children differently; as a result, each comes up with different labels and treatment programs.

The Medical Framework

The medical model is heavily used by speech-language pathologists, the specialists whose job it is to identify and improve communication of those labeled communicatively handicapped. Speech-language pathologists work in both medical settings (hospitals, clinics) and educational settings (universities, public schools). Their affinity for the medical framework is strongest in the medical context, however, as can be surmised from their chosen title, pathologist. Evidence for the medical focus is found in the use of medical terms to describe aspects of the profession. For example, the term *etiology* is used to refer to the biological or psychological origins of a communication problem; speech and language problems are referred to as disorders or pathologies that can be diagnosed; people are viewed as having the disorder in the same way medical doctors see people as having diseases; communicatively handicapped people are called patients, and their symptoms are treated in speech and hearing clinics; and the work done is called therapy or treatment, and different prescriptions of treatment are offered for different kinds of disorders. While the medical framework is applied to all communication disorders, there are a few to which it lends itself best—the physically caused disorders of cleft palate, cerebral palsy, and hearing impairment.

Cleft Palate.   One in 750 or so babies is born with a cleft (opening) in either the lip or palate (or both). The etiology of this disorder is from a variety of sources. Clefting tends to run in families, suggesting a genetic origin, or it can be caused by nongenetic factors, such as German measles or thalidomide, that interfere with the developing embryo between six to nine weeks after conception (Fraser, 1971, 1973).

Although clefts are repaired surgically, within the first year of life 30 percent of the children with repaired lips and palates have problems with their speech and language once they begin talking (Moll, 1968). The most common symptom is nasality, in which the air used for speech production leaks through the nose because of insufficient closure between the oral and nasal passages. The problem is described medically as insufficient velopharyngeal closure, or velopharyngeal incompetence.

Velopharyngeal incompetence selectively affects the speech sounds that require air pressure to be built up in the mouth. It is the mispronunciation of these sounds (stops: *p, b, t, d, k, g*; fricatives: *f, v, s, z, sh*; and affricates: *ch, j*) that characterizes the speech of many cleft palate children.

Therapeutic prescriptions for improving cleft palate speech are readily available and frequently carried out by speech-language pathologists. They entail exercises for building up velopharyngeal closure (Shprintzen, McCall, & Skolnick, 1975), as well as lessons for teaching children the correct production of the speech sounds they are misarticulating (Wells, 1971).

Cerebral Palsy.   There is a family of neuromuscular disorders whose effect results in various types of motor disabilities all falling under the rubric of cerebral palsy. Problems with muscle control originate from damage to the motor control centers of the brain and produce paralysis, weakness, or incoordination (Perlstein, 1949). The damage often occurs before the child is born (four out of every thousand births—Nelson & Ellenbert, 1977), but also can result from brain disease or brain trauma during or after birth. The cerebral palsies range considerably in severity and type of motor disability, depending upon the age of onset and the degree and location of the damage. A cerebral palsied person may have mild or severe muscular spasticity in which the muscles are rigid, or may have mild or severe athetosis in which the muscles are uncontrollable and look as if there is an overflow of movement.

Because nervous tissue does not regenerate, the condition of cerebral palsy is irreversible; thus it must be treated through compensatory techniques. Speech-language pathologists may place a child in physical postures to reduce muscle spasms, thereby facilitating speech production (Mysak, 1968; Bobath & Bobath, 1952); they may teach compensating movements for producing understandable speech (Crickmay, 1966); or they may train the child to communicate via means other than speech, such as with electronic communication boards (McDonald & Schultz, 1973).

Hearing Impairment.   Hearing loss is the source of communication problems for 5 percent of the population. Losses can range from mild (27 to 40 dB) to profound (91 or more dB) and can vary in the degree of sound distortion as well as in the degree of reduced sensitivity. Hearing losses can be caused by a genetically inherited defect, by certain medications, by disease (e.g., middle ear infections or tumors of the auditory nerve); or by acoustic trauma from loud noises. Some types of losses are surgically operable or medically treatable; others, such as those involving the neural transmission of the acoustic signal, are not medically remediable. Hearing losses are diagnosed by audiologists who use specially designed tests. Audiologists also have expertise in prescribing hearing aids for children and adults with hearing losses.

People with hearing problems sometimes have accompanying speech problems, depending upon when the loss began, what type of loss it is, and its severity. Those with severe losses are considered to be deaf. Because they miss so much of the acoustic signal, the severely hearing impaired often learn and communicate best through the use of sign language.

Speech and language therapy for hearing-impaired children may involve teaching them how to say speech sounds by attending to how the sounds look and feel, rather than how they sound. Speech-language pathologists and audiologists also provide aural rehabilitation to hearing-impaired people to teach them how to make the best use of their residual hearing and to use other cues (auditory, visual, linguistic, or situational) to understand language.

The medical framework not only is applied to the types of handicap that have obvious biological causes, such as cleft palate, cerebral palsy, and hearing impairment, but also is applied to other handicapping conditions with intangible biological origins, such as learning disabilities and stuttering. Under the medical framework, learning disabilities and stuttering would be viewed as originating from neurological malfunctioning and cast as health-related problems (Goldstein, 1978; Carrier, 1983).

The communication disorder specialists who work within the medical framework are often trained in medically affiliated masters degree programs. Communicative disorders departments with medical philosophies tend to be located in medical schools along with other allied health training programs, such as nursing, occupational therapy, and physical therapy. Students majoring in communication disorders take a course of study specializing in either audiology or speech-language pathology. The training of audiologists emphasizes differential diagnosis of various types of hearing disorders; thus the audiologist learns to administer audiometric tests that differentiate the physical or medical source of hearing problems. Such specialists are called clinical audiologists.

Medically oriented speech-language pathologists learn to associate the various types of speech and language disorders with different neurological disorders. Indeed, medical diagnoses can often be made from the speech or language characteristics of the patient (Darley, Aronson, & Brown, 1975). Speech and language therapies are prescribed as well as carried out by speech-language pathologists and are often different depending upon the medical diagnosis.

The Developmental Psychology Framework

While the medical framework defines communication disorders in terms of the underlying pathologies, the developmental psychology framework concentrates on the degree of departure from normal in order to identify the communicatively handicapped. Normal is considered to be what most people of that age do in a particular culture. To determine which people are abnormal requires that measures be taken of how people of different ages perform on particular tasks. These measures result in the establishment of developmental norms, which provide a standard for determining whether or not people are normal or whether they exhibit a developmental delay. If the delay is significant, those being tested qualify as developmentally delayed.

Professionals subscribing to the developmental framework use tests to determine whether children or adults meet the standards of the test norms. Standardized tests serve the speech-language professional in several ways. There are general developmental tests, such as the Bayley Test (Bayley, 1969), which are designed to measure children's developmental level in many areas. These tests allow specialists in communication disorders to judge whether a child's communication problem is the only problem or part of a general developmental delay.

Developmentalists also use tests that are more specifically related to the child's communication problems. For example, the Uzgiris and Hunt scale, (Uzgiris & Hunt, 1975) includes subtests of skills that have been found to be highly correlated with the onset of language in normal one- to two-year-old children (Bates, 1979).

Finally, there are a large supply of tests that have been designed to measure children's communication competence directly (Darley, 1979). These tests may include measures of children's speech sound production, their knowledge of vocabulary, how they combine words, or their level of language comprehension. Children are considered to have a speech or language delay if they depart significantly from the norms on any of these measures of communication.

Delayed Speech.   The normative framework assumes that children progress through distinct stages in their speech and language development. Researchers have followed children's acquisition of the sound system of English and have published norms on what age normal children say each of the sounds of English. They have found, for example, that *p*, *b*, and *m* are early developing sounds and that *r* and *l* are much later (Templin, 1957; Prather, Hedrick, & Kern, 1975).

Children with delays in speech sound development traditionally have been described as having articulation disorders. Speech-language pathologists with the normative approach identify which sounds are not yet developed and then teach the child those sounds in the order in which normal children acquire them. Less strict adherents to the normative approach might examine the child's speech in more detail and perhaps work on those sounds that are most easy for that child to produce, regardless of what normal children do.

The developmental framework, in its strongest form, leads to a disregard for the peculiarities of particular disorders and concentrates instead on determining the developmental levels for handicapped children. Those using the developmental approach might first assign children to a developmental level, and then if the level is below that of other children their age would conduct therapy with the aim of speeding up the children's progress. For example, Miller and Yoder (1982) recommend that language impaired children be taught language structure following the sequential developmental stages found in normal children, such as working from single words to two- and then three-word utterances.

The Linguistic Framework

The medical framework uses pathology for its classification categories; the developmental psychology framework uses areas of developmental delay. The linguistic framework, by contrast, bases its classification system on the linguistic patterns that exist in the child's language performance. Thus children with communication disorders are described under the same categories that linguists use to describe the language of the culture. They are said to have problems with phonology, syntax, or semantics.

Phonological Problems.   Languages are made up of individual sounds that combine in allowable ways to make up words. The same sounds are pronounced in many different ways and listeners still recognize them as being the same. For instance, they can be pronounced sloppily or carefully, slow or fast, loud or soft. Sounds of the language are abstract in the same way that we have abstract ideas, such as that the word *house* means more than an amalgamation of the houses we have seen. These abstract categories of sounds are *phonemes*.

Phonemes make up only part of phonology. Another aspect of phonology is our ideas about how phonemes are allowed to combine into words. Languages dictate these combinatorial rules. English, for example, allows the consonants *b* and *l* to combine (blink), but not *b* and *n*. Some languages, such as Japanese, do not have consonants at the ends of syllables or words.

Children who have phonological problems are identified as being different because they violate the phonological rules of the adult language. The violations are usually predictable in that the same child makes the same sort of mistakes whenever he or she talks. Violations of the adult phonological system can be studied as a language governed by rules, in the same way the adult language is studied by linguists (Ingram, 1981; Edwards & Shriberg, 1983). This attempt to discover the patterns in children's language differences is characteristic of the linguistic approach to communication disorders and has created techniques for evaluating the speech and language of children (Crystal, 1982; Lund & Duchan, 1983). The techniques are different from diagnostic approaches and from normed tests in that they analyze the language structure of the child's everyday language. The procedure is to do *language sample analysis* by recording the child's talk, transcribing the recording, and eventually analyzing it for its language patterns.

The linguistic approach to helping children with phonological disorders learn the adult form of the language is to teach them the phonological rules. This differs from the articulation approach in that for the linguistic approach there may be a focus on several sounds at one time, and the emphasis is to teach abstract linguistic understandings rather than better pronunciation of individual sounds.

Syntax Problems.   Not only do children learning language have to figure out a complicated sound system, but also they must learn about how words combine into phrases and sentences. That is, they must learn the syntactic rules.

Linguists have demonstrated that languages do not work by simply stringing sounds into words and then words into sentences, as if one were making a beaded necklace. Rather, the words are arranged more like twigs on branches that then fit together into larger branches, finally emerging into the trunk, which constitutes the whole sentence. It is no accident that linguists refer to the hierarchical organization of sentences as tree structures.

Children who have problems with syntax are unable to decipher the intricate hierarchical relationships among the words in the sentences they hear. They are not able to say sentences with complex syntactic relationships. Their mistakes may be such that they cannot follow multiple clauses; thus they make a series of simple sentences out of more complex ones. They may interpret "The man who kissed the child drove away in the car" as "The man kissed the child and the child drove away in the car."

Speech-language pathologists with linguistic orientations will analyze a child's syntax to see what types of sentences they understand and say and will then provide the children with models of the sentences they have trouble with. They may describe a scene, for example, in which the child sees the man kissing the child and then driving away, thereby showing the children how the complex sentences fit with their real-world understandings (Lee, Koenigsknecht, & Mulhern, 1975).

Semantics Problems.   Children may have good knowledge of phonology and syntax but still have trouble interpreting the meanings conveyed by the language. This may be due to a semantics problem in which they do not know meanings of individual words, or the semantic relationships between words in phrases, or sentences, or topical relationships between sentences. Semantics problems are more difficult to identify than phonological or syntactic ones because they are less observable. For example, when a child uses the word *cat* to refer only to her cat and none other, the error does not become apparent. We do not know that she understands the word in such a limited way because we assume our own meanings when she says cat in reference to her pet.

Some semantic problems stem from conceptual difficulties in particular areas of knowledge. Often children who do not know the meaning of left and right use both hands equally well and, in fact, do not make the distinction conceptually.

The specialists' approach to teaching semantics of single words has been to associate words with their referents through the use of techniques such as having the child find the named picture card, or get a named object, or name a designated object or picture. Semantics of word domains are often taught as parts of thematic units such as names for foods, animals, and people, and the semantics of sentences and paragraphs are presented through story retelling perhaps accompanied by questions about the story.

Verbal Processing Problems.   If children are unable to express themselves by speaking, or are unable to understand verbal communication, the linguistic orientation allows that they may still have a language competence. The problem may be that they cannot express or understand language in spoken form. In these cases, the therapy is to explore alternative modes and modalities for children to use for their communication (Yoder, 1982). Among the various choices for the clinician are sign language, picture boards, spelling systems, or electronic communication devices (Fristoe & Lloyd, 1978). The language pathologist chooses the system that best fits the child's language and physical competencies and tailors the language system to meet the particular child's communicative needs (Vanderheiden, 1978; Shane & Bashir, 1980).

To summarize, those speech-language pathologists with linguistic orientations treat each child's language as if it were an internally consistent exotic language spoken in a foreign country. Like linguists, the pathologists talk or interact with the native speaker, in this case the child, record what the child says, and then study the recording to discover the consistencies in the language. The procedure has been called "language sample analysis" or, for the nonvocal child, "action analysis" (Lund & Duchan, 1983).

Once the idiosyncracies are discovered, the clinician then works with the child as if he or she is learning a second language, the language spoken by the child's peers or adults. The techniques of instruction may be direct, using imitation, pattern practices, or correction, or they may be more indirect, exposing the child to examples of the language structure in everyday naturalistic contexts.

The Educational Framework

One prevalent educational approach to handicapping conditions has been to classify the children according to the special education classes and teacher specialties that are available in the school. The classes are often taught by teachers who have majored in that specialty in college, within a department of special education. The specialties most prevalent are those that involve educable mentally retarded (EMR) children, trainable mentally retarded (TMR) children, severely and profoundly mentally retarded (PMR) children, learning disabled (LD) children, and, in some places, with autistic children. The emphasis in the teacher training program is on the curriculum, where teachers learn about techniques for teaching and managing children who have those disabilities.

Speech-language pathologists working in the schools usually select the children from these special classes who are communicatively handicapped and work with them in small groups or individually. The pathologists in educational settings are usually called speech teachers or speech therapists, and they conduct their speech lessons in a speech room.

Like the special education teachers, the speech therapists who subscribe most enthusiastically to the educational framework develop different ways of working with children depending upon the child's educational label. They may, for example, group the EMR children together and design speech or language lessons for them.

Educable Mentally Retarded Children.   Children of this classification are usually first identified as deviant by the classroom teacher who finds that they are not keeping pace with the others in the classroom or are not conforming to classroom rules and rituals. These children are often not recognized as being different except in the academic setting of the classroom (President's Committee on Mental Retardation, 1970). The teacher refers the child to the school psychologist, who evaluates their intellectual competence by giving them an IQ test. If the children score between 50 and 75 on the

Disabled and nondisabled students can be placed together in skill groups. Here the teacher clarifies the purpose of the activity. (Photograph by Mima Cataldo.)

test, they are typically classed as educably retarded and placed in a special class with other children so labeled (Goldstein, Arkell, Ashcroft, Hurley, & Lilly, 1976). Only 10 percent of these children are ever returned to a regular classroom (Gallagher, 1972).

Curricula for EMR children include academic teachings such as reading, writing, arithmetic, and social studies, but not at the pace or level of depth of the curriculum for normal classrooms. Most often the children are regarded as slow learners by their teachers, rather than children who are different learners.

Speech and language programs for EMR children may involve programs similar to those used for communicatively handicapped with normal intelligence, but slowed down. Speech therapists who work from a developmental normative framework thus assess the EMR children for their developmental level and then teach them to perform at the next developmental step. Those speech therapists who work from a linguistic framework analyze the linguistic rules governing each child's language and teach the linguistic rules required to have them conform to adult competencies. Other speech therapists may use commercial materials that have been specially designed for accelerating the speech and language acquisition of EMR children.

Trainable Mentally Retarded Children.   Children whose IQ scores range from 25 to 50 are considered to be trainable retarded. The curriculum in TMR involves developing the children's skills for independent living. These skills sometimes come under titles such as self-help, social adjustment, or occupational training and are designed to prepare the children for an adult life in which they will be able to live and work in supervised settings.

Speech therapists working with TMR children often structure their lessons to build the children's functional language for meeting their basic wants and handling simple social interactions. Core vocabularies include common everyday objects and actions (Lahey & Bloom, 1977). TMR children who are unintelligible or nonverbal are sometimes taught an alternate means of communication such as using picture boards or signs and gestures to communicate.

Profoundly Mentally Retarded Children.   Children of this category have an IQ test score below 25. Until recently they had been institutionalized and offered no educational program. Instead, their daily lives involved basic caretaking. A recently developed training program in special education was designed to teach teachers to work with profoundly mentally handicapped students. With this program and the move to deinstitutionalize society, the public schools are adding special classes for profoundly retarded children to their school organization.

The curriculum for PMR children consists of breaking down daily tasks and rehearsing the steps so that the children can learn the actions and their sequences. The tasks are classified under categories such as social skills, motor skills, independent living skills, and vocational training (Sternberg & Adams, 1982).

Just as for the TMR children, speech-language therapists working with PMR children in public schools and in institutions are experimenting with alternative modes of communication, rather than relying solely on the children learning verbal language. Speech therapists with a developmental-normative framework have drawn from developmental psychology using the stages that normal children go through prior to learning language as a way to teach PMR children to communicate. The approach involves teaching nonverbal children to use a symbol system. Training may begin with teaching skills prerequisite to symbol formation. Speech therapists have recently been designing lessons such as looking for hidden objects or anticipating events. The lessons require that the children learn to keep things in mind without the help of their physical presence—that is, they must learn to re-present them.

Learning Disabilities.   Children who are learning disabled differ from the retarded in that they show competencies that they do not live up to. Sometimes called underachievers, they have been officially defined in the Children with Specific Learning Disabilities Act of 1969:

Children with special learning disabilities exhibit a disorder in one or more of the basic psychological processes involved in understanding or using spoken or written language. These may be manifested in disorders of listening, talking, reading, writing, spelling or arithmetic. They include conditions which have been referred to as perceptual handicaps, brain injury, minimal brain dysfunction, dyslexia, developmental aphasia, etc. They do not include learning problems which are due primarily to visual, hearing, or motor handicaps, to mental retardation, emotional disturbance, or to environmental disadvantage (Federal Register, 1975, p. 42478).

Their deficits are often cast in a framework of information processing theory, which locates the problem as occurring in the process of gathering and organizing knowledge. Thus, learning disabled children who are found to be hyperactive and inattentive are viewed as having auditory or visual perceptual problems or problems with memory. These processing problems are seen as the major source of their underachievement.

Others who work with learning disabled children see them as having knowledge problems that interfere with their ability to process information. The children are regarded as attentive because they lack the knowledge background from which to organize the incoming information.

This processing versus knowledge debate is a healthy one in the literature on learning disabilities. It has sometimes been referred to as the process-product difference and has recently been described as the bottom-up versus top-down views of learning (Duchan & Katz, 1983). In the bottom-up view, learning is regarded as a process in which information is taken in through the senses, processed, organized, and stored for future use. In the top-down view, learning is regarded as the ability to use an already formed knowledge system for gathering knowledge. The bottom-up approach to learning disabilities leads to the use of programs to enhance information processing. These process training lessons include discrimination training, perceptual training, memory training, and training to sequence.

Speech therapists have a special version of the processing-training approach that concentrates on auditory processing because the auditory modalities seem more closely allied with verbal language. The processing-training approaches involve teaching the learning disabled child to tell the differences between sounds, listening for sounds in a background of noise, and sequencing sounds and words (Butler, 1981; Goldman, Fristoe, & Woodcock, 1974). A particular form of the processing model is one explicated in the Illinois Test of Psycholinguistic Abilities (Kirk, McCarthy, & Kirk, 1968). The ITPA test is intended to diagnose a child's auditory and visual processing difficulties and to lead the therapist to a training program that fits the child's test profile.

Those who view learning disabilities as a top-down problem focus their curriculum on conceptual understandings. For example, reading programs have been designed to emphasize language understandings rather than visual processing of the symbols (Vellutino, 1978; Spiro, Bruce, & Brewer, 1980).

Speech therapists who take the top-down view of learning disabilities see children's language knowledge as pivotal in their learning school subjects and concentrate their efforts on teaching the children language structure (Stark & Wallach, 1982). Recently there has been a trend toward combining top-down with bottom-up approaches, and language forms and rules are taught alongside exercises for processing that knowledge (Hubbell, 1981; Wiig & Semel, 1980).

The Sociological Framework

The medical, developmental, and educational frameworks locate the problem of deviance in the children—in their biology, slow development, or learning competence. The sociological framework asks how people get identified as deviant in the first place. Proponents of this view look to the society for the origins of deviance. There are several strands of research in sociological theory that have attempted to outline answers to this question. One strand examines who gets labeled, another examines who does the labeling, a third examines the influence of the label on the child, and a fourth examines why society needs to identify people as deviant. Sociologists study these aspects of deviance for groups beyond the handicapped (criminals, drug addicts) and build their theories to account for all types of deviance. The focus here will be on how the sociology of deviance relates to handicapped children.

Who Gets Labeled?   The medical perception of handicaps has in it the possibility that children can be handicapped yet go undiagnosed, in the same way that diseases can exist without being detected. The sociological view of deviance views handicaps operating like status designations where the label is given someone. Without that category label the person remains of normal status. The influence of social labeling has been most studied in relation to educably mentally retarded children with the clear result that those labeled EMR are disproportionately poor and black and male (Mercer, 1973). The preponderance of low-status children in EMR classes is evidence that they are differentially treated by virtue of their status rather than their inherent ability, and that the schools and measuring instruments do not accept or accommodate children from low-status groups.

In contrast, until recently, one found a disproportionate number of middle- and upper-class white children among the learning disabled and autistic population. These handicaps are higher status handicaps, carrying with them more positive stereotypes. Families who can afford it often have their child evaluated by a variety of professionals and are more likely to have their child assigned to more prestigious diagnostic categories (Hood-Holzman, 1982).

Who Does the Labeling?   Different professionals have the authority to designate children as abnormal. The authority of the professional differs depending upon the category the children are to be assigned to. Medical doctors, for example, have the authority to diagnose children autistic, emotionally disturbed, or neurologically impaired; school psychologists can determine their intelligence quotient for educational placement into educable, trainable, or profoundly retarded classes; educators can identify their learning problems as learning disabled or as reading, writing, or math disabilities on the basis of achievement tests; audiologists can ascertain the degree of hearing loss; and speech-language pathologists can decide whether or not the child is classified as communicatively handicapped and what sort of handicap he or she has.

The professionals as a group have middle-class status and are placed in a position of judging those who are in a different class from them (Tomlinson, 1982; Larson, 1977). Professional groups have devised assessment procedures of two general types, medical and normative. The medical assessment approach allows the professional, usually the medical doctor, to examine the child for symptoms and to arrive at a judgment based on professional expertise. The normative model relies on statistical measures for defining children as deviant, so an IQ within a certain range qualifies a child as normal or retarded, and language tests qualify children as having normal language or as being language impaired. The normative judgment is made on the basis of test scores and is thus considered to be an objective measure, although it has been found to be culturally biased and subject to the scorers' interpretations.

The Influence of Labels.   The influence of a label on a child and interactants varies with the circumstances. For those who are misdiagnosed, the result of the diagnosis may be self-fulfilling, that is, the child becomes socialized to act like the group for which he or she is labeled. Johnson (1961) has argued, for example, that stuttering begins in the adult's ear and from there makes its way to the child's mouth. That is to say, labeling the child a stutterer results in making him or her a bona fide stutterer.

For those who do have problems, the diagnosis can add to their sense of being different and create a life of overcoming or hiding that difference. Edgerton (1967) has reported how deinstitutionalized retarded people try to pass as normal by scattering reading material throughout their house to look as if they can read and by parking a car in front to look as if they can drive. Children who have once been in classes for the educable retarded do not tell their friends of their earlier placement (Jones, 1972). Handicapped children who do not know the answer to what they are asked develop elaborate guessing strategies (Duchan, 1983). Stutterers do not volunteer to speak in public and try to pass as shy in face-to-face interactions.

For those children who are more noticeably different before the diagnosis, the actual labeling and placement in treatment contexts such as special classes can accentuate the problem. They become stigmatized and differentiated from others even more. The curricula in the special classes are different from what is going on with normal children, resulting in the child being more different from normal children. The different kind of education along with the stereotyping as handicapped follows the child throughout his or her life, resulting in fewer employment opportunities.

Why Do We Label People Handicapped?   The sociological view points to the importance of deviance as a social safety valve that relegates potential troublemakers to positions in which they can no longer make trouble. Thus, children who do not comply in classrooms are designated as offenders and are removed from that context. Incompetent people or those who cannot be cared for by their families are placed in institutions away from the mainstream society.

A second reason we are labeling more and more children handicapped has to do with the emerging professional class. Like workers in any business, professionals have made a place for themselves in our society by increasing the number of people who need their services. Thus, we have newly defined handicapped groups such as learning disabled who require special education and related professional services.

The sociological framework, then, changes the view of handicap from one that is a social problem to one that is a sociological problem, and from one that originates in the handicapped person to one that originates in a society that designates so many of its members deviant.

Summary: A Case Example from Autism

Before considering a sixth framework as a candidate for viewing communicatively handicapped people, it may be helpful to review the first five frameworks to concretize their influence. We will take as our point of departure the various views of the communication problems of autistic children.

Specialists with a medical approach to autism emphasize diagnosis and in so doing identify symptoms that are characteristic of an assumed disease. Historically, the emphasis has been to differentiate autism from emotional disorders. The American Psychiatric Association published a list of symptoms designed to distinguish childhood autism from other disorders such as childhood schizophrenia. The list outlined in the Diagnostic and Statistical Manual of the American Psychiatric Association (1983) has come to be called DSM III and includes symptoms such as "pervasive lack of responsiveness to other people" and "gross deficits in language development."

Symptom check lists have replaced neurological or physiological tests for diagnosing autism because to date there are no known or consistent neurophysiologic indicators of the disorder. That is to say, autistic children are distinguishable from other children only by their behaviors. Medical doctors or psychologists are usually the ones to diagnose children autistic, and they usually rely on the DSM III to do so.

In keeping with the medical framework, medically oriented professionals design their approach to autism to get rid of the symptoms of unknown origin prevalent in autism. Symptom-oriented treatment programs call for eliminating behaviors that were used to diagnose the children autistic. In this case

Nonverbal communication skills are important precursors for expanded language skills. These two young children have been placed together in front of a favorite toy and the teacher is there to encourage interaction. (Photograph by Mima Cataldo.)

the therapy may be a set of lessons prescribed and designed by the speech-language pathologist to eliminate symptoms such as echolalia or self-stimulatory behavior.

Whereas the medical framework views autism as a disease whose symptoms are manifest in the communication disorder, the developmental psychology framework regards autism as a developmental disorder with the communication disability being one of the significant areas of developmental delay. The developmental emphasis is not geared to identify which children have the disease, but rather asks which are the areas of developmental delay and what is the degree of the delay.

Developmental specialists in speech-language pathology administer tests that are norm-referenced on normal children. Some pathologists use broadly focused tests to identify a variety of areas of developmental delay to arrive at a profile of competence levels. Others use more specific tests to identify areas of knowledge that the child needs to learn in order to communicate. Still others use very specific tests to determine the children's competencies in various areas of communication.

Severely handicapped autistic children often do not perform on the tests well enough for the tester to ascertain a developmental level; as a result, the children earn the undignified label of untestable. In the not-so-recent past, autistic children carrying such a label were not eligible for speech or language therapy (Siegal, 1983). The inclination not to help the untestable children follows from a strict developmental framework that requires that children be assigned a developmental level before decisions can be made about what to teach.

Strong developmentalists design their language training for testable autistic children with an eye toward having them progress through the same stages as would normally developing children. Thus there are language training programs that begin with the child's practicing early emerging speech sounds such as *p*, *b*, and *m*. From there the lessons progress to later developing speech sounds such as *r* and *l*. Typically, developmental teaching is arranged along a preestablished developmental progression from simple to complex. For the preverbal autistic child, there are language programs that train them to progress through the six sensorimotor stages that Piaget found in the development of normal preverbal children.

Some speech-language developmentalists take a linguistic developmental approach and concentrate on evaluating and teaching autistic children linguistic structures. Linguistic-developmental evaluations involve determining at what developmental stage the autistic child is performing and then helping the child to proceed to the next step in the progression.

Other speech-language pathologists less committed to the developmental framework examine the autistic child's language for its own structure, allowing for the possibility that autistic children's language is not developmentally delayed but is following a somewhat different course from that of normal children's language development.

For example, Hurtig, Ensrud, and Tomblin (1982) have evaluated the repetitive language of older verbal autistic children and found that the repetitions of questions are bids from the autistic speaker for the listener to respond in particular ways. If the desired response is not obtained, the overture is repeated. Similarly, Prizant and Duchan (1981) found through language sample analysis of videotapes that autistic children's echolalia serves different communicative functions, among which are to rehearse what was just said or to acknowledge or affirm it. Further, Bruce and Duchan (1983) and Park (1982) found from their study of individual children that some autistic children rely heavily on the melody of language to convey their meanings and less heavily on the particular words tucked into the melodies. Prizant, in an overview article about how autistic children may be processing language, has used evidence such as autistic children's preference for intonation and their tendency to repeat a whole phrase; from that evidence he has argued that the children may be organizing their language into larger units than do most normal children. So, instead of autistic children thinking about language as combinations of individual words, where words are learned individually and then combined, they think first about language as unanalyzed sentence-sized tunes and proceed to adult use by breaking down those large linguistic sentence tunes into word constituents (Prizant, 1983).

The preceding researchers arrived at their notions about autistic language as a different language by thinking as a linguist would (how is this person's language organized?) rather than as a developmentalist (how does this person's language compare with normal language?) or a "medicalist" interested in differential diagnosis (what aspects of autistic children's language are unique to them as a group?).

A linguistic approach to training begins by identifying the language structures that the child has and then working toward those that are lacking. The methodology may involve treating the child as one who is aware of language, much as one would deal with a second language learner, and teaching them what they want to say in a more appropriate way. The format of such a metalinguistic approach is to conduct language lessons. This method of teaching follows what teachers in our culture often do (Mehan, 1979). Others taking a linguistic approach might operate on the assumption that children do not understand language as an abstract system, but rather as a tool to think with or to get things done. Under this framework, the speech-language pathologist is more likely to spend time translating what the child says and does into conventional linguistic forms. This more child-centered approach is called modeling and is what parents in our culture often do (Ferguson & Snow, 1977).

For the children who are unable to master conventional spoken forms, speech-language pathologists are currently experimenting with other means besides talking for communicating with them. For example, clinicians have encouraged autistic children to use natural gestures to communicate (Silverman, 1982). Others have offered the children pictures of what they may want in hopes that the children will learn to point to the picture to express their intent (Schuler & Baldwin, 1981). Natural sign language has also served as a vehicle for communicating with autistic children (Bonvillian, Nelson, & Rhyne, 1982; Fulwiler & Fouts, 1976; Casey, 1978). Finally, special systems such as electronic communication devices, or written symbol systems such as words or pictographs, have proven successful for communicating with some autistic children (LaVigna, 1977).

A metalinguistic lessonlike approach to language training is frequently found among speech-language pathologists who use the educational framework to teach language to autistic children. Those who use the educational classifications will organize and select lessons depending upon educational classifications of the children. Thus, autistic children might receive one type of language training if they are placed in classes for learning disabled children, and another if they are placed in classes for retarded children. In many places attempts have been made to group autistic children together in the same class, and in these cases the educational specialists in the area of speech-language pathology are inclined to design or use language programs specifically designed for autistic children (Lovaas, 1977).

The language programs for autistic children differ from those used for other groups of children in that they are heavily influenced by behavior modification techniques. Behavior modification owes its heritage to B. F.

Skinner, a psychologist whose ideas developed from an older version of behaviorism known as classical conditioning. Both pre-Skinnerian and post-Skinnerian behaviorists believe that thinking and understanding can be reduced to a set of stimulus-response associations. Not unlike reflex reactions, learning is seen to take place by associating responses with stimuli present in the environment. Skinner's contribution to behaviorism was to focus on what followed a particular stimulus-response chain. The following event, or reinforcer, may result in an increase in the number of times an organism gives a particular response when presented with a particular stimulus. In such cases where subsequent events increase the likelihood of a preceding response occurring, positive reinforcement is said to have taken place. If, on the other hand, the following event results in a decrease in the tendency for the organism to associate a particular response with a given stimulus, the event is said to be negatively reinforcing (Skinner, 1957). Skinner's addition of reinforcement to behaviorism is now referred to as operant conditioning, a technique that serves as a basis for behavior modification.

The method of behavior modification includes techniques for determining which events are reinforcing, when to reinforce, and how to break a task down so the child can be positively reinforced along the way of making successive approximations to the more complex responses (Sloane & MacAulay, 1968).

Programs using behavior modification have become widely used in classrooms with autistic children. Lovaas (1977), a pioneer in developing such programs for use by teachers, was one of the first to assume that severely autistic children were capable of learning. His early use of behavior modification techniques involved conditioning autistic children to attend to tasks and to eliminate their self-stimulatory behaviors.

More recently, behavior modification techniques have been developed to teach language to autistic children (Hinerman, 1983). The language lessons are usually highly organized, beginning with the teacher presenting a stimulus (a picture to be named; a word, phrase, or sentence to be imitated), followed by the child's response and then the teacher's reinforcement. The teacher proceeds to a new round by presenting a new stimulus. If the child fails, the task is broken down further or the teacher cues the child, using some sort of verbal or nonverbal prompt. Attempts are made by the behavior modifier to make the child successful, to give him or her positive reinforcement. Lessons are under control led by the teacher, and the language produced by the child is regarded as correct or incorrect, depending upon what the teacher wants for the response.

Children who are grouped together in classes whose educational programs are based on behavior modification principles have more in common with one another than their symptoms and curriculum. They have a common sociological history. They tend to have a history of being labeled many things: deaf because they have not responded to sound; retarded because they have not progressed along the prescribed developmental milestones; emotionally disturbed because they do not relate normally to others; and, for those more competent, learning disabled, if they have high-level competencies along with severe learning problems.

Autistic children also tend to be from families who have been persistent in taking their handicapped child to different professionals (Hood-Holzman, 1982). This shopping for different and more acceptable diagnoses and educational classifications is more common for middle-class families who have the financial means for having their child evaluated. Along with higher status, because of the prestige of the label, autistic children are more likely to receive special services such as occupational and speech-language therapies than are their retarded counterparts.

But what about the children whose families have not been able to act as their full-time advocates? One of their most common fates has been to be placed in residential institutions such as developmental centers, where they may or may not receive schooling or even vocational training.

Social efforts to counter ostracism of autistic children have been evolving over the last twenty years or so. The deinstitutionalization movement has emerged with the aim of removing people from the institutions and placing them in the community. Those autistic children who are deinstitutionalized usually live in group homes in transient neighborhoods of large cities.

To summarize, children diagnosed autistic are treated differently by professionals and their treatment will depend in part upon whether the professionals display a medical, developmental, linguistic, educational, or sociological orientation. What still needs to be examined in detail is how different professionals from different orientations bring those theoretical orientations into their interactions with autistic children.

A Sixth Framework: The Handicap Is in the Interaction

This chapter began with a discussion of the important role interaction plays in determining a handicapped child's quality of life. We now return to that theme and discuss the interaction framework in light of the more prevalent five frameworks that are used to identify and handle handicapped children. The five frameworks exist because of the various orientations of professionals who are identifying and teaching handicapped children. They continue to exist because in varying ways they help explain and understand handicapped children. There *are* some conditions that have tangible diseaselike origins, which lend themselves to classifications and treatment under the medical framework. There *are* developmental differences between handicapped children and normal children that allow us to scientifically distinguish normal from abnormal and to identify areas of abnormal development under the developmental psychology approach. There *are* children whose learning and communication problems originate in their linguistic understandings. There *are* children who have trouble succeeding in regular classrooms and who do better in special classes with specially designed curricula. And there *are* sociological considerations for understanding how children come to be designated and treated as handicapped. Thus, in certain respects all these frameworks can be brought to bear on understanding different aspects of different handicapping conditions. In other respects the understandings can be gained from the frameworks' lead to conclusions that are at best uninsightful and at worst damaging. We now turn to an emerging sixth framework that can help point out some of the problems with the first five.

The sixth framework, the interaction framework, is one that views the handicapped child as but one member of an interaction. The other members of the society with whom the child interacts are seen as equal contributors in determining the degree of handicap and the quality of the interaction.

The interaction framework holds that when two people come together they must find something to do and to talk about. They must choose from what they know those things that are of mutual interest and that will allow the interaction to move forward. Each interactant often comes to the interaction with a predetermined agenda. Sometimes the agendas are incompatible and must be negotiated; other times they are controlled by one member of the interaction and need not be negotiated, if the arrangement is agreeable to the other member. Still other times the agendas are compatible, in which case they also need not be negotiated.

This view that what is going on is a two-way interaction between handicapped children and adults leads away from the view that there is a deficit in the child to one where it is the responsibility of both child and adult to find a way to be together to fulfill one another's goals. It also moves from a view that handicapped children's problems originate with a cause outside the here and now, such as medical or learning problems or problems in the society, to a view that says the degree of the problem depends upon how well the current interaction is going. Under the interaction view, the handicap is felt by both adults and children when the children are unfavorably compared with others—either with normal children or as members of the handicap group—and asked to engage in interactions that they are not capable of or ones that are beneath their dignity, or ones that highlight the handicap (see Box 7). This view does not regard children as once-and-for-all handi-

---

Box 7
From "Do You Like Your Larynx?" (Creech, 1980)

There is a great need for educating the public on how to treat physically limited people. People are still under the misconception that somehow the abilities to speak, hear, see, feel, smell and reason are tied together, that if a person loses one, that person has lost the others. The number one question people ask my parents is, "Can he hear." When they reply that I can, they bend down where their lips are not two feet away from my eyes and say very loudly, "How are you? Do you like that talking machine?" . . . (That) is like a person walking up to another and asking, "Do you like your larynx?"

Box 8
Vocabulary for the Interaction Framework

Intent: What the speaker wants to have happen for each
                               utterance.

Function: The outcome of the intent.

Agenda: The goal for the event, according to each partic-
                               ipating member.

Event: The overall game plan, as conceptualized by
                               those in the interaction.

Negotiation: How partners vie for what is happening, who gets
                               to talk, who chooses the event, and who deter-
                               mines what happens next.

*Strategic
contextualization:*   A positive interpretation of an act.

Negative sanctions: A negative interpretation of an act based on a pre-
                               conceived idea that the person is, after all,
                               handicapped.

Breakdowns: An intent that fails to achieve its function, an
                               agenda that does not get achieved, or a misun-
                               derstanding in the interaction.

Repairs: The process of mending breakdowns so that the
                               interaction can continue.

Sense making: What people think is going on.

Fine tuning: The adjustment of a turn in an interaction toward
                               the communicative competencies and expecta-
                               tions of the partner.

---

capped, but only handicapped when interacting with someone who does not apply false expectations or misconceptions to the interaction. Nor does this view lead to a planned curriculum for children with particular types of handicap. Rather, it leads to a view that education is a negotiated event subject to fluctuations in interests and to the communicative abilities of the child and of the adult as they interact during a particular event. This view that the interaction is what should be focused on when evaluating and educating handicapped children has exciting potential for changing the everyday lives of handicapped children and those of us who deal with them every day (see Box 8).

Education from an Interactional Perspective

The interactional framework allows us to evaluate educational projects in terms of the quality of the child's everyday interactions. To make the point, it will help to discuss interactions that are not going well, and those that are, and to discuss current ideas in educational programming for handicapped children in terms of the quality of interactions they foster.

American education for handicapped children, as well as for normal children, tends toward authoritarianism (Bruner, 1982). That is, teachers and curricula are prescribed, with little room for children's negotiation of the event and the participants' roles within them. Some lessons are explicitly laid out so that they define what people will say and do, and when they will say and do it. Explicitly prescribed lessons tend to be even more characteristic of curricula for handicapped children than for normal children. Under these regimented lessons, the interaction fails to go well when children fail to conform to stipulated or assumed rules governing the event, or when children conform but respond incorrectly thereby accruing negative sanctions from the onlookers and the teacher. From a long-range perspective, prescribed interactions that lead to continual failure produce an attitude in children of "learned helplessness," in which they come to understand that they have no control over their school performance (Weisz, 1979).

Even when interactions are less prescribed in that they are more controlled by the handicapped child or more negotiated, negative sanctions might apply. When the child does something unconventional, adults may judge the act inappropriate and try to divert them or dissuade them from continuing with little regard for the intent behind the child's action. The likely result is that children fail to satisfy their intents.

Negative sanctions also occur indirectly when handicapped children are left out of activities because of assumed incompetence, or when they fail in the activities because of misassumed competence. Finally, and perhaps the most negative of all, is when handicapped children are ignored and cut out of what is happening as though they were not even there (Helm, 1981).

On the more positive side are the nonauthoritarian and accepting interactions, ones in which the interactant interprets the child's actions by using strategic contextualization. During these times the children's errors are viewed as legitimate and the source of their wrong answers are seen as originating not in the child's inappropriateness or handicap, but in their sensible and legitimate understanding of the event.

Along with strategic contextualization, the key to successful interaction is in appropriate fine tuning where the adults and children engage in and create events that produce growth in both and fewer "mistakes" on the part of either.

These constructs of negative sanctions, of strategic contextualization, and of fine tuning are potentially useful for thinking about children's everyday life in the classroom. There is a movement afoot in special education for changing the current way of educating handicapped children. The effort is to integrate handicapped with normal children rather than to place the handicapped children in special classes or special schools or institutions. When integration is not feasible, the effort is to change the physical environments to be more like those encountered by normal people. The integration movement is called mainstreaming (Knoblock, 1982); the environmental change is called normalization (Wolfensberger, 1972). From an interaction perspective, mainstreaming and normalization may be either good or bad, depending upon the interactions that take place in those new classrooms or new physical arrangements.

Imagine, for example, a child in a special classroom where he or she receives positive sanctions and where the fine tuning is working, but where there is no exposure to normal children. Imagine, then, that the child is removed from this comfortable nurturing environment to a class with normal children, replete with negative sanctions and no fine tuning on the part of the teacher or normal peers. This child is likely to fare best in the isolated class, even though he or she may fail to develop skills for getting along with normal children of the same age or ability level.

Similarly, imagine a handicapped adolescent who likes to play with dolls or infant toys, and who is not given these things because of his or her efforts to normalize his or her setting and make it like that of other teenagers.

Speech-language pathologists working within the interaction framework are beginning to borrow and develop evaluation procedures for measuring how well people negotiate agendas with communicatively handicapped children, how interactions are constructed with those children, the degree of authoritarianism inherent in the interaction, and the sorts of interpretations adults place on unconventional communicative acts. These procedures differ from ordinary ones in that their focus is not on the child but on the quality of the interaction.

An example is the AIM procedure (Duchan, 1983) for assessing the interaction mode between adults and language-impaired children. Assuming a continuum of interaction with authoritarian teaching at one end and following the child's lead at the other, the procedure analyzes interactions for where they fall along the continuum. The procedure is modeled after language sample analysis in that it has the analyst videotape an interaction, transcribe it, and analyze the tape and transcript for relevant patterns. In this case the analysis involves examining the activity going on and how it is organized. Once the structure of the event is determined, the relative contribution of the interactants in organizing the structure is traced (e.g., who initiated the event, how well the interactant responded to the other's initiations, how breakdowns in the interaction are repaired). The placement of the particular interaction along the authoritarian-nurturing continuum is then assigned, based on the amount of work and degree of control of each interactant. Finally, there is a step in the procedure where the interaction mode of the event is evaluated for whether it was effective in achieving what the participants intended.

While a beginning, the AIM procedure only touches the surface of what can be done to study interactions. What is needed are more measures of the quality of interaction—measures for how well teachers and normal students fine tune to those who are different, and measures for what the impact of normalization is on the quality of life and interactions of handicapped children. What is needed is a change in attitude of professionals that focuses not on what is wrong with the person who is different, but on the mismatch between the child and the interactant that makes that difference negative enough to exclude the children from positive participation.

> The viewpoint must switch from the present fix on pathology which points the accusing finger of cause at the child to approaches which emphasize the fact that the problem is not in the child but in the mismatch which exists between the child's needs and the opportunities we make available to nurture his self realization (Deno, 1970, p. 229).

What is needed is a change in society that results in less concern for specifying groups as deviant and more concern for strategic contextualization of differences regarding them as legitimate and understandable. It is a herculean task that will require much special education, not only for handicapped children, but also for those who interact with them.

Summary

We are accustomed to thinking of handicaps as being in people and as being fixable by professionals who have a common philosophy about what to do. In this chapter, we show that special education specialists, in this case speech-language pathologists, have different frameworks and that the frameworks dictate what they think and do to help handicapped children. The particular focus of the chapter is on the communicatively handicapped—those children who have trouble with their speech and language. Children's speech and language problems are described, cloaked in medical, psychological, linguistic, educational, and sociological perspectives. An example of how frameworks affect people's reactions to autistic children is given to illustrate the importance of perspectives. The chapter concludes by arguing for a new framework, the interaction framework, which prescribes working toward more egalitarian relationships with handicapped children, and asks that adults and peers assume more communicative responsibility in interacting with communicatively handicapped children. The interactive framework, in order to have an impact, requires that society change. The changes will not only benefit handicapped children, but also those who learn to interact with them.

Chapter 5

Peter Knoblock

Peter Knoblock is a professor of special education in the Division of Special Education and Rehabilitation at Syracuse University. His primary interest is developing school programs that integrate disabled and nondisabled students. In 1970 he helped to create Jowonio School, an integrated preschool program that has been used as a model for developing a continuum of integrated classrooms in the Syracuse City School District. At Syracuse University he teaches courses in emotional disturbance and autism and is the author of Teaching Emotionally Disturbed Children *and* Teaching and Mainstreaming Autistic Children.

Integrating Areas of Development: Implications for Socioemotional Development

After reading this chapter, you should be able to:

1
Define socioemotional development.

2
Recall important developmental tasks to be mastered by all children and describe unique problems faced by children with disabilities.

3
Define stress and discuss its application to understanding the school experiences of students with disabilities.

4
List the ways teachers can facilitate the socioemotional development of students with disabilities.

Understanding children and adolescents with disabilities requires an appreciation of each area of development described in the previous chapters: physical development, cognitive development, and communication; how these areas are related; and how socioemotional development is facilitated by the satisfactory development of skills within each area.

Early efforts in special education emphasized the discrete needs of children with particular disabilities. A child with a learning problem was tested for cognitive deficits; those with visual impairments had programs devised to minimize their sight limitations, and so on. Specialized programs and interventions were developed to respond to the unique needs of each of these "types" of students. Now, after several decades of program development, we are gaining a new appreciation of the reciprocal nature of physical, cognitive, communication and socioemotional functioning, and how children's school programs can be enhanced when this reciprocity is taken into consideration and the child is viewed as a whole person. This chapter describes the many connections between these areas, particularly as they influence a child's relationships with adults and children.

Children's opportunities for healthy relationships are enhanced by a society that minimizes social and economic barriers to growth. As Chapter 1 points out, however, previous social policies toward those with disabilities have contributed to the creation of facilities and programs that limit those opportunities by isolating children and adolescents from their peers and communities. Conversely, newer policies that encourage economic and social support for families and the integration of disabled students with their nondisabled peers have positively influenced their socioemotional development. This chapter will also discuss approaches used by communities and schools to implement these policies.

The Many Facets of Socioemotional Development

Educational psychologist, Philip Jackson, writing on life in classrooms, observed that a teacher has hundreds, even thousands, of daily interactions with children (1968). These interactions involve a variety of relationship concerns. This range is addressed by Anastasiow (1981) when he states:

> Socioemotional development means the development of emotions, the ability to get along with peers, the development of ego and superego, the ability to form attachments and affiliations with caregivers and peers, and the ability to grow and develop as a person—in other words it is a confusing puzzle (p. 2).

Each of the developmental milestones and tasks referred to by Anastasiow in the above quotation is influenced by children's physical, cognitive, and language development. Albert Ellis, a child therapist specializing in work with disturbed children and adults states, "Rarely, if ever, do disturbed emotions exist independently of cognitions" (Ellis, 1985, p. 471). Children's understanding of inner experiences, such as feelings, has become a major area of interest in child development and more recently in special education. This blending of affect and cognition, referred to as cognitive behavior modification, has encouraged teachers to create social skills training approaches in which children are taught to think through a problem as one way to interact more effectively with others. This approach is described later in this chapter.

In turn, physical development is dependent to an important degree upon the communication between adult caregiver and infant. The ability of a caregiver to accurately "read" and to react to infants' emotionally expressive behaviors such as crying, smiling, and laughing may be necessary for meeting the physical needs of babies, and skilled adult behavior also contributes to social and cognitive growth. Duchan's chapter in this book emphasizes communication as social interaction and discusses the importance of making adjustments in what is communicated by adults, or "fine-tuning" one's expectations of what a child can reasonably be expected to do. It is likely that infants respond positively to accurate responses to their basic needs for touch, food, and warmth, thus highlighting the importance of communication between infant and adult.

The influence of one area of development upon other areas and the impact on children's progress of stimulating adult interactions is supported by the research of child development specialists and the observations of parents and teachers. A child's successful entry into the larger world of peers and schools is dependent to a large degree upon the functioning within and between these areas of development, and the response of parents, teachers, peers, and other members of the community who may hold particular value positions about children and disability despite having considerably less contact with them than teachers and peers. All these factors are present as children attempt to master important developmental tasks.

Important Developmental Tasks for Disabled Children

Children and adolescents with disabilities are faced with the same developmental needs and tasks confronting all children. By using normal development as a yardstick we can trace variation in children's progress with a degree of accuracy. In addition, the study of children with disabilities can provide us with further evidence of the interaction between developing affective, cognitive, and physiological systems. Each of these points is highlighted in a longitudinal study conducted over seven years with infants with Down's syndrome (see Chapter 2 for a description) by Cicchetti and Pogge-Hesse (1982). Their findings support the similarities in the developmental process in Down's syndrome infants and nonretarded infants. They report the achievement by Down's syndrome infants of various developmental milestones at a slower rate and generally retarded cognitive development. They also support the premise of this chapter that systems are connected when they state: "Affect and cognition are viewed as inseparable as two aspects of the same developmental process. Our research offered clear support for the premise that affective and cognitive development of infant affective expression is clearly integral for understanding emerging cognitive capacities" (p. 298).

This interrelationship is seen clearly in the early emotional expression of infants with Down's syndrome. Emde, Katz, and Thorpe (1978) have studied the smiling behavior of Down's syndrome infants to see if there were any differences in their emotional signaling as compared to normal infants. They have summarized their findings as follows:

> First, our MDS (multidimensional scaling) analysis suggests that there is more uncertainty or noise in the emotional signaling of the Down's infants and that this uncertainty arises from the infant rather than from the mother (although the latter undergoes a difficult adaptation of her own).
> Second, the onset of the social smile in the Down's syndrome infant, although slightly delayed, is chiefly deviant by its dampened intensity, poor eye-to-eye contact, and lack of "crescendoing" activation. Instead of rewarding a social interaction, instead of engaging and "being fun," it tends to disappoint because it is so different from what is expected.
> Third, our experience with the longitudinal study of six families with Down's syndrome infants highlights the importance of these phenomena in the context of social development. The parents, who have to do psychological grief work following the birth of a defective infant in the first two postnatal months, often experience renewed disappointment in the face of the dampened social smile at 4 months, and this disappointment can inaugurate a second wave of grieving for the normal infant they had expected (pp. 359–360).

The study cited above also included photographs comparing smiling behaviors of normal versus Down's syndrome 3½-month-old infants. The infants with Down's syndrome are indeed smiling and responding, but in comparison to the normal infants their responses are not nearly as clear and dramatic. It would be necessary for an adult to attend quite closely to such subtle responses in order to reinforce smiling behavior. This is a good example of the influence that infants can have on their caregivers. This influence is in evidence in each of the developmental tasks described: social interchange, ability to form attachments, and the development of friendships.

Social Interchange

The study of disabled children's early development can begin with an examination of the behaviors of adults and children as they contribute to the socialization process. Adults teach social skills by modeling and direct instruction, provide children with opportunities to develop and expand their contacts with other adults and children, and help children learn to cope with inevitable frustrations. On the other hand, recent research points to the impact infant behaviors have on the quantity and quality of adult interactions.

Children need opportunities to play together. Social interactions, like the one between these two children, can lead to the development of friendships. (Photograph by Mima Cataldo.)

In schools, for example, teachers can describe the numerous ways that children in their classrooms influence how they respond to those children—and so can parents. Gradually, child development researchers, teachers, and parents have begun to recognize children's power in relationships. Another way to view this phenomenon is to acknowledge how much we can learn from children. For teachers it means that along with focusing on what we can do to modify children's behaviors for purposes of helping them acquire skills we can also focus on how interactional the teaching process is. Teaching is not a process of doing things to a student, but rather one of engaging a learner in meaningful goals and activities. This theme of mutuality—our assisting children and our learning from them—is central to an understanding of children's development.

Reciprocity.   Infants are no longer viewed as passive recipients of adult interventions: their behaviors can elicit adult responses by influencing expectations of caregivers. That is, adults may read into certain expressions and behaviors of infants, thus ascribing intentionality to what they observe. This social interchange perspective maintains that behaviors of infants and caregivers are jointly regulated by a variety of conditions including the affective, cognitive, and communication skills of each.

For example, if effective social interaction is to occur an infant must be able to understand the meaning of a caregiver's emotional response and to respond emotionally. Similarly, if reciprocity is to occur the caregiver must be able to communicate needed emotional expression to an infant who seeks such support. The turning to one's caregiver in moments of need is referred to as maternal referencing. This back-and-forth looking from infant to mother occurs in normal infants during the second half-year of life and somewhat later in development for infants with Down's syndrome (Sorce, Emde, & Frank, 1982).

In school, efforts to teach children with disabilities to engage in reciprocal interactions typically emphasize their social skills deficits. Assessment procedures using observations, social skills check lists, sociometric ratings, and other approaches are designed to highlight disabled children's social deficits. If our goal, however, is to foster social reciprocity, then we must be certain to include nondisabled peers in our teaching and assessment procedures.

Teaching functional skills, or those skills needed to function effectively in a range of community environments including school, is crucial for students with severe disabilities, and indeed for all learners (Brown et al., 1978). A second grade teacher of an integrated classroom for severely disabled and nondisabled children surveyed the nondisabled students for information about what they did after school and with whom they interacted. She asked them questions about self-care and home organization (using an alarm clock, brushing one's teeth, waiting for the school bus alone or with a friend); about beginning job skills (setting the table, feeding pets, cleaning their room); about community functioning (going out or meeting friends or parents at parks, the library, shopping malls); about leisure and recreation (activities inside their homes and whether done alone or with friends). The teacher was hoping to get a clear sense of how nondisabled peers spend their time and what the expectations are for them outside school, and to then begin structuring the school curriculum to include these skills and activities for the students with disabilities. The teacher, in effect, was using the functioning of the nondisabled peers as guidelines for developing skill approaches and activities for students with disabilities. This systematic surveying or observing of what skills are called for in a particular situation is known as taking an ecological inventory (Evans & Meyer, 1985). If you are preparing a child to eat in restaurants, then you can observe what it is that people in that restaurant are required to do for effective participation.

Thus, we see the importance of reciprocity in the socioemotional development of infant and school-age children. Infants and caregivers, and students and teachers who are able to "successfully" interact, that is, to jointly regulate, increase the likelihood of more normal socioemotional development. Some disabled children, however, may demonstrate behaviors that interfere with this important interaction cycle. One such behavior is the ability to function in synchronization with others.

Synchronization.   Observations of the timing of infant and adult actions provide support for the contention that joint regulation is a crucial aspect of social development. In normally developing infants, synchronization, or the fluid timing of interactions, is well documented for behaviors such as vocalizations, eye gaze, facial expression, and early speech. For some children, however, their responses to cues, their response to rhythm, and the sequence they follow may be deviant. In other words, the timing of their affective interactions may be as important to understand as what infant and caregivers do and the intensity of their interactions (Massie, 1982).

An example of the importance of synchronization is seen in the movement therapy film *Looking for Me.* Janet Adler, a dance therapist, is shown attempting to elicit responses from two young girls. Initially, they are extremely unresponsive and aloof, seemingly ignoring her presence. Adler's work with these youngsters, described as psychotic, reflects a gentle but insistent form of intrusion. She begins by sharing the physical space with each child, then moving closer, and eventually imitating their exact movements. In one dramatic scene Adler and one of the girls are shown dancing around the room holding hands and moving in perfect synchrony. She makes the point that it is important to reach a level of mutuality in which no one leads and no one follows.

William Condon and his colleagues (Condon, 1975; Condon & Sander, 1974) have been studying the possibility that rhythmicity and precision in handling auditory input are disturbed in some children (thoses with autistism, cerebral palsy, learning disabilities, and aphasia). In a series of ingenious studies, Condon filmed the precise body movements of neonates in response to auditory input. Utilizing frame-by-frame film analysis, the investigators studied the "entrainment" process—the connection between an infant's body movements and the articulatory pattern of adult speech. The body movements of dysfunctional children were found to be "dysynchronous" with the auditory input from adults, that is, they responded in a delayed fashion to the input. To date, Condon's findings have not been replicated, but the possibility that some disabled children experience auditory processing problems—thereby creating a delay and lack of responsiveness—is intriguing and worthy of further study (Oxman, Webster, & Konstantareas, 1978). The ability to engage in reciprocity and to respond in a synchronous manner to the behaviors of others can influence one's ability and opportunities to form attachments.

Ability to Form Attachments

Child development specialists emphasize the importance of an infant's ability to respond to parental care and the capacity of caretakers to provide a nurturing and growth-enhancing environment. It is likely that a disruption in the ability to respond of either child or parent can significantly disrupt the development of an attachment. The assumption is that the infant must form an attachment with primary caretakers if further development and mastery of emotional tasks are to occur. On the other hand, the long-term goal for all children, including disabled children, is to become a separate, independent individual. In child development theory, this is referred to as separation and individuation. Mahler, Pine, and Bregman (1975) have described four phases of this process. Note the interaction of emotional and cognitive factors and the social contexts in which this process is embedded.

1. Differentiation (five to ten months). The child begins to discriminate differences in people and the environment and explores the world by sight and reaching. Cognitive maturity and increased motor skills for exploration and movement (crawling) allow the child to move from close physical contact with the caregivers.
2. Practice (ten to fifteen months). This child normally learns to walk; greatly expanded exploration is done with excitement and enthusiasm. The child now returns periodically to the caregiver for emotional refueling and reassurance that the caregiver is there and dependable.
3. Rapprochement (fifteen to twenty-five months). The child now expands exploration and movement away from the caregiver but at the same time becomes more aware of his or her helplessness and dependence. This results in ambivalence with more extremes of alternate closeness to and rejection of the caregiver (for example, saying "no," and temper tantrums of the two-year-old). The child's ambivalence and what appears to be regression is seen as communication. Although words are used in this phase, the frustrated use of gestures when the child is not understood is also seen.
4. Partial Object Constancy (twenty-four to thirty-six months). The image of the caregiver is now internalized and the child can function independently. Because the child is struggling for autonomy, there is some conflict when parents make demands. While the child is working through the conflict of limits placed by parents and his or her own striving for independence, the child is also aware of his or her helplessness and dependence on the parent (Ulrey, 1981, p. 40).

Ulrey (1981) has described the separation-individuation phase of early emotional development as an extension of the attachment process. He has stated: "The attachment-separation-individuation process (ASI) provides a conceptual framework and observable developmental milestones. The factors that influence ASI can be understood only as a complex system. The clinician should be aware that abnormalities in any part of the process, such as in parental attitudes or in the child's behavior, will change the system" (p. 40).

The point is that the presence of a developmental disability can create stress in the ASI process and thereby increase the problems for both child and caregiver. The nature of the stress placed on each will undoubtedly differ as will the coping strategies adopted by child and adult to respond to a potentially difficult situation. In a study of fifteen handicapped infants in an intervention program, Stone and Chesney (1979) found disturbances in one or more attachment behaviors. One of their hypotheses was that the infants' difficulties in expressing affective states prevented their caregivers from accurately understanding the child's messages. The nature of the infant's be-

Table 1
Disabled Children's Behavior and Adult Response

Disability	Implications for adults
Motor Deficits	
Infants with Minimal Brain Dysfunction with abnormal muscle tone (hypertonia) (Prechtel, 1963).	Difficulty handling child because baby cannot relax.
Mentally retarded young children can show delays in postural adjustments to caregivers (Molner, 1978).	Parent may feel rejected or inadequate.
Children exhibiting abnormal muscle tone or primitive reflexes may be at risk.	Caregiver may reduce physical contact due to inability of child to adjust to physical comforting.
Children with cerebral palsy may have delayed expressive language (de Hirsch, 1973).	Parent may not have a clear understanding of child's needs and child is prevented from eliciting positive reactions.
Some infants may respond in a delayed fashion to adult initiation (Condon and Sander, 1974).	Parent messages may not be synchronous with infant response.
Visual Handicaps	
Blind and visually handicapped infants are not able to show preference for a familiar face.	This may impede early attachment behavior.
Autistic children exhibit gaze aversion.	The lack of eye contact may interfere with parent motivation to respond with enthusiasm.
Smile behavior of blind children does develop but is often delayed.	Caregivers may try to respond but are thwarted by child's lack of vision feedback.
Recognition of caregivers and discrimination of strangers is delayed for blind children (Adelson & Fraiberg, 1973).	Attachment to relationships may be delayed.
Blind children may be dependent on close proximity to caregivers.	This may delay the separation-individuation process.

(continued)

havior and disability can interact with parental expectations and needs to thwart the development of an adequate two-way interaction process. This relationship is depicted in Table 1. For example, a parent may feel rejected by an infant's unresponsiveness, which may be due to the child's temperamental qualities or to an actual deficit in motor development.

Table 1
(continued)

Disability	Implications for adults
Hearing Loss	
Children with hearing loss may not vocalize properly.	Caregivers may not be able to discriminate sounds and identify particular need (e.g., crying, hunger).
Verbal skills may be impaired due to hearing loss.	Development of autonomy as part of the ASI process may be delayed (verbal language can increase child independence).
Delayed verbal skills may cause child frustration and adoption of other means to elicit desires.	Power struggles can occur between child and caregiver due to child's disruptive behaviors.

Source: From Ulrey, 1981.

Each disabled child faces the dual risk of dealing with his or her handicap and receiving messages and care from adults that may not be as facilitative as desired. Caregivers face a similar dilemma: they must contend with their child's disability and their own attitudes and needs as parents. As professionals we can recognize the interaction effects that a disability creates and develop responsive helping environments. For example, we may exacerbate the problems parents of mentally retarded children face by our focus on the "sick" child. This can contribute to lowered expectations and withdrawal of time and energy by parents. We can no longer treat the child in isolation from the social system of that child. We must attempt to understand the needs and vulnerabilities of families as well as those of the disabled child. Parental concerns and attitudes about having a disabled child must be acknowledged and we can respond by changing our language, attitudes, and interventions to avoid the notion that these children are defective.

Ability to Develop Friendships

The ability to develop and maintain friendships is a central task of childhood and adolescence because it can set a pattern for future relationships.

Caution is called for in assessing disabled children's interpersonal relationships. As a group, mentally retarded children, for example, may suffer exclusion by peers and be assigned a lower social status. There is nothing inherent in mental retardation or in other disability groupings to preclude their effective functioning with peers. Any child's ability to make friends is influenced by particular behaviors, and disabled children can be taught skills to help them interact successfully with peers. These are described in a later section.

Erikson's (1950) observations of the psychosocial stages through which a child must pass by satisfactorily negotiating the tasks demanded at each phase can help us understand the crucial role that expansion into the world of peers can have in a child's development. For example, in Erikson's "Play age" the child begins to explore boundaries beyond himself, now that he has mastered basic control over himself and the environment. Maier (1965) has summarized the tasks required at this stage:

> The child now faces a period of energetic learning which leads him through his limitations to future possibilities. The child associates, much of the time, with children of his own age. He enters actively into the lives of others and, thus, into a multitude of new experiences. Above all, he sees himself—he learns, associates, and experiences—as a boy or as a girl. At the same time, the child cannot escape the fact that his learning, his social contacts, and his experience introduce new thoughts, feelings, and imagined or accomplished deeds which will provide a new area for a sense of guilt. The child frequently fears he has gone beyond his rights, which, in fact, he frequently does. He continuously questions his sex role: is his behavior in line with what is expected of his sex? is it all right that, in many ways, he still feels and acts like a child of the opposite sex? is it all right that, in the matter of his sexual desires, he no longer feels like a child? Thus, this phase provides moments of feeling a sense of real accomplishments, and moments when the fear of danger and a sense of guilt are engendered (p. 46).

Anyone observing children interacting, whether very young children engaged in parallel play, or older ones interacting around a social task, recognizes the subtle cues children use to help them respond to others, how they go about the business of representing their own needs and interests, and how they find a way to tolerate the presence of others or to actively incorporate peers into an activity. Most agree that the development of friendships assists in learning a variety of social skills, facilitates social comparisons, and fosters a sense of belonging. Children can become social resources for one another. Experts also agree that a variety of skills are embedded in successfully acquiring those benefits.

What are some of the social skills necessary for successful peer interaction? To begin with, children need to know how to *communicate* with each other. Young children can communicate very effectively in a nonverbal fashion, while older ones use body language and verbalizations. In order to want to communicate, which implies sending and receiving messages, a degree of *empathy* must be present so that a child can understand others and care about them. It is not sufficient, however, to want to communicate and to understand others. It is also necessary to have *socially acceptable techniques* for engaging others and to do so tactfully. Obviously, children's relationships, as is true of all relationships, run aground at times. So the ability to resolve conflicts becomes a needed part of a child's repertoire of skills. Finally, friendship skills often require a child to *represent* himself or herself as an equal or peer on some level.

Drabman and Patterson (1982) have summarized the ways exceptional children are viewed:

> From descriptions of the different types of exceptional children and from research that seeks to determine how others view them, a general picture of the exceptional child emerges. Gifted and creative children are seen as excelling in academic pursuits and social adjustment and as being industrious. Excluding the gifted and the creative, exceptional children are viewed as unattractive and as likely to have difficulty learning material presented to them. They are also thought to behave inappropriately, to appear unhappy, to be nonconforming, to require supervision, to be withdrawn, and to oppose peers (p. 47).

This is a rather imposing list of deficits, not all of which need to remain true if we can develop environments that reduce the negative perceptions of normal peers and institute social skills training to foster the interpersonal development of exceptional children. A later section on the role of the school in fostering social and emotional development provides a number of ways disabled children can be assisted to develop friendships by acquiring specific skills. We can also create caring environments in which scapegoating and stereotypes are reduced. For now, let us examine the problems several groups of disabled children encounter as they interact with their peers.

Mentally Retarded. These children are characterized by poor cognitive abilities and/or a history of school failure due to their actual deficits or to lowered expectations of their capacity and motivation to learn. The difficulty these children have in grasping and using concepts may severely hinder their learning social rules. There is every reason to assume that individuals who are classified mentally retarded need friendship and social interaction. However, their problems in communicating interests and needs may prevent others from understanding them. Again, these are skills that can and should be taught despite any cognitive impairments or limitations.

In addition to cognitive and communication difficulties, this broad group labeled mentally retarded may exhibit poor adaptive behaviors that can include interpersonal and self-help deficits (Grossman, 1973). A child is viewed as different or deviant, and sometimes rejected by normal peers, based on lack of certain self-help skills and presence of abrasive interpersonal behaviors.

Behavior Disordered. Many types of children are grouped under this broad heading, with disruptive behavior being one of the primary descriptives used to characterize this population. Such behavior is not one of the personal attributes that attracts other children to them; in fact, unpleasant and unhelpful responses can reduce a child's likability in the classroom. The reciprocal nature of such behaviors is highlighted in a study by Charlesworth and Hartrup (1967). They employed classroom observation procedures and found that children who responded positively received a great deal of positive social reinforcement back for their efforts.

Many of the behaviors of behaviorally disordered children and youth interfere with the social skills outlined at the beginning of this section. Violations of classroom rules and norms, off-task behaviors, and physical and verbal assaults on others serve to isolate them from their peers rather than move them closer. These are not appropriate techniques for engaging peers in social interactions, at least not positive ones. Teachers often describe the efforts made by one of their pupils to involve others by engaging in disruptive behaviors. Some are remarkably successful at "contaging" the rest of the group and even appearing calm once the damage is done. The solution to this complex issue is to teach such children appropriate skills that foster acceptance by others and to create classrooms that include rather than isolate children who are different. Many of these children, based on their needs and learned social behaviors, tend to focus on themselves to a degree that inhibits their empathy and understanding of others. Finally, they may need help in learning to resolve conflicts in ways that do not escalate classroom disputes.

Autistic.   These children are distinguished by poor social relations, difficulty using language for social purposes, and a variety of behaviors that interfere with learning including self-stimulation, and poor eye contact. Currently, these are thought of as skill deficiencies rather than deficits, and the development of school programs, particularly the implementation of mainstreamed programs in which autistic children are educated with their nondisabled peers, has lent credence to their educability (Knoblock, 1982; Certo, Haring & York, 1984). This realization was slow to develop because of the consistent observation that autistic children rarely initiated social encounters. However, once placed in supportive and stimulating classrooms, many children accept and even enjoy physical contact and social initiations by adults. Howlin (1978) has reported that autistic children may look less at everything, not just human faces. Placing autistic students in learning environments with nondisabled peers may provide them with models to imitate and with children who communicate effectively. However, such placements do not guarantee positive social interactions. Strain, Kerr, and Ragland (1979) have advocated training of peers to prepare them for roles as helpers in autistic children's acquisition of social skills. They provide peers with specific instructions and skills for their helping role. In addition to targeting specific behaviors of disabled children that are in need of modifications (such as turning away from social initiations), advocates of this approach recognize the importance of designing environments, schedules, and materials to encourage interactions. Thus we see that in contrast to earlier beliefs that these children were incapable of changing, current teaching approaches are building on existing skills not previously tapped as well as adding new ones to a child's repertoire.

Physically Disabled.   Their acceptance or rejection by peers is influenced by several factors, including their appearance. Sensory and motor handicaps may cause anxiety and withdrawal on the part of some nonhandicapped children. These concerns can be responded to by providing information to non-disabled peers about disabilities, designing pleasurable classroom activities that bring all children together, and by maintaining reasonable expectations for all children. Social status is also affected by behaviors of disabled students. For example, some may have difficulty realistically appraising their social status, assuming they are more liked than is the case. Such inaccuracy can further alienate nonhandicapped peers, causing them to see the student as oblivious to reality. Again, a sensitive teacher can help special needs students recognize cues and behaviors of their nonhandicapped peers and at the same time provide them with social skills to assist in successful interactions. Finally, a school can create a positive climate for understanding disabilities. One way to begin is to highlight or "celebrate" persons with special needs. Kahan and Cator (1984) have described creating a handicap awareness showcase that included items depicting a variety of disabilities, such as mental retardation, visual impairment, orthopedic impairment, and learning disability. The items ranged from displaying braces, crutches, and hearing aids to samples of printed alphabet with corresponding Braille and finger-spelling alphabets. Explanations were provided for each of the above. A different approach is seen in the Special Friends Program in Hawaii, where nonhandicapped students are taught to interact with their disabled peers, not as helpers but as friends (Voeltz et al., 1983). This attempt to foster reciprocity reduces the likelihood that students with disabilities will be viewed in a condescending manner—as individuals to be helped.

Ideally, it is diversity that should be highlighted, with disabilities only one focus. Each school is comprised of many persons and interests. This diversity can be viewed as an asset to be understood, appreciated, and capitalized upon.

In summary, the development of meaningful friendships and social relations requires a number of skills that, to varying degrees, many exceptional children have difficulty mastering. Among these are sustained attention, taking turns, assuming responsibility for one's own behavior, and sharing responsibility for what occurs while with others. Friendships develop from increasing social awareness. Such awareness implies gaining control over one's own behavior and the ability to understand social encounters and respond constructively. Becoming a friend requires experience with peers, a level of understanding or intelligence, and the ability to modify one's behavior to avoid conflict, or when that is not possible, to engage in problem-solving behaviors designed to reduce conflict.

The problems disabled children face are compounded by attitudes and expectations of others. The solution goes beyond providing these children with skills to that of understanding the barriers they face. It is hoped that a recognition of environmental variables that impinge on their functioning will allow each of us to contribute to society's awareness of such barriers and to move toward overcoming them.

Barriers Faced by Disabled Children and Adolescents

Are the experiences of disabled children and youth sufficiently different from those of nondisabled children so that additional stress and disorders result? The answer is complicated because existing research and anecdotal material on the lives of disabled children has failed to show a direct correlation between disability and specific response patterns. Disabled children show a range of behaviors, some adaptive and others maladaptive, and these are described in the following sections. Nevertheless, they must contend with many complex psychological and environmental variables as they develop. British social psychologist David Thomas (1978) has offered a compelling argument for understanding disabled children's responses to and effects upon their social environment.

> Perhaps it would be more correct to say that a disability may be evaluated objectively, in the sense that constraints on mobility, manipulatory skills, hearing, etc., can be quantified, but that the handicapping nature of the disability cannot be so accurately assessed. This will depend on the individual person's perception of his difficulties and whether the social climate either encourages or inhibits his striving to compensate for them. It is both a social value judgement and a personal one—a self-value judgement which is, of course, powerfully affected by the attitudes of, and interaction with others, but is not totally conditioned by them. Any loss of physical function is likely to be viewed negatively, and the negative values derive from three sources: the nature of the disability, negative values imposed by the self, and negative ones imposed by society (pp. 9–10).

Based on the above analysis, a variety of factors contribute to a disabled child's adjustment and to the community and school's response to that child.

Personal Meaning of the Disability.   Increasingly, we are accumulating first-person accounts by disabled persons describing how their lives are affected by their disability. Some view themselves as damaged individuals; others see the disability as a challenge, an obstacle to overcome; and, of course, there are some children so disabled that it is not likely they have any conscious understanding of the nature of their disability or its impact on others. However, such an assumption may need to be challenged. For example, there is a fascinating report of a 31-year-old man who has recollections of growing up as an autistic child (Bemporad, 1979). Contrary to the usual assumption made by practitioners, this man was able to recall and describe some of his feelings and concerns during those difficult growing-up years.

Community Attitudes.   Each child's understanding of his or her disability is influenced by community acceptance and tolerance. Historically, there was a time when an individual whose behavior was different could be assimilated more easily into the ongoing life of a community. Today, the increasing tendency to label children has led to a singling out of persons who "fit" and those for whom separate facilities and services must be found. This paradox of defining and labeling children in order to help them has led investigators to study community tolerance for certain behaviors (Eyman & Call, 1977).

Child's Impact on Family. Each disabled child has a profound impact on the dynamics and social system of a family. How each family attends to the changes wrought by a disabled child influences the child's adjustment. In turn, this impact influences how family members respond to the needs of each child. Helen Featherstone (1981), a mother of a multiply disabled child, has written a wise and thought-provoking book describing the impact her child had on the family. She describes life with her disabled son by detailing the impact their child had on the family as a system (marital stress, brothers and sisters) and the feelings engendered by his presence (anger, frustration, acceptance, guilt, and self-doubt).

Episodic Nature of Disability. The symptoms of conditions such as epilepsy and other seizure-related disorders may occur infrequently, and this unpredictability can create tension for all concerned (Yard & Thurman, 1982). Children may feel powerless at the prospect of losing control. The ambiguous nature of such disorders can increase a child's apprehension at not knowing when and under what circumstances his or her behavior will become visible to others. On a less dramatic level, perhaps, are those children who experience difficulty functioning under certain conditions or performing particular tasks, or who have problems learning through one modality. These children, while admittedly less impaired than those who experience seizures, may nevertheless protect themselves from having to confront potentially threatening learning experiences. Each child may adjust differently, and the response of significant adults and community representatives can influence the direction of their adjustment. With the increasing emphasis on educating the general population to understand disabilities, it is hoped that there will be less stigmatizing of those whose problems are neither obvious nor predictable. However, until there is greater understanding of disabled children's emotional responses to the stresses these barriers present, we may hamper their adjustment.

Stress and Disabled Children

Understanding stress in children's lives requires focusing on their bodies and their emotions. Hans Selye (1978) alerted professionals and the general public to the bodily changes brought about by life conditions perceived as stressful by individuals. Seyle (1978, p. 74) has said, "stress is the nonspecific response of the body to any demand, whether it is caused by, or results in, pleasant or unpleasant conditions." Since his pioneering discovery, a variety of links between stress and physical and mental health continue to be found, including physiological changes in the nervous, endocrine, and immune systems (Asterita, 1985).

The concept of stress has been summarized by Schultz and Heuchert (1983, pp. 21–22):

1. All life events carry the potential for introducing stress into a person's life.
2. In a psychological sense, any life event, in and of itself, is neutral. It is how we interpret, react to and act upon the life event that determines the effect it will have on us.
3. There are two forms of stress distinguished: physical and psychological; but in practice they tend to interact with one another, to an extent equal to an individual's capacity to integrate the stressor.
4. Psychologically, we react to threatening situations in ways that have been successful to us in the past to reduce stress. Such reactions, however, may not always be consciously available or fully comprehended by us.
5. Physiologically, we react to life events we perceive as potentially threatening in a standard manner. We call this the general adaptation syndrome. It includes: (a) the *alarm reaction* in which the body's defense system is mobilized; (b) the *stage of resistance and adaptation*, in which we strive to ward off or adjust to the stressor; and, (c) the *stage of exhaustion* which occurs as the final phase of reaction to a stressor or to stress over a prolonged period of time. This sequence always occurs in any reaction to stress and is quite predictable (Selye, 1956).
6. The outcomes of stress reactions are of two types: (a) *eustress*—the result of proactive, positive, or adaptive responses to stressful life events; and (b) *distress*—the result of negative, nonconstructive, or maladaptive responses to stressful life events.
7. How we learn to manage life events will govern the ratio that will obtain between eustress and distress in our life.
8. There is a functional relationship between the life events (positive or negative) we find stressful, the types of stressors involved (physical or psychological), and the outcomes of such stressful situations (eustress or distress).
9. Chronically inadequate reactions to life events will generally lead to organic dysfunctioning, and ultimately to organic debilitation or death. Maladaptive reactions to life events contribute to and probably hasten this general physical and mental deterioration.
10. We have the gift of personal power to alter the way we are. Our power can emanate from many sources, such as a belief in our abilities, a religious orientation, supportive friendships, and the like. Thus, we can learn more functional and adaptive methods for helping us meet and successfully act upon life events.

The concept of stress has remained an elusive one despite considerable research efforts to operationally define stress, identify which life events and aspects of those events lead to which type of disorder, and which underlying mechanisms could account for the path from a stressful event(s) to a particular disorder. The effort remains important because of the variety of stressors that exist in the development and daily functioning of disabled children and youth. Much of what disabled children experience fits the general components of Seyle's syndrome: there is one or more stressor or life event that creates or has the potential to create some form of disequilibrium, which leads to a mental state thought of as distress.

Stress and Psychiatric Disorders

The methodological problems involved in clearly defining the concept of stress and in measuring psychiatric disorders make it difficult to conclude that there is always a direct relationship between stress and psychiatric disorder. Despite these issues there is some evidence from empirical studies and clinical contact with children to support the belief that stress experiences may contribute to short-term disturbances. Early studies of children reared in institutions (Spitz, 1950), investigations of maternal deprivation (Rutter, 1981), and interruption of emotional attachment opportunities (Bowlby, 1969) revealed that in such situations children showed an increased risk of psychiatric disorders. Those studies examined rather chronic and long-lasting adverse experiences, and it is understandable that children could be significantly affected. The impact of acute stressful experiences on children's development is less clear. The studies that exist to show a link between stress and psychiatric problems do not specify the type of stress event. Hudgens (1974) found a relationship between stressors and depression in adolescents with medical problems; Heisel, Ream, Raitz, Rappaport, and Coddington (1973) found a higher number of stresses in children with psychiatric disorders compared to a control group in the general population. If we want to understand the impact of stress on disabled children and adolescents, it is useful to look at specific events and highlight the potential concerns they raise.

Hospital Admission.   Placement in hospitals and exposure to medical treatment is one of the unfortunate facts of life for many disabled children. Certainly, those with physical disabilities and chronic medical problems are often required to work their way through the medical maze for evaluation and treatment. Here is how one mother describes the experience.

> If I felt like a chicken, Jeff looked like one. The first day his bandages were off, I found him baking under a regular incandescent light with the wiry black stitches curving low across the base of his spine and upward along one side, branching out to a Y and then one further branch. This, I could understand, was how the neurosurgeon freed up good skin, pulling it down this way and that until he could cover the lesion without a skin graft. With his little legs tucked up under him, Jeff looked like a plucked and skewered fowl. He was a sad sight, and obviously felt pain, judging by his fitful behavior. Sometimes we could recognize his bleating little cry from down the hall. I called him "little lamb." He also had a good, lusty, distinctly angry cry on occasion, which had such well-timed expression as to provide everyone with a few good laughs. He had a real personality already, and I could not wait to take him home (Pieper, 1978, p. 12).

Many preschool children exhibit signs of emotional disturbance when placed in hospitals, and the behaviors may persist for weeks or months after returning home, but a stay of one week or less has not been found to cause risk of longer-lasting problems. Such may not be the case for children with chronic illness, some of whom have experienced personality changes over a period of time (Barton & Cattell, 1972). No assumption should be made that hospital experiences alone can account for such changes. On the other hand, it is encouraging to note that changes in hospital policies related to parental visitation privileges (including sleeping-over arrangements), the presence of child advocates, more direct inclusion and feedback to the sick child, designing child-care units to respond more therapeutically to the needs and interests of children, play and play therapy units are testimony to the growing awareness that a child's hospital stay can be made more therapeutic and potentially less stressful.

Divorce.   Those working with disabled children and their families recognize the impact such a child can have on family dynamics. In some instances the presence of a disabled child places additional strain on the relationship between the parents. By the same token, parental discord, sometimes leading to divorce, can have an immediate and profound effect on the child. Certainly at a very basic level a child's support system is changed: the nature of child-care provisions may change due to the absence of one parent; the routine is disrupted; and depending on the child's ability to understand the situation, there may be feelings of confusion, anxiety, or anger. Usually divorces and separations take place in the context of prolonged periods of discord in the home. How the child has reacted to those experiences and the ways in which parents and other child-care persons have been supportive will influence the child's adjustment. There have been studies to show that emotional problems increase immediately following a divorce and that children face a number of psychological tasks (Wallerstein, 1983). Again we can see the importance of recognizing a child's needs at such crisis times, and once acknowledging them we can move to minimize the stress. Unfortunately, there are still many examples of our insensitivity to family stress patterns. There was, for example, the incident of a school calling home to tell a father that he would have to come and take his autistic child home for misbehaving; the call was made despite their awareness that the mother had just experienced a major heart attack.

Birth of a Sibling.   The birth of a sibling can be a stressful experience for a disabled child. Again, its impact depends on many factors: the nature of parental support, the type of disability, the child's ability to understand the nature of the event, and so on. Moore (1975) has studied the reactions of children to the birth of a sibling and has found that 15 percent of the children in his small-scale longitudinal study of London children demonstrated "problem" behaviors. In another study, Dunn (1981) detailed problems such as sleeping difficulties, toileting problems, and crying after the birth of a sibling in two- to three-year-old children. Many families of disabled children work toward establishing a pattern of communication and management to respond to their child. The birth of a child can upset that equilibrium, at least on a temporary basis. How the family handles the experience can reduce or increase the stress for the disabled child. Fortunately, there is growing recognition that interactions between normal and disabled siblings are significant ones and worthy of study and understanding.

Environmental Perspectives on Stress

In each of the foregoing sections on potential stress events for disabled children—divorce, hospitalization, and birth of a sibling—there has been some environmental change that could contribute to stress or reduce potentially harmful effects. In studying the newborn nursery as an environmental stressor, Leiderman (1983) has asked:

> What is the nature of "environment," in which change leads to stress reactions? Certainly it can be physical, though for a person it may more often involve changes in psychological and social circumstances, such as the loss of a close companion, loss of self-esteem, loss of a job or retirement, or loss of social status. Quantification of the physical and social environment, as it impinges on the individual, does not lend itself to simple physical measurements or even to assessment by outside observers. It depends upon an individual's appraisal of a particular situation, and is influenced both by current perceptions and prior experiences. The individual and his or her reactions to environmental conditions are inextricably linked. A quantitative determination of this relationship remains a basic problem for researchers in the area of stress and coping (p. 136).

Leiderman, to highlight the influence that environmental change can have on stress, has explored the impact of separating a mother from the care of her preterm infant; he also has examined how that influence is processed through individual perceptions and experiences.

Before 1900 most premature infants died. In the early 1900s Budin (1907) developed a system of hygienic care for such infants by placing them in separate care facilities in the hospital in heated, clean rooms and by providing routine care. Thus we see how environmental change significantly altered infant mortality rates. By the late 1960s, however, observers of infant development were concerned that under the existing system of newborn nurseries mothers regained contact with their babies several days or weeks later, depending on infant health and weight. Particularly disquieting was the observation that mothers had difficulty adjusting to their newborn—both physically and psychologically. Some could not respond to the physical needs; others could not accurately "read" their babies needs. Despite what was once considered optimal care after discharge some infants did not thrive and presented severe problems. Some concluded that the problem rested with inadequate mothering skills in conjunction with the multiple causes that could be attributed to high-risk infant development (genetic, intrauterine, prenatal, and perinatal causes); others observed that the institutional arrangement of separating mothers from infants for extended periods while in the hospital may have functioned as a stress factor. So, by the early 1970s, what was once seen as a positive environmental intervention early in this century began to be thought of as a potential hazard to some infants' development. In both instances the environment played a major role in children's development.

The birth of a premature infant in and of itself can create disequilibrium for all concerned. Prematurity can account for delayed development in some children and even brain damage and retardation in others. Although the existing studies on hospital care of premature infants and patterns of hospital and home care are not conclusive, many hospitals have modified their practices to involve parents in the care of their infant while in the hospital. These studies point to the many factors influencing infant development: adequate social supports and parent socioeconomic status and social class. On the other hand, the responsiveness of the environment and the people in it can reduce the risk of further problems.

Schools, as another example of an institutional structure, can influence children's behavior and development. Schools, just as hospitals, can play an important role in a disabled child's life, for it is in school that many children acquire their labels. Some believe school is where they acquire the behaviors that contribute to their being labeled deviant. A recent large-scale study of the relationship between school organization practices and disruptive behaviors and absenteeism found differences that could be related to varying school characteristics (Rutter, Maughan, Mortimore, Ouston, & Smith, 1979). Children respond to stressors in a variety of ways, and the next section describes four frequently observed behavioral styles of responding to stress.

Stress: Relevance to Behavior Disorders

The various forms of stress that children are exposed to and in some ways contribute to are well documented and described in the previous sections. This litany of potential stressors in childhood and adolescence reminds us that while all children are subject to stress, the deviant behavior shown by some disabled children can be viewed on a continuum: these behaviors may reflect styles of responding to stress, with behaviors ranging from normal to less acceptable or deviant in society's view.

Chandler and Lundahl (1983) have summarized a variety of diagnostic classification schemes including traditional psychiatric-descriptive approaches (Ceretto & Tuma, 1977) and more recent efforts to utilize statistical-empirical approaches (Wiggins, 1980). The former relies on the application of a theoretical framework such as psychoanalytic theory to help explain psychological phenomena; the latter utilizes observable behavior to form a cluster or syndrome of behaviors that is then assigned a designation—Kanner's labeling the behaviors of children in eleven case studies as "early childhood autism" is an example of an empirical approach (Kanner, 1943).

Based on their analysis of the above approaches, Chandler and Lundahl (1983) concluded that there is "support for an active-passive dimension and for an introversion-extroversion dimension. The model presented here depicts two dimensions of personality functioning and proposes that deviant behavior can be seen on a continuum of normal styles of responding to stress" (p. 461).

One or more of the four response patterns depicted in Figure 1 may be seen in the behaviors of many disabled children. These patterns may be useful in helping to understand the needs and concerns of children as they respond to their disability and to the attitudes of others in the home, school, and communities in which they find themselves. Throughout the following discussion of each response pattern it is important to remember that *all* children respond with one or more of these sets of behaviors and that in their more extreme form these are attempts to respond to stress.

The Dependent Child.   There are children who, for a variety of reasons, have not assumed responsibility in one or more areas of their development for mastering tasks appropriate to their age or level. They may fail to take

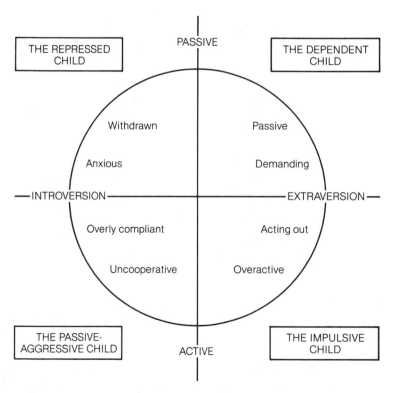

Figure 1. *Four common response patterns to stress.*

Children can be resources for one another in classrooms. These students are working on a reading assignment together. (Photograph by Mima Cataldo.)

the initiative in learning or responding to self-help skills, and such failure can generalize to learning social skills as well. This orientation to life can come about for a variety of reasons. For example, the nature of the child's disability may sufficiently restrict him so that learning to take care of himself and to acquire new skills may require extra effort on his part.

At the other extreme of this response pattern are those children who become insistent on having their dependency needs taken care of. The ways significant adults in the environment respond will affect the child's progress. Teachers and parents may take the path of least resistance and continually respond to the demands of the child, thus reinforcing that pattern. It is not simply a matter of blaming these adults for reinforcing nonproductive child behaviors; such children can be very temperamental and insistent.

An environment—home or school—would have to find ways to remain consistent and still hold up under such children's persistent demands. Their demanding nature may resemble the behaviors of impulsive children. Thus we see that none of these response pattterns is completely independent of the others.

The Impulsive Child.　　These children also fall on the extroversion dimension, but they are active and their activity is frequently directed at others, peers as well as adults. They are considered to have control problems, that is, they experience difficulty monitoring and modulating their needs and impulses. Children with a variety of disabilities can demonstrate these behaviors. For example, a large number of children and youth are considered "hyperactive," and many children labeled as such represent a variety of problems; brain damaged, emotionally disturbed, autistic, and even some gifted children are characterized as overactive. It is helpful to think of these children as being unable to handle frustration.

Impulsive children, when thwarted, may respond with forms of aggression toward others. Again, the nature of their disability can contribute to the extent and nature of their acting-out behaviors. There are deaf children who experience frustration at not comprehending others or who find themselves in environments that are indifferent or hostile to their needs; thus they may strike out at the world and the people in it. Physically disabled or frail children may become verbally abusive toward others rather than physically assaultive. Again, the manner in which adults respond can influence such behaviors. Verbally abusive youngsters who find an adult's weak points present that adult with a challenge, namely that of resisting the temptation to retaliate in kind. To avoid retaliating against children it is necessary to understand the nature of children's assertiveness and the role environmental structures play in helping children feel more competent.

The Repressed Child. At one extreme are those children and youth who are depressed. Others are shy, anxious, and introverted. All of those falling somewhere along this dimension are in need of support from adults and social skill development. As we have seen in the preceding descriptions of response patterns, many characteristics are found in each pattern: there is difficulty in school; anxiety reactions are present; actions are directed toward peers or adults directly or indirectly; and there is a lack of appropriate social skill development. Many disabled children exhibit one or more forms of behavior falling within the repressed child dimension. Childhood depression is being increasingly studied and recognized as a mental health problem of large proportions. Children with chronic health and physical disabilities may withdraw because of schools, homes, and communities that fail to provide early and ongoing stimulation. Down's syndrome children and youth with the ability to recognize some of their skills and the social awareness to understand unsupportive social and academic environments may pull back and withdraw.

The Passive-Aggressive Child. While these children turn their feelings inward they expend energy toward developing strategies that allow them to cope in school. These coping strategies usually involve an orientation to failure (Holt, 1964). They may appear to comply with a request, but never follow through. One has the impression that they are warding others off as opposed to getting closer. It is possible that some disabled children lack the necessary skills to successfully negotiate their own needs with the demands of others. Teachers and parents can aid these children by teaching them appropriate social skills.

Each type of child described in this section may be labeled by the school and community. The particular label may have implication for placement and may influence how the child is viewed by others. The use of the term *behavior disorders* is an attempt by practitioners and researchers to broaden our definition and awareness of children's needs and concerns. Until recently, special educators have been inclined to think of these children as emotionally disturbed, carrying the implication of a serious clinical disorder, usually involving intrapsychic or internal conflict. In addition, the cause of the problem is believed to reside in the nature of the parent-child interaction: a failure in emotional attachment between parent (often assumed to be the mother) and the child. This view of disturbance and its assumed origins derives from the *medical model*. This model is described in other chapters in this book by Duchan and by Taylor and Searl and is an effort to apply diagnostic and treatment approaches used by physicians in treating physical disorders and a wide range of mental health problems. Critics of the medical model contend that the direct translation of a disease-oriented diagnostic and treatment model does not fit the diverse populations of children who could be considered behaviorally disordered or troubled.

This move to restrict the use of the psychiatric label of *emotional disturbance* to those children who display systematically documented syndromes such as childhood depression or school phobia and to classify children displaying a wide range of behaviors and problems as *behaviorally disordered* has been initiated by the federal government and professional groups such as the Council for Children with Behavior Disorders, a division of the Council for Exceptional Children. In the meantime, children displaying aggressive behaviors and those who show signs of depression command the attention of teachers and parents. The following section describes children and youth demonstrating these extreme forms of behavior and examines the interaction of psychological and environmental factors as we attempt to respond to such troubled individuals.

The Extremes of Behavior

Many adults working in schools view assertive behavior as "problem" behavior. One word of caution is in order. Duchan, in her chapter on language and communication, makes the point that by labeling some children with a specific designation, such as emotionally disturbed or language impaired, we automatically ascribe certain behaviors to them: emotionally disturbed children are aggressive, language impaired children do not communicate properly, and so on. In an effort to avoid such circular reasoning, this section describes a range of behaviors engaged in by disabled children and youth to *represent* themselves in their encounters with others. The point is made again: the lives and issues of children, parents, and teachers are too complex to fix blame. There are reasons for children engaging in particular behaviors, and it is to everyone's advantage to understand the many possible interactive causes of assertiveness. Because the majority of teachers are focused on discipline problems, we can begin with a discussion of children's aggression.

Aggression in Childhood and Adolescence

Aggression, or the physical and/or verbal attacking of others, is observed in normal children and is even considered acceptable in certain subcultures in this country and in some other cultures. On the other hand, there are cultures that attempt to create environments that are nonaggressive in nature, reminding us again of the influence that environment has on behavior (Montagu, 1978). In the United States, aggression and delinquency are often equated; despite the fact that we have overwhelming evidence to show the relationship between certain environments and child aggression, we remain focused on blaming the child for his or her transgressions.

This chapter opened by describing the child as an active participant in the social interchange with caregivers. This perspective can be useful in our understanding of the child's contribution to his or her aggression. One implication is that educational and behavioral approaches such as social skills training can be utilized to assist children to modify their own behaviors. The other perspective emphasized throughout this chapter is that disabled children are responded to by peers, adults, and communities based on attitudes, perceptions, and previous experiences that may not be directly related to a particular child. In other words, disabled persons often are viewed as members of a group and not as unique individuals subject to the same complex and contradictory behaviors as others. Thus, a child's aggression must be viewed in the context of the interaction of his or her behavior with environments and the people in them.

Childhood Depression

The existence of an entity called childhood depression remains a question in the field of child psychopathology. The standard resource in the field— the Diagnostic and Statistical Manual of the American Psychiatric Association—does not include childhood depression as a separate category. Psychoanalytic theory maintains that it is only during adolescence that depression is seen, for it is at that point that superego, or the development of conscience, is complete.

The Debate. In contrast to childhood autism, in which there is some agreement that there is a syndrome of behaviors that distinguish autistic from nonautistic children, no such agreement exists for childhood depression. Issues such as whether symptoms reflect developmental concerns and disappear with age rather than reflecting a clinical syndrome, whether there is a distinction between moods of unhappiness as normal reactions to life circumstances and persistent depression, and whether depression is the cause or the result of behavior problems continue to perplex practitioners and researchers. It is conceivable, for example, that children who are hyperactive or aggressive toward others may in fact suffer from depression. On the other hand, it is also possible that children who experience failure in school, diminished self-concepts, and unsatisfying home and peer relationships can become depressed.

Despite this debate, there are many exceptional children who exhibit symptoms thought of as depressive in nature. These symptoms are considered to represent a disorder of *affect*, a child's emotional state, and can reflect a disruption in a child's thinking, emotions, behavior, and physical functioning. Again we see a condition that involves a combination of organic and psychological determinants.

Achenbach (1982) believes that some of the preceding conceptual issues could be clarified if we knew the prevalence of depressed affect in normal as compared to disturbed children. One confounding factor is that depressive affect alone rarely accounts for a child's referral for assistance. In one study of clinically referred and nonreferred children, no more than 13 percent of the nonreferred children ages 4 to 16 were described by parents as unhappy, sad, or depressed (Achenbach & Edelbrock, 1981). The rate at which these descriptors were used for referred children was much higher—ranging from 43 percent of 4- and 5-year-old boys to 86 percent for 12- and 13-year-old girls.

Teachers of exceptional children and certainly parents of those who are physically disabled or chronically and terminally ill recognize many behaviors that manifest a flattened and depressed affect.

These behaviors, found for 6- to 11-year old boys and girls, include the following (Achenbach, 1975; Achenbach & Edelbrock, 1978):

- · Complaining of loneliness
- · Fearing he/she might do something bad
- · Feeling he/she has to be perfect
- · Feeling or complaining that no one loves him/her
- · Feeling others are out to get him/her
- · Feeling too guilty
- · Feeling worthless or inferior
- · Acting nervous, high-strung, or tense
- · Acting self-conscious or easily embarrassed
- · Sulking a lot
- · Acting too fearful or anxious
- · Being unhappy, sad, or depressed
- · Worrying

Adolescent Suicide.   Each child's developmental stage, in addition to the above factors, can influence adjustment to a particular life situation. An extreme consequence of depression is adolescent suicide, although not every suicide is necessarily preceded by depression. The preceding Achenbach (1975) study—a factor analysis of behavior problems—showed that 6- to 11-

year-old boys scored higher on items reflecting "deliberately harms self" or "attempts suicide" and "talks about killing self." In contrast, adolescents did not respond to these items in a particular pattern. Clinicians experienced with adolescents report that adolescent suicidal behavior may be more likely to result from conflicts with others, crises related to their developmental stage, failed love and dating relationships, and frustrations that seem unmanageable.

The magnitude of adolescent death by suicide warrants serious attention and concern, and we should recognize that the number of attempted suicides is much higher. Klagsbrun (1977), in her book, *Youth and Suicide: Too Young to Die*, has stated the problem:

> How many people know that suicide kills far more teenagers and young adults than do such dread diseases as cancer and heart ailments? Each year more than 4,000 young people between the ages of fifteen and twenty-four die as suicides. Only accidents and homicides claim more young lives. And the ratio of suicide to these other causes of death may be much higher than now known because many suicides are hidden by family and reported as accidents or even murders.
>
> How many people know that the suicide rate among young people in the 1970s was almost three times higher than it had been in the 1950s? It was almost twice as high as it had been in the 1960s (p. 23).

The interactional framework utilized in this chapter can also be applied to our understanding of suicide. There is evidence to support the contention that an early disruption in the ASI process can contribute to later depression (Parkes & Stevenson-Hinde, 1982). It is conceivable that the nature of a child's early relationship can lead to a sense of loss and feelings of helplessness, perhaps culminating in suicide or attempts to take one's life. Thus, we see how many aspects of a child's physical, psychological, and social development (including family stability) may interact to influence the onset of depression and even suicide.

Understanding the world children grow up in and their responses to it is crucial. The concluding section focuses on our social policy goals for children with disabilities and how these are translated into supports for families of disabled children and into programs emphasizing education in the least restrictive environment.

Disabled Children in Today's World

Today's world can be seen as challenging or frightening by children and youth. It is challenging because change is everywhere and frightening because not all those changes are positive. We are raising children at a time when community support services are facing reductions; when increasing numbers of children are growing up in single-parent households; and when large numbers of men and women are experiencing problems providing for the basic care, feeding, and general well-being of millions of children.

Children's socioemotional development must be understood in the context of the world in which they live. Sybil Escalona (1982), a child development specialist, has advised us to recognize the impact that current world and national problems can have on children's personality development:

> Growing up in a social environment that tolerates and ignores the risk of total destruction by means of voluntary human action tends to foster those patterns of personality functioning that can lead to a sense of powerlessness and cynical resignation. . . . In short, I believe that growing up fully aware that the adult world seems unable to combat the threat of total destruction can render the next generation less well equipped to avert actual catastrophe than they would be if the threat existed in a different social climate (p. 601).

The concepts of hope versus despair are relevant to our understanding of disabled children's functioning and to how they see themselves and those around them. Survey data obtained by the Institute of Social Research at the University of Michigan indicated that 47 percent of the high school seniors surveyed felt powerless about the world situation and doubtful about any personal impact they might have on changing those conditions (Smith, 1983).

In a large-scale study of special-class programs for emotionally handicapped pupils (Morse, Cutler, & Fink, 1964), children revealed that the pattern of expectations for their future was a mixture of optimism and concern. In the sample of 519 pupils, 45 percent indicated that they expected to return to regular class soon, while 32 percent indicated that they would return in a few years. This degree of optimistic personal prognosis matched their satisfaction with the programs in which they were enrolled. On the other hand, 54 percent of these same pupils anticipated academic difficulty when they returned to regular classrooms. Cameron, Titus, Kostin, and Kostin (1973) attempted to study the quality of life and satisfaction with life perceptions of adolescents and adults with various disabilities compared to normal subjects using semistructured interviews. They concluded, "The handicapped judged their lives as more difficult and likely to stay that way as compared to normals' judgments" (p. 212).

While the above picture is painted rather darkly, there are many efforts to design therapeutic efforts to modify an individual's feelings of helplessness and increase their expectations for success (the subsequent section on fostering competence provides an example of "empowering children" to gain control of their feelings). Seligman (1975) has discussed the importance of helping individuals to avoid learned helplessness, the perception that one's actions are futile. However, teachers and other adults (and peers) can provide feedback to help children recognize that responding produces positive reinforcement.

In addition, the social policies we create can contribute to the empowerment of families and children by setting clear national priorities to support the physical, mental, and emotional development of all children. Chapter 1 emphasized the importance of Public Law 94–142, the Education for All Handicapped Children Act. For the first time children with disabilities were guaranteed a free, appropriate education in the least restrictive environment. While much remains to be accomplished in the implementation of this federal law, a feeling of hope and a sense of purpose exist for many professionals, families, and students with disabilities. In addition, it is increasingly recognized that we must also create a national policy for children and families that will respond to existing crises such as poverty, catastrophic illness, and shifting economic conditions and will provide for a preventive focus—one that works to reduce birth injury, responds to the growing numbers of teenage pregnancies, and treats the root causes of emotional disturbance and mental illness in our society, as opposed to treating each case as a unique situation (Cowen, 1985).

This concluding section argues for social policies and educational practices that foster adaptation, coping, and growth in our children and adolescents with disabilities. As we learn more about what contributes to successful functioning in schools and communities we can act on those factors. To date, there is encouraging evidence that supporting families of children with disabilities and developing mainstreamed programs enhances the socioemotional development of those with disabilities.

Adaptation, Coping, and Growth

Throughout this chapter you are encouraged to consider the wholeness of each disabled child. A child's label, as this book stresses, often fails to convey the diversity between children with the same condition or designation; the interaction of socioemotional, cognitive, and communicative skills; and the child's impact on others. This section attempts to put the child back together, so to speak, and to highlight the need to view exceptional children in the context of their environments. The child's unique psychological characteristics and educational needs always interact with the expectations of others. Sometimes a mismatch occurs between environmental demands and expectations and the capacity of the individual to respond. Ideally, what is needed are flexible environments, capable of bending and reorganizing to meet the unique needs of children (Hobbs & Robinson, 1982). While we work toward that ideal we can increase our efforts so that disabled children might acquire skills designed to help them cope and thrive in their families, schools, and communities.

The "Life-Space" Viewpoint

Viewing children as "being-in-the-world" is a perspective that Erikson (1982) advocates when he tells us that children acquire social and emotional skills in the context of their environments, and that they must develop ways of responding to crises that are appropriate to their developmental level. This life-space viewpoint argues for studying persons, their psychological environments, and *their* perceptions of their situation (Lewin, 1951).

Each aspect of a child's social system—home, school, and community—interacts with a child's own personality disposition; taken together, they contribute to an individual's socioemotional development. Of course, the interaction of these factors is exceedingly complex, thus making it difficult to draw clear conclusions from several patterns of developments. As teachers and program developers, we are called upon to individualize instruction and to design programs that are responsive to each child's needs. Every effort can be made, then, to understand each child within the context of a particular social system. This concluding section combines the earlier emphasis on recognizing the child as an active participant in the learning process with an understanding of how various parts of the child's world can facilitate development.

Sroufe (1979) has summarized the central role of adaptation in child development:

> At the individual level, adaptation refers to children's active engagement of the environment, fitting and shaping themselves to that environment and effecting changes in the environment to satisfy needs. The child does not merely react to environmental events but seeks stimulation and selects and organizes behavior in terms of his or her own goals (p. 834).

Preceding sections described a variety of deficits exceptional children show in their development compared to normal children. At the same time, there are many disabled children who engage in coping behaviors that give testimony to their resilience and to the importance of structuring environments that build on children's strengths, not weaknesses.

Katherine, a nineteen-year-old woman, had to face the amputation of her leg due to osteogenic sarcoma, a life-threatening illness. Faced with her own fears and the concerns of her family, she struggled to maintain her perspective while its impact threatened to overwhelm her:

> It's not just physical things like running or skiing. You can't even *daydream* that you're running down the stairs or on the beach, because you can't do those things anymore. It's all right to daydream and get away from reality a little. But when you start to ignore a physical disability, it's hard to keep yourself in perspective. It was very awful. For a long time I was just thinking about my leg and my doctors and the pain and all the bad things, so for awhile I didn't even daydream. It affects you in so many ways. You're always haunted by it (Sourkes, 1982, p. 96).

Katherine's obvious fears are combined with healthy insights in the way she is reacting and an awareness of what she must do to maintain her equilibrium. How does such adaptation come about under such difficult circumstances?

Invulnerable Children

The litany of stress situations faced by today's children is rather extensive. Despite what appear to be overwhelming odds against further development, we have ample evidence, as in Katherine's statement, of children and young people who struggle to maintain their perspective and who continue to develop despite adversity. Garmezy (1983) has summarized conclusions on resiliency in children from five different approaches:

1. An epidemiological study comparing family variables associated with increased incidence of psychiatric disorders in childhood and protective factors that tempered children's risk factors (Rutter, Cox, Tupling, Berger, & Yule, 1975).
2. A literature survey of studies of competent black children exposed to stressors of poverty and prejudice in urban ghettos (Garmezy, 1981).
3. A longitudinal-developmental study—birth to early adulthood—of children born on Kauai in the Hawaiian Islands. These were children at risk due to perinatal stress, poverty, parental mental health problems, and family instability (Werner & Smith, 1982).
4. A study of "ego resilience" in children viewed from the perspective of infants' response to environmental change (Block & Block, 1980).
5. Studies of children's response to the stress of war (Rosenblatt, 1983).

Results from these studies led Garmezy to conclude that several factors contributed to children's resiliency:

1. Positive personality dispositions.
2. A supportive family milieu.

Imaginative play, like this puppet role-playing activity, can foster symbolic thinking and social interaction. (Photograph by Mima Cataldo.)

3. An external societal agency that functions as a support system for strengthening and reinforcing a child's coping efforts.

The successful adaptation of children raised in a home in which one or both parents are mentally ill appears to confirm the importance of these protective factors. The availability of a supportive parent or other adult has been shown to contribute to a child's adaptation to difficult situations and to increase competency (Clausen & Huffine, 1975). In addition, those children appearing less vulnerable to a difficult family living situation were also more socially skilled with adults and peers and tended to have a reasonably sound self-concept. Despite adversity, they have a type of inner confidence that indicates a reflective rather than an impulsive orientation to regulating their behaviors (Garmezy & Nuechterlein, 1972). Thus we see the interaction of an individual's personality and environmental influences. The following sections highlight the role families and schools can play in providing these protective factors for children.

Supporting Families of Exceptional Children

Child advocates recognize the possibility that children with special needs can contribute to family stress patterns along with bringing happiness to the adults in their life. There are also situations in which parent interactions can influence how disabled children function. Vogel and Bell (1968) have argued for treating the interaction of parents as an independent variable influencing children's development. They studied a small group of "disturbed" families, each with a child identified as emotionally disturbed, and compared them to a control group of families without a child so identified. By studying the family as a social system and, in particular, the conflicts between parents, they made the observation that children can be scapegoated as a result of needs and tensions of other family members.

Studying the family as a unit that influences the roles and behaviors of its members has gained credence since the 1960s and has largely replaced the earlier, less constructive blaming-the-parent approach that characterized diagnosis and treatment of childhood and adolescent mental health problems. This less punitive approach has contributed to our understanding of why parents and families behave as they do toward their children. With increased knowledge we can move toward prevention of potentially harmful environmental effects and to the development of supportive services for families.

An example from the child abuse literature highlights the changing orientation described above. Newberger and Cook (1983) studied the social cognition or parental awareness patterns of parents with a history of child abuse and neglect. By analyzing parental conceptions of children and the parent-child relationship, they found significant differences between parents with abused children and a control sample of nonabusing parents. If we could assess how parents think about their children, and if those conceptions are inappropriate, then perhaps we could design interventions that help parents think and respond in a manner appropriate to the needs of their children (Holman, 1983).

Considering the Parent's Perspective. An advantage of attempting to unravel a parent's perspective, understanding, and knowledge base is that remedial efforts and interventions can be of a pedagogical nature, that is, we may be able to teach and assist parents to function more effectively.

> A shift in orientation from what is correct (and incorrect) to what is cognitively and developmentally available can serve to liberate the interpretation of the parental role in parental dysfunction from a reliance on deficit formulations (such as lack of love or early bonding; parental psychopathology; inappropriate expectations; or faulty practices). Such a liberation is urgently necessary, as parents who abuse or neglect their children do love them, and cultural variations in parental practices may contribute to differential and inappropriate labeling. Parental care is not dependent on maturity of reasoning, nor does any level of awareness dictate a static formulation of "appropriate behavior." One might argue, however, that identifying a parent as reasoning at less mature levels of awareness can become another form of onerous labeling, and this is certainly a danger with any scale. What the developmental model offers implicitly, however, is an orientation toward the natural process of adaptation to the vicissitudes of relationships in which levels of competence—and not simply islands of pathology—can be identified (Newberger & Cook, 1983, p. 523).

We can increase parental competence, as Newberger and Cook's statement suggests, by increasing our knowledge of children's needs and disabilities, by communicating this information to parents at a level they can understand and use, and by providing support as they respond to their children. An example of translating theory and information into practice is found in the growing body of literature on adolescent depression. McCoy (1982) has written a guide to help parents understand and respond to their teenager's concerns; in it she covers depression, school phobia, truancy, sexuality, substance abuse, and suicide. Her balanced approach offers parents guidelines to detect problems, questions about their communication patterns, and suggestions for monitoring school programs and seeking outside help. Table 2 provides a list of questions parents can ask themselves about their teenager's vulnerability to depression. Many of these questions are relevant for teachers to ask about youngsters in their classrooms.

Viewing Parents as Partners. Viewing parents as partners with whom we can share our skills while avoiding treating them in a condescending fashion is exemplified by recent efforts to assist families of limited intelligence. Hospitals, clinics, and schools are recognizing the value of teaching families a variety of ways they can care for their children. For example, one urban mental health center has trained its staff in procedures to facilitate involvement of parents with limited intelligence. Such efforts are designed to help parents maintain their children in agency activities, such as well-baby

Table 2
How Vulnerable Is My Teen to Depression?

1. Has anyone in your immediate or close extended family died during the past year?
2. Has a family pet died or been lost?
3. Has your child lost a friend through death in the past year?
4. Have you and your spouse had significant marital problems recently with an increase in the number of arguments and tensions?
5. Have you and your spouse separated or divorced this past year?
6. If you are divorced, has your child seen a great deal less of you or your spouse during the past year?
7. Has your family moved within the past twelve months?
8. Has your child changed schools this year—either due to a move or due to progressing on to junior high or high school?
9. Has another child in your family left home for college, marriage, or independent living?
10. Has a friend or romantic interest of your teenager moved away recently?
11. Have you or your spouse experienced serious depression recently?
12. Do you or your spouse have a drinking or drug abuse problem?
13. Has anyone in your family had a serious illness or injury during the past year?
14. Does your teenager have a chronic illness such as diabetes or epilepsy that sometimes limits his or her participation in normal teenage activity or that is a source of conflict between you and your teenager?
15. Has your teen had a serious or prolonged illness this past year?
16. Has your child sustained an injury that required curtailment of his or her normal routine and activities recently?
17. Has your child experienced significant physical changes in the past year, for example, a growth spurt, breast development, voice change, beginning of menstruation?
18. Is your child lagging behind peers in physical development, and is he or she possibly the object of teasing because of this?
19. Has anyone in your extended families, including parents, grandparents, siblings, aunts, uncles, ever suffered from significant depressive illness?
20. Has your family had a significant change of life-style recently, for example, financial hardships, a parental job loss, a parent reentering the job market?
21. Does your child seem to have low self-esteem and be highly self-critical?
22. Do you have high expectations of your child and find yourself extremely disappointed—showing this disappointment openly—when your child's performance falls somewhat short of these expectations?
23. Is someone in your family, especially a parent, extremely critical of this particular child? Is this teen regarded as the family misfit or seen to be the focus of a lot of family conflict?
24. Have you felt distance growing between you and your teen during the past year? Is it difficult or impossible to communicate these days?

(continued)

Table 2
(continued)

25. Do you find yourself increasingly unable to spend as much time with your child as you or he or she might like?
26. Are you quite permissive, with few rules and regulations for your teenager?
27. Are you a strict parent, with many rules and a low tolerance for conflict or disagreements? Do you hear yourself saying, "Because I said so!" or "Don't you dare talk back!" quite often?
28. Is openly expressed anger taboo in your home?
29. Do you have trouble trusting or expressing trust in your teenager?
30. Has your teen suffered through a significant romantic breakup recently?
31. Has he or she experienced estrangement from an important friend?
32. Does it seem to you that your teenager is often the target of teasing and ridicule from peers?
33. Does your teen seem unusually sensitive to teasing, criticism, or indifference from peers, teachers, relatives, or friends?
34. Does your teenager seem to have difficulty making and keeping friends?
35. Is your child prone to either-or, black-and-white thinking, such as feeling like a failure if he or she isn't always the best?
36. Does your child have a learning disability?
37. Is your child having difficulty with a particular teacher this year? Does he or she feel picked on, intimidated, or put down by his or her teacher and complain more than usual about difficulties at school?
38. Has your family had an addition—birth of a baby or adoption of a child, grandparents or other relatives moving in—that has increased your teen's responsibilities or decreased his or her privacy?
39. Has another child in your family made significant achievements in the past year or so? Have there been any comparisons made between siblings, always in favor of the achiever?
40. Has your teenager achieved a significant goal recently—for example, graduated, won an award, made a team, perfected a skill, or otherwise achieved unusual positive recognition?

clinics, child therapy, and family and child recreational opportunities. Staff in-service experiences aimed at improving attitudes toward these families and the modification of agency procedures to assist parents in filling out forms, simplifying them, and even reducing the required paperwork can contribute to increasing and enhancing contact with hard-to-reach families. Increasingly, programs now respond by establishing services in neighborhoods or assisting parents in finding their way to an agency that may be located at a great distance from the family home. Rather than faulting parents for not showing up for scheduled appointment times, an agency worker may meet the family at a designated midway point until the family and child can learn the travel route.

The National Resource Center on Family Based Services, established in 1977 to develop family based alternatives to foster care, is another example of a family support service. It was developed in response to the dissatisfaction with a social policy that perpetuated foster care as the primary placement option for abused and neglected children, status offenders, and other children with special needs. We are all familiar with children who have been placed in a succession of community placements. In such a process the family is removed from the picture and the costs to all concerned are high: children experience long-term adjustment problems, communities expend considerable amounts of money, and parents do not learn the needed skills to either maintain such children or to absorb them back into the home at a later time. Creative efforts to develop in-home family service delivery systems that respond to children, ranging from those who are aggressive to those who are chronically ill, are now being developed (Maybanks & Bryce, 1979; Bryce & Lloyd, 1981).

The Concept of Social Support.   The challenge is to find ways to structure human interactions and attachments so that support is provided to those who are in need and resources are exchanged among families, relatives, community members, and voluntary associations (Gottlieb, 1981). The concept of social support has been characterized by Cobb (1979):

> Social support . . . has beneficial effects on a wide variety of health variables throughout the life course from conception to just before death, and on the bereaved who are left behind after a death. . . . One cannot escape the conclusion that the world would be a healthier place if training in supportive behaviors were built into the routines of our homes and schools, and support worker roles were institutionalized (p. 113).

Applied to families of exceptional children, social support can take tangible form in the following ways.

- Assisting families in working their way through the special education maze so they find the services appropriate to the needs of their children (Cutler, 1981).
- Providing respite care services for families to enable them to seek leisure and recreational opportunities away from the constant pressure of child care for their special child (Salisbury & Griggs, 1983).
- Assisting families to obtain available financial aid for their children, particularly those with physical disabilities and life-threatening conditions or chronic disabilities—conditions that may require special programs, equipment, and care (McAndrew, 1976).
- Developing a school-based informational model to formalize parent involvement. In such a process, parents would be included in the construction and implementation of their child's individualized education plan (Clements & Alexander, 1975).

The availability of psychological and social support is equally important. This level of support can also take many forms.

- Recognizing the sources of stress experienced by families of disabled children and communicating to them our recognition of their situation (Gallagher, Beckman, & Cross, 1983).
- Including siblings of disabled children in our efforts to deliver a more thorough model of family centered care (Bodenheimer, 1982; McKeever, 1983).
- Recognizing the value of parent self-help groups and offering our support as professionals to their efforts to develop networks that provide opportunities to share information, to discuss feelings and create services for their disabled children (Gartner & Riessman, 1983).
- Advocating improved frameworks for the delivery of services to children. These include provision of supportive services to families and the development of service delivery systems (education, mental health, social services, correctional, and medical) that go beyond a deficit model of intervention to one of prevention, restoration, and development (Goffin, 1983).

The Importance of Schools in the Socioemotional Development of Disabled Students

In 1975 handicapped chidren were guaranteed a free appropriate education with the passage of Public Law 94–142, "The Education for All Handicapped Children Act" (see Chapter 1 for a discussion of the rights of disabled children). Since then, parents, teachers, and schools have struggled to translate this federal law into meaningful practice on a daily basis in schools. It is hoped that school programs will help disabled students cope with the variety of stressors described in this chapter by teaching them skills to understand and manage their feelings and behaviors.

The impact of the schools on socioemotional development is potentially far-reaching. Busch-Rossnagel and Vance (1982) have cited the influence schools have in terms of the numbers of students (approximately 65 million) and the number of hours (up to 10,000) spent in classrooms over the course of a child's school life. The challenge is to set clear priorities and goals for the education of disabled children and then to find ways to achieve those goals.

The barriers and issues faced by disabled children and youth (see the preceding list derived from Thomas, 1978) can contribute to diminished feelings of self-confidence and worth. Depending on the disability, the concerns may vary; disabled children will often internalize the concerns of others and blame themselves for the disability and the "unacceptable" behavior.

> When I was young, I always thought that it would be a big deal to have nondisabled friends other than my brothers and sisters. When I grew up, I found that such friends were very difficult to have. I often had embarrassing experiences because I felt too uncomfortable with nondisabled per-

sons to ask for help. I even thought, at one time, that I had to agree with everything nondisabled friends said if I wanted to keep their friendships. In fact I played rather dishonest games with both them and myself (Stephen Hofman, 1983; an educational consultant to parents of disabled children writing from his perspective of how others saw his condition of cerebral palsy).

Because of my deafness there were obvious attitude changes among my peers. A lot of them just couldn't cope with the fact that I was deaf, or going deaf. I couldn't talk on the phone anymore. On summer nights I stopped playing my favorite neighborhood game of hide and seek because it was just too dark and I couldn't lipread.

Some of the kids I knew began to make fun of my speech, too. I didn't sound the same anymore. I can remember them asking each other "What did she say?" "I don't know!" Giggles. I would crumble inside, I was so ashamed and hurt. I found a solution to all this. I just stopped associating with most of my peers. I began to withdraw. I took all this inner agony with me into books. I'd shut myself up in my bedroom and read. I only spoke when spoken to. I stopped being open with people. I just read and read (Zannet Coleman, 1983; instructional counselor, California School for the Deaf, Fremont).

These thoughtful and anguished descriptions by two adults recollecting childhood experiences are examples of how one's self-confidence can be diminished. The individuals cited above are obviously articulate, but there is research to support the likelihood that some retarded children also have the skills and insight to accurately perceive and report their feelings (Wylie, 1979).

How can disabled children's school experiences be made more constructive so they come to see themselves as active persons with power and control over their relationships and experiences? This personal view of self-concept is considered to be an important perspective along with helping individuals develop positive categories by which to define themselves in the external world (Dickstein, 1977; Lewis & Brooks-Gunn, 1979).

Teachers and schools can strive to include disabled children so they feel confident and become an integral part of the school environment. In several studies, Jones (1972) has reported the stigma experienced by mentally retarded junior and senior high school boys. In fact, a follow-up study of 269 students who had been labeled educable mentally retarded found that 65 percent of the adults had disclosed to very few that they had once been in a special class placement.

Placing disabled children with their nondisabled peers is another effort to help them experience school more fully. The mainstreaming movement continues to gain momentum as program designs improve and the benefits to all children become more obvious.

Mainstreamed Programs.   Classrooms and programs that maximize the amount of time that disabled learners spend with their nondisabled peers have increased during the past decade. The concern with providing equal educational opportunity developed from instructional, psychological, and ethical-legal considerations. Chaffin (1974) has offered the following list of contributing factors: (1) equivocal results of efficacy studies of special classes; (2) inappropriate placement of children in classes for the retarded as a result of the cultural bias of many diagnostic instruments for identifying the retarded; (3) recognizing the debilitating effects of labeling a child; and (4) litigation related to placement procedures and the right of all children to education (Paul, 1977, p. 4).

In addition to the preceding factors supporting mainstreaming, teachers and school administrators now have a variety of models to utilize in the implementation of a mainstreamed program (Anastasiow, 1978; Knoblock, 1982) as well as having curriculum materials and assessment procedures available to assist in the instructional process (Hart, 1981; Barnes, Berrigan, & Biklen, 1978). The Syracuse City School District has designed a sophisticated program that offers mainstreamed classrooms at the elementary level and partially integrated classes at the junior and senior high schools. In Syracuse a continuum of mainstreamed services is being developed beginning with a preschool program (Knoblock & Barnes, 1979) and continuing into high school; it is hoped that area vocational education and counseling resources can be marshalled to build on children's skills already attained so that those skills can be implemented in the world of work. The classroom model at the elementary school level is described in detail elsewhere (Knoblock, 1983), and it has since been expanded to provide integrated classrooms at the kindergarten through sixth grade levels. All children, disabled and nondisabled, interact to a degree that is instructionally sound and participate in school activities.

Now that mainstreaming models are in place, school *practices* to facilitate the full participation of disabled children are being explored. In fact, the argument is made that if we expect disabled students to function as contributing members of society when their schooling is over they must be allowed access to the life of schools while in them.

> Severely handicapped students should be allowed life spaces that both require and ensure *maximal participation*. That is, as many minutes per day as possible should be spent in constructive and clearly habilitative environments and activities, and as few minutes as possible per day should be spent in restrictive, neutral, or antihabilitative environments and activities. Many classrooms contain one teacher, a full time aide, and from six to ten severely handicapped students. Because it is often assumed that most can develop or function best with one-to-one instruction, it logically follows that at any point in time several students will not be receiving direct instruction. This phenomenon often results in large amounts of dead time. Or, as is often the situation with students with severe motor difficulties, many time periods are occupied with zero or close to zero response levels. In regular schools, nonhandicapped student volunteers can be used extremely effectively to minimize dead time and to increase the proportion of direct instruction (Brown, Ford, Nisbet, Sweet, Donnellan, & Gruenewald, 1983, pp. 18–19).

Practices that benefit severely handicapped students in regular schools (Brown et al., 1983) include *proximal interactions*, in which some form of sensory contact is made between a severely handicapped student and a nonhandicapped peer; *helping interactions*, in which experiences are structured to permit nonhandicapped students to assist or instruct their handicapped classmates; *service interactions*, in which a nonhandicapped student provides a service; and *reciprocal interactions*, in which handicapped and nonhandicapped students are engaged in activities of a mutual nature, such as playing, learning together, or attending school functions. A growing repertoire of practices is becoming available to educators (Knoblock, 1982; Wilcox & Bellamy, 1982; Sailor, Wilcox, & Brown, 1980).

Proponents and critics of mainstreaming agree that merely placing disabled and nondisabled students together in the same classrooms will not necessarily change attitudes and enhance learning. This "contact hypothesis," according to Gottlieb and Leyser (1981), will only prove of value if disabled students are taught socially appropriate friendship skills. Writing about retarded students, they have stated:

> The implication of our research, then, is that contact between retarded and normal children will not produce positive attitude change unless the retarded children can be taught to exhibit behavior that conforms to the standards expected by their nonretarded peers. In other words, placement of retarded children with nonretarded children must follow or coincide with efforts to modify the retarded children's inappropriate behavior patterns, assuming that retarded children are more apt to be accepted by their nonretarded peers when their behavior meets an acceptable standard of appropriateness or competence (p. 158).

What are some of the social skills and competencies that can be focused on in mainstreamed classrooms? The following sections describe approaches that teachers can use to foster competence and social relationships. If contact between students is no guarantee of positive interaction, neither is it adequate to focus exclusively on expanding the disabled child's skill repertoire; that is necessary but not sufficient. Adults and peers need to make changes also. Essentially, what is needed are teachers who respond to the unique needs of all children in their classrooms, and school administrators who are committed to developing a cohesive school environment that fosters the personal growth of students and staff.

Fostering Competence. Interactions between teachers and students are increasingly viewed as reciprocal. As was the case with parent-child interactions, this current emphasis on the transactional nature of the relationship between teacher and student has been slow to gain recognition. The implication is that students have expectations for teachers and insights into their behaviors just as teachers have of them. Thus, if we view students as active participants and critical consumers in school programs, then we will need to develop responsive services, anticipate their needs, and solicit their input.

Takanishi and Spitzer (1980) interviewed children, ages four to twelve, in multi-age rooms and asked to whom they would go for different purposes (if help was needed on a task, if they felt sad). Children made distinctions among their teachers and peers. Fiedler (1975) has observed the classroom interactions of seventh and eighth graders and asked them to indicate the degree to which their teachers encouraged them to feel in control of their behavior. These studies and others remind us of the importance of soliciting children's perceptions of their classroom experiences.

Involving children in the context of fostering personal adjustment can mean providing them with skills and techniques to manage their own behaviors. Becoming more independent is a long-term instructional goal for all disabled children, and it is just as important to focus on independence training in personal adjustment as it is on the learning of academic tasks. In fact, teaching children self-control is gaining widespread interest as one means by which they gain mastery over their environment in positive ways.

Fagen, Long, and Stevens (1975) have developed a psychoeducational curriculum to teach children the necessary skills for satisfactory adjustment to the task and social demands of schools. The objectives in Table 3 reflect the skills needed to manage one's behaviors and the curriculum approaches teachers can utilize to construct activitites and materials responsive to each curriculum area.

Utilizing a combination of behavioral and psychoeducational procedures, Goldstein, Sprafkin, Gershaw, and Klein (1980) have developed a process that can be utilized to teach adolescents positive interaction skills. They have described their process as structured learning, which consists of four behavior change procedures: modeling, role playing, feedback, and transfer training.

In structured learning a skill is decided upon, hopefully in consultation with the youngsters involved, and the appropriate behavior is demonstrated, or modeled, by adolescents using the skill correctly. Role playing, or behavioral rehearsal, is the next step and is designed to give the youngster practice in learning the new skill. Feedback is then provided, based on an evaluation of the role-playing performance. The last step is transfer of training and is crucial in aiding students to generalize their skills to new situations and persons.

Examples of skills for dealing with feelings are as follows:

Knowing your feelings
Expressing your feelings
Understanding the feelings of others
Dealing with someone else's anger
Expressing affection
Dealing with fear
Rewarding yourself

Each of the above skills (or others designed by a teacher) can be broken down into small behavioral steps. The following steps in understanding the

Table 3
The Self-Control Curriculum: Overview of Curriculum Areas and Units

Curriculum area	Curriculum unit
Selection	1. Focusing and concentration 2. Mastering figure-ground discrimination 3. Mastering distractions and interference 4. Processing complex patterns
Storage	1. Developing visual memory 2. Developing auditory memory
Sequencing and ordering	1. Developing time orientation 2. Developing auditory-visual sequencing 3. Developing sequential planning
Anticipating consequences	1. Developing alternatives 2. Evaluating consequences
Appreciating feelings	1. Identifying feelings 2. Developing positive feelings 3. Managing feelings 4. Reinterpreting feeling events
Managing frustration	1. Accepting feelings of frustration 2. Building coping resources 3. Tolerating frustration
Inhibition and delay	1. Controlling action 2. Developing part-goals
Relaxation	1. Developing body relaxation 2. Developing thought relaxation 3. Developing movement relaxation

feelings of others is an example of such a task analysis approach:

1. Watch the other person.
2. Listen to what the person is saying.
3. Figure out what the other person might be feeling.
4. Think about ways to show you understand what he or she is feeling.
5. Decide on the best way to do it (p. 102).

These approaches may not be as appropriate for disabled children who need direct interventions by teachers or who require stimulation of various sensory modalities (Nickerson & O'Laughlin, 1982). Such action-oriented approaches include play approaches that are intrusive and attempt to stimulate unresponsive children (Jernberg, 1979); music therapy approaches to increase children's pleasure, creative development, and communication (Purvis & Sammet, 1976); storytelling techniques to assist children's expressions of feelings (Gardner, 1972); and paraverbal techniques that use various media including dance, mime, and drama as channels for communication (Heimlich, 1972).

School programs can contribute to children's feelings of competency by offering them the opportunity to develop a larger repertoire of responses to frustrating situations other than being aggressive toward others. Efforts to provide children and adolescents with methods to control their anger represent one approach to competency training.

Stress inoculation, a coping skills approach, has been advocated by Meichenbaum (1975) and Novaco (1978). In using the metaphor of inoculating a child against quantities of unmanageable stress, a learning environment can be structured so that stressors that arise do not overwhelm the learner. The range of behaviors and needs of disabled children and youth dictates that a variety of cognitive and behavioral coping skills be taught to respond to particular stress experiences. This approach involves cognitive preparation, skill acquisition, and application training.

Teaching children prosocial behavior is another broad set of skills to move children away from being aggressive to others and toward responding in socially acceptable ways (Mussen & Eisenberg-Berg, 1977). A variety of positive behaviors have been grouped under this broad heading *prosocial*: sharing, helping, cooperation, empathy, and perspective taking. Assertive and aggressive students may appear deficient in one or more of these behaviors. By designing structured classroom environments to teach children to understand and use these behaviors, teachers can foster positive interpersonal behaviors. The structure would need to represent a democratic and cooperative classroom environment so children could experience positive behaviors and hopefully model them.

Ringness (1975) has raised the question of whether the schools should teach or stimulate attitudes and values. These could include responsiveness to others, good work habits, liking teachers and peers, following directions, taking care of property, and similar attitudes that could contribute to a student's good citizenship while in school.

These approaches to fostering competence and teaching prosocial behaviors are preventive in nature, or at least represent what should be ongoing emphases in classrooms and schools. However, there are children whose behaviors are so extreme that we are required to respond immediately to avoid a crisis. Redl and Wineman (1951, 1952) have described the disorganization and breakdown of behavior controls in "children who hate." Unfortunately, schools and communities are filled with angry and alienated children and youth who cannot manage their feelings or their negative reactions. These children are characterized by faulty control or impulse systems that cause them to react to events and people on the basis of impulse gratification. There are those who have such a low frustration threshold that they cannot tolerate the feelings produced by moderate levels of frustration, or those who are overstimulated by situations and consequently lose control of their feelings. Teachers and children's workers are encouraged to develop crisis management interventions in the context of supportive environments to strengthen children's control systems or deficient ego function. Redl and Wineman (1952) have referred to this approach as "programming for ego support."

Fostering Social Relationships.   Teachers and schools can structure classroom practices and procedures to increase the positive interactions between disabled and nondisabled students. Approaches such as affective education or social skills training have been used to accomplish this by utilizing curriculum materials and classroom management techniques. The choice of one designation over another reflects one's bias. Wood (1982) has raised the following questions: "What are the differences between these two approaches to helping children and youth grow into happy, productive adulthood? Is one more 'humanistic' than the other? More 'scientific'? Or demonstrably greater effectiveness?" (p. 212). He has pointed out the value of both approaches: providing experiences in which emotional and cognitive development are interrelated and teaching children appropriate social behaviors. Again we see the value of integrating viewpoints to accomplish specified outcomes.

Irrespective of our theoretical bias, it is well established that teachers have an impact on classroom social interactions. Rist (1970) reported observing a classroom in which children were assigned seats at three different tables: one for "fast learners" and those whom the teacher described as having no idea of what was going on in the classroom. Rist observed that the children seated at tables 2 and 3 were ridiculed by the children at table 1 and by themselves, and those at table 1 viewed themselves more positively than the others. This is a state of affairs not to be emulated. What practices can teachers engage in to avoid such damaging social relationships?

Creating Cooperation.   Teachers can strive to foster cooperation rather than competition in classrooms. Merely placing children together, whether in segregated or mainstreamed classrooms, does not guarantee positive interactions. Structuring activities to enhance cooperation is one positive practice available to teachers. Cooperative learning situations can occur during many time blocks during a school day. Knight, Peterson, and McGuire (1982, pp. 234–235) have offered the following guidelines for the teacher's role in setting up cooperative instruction.

1. Specify the instructional objective.
2. Select the group size most appropriate for the lesson. Size will vary according to the type of materials and resources needed to complete the lesson, the cooperative skills of the members, and the nature of the task.
3. Arrange the classroom. Teachers will want to cluster the groups so that they will not interfere with each other, yet so that all can share materials and ideas within their own group.
4. Provide appropriate materials. When students are not skilled at cooperation, it may be advisable to arrange the materials like a jigsaw puz-

zle so that each member will have something to contribute to the whole project.

5. Explain the task and the cooperative goal structure. After specifying the task, the teacher will need to describe the group goal, explain how goal achievement will be evaluated, and indicate that all group members will be rewarded on the basis of the quality of the group's work.

6. Observe student-student interactions. Much of the teacher's time will be spent observing the groups and the problems they encounter as they function cooperatively.

7. Intervene as a consultant to help the group solve problems and work together effectively. Help group members learn and practice the interpersonal and group skills necessary to achieve the final product.

8. Evaluate the group product, using the criterion-referenced evaluation system.

Social Interaction. Studies of children's attitudes toward their disabled peers reveal attention paid to differences. Gerber's (1977) interview and sociometric study of preschool children in an integrated program found that differences were cited by 88 percent of the children when describing autistic, hyperactive children; 68 percent described something different about children in a body brace; and 50 percent noted some difference in a child with cerebral palsy. The important question is whether the awareness of disabled children's differences lead to acceptance or social avoidance by nondisabled students.

The structuring of classroom practices can turn perceptions of differences into bases for positive social interactions. In a study of classroom interactions of autistic and nondisabled peers, Barnes (1982) described a number of teacher behaviors that promoted integration and led to the development of a sense of community.

· Utilizing a teacher's presence in an activity as an attraction for nondisabled children to move toward the special children involved in that activity.
· Teachers spontaneously incorporating children into a joint activity.
· Planning activities appropriate for all children.
· Directing children toward each other.
· Intervening to decrease the deviancy of certain behaviors.
· Providing explanations to the questions asked about disabled children and their behaviors.
· Modeling appropriate ways to respond to and interact with disabled children.

The following statement by a teacher represents a goal toward which we should strive:

I think basically what I've seen here is typical kids together and interacting as human beings would—not a situation where you force an interaction but you do try to help an interaction occur, where kids have questions answered about differences. They learn to appreciate the differences and those differences that they don't like they can say they don't like and that's okay. They can feel better about themselves. Special kids get to be with kids that have not been so severely injured by life as they've been and they can grow from that and open up from that. That's what I see— not forcing something or staging relationships, but helping people" (Barnes, 1982, p. 256).

Peer Acceptance.   Designing cooperative activities is one method that can be used to help children feel more positively about each other. Increasingly, special educators and regular educators are recognizing the long-term value of increasing peer acceptance of handicapped children. Some disabled children with pronounced physical differences or who demonstrate aggressive behaviors toward other children can be judged less acceptable by peers. Of equal concern is the possibility that peers (as well as parents and teachers) may have lowered expectations of those children who are less physically attractive. In addition, the importance of structuring experiences to foster peer acceptance of handicapped students is underscored by the likelihood that many disabled children have very different socialization experiences than their nondisabled peers. These differences may include less time with peers and underdeveloped social skills.

Susan Bookbinder (1978) has described a curriculum utilized at the Meeting Street School in Providence, Rhode Island, to enhance peer acceptance. The development of a curriculum at this center for multiply disabled children has as its central purpose: "When ordinary children understand the causes, visible effects and consequences of disabilities, they will try to treat disabled children as they would anyone else" (p. 3). To achieve this goal teaching units are developed for the disability areas of blindness, deafness, physical disabilities, and mental retardation. Each unit is designed to provide nondisabled elementary school students with experiences that sensitize them to their disabled peers. Here is a list of activities to assist in the appreciation of physical disabilities:

1. Many opportunities to look at slides, photographs, and movies of children with different kinds of physical disabilities, so that the visible, manifest aspects of these disabilities will be "demystified." Once children realize that, except for the pain and awkwardness of their disabilities, physically disabled children are very much like themselves, the appearance of a child with a physical disability will not be so alien or frightening.
2. Ample time to investigate and use all the equipment that physically disabled children need to get around.
3. Ample time to handle and use all sorts of aids and devices that physically disabled children may use for protection, communication, and relaxation.

4. Some understanding of what goes on in physical therapy, speech therapy, and occupational therapy.
5. Stimulation activities and experiences that help the children imagine how it feels to have a physical disability.
6. Time to talk about their preconceptions, feelings, and fears concerning physically disabled people (p. 57).

Teachers can contribute in significant ways to children's socioemotional development, and this section has described several approaches that teachers have used. Hopefully, this material will stimulate you to try these and other interventions that respond to the needs and growth potential of all children.

Summary

This chapter has emphasized the importance of understanding disabled children's socioemotional development. Their development is best understood in the context of studying the world in which we live and the particular social environments in which they interact with peers and adults. The unique characteristics of some disabled children may increase their vulnerability to stressors that exist for all children in today's complex world.

We first examined the observation that infants can influence the quantity and quality of adult interactions. Studying social interchange can help us understand early socialization and personality development. Discussions of reciprocity and synchronization, or the timing of infant and adult interactions, provided examples of two ways in which infant behaviors and characteristics can affect adult responses.

Disabled children's unique characteristics may influence their mastery of important developmental tasks such as the ability to form attachments and to develop friendships. Attachment, or bonding between children and their caregivers, can be viewed in an interactional context. For example, particular behaviors such as lack of eye contact or difficulty moving limbs in response to adult initiatives may make it more difficult for some caregivers to attend to children or to sustain their own level of involvement. Similarly, a variety of social skills are often required for successful peer interaction; depending on a child's disability, friendships may be difficult to achieve. Mastery of these developmental tasks is also influenced by behaviors and attitudes of others. Examples of differing attitudes can be seen in children's responses to physically disabled children in contrast to their perceptions of less obviously impaired peers.

A range of barriers confronts disabled children. These barriers are often expressed in first-person accounts by disabled persons and include descriptions of community attitudes, family dynamics, and the nature of the disability—whether it is chronic or episodic. The presence of barriers to personal adjustment and social acceptance can cause varying degrees of stress. The role of stress in the lives of disabled children was examined in a discussion of stress and psychiatric disorders. These children may be subject, for example, to a higher degree of hospitalization. One could argue that they may be less able to cope with that stressor and others, such as parents' separation and divorce. It may be necessary to provide support to them, as well as to the family, at that time.

The concept of stress can help us understand a range of children, including those with behaviors labeled dependent, impulsive, repressed, and passive-aggressive. Rather than labeling such children as deviant, it may be more useful to focus on their behaviors as responses to one or more stressors in their lives. Children who show extreme behaviors—those who are aggressive with others and those who are depressed and suicidal—demand careful and immediate responses by teachers, parents, and communities. Fostering competence in aggressive students and helping parents learn to detect danger signs of depression and suicide in their children are examples of responses that reflect a social-interactive perspective.

By viewing disabled children in that perspective, we may learn why some children remain invulnerable or less vulnerable to stress. In other words, is it possible to create environments that are supportive to children and preventive in nature? The chapter concludes with suggestions for supporting parents of disabled children and with a discussion of how schools can foster competence and social interactions. These two aspects—constructive family behaviors and a supportive school environment—are major conditions for the development of more competent and less vulnerable children.

Chapter 6

Raymond Glass

Raymond Glass is professor and chair, Department of Special Education, University of Maine at Farmington. His areas of interest include helping regular class teachers work with children who exhibit problem behaviors, using cooperative learning to enhance social integration, and applying research on effective teaching practices.

Planning and Organizing Instruction for Exceptional Students

After reading this chapter, you should be able to:

1
Recall the basic information contained in a written IEP.

2
Describe effective learning principles and their application when teaching students with disabilities.

3
List instructional approaches and discuss their usefulness when individualizing instruction.

4
Critique time-out procedure as a way to improve student behavior and describe positive alternatives.

Being an effective teacher is an art as well as a science. The scientific aspect requires knowledge and skill in a variety of areas, including assessment, curriculum, teaching methods, and working with parents and other professionals. The artistic aspect involves knowing when and how to apply the vast array of knowledge and skill to maximize student growth. In different terms, effective teachers learn how to tune in to their students. They plan and organize instruction that is responsive to the learning needs of their students. They use a variety of instructional techniques known to be successful through research and experience, and they develop constructive ways to motivate students to behave in increasingly appropriate ways.

This chapter is divided into three sections that parallel the preceding description of effective teachers. The first part presents planning and organizing instruction for exceptional students. Ways to tune in to students by using informal assessment techniques are reviewed. Then, the process of converting assessment data into teaching goals and objectives is reviewed. Included in part one is a discussion of Individualized Education Programs or IEPs, which provide a step-by-step framework for planning instruction for exceptional students. The second part introduces ways to modify instruction to maximize learning for exceptional students. Various techniques used by skillful teachers are demonstrated. Finally, the third part presents approaches to helping reduce disruptive or inappropriate behavior and learning more effective and constructive ways of interacting.

As you read, keep in mind that nearly all the approaches presented in this chapter cut across specific categories of exceptionality and degrees of impairment and are appropriate for any student who demonstrates special needs in learning or classroom behavior. Thus, whether the student is labeled emotionally disturbed, developmentally delayed, learning disabled, health impaired, partially sighted, or hearing impaired, similar, if not identical, principles need to be considered in planning and carrying out instruction.

The IEP: A Framework for Planning

Few educators would argue with the assertion that careful planning is a key element in developing effective instruction. Indeed, research on effective teaching practices clearly suggests that teachers who develop specific learning objectives and who plan, organize, and deliver instruction to accomplish their specific objectives are more likely to meet with success than their less purposeful colleagues (Rosenshine, 1983; Rosenshine & Stevens, 1986). In this section, we will examine some of the critical dimensions along which many successful teachers of handicapped children plan and organize their day-to-day instruction.

Prior to 1975, handicapped students could be placed in special education programs with little assurance that their special needs would be addressed or that the effectiveness of their program would be routinely evaluated. The right to receive a carefully planned instructional program was crystallized with the passage of Public Law 94-142, which requires that an Individual Education Program (IEP) be developed for every handicapped student. Developed by a school's child study or pupil evaluation team (the name of the team may vary among school districts), the IEP is a written statement of the unique needs and special education services a student is to receive. Although specific items vary somewhat among states, IEPs address the following concerns:

1. *Present level of educational performance.* The student's present level of educational performance is described by a summary of relevant test scores, classroom work samples, and teacher observations. This information is then condensed into a list of strengths and weaknesses that characterize the student.
2. *Annual goals.* Academic, social, behavioral, language, motor, and other listed weaknesses and some strengths are converted into annual program goals for the student. These goals indicate the areas to be addressed by the special education program and set the stage for day-to-day instruction.
3. *Short-term objectives.* Annual goals are broken down into specific short-term objectives, which are usually written in behavioral terms. Since these objectives are often difficult to develop in a pupil evaluation team meeting, one or more teachers who work closely with the student may be assigned the responsibility of writing these specific objectives. In many school districts, specific objectives are written for each new marking period or grading period. These objectives are stepping-stones toward the accomplishment of annual goals. It is toward these short-term objectives that day-to-day instruction is geared.
4. *Services.* The nature and amount of special education services and aids the student is to receive must be described (e.g., three twenty-minute sessions a week of articulation therapy; thirty minutes a day of instruction to increase sight vocabulary and word recognition skills, mobility training). In addition, the setting where the student is to receive the services as well as persons responsible for delivering the services must be listed.
5. *Evaluation.* Both procedures and timetables for evaluating the effectiveness of the special education services are specified. As mentioned previously, the IEP must be reviewed at least annually.

The preparation of IEPs most often lies in the hands of special education teachers (Price & Goodman, 1980). Though time consuming to develop, a well-written IEP offers distinct advantages. Because goals, objectives, and services the student is to receive are put into writing, parents can be better informed about their child's program. For example, it is no longer sufficient to say a student will receive special help or special education or will be placed in a resource program. These terms convey no information regarding the specific kinds of assistance the student is to receive. Instead, the kinds of help the student is to receive must be spelled out in detail. Teachers and students can also benefit from clearly written IEPs since they provide a concrete set of goals and methods to follow, thus helping to insure that a student's specific educational needs are addressed each day. A partially constructed IEP appears in Box 1.

Assessing Learner Strengths and Weaknesses

One of the initial steps in planning an educational program for handicapped students is to assess their strengths and weaknesses. This seemingly uncomplicated task has generated considerable controversy among teachers and administrators because there is a wide variety of tests with different purposes. Disagreement sometimes occurs regarding how much testing is needed, what tests should be used, and who should conduct the tests. Although it is beyond the scope of this chapter to provide a detailed discussion of assessment issues and practices, a brief review of assessment tools and their purposes will help you understand how strengths and weaknesses are assessed.

As mentioned in chapter 3, standardized achievement, intelligence, and diagnostic tests may be administered by psychologists and well-trained teachers to determine whether a student qualifies for special education services because his or her skills and abilities differ markedly from the norm. Commonly used tests include the Wechsler Intelligence Scale for Children (Wechsler, 1974), the Stanford Binet Intelligence Test (Terman & Merrill, 1960), the Woodcock-Johnson Psychoeducational Battery (Woodcock & Johnson, 1977), the Peabody Individual Achievement Test (Dunn & Markwardt, 1970), the newly developed Kaufman Assessment Battery for Children (Kaufman & Kaufman, 1983), and the Woodcock Reading Mastery Tests (Woodcock, 1973).

While one or more of the preceding tests can be used to help determine whether a student is eligible for special education services, their results offer teachers little useful information for planning day-to-day instruction. That is, assessment for the purpose of identifying exceptional students is not the same as assessment for teaching them. When it comes to determining specific strengths and weaknesses and establishing specific day-to-day teaching objectives, teachers often use a combination of informal tests, criterion-referenced tests, observation and rating scales.

Informal Teacher-Made Tests.   Many special education teachers construct their own tests to help determine particular strengths and weaknesses in academic areas. For example, if one wished to determine what math skills a second grader had mastered, it would be possible to consult teachers' manuals from a math series used in the child's classroom to determine what skills are typically developed in the second grade. Then, test items to determine whether the student has acquired the specific skills could easily be developed as indicated in Figure 1. By giving such an informal test, one could determine what specific skills the student already knows and what skills the student has not yet mastered relative to the specific curricular series used in the student's

Box 1
An Individual Education Program

I. General Information

Name: Brian P.　　　*Birth date:* Nov. 1, 1976
Current placement: 2nd Grade, Weld Elem. School
Reason for referral: Brian was referred because of disruptive, disorganized classroom behavior and his unwillingness to work alone in all skill areas.

PET members: Mr. Gill, Principal
　　　　　　　 Mrs. P., Parent
　　　　　　　 Mrs. Latham, Teacher
　　　　　　　 Mr. Frank, Special education teacher

II. Present Level of Educational Performance. Based on classroom observations, teacher reports, and informal tests, the following strengths and weaknesses are apparent:

A. *Strengths:* Brian . . .

1. Knows the basic addition and subtraction facts and can add and subtract when renaming is not required.
2. Reads on grade level and applies basic word attack skills in sounding out unfamiliar words.
3. Learns rote information such as spelling words and math facts quickly.
4. Enjoys attention from teachers and peers.
5. Can complete some independent seatwork (5–10 problems) when he understands and the tasks are simple.

B. *Weaknesses:* Brian . . .

1. Does not know how to rename in addition and subtraction or how to count change.
2. Reads orally at a slow rate (50 words per minute).
3. Prints using letters that are too large and words that often are not on a straight line with many erasures.
4. Is easily distracted by other students, gets out of his seat to sharpen a pencil 2–3 times in a 30-minute work period and fails to complete many seatwork assignments unless he is reminded to "get to work" every 3–5 minutes.
5. Gets easily confused and then frustrated when faced with math problems that require more than one step, comprehension questions that require inferential thinking, or writing tasks that require him to identify, organize, and then write his ideas.
6. Uses unconstructive behavior such as excessive talking, laughing, or grabbing materials during group activities.

(continued)

Box 1
(continued)

*Date
Completed*

Goal: Improve handwriting and spelling.
1. Given a 5–6 word sentence to copy, Brian will reproduce the sentence by writing each word on a line, and placing ½ inch between each word.   _____
2. In daily assignments, Brian will complete at least one spelling paper with no more than two erasures.   _____
3. Spell at least 95 percent of 150 new words from a second grade spelling list.   _____

Goal: Improve task attention and work completion skills.
1. Begin at least 4–6 daily written tasks within one minute after being requested.   _____
2. Complete at least 2 brief written assignments each day within a 15-minute time period and without talking or leaving his seat more than once.   _____

Goal: Improve ability and willingness to engage in inferential and creative tasks. Brian will . . .

1. Accurately write and spell three 6-word sentences presented by dictation (e.g., the teacher says and then Brian writes "The man went to the city") without saying "I can't do it" or "This is too hard."   _____
2. With the help of a tutor, dictate an experience story that contains at least 5 sentences, without making negative statements such as "I don't want to do this."   _____

Goal: Improve ability to work in a group setting. Brian will . . .

1. When in a group activity, reduce the frequency of laughing or talking out of turn to 2 per 10-minute period.   _____
2. Reduce instances of shouting, screaming, or grabbing materials from others during play periods to no more than 2 per session.   _____
3. Share a material or wait to take a turn without shouting "my turn" at least once during a play period.   _____

(continued)

Box 1

(continued)

III. Annual Goals: Long-term goals for Brian are to:

1. Increase math skills, particularly renaming, word problems, and counting change.
2. Increase reading skills, particularly oral reading rate and comprehension.
3. Improve handwriting.
4. Improve task attention and work completion.
5. Increase his ability to engage in complex tasks such as word problems, influential thinking, and producing written sentences or stories.
6. Increase his ability to share, take turns, and work in a group setting.

IV. Short-Term Objectives:

The following list of objectives was developed by Brian's teachers shortly after Brian began to attend his special education classroom.

Goal: Increase math skills, particularly renaming counting change and word problems. Brian will be able to . . .

	Date Completed
1. Subtract any 2-digit number from another 2-digit number using regrouping (e.g., 56–29) at a rate of 3 per minute and with 90 percent accuracy.	_____
2. Add any 2 double-digit numbers that require renaming at a rate of 3 per minute and with 90% accuracy.	_____
3. Add any combination of pennies, nickels, and dimes with sums to $.95 with 90 percent accuracy.	_____
4. Accurately answer at least 80 percent of any series of simple word problems requiring addition or subtraction.	_____

Goal: Increase reading skills, particularly oral reading rate and comprehension. Brian will . . .

1. Complete Level 9 of the *Holt Basic Reading Program*, being able to read any passage with 95 percent accuracy.	_____
2. Orally read any Level 9 passage at a rate of 60 words per minute.	_____

(continued)

Box 1
(continued)

3. Correctly answer (orally or in written form) at least 4–5 simple recall questions presented at the end of any reading passage. _____

4. When given 3 possible answers to an inferential question, select the correct answer on at least 7 out of 10 occasions. _____

V. Educational Services: *Persons Responsible*

   A. *Regular Classroom:* Brian will attend his regular second grade each afternoon where he will participate in science, social studies, art, and other activities. Brian will receive free time and other privileges for completing modified assignments. A daily performance card will be sent home at the end of each day.   Mrs. Latham

   B. *Special Classroom:* Brian will be placed in a self-contained class each morning where emphasis will be placed on increasing reading, math, handwriting, task attention, and group participation skills.   Mr. Frank

   C. *Home-School Coordination:* A daily performance chart will be sent home each day. Mrs. P. will praise Brian for his efforts and play a game of checkers with him for appropriate in-school behavior.

   D. *Coordination:* Mr. Frank and Mrs. Latham will meet bi-weekly to discuss Brian's program along stated objectives and revise strategies as needed.   Mr. Frank

VI. Evaluation:

The effect of the placement will be evaluated by determining Brian's progress along his goals and objectives. Criterion-referenced tests and direct observation of classroom behavior will be used. This information will be presented at a PET to be conducted 3 months from today.

(continued)

Box 1
(continued)

VII. Justification for Educational Placement:

1. It is believed that Brian can succeed in most regular class assignments provided the work and evaluation procedures are adjusted to his strengths.
2. Removal from class for half a day is necessary to provide intensive individual and small group instruction in academic and social-behavioral areas.

I have had the opportunity to participate in the Pupil Evaluation Team and to help develop this Individual Education Program.

I agree with this program. (   )

I disagree with this program. (   )

Parent's signature _____

---

regular classroom program. Similar informal tests can also be developed in reading.

Criterion-Referenced Tests.   Criterion-referenced tests are usually teacher constructed tests designed to determine whether a student has obtained a predetermined level of mastery or standard of performance along a very specific learning objective. For example, if a teacher wanted students to add basic addition facts from memory, a test could be developed in which the student was expected to add twenty simple addition problems (problems with sums to 20, such as $5 + 6$) within one minute with at least 95 percent accuracy. If the student was able to pass this informal test according to the stated criteria (within one minute and with at least 95 percent accuracy), then the teacher could conclude that the student had reached mastery on this particular skill. Similarly, a teacher may want students to learn to follow ten simple, one-stage directions presented verbally and through signing and may decide that mastery of this objective would be the ability to comply with at least nine out of ten directions on three successive days. A criterion-referenced test in which students are presented with ten simple directives (e.g., sit down, stand up, look at me, get the block) and are expected to accurately carry out nine of them on three successive days could be used to determine whether mastery was achieved.

As each new objective is introduced and developed through daily instruction, a criterion-referenced test can be administered to evaluate student progress and, not incidentally, the effectiveness of the teacher's instruction. Criterion-referenced tests can be developed for a variety of skills as indicated by the following examples.

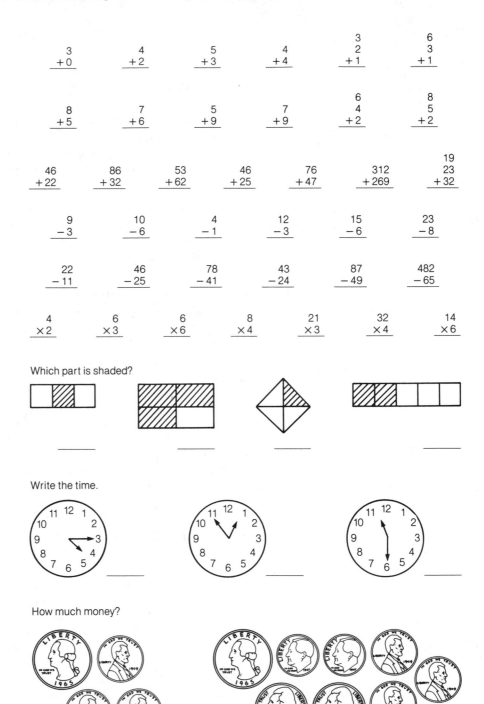

```
  3        4        5        4        3        6
+ 0      + 2      + 3      + 4      2        3
                                   + 1      + 1


  8        7        5        7        6        8
+ 5      + 6      + 9      + 9      4        5
                                   + 2      + 2

                                                     19
 46       86       53       46       76      312      23
+22      +32      +62      +25      +47     +269     + 32


  9       10        4       12       15       23
- 3      - 6      - 1      - 3      - 6      - 8


 22       46       78       43       87      482
-11      -25      -41      -24      -49      -65


  4        6        6        8       21       32       14
×2       ×3       ×6       ×4       ×3       ×4       ×6
```

Which part is shaded?

_____   _____   _____   _____

Write the time.

_____   _____   _____

How much money?

_____   _____

Figure 1. *Informal test of second grade math skills.*

Objective	*Criterion-Referenced Test*
Reading basic sight words.	The student is presented with the Dolch Basic Word List and is expected to read at least 90 percent of the words on the list.
Fluently reading third grade level material.	The student is presented with a randomly selected 100-word passage from a third grade level reader and is expected to read at a rate of 65 words per minute with less than 3 errors.
Spelling single syllable words containing the vowel-consonant-vowel pattern (e.g., bike, take, gate).	The student is presented 25 single-syllable VCV words to spell and is expected to obtain a score of at least 22.
Multiplying any double digit by a single digit number with renaming (e.g., 32 × 6).	The student is expected to solve at least 18–20 problems within 5 minutes.
Naming 10 basic parts of the body.	When asked to point to a particular body part (e.g., head, arms, legs, feet), the student accurately points to the appropriate body part.

The major advantage of criterion-referenced tests is that they can be keyed to goals and objectives contained in a student's IEP. Thus, criterion-referenced tests assess exactly those skills the teacher wants to develop. Students who do not reach the criteria can be given additional learning activities until they reach the desired standard of performance.

Observation.   Directly observing how a student interacts with teachers, peers, and learning tasks represents a rich source of diagnostic information that cannot be easily acquired through formal or informal tests. With good observation skills, teachers are in a unique position to obtain information such as the following:

- *Attention span:* How long can the student work with sustained attention, stay in his or her seat, and maintain interest in a topic?
- *Group participation skills:* Can the student share materials, take turns, wait for others, and offer constructive help to other students?
- *Responses to stress:* Does the student use self-control when frustrated? How does the student respond when asked to delay gratification of impulses?
- *Reactions to adults:* How does the student react to teacher offers of help, suggestions, praise, directions, and commands?

· *Academic interests and attitudes:* What level of interest and confidence is shown in various academic subjects?
· *Needs for clarity and structure:* How specific and organized must directions and assignments be for the student to understand them?
· *Adaptive learning:* What everyday skills, such as dressing, toileting, and feeding, has the student learned?

Just as in academic assessment, there are different observation procedures. Frequency counts can be used to record the number of times an identifiable behavior—such as hitting, swearing, talking out of turn, or getting out of one's seat—occurs in a given period of time. If a student appears to exhibit troublesome behaviors such as those just mentioned, it may be useful to find out how often these behaviors occur and whether they occur more frequently in one setting versus another (e.g., playground versus reading period). Frequency counts (Box 2) can usually be maintained while the teacher is working with students; thus they are a relatively easy and useful observation tool.

Duration records measure the length of time a specific event such as crying, reading silently, or engaging in appropriate peer play occurs. Such records are kept when it is important to know how long a critical event typically occurs. As in frequency counts, it is important to note the time, date, and setting when conducting a duration record. Keeping such a record can be a normal part of teaching. For example, one can note and write down when a crying outburst began and ended as a natural way of responding to the incident.

Anecdotal records provide brief accounts of meaningful events that occur from time to time and that lend insight to the student or the teaching-learning process. Consider the value of the following anecdotal record:

November 10: During morning recess I played a game of freeze tag with my group of five boys. It was a zestful game, with little anger or frustration shown by anyone. When the bell rang, everyone went into the room smiling, out of breath, and talking about the next game. Mike was the only

---

Box 2
Teacher's Frequency Count, Listing Time and Setting, Behavior(s), and a Mark for Each Time the Behavior Occurred

Student	Joe	Date	October 6
Setting	Reading	Time	10:15–10:45

1. Out of seat without permission: //
2. Talks out without raising hand: ////

one who could not settle down. He seemed charged with energy which he could not contain. When I read a story, he sat quietly; but he refused to do any work for the rest of the morning. Instead, he paced around the room looking for toy cars or other objects to play with, made paper airplanes, or simply sat at his desk, despite my three or four reminders to do his work. Fortunately, he did not talk to or distract other students as he has sometimes done. Although Mike came to school in a good mood and seemed to enjoy the game, I think it was far too stimulating for him. This fits a little with my hunch that once Mike gets angry or excited, it takes him a long time to regain composure.

In preparing anecdotal records, it is important to present as much observable, factual detail as possible and to separate factual from judgmental statements. Instead of writing descriptive anecdotal records such as the one just presented, some observers make the mistake of presenting interpretations and conclusions instead of facts, as the following record indicates.

Mike had another anger outburst today in which he became obstreperous. He is a difficult, unmanageable youngster who is frustrating to teach. I am at a loss as to what to do.

Wright (1967) has provided a number of useful "rules for reporting" when using any type of observation, especially anecdotal records. He reminds us to (1) observe and report as fully as possible on the subject's situation, (2) present descriptions instead of interpretations or conclusions, and (3) describe exactly what the subject does as well as what others who interact with the subject do.

Rating Scales. Rating scales are useful for obtaining and reporting perceptions of teachers, parents, and other professionals. Rating scales usually elicit judgments regarding the attitudes, conduct, and general development of students. Informal rating scales can be designed by professionals to yield information useful in their work. A physical therapist, for example, could ask parents to respond to a series of questions about the degree of fine and gross motor coordination exhibited by a physically disabled child. Box 3 shows an author-constructed list that is used to help the regular classroom and the special education teacher develop a clear set of mutual goals.

Many commercially prepared lists are also available, including the Behavior Problem Checklist (Quay, 1967), the Devereux Adolescent Behavior Rating Scale (Spivack, Spotts, & Haimes, 1967), the Pupil Behavior Rating Scale (Lambert, Hartsough, & Bower, 1978), and the Adaptive Behavior Scale (American Association on Mental Deficiency, 1974). Some of the commercially developed scales present normative data so that an individual's score can be compared with a broader sample.

Purposes of Assessment

As you can see, a variety of assessment instruments and procedures are available to teachers and consultants of exceptional students. In considering the

Box 3
Goal-Setting Profile

Directions: This is an instrument to help describe the needs and goals for students with behavior problems. After completing the general identifying information, read each item and circle the response that best characterizes how the student behaves or performs. Circle 1 if the student demonstrates the behavior not at all or does the opposite of the behavior. Circle 2 if the student demonstrates the behavior occasionally or with repeated help or warnings. Circle 3 if the student demonstrates the behavior at least sometimes on his or her own initiative. Circle 4 if the student willingly demonstrates the behavior.

Student's name _____   Grade _____

Teacher _____   Date _____

1. *Academic Behaviors*

   1.1 Arrives on time for class   1 2 3 4

   1.2 Begins tasks on time   1 2 3 4

   1.3 Completes tasks on time   1 2 3 4

   1.4 Works independently   1 2 3 4

   1.5 Pays attention while teacher is delivering   1 2 3 4
       information

   1.6 Follows written directions   1 2 3 4

   1.7 Organizes work carefully   1 2 3 4

   1.8 Other _____   1 2 3 4

2. *Group Participation Skills*

   2.1 Offers opinions and answers when asked   1 2 3 4

   2.2 Enjoys group activities   1 2 3 4

   2.3 Takes turns and shares   1 2 3 4

   2.4 Complies with basic rules for group   1 2 3 4
       participation

   2.5 Shows concern for others' feelings and   1 2 3 4
       property

   2.6 Solves conflicts without shouting, fighting,   1 2 3 4
       or intimidating

   2.7 Makes constructive contributions during   1 2 3 4
       group activities

   2.8 Other _____   1 2 3 4

(continued)

Box 3
(continued)

3. *General Coping Skills*

3.1 Follows classroom rules and routines	1 2 3 4
3.2 Follows rules and expectations during unsupervised periods	1 2 3 4
3.3 Accepts constructive criticism/feedback	1 2 3 4
3.4 Takes part in classroom housekeeping	1 2 3 4
3.5 Seeks help when necessary	1 2 3 4
3.6 Accepts help from teachers	1 2 3 4
3.7 Accepts help from peers	1 2 3 4
3.8 Is confident of own abilities	1 2 3 4
3.9 Seeks constructive or legitimate peer attention	1 2 3 4
3.10 Asserts own rights when appropriate	1 2 3 4
3.11 Is willing to try new activities	1 2 3 4
3.12 Maintains composure under mild frustration	1 2 3 4
3.13 Considers consequences before acting	1 2 3 4
3.14 Is physically alert and active	1 2 3 4
3.15 Changes assignments within class smoothly	1 2 3 4
3.16 Can work with normal distractions	1 2 3 4
3.17 Is generally positive about self	1 2 3 4
3.18 Other _____	1 2 3 4

To determine high priority behaviors, look over the behaviors you circled with 1 or 2 and select the two or three behaviors that you feel are most in need of immediate attention. Write each behavior down.

1. _____

2. _____

3. _____

value and application of these tools, it is useful to remember that most assessment instruments serve one of two broad purposes: to identify exceptional students or to plan instructional programs for these students once it has been decided that they qualify for special education services. To illustrate this point, the sequence of tests used with Jane, a third-grade student who now receives two hours a day of special education services, is presented.

> By early October, Mr. Brown, Jane's third grade teacher, sensed that Jane was unable to keep up with even the slowest reading and math groups in his classroom. Mr. Brown's initial observations and impressions about Jane's low performance were confirmed by results from standardized achievement test scores which were administered in late September.
>
> On the basis of Jane's classroom performance and achievement test scores, Mr. Brown referred her to the school's Pupil Evaluation Team to determine whether she qualified for special education services.
>
> With parental permission, a school psychologist administered the Wechsler Intelligence Scale for Children, an individual intelligence test, and found an overall score of 65. Since the average IQ score falls between 85 and 115, this score put Jane into the range identified by the American Association on Mental Deficiency as "Mild Mental Retardation." To determine Jane's general level of achievement, the achievement section of the Woodcock-Johnson Psychoeducational Battery was administered. In nearly all areas of achievement (e.g., Science, Social Studies, Reading, and Math) Jane scored at the middle of the first grade level, indicating that she was performing well below her grade level, and confirming the validity of the IQ score. Finally, the psychologist interviewed both the teacher and parent to determine Jane's general social functioning. The mother reported no serious difficulties other than the fact that Jane demonstrated a short attention span and quickly lost interest in many activities. Although she needed continual reminders to wash, dress, and get ready for school, she was able to do these tasks quite easily.

The tests administered thus far, the SRA Achievement Tests, the WISC, and the Woodstock-Johnson Psychoeducational Battery, are all examples of standardized tests that indicate where a student's score falls in relation to a norm group. Such scores are particularly useful for identifying which students appear to be sufficiently different as to require special education services. In Jane's case, the scores suggest that she is functioning at a level indicative of mild mental retardation and, therefore, does indeed qualify for special education services. At a subsequent pupil evaluation team meeting, it was decided that Jane should spend two hours each day in a resource room program in which she would receive special help in reading, language, and math.

With this decision to give Jane additional help, her special education teacher, in consultation with Mr. Brown, had to decide what specific learning objectives and methods should be established. That is, assessment for the purpose of instruction was conducted. Jane's special education teacher could have begun a new testing cycle by administering standardized diagnostic tests in reading, spelling, and math. However, not wishing to burden Jane with more testing, she was included in many of the ongoing learning activities in the special education classroom. Jane's performance on these tasks and on informal tests that were introduced as part of her daily work were then used to determine specific strengths and weaknesses.

The approach used by Jane's teacher moves away from a once traditional practice in which a formal assessment period was observed prior to the initiation of any teaching. Although some teachers still follow this diagnostic format, many have moved to a more functional approach to assessment. Such an approach minimizes the use of standardized tests and relies more heavily on informal and criterion-referenced tests, which are often introduced to the student as a learning activity rather than a test. Results from these informal procedures are combined with the rich source of information that can be obtained by carefully observing student responses to daily academic and social tasks. Thus, rather than administering a series of tests and attempting to make important conclusions about a student's instructional needs within a brief time period, assessment can be viewed as a continuous process in which diagnostic information is revised and refined as a normal part of the teaching-learning process.

Developing Goals and Short-Term Objectives

Once a clear understanding of student strengths and weaknesses is determined through the assessment procedures described in the previous section, goals and objectives are then developed. Typically, for every significant weakness that is detected, a broad goal can be developed; correspondingly, for every broad goal, a series of more specific short-term objectives can be constructed. It is toward the accomplishment of these short-term objectives that daily instruction is geared.

Although somewhat time consuming to develop, the payoff for developing clear teaching goals and objectives is substantial. As we have already noted, there is a significant relationship between the clarity of teacher's objectives and the amount of learning that takes place. That is, effective teachers have a clear picture of the specific skills and understandings they want their students to accomplish, and they make systematic efforts to achieve these goals. Keeping this crucial relationship between clear goals and student learning in mind, let us examine how goals and objectives are actually developed.

Formulating Goals.   Goals are derived from both formal and informal assessment procedures and are broad, long-range statements that identify the general academic, social, and adaptive areas in need of attention.

The following are examples of long-range goals established for different students in various skills areas.

Reading
1. Improve ability to use phonic principles to decode words.
2. Increase overall reading skill to the third grade level.
3. Increase oral reading rate to at least 100 words per minute.

4. Improve ability to comprehend written material presented in sixth grade science and social studies texts.

Arithmetic

1. Master the basic multiplication and division tables.
2. Learn to tell time by the hour and half hour.
3. Learn to solve simple word problems.

Written language

1. Improve ability to describe one's experiences through writing simple sentences.
2. Be able to read and correctly complete a simple job application form.
3. Be able to use appropriate punctuation when writing a paragraph.

Adaptive behavior

1. Demonstrate proper toileting behavior.
2. Demonstrate proper use of table utensils while eating.
3. Put on and take off shoes and overcoats without assistance.

Social-emotional behavior

1. Improve ability to start and complete academic tasks on time.
2. Decrease aggressive responses to authority.
3. Increase use of self-control when frustrated or angry.

Goals are usually formulated during the pupil evaluation team meeting. Ideally, weaknesses, which have been determined through formal and informal assessment procedures, are discussed by the team members. Weaknesses that need immediate attention are then converted to long-range goals, which beome the foundation of a student's special education program. In some cases, particular strengths, such as interest in art, music, or athletics, are also used to establish goals. While this decision-making procedure represents the ideal, Ysseldyke and his colleagues, in their study of how pupil evaluation teams actually function, noted that far too much time is spent discussing test results that are unrelated to the development of goals and services needed to teach these goals (Ysseldyke, Algozzine, Rostollan, & Shinn, 1981). This tendency to spend too much time discussing test results at the expense of more practical considerations, such as what should be done to help the student, should be kept in check by all team members, especially those responsible for planning and conducting team meetings.

For more severely handicapped students, goals must stress the development of functional life skills to help the individual become as independent as possible (Brown, Nietupski, & Hamre-Nietupski, 1976). Parents play a critical role in the goal-setting process, as they are in an excellent position to identify specific skills the student needs to function more independently on a day-to-day basis (Stith, 1984).

Formulating Short-term Objectives.   Short-term objectives (see Box 1) represent logical stepping-stones toward the accomplishment of long-range goals. That is, each goal can be subdivided into several more precise, short-range objectives. Mastery of these more specific objectives indicates progress toward the accomplishment of the larger goals. Because writing short-term objectives requires considerable thought, they are rarely formulated at the pupil evaluation team meeting. Rather, they are usually developed by the special education teacher or other specialist (e.g., speech therapist, physical therapist) who is responsible for delivering instruction.

It should be noted that short-term objectives are written in the form of behavioral or performance objectives. That is, each objective should contain a *behavior* that can actually be observed, a *standard or criterion level* that indicates the desired level of achievement regarding the objective, and a *condition* that indicates the time, place, or circumstances under which the behavior is to be demonstrated.

Objective:	Spell at least 95 percent of 150 new words from a second grade spelling list.
Behavior:	Spell 150 words.
Condition:	From a second grade level text.
Criteria:	With 95 percent accuracy.
Objective:	When in a group activity, reduce the frequency of inappropriate laughing or talking out of turn to two or fewer instances per ten-minute period.
Behavior:	Reduce talking out of turn or inappropriate laughing.
Condition:	During group activities.
Criteria:	Two or fewer instances per ten-minute period.

Short-term objectives identify what we will teach and the desired level of proficiency we wish to obtain. They provide the basis for day-to-day planning and instruction geared toward the achievement of each specific objective. Similarly, the effectiveness of our teaching methods and the value of the overall special education program that is provided can be evaluated by analyzing the degree to which the short-term objectives are met (Deno, Mirkin, & Wesson, 1984). Informal and criterion-referenced tests are particularly useful in this respect as test items or observation procedures can be designed to assess each short-term objective. For example, to determine whether the student has indeed reduced talking out to fewer than two instances per ten-minute period, a frequency count of the number of talk-outs during a ten-minute group activity could be taken on a weekly basis.

Modifying Instruction

Once clear behavioral or short-term objectives have been identified, the next logical step is to develop an instructional program to accomplish the stated goals and objectives. In this section we will examine two related questions:

What are some learning principles that seem to be particularly applicable to exceptional students, and what are some promising instructional approaches? As you read this section, keep in mind that the learning principles and instructional programs apply to students from all categories of exceptionality. Any student who demonstrates difficulty learning will profit from a carefully designed instructional program based on the principles introduced in this section.

Effective Learning Principles

Regardless of the textbooks, workbooks, and other materials one selects or constructs for students, there exists a set of principles that helps to maximize student learning. Put in different words, it is not so much the particular textbook or teacher-made material we use to help a student learn reading, writing, mathematics, or how to use self-control, but the learning principles we apply when using these materials that seem to make a difference in how students learn. Several critical learning principles are introduced in this section: (1) planning for small increments of change, (2) using modeling and self-instruction, (3) providing feedback and practice, and (4) using effective communication skills.

Plan for Small Increments of Change.   Nearly twenty years ago, Frank Hewett (1968) advised us to look for "thimblefuls" instead of "bucketfuls" of change when developing programs for emotionally disturbed children. This advice holds as true now as it did in 1968 and is applicable to all exceptional students, not just those with emotional problems. Indeed, the idea of planning for small, step-by-step increments of change represents a cornerstone of instructional planning. To help students experience success, one should break down learning into a series of small, accomplishable steps that can be more readily mastered. These smaller steps become objectives for daily or weekly instruction. Teaching toward these objectives provides a sense of clarity and structure for teacher and student alike (Glass, Christiansen, & Christiansen, 1982).

A clear example of the value of planning for small increments of change is provided by Bryant, Drabin, and Gettinger (1981), who have examined the effects of varying the number of spelling words given to children identified as learning disabled. Over a three-day period, one group of students received three new words a day to learn, another was given four, and another received five new words to learn. Thus, the first group had a total of nine new spelling words, the second group had twelve, and the third group had fifteen. In each group the same methods were used to teach the words. At the end of the three-day period, a spelling test was administered. Bryant found that the average number of words spelled correctly was between six and seven regardless of how many words the student was given. That is, students who received only three new words a day learned as much as those who were given five words a day and obviously experienced less failure in doing so.

The same principle of planning for small increments of change can be applied to learning just about any skill. For example, we may want a student who has difficulty paying attention and completing math to initially finish only five problems in a ten-minute time period. Once the student can routinely fulfill this objective, expectations can be increased bit by bit. Applied to students with more severe handicaps, planning for small increments of change is often accomplished by conducting a task analysis. In conducting a task analysis, a specific task or skill—such as tying one's shoes, using a spoon at the dinner table, making a purchase at a store, or completing a job-related task such as assembling a piece of equipment—is carefully analyzed to determine the component or subskills needed to accomplish the task. Task analysis is most often accomplished by observing someone engaging in the task and then logically analyzing each step and/or skill needed to complete the entire task. For example, in teaching a severely handicapped individual who has not learned to use utensils to use a spoon, a task analysis may reveal the following subskills:

1. Coming to the dinner table and sitting down when asked.
2. Being able to distinguish a spoon from other utensils.
3. Being able to grasp and properly hold the spoon.
4. Being able to place the spoon in a bowl, pick up food, and bring the spoon to one's mouth.
5. Remembering to chew and swallow food before taking another spoonful of food.

The student is then observed to determine which subskills need to be developed, and daily instruction is then geared toward the accomplishment of each specific subskill.

One can see how much influence teachers have on how successful students will be simply by controlling the amount of learning or change in behavior that is expected. Demanding too much change can lead to feelings of frustration, anger, or discouragement, which can cause a student to look for ways to avoid learning. On the other hand, expecting too little can lead to feelings of boredom or a lack of progress.

Use Modeling and Self-Instruction.

How does one actually go about teaching a student a new skill or behavior? Simply telling a student what to do is usually not enough. Instead, it is best to explain to the student what is to be learned and then model or demonstrate the correct procedure, such as how to say a new word, use a particular process in arithmetic, or ask another student to share in the use of learning materials.

The impact of providing a model can be further strengthened by using self-instruction. In self-instruction, the student watches a model (usually a teacher) perform a task or solve a problem. While performing the task, the model verbalizes the steps being followed in solving the problem. Students are then asked to follow and say aloud the same steps demonstrated by the model.

A practical example of the use of self-instruction is provided by Albion and Salzberg (1982) in their study of the effects of self-instruction on the arithmetic performance of educable mentally retarded children. Such children often experience difficulty in learning complex procedures such as renaming in addition and subtraction. Teachers need to apply all their skill in helping many children, not just those who are retarded, learn these and other complex procedures. Instead of simply telling students how to use renaming, Albion and Salzberg provided a model who demonstrated and said out loud the steps observed in solving several addition problems requiring renaming. Students were then taught, through repetition, to verbalize the same steps in completing similar problems. For example, in solving the problem

$$\begin{array}{r} 68 \\ +46 \\ \hline \end{array}$$

the students learned to say the following:

> "First, I look at the two numbers in the right column (point with finger). Let's see, 8 + 6. Which is the top number? Eight! I write an 8 down on my scrap paper." The next step was verbalized in the following manner: "I place six marks next to the 8. Good! Now I start counting from the 8: 9, 10, 11, 12, 13, 14 (touching each mark with a pencil point as it is verbalized). Now I write down the 4 under the first column and put the 1 over the next column. Now what numbers do I add? I add 6 + 4 and the 1 I carried. I write down the 6 on my scrap paper" (p. 126).

In a similar, but less complicated procedure, students with learning disabilities were taught to improve their reading comprehension through modeling and self-instruction (Rose, Cundick, & Higbee, 1983). The students were taught to pause after reading three to four sentences and ask themselves questions about what they had just read. After answering the questions in their minds, they read the next three to four sentences and again asked themselves questions. The procedure of pausing and asking questions was modeled by the teacher and then practiced frequently by the students.

The use of modeling and self-instruction is a powerful tool and should be considered when teaching students any new skill as it often leads to more effective learning (Albion & Salzberg, 1982; Omizo, Radner, & McPherson, 1983). The technique seems to be particularly useful for students who approach tasks in an impulsive manner or who often forget to complete steps in solving a problem despite frequent reminders.

Provide Feedback and Practice.   Simply because a student supplies the correct answer to a problem, decodes a word correctly, or uses the correct sequence of steps in solving a problem, does not mean that the student has thoroughly learned the skill and is capable of demonstrating it consistently and in a variety of settings. In helping students master skills, we must provide ample feedback and practice.

These children are playing an alphabet bingo game and the teacher is assisting by prompting and providing cues. (Photograph by Mima Cataldo.)

Feedback is information that tells the learner how well he or she has performed or what aspects of a task have been performed correctly or incorrectly. Feedback is used in a variety of ways as a natural part of the teaching-learning process as demonstrated in the following examples.

1. In teaching reading to a group of students who have experienced considerable difficulty retaining and learning how to decode words, Mrs. Smith introduces carefully each new word that will appear in the story to be read. She first reads the new word to the group (modeling), then asks the entire group to say the word out loud, and then asks selected individuals to say the word, providing feedback where appropriate as indicated below:

Teacher: Here is the first new word. The word is "clock." A clock can hang on the wall or sit on a table. A clock tells us what time it is. Everyone, say the word "clock."

Group: (In unison says clock.)

Teacher: Good, you said it the right way (feedback).

Teacher: (Pointing to the word "clock," which is written on the chalkboard) Tom, would you please read this word?

Tom: Lock.

> *Teacher:*   Almost, Tom. The word is clock. Remember the first sound
> "C-l-o-c-k" (corrective feedback). Say it again, Tom.

2. Mr. Jones is just beginning to teach a group of boys how to add with renaming. After modeling and verbalizing the correct solution to several problems, he asks each student to come to the board to solve two problems using the same procedure he demonstrated. As the student completed each step, Mr. Jones provided appropriate feedback. When he was reasonably sure that each student could follow the process, he gave them five problems to complete at their seats. While the students were completing the problems, Mr. Jones circulated among the students, praising them when they followed the correct procedure and demonstrating the procedure again to individuals who seemed confused.

3. At the end of each morning, Mrs. Harris conducts a five-minute meeting in which she reviews everyone's classroom behavior. Each student has a particular, daily objective to work toward, such as completing work on time, not getting out of one's seat more than two times, or asking for help when frustrated. As indicated by the dialogue, Mrs. Harris provides feedback to each student in a direct manner.

> John, your objective for the morning was to keep working and not get out of your seat more than two times. I noticed that you got out only once. Good job!

> Sara, your goal was to complete at least ten math problems. You finished eight today so you came close, but didn't reach the goal.

In providing feedback, it is important to make sure it is specific and offered immediately, particularly when a student is first learning a skill. Saying to a student, "That's wrong, do it again," fails to indicate what the student did well and what the student needs to correct. Furthermore, the statement is somewhat negative and can be perceived by some students, particularly those who resent authority, as confrontational or punitive. Instead, the teacher might say, "OK, you added the first two numbers correctly, but then you forgot to carry. How about fixing these problems?"

In addition to providing feedback, ample opportunity to practice new skills is critical, especially for students who require extensive practice and review to learn new skills and concepts. Practice typically involves some form of drill or repetition, such as completing ten addition problems that require renaming each day until the student demonstrates the skill at a high rate of accuracy, or reading aloud a list of words with a particular vowel-consonant-vowel pattern (e.g., cake, bike, time) over successive days until a predetermined level of accuracy is reached. The desired levels of accuracy are usually specified in the short-term or behavioral objectives constructed by the special education teacher.

In providing practice activities for students, several considerations should be kept in mind. First, it is important to review the correct procedure before allowing a student to practice on his or her own. If you recall, Mr. Jones first required his students to come to the board to demonstrate their understanding of addition with renaming before he allowed them to complete problems on their own. Used wisely, this procedure will help students review basic procedures and engage in practice activities with a minimum of errors and frustration.

A second consideration is to provide a wide variety of practice activities to help insure that the student will generalize learning to new situations. Many teachers are frustrated at the seeming inability of students to apply skills in new settings. Being able to read words when presented on flash cards but failing to read them when contained in paragraphs, being able to add math problems when presented on a page but not knowing when to use addition when given a word problem, and the ability to raise one's hand only when closely watched by one particular teacher all represent problems in generalization. Admittedly, teaching for generalization is a difficult and complex problem. As a rule of thumb, we would do well to understand that generalization is not likely to occur by itself and that we must create learning activities with generalization in mind. For example, in helping a student learn to share materials and possessions, we might develop the following sequence of learning activities over a period of several months:

1. Include the student in a small group of individuals who are learning social behaviors such as sharing.
2. Provide a model by having the student watch several students demonstrate sharing.
3. Have the student imitate the models and then role-play the use of sharing in a variety of situations.
4. Help the student use self-instruction when confronted with situations in which sharing can be used (e.g., teach the student to ask himself, "Is this a good time to share?").
5. Engage students in a discussion of the value of sharing. Consider how sharing can build feelings of trust and caring.
6. Ask the student to make a commitment to try to share something once during the day.
7. Provide feedback and praise to the student when seen sharing.
8. Conduct a discussion at the end of certain days in which you ask students to recall a time when they shared during the day and how it made them and others feel.
9. Discuss value issues surrounding sharing. Must we always share?
10. Ask students to look for opportunities at home and on the playground when they used sharing.

Teaching for generalization or skill transference is especially important for moderately to severely handicapped learners who do not readily transfer learning to new settings. Once a new skill—such as feeding oneself with a spoon, asking for directions, starting a conversation, or making a purchase in a store—is learned in the classroom setting, the skill must then be practiced in as many different settings and with as many different people as possible (Stith, 1984). Failure to teach for transfer is likely to result in a situation in which the learner can perform a skill in the presence of only one or two people, usually those who provided the initial teaching, or in only one specific setting.

Use Effective Communication Skills.   While planning for small increments of change, using modeling and self-instruction, the teacher should provide feedback and practice, which represent important mechanical aspects of effective teaching. The quality of the teacher-student relationship is a factor in learning that cannot be overlooked. Indeed, a positive teacher-student relationship lies at the heart of effective learning. As a student feels valued as an individual and understood for his or her own qualities, then possibilities for growth and change emerge. If a student is made to feel demeaned or insignificant by an insensitive teacher, alienation is likely to occur. This alienation may render less effective even the most skillful application of the mechanical aspects of teaching.

How can the teacher-student relationship be enriched? Carl Rogers (1969) identified three conditions that are vital to any helping relationship— genuineness, positive regard, and empathic understanding. *Genuineness* is a willingness to be oneself with students, to be sincere, and to express one's feelings, likes, and interests in a way that will not be harmful. *Positive regard* signifies a respect for the student as a person with feelings, not just someone to fill with facts. The teacher who practices positive regard listens to student's thoughts, ideas, and concerns while still placing limits on misbehavior. *Empathic understanding* represents the teacher's ability to understand experiences or feelings from the student's point of view.

Thomas Gordon (1970) has provided concrete suggestions for enriching the teacher-student relationship by paying careful attention to how we talk with children. When we discuss students' behavior or conduct or listen to their opinions or feelings, how we respond has a direct influence on how students feel. Certain teacher responses such as commanding, threatening, blaming, or criticizing can have a provocative effect, as revealed by the following dialogue between Bob, a sixth grader in a class for students with emotional problems, and Mr. Wing, his teacher.

> *Mr. Wing:*   All right, class, let's begin our independent work. Each of you has a math card to complete. Those of you who don't begin right away will receive a minus grade. (Threatening.)
>
> *Bob:*   (feeling fearful of his math abilities) I hate this stuff. I can't see why we have to work alone.
>
> *Mr. Wing:*   Bob, why do you always have to be the complainer? (Criticizing/name calling.)
>
> *Bob:*   Who's complaining! I just think working alone is dumb.

> *Mr. Wing:* (a little angered) Bob, get to work now! If you don't, you'll be doing the work after school in detention. (Ordering/threatening.)
>
> *Bob:* (angrily) Good! I love detention and you can bet I won't do your lousy work there.
>
> *Mr. Wing:* (loudly) Bob, it's too bad things had to go like this again. Again, your temper got the best of you. (Blaming.) Please go down to the office and finish your work there.

From this brief dialogue you may note that Mr. Wing used a variety of techniques that not only blocked communication, but also created a cycle of stress. The real issue of Bob's feelings of inadequacy was never considered, and Mr. Wing never got the opportunity to use his skills and experience to help Bob with his math. To minimize such fruitless and frustrating encounters, Gordon suggests that teachers use more positive techniques.

1. *Listen carefully.* Demonstrate a genuine concern about the student's ideas, opinions, and feelings. Maintain eye contact with the student and provide nonverbal cues that you are giving full attention (e.g., head nodding to show understanding).
2. *Reflect feelings and ideas.* By taking time to restate, paraphrase, or summarize a student's concerns, you not only show your interest, but also demonstrate your understanding of the student's point of view. Such techniques help build acceptance and understanding and encourage the student to continue sharing thoughts and feelings in a constructive manner.
3. *Use "I-messages."* "I-messages" tell students how you are feeling or reacting to what they are saying or doing, without trying to establish blame. For example, you might say, "I feel frustrated when you say you can't do the work, because I know you can." Such messages describe your own feelings and are less likely to promote stress then "you-messages," which blame or criticize ("You make me angry," "Your attitude is unconstructive," "You are lazy").
4. *Encourage problem solving.* Ask students to identify ways they can solve particular problems instead of telling them what to do (e.g., "What can you do when you get frustrated and need help?"). By asking students to help solve their own problems, you can minimize power confrontations.

In addition to adopting the communication techniques suggested by Gordon, it is important to recognize the effect of nonverbal communication on students. Eye contact, for instance, can convey a message of acceptance and caring or tell a student that the behavior being demonstrated is inappropriate. A hand on a shoulder can communicate awareness of and concern for a student's personal difficulties. Physical proximity, or moving toward a student about to create a disturbance, can be used to prevent potentially disruptive classroom situations. When nonverbal communication is combined with communication techniques like those suggested by Gordon, the student is likely to receive a consistent, positive message from you.

Let us look back for a moment at Bob and Mr. Wing and examine how some of these skills might be applied to promote more positive communication.

Mr. Wing:	All right class, it's time to begin independent work. Each of you has your math card to complete. Raise your hand if you need help getting started. (Instead of issuing a threat, Mr. Wing offers his assistance.)
Bob:	(feeling fearful of his math abilities) I hate this stuff. I can't see why we have to work alone.
Mr. Wing:	(recognizing that Bob's fear of failure causes stress) Bob, can I help you get going?
Bob:	I hate this kind of work. Do I have to do it?
Mr. Wing:	(speaking privately) Bob, I guess you are a little worried about whether you can do this. (Reflecting feelings.)
Bob:	(looking sheepish) Yeah.
Mr. Wing:	Remember how you got over the same hurdle last week? (Problem solving.)
Bob:	Oh, yeah. I took it one problem at a time. When I got stuck on one I asked you for help.
Mr. Wing:	Beautiful! Even though your were frustrated, you didn't let your feelings get the best of you. (Careful listening; reflecting feelings.) I think you can do it again. How about it? (I-message.)

While not all dialogues end in such a positive manner, the advantages of Gordon's effective communication skills are clear. Listening carefully demonstrates a regard for the student as a unique individual with legitimate concerns, feelings, and perceptions. Reflecting feelings can help clarify what may be causing students discomfort. It can also help to avert or defuse a potentially explosive confrontation by providing a chance to drain off feelings of frustration, fear, or anger. Involving students in the process of solving problems indicates your interest in sharing responsibility, and reduces the potential "battle of the wills" (Dreikurs, Grunwald, & Pepper, 1971). In short, these communication techniques help to establish a tone of "teacher with student" rather than "teacher against student." Even if a particular problem is not immediately resolved, the door will be kept open for constructive dialogue at a later time.

The same careful attention to the communication process needs to be paid when working with less verbal and/or more severely impaired students. As adults, we need to recognize nonverbal signs of frustration, discomfort, or excitement and respond to them with physical proximity and clear, direct messages of recognition and support. In addition, it is important to learn what words the student does understand and use them appropriately. Using too many words or providing lengthy explanations may only serve to confuse a youngster who already has difficulty understanding directions and following procedures. In some instances reducing our vocabulary to single words or short phrases will help children better understand our expectations. For example, saying "look at me" or "eyes on me" may be a clear way of communicating the expectation to make eye contact and get ready to receive information or instructions.

Instructional Approaches

The learning principles just introduced are fundamental to any instructional program for any student, regardless of the label or handicapping condition. In this section, a variety of prevalent instructional approaches will be reviewed. Each approach incorporates the learning principles in a different way with some, such as "direct instruction," adhering to the principles in a systematic fashion. As you read each description, it will be helpful to think about how the learning principles are used and what types of students are likely to benefit from the approach.

Direct Instruction.   Direct instruction relies heavily on the learning principles discussed in the previous section. This approach is based on the assumption that learning can be best accomplished by breaking tasks into small parts and then teaching directly toward the acquisition of each step via the systematic use of models, feedback, and extensive practice until the learner reaches a predetermined level of mastery. Criterion-referenced tests are used frequently to determine whether a student has reached mastery or whether additional teaching and practice are needed. This approach is the opposite of discovery learning or student-directed learning, as it leaves little to chance or student choice. The teacher decides what the student is to know, establishes specific objectives, and uses direct methods to accomplish his or her objectives.

An excellent illustration of the direct instruction approach is provided by Pany, Jenkins, and Schreck (1982), who have examined the effects of three different instructional procedures on the vocabulary acquisition of children with learning disabilities. Of the three methods studied, the first two closely paralleled those used by many classroom teachers while the third method represented a direct instruction approach.

1. *Meanings from context.* No direct instruction was provided on word meanings. Instead, students read two sentences, the first containing a target word, the second, which was related to the first, containing a synonym of the target word.

   Student reads: Dan is a real buffoon. He is the funniest clown in the circus.

2. *Meanings given.* Students read a sentence containing a target word. Next, the experimenter provided both the meaning of the target word and a sample sentence using the word as the student might hear it in his/her daily experience.

Student reads: Dan is a real buffoon.

Experimenter says: Buffoon means clown. Teachers do not like their students to behave like buffoons or clowns in school. Read the sentence again to yourself.

3. *Meanings practiced.* Students read a single target word. The experimenter stated a synonym and a sample sentence using the target word. The students then repeated the target word and the synonym.

Student reads: Buffoon.

Experimenter says: Buffoon means clown. Your teacher may become angry if you behave like a buffoon in class. What does buffoon mean?

Student says: Buffoon means clown.

Experimenter says: What does buffoon mean?

Student 2 says: Buffoon means clown.

In this condition, two additional words were presented with the target words to increase the task difficulty and to ensure that students attended to each word. Students were not told that they would be tested on only the two target words. When all four words had been presented, they were reviewed, and the index cards were shuffled. Then the experimenter presented all four cards, one at a time. One student read the word and attempted to state its meaning. The experimenter supplied corrective feedback when necessary. This procedure continued until the student had given correct meanings for all target words on three consecutive trials. The experimenter then repeated this procedure for the second student. (Pany, Jenkins, & Schreck, 1982, pp. 204–205).

On tests to determine how many new words students could read and define, those learning disabled students who were taught via the direct instruction approach (meanings practiced) learned significantly more than those who were taught by either of the first two approaches.

Careful examination of these three experimental conditions reveals that students in the direct instruction condition spent considerably more time practicing the words to be learned than students in the first two approaches. This fact represents an essential feature of direct instruction: that students continue to practice until they reach a predetermined level of mastery. This reliance on practice, with appropriate feedback, is consistent with findings from recent research on effective teaching practices that suggests a link between the amount of time students practice reading or other academic tasks and achievement (Rosenshine & Stevens, 1986). Direct instruction appears to be particularly well suited to helping students master basic skills including initial reading, spelling, math operations, vocabulary development, and basic writing. Direct instruction is the method of choice in teaching basic skills to moderately and severely handicapped learners because it provides the clarity, precision, and repetition these learners require.

DISTAR is an acronym for Direct Instruction Systems for Teaching Arithmetic and Reading (Haring & Bateman, 1977). Originally developed by Carl Bereiter and Sigfried Engelmann for use in head-start programs for disadvantaged preschoolers, the program has extended to teach basic skills in reading, math, and language to elementary-aged children. DISTAR embodies all of the features of the direct instruction approach with the added advantage that all objectives, lessons, and materials have been prepared for the teacher. Thus, rather than designing his or her own lessons, the user follows the detailed *Teacher Presentation Booklet,* which contains daily lessons, including an actual script to follow in presenting examples, questions, and directions to students (Figure 2).

As you can see, the teacher models the correct response, gives students ample practice in making the correct response, and, when needed, provides corrective feedback. Each new skill is carefully introduced and continually reviewed in this step-by-step approach.

All DISTAR lessons are fast paced and designed to elicit frequent student responses, as indicated by the following description:

> A visitor to a typical direct instruction classroom during academic work time probably would observe a small group (4 to 10) of the children engaged in quick, enthusiastic verbal exchange with a teacher or aide. The teacher or aide holds a teacher-presentation book and is presenting tasks (arithmetic, language, or reading) to which the children often respond in unison. The pace is fast and both children and teacher stay on the task. The teacher may be using hand signals somewhat reminiscent of a choir director. Visitors often comment on the enthusiasm, the business-like schedule, *and* the noise level (Haring & Bateman, 1977, p. 168).

DISTAR seems uniquely suited to students who need a great deal of modeling, repetition, and reinforcement to help them learn. This includes many nonhandicapped students who learn at a slow rate, as well as many students who are educable mentally retarded, learning disabled, and emotionally disturbed.

Multisensory Approaches.   If you think about how instruction takes place, you are likely to observe that most academic instruction relies almost exclusively on the visual and auditory senses. The visual channel is used when students are told to look at words, pictures, or demonstrations and then expected to remember what they have seen. The auditory channel is used when students are asked to listen to descriptions or explanations and then

Lesson 1

Before beginning the program, be sure to administer the placement test that is found in the test booklet. Children who make two or more mistakes on the placement test begin with this lesson.

SOUNDS

TASK 1 Teaching a as in and

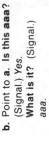

a. Point to a. **You're going to learn this sound.**

b. **My turn. When I touch it, I'll say it. I'll keep on saying it as long as I touch it.** (Pause.) Touch a and say: **aaa.** Lift your finger.

c. **(Pause.)** Touch a and say: **aaa.** Lift your finger.

d. **Again.** Touch a for a longer time and say: **aaaaaa.** Lift your finger.

e. **Again.** Touch a for a shorter time and say: **aaaa.** Lift your finger.

TASK 2 Children identify a

a. Point to a. **Your turn. When I touch it, you say it. Keep on saying it as long as I touch it.** Touch a. The children say aaa. Lift your finger.

b. **(Pause.) Get ready.** Touch a. The children say aaa. Lift your finger.

To correct	1. Say the correct sound immediately. **aaa.**
	2. **Say it with me.**
	3. Point to a. **Get ready.** Touch a. Say **aaa** with the children.
	4. **Again.** Repeat step 3.
	5. Repeat a and b.

c. **Again.** Repeat b two times.

TASK 3 Children discriminate a

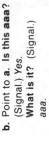

a. Point to the dog. **Is this aaa?** (Signal.) *No.* **What is it?** (Signal.) *Dog.*

b. Point to a. **Is this aaa?** (Signal.) *Yes.* **What is it?** (Signal.) *aaa.*

c. Point to the tree. **Is this aaa?** (Signal.) *No.* **What is it?** (Signal.) *Tree.*

d. Point to a. **When I touch it, you say it. Keep on saying it as long as I touch it.** (Pause.) **Get ready.** Touch a. aaa.

TASK 4 Individual test

Call on different children to do task 3. Have them do a, b, c, or d.

Figure 2. *The first page of lesson 1 of the Teacher Presentation Booklet of DISTAR Reading I (Engelmann & Bruner, 1974), in which beginning readers are introduced to one sound made by the letter a.*

remember what they have heard. In many cases both sensory channels are employed concurrently, as when a teacher asks students to look at a word on the chalkboard as he or she sounds it out.

Of course, other sensory channels can be employed when teaching students. The tactile sense is used when blind people are taught to read via Braille, which relies on touch. The same tactile sense is used when a teacher asks a student to touch and feel a word that has been constructed from sandpaper letters. The kinesthetic sense involves movement such as tracing words, writing new words in a shallow box filled with salt or sand, or actually walking the shape of large letters or words printed on the floor.

While most of us learn through traditional approaches that rely on the visual and/or auditory channels, a number of theorists believe that the tactile and kinesthetic senses should be used when teaching students who demonstrate severe learning problems (Fernald, 1943; Cruickshank, Bentzen, Ratzeburg, & Tannhauser, 1961; Kephart, 1971). These additional senses are employed not to replace the visual and auditory modes, but to supplement them, as it is believed that some students with severe learning difficulties may perceive adequately via the auditory and visual channels.

The original and probably best known multisensory approach was developed by Grace Fernald and described in her text *Remedial Techniques in Basic School Subjects* in 1943. Fernald's approach is called the VAKT approach because it employs the visual, auditory, kinesthetic, and tactile modalities in teaching reading to students who have failed to learn via traditional methods. Her approach was developed at the Los Angeles clinic school of the University of California, which served children with at least normal intelligence who had severe educational problems, particularly in reading and spelling. In today's lexicon, many of these children would likely be identified as learning disabled.

Fernald's VAKT approach requires that the teacher and student work on an individual basis. In an effort to create a positive expectation, the teacher explains that a new method, which has been successful with other students who have had similar reading problems, will be used. The student is then asked to select any word he or she wants to learn, regardless of its difficulty. The teacher then observes the following steps in teaching the new word.

1. The teacher writes the word on a card in letters about one to two inches high. Cursive writing is used so the student will view the word as a single entity.
2. The student then traces the word with his or her fingers, saying the word aloud as it is being traced. The student traces and says the word aloud repeatedly, until it can be written from memory. This may require saying and tracing the word five to ten times.
3. The student demonstrates that he or she has learned the word by writing it several times without the use of the original model. Then, the word is written on a card, which belongs to the student and will be used often in reviewing that and other words that have been learned.

4. After several words are taught in this fashion, the student is encouraged to write a short story or several sentences using the new words. (The author recalls one student, a complete nonreader, whose first sentence was "My father is an electrician." This was learned in the first session.) The student either writes the story with the teacher supplying the spelling of words that have not yet been learned or the student dictates the story to the teacher.

5. After the story is written, the teacher types it immediately or returns it the next day for the student to read. Words that the student cannot read are written on cards and taught using the tracing-sounding method.

6. Each day, the student reviews the growing list of word cards, rereads stories, and writes new ones, which are subsequently typed and returned by the teacher.

7. In most cases, the need to trace new words gradually diminishes as the student becomes more able and confident.

Fernald's approach is not incompatible with the preceding direct instruction format. Notice that both approaches leave little to chance in that they provide continuous practice and review until learning has been demonstrated. The approaches do differ in the respect that teachers who use VAKT encourage students to select their own words and write their own stories, something that can be more easily accomplished when one teacher works with one student. Nonetheless, it would be possible, and in some cases highly desirable, to combine elements of both approaches. For example, the teacher who uses direct instruction and who has preselected words and stories for students to learn could easily have students trace and sound out the new words several times. Using the new words, the students could also be encouraged to write a group story that could be typed and read the following day.

Students as Tutors.   Whether they are classmates or from a higher grade, students can be a powerful resource in teaching exceptional youngsters. In most cases, students are enlisted to provide extra practice and drill, an activity many teachers cannot always provide to their students. Student tutors often review reading words, math facts, and spelling. They may also read stories, listen to others read, play instructional games, and help in art and gym activities. Typically, student tutors work on a one-to-one basis.

The advantages of using peers as tutors have been well established. Peers appear to be more readily accepted by mentally retarded youngsters than adult aides (Vacc, 1978). Academic skills also improve markedly in peer tutoring programs that are well planned and conducted on a regular basis (Mandoli, Mandoli, & McLaughlin, 1982). There are advantages for the tutors as well. In addition to feeling a sense of heightened responsibility, tutors often improve in their self-confidence and academic skills. Finally, the attitudes of peer tutors who work with handicapped students often improve markedly. For example, in one program older elementary-aged volunteers worked with moderately retarded students. After an orientation period that focused on the needs of retarded children, the volunteers helped in a variety of activities, such as putting puzzles together, playing ball, and working on self-help skills like eating, dressing, and grooming. The volunteers were noted to demonstrate more positive attitudes toward the retarded as a result of this direct interaction program (Poorman, 1980).

While the impact of peer tutoring programs has been well established, the effect of any program can be diminished if there is inadequate planning and supervision. In successful programs, tutors generally serve on a voluntary basis, go through an orientation or training period, have clear tutoring objectives and adequate materials, and receive ongoing supervision. In addition, tutoring sessions are conducted according to a regular schedule and occur at least three times a week to yield maximum results.

Cooperative Learning.   In cooperative learning, students work together in small groups of three or four to accomplish a common academic task such as a math worksheet or practice for a spelling test. While students receive grades for their individual performance on informal tests, they can earn bonuses if their group score reaches a predetermined criterion (i.e., if the average spelling test score for the group is 85 percent). Thus, students are encouraged to tutor, drill, monitor, and reinforce each other with the classroom teacher actively helping students learn positive interaction skills through demonstration, reinforcement, and discussion.

The impact of cooperative learning activities on academic achievement and social interaction skills is positive. Typically, students learn as much or more academic content than students who are taught through traditional approaches, while the interactive nature of cooperative learning enhances social interaction skills and acceptance of handicapped learners (Johnson & Johnson, 1981; Slavin, Madden, & Leavey, 1984). Cooperative learning activities seem to be particularly well suited for exceptional students who are placed in regular classrooms. Here, teachers can carefully structure cooperative learning groups to include handicapped and nonhandicapped learners, thus insuring more active participation of handicapped learners in mainstream settings.

Parallel Alternative Curriculum.   In a parallel alternative curriculum (PAC), students learn the same information as their nonhandicapped classmates, but use different materials and learning activities. This relatively new approach enables many secondary-level students with learning problems to take English, science, social studies, and other subjects even though they may not be able to read the text and other materials associated with the class because of low reading skills (Swart, 1979). In the PAC method, it is assumed that reading is an ineffective method of acquiring information. The purpose of the PAC is to provide information through additional senses and to bypass the disability of the student.

Wiseman and Hartwell (n.d.) have provided a thorough list of considerations for a teacher who is preparing a parallel alternative curriculum.

1. Identify precisely what the students will be expected to know and what skills they will be expected to demonstrate. Arrange these expectancies in the desired sequence and develop a list of instructional strategies that will accommodate a multistrata group of students.
2. Compile a list of alternative methods for presenting course content, such as class discussion, group discussion, lecture, student panels, reading text aloud, cassette tapes of class lecture, methods and comprehensiveness of introducing film/video tapes, methods for reviewing films, discussions, lectures, etc.
3. Prepare the desired software before the class begins and have it readily available for use. Software could include tapes of text chapters, transparencies of class notes, video tapes, movies, filmstrips, study guides, etc. Set up a central storing place in the classroom for easy retrieval of software.
4. Identify the audio-visual equipment needed to present the many lessons and determine its availability.
5. Using an established readability formula, determine the readability level of handout materials, the course text, and examinations. Most course textbooks are written at a readability level that is higher than that necessary to express the content area.
6. Compile a list of alternative methods for evaluating student growth, such as reading tests aloud to the class, presenting tests to individuals or small groups of students, having peer tutors administer tests, giving open book/note tests, providing tests in which several students complete the exam together, etc.
7. Identify the entry level achievement skills of your students, such as in reading, writing, spelling (if relevant to the class), note-taking ability, etc. There is no defensible reason for administering an essay exam to a student who has difficulty writing, or a written test for a student with poor reading skills.
8. Identify and match the students' preferred style of learning to the different presentation methods that will be employed. For example, if a poor reader prefers learning textbook material auditorially, provide cassette tapes of the required chapters.
9. Evaluate and teach the study skills necessary for your class, such as structure and usage of the text, note-taking ability, organizing materials, strategies for memorizing, learning vocabulary, etc.

Regular classroom teachers may not be responsible for the entire development of a parallel alternative curriculum. The secondary-level special education teacher is in an excellent position to provide assistance in this area. However, a thoroughly designed parallel alternative curriculum may require a small task force of teachers and curriculum specialists, as there are many materials and alternative learning activities to be developed.

The special education teacher, working alone or in conjunction with a content teacher, can take a less elaborate approach than that proposed by Wiseman and Hartwell and still create a parallel alternative curriculum. For example, using a basic text in any subject area, one could:

1. Highlight, through underlining, important passages the student is to read. This process would enable the student to read only the most critical information contained in the text.
2. Condense and rewrite, in language the student can easily understand, each chapter in the text.
3. Employ a student who is a fluent reader to tape the written (or highlighted or condensed) material.

Microcomputers.   The use of computers in education dates back to the 1960s, when supplemental instruction was provided to students through large, main-frame computers connected to school-based terminals by long-distance telephone lines. The high cost of such systems—in combination with frequent breakdowns, workbooklike programs, and the need for specialized personnel to implement and monitor computer assisted instruction (CAI) programs—led to a low rate of utilization of CAI by schools (Budoff & Hutten, 1982). Today's microcomputers, on the other hand, offer a less costly and more reliable way to individualize instruction than their unwieldy ancestors.

Microcomputers have a wide variety of actual and potential applications, the most common of which is in the area of drill and practice. Drill-and-practice programs have been demonstrated to increase student learning significantly when they are used to supplement, not replace, the teacher's instruction (Burns & Bozeman, 1981). Thus, vocabulary development, math facts, grammar, and any other informational learning can probably be increased significantly by using drill-and-practice programs to supplement teacher-directed learning. Drill-and-practice programs are effective because they require students to make frequent responses and they provide immediate feedback, both of which are conditions related to efficient learning. Some drill-and-practice programs are also designed to stimulate by using formats similar to those found in video games (Chaffin, Maxwell, & Thompson, 1982). Students who might resist spending time memorizing math facts and other information are sometimes attracted by the challenge and novelty of these gamelike programs.

A number of educators assert that drill-and-practice programs, although valuable, fail to realize the potential of microcomputer applications. For example, Hofmeister has suggested that special education students have great difficulty learning concepts and that computers should be pointed toward solving this problem.

Special education pupils are often "special" because of their inability to learn easily from the haphazard structure of the environment. In order to teach concepts to special education populations, we need to have on hand a rich reservoir of examples and nonexamples of the concept we are teaching. These examples and nonexamples need to be carefully matched, and carefully managed. The management and selection of these examples and nonexamples is a complex task well suited to the memory capacities and interactive responsiveness of the computer (Hofmeister, 1982, p. 117).

Microcomputers have already made vital contributions to those with moderate to severe impairments. For example, word processors can be used by children who do not have sufficient fine motor control and/or attention spans to write and rewrite creative stories. The Kurzweil Reading Machine (Kurzweil Computer Products, 1979) has opened new avenues to the blind and the severely reading disabled. This device immediately converts printed matter such as books, magazines, and typewritten text into speech that can be understood by the user. The Type-N-Talk machine by Vortrax allows those unable to speak to type any measage into a microcomputer and then have that message translated to speech. Adaptations can be made for physically disabled individuals who are unable to use a keyboard. Furthermore, individuals with limited language development can make their needs known by pointing to a series of symbols on a board (Bliss, 1965). Recent adaptations now provide computerized, talking "Blissboards" that allow users to communicate with a greater number of people, including those who are not trained to understand Bliss symbols (Bennett, 1982).

In addition to their value in helping individuals learn and communicate, computers are being used to help teachers and administrators cope with growing demands for record keeping and report writing. Computer programs have enabled school personnel to develop extensive lists, specific goals, and objectives that can serve as a pool from which specific goals and objectives can be retrieved for use in developing individualized educational program plans for students. In some cases, teaching strategies, suggested materials, and evaluation procedures are also keyed to specific goals and objectives, thus reducing significantly the time it takes a teacher to construct a written individualized education program. On the other hand, care must be taken to make sure such programs do not merely present the illusion of an individualized program by virtue of their high-technology format. Teachers and administrators must be certain that the goals and objectives reflect specific needs of students as indicated by their unique strengths and weaknesses.

While it is true that microcomputers will likely have a significant impact on the schools, their potential has not yet been fully realized. One survey revealed that, in schools where microcomputers are present, the average use by an elementary age student is less than thirty minutes per week (Center for Social Organization of Schools, 1983). On the other hand, teachers who frequently employ microcomputers in their classrooms suggest that the greatest impact has been in the social organization of the classroom.

Substantial numbers of microcomputers using teachers believe that micros have lead to increased student enthusiasm for schooling; to students working more independently, without assistance from teachers; to students helping one another and answering each other's questions; and to students being assigned to do work more appropriate to their achievement level (Center for Social Organization of Schools, 1983, p. 3).

Like most other innovations, microcomputers will not be a panacea for all of the needs of special students. Rather, used wisely, microcomputers will likely become a useful tool that will allow teachers to provide more intensive and more individualized instruction to students.

Toward Individualizing Instruction.   Individualized instruction is not a concept with one simple meaning. To some, individualized instruction brings forth an image of students seated at individual work stations proceeding at their own pace on computer-assisted instruction or self-paced workbooks. To others, the term implies tutorial or small-group instruction with ample time for questions and answers; for others, individualizing instruction implies a philosophy in which students exercise considerable choice in what they will learn. Although these images represent legitimate examples of individualized instruction, they offer little help in determining what type of instruction is best for a student. That is, simply having students work at their own pace is no guarantee that efficient and effective learning will take place. How then does one decide what may be the best approach for a given student?

Individualizing instruction is not merely a way of presenting instruction

Independent functioning is an important goal of education. This student is learning a skill that can assist her in finding work opportunities. (Photograph by Mima Cataldo.)

to students; it is a process or series of decisions to be made, which reflect upon the most effective way to accomplish goals and objectives established for each student. Therefore, the process of developing an individualized program involves a series of questions about the learner that a teacher must ask, make tentative decisions about, and then test and refine as he or she teaches the student on a day-to-day basis. Although many of these questions have been introduced throughout this section, they are restated to help illustrate the decision-making process.

1. *What are the student's unique strengths and weaknesses?* This question helps us determine basic information about the student, including the current level of skill development in academic, social-emotional, psychomotor, and life-skill areas. Typically, formal and informal assessment procedures, including observations and parental interviews, are used to acquire information about strengths and weaknesses.

2. *What goals and short-term objectives should be established?* No program can be considered to be individualized unless a significant portion of its goals and objectives relates to the student's unique strengths and weaknesses. Goals and objectives are derived from information acquired through the assessment process, but can be revised as new information is acquired.

3. *What specific learning principles seem to be especially relevant for the student?* Students learn at different rates and in different ways. Some learn rapidly and require relatively little practice and reinforcement, while others require carefully sequenced material. As we design instruction for a student, we should consider the following questions:
   a. Does this student need to have instruction delivered in especially small pieces or steps?
   b. Does this student require a great deal of modeling by the teacher, instruction geared to many sensory modalities, and/or self-instruction to help learn new skills and procedures?
   c. Will frequent, carefully introduced practice sessions with immediate feedback need to be provided?
   d. Must I be especially sensitive to possible feelings of frustration, fear, or anxiety when the student is asked to engage in new or unfamiliar tasks?

4. *What instructional approaches may be most compatible with the student's need for small increments of change, modeling, practice, feedback, and other learning principles?* Some of the instructional approaches described in this section may be more or less appropriate for different students. For example, a student who requires a high degree of repetition, modeling, and the slow, careful introduction of new skills would probably learn to read more efficiently and with greater success with the use of a direct instruction approach. The same approach may stifle or frustrate a student who learns rapidly or

who is interested in reading material based on a clearly defined interest. Similarly, an aggressive, self-conscious youngster may refuse to participate in group math lessons but may be more than willing to use a computer program that provides drill and practice through a game format.

The determination as to what instructional approaches are best for individuals often comes about through trial teaching and is not necessarily made during the first week or weeks of school. This point is illustrated in the following teacher's account of how a reading program was developed for two emotionally disturbed, seven-year-old students who began the school year as nonreaders.

> Although seven, Brian and Rene were unable to recognize words or letter sounds or names. Both students had difficulty maintaining attention and were easily distracted by sounds made by other students. Since I had success in teaching several non-readers using a word family approach, I decided to use the following strategy with Rene and Brian during our daily 30-minute reading sessions: I would teach both boys an initial sight vocabulary of about twenty words using a modified Fernald Approach. That is, they would dictate to me several simple sentences in a story which I would then teach them to read using tracing, sounding, and many repetitions. When the students would acquire at least 20 words and some success with reading, I would then teach them to read a word such as "at" and then blend the "at" with a variety of initial consonants such as h (hat), f (fat), and so on. Then, I planned to enter them into the first book of the Merrill Linguistic Reading Series where the very first sentence in the book is "Nat is a Cat" and words with the "at" ending appear frequently.
>
> My strategy worked well for Brian, who remembered each word and began to decode new words on his own. Brian quickly acquired confidence in his ability while Rene seemed overwhelmed with the approach. He never really learned to analyze a word but merely made a guess if the word looked familiar to him. I decided that a more basic approach that would start by teaching Rene to focus in on and identify individual letters and then gradually blend these letters to form simple words was needed. He also needed a great deal of repetition and immediate feedback so I decided to use Distar I. Since Brian did not want to remain at his seat while I introduced each daily Distar lesson to Rene, Brian was invited to participate with Rene, which he did with great enthusiasm. Rene made steady progress in DISTAR and looked forward to each daily lesson as he knew he would experience success. In the meantime, Brian and I continued using the Merrill Linguistic Readers until the end of the school year. Both boys were quite successful. Although outpaced by Brian, Rene learned over 120 words and was able to read simple stories by the end of the year.

A remaining variable in the process of individualizing instruction for students is to determine how to maintain appropriate student behavior and, when necessary, how to improve behavior. These topics are considered in the following section.

Improving Student Behavior

Regardless of their label, many exceptional students have difficulty coping with the demands of everyday living. For these students and their parents and teachers, learning how to delay gratification, share, take turns, engage in daily chores and routines, accept direction from authority figures, interact with peers in acceptable ways, and feel positive about themselves represent goals as important as learning to read and write. The challenge for teachers is to learn effective skills for responding to and managing disorganized or otherwise inappropriate student behavior in a positive, caring way and to help these students develop increasingly more appropriate coping skills. In this section we will examine a number of approaches related to accomplishing these ends.

Provide Structure.   Central to any effort to help exceptional students is the establishment of adequate levels of structure. Many students, particularly those with learning and behavior problems, can perform better when expectations are spelled out in a simple, direct manner and when a daily routine is observed (Hewett & Taylor, 1980).

Clear expectations convey concise, easily understood guidelines for students who may have difficulty understanding directions or paying attention. We communicate our expectations both by the specific requests we make of students on a moment-by-moment basis and by the rules we develop for individuals or groups of students. For example, instead of asking a young, overactive student who has difficulty paying attention to "settle down" or "be good," we may get close to the student, put our hands on his shoulders, kneel down, and look directly into his eyes, and say "sit down now, please." Similarly, a teacher might ask a student to repeat a direction or demonstrate how to do a task before allowing the student to work alone, or ask an impulsive student to finish five problems before engaging in a play activity.

Classroom rules present another opportunity for presenting clear expectations. Again, instead of vague, ill-defined rules such as "follow directions," "work hard," or "be a good citizen," we can develop more precise guidelines:

> Stay in your seat during work time.
> Raise your hand before talking.
> If you get frustrated ask for help.
> Follow the teacher's directions without complaining.
> Line up for recess without running.

If needed, rules and expectations can be personalized by using a check list (Box 4). At the end of each activity period the teacher and student determine whether the stated objective was met and mark the appropriate place.

Because most students with behavioral difficulties have a history of failure in academics as well as in coping with rules, routines, and stress, it is important to develop expectations that are clear and easily achievable. To help

---

Box 4
A Check List of Important Behaviors the Student Is to Demonstrate

Name _____ Date _____

Important behaviors to remember:	Yes	No
1. Complete math seatwork with at least 80 percent correct.	X	
2. Stay in your seat during math. Do not get out without permission more than once.		X
3. Line up during recess without hitting, running, or pushing.	X	

---

students achieve success, think in terms of small, daily steps of improvement rather than dramatic, global changes. Daily accomplishment of such objectives will help bolster self-confidence and develop a commitment to appropriate classroom behavior rather than inappropriate behavior to gain attention.

Another way to provide structure is to develop a predictable, consistent daily routine. Many exceptional students have not learned how to follow a daily schedule of activities or work at one task with sustained attention. These students act before considering the consequences of their actions and have difficulty observing rules. Some may come from chaotic backgrounds in which mealtime, bedtime, and other routines are virtually nonexistent. Others may have impulsive models at home or simply have not yet developed good learning habits. These students need a consistent, carefully established set of procedures to help them become less impulsive. Some suggestions for developing consistent expectations are listed below.

- Develop and follow a daily schedule of class activities. Post the schedule in view of the students.
- To help students become aware of a sense of routine, review the schedule periodically.
- Review class rules prior to beginning each new activity.
- To help students prepare for transitions from one activity to another, remind them that the activity is going to end in a few minutes. Such reminders will help students finish their work or their thoughts and begin to get ready for the next activity.
- To help students start each new activity with a feeling of success, begin with several verbal or written problems that the students can solve with ease.
- When students follow rules or comply with expectations, recognition can come in many forms: a smile, a thank-you, a pat on the back, or a positive note to the students.

While the establishment of a well-structured environment will go a long way toward reducing misbehavior, some students will engage in minor disruptions to gain attention, assert their power over others, or make others feel hurt or devalued (Dreikurs, Grunwald, & Pepper, 1971). Other students may misbehave simply because they are momentarily frustrated and do not know how to manage their feelings in acceptable ways. Long and Dufner (1980) have described an escalating stress cycle that can occur when adults respond to misbehaviors in unthoughtful ways.

1. *Stressful incident.* The stress cycle begins with a painful incident, such as being called a name, feeling incompetent as a result of not knowing how to do an assignment, being reprimanded for misbehavior, or being criticized by a parent or other authority figure.
2. *Feelings.* Stressful incidents, by definition, cause a variety of feelings, such as anger, hatred, revenge, guilt, jealousy, powerlessness, sadness, isolation, and rejection. Although it is entirely normal to experience these feelings, many students with learning and behavior problems experience overwhelming degrees of these emotions, which lead to overt behaviors.
3. *Overt behavior.* Students with persistent behavior problems often lack self-control and vent stress-induced feelings through inappropriate behaviors, such as shouting, arguing, swearing, hitting, withdrawing, teasing, tearing up papers, or becoming sullen.
4. *Teacher reactions.* How you react to the overt behavior is the final component of the stress cycle. If, for example, you overreact to certain misbehaviors, additional stress is likely to result, and the stress cycle begins again on a more intense level. Thus, inappropriate teacher reactions to misbehavior may only serve to further intensify student feelings, behavior, and teacher reactions to the behavior. The cycle may continue until a shouting match or other type of confrontation occurs, in which case both the teacher and the student are likely to experience anger, frustration, or guilt.

Avoiding the Stress Cycle.   How can the stress cycle be avoided? Instead of becoming personally offended or threatened when a student becomes upset, you should remember that the student is probably experiencing strong emotions that need to be reduced. One way to respond is to use some of Gordon's communication skills presented in the previous section. If you recall, Mr. Jones was able to help cope with his frustration by listening carefully, reflecting feelings, and engaging in problem solving. Use of these techniques in a calm, accepting manner enabled the student to begin his work and Mr. Jones to carry on with his lesson.

Not every instance of student misbehavior requires such an involved response as that made by Mr. Jones. Techniques to help you respond constructively to momentary student misbehaviors, which were developed by Redl and Wineman (1952) in their work with aggressive students, have been refined by Long and Dufner (1980). The significance of these techniques is that they offer concrete steps for minimizing misbehavior during ongoing learning activities. The first three techniques are the easiest to implement in that they can be used without stopping the lesson and do not give undue attention to the misbehaving student. The remaining five techniques require more direct efforts.

1. *Planned ignoring.* Certain students misbehave in an effort to gain attention or "get the teacher's goat." Some minor misbehaviors such as talking or whispering, complaining about an assignment, or making inappropriate noises may best be ignored if past experience suggests that the misbehavior will not spread to others and will cease after several moments if not confronted. Ignoring such behaviors has at least two advantages. No attention is paid to the misbehavior, and arguments or confrontations are avoided over relatively minor misbehaviors. These misbehaviors, however, may also be a cue that the student is frustrated and needs help. In such cases, the misbehavior should be ignored but help should be provided as soon as possible.

   The value of ignoring misbehavior is sometimes confused and overstated. Clearly, some misbehaviors may cause harm to others, disrupt the lesson, or set off a chain reaction of similar misbehaviors from other students. These should definitely not be ignored. On the other hand, experimentation with this technique may lead to the understanding that some minor misbehaviors stop when left unrecognized.

2. *Signal interference.* Some misbehaviors can be quietly stopped through a variety of nonverbal signals to the student. These may include eye contact, gestures such as signaling for quiet, facial expressions, and acts such as turning off the lights. These signals can be particularly effective if the student is just beginning a minor misbehavior (pencil tapping, talking to others) and if the student is responsive to your attention.

3. *Proximity control.* Standing near some students can help them maintain composure, keep task oriented, and feel supported. Circulating about the room and offering help or checking work is one example of proximity control. Other examples include placing the student's desk close to your primary work area, sitting near the student during group activities, or sitting or standing next to the student as signs of fatigue, stress, or frustration are noticed.

4. *Tension decontamination through humor.* Humor can occasionally be used to defuse a tense situation and get students back to work. Consider the following example provided by Long and Dufner (1980, pp. 237–238).

   > I walked into my room after lunch period to find several pictures on the chalk board with "teacher" written under each one. I went to the board and picked up a piece of chalk, first looking at the pictures and

then at the class. You could have heard a pin drop! Then I walked over to one of the pictures and said that this one looked the most like me but needed some more hair, which I added. Then I went to the next one and said that they had forgotten my glasses so I added them, on the next one I suggested adding a big nose, and on the last one a longer neck. By this time the class was almost in hysterics. Then, seeing that the children were having such a good time and that I could not get them settled easily, I passed out drawing paper and suggested that they draw a picture of the funniest person they could make. It is amazing how original these pictures were.

Note that the teacher had to feel self-assured to use this technique. Some teachers take things personally and are quick to levy punishment on the entire class or demand a confession from the guilty student. Though tempting, such tactics usually only serve to increase tension and conflict and may result in overly harsh punishment. Use of humor need not be construed as tacit approval of the misbehavior. You can remind students that certain behaviors are inappropriate after the tension has been reduced. Of course, other techniques can be used if the misbehavior persists.

5. *Hurdle help.* For some students, momentary frustration with academic tasks can begin a cycle of stress. Not knowing how to begin a task, becoming stuck on a difficult problem, or being faced with a long series of problems can be a genuine source of anxiety. Knowing in advance how a particular student is likely to react under these conditions, you can take effective steps to help overcome the hurdle and prevent a more serious outburst. Helping the student do the first few problems, assisting the student with difficult problems, or carefully explaining directions to the student are all examples of this technique.

6. *Restructuring the activity.* While it is true that structure and routine are important, occasionally it is helpful to vary an activity in response to the mood or general tone of the classroom. Again, an example may help (Long & Dufner, 1980, p. 238):

The children were just returning to the room after the recess period. Most of them were flushed and hot from exercise, and were a little irritable. They were complaining of the heat in the room, and many of them asked permission to get a drink of water as soon as the final recess bell rang. I felt it would be useless to begin our history study as scheduled. So I told all of the children to lay their heads upon their desks. I asked them to very silent for one minute and to think of the coolest thing they could imagine during that time. Each child then told the class what he had been thinking. The whole procedure lasted roughly ten minutes, and I felt that it was time well spent. The history period afterward went smoothly, the atmosphere within the room relaxed, and the children were receptive.

Note that in this case the orderly transition from one type of activity to another was threatened. Rather than attempting to force the students to comply with the original activity, a slight variation in the structure was used. Another example is switching from a discussion activity to a seat-work activity or vice versa if the activity seems to be provoking confusion or frustration.

7. *Direct appeal.* Direct appeals or requests can be made for students to correct their own behavior. One way to issue an appeal is to simply ask the student to stop the misbehavior ("Please sit down now.") At times your appeals can have greater impact if you provide a basis for the appeal. For example, you can make an appeal on the basis of reality consequences ("If you continue to talk you won't get your work done, and then you won't have time to read your magazine.") This type of appeal reminds the student, in a nonthreatening way, of the consequences of continued misbehavior. You can also make appeals on the basis of peer reactions ("How do you think other students will feel about you if you continue to interrupt them while they are talking?"), preestablished rules ("We have a rule that says only two people at a time can be at the listening center"), or a personal relationship ("All that noise is giving me a headache. Please tone it down."). The basis on which you make an appeal should have meaning to the student. For example, appealing to peer reactions would have little impact on the student who was unaware of or unconcerned with peer reactions.

8. *Physical restraint.* On very rare occasions, a student may become so upset that all self-control is lost. The student may hit himself or herself, throw objects, or begin running about the room with every indication that the misbehavior will continue to accelerate. Firm restraint should be used to prevent the student from doing serious harm to himself and others. A supportive, nonpunitive form of restraint can be used by standing behind the student, crossing his or her arms around the sides and firmly holding onto the wrists. During this episode, sincere concern should be expressed. You should reassure the student that as soon as he or she regains composure, the student will be released. Long & Dufner (1980) suggest that many students go through a cycle from initial anger and rage, to crying and sobbing, to silence, at which point that student may ask to be let go. If you believe that the student has regained sufficient self-control, the student may be released. Obviously, your own physical stature may be a factor. With older students, you may need to call the building principal or other teachers for additional help.

Needless to say, the use of physical restraint is a dramatic and exhausting tactic. It may even have legal consequences. As a rule, advantages and disadvantages of restraint for particular students should be considered at pupil evaluation team meetings. If such a technique is believed to be necessary for a particular student, decisions should be made beforehand as to whether you or other persons will do the actual restraining and whether it will occur in the classroom, hallway, or a quiet office.

The behavior management techniques just reviewed will not be equally effective for all students. Some students may be quite amenable to proximity control, while others will become embarrassed by such closeness. Hurdle help may prove useful for students who need immediate assistance, whereas others can be ignored with the knowledge that their misbehavior will not influence other students and will quickly subside. Indeed, part of the challenge of building a repertoire of constructive behavior management techniques is to identify which techniques work best for specific students.

Rewarding Positive Behavior

Many students, particularly those who have been labeled emotionally disturbed, mentally retarded, or learning disabled, need to learn that it is more rewarding to complete academic tasks and behave appropriately than it is to misbehave. Although most students are rewarded by the satisfaction of completing a task or by the anticipation of a good trade, those who have experienced failure are not so self-directed. For these students, the systematic application of rewards such as praise, special privileges, and tangible items has lead to improved classroom behavior, task attention, and academic performance (O'Leary & O'Leary, 1977).

Praise and Attention.   The careful applications of praise, proximity and approving smiles, and gestures can often serve as a powerful yet subtle reinforcer (Becker, Madsen, Arnold & Thomas, 1967) in the process of developing appropriate student behavior. Thanking a student for raising his or her hand before talking, kneeling down and hugging a child for using an appropriate word or gesture or for demonstrating a new skill such as tying shoes, as well as warmly praising a student for sharing an item or finishing work on time are all examples of the application of praise and attention to reinforce appropriate behavior.

To use praise effectively, the teacher must develop a clear, well-thought-out strategy. First, specific behaviors to encourage and develop must be identified. Then, the teacher must look for or create instances when students can demonstrate the desired behavior. Finally, the teacher must be willing to provide warm and enthusiastic praise when students exhibit the desired behavior. At the same time, paying too much attention to misbehavior must be avoided; otherwise, it may be unknowingly reinforced through attention. Thus, planned ignoring and other management techniques must be used in an effort to pay as little attention as possible to misbehavior.

Feedback.   Closely related to praise is the use of feedback or knowledge about one's performance. Students who have an awareness of their misbehavior as well as their daily objectives are often interested in knowing how well they performed along specific objectives. Thus, we can tell students how many words they spelled correctly, how many math problems they completed in a fixed time period, how many times they talked out of turn, or how often they remembered to raise their hand before talking. In using feedback, the teacher keeps a tally of a particular behavior and then informs the student of his or her performance. Indeed, once students realize that some form of scorekeeping is being used, many are motivated to improve their performance.

Another form of feedback is a good behavior chart or check list, which is completed by the teacher or both teacher and student. Charts such as the one presented in Box 5 list the behaviors the student is trying to improve and provide feedback from the teacher.

Good behavior charts can be reviewed periodically. At logical points, such as the end of a seat-work period, after recess, and after a particular class, the teacher may spend a moment with the student to enter the appropriate code onto the chart. Enthusiastic praise is provided along with the marks that are entered onto the chart. Lower ratings are entered in a matter-of-fact way with encouragement to improve during the next activity.

Students can take increasing responsibility in completing charts as their skill and reliability improve. At the beginning of the charting program, teachers may complete all ratings to insure continuous attention and consistency. As behavior improves, the student may take increasing amounts of responsibility until, finally, the student rates his or her own behavior with you endorsing the student's self-rating. Such a procedure fosters the development of responsibility and self-control.

Box 5
Good Behavior Chart

Student _____ Date _____

1. Reading seatwork completed by 10:15. _____

2. Stayed in seat during seat-work time (9:30–10:15). _____

3. Lined up for recess without pushing, running, or hitting. _____

4. Raised hand before talking during social studies or science class (11:00–11:40). _____

　　　　3 Excellent—All tasks or behaviors completed.
　　　　2 OK—Most tasks or behaviors completed.
　　　　0 Needs improvement—Some tasks or behaviors completed.

Good behavior charts can be easily adopted for use as home-school notes, which often have a positive effect on student behavior (Imber, Imber, Rothstein, 1979). To initiate a home-school note program, a phone call or personal conference between parent, teacher, and student should be conducted to determine whether the parent is interested in this type of program. If so, procedures must be clarified, such as how often the note is to be taken home, what happens if the note is lost or destroyed, what types of ratings or points the student must earn to receive a reward, and what types of rewards will be used. Parents should be reminded to provide the reward only when earned and not to punish the student for poor performance.

Other, less formal home-school notes such as the one presented in Box 6 can be used to bring outstanding achievements or efforts to the attention of parents. Such notes have a distinct advantage in that they emphasize positive student behavior. Notes are generally issued somewhat less frequently than daily performance charts and are used to single out and reward outstanding behavior, attitudes, or good academic progress.

Privileges.   In some cases praise, attention, and feedback may not be powerful enough to change misbehavior. More substantial incentives such as privileges or activities that students may earn for accomplishing predetermined objectives may need to be instituted. The following list represents only a few of the many privileges or activities typically available to elementary and secondary students:

Feed or water animal	Receive extra recess
Pass out papers	Work on a special project
Play a game	Have a class party
Use the class computer	Have TV time at home
Receive a library pass	Read magazines
Listen to a record	Go on a class outing or field trip
Play a game with a friend	Take a spelling test
Read a story to a lower grade	Have no homework

Privileges or special activities should not be given haphazardly. They can be used to reward responsible student behavior according to a carefully worked-out plan. You first identify specific behaviors the student should demonstrate and then privately review them with the student. Privileges or activities that appear desirable are selected by you and the student, and a clear agreement is reached as to what the student must do to earn the privilege. ("After your math is completed you may listen to a record." "If you participate in discussion without yelling or making fun of someone, you may use the computer.") As a general rule, privileges should be offered as soon as possible after the desired behavior occurs. This usually means at the end of an assignment or class period. In some cases, however, substantial privileges, such as attending a special event, may occur at the end of a week or longer. In these cases, care must be taken to reward the student with praise or attention on a more frequent basis. Indeed, the use of privileges does not

---

Box 6
An Informal Home-School Note

Good behavior-gram

To: Mrs. Smith

From: Mrs. Dodge

This note is to recognize outstanding effort by your child in the following areas:

1. Mike has completed all his math and reading work this week. _____

2. Mike has avoided fighting all week. _____

_____

_____   *June Dodge* _____
Signed

---

negate the use of praise. Praise should always accompany the administration of privileges. ("Jack, you did a great job getting your work done on time. Now you have earned ten minutes of free time.")

Tangible Rewards.   When it is determined that praise or privileges are not powerful enough to change behavior, tangible rewards such as popcorn, crackers, juice, stickers, posters, and other items the student can consume may provide the incentive to help a child learn a new skill or behavior. Autistic and other severely and moderately impaired youngsters who are learning fundamental skills such as maintaining eye contact with an adult, imitating sounds or words, pointing to and/or naming objects, completing simple academic tasks, or staying in one's seat for a brief period of time often perform more willingly and learn more quickly when they receive a tangible reward along with enthusiastic praise as soon as they demonstrate a desired behavior. For example, when teaching a child with delayed language development to speak, one may encourage a child to imitate sounds or words in the following manner:

Teacher: (Looking at student) "Say 'ma' . . . 'ma.'"

Student: (Immediately) "Ma."

Teacher: "Great!" (Enthusiastic praise.) (Hands child a piece of popcorn, a tangible reward.)

"Say 'ball' . . . 'ball.'"

Student: (Looks away and does not respond.)

Teacher: (Gently moves child's face toward hers) "Say 'ball' . . . 'ball.'"

Student: "Ball."

Teacher: "Great job!" (Rubs child on back and hands him a piece of popcorn.)

With more skillful students, tangible rewards can be administered after completing predetermined tasks. Indeed, some teachers employ point systems in which desirable behaviors such as finishing a paper on time, working quietly, and helping another student are assigned point values. At the end of the day or week, points are cashed in for specific privileges or tangible items. In some cases, teachers levy fines (response cost) by subtracting a predetermined amount of points for particularly disruptive misbehavior such as fighting, name calling, or arguing with the teacher.

Providing Consequences for Persistent Misbehavior

Successful behavior-change programs place far greater emphasis on rewarding appropriate student behavior than on paying attention to misbehavior. However, some misbehaviors cannot be completely ignored, particularly if they disrupt learning. In these cases, consequences for inappropriate behavior must be spelled out and applied in a consistent manner.

Consequences may vary in degree and complexity. Simple consequences for misbehavior involve the failure to earn part of all the agreed-upon reward or privilege. A consequence for not completing assigned work, for example, would be the failure to earn the specified reward. More serious misbehavior may require additional consequences such as a note or phone call to the student's parents describing the misbehavior, exclusion from class for a short time, or being removed from school for the day. Since some consequences may be relatively drastic, they should first be worked out with the student, building principal, and parents. The following techniques are sometimes used by teachers and administrators.

Time-Out.   Time-out is a flexible procedure in which the student is removed from a desirable activity for brief periods of time (Gast & Nelson, 1977). The most simple application, which may be quite useful for younger students, is to require the student to lower his or her head and rest for two or three minutes. More elaborate procedures may involve moving the student to an isolated area of the room for a specific period or moving the student to the principal's office or similar location. The central purpose behind the use of time-out is to present an immediate consequence, removal from the group or the learning activity, for persistent misbehavior. The assumption is that such a brief period of removal will help the student learn what behaviors cannot be tolerated and will also help the student regain composure so that he or she can participate in the remainder of the learning activity.

Planned Suspension.   A more drastic consequence for persistent misbehavior is sending the student home for the remainder of the school day. This procedure cannot be arbitrarily applied; rather, careful planning between parents and the building principal should be developed. Specific misbehaviors that require suspension must be listed. These behaviors are generally those that threaten the safety of that student or others (fighting, throwing desks or chairs, hitting others, and so on). Procedures for notifying parents need to be established, including who will call home and who will take the student home. Also, parents should be encouraged not to levy severe punishment at home in addition to the suspension, which by itself is a relatively drastic punishment. Loss of some privileges for the remainder of the day may, however, be applied. An example of the effectiveness of planned suspension is illustrated in the case of Bob Jones, an emotionally disturbed student.

> Bob Jones spent half-days in a regular third-grade classroom and a self-contained class for emotionally disturbed children. The use of good behavior charts and privileges helped him to complete assigned work on time and without talking out of turn. However, on several occasions, Bob entered the regular classroom after recess in a rage, throwing chairs and flipping over several students who were already seated at their desks. On each of these occasions, the special education teacher was summoned to restrain Bob. These outbursts continued and his parents were consulted over the telephone. A plan was worked out that involved Bob's removal from school for the remainder of the school day if he demonstrated chair or desk throwing or attacked any student. The special education teacher was to remove Bob from the classroom and then call the parents, who were to come to school and take him home for the day. These consequences were discussed with Bob, who indicated his understanding of the limits. On the very next school day, Bob again threw several chairs upon entering his classroom at the end of recess. The special education teacher removed him and called his parents. Bob became very anxious and promised not to throw chairs again if he could stay in school. Despite Bob's apologies, the consequences were carried out in as calm a manner as possible. The special class teacher emphasized that Bob knew the limits and consequences. As a result of this suspension, Bob did not throw chairs, desks, or any other objects for the remainder of the school year.

A related form of planned suspension is in-school suspension. Here, the student may be sent to a particular rom that is designated for such a purpose and monitored by a teacher, administrator, aide, or secretary. The student is afforded little opportunity to interact with other students or adults, the message being that time to think about appropriate behavior and consequences for misbehavior is needed. This procedure lies between time-out and removal from school for the entire day. The procedure may be a useful compromise if parents are unable or unwilling to participate in a planned suspension program.

Several points about the use of consequences for persistent misbehavior need to be stressed. First, consequences should not be used in the absence of incentives for positive behavior. Remember, an important goal is to help students learn that appropriate behavior is more likely to receive attention and recognition than inappropriate behavior. Second, consequences should be clearly spelled out to the student at the beginning of a systematic behavior change program. The student should not only know what behaviors he or she is expected to demonstrate and what rewards there will be, but also what consequences will be applied for serious misbehaviors. Third, a system in which the student receives one or two warnings or reminders before applying the consequences may be instituted, except in cases of harmful behavior. However, keep in mind that too many reminders may result in too much attention being paid to misbehavior. Finally, if the student exceeds the limit and the consequence must be applied, do not accept pleas, promises, or requests for another chance. Giving in may inadvertently teach students that they are not responsible for their own actions.

Teaching Children Social Skills

Although rewarding students for demonstrating appropriate behavior is an effective behavior management technique, the use of rewards alone is not always an efficient way to develop new social skills. Some students need specific instruction in how to interact constructively. A relatively new area of attention is the development of social interaction skills through direct instruction techniques of modeling, guided practice, reinforcement, and discussion. The use of these techniques is based on the assumption that children with poorly developed social skills and low self-control need careful and systematic instruction in learning how to behave and interact with others just as some children with specific academic deficiencies need direct instruction in academics.

An excellent example of the use of direct instruction techniques to develop social skills is the comprehensive curriculum developed by Jackson, Jackson, and Monroe (1983). In their program, seventeen social skills are identified and then developed in a series of well-organized lessons. The skills are listed in Box 7. Each lesson proceeds in a rather straightforward manner. In teaching students how to offer help (skill 10), the teacher describes and then demonstrates ways to offer help. Students are then asked to identify constructive behaviors demonstrated by the teacher to make sure they have focused on the correct behaviors. Then students are given various role-playing situations in which they practice the skill of helping others (e.g., A kid you don't like is on crutches and trying to carry his lunch box and library books). The teacher engages students in a discussion regarding the merits of offering to help others by asking questions such as, "Why do you think it is important to offer help to others?" The teacher then helps students consider ways in which they can demonstrate the behaviors in school and home situations.

Box 7

Core Social Skills (From Jackson, Jackson, & Monroe, 1983, pp. 11–12)

Skill 1: **Introducing**
To introduce yourself to someone, you:
—Use a pleasant face and voice.
—Look at the person.
—Tell the person your name.
—Ask for the person's name.

To introduce two people who don't know each other, you:
—Use a pleasant face and voice.
—Look at each person.
—Tell each person the other's name.

Skill 2: **Following Directions**
To follow directions, you:
—Use a pleasant face and voice.
—Look at the person giving the directions.
—Say "OK."
—Start to do what was asked right away.
—Do it satisfactorily.

Skill 3: **Giving and Receiving Positive Feedback**
To give positive feedback, you:
—Use a pleasant face and voice.
—Look at the person.
—Tell exactly what you like about what the person did.
—Tell the person right after it was done.

To receive positive feedback, you:
—Use a pleasant face and voice.
—Look at the person.
—Acknowledge the feedback by saying, "Thanks" or, "You're welcome."

Skill 4: **Sending an "I'm Interested" Message**
To send an "I'm interested" message, you:
—Use a pleasant face.
—Look at the person.
—Keep your hands and body still.

Skill 5: **Sending an Ignoring Message**
To send an ignoring message, you:
—Keep a pleasant face.
—Look away or walk away from the person.
—Keep a quiet mouth.
—Pretend you're not listening.

Skill 6: **Interrupting a Conversation**
To interrupt the right way, you:
—Use a pleasant face and voice.
—Wait for a pause in the conversation.
—Say, "Excuse me."
—Look directly at the person.
—Then talk.

Skill 7: **Joining a Conversation**
To join a conversation, you:
—Use a pleasant face and voice.
—Look at the person.
—Wait for a pause.
—Say something on the topic.

Skill 8: **Starting a Conversation and Keeping It Going**
To start a conversation and keep it going, you:
—Use a pleasant face and voice.
—Look at the person.
—Ask questions about the other person.
—Tell about yourself.

Skill 9: **Sharing**
To share, you:
—Use a pleasant face and voice.
—Divide up something there's not much of, so others can also have some (if appropriate).
—Take turns (if appropriate).

Skill 10: **Offering to Help**
To offer to help, you:
—Use a pleasant face and voice.
—Notice something that you can do for someone.
—Ask if you can help.
—If that person says "yes," then you do it.

Skill 11: **Compromising**
To compromise, you:
—Use a pleasant face and voice.
—Think of a way both people can get something that they want.
—Suggest it.

Skill 12: **Asking for Clear Directions**
To ask for clear directions, you:
—Use a pleasant face and voice.
—Look at the person.
—Ask for more information.
—Repeat the directions to the person.

Skill 13: **Problem Solving**
To solve a problem, you:
—Take a deep breath to get a calm body and good attitude.
—Think of at least three different things you can do.
—Pick the best one for you.
—Try that one first.

(continued)

Box 7
(continued)

Skill 14: **Using Positive Consequences**
To reward someone, you:
—Use a pleasant face and voice.
—Do something nice for the person.

For example, you could do the person a favor, thank the person, give the person a hug, or share something.

Skill 15: **Giving and Receiving a Suggestion for Improvement**
To give a suggestion for improvement, you:
—Use a pleasant face and voice.
—Say something nice on the topic.

—Make the suggestion.
—Thank the person for listening.*

To receive a suggestion for improvement, you:
—Use a pleasant face and voice.
—Listen to the suggestion.
—Make no excuses.
—Thank the person for the suggestion.

Skill 16: **Handling Name-Calling and Teasing**
To handle name-calling and teasing, you:

* When using with young or low-functioning children, substitute these components: "I like the way you . . . ," "It might be better if you . . . ," and "Thanks for listening."

—Keep a pleasant face.
—Take a deep breath to get calm.
—Look away, or walk away if you can.
—Use positive self-talk (say to self, "I am calm," etc.).

Skill 17: **Saying "No" to Stay Out of Trouble**
To say "no," you:
—Use a pleasant face and voice.
—Take a deep breath to get calm.
—Look at the person.
—Keep saying "no."
—Suggest something else to do.

If suggesting something else doesn't work, you:
—Ignore and walk away.

Summary

Three broad areas related to effective teaching practices have been discussed: (1) planning and organizing instruction, (2) modifying instruction, and (3) improving student behavior. Central to these areas is the IEP, which serves as a critical tool in planning, organizing, implementing, and evaluating a student's program. The IEP requires teachers to provide a clear description of their goals, objectives, and methods. Although the need to develop a written IEP early in the school year or soon after a child has qualified for special education services puts teachers under pressure to quickly determine goals and methods, skillful teachers continually assess student strengths, weaknesses, and learning patterns and revise their teaching strategies as they become more in tune with their students. It is this dynamic process that can be referred to as the artistic aspect of teaching.

These teaching practices are appropriate to students regardless of their category of exceptionality. The practices reviewed are not meant to be exhaustive. Rather, they have been presented to illustrate a variety of techniques available to help students who demonstrate difficulties learning academic skills and behaving appropriately.

Individualizing instruction for students can be accomplished by focusing on several key questions, including:

1. What are the student's unique strengths and weaknesses?
2. What annual goals and short-term objectives should be established?
3. What specific learning principles seem to be particularly relevant for a student? In particular, how specific must day-to-day instruction be in terms of increments of change, modeling, reinforcement, practice, and feedback?
4. What instructional approaches are most compatible with the student's learning needs?

These questions can begin to be addressed through completing an IEP. This point of view indicates that there is a clear strategy related to effective teaching. Developing clear, concrete learning objectives and then selecting approaches that most efficiently accomplish objectives is clearly related to student progress.

Chapter 7

James W. Black

Joy Casey-Black

James W. Black is a doctoral student in the Division of Special Education and Rehabilitation, Syracuse University. He has been a teacher of students with mild, moderate, and severe disabilities within the Syracuse City School District. He is presently involved in developing curricula and working with parents and teachers to prepare students for active participation within integrated school and community environments.

Joy Casey-Black is currently a preschool teacher at Jowonio School in Syracuse, a preschool program that mainstreams children with a variety of disabilities alongside their typical peers. She is also a student in the master's degree program at Syracuse University, in the Division of Special Education and Rehabilitation. Joy's present interests focus on issues of functional curricula for preschool-age children.

Technology and Practice

After reading this chapter, you should be able to:

1
Discuss the importance of envisioning student outcomes.

2
Define the criterion of ultimate functioning.

3
Describe the advantages of using technology with students with severe disabilities.

4
List teacher behaviors that facilitate multidisciplinary team decision making.

Can Johnny learn? Yes, and we can answer without even knowing him. This essential assumption, that all people can learn, is also implicit in the Federal Education for All Handicapped Children Act (Public Law 94-142 of 1975). Not only are all people educable, but also they are capable of achievement beyond what we, as educators, ever previously imagined. For example, envision the following educational achievements.

- Ronald will be a poet. He has cerebral palsy, which limits his hand movements, but he has learned to do word processing on his Apple IIe computer with special software. He painstakingly composes his poetry by selecting one letter at a time by slight movements of his head.
- Kathy will be a lawyer. She is blind and has learned to review textbook materials on audio tape to stay at the top of her high school class.
- Brian will be a cook's helper. After experiencing severe mental retardation and having been locked up in an institution for fifteen years, Brian received community-based vocational training through his home school district. He just landed his first job at Pizza Hut at the minimum wage rate.
- Missy will talk. Her new hearing aid, auditory training, and early intervention have begun to improve her oral language development. She attends an integrated preschool program.

Ronald, Kathy, Brian, and Missy are symbols of recent achievements in special education. They have benefited from the advancing frontiers of learning and teaching. They represent a model for comprehensive educational efforts, ranging from preschool through postsecondary programs. Within this model, programs for handicapped individuals will begin early and will provide intensive curricula and technologies to maximize each learner's potential.

This chapter reviews innovative instructional issues and practices used in the education of children and young adults with unique and individualized educational needs. It examines educational programming for children who experience hearing impairments, severe mental retardation, visual impairments, and impairments to motor functioning. Because of the individualized nature of students' disabilities, we will be reviewing educational practices of teachers working with very divergent groups of students. The theme that unites Ronald, Kathy, Brian, and Missy is one of positive learner outcomes through the use of innovative technology and appropriate curriculum. These positive outcomes can be achieved within integrated educational settings.

Throughout the country, children with even the most severe disabilities are receiving their education alongside their nondisabled peers within regular schools, classrooms, and community environments. Intensive services designed to meet children's individualized educational needs are being delivered within the mainstream of school and society. There, children with all types and degrees of disability benefit from ongoing opportunities to interact with, observe, model, and develop friendships with other less disabled and nondisabled citizens.

Envisioning Student Outcomes

Consider an example of an instructional program for a multiply disabled adolescent who experiences severe mental retardation and motor impairments. As part of her educational program at her neighborhood middle school, Linda has begun to receive instruction in life skills within the community. The following narrative, occurring in a grocery store near Linda's school, describes an example of community instruction.

> With help, Linda places her apricot juice and granola bar on the checkout counter at the P&C grocery store. Her teacher, Dana, guides Linda's hands back to the open purse that is hooked on the side of Linda's wheelchair. Linda is learning how to purchase a snack in the community. Her head shakes side-to-side as she lets out a brief screech.
>
> The cashier looks up and smiles. About this time every Tuesday and Thursday, Linda, Dana, and another student from the middle school pass through her checkout line. She wonders how Linda will do today. After totaling both items she looks over and says, "Okay Linda, that will be eighty-seven cents today."
>
> Linda glances at the cashier's face but makes no movement toward the money in her purse. The cashier tries again and says, "Linda, that's eighty-seven cents please." Dana lightly prompts Linda's right hand toward her purse. Linda responds by grasping the envelope lying just inside her purse. The envelope has a dollar bill paper-clipped under the flap. On the other side of the envelope the following message is printed: Please put my change back into this envelope and paper-clip it closed. Thank you! As Linda pulls her hand out with the envelope, Dana positions herself to provide physical assistance if needed. But today, Linda hands the money to the cashier *on her own*. The cashier grins at Linda and Dana. As she hands the change back to Linda she says, "You're doing great, Linda!" Although her school records and reports state that she is severely retarded and has no language comprehension, Linda's face appears to beam with pride and pleasure.

This brief four-minute period of instruction represents an array of instructional decisions and efforts on the part of significant others in Linda's life. Her parents, special education teacher, speech-language therapist, physical therapist, and occupational therapist had cooperatively made the following educational decisions and efforts.

1. All team members agreed that Linda should learn to more actively participate in a community shopping routine. Her parents suggested the Big M grocery store near their home and the school.
2. The special education teacher and the occupational therapist went to that store and engaged in purchasing a two-item snack. They broke

down the sequence of steps into small parts and adapted them for Linda's physical disabilities. For example, they knew that Linda would have great difficulty receiving and holding change in her hand; thus the occupational therapist suggested the idea for the change envelope adaptation.

3. The special education teacher began to provide instruction in the identified skill sequence. She assessed Linda's performance, targeted specific skills (e.g., reaching into purse and handing money to the cashier), and gradually decreased the amount of assistance she provided to Linda. Other multidisciplinary team members shared in the problem-solving process during weekly review meetings.

This example has illustrated the educational outcomes that can be attained through a process of envisioning a student's fullest participation in an environment of concern, engaging in an ongoing decision-making process, and generating curricular content and individualized adaptations in order to achieve the envisioned outcome.

An Instructional Perspective on Disability

Because of her intellectual and motor impairments, Linda required extra instruction and assistance from society to learn grocery-shopping skills. Most of us probably learned shopping skills incidentally by observing others and applying the math and reading skills that we learned at school. What characterizes people with cognitive, motor, and/or sensorial impairments is not what they can and should learn, but rather the intensity of the instructional technology and societal support that they require. Gold (1980) has argued that "the mentally retarded person is characterized by the level of power needed in the training process required for her to learn, and not by limitations in what she can learn" (p. 148). Gold offered the field of special education a powerful reconceptualization of mental retardation when he proposed an alternative definition:

> Mental retardation refers to a level of functioning which requires from society significantly above average training procedures and superior assets in adaptive behavior on the part of society, manifested throughout the life of both society and the individual (Gold, 1980, p. 148).

From this sociological perspective, disability does not reside solely within the individual, but is found in the interaction of an individual and the levels of instructional technology and assistance made available to that individual by society. Fortunately, instructional technologies and adaptive devices for people with disabilities are rapidly evolving and being disseminated. For example, we presently have the instructional methodology to shape and increase the rate of vocational production (Bellamy, Peterson, & Close, 1975; Gold, 1976; Wehman & Hill, 1985). Applied researchers have documented nonpunitive educative procedures to decrease aggressive and self-abusive behavior patterns (Horner & Bud, 1983; Whitman, Sciback, & Reid, 1983;

Whitman, Hurley, Johnson, & Christian, 1978). We now have adaptive technologies that enable people with severe disabilities to control their living environments via personal computer systems and robotics (Behrmann & Lahm, 1984), attain independent mobility via electric wheelchairs (Stout, 1979), drive automobiles (Less, Colverd, Demauro, & Young, 1978), participate in sexual relationships (Mooney, Cole, & Chilgren, 1979), and communicate their thoughts using only a single voluntary movement (Vanderheiden, 1978). This is truly an exciting time for educators.

This chapter explores a process of envisioning the maximum participation of all students within valued lifestyles. It examines the nature of educational decision making with particular emphasis on the use of a multidisciplinary team approach. Finally, it reviews examples of innovative curriculum design and state-of-the-art technology for children and young adults through case studies of students with identified hearing, intellectual, visual, and motor impairments.

Throughout the discussions are illustrations of the concepts presented through case studies and examples drawn from the authors' work in education and from the experiences of other professionals, parents, and consumers of special education services. Within the case studies, descriptive information (name and sex) has been changed to maintain students' confidentiality. In some instances, situations have been modified or combined to highlight a relevant point.

The first important step in designing instructional programs for students is to envision desired outcomes. As educators, we need to create ideals of excellence for all students, including those with the most severe disabilities.

Maximum Participation for All

We envision disabled children and young adults assuming significant social roles within their communities. Alongside their nondisabled peers they will be workers, citizens, consumers, friends, and lovers. As educators, we can help make these valued roles attainable.

Valued Social Roles

Wolfensberger (1983) has stated that "the most explicit and highest goal of normalization must be the creation, support, and defense of valued social roles for people who are at risk of social devaluation" (p. 234). Wolfensberger has shown that two types of intervention strategies are basic to effective human services. He has proposed the term *social role valorization* to describe this ideal human service model. As educators striving to provide valued social roles and life conditions for our students, we may engage in these two types of related intervention activities by developing students' competencies and by enhancing students' images (Wolfensberger, 1983).

The most frequent type of intervention within educational programs seeks to increase students' competencies. We teach students to read, write, reach, grasp, walk, communicate, work, purchase items, and to perform a wide range of other functional skills. In an attempt to increase students' competencies, we may teach them to appropriately use technological aids such as electric wheelchairs, augmentative communication devices, or pocket calculators. We may also use specialized instructional procedures. We break down learning tasks into very small units (task analysis), gradually reduce the level of assistance (fading), and ignore some types of misbehavior (extinction). These are just a few specialized instructional procedures. Others will readily come to mind.

Many children in our society will achieve valued social roles and life conditions without specialized educational services. They progress, more or less steadily, through the regular education system. They may graduate and go on to employment or higher education. Other students require specialized and powerful educational interventions to maximize their potential. They may require the expertise of specially trained instructional staff, more intensive staffing allocations, instruction within the community, and/or prosthetic technologies. The next section examines the nature of the decision-making process in making these critical choices.

Integration with nondisabled peers provides opportunities for interaction, friendship building, and skill development. Nicole, who experiences a severe hearing impairment, attends a regular kindergarten class. (Photograph by James W. Black.)

An equally important class of actions to consider when striving to create valued life conditions for disabled students is the enhancement of the students' images within the perceptions of others. To enhance students' images in the perceptions of others, we try to avoid stigmatizing them by our interventions. Consequently, we try to provide educational services within regular schools and community settings, avoid congregating large groups of disabled individuals, and demonstrate and model a high degree of respect for students by treating them in a manner appropriate to their chronological age. Again, these are just a few of many possible examples of means of enhancing students' images and competencies.

Consider the following principles in envisioning futures for all children, regardless of the type or degree of their disability.

- All citizens should be actively prepared for, and have available to them, homes, jobs, and the opportunities to develop relationships and friendships with a wide range of other disabled and nondisabled citizens.
- We now have instructional methods and technologies that will allow children who were previously regarded as "ineducable" to become participating members of society.
- As teachers and practitioners, we can have a powerful impact on the lives of the children, young adults, and adults whom we teach.

Parents typically have powerful visions for their nonhandicapped children. They may want their children to become doctors, lawyers, or mechanics. Most of all, they want their children to be happy and productive. Within the new educational partnership between parents and teachers, we need to support the visions that parents possess. The fact that their child has a severe disability does not preclude their achieving a valued and rewarding lifestyle. Consider one parent's experience.

A Parent Perspective

"They told me to put Alex in an institution when he was only 11 months old. My pediatrician said that he would never learn to walk, talk, or be independent. Thank God, I ignored that advice. The doctor was right about his walking and talking. But Alex is becoming more independent in many other activities. He helps me in the kitchen by putting away the silverware, he plays video games with his brother, he is even learning to work in a supervised vocational training site within our community as part of his special education program." Sharon is speaking about her sixteen-year-old son who has multiple handicaps and who currently attends a regular public high school within his school district.

It was difficult during most of his early school years. The only choice of placements offered to us then was a special school for other children like him, about twenty miles away from our community. Even though they seemed to have a nice facility, and large numbers of specially trained staff, Alex never seemed to learn things that he could do at home. During those years I almost gave up hope that Alex could someday do many of the things that other kids did.

I'm satisfied with his school program these last few years. Our school district finally started a program in a regular high school for students with multiple disabilities. Now Alex goes to the same school as his brother. He spends part of his school day in a special class, part in regular classes like homeroom, industrial arts, and home economics, and part in the community. He's learning to cook, have friends, go shopping, and to work in the real world. I know that Alex will always need a lot of help, but I still want him to have the kind of life that we all enjoy. It's not only a matter of teaching him to be more independent, but also a matter of getting others to accept him for what he can do, and not judge him by the many things which he can't do. My hopes for his future are getting even stronger.

It's clear from Sharon's experience that when parents, educators, and society share similar visions for children with disabilities, those visions begin to become realities. As with most change the process happens slowly, a little bit at a time. Educators' intervention practices can facilitate positive growth in students. Our daily, long-range decisions greatly influence the achievement of our educational visions.

Making Educational Decisions

Teachers, related service providers, and parents regularly face critical decisions about the design and implementation of educational programs. Should we teach Terry to use sign language or to use a communication board instead? Will John learn needed vocational skills best in his classroom or in a community-based vocational training site at a real workplace? How much of her school day should Karen be integrated with her nonhandicapped peers? Is a segregated school for only handicapped children an appropriate educational setting for Kevin?

As we participate in an ongoing educational decision-making process, we are challenged by an increasing array of choices. How do we know we are fostering the maximum potential for participation of each child or young adult? After all, children vary considerably in their abilities, motivations, and preferences. By what standard can we evaluate our educational interventions with students who experience severe disabilities?

One option is periodic evaluation of a student's progress toward long-term educational outcomes. Typically, the outcomes involve active participation in a variety of natural school, family, and community environments. This has been conceptualized as the "criterion of ultimate functioning." Because of the range in ages, skills, and abilities of the students we are considering in this chapter, ultimate functioning has a broad range of meanings.

The Criterion of Ultimate Functioning

In a critical analysis of many accepted educational practices of the period, Brown, Nietupski, and Hamre-Nietupski (1976) formulated the "criterion of ultimate functioning." Based on an analysis of the educational outcomes of programs for students with severe disabilities, the criterion of ultimate functioning offered a new standard by which to evaluate the outcomes of our special education services.

> The criterion of ultimate functioning refers to the ever changing, expanding, localized and personalized cluster of factors that each person must possess in order to function as productively and independently as possible in socially, vocationally, and domestically integrated adult community environments (Brown, Nietupski, & Hamre-Nietupski, 1977, p. 8).

Based on this criterion, we would no longer evaluate our educational programs on the numbers (rather than importance) of the skills learned by students, the amount of direct therapy time available, or the staff-to-student ratio provided. Instead, we would begin to reference our educational progress to the requirements of the typical integrated environments found within our communities. Because of the significance of this principle to the concept of meaningful and preparatory education, we will look at each of its components in more detail. In the following text, major sections of the "criterion" are repeated and then discussed in more detail.

Let us begin by examining the first section of the definition of the criterion of ultimate functioning: "the localized, and personalized cluster of factors that each person must possess." The skills required for participation in community life by individuals vary. They change over time and are strongly influenced by local conditions and factors. They vary from city to city and individual to individual relative to a person's age. For example, the requirements for independent travel vary widely from community to community. In one city, use of public buses must be learned. In another, the subway system is the best means of transportation. In still another primarily rural area of the country, no bus and subway system is available, thus requiring walking (or bicycling) or use of a private taxi service.

Next, we consider the section of the definition that states: "in order to function as productively and independently as possible." Notice that the emphasis is again on the individual, and his or her ultimate functioning. The inclusion of "as possible" is an important concept. The criterion of ultimate functioning acknowledges the fact that individuals will differ in their levels of achievement in particular skill areas, in this case their levels of production and independence. However, Brown and his colleagues were asserting that *all* people can attain some degree of production and independence and that this has value. Furthermore, this attainment can be achieved dramatically with the provision of appropriate educational services.

Finally, the criterion of ultimate functioning refers to "integrated adult community environments." In the recent past (and in many locations today),

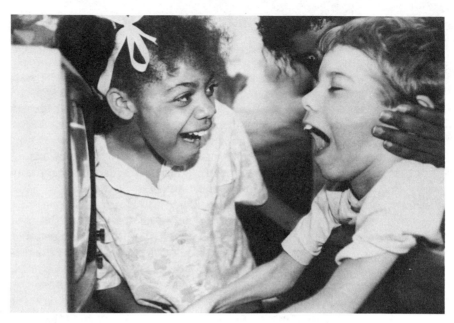

Personal computers can enhance the academic and communication skills of children with severe motor disabilities, as well as foster interaction between children. During their year together in second grade, Marc and Wilcreshia developed a close friendship. (Photograph by James W. Black.)

people with disabilities were restricted to special schools, sheltered workshops, adult daycare institutions, or recreational programs for only handicapped individuals. "Functioning" in these environments refers to acceptance by, interactions with, and equal access to the places used by nondisabled individuals in the community. Integrated adult community environments include real work sites, grocery stores, restaurants, shopping malls, public transportation, and homes in the community. For many individuals with visual, hearing, or motor impairments, integrated environments of concern also include postsecondary education and professional careers. An emphasis on teaching students the age-appropriate skills required to access and participate in a broad range of integrated community environments is an important corollary to the "criterion of ultimate functioning."

In order to achieve the criterion of ultimate functioning, many students will require the expertise of specially trained instructional staff, more intensive staffing allocations, community-referenced curricula, and/or prosthetic technologies. Individuals in diverse roles will need to function cooperatively to help students achieve their goals. The next section examines the nature of decision making within a multidisciplinary team approach.

Multidisciplinary Team Decision Making

Public Law 94-142, in establishing the right of all children to a free, appropriate public education, dictates the provision of related services by public educational agencies as necessary to enable each handicapped child to benefit from his or her educational program and to achieve those individualized educational goals targeted in the student's individualized education plan. The provision of such related services is critical for the success of educational programming for many students with sensory, motor, cognitive, or multiple disabilities. Without a combined team approach that responds to the full range of a student's needs, educational services become fragmented, rather than planning for the total student.

What are such related services comprised of? Related services refer to noninstructional, supplemental services such as special transportation, psychological services, as well as physical, occupational, and speech-language therapy, "interpre-tutors" for students with hearing impairments, and mobility instructors for students with visual impairments. This cast of characters who share responsibility for designing and implementing an educational plan for a student may appear overwhelming. How does one coordinate and integrate the information content and growth strategies, in short the perspectives, of such a variety of practitioners to provide a holistic educational program for a student? This is the challenge and the responsibility of all members of a multidisciplinary team.

Team Members and Their Roles

Special Education Teacher.   The major responsibility for coordinating and orchestrating educational programming for a student lies with the special education teacher. The degree of direct involvement in instruction in which the special education teacher engages is dependent on the needs and the placement of the student. For a student with a hearing impairment who is placed in a regular education classroom, the special education teacher's role may consist of ongoing consultation with the classroom teacher about particular teaching techniques and materials that would support the student's successful class participation. For a student with multiple disabilities placed in a self-contained classroom, the special education teacher's role may involve delivery of direct instruction, supervision of teaching assistants, coordination with regular education staff to orchestrate student placement in particular mainstream classes, as well as brainstorming with related service personnel to integrate their knowledge and contributions for the creation of an educational program that is responsive to the total student. In addition, the special education teacher is often the primary parent contact person, conveying information and questions from the team to the student's parents, and from parents to team members.

Speech-Language Therapist.   The speech-language therapist has responsibility for delivering direct service to students and providing ongoing classroom observation and consultation to support the student's functional use of his or her language skills. Consider a student using a non-oral communication method such as sign language. For this to be a functional language system within the classroom (and, by extension, within the student's home), the speech-language therapist must ensure knowledge of sign language vocabulary by classroom personnel, the student's family, and, as much as possible, other peers with whom the student will come in contact. When there are additional personnel directly involved in the speech-language aspect of the student's educational program (e.g., a sign language interpre-tutor), the speech-language therapist has responsibility for coordinating with the classroom teacher and the additional personnel to plan for the best utilization of such resources in the student's program.

Physical Therapist.   The physical therapist is primarily responsible for assessment and evaluation of a student's motor functioning in the areas of locomotion, balance, body awareness and management, coordination, postural tone, and strength. Given information about student functioning obtained through a complete assessment, the physical therapist makes recommendations for the type and frequency of direct therapy services and provides training for classroom staff and parents in proper handling and positioning of the student for optimal classroom participation and performance. In addition, the physical therapist acts as a resource person in finding and designing assistive or adaptive devices to complement the student's abilities and to allow for greater participation and independence (e.g., customized wheelchairs, leg braces, and appropriate seating for table tasks). Finally, the physical therapist may provide additional consultation and demonstration for other disciplines that deliver services based significantly on motor abilities (e.g., adaptive physical education and mobility instruction for students with visual impairments).

Occupational Therapist.   Since both physical and occupational therapists focus on a student's motor abilities and functioning, the degree of distinction between what the two professions look at and respond to is dictated by the needs and abilities of the particular student. There may indeed be areas of overlap between the goals and objectives as well as the therapy techniques utilized by both physical and occupational therapists. In general, however, an occupational therapist is primarily responsible for assessment, evaluation, and developing strategies for skill improvement in the areas of reach, manipulation, unilateral and bilateral coordination, motor planning, and motor accuracy. The occupational therapist will make recommendations for direct therapy services if needed, provide ongoing classroom consultation to convey information around the student's progress in therapy, receive feedback from classroom staff on suggestions he or she has made to enhance the student's functioning within the classroom, and offer new ideas for translation of therapy goals and strategies to the classroom setting. Additionally, the occupational therapist will provide assistance in brainstorming and in finding and individualizing any adaptive or assistive devices needed by the student to enhance his or her full participation and independence.

Instructional Assistant.   Instructional assistants are paraprofessionals who support and extend the instruction of the special education teacher by performing a wide range of duties and responsibilities. Depending upon the educational model and the needs of particular students, instructional assistants may fill diverse roles such as leading instructional groups within the classroom (planned in conjunction with the teacher), accompanying and supporting students within mainstream classes, delivering individualized instruction in toilet training, maintaining student performance records, participating in team meetings, and communicating student issues directly to parents. The addition of instructional assistants to teams greatly facilitates the individualization of educational programming for students.

Team Decision Making

Given the number of personnel potentially involved in designing and implementing a student's educational program, it is critical to have a generally acknowledged and accepted forum for discussion and decision making around the changing issues and strategies affecting that student's school experience. Specifically, multidisciplinary teams function best when both informal and formal means of communicating about students are in place.

Team Communication.   Informal communications convey relevant questions and information on an immediate basis, when such questions and information require on-the-spot actions or decisions that cannot be delayed until the next planned team discussion. Many teams have been creative about their methods of informal communication. For example, one team routinely attaches brief notes to its members' plan books to outline new developments and observations; another team has a bulletin board by the classroom door with pockets attached for interteam communication; still another team involves students directly in conveying information (in a positive and respectful fashion) by assigning the job of messenger, to deliver communication either verbally or in written form.

In addition to such informal methods of interteam communication, there is a strong need for a more structured, formalized means of team sharing, in which all team members have an opportunity to hear from and be heard by the other professionals and paraprofessionals involved in a student's program. Such team meetings should not be limited to a member's report on his or her perspective and view of student accomplishments and future goals, but should be structured to invite and encourage active discussion, brainstorming, and problem solving around issues of concern. Maximum participation by all team members in the sharing process ensures an integrated and cohesive educational program that responds to the student in a holistic rather than piecemeal fashion. To promote maximal participation by all members, each individual within the team must be willing to engage in (1) active listening to others' ideas and concerns, (2) summarization and clarification of what he or she has perceived was said by other group members, and (3) giving and receiving feedback (both positive and negative) in the search for the most beneficial outcome for the student. With such mechanisms for interteam communication in place, the task of translating team decisions into practice is greatly facilitated.

Translation into Practice

The amount and degree of integration and assimilation of related services personnel into the student's primary classroom environment is one of the significant decisions team members must make. Should the model of service delivery be one of consultation only, with the respective therapist(s) providing classroom observations and recommendations to teachers about specific strategies for student growth? Should the therapist(s) provide direct service to the student in an intensive, one-to-one therapy session; in a partnered or small group therapy session; or within the context of the total classroom group? If direct service is decided upon, should it take place in a separate therapy room, in a specially designed location within the primary classroom, in the student's classroom, within the context of regular classroom activities, or in the community? Finally, who should be responsible for ensuring that the targeted goals and objectives are implemented—individual therapists for their particular domain, classroom teachers and paraprofessionals, parents, the students themselves, or all participants in the home-school team concerned with students' growth? Theoretically, the coordinated plan of action drawn up through team discussion to respond to each student's needs and abilities will utilize a variety of the above scenarios in creating the best "fit" for a student. The following case study illustrates some of the issues and team responses highlighted in this section on multidisciplinary team decision making.

A Case Study: Bobby

At the age of three, Bobby was referred to a full-day, private preschool program serving typical children aged three to five, as well as their disabled peers. He had been previously enrolled in a half-day parent-infant program sponsored by his local school district, which served children labeled as having a variety of handicapping conditions. Bobby had been labeled by his school district as multiply handicapped. Since Bobby's referral came near the end of the summer school term, it was decided that various team members would utilize some of the remaining summer time to conduct observations of Bobby, both at home and at school, to interview his parents, and to evaluate his performance in specific skill areas using a variety of developmental check lists. Throughout the weeks of evaluation, team members met on a weekly basis to share their experiences with Bobby: what he liked and didn't like and what strategies for engagement seemed to work best. They also developed a profile of what his current skills looked like in various domains (e.g., communication, socialization, cognition, and motor skills). The team members involved throughout the evaluation process included a special education teacher, a speech-language therapist, a physical therapist, and an occupational therapist. The comprehensive evaluations enabled team members to generate preliminary recommendations for the types of related services Bobby would need to receive maximum benefit from his educational program. These recommendations would be translated into actual practice during the first few weeks of the fall term, when specific classroom activities and schedules would be more clearly delineated.

When the fall term began, team members met during two in-service days to develop a comprehensive schedule of weekly activities, designed to respond to the needs and interests of all students. Related services personnel negotiated with classroom staff to spend the initial two weeks of school observing and supporting targeted students (e.g., Bobby) within regular classroom activities. At the end of the observation period, all team members would meet together to define the parameters of each student's program.

At the end of the two-week observation period, team members met as a group to finalize Bobby's schedule. His classroom was a heterogeneous grouping of sixteen three- and four-year-olds, with ten "typical" children and six children labeled as having special needs. The classroom staff consisted of a special education teacher, an assistant teacher, and two graduate student interns. The multidisciplinary team decided that Bobby should receive both classroom consultation and direct service from the speech-language therapist (5 times per week for ½ hour); the physical therapist (2 times per week for ½ hour); and the occupational therapist (2 times per week for ½ hour). In determining the location and grouping for direct services, all therapists looked first at the classroom schedule to figure out which classroom activities would be most conducive to achieving their goals. With an ideal schedule in mind, related service personnel then met with the other classroom teams they served to prioritize goals and develop workable schedules. A final team meeting was held (with Bobby's team) to come up with a mutually agreed-upon schedule. The final schedule for related services for Bobby looked like this:

> *Speech-language therapy*—Five half-hour sessions per week: two times per week in an integrated skill group with three peers in the classroom; two times per week one-to-one in the resource room with the speech-language therapist; and once per week in a partnered community outing to nearby grocery stores, bakeries, playgrounds, etc.
> *Physical therapy*—Two half-hour sessions per week: once in the resource room one-to-one with the physical therapist and once as part of the classroom's weekly swimming program at a local recreation center.
> *Occupational therapy*—Two half-hour sessions per week: once in the resource room one-to-one with the occupational therapist and once during the classroom's lunch time, at a table with four peers.

In addition to direct services, Bobby's classroom team received ongoing consultation from the therapists involved in his program through on-the-spot demonstration of techniques and strategies during in-classroom therapy times (e.g., skill times, lunch times, and swimming lessons), through informal communications, and through weekly multidisciplinary team meetings. Team meetings served as a forum throughout the year for sharing information about Bobby's growth, raising questions and issues of concern, and brainstorming new activities and approaches.

This case study illustrates the major components of multidisciplinary team decision making: outlining who may be involved in designing and implementing a particular student's educational program; deciding whether to provide consultation only, or consultation in conjunction with direct service by related services personnel; answering questions of the location and grouping for therapy as related to participation in the functional context of the student's classroom; and arranging for informal and formal communication among multidisciplinary team members.

Educational Interventions with Students Who Experience Disabilities

The following sections present issues and practices in the education of students with hearing impairments, visual impairments, severe mental retardation, and motor impairments. You will read about Nancy, Shanon, Maria, and Derrick, whose case examples illustrate many important issues surrounding educational placement, team decision making, adapting curriculum and learning environments, working with parents, and planning for the future. Examples of teaching and program development should give you a feeling for working with children and young adults within integrated settings.

To help you understand these students' educational needs, we have provided some preliminary information on disability categories. Prior to each student's case study, we have provided the current definition and prevalence figures for the specific disability that the child experiences. However, despite the convenience of this approach, we also recognize the danger of thinking about children in categories, not as unique individuals with special needs.

Students with Hearing Impairments

Hearing impaired is a broad, generic term for any hearing disability, regardless of severity, and without reference to etiology, age of onset, or educational programming. A 1975 study published by the U.S. Office of Education estimated that students with hearing impairments made up approximately 0.6 percent of the total population of school-aged children. Of this group, the Office of Education study showed that roughly 0.075 percent were students labeled as deaf, while the remaining 0.5 percent were labeled hard of hearing. For educational purposes, the following definitions describe the range of disabilities experienced by people with hearing impairments:

> A *deaf* person is one whose hearing disability precludes successful processing of linguistic information through audition, with or without a hearing aid.

> A *hard-of-hearing* person is one who, generally with the use of a hearing aid, has residual hearing sufficient to enable successful processing of linguistic information through audition (Report of the Ad Hoc Committee to Define Deaf and Hard of Hearing, 1975, p. 509).

The level of hearing loss, or the detectable reduction in auditory acuity, is described in units called *decibels* (dB), a measurement of the intensity or "pressure" of a sound. Audiometric testing is used to determine the threshold, or lowest level of intensity at which an individual is able to detect the presented sound. A person with normal hearing is able to detect the presented sounds at zero dB. The probable impact on language acquisition and communication is referenced to the degree of hearing loss a person experiences, and is described in terms of its severity. A person whose hearing threshold is 26–54 dB is expected to experience a mild impact on language learning and communication; one whose threshold is 55–69 dB, a moderate impact; a threshold of 70–89 dB is likely to cause a severe impact on communication; and a hearing threshold of 90 dB or greater is described as creating a profound impact on communication.

Many changes have occurred in the past decade with respect to educational intervention models for students with hearing impairments. Although there are differing opinions about the best practice regarding student placement (e.g., segregated, homogeneous groupings versus integrated, heterogeneous groupings), the educational tide for students with varying types and degrees of disabilities seems to be turning toward preparation for life integrated within one's community, through participation in an integrated educational community. Perhaps the following case study best illustrates the issues and interventions currently encountered in the education of students with hearing impairments.

A Case Study: Nancy.   Nancy is a bright and beautiful five-year-old, tall for her age and strong. She climbs to the top of her classroom's gym and straddles the bars before flipping over and jumping to the mats below. A friend gestures to Nancy to come to the playhouse, and they begin to "cook" together a "soup" made of brightly colored wooden blocks. After five minutes, the balloon math group is called to a work table, but Nancy does not respond. One of her friends leaves the table, walking over to where Nancy still plays, tapping her on the shoulder and signing while saying "work time" to her. She accompanies her friend to the work table, where her teacher has donned the microphone portion of Nancy's phonic ear (a specialized hearing aid). Nancy wears a small amplifier strapped to her chest, as well as a receiver, barely detectable, in her ear. To supplement the limited auditory information that amplification makes accessible to Nancy, classroom team members have implemented a total communication approach to language learning and processing, involving (1) speech reading (decoding spoken language by watching the speaker's lips), (2) sign language (a form of manual communication illustrated in Figure 1), as well as (3) assisted auditory processing (through sound amplification with the hearing aid). A sign language interpre-tutor sits with the group, signing fluently while the teacher gives directions for the day's lesson. Nancy attends primarily to the teacher, casting subtle glances toward the interpre-tutor when she needs more information than she is able to glean through listening and speech-reading. Directions completed, the students begin their work with occasional assistance from both the teacher and the interpre-tutor when they appear stuck or confused. Nancy blends into the group, noticeable only by the amplifier strapped to her chest.

Nancy entered this full-day, regular education kindergarten in September, after having attended a private preschool program for children with severe hearing impairments for two and a half years. Many factors contributed to Nancy's placement within this integrated setting, including strong parent advocacy; a commitment by her local school district to serve all its students in the most normalized environment possible; the willingness of individual teachers and administrators to "stretch" their abilities and creativity to respond to a child with differing needs; as well as the availability of resources, both human and technological, to supplement the regular education curriculum and experience for Nancy. Let us examine some of the above factors in greater detail.

1. Nancy's parents had witnessed a willingness and commitment by their local school district to educate students with severe disabilities within the mainstream of education. The educational model for integration into the mainstream varied for particular students, depending on the intensity of their need as well as the types of resources available to support their success within the regular education classroom. Nancy's mother and father advocated strongly for her placement within a regular education kindergarten, with supports. Their feeling was that such a classroom would be most appropriate for their daughter with respect to curricular content and social development, and would provide a stimulating, if challenging, language environment for Nancy.

2. After thoughtful consideration, the school district agreed with Nancy's parents that a regular education kindergarten would be most appropriate for Nancy. Although a few district representatives felt that a self-contained class for hearing-impaired students would better serve Nancy's needs by providing her with an intensive communication environment in which all students and staff utilized both oral and manual means of communication (sign language), the majority chose to create an intensive communication environment within a regular education classroom.

3. To formulate such an intensive language environment for Nancy's

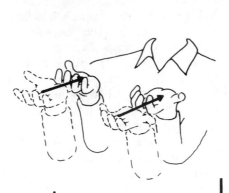

want
Five shape both hands palms up, fingers slightly curved. Draw back to body.

warm
Place tips of right claw at mouth then open up fingers into five shape.

wash
Rub right S in circular motion on upturned left palm.

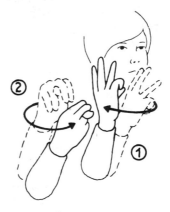

wasn't
Place index finger of right W on lips and move back to right cheek. Then form N shape and twist in.

Figure 1. *Sample vocabulary of the American Sign Language (ASL) system. (From Bornstein, Hamilton, Saulnier, & Roy, 1975, p. 227.)*

classroom, the district set about creating a multidisciplinary team to support and consult with the regular education teacher. The regular kindergarten teacher had been identified as the best choice for Nancy based on (a) her previous experiences teaching children with various special needs, (b) her willingness to devote both the time and energy required to adapt her instruction to Nancy's needs (e.g., participating in an in-service course in sign language), (c) her ability to work effectively within a team framework, and (d) her ability to help each child in her classroom both feel and be perceived by others as uniquely valuable for his or her special qualities.

The multidisciplinary team designed to support the classroom teacher was composed of a speech-language therapist, a sign language teacher, and a sign language interpre-tutor. After an initial week of observation and assessment of Nancy in her classroom, the team decided on a combination of direct therapy services and classroom consultation. At the outset, related services planned for Nancy were comprised of: speech-language therapy, focused on speech production, articulation, and speech reading, for one-half hour, five days a week; and one-to-one sign language instruction with the sign language teacher for one-half hour, three days per week (both occurring in a small room off the main classroom). The team decided that the most advantageous way to utilize the interpre-tutor's skills was to regard him as another classroom teacher. To this end, he assumed responsibility for various portions of general classroom programming, as well as for specific portions of Nancy's program. For example, to assist in building an intensive classroom language environment, the interpre-tutor taught a sign language group to the entire class two days a week at Circle Time. The children both enjoyed the group and learned from it. Many of them spontaneously used the sign language vocabulary they had learned when talking to Nancy. When the regular kindergarten teacher was leading the group, the interpre-tutor signed the words to the accompanying song, game, or directions. In addition, he assumed responsibility for implementing instruction (planned in conjunction with the teacher) for a daily reading group, of which Nancy was a member. Throughout the school year, the team met on a weekly basis to plan for, evaluate, and restructure Nancy's program.

4. Although Nancy experiences a severe hearing loss, consultation with her physician indicated that her ability to process auditory information could be assisted by use of a hearing aid to amplify spoken language. Upon her entrance into kindergarten, Nancy was fitted with a different type of hearing aid, called a *phonic ear*. This device was more powerful than her previous hearing aid, which fit completely within her ear. The phonic ear consists of an individually molded, transistorized earpiece that fits within the ear and is attached to a radio-sized box, worn on Nancy's chest. This unit acts as a powerful amplifier, which transmits sound spoken through a microphone to the

earpiece Nancy wears. The microphone, which is wireless, is worn by the teacher, but is easily put on and taken off to allow for use by other persons.

The success of Nancy's placement within the regular education kindergarten was made possible by a creative orchestration of multiple factors, including classroom structure, curricular content, human resources (classroom team members and related services staff), and the use of technological assistance. These factors come together to create a variety of models of educational intervention, as the following case studies reveal.

Students Who Experience Severe Mental Retardation

Our introductory section presented Gold's (1980) alternative definition of mental retardation. He has urged us to commit the power of our instructional technologies and social supports to the development of the competencies of individuals who need our superior assets. Before examining some current practices in the field of special education of individuals with severe mental retardation, we will examine a more widely adopted perspective on the issue of definition.

The American Association on Mental Deficiency (AAMD) has formulated a definition of mental retardation that has gained wide acceptance and influence within education. For better or worse, educators frequently employ the AAMD definition for labeling and classifying children. As with other definitions of disability categories, the AAMD definition benefits children when it is used to identify needs and provide the extra social supports, adaptive assistance, and instructional intervention required by a child to succeed within an integrated educational environment. On the other hand, when definitions are used in a manner that results in exclusion and homogeneous grouping of children with similar types and degrees of disability, they tend to degrade the quality of children's school and postschool lives. Because of the general requirement of labeling children for the purpose of funding necessary educational interventions, we present the current AAMD definition: "Mental Retardation refers to significantly subaverage general intellectual functioning existing concurrently with deficits in adaptive behavior, and manifested during the developmental period" (Grossman, 1977, p. 11).

The three important components of this definition are its reference to manifestation of the condition during the developmental period, impaired intellectual functioning, and deficits in adaptive behavior. Manifestation of a condition during the developmental period means that the condition exists prior to one's eighteenth birthday. Intellectual functioning is typically measured by a person's performance on a standardized, individual measure of intelligence. Adaptive behavior refers to the degree to which an individual is able to meet the societal expectations and norms for his or her age group. These norms vary widely with age. During infancy and early childhood, adaptive behavior is reflected in the achievement of sensory-motor, communi-

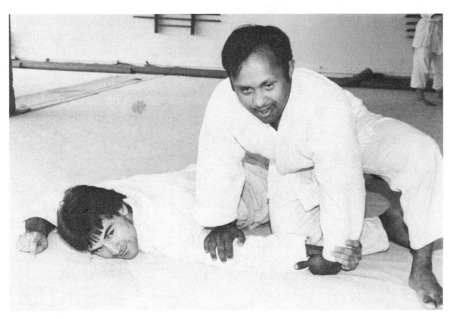

Montez is a recent graduate of a public school program for students with severe mental retardation. He has practiced the martial art of Aikido three times a week for the last three years. Although he is nonverbal, and has been awarded an IQ in the low 20s, he is an active and valued member of his martial arts school. (Photograph by James W. Black.)

cation, self-help, and socialization skills and abilities. During the school years of childhood and early adolescence, adaptive behavior is reflected in the mastery of academic skills, daily living skills, reasoning, and judgment, as well as group and interpersonal social skills. Finally, adaptive behavior during late adolescence and adulthood is referenced to social responsibility and vocational independence.

The AAMD definition includes different levels of mental retardation based on the degree of impairment of *both* intellectual and adaptive behavior as compared to the average person. Accordingly, people are labeled mildly, moderately, severely, or profoundly retarded based on their perceived deviation from average intellectual and adaptive achievement. However, the focus of this section is on individuals who function in the severe to profound range of mental retardation. These children, young adults, and adults experience major challenges to successful adaptation and present intensive instructional and technological needs in order to meet the intellectual and adaptive demands of their homes, schools, and communities. Children with severe mental retardation often experience additional handicapping conditions like motor and/or sensory difficulties.

How many children in our schools and communities experience severe and profound levels of mental retardation? *Prevalence* refers to the number of individuals experiencing a specific disability within the population. It is frequently expressed as the number of disabled individuals per thousand, or as a percentage. Overall, estimates for the prevalence of mental retardation in school-age populations range from 1 to 3 percent (Brewer & Kakalik, 1979). Statistically, we would expect individuals with severe to profound levels of mental retardation to comprise about 0.15 percent of the population.

The following case study illustrates an approach to the design of educational services that promotes maximum participation in school and society by children who experience severe mental retardation. Look for examples within the case-study of the creation of integrated classroom models, ongoing educational decision-making efforts, specialized equipment and adaptations, and the instructional methods required to promote skill mastery.

A Case Study: Shanon.   Shanon is eleven years old, attends his neighborhood elementary school, and experiences severe mental retardation. He has obtained an IQ score of 30 on a recent evaluation and has the genetic condition of Down's syndrome. (Note, many individuals with Down's syndrome function in the moderate and mild range of mental retardation.) He can walk, count up to three objects, and use gestures and a few picture-symbols to communicate his needs. Shanon is popular with both his disabled and his nondisabled peers.

At the end of the last school year, Shanon's school district proposed to continue his placement within the self-contained special education class for Shanon and eight other children with severe disabilities. His parents refused to agree with this continued placement and argued for placement within a regular fifth grade class. They wanted the intensive services to be provided to their son within the mainstream. They felt strongly that an ongoing opportunity for Shanon to be around other children his age without severe disabilities was critical for his social and communication development. After a number of meetings, both sides compromised: Shanon would spend mornings in the fifth grade class but return to the special education class in the afternoons. One of the instructional assistants from the special education room was assigned to help Shanon *and* the other fifth grade students.

During the summer, the regular education, special education, and related services staff participated in a series of team meetings. The team designed an individualized educational program for Shanon within an integrated educational setting. Initially, some team members had difficulty envisioning Shanon's active participation within the regular classroom. The academic curriculum was clearly not appropriate for his present and future needs. The label "severe mental retardation" was neither informative nor helpful.

The team thus decided to target *instructional domains* (another term for instructional areas) based on (1) parental interest and input, (2) Shanon's interests and strengths, and (3) an analysis of the skills Shanon would need for more independent functioning within the school and community, now and in the future. After much discussion, brainstorming, and input from Shanon's parents, the multidisciplinary team prioritized the following skill areas

Table 1
Educational Goals Established by Shanon's Multidisciplinary Team

Educational domain	Long-range goals	Rationale
Communication	1. Indicate what he wants by pointing to his picture communication booklet (symbols) without any reminders.	Shanon does not regularly use his picture-symbol book in order to get across his message.
	2. Shake his head no in order to indicate that he doesn't want a particular task, item, or service.	He has started to show frustration about his ability to make his needs known.
Social	1. Develop one friendship and eat lunch with this student in cafeteria.	Both Shanon and other nonhandicapped children will grow in respect and understanding within a relationship.
	2. Play computer and board games with a peer.	His parents would like him to do this at home, with family and neighborhood kids.
School routines	1. Morning routine: Bus, Locker, Pledge of Allegiance, Announcements and attendance	Increased independence within these routines will enhance his social role as a student. It will also build his self-concept.
	2. Lunch routine: Preparation, Negotiating hallways, Lunch line, Eating and interacting	
Domestic	1. Shower and dress more independently after swimming class.	These were the activities and skills that Shanon's family felt were important at home for now.
	2. Fix simple snacks: Toast, Cereal	

for instruction: communication, social and leisure activities, school routines, and domestic skills. For each instructional area long-term, annual goals were identified (see Table 1).

After a few weeks of working with Shanon, the team reached the following conclusions about his individual learning style:

1. To understand what was expected of him, Shanon needed a consistent schedule. During the first weeks, teachers had sometimes inadvertently changed the sequence of his routines. After lunch he was usually expected to use the bathroom, where he would wash his face and hands on the way back to class. When in a hurry, some staff members skipped this step, thus confusing Shanon. It was as if he were saying, how can I learn this routine if you change it every few days?

2. Shanon clearly learned best when complex skills were broken down into smaller steps for the purposes of instruction. The following list is a task analysis, in which "using a hall locker" was broken down into fifteen smaller steps.
   a. Locates locker with his picture on it.
   b. Grasps handle.
   c. Lifts handle.
   d. Swings open door.
   e. Grasps large ring on coat zipper.
   f. Pulls ring down, unzipping coat.
   g. Pulls out right arm.
   h. Pulls out left arm.
   i. Maintains grasp on coat.
   j. Grasps hood.
   k. Locates hook in locker.
   l. Places coat hood on hook.
   m. Grasps locker door.
   n. Pushes door closed until it latches.
   o. Turns toward classroom door.

   Shanon received instruction at his locker twice each day at the beginning and end of the school day. His teachers gradually reduced the amount of assistance they provided on each step, as Shanon became more independent.

3. Shanon often required more time than other students to complete an activity. During his morning routine he would usually take five minutes longer than the other children to hang up his coat. While a long-term goal of increasing his speed within the morning routine could be considered at some point, the team felt that he should not be rushed at this time.

4. The other nonhandicapped children within the class were often effective models for Shanon. They enjoyed being with him; in the halls, going to lunch, and sharing the computer. A few children had to be reminded that they were his friends and not his teachers. The educational team felt that it was most important to help Shanon be perceived as an equal member of the class.

5. Shanon utilized a picture-symbol daily schedule to organize the sequence of activities throughout the school day. His daily schedule was represented by a series of simple line drawings paired with sight words. Shanon was taught to discriminate and interpret the new pic-

tures on his schedule, over a two-month period. The use of a picture-symbol system as an instructional aid within functional activities seemed to hold great promise for Shanon. This cheap, readily available technology could be used in order to promote his independence within activities, for example, in the complex sequences of tasks involved in meal preparation (e.g., making soup) or a future vocational routine (e.g., cleaning a motel room).

6. The Apple IIe microcomputer within the classroom proved to be a stimulating learning center for Shanon, as well as for the other typical children in the classroom. Shanon preferred educational and recreational software that provided lots of color graphics and sound as reinforcement for correct responses. Activities at the computer improved his attending, fine motor, discrimination, and age-appropriate leisure skills. Typically, he was paired with two other children, whom he would observe and take turns with.

7. Teachers learned to structure parallel learning activities for Shanon during academic skill times in the classroom. While other children were in reading groups, Shanon was assigned to a reading group in which he matched and discriminated new picture symbols for his schedule. When math instruction was taking place, he joined his assigned math group, in which he was learning to match numbers and use a calculator in preparation for future grocery shopping instruction.

As the school year progressed, it became increasingly evident that Shanon's program had liberated much of his hidden adaptive potential. He remained severely retarded as measured, defined, and classified by the AAMD definition. He demonstrated, however, that he could become a valued member of the fifth grade classroom. For Shanon and other severely disabled students, intensive services do not require a separate learning environment or totally different curricula and instructional methods. How many other disabled children are waiting for a similar opportunity?

Students with Visual Impairments

The experience of a visual impairment by a student has a greater effect on the strategies and methodologies used for instruction than on the curricular content to which the student is exposed. Specialized instructional strategies facilitate the visually impaired student's successful participation within regular education classrooms. The degree of specialized intervention needed depends upon the intensity of the student's impairment. The following definitions describe generally accepted educational terms for the range of visual impairments.

Legal blindness is defined as visual acuity of less than 20/200, or a visual field of less than 140 degrees, despite the best correction with glasses.

A *partially sighted* person is one who has visual acuity ranging from 20/70 to 20/200 despite the best correction with glasses. (National Society for the Prevention of Blindness, 1966).

Visual impairments may be *congenital* (present at birth) or *adventitious* (of accidental as opposed to hereditary origin).

Students who are legally blind or partially sighted may need instruction in independent mobility, as well as support in gaining access to academic books and materials and in expressing their thoughts and ideas in written form. It is estimated that among students with visual impairments, approximately 25 percent are totally blind, another 25 percent have some light perception (useful for mobility but not for reading), and the remaining 50 percent have enough residual vision to read enlarged print books. What type of educational model best serves the needs of the 0.1 percent of students who experience visual impairments? The case study of Maria, which follows, describes both an educational model and a few technological aids utilized in supporting the school experience of students with visual impairments.

A Case Study: Maria.   Maria, aged thirteen, is a seventh-grade student at Washington Junior High School. She is a serious and determined student, working hard to maintain her B average. Maria's after-school hours this time of year are filled with rehearsals for the school play, for which she has a part singing with the chorus. Moving on and off the stage at the appropriate times presents a special challenge to Maria, for she is legally blind. In order to move fluidly with the rest of the group, Maria simply places her hand on the elbow of her friend, Martina, to her right, and walks to the appropriate place.

What other kinds of challenges does Maria encounter in her school experience? What are the ways in which her school system responds to the unique needs Maria presents as she moves through junior high school? Let us examine some of the issues raised by Maria's visual impairment, as well as the strategies offered by her school system to maximize her success in junior high.

1. We began this section on visual impairments by stating that the experience of a visual impairment by a student has implications for the strategies and methodologies of instruction more than for curricular content. That, indeed, has been Maria's experience. Since entering kindergarten at the age of five and a half, Maria has always attended regular education classes. The curriculum content she has studied has been appropriate to her grade level. This, at times, has presented quite a challenge to both Maria and her teachers, particularly in early elementary school, around the teaching of reading. In addition to the issues of academic programming for Maria, her curriculum needed to include a focus on instruction in independent mobility. To respond to these unique needs, Maria received supplemental support from various related services and support staff.

2. From kindergarten on, Maria has received additional support from an itinerant special education teacher, who specializes in working with students with visual impairments. The itinerant teacher is not assigned to any particular school within the district, but travels from school to school as dictated by the needs of students. Throughout elementary school, Maria's itinerant teacher visited her classroom for a half day, on a twice-a-week basis. In elementary school, with the consistency of one classroom and one teacher, her itinerant teacher functioned primarily as an in-classroom consultant and materials resource person. In addition, she delivered direction instruction to Maria in the areas of orientation (establishing an awareness of one's position within the environment with relation to significant objects) and mobility (the ability to move safely and efficiently within the environment). As Maria entered junior high with its more complex schedule of classes, each having a different instructor, the job of connecting with each of Maria's teachers was more than the itinerant teacher's schedule could handle. Because of this and the increased academic pressure of junior high, it was decided that Maria needed the ongoing support of a consistent person within the school building. Therefore, Maria began to receive services from the resource teacher, a special education teacher who assists students with special instructional needs on a part-time basis. The resource teacher would receive consultation from the itinerant teacher and coordinate the sharing of information, materials, and resources with Maria's content area teachers (e.g., math, science, social studies). In addition, the resource teacher would see Maria for one forty-minute period per day to supply supplemental instruction in the content areas, as needed.

   One additional member of the multidisciplinary team involved with Maria was a half-time teaching assistant who was responsible for transcribing Maria's written work, done in Braille, to typewritten copies, readable by her teachers, and rendering Braille copies of printed handouts given by Maria's teachers. The teaching assistant also participated in the process of test taking with Maria, reading test questions aloud to Maria and recording her oral responses.

3. Throughout her school experience, Maria has utilized a variety of technological aids to facilitate her success in school. Such aids do not replace, but support, the critical skills Maria had been developing during elementary school (e.g., listening skills, organizational skills, etc.). These technologies serve as important aids to academic and personal success.

   a. Tape recorder. Maria records all classroom lectures in her major content areas. She uses these tapes in place of notebooks to review and study important concepts.

   b. Texts on tape. Maria's itinerant teacher acts as a resource person for locating and securing textbooks and related materials on audio tape for use in place of written texts.

   c. Optacon. For those written materials not available on tape, Maria uses an Optacon—a portable electronic reading aid that converts print to tactile vibrations in the image of the print via a small, hand-held camera. Since the Optacon must be used letter by letter, its use is very slow (five to eleven words per minute), and is usually used only when other means of getting the printed information are unavailable or impractical.

   d. Perkins Brailler. The Brailler is a typewriter with six keys containing dots, which leave an embossed print on paper, representing letters of the alphabet. The embossed print created by the Brailler is read tactilely by running one's fingertips over the sequence of raised dots. Codes are also available for math, science, and foreign languages. Maria uses the Perkins Brailler to complete written assignments (later transcribed by the teaching assistant) as well as to make study notes for herself.

   e. Hoover cane. Maria uses this long cane as a mobility aid, sweeping it in an arc and tapping the ground in front of her to locate obstacles and detect changes in the terrain.

As students move through school to increasingly more complex educational environments, they are challenged to meet higher academic standards as well as higher expectations for independence. For students with visual impairments, the challenge of academic success and independence can best be supported through the provision of supplementary human resources and a variety of technological aids, within the context of mainstream education.

Students with Motor Impairments

Motor impairments refer to nonsensory physical limitations or health impairments that interfere with a student's educational performance and/or attendance and that necessitate the provision of specialized services, training, equipment, and materials for children to achieve their maximum potential. Because much of our early learning experiences take place through interactions with objects, events, and stimuli in our environment, motor impairments may interfere with a child's ability to explore his or her environment, therefore affecting the development of children's skills, attitudes, and abilities. Such motor impairments may result from accidents, disease, or physical defects present at birth. The most common motor impairments experienced by students result from the following medical conditions: cerebral palsy, a class of nonprogressive disorders of movement and posture caused by brain damage; muscular dystrophy, a progressive degeneration of musculature; and spina bifida, a congenital birth defect in which the bony units of the spine fail to develop fully, leaving a defect or cleft in the spinal canal that affects central nervous system functioning. The U.S. Department of Health, Education and Welfare (1975) estimated that five school-age children in one thousand (0.5 percent) experience physical handicaps.

Students with severe intellectual and motor impairments can enjoy recreation and leisure activities using personal computers with adaptive software and switches. Jim is using a drawing program that changes the shape and color of the design on the screen by pressing a single plate switch attached to the arm of his wheelchair. (Photograph by James W. Black.)

The term *motor impairments* refers to a divergent group of individuals with unique needs and abilities with respect to physical movement. As with any categorical discussion of impairments, we must be careful to acknowledge the individuality and uniqueness of all children. For example, many children with motor impairments do succeed within the typical regular education curriculum when provided with appropriately coordinated services and assistance (specialized transportation to and from school, a personal aide). Other children may experience such profound physical and multiple disabilities that they may require specialized curriculum and instructional procedures to participate fully within integrated school and community environments (community-referenced instruction). Sometimes, children's greatest obstacles are the negative attitudes, perceptions, and prejudices of others.

Imagine that you have cerebral palsy. It takes an incredible effort and concentration for you to move your right arm. You cannot effectively move your other limbs or change your position at all. Because of the effects of brain damage on your control of voluntary muscles, you cannot say more than a barely recognizable yes and no. People do things for and to you all day long: they scrub your face, push around your wheelchair, feed you, and make virtually all choices for you. Consequently, after many years you have almost given up attempting to act on your environment and do things independently. You have learned to be helpless (Seligman, 1975). A disturbing thought, isn't it? Unfortunately, this scenario is similar to the experiences provided to a student named Derrick over many years.

A Case Study: Derrick.   Derrick is a seventeen-year-old young man who experiences spastic quadriplegic cerebral palsy. In other words, he experiences abnormally tense and variable muscle tone (spasticity) on all four extremities of his body (quadriplegic) due to brain damage that affects his motor functioning (cerebral palsy). Derrick uses a wheelchair. With great difficulty Derrick can move his right arm to point to, grasp, or manipulate objects in his environment. Motor deficits in his oral area make eating a challenging and rather sloppy endeavor and limit his verbal output to a few barely intelligible utterances.

For many years professionals have failed to recognize Derrick's true potential. His primary motor impairment has deprived him of many crucial early interactions with his environment. This experiential handicap was greatly exacerbated by years of inadequate and inappropriate educational programming. From ages four through sixteen, Derrick spent hours each day rotating through passive positioning activities on the mats in his classrooms. Innumerable wasted hours were spent smelling things, tracking flashlights and other shiny objects, and stacking preschool rings. Derrick spent years getting ready to learn meaningful things. The proof of the failure of this educational approach is in the fact that these activities stayed the same year after year. Derrick merely moved to a new classroom for older children every few years.

A reality for many teachers of older students is their urgent need to make the best of the few remaining years of school their students have. When Derrick joined his new teacher, he had only five years of publicly supported education left. He had no communication system, no means of independent mobility, and almost nonexistent social, community, and vocational skills. Derrick was generally passive with occasional periods of stubborn and noncompliant behavior. Derrick's new class, located within a regular high school, was a heterogeneous, noncategorical mix of eight students with mild and moderate disabilities. Consequently, Derrick's new classmates range from Carol, a student with learning disabilities, to Donald, a student who experiences moderate mental retardation. Derrick is the only student in the group who has a severe motor impairment and uses a wheelchair for mobility.

An educational team comprised of Derrick's teacher, Kevin; the two classroom instructional assistants; and the speech-language, physical, and occupational therapists met weekly to plan and implement Derrick's new educational program. Derrick's teacher obtained input from his family detailing his activities at home, his likes and dislikes, and the family's major concerns.

Based on the team members' experiences with Derrick during the first weeks of school, they reached the following conclusions. First, it was past time to move beyond a readiness model of educational intervention. The team focused on the functional, age-appropriate skills that would assist Derrick in participating in future least restrictive environments. Parents and team members thought that these future environments should include a supervised apartment-living arrangement, a supported work placement within an integrated work site, and the use of a variety of community restaurants, shopping malls, grocery stores, and recreational facilities. Second, Derrick's priority needs fell into a few critical skill areas: communication skills, mobility skills, school and community skills, and maintenance and improvement of physical health, posture, muscle tone, and movement patterns.

The team was most concerned with Derrick's lack of a systematic means of communication. Despite the fact that he was currently able to identify over fifty pictures of common foods and household items, he had no augmentative communication system to facilitate his nonvocal interactions with others. The team settled initially on a picture-symbol notebook incorporating simple line drawings. The first symbols incorporated into his system included: want, yes, no, more, bathroom, eat, drink, mad, McDonald's, video arcade, Apple computer, tape player, book, bus, sick, work, money, his daily/weekly schedule, and pictures of his classmates, teachers, and family. Symbols were added a few at a time to his notebook. The use of plastic slide archive pages with pockets facilitated the ongoing addition to and modification of his picture-symbol vocabulary. Because of the rapid success that Derrick experienced with this inexpensive direct selection communication system (he directly chose symbols), the team began to investigate a number of more sophisticated technological devices for augmentative communication. They are currently considering a number of devices that would scan Derrick's current vocabulary (e.g., via a light flashing and moving over available choices, which can be stopped via a simple switch) and would generate speech output.

For many years, Derrick's parents had advocated an electric wheelchair, but professionals had been skeptical about his intellectual ability to handle it. One month after school started in his new program, Derrick finally got his electric wheelchair. He received instruction on using it within the hallways, classrooms, and in the community. A mere five weeks after receiving his wheelchair, Kevin handed Derrick the classroom attendance cards and said, "Derrick, take these down to the office, please." Without another word, Derrick, with the cards on his lap, spun around and exited the classroom. He negotiated the maze of hallways and arrived independently at the office, to the utter amazement of the secretarial and administrative staff. Derrick's mother broke down and cried when told of the achievement. Everybody began to notice changes in Derrick, who seemed more alert and involved with life now that he could communicate and move around under his own volition.

Within the high school environment, Derrick was scheduled into a regular homeroom period each day. Communication and social skills related to using his new communication system were worked on in a study hall and student lounge where Derrick could interact with his nonhandicapped friends. Additionally, he was enrolled in beginning swimming and typing classes. In the typing/computer lab, he was learning to use a computer primarily for leisure skills. The classroom teacher and assistants modified the curriculum and activities and provided the necessary supervision within the mainstreamed classes to focus on Derrick's individualized educational goals.

Community-based instruction during the afternoons initially involved learning to order and hand over payment in a fast-food restaurant, making purchases in a grocery store from a five-item picture-symbol list, and nonpaid work-study vocational training in a local hospital's central supply department. Derrick and two nonhandicapped students from the high school's alternative program received vocational training three afternoons each week. Derrick is learning to package and sterilize hospital supplies.

Derrick's physical needs required continued consultation with medical and therapy personnel. Without prescriptive exercises and movement, Derrick's muscles will continue to contract, further limiting the movement in his joints and causing serious health problems. The team's physical and occupational therapists provided valuable consultation regarding the best positioning for Derrick and the best arrangement of equipment and materials within the community shopping activities, as well as in the typing class and at the hospital work site. For example, the occupational therapist designed and built an adaptive device that helped Derrick slide items to be sterilized into a plastic bag.

Derrick's case study illustrates important points that are applicable to educational interventions with students experiencing significant disabilities:

1. Getting ready to learn meaningful skills is a dangerous approach to educational intervention. Students with severe disabilities have little time to waste with nonfunctional activities. If a student fails to make significant and functional progress within a skill sequence and consequently tends to be required to engage in the same activities year after year, we must seriously question the appropriateness of that activity, skill, or curriculum. As a student gets closer to graduation, the curricular choices we make become increasingly critical and irreversible. At the secondary level, as students approach graduation, instruction in the community environments within which the student will function becomes critical.

2. Even at the high school level, there are valuable integrated educational experiences for students with all degrees of disability. Creative exploration of school environments will reveal times and settings that are appropriate for both integration and functional skill development. An integrated typing and computer lab provided an ideal setting for Derrick's leisure skill development. While other students were working independently on word processing and secretarial skills, Derrick learned to use a variety of educational and recreational software programs. During the last five minutes of class, two or three of his nondisabled peers would challenge him to a game of "Space Invaders."

3. When appropriately selected and used, technological aids and devices

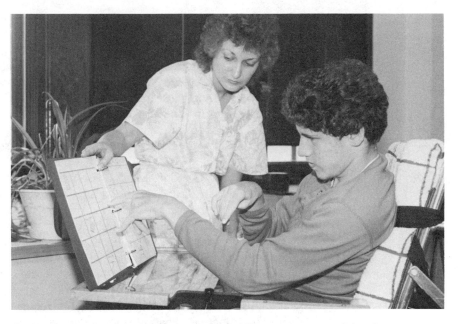

Students without verbal communication skills may use a variety of augmentative communication systems to interact and converse with others. Tony is pointing to simple line drawings and symbols in his booklet to indicate his next scheduled activity. (Photograph by James W. Black.)

will make the difference between passivity and participation, helplessness and competence. All team members agreed that Derrick would never learn to wheel a nonelectric wheelchair independently, or to communicate in a verbal mode. Nevertheless, Derrick has functionally achieved these outcomes via instruction on using an electric wheelchair and via an augmentative communication system. We can only speculate on his level of achievement if these devices had been provided to him at an earlier age.

Summary

In this chapter we have reviewed some of the issues and practices in school programs for students who experience hearing impairments, severe mental retardation, visual impairments, and motor limitations. We examined some of the philosophical, curricular, and technological dimensions of current educational models and intervention strategies.

We began by considering the critical process of envisioning the ultimate goals of our educational efforts with children. In all educational endeavors, whether with disabled or nondisabled individuals, we need to formulate a vision of our desired outcomes. Parents and educators can share in these visions for youth. We suggested that the full participation in life was the general goal of educational programs for student's who experience significant disabilities. Full participation is achieved when a disabled citizen assumes a valued social role as a member of his or her community.

Next, we considered the importance of educational decision making as a means of achieving these desired visions of outcomes. We presented a model of decision making that utilized a multidisciplinary team approach. We outlined the important team contributions of teachers, speech-language therapists, physical therapists, occupational therapists, and instructional assistants.

Finally, we presented a series of case-study examples and discussed the individualized curricula and technologies that are found within programs for students who experience serious impairments. We met Nancy, a hearing-impaired student who attends a regular education kindergarten; Shanon, a fifth grade student with severe mental retardation; Maria, a middle school student with visual impairments; and Derrick, a high school student who experiences cerebral palsy. Despite the highly individual nature of each student's abilities and disabilities, and their wide age span, all four students' case studies shared common elements. Their teachers and parents had shared visions of their increased participation and independence within their school and community. Each student had regular opportunities to interact with and develop relationships with their nondisabled peers. Ultimately, many human and technological resources were applied to assist each individual in achieving a valued and meaningful lifestyle.

Resources

Suggested Additional Readings

Behrman, M. M. (Ed.). (1984). *Handbook of microcomputers in special education.* San Diego: College-Hill Press. This book provides a comprehensive overview of current applications of microcomputer technology in special education.

Biklen, D. (1985). *Achieving the complete school: Strategies for effective mainstreaming.* New York: Teachers College Press. Biklen and contributors present a description and analysis of current mainstreaming models and strategies in American schools.

Brightman, A. J. (Ed.). (1984). *Ordinary moments: The disabled experience.* Baltimore: University Park Press. This is a collection of very powerful autobiographical stories by persons who experience physical and sensory disabilities.

Organizations and Professional Associations

American Occupational Therapy Association
1383 Piccard Drive
P.O. Box 1725
Rockville, MD 20852
(301) 948-9626

American Physical Therapy Association
1111 Fairfax St.
Alexandria, VA 22314
(202) 684-2782

American Speech-Language-Hearing Association
10801 Rockville Pike
Rockville, MD 20852
(301) 897-5700

Association for the Education and Rehabilitation of the Blind and Visually
    Handicapped
206 North Washington Street, Room # 320
Alexandria, VA 22314
(703) 836-6066

The Association for Persons with Severe Handicaps (TASH)
7010 Roosevelt Way, N.E.
Seattle, WA 98115
(206) 523-8446

Council for Exceptional Children
1920 Association Drive
Reston, VA 22091
(703) 620-3666

Catalogs and Suppliers

American Foundation for the Blind, Inc.
15 West Sixteenth Street
New York, NY 10011

Computers for the Physically Handicapped
7602 Talbert Avenue
Huntington Beach, CA 92647

Fred Sammons, Inc.
Box 32
Brookfield, IL 60513-0032

Technical Aids to Independence, Inc.
12 Hyde Road
Bloomfield, NJ 07003

Part III

Understanding Disabled Students in Context

Disabled Persons in the Community

This final section describes the importance of understanding the placement of disabled children and adolescents in community programs, including the necessity of training them for effective functioning in the community, and the need for professionals, including teachers, to understand parents of disabled students. We hope that the advocacy perspective Taylor and Searl described in Part I and the material presented in Part II detailing important areas of functioning have contributed to your recognition of the need for community placements and programming and provided you with information to facilitate such placements.

The chapters in Part III—Murphy and Nisbet on disabled adolescents in the community (chapters 9 and 10) and Ferguson and Ferguson on parents and professionals (chapter 8)—are related because an increasing number of parents of disabled persons look to the time when their child will become a valued member of the community, beyond the school and home. Also, it is becoming increasingly clear to professionals that community placement requires parent involvement and assistance.

As teachers of disabled students you will be asked to look beyond the confines of your classroom to consider the broader worlds of your students—a difficult task considering the complex behaviors of many students and the instructional dilemmas they present. As you respond to them on a case by case basis, using much of the material presented in Part II, you will need to consider their long-term needs, and one of the most crucial of these is the ultimate ability to function independently in the community. Brown, Nietupski, and Hamre-Nietupski (1976) advocate applying the "criterion of ultimate functioning" as we plan instructional programs for young disabled children. They recommend that we ask the following questions prior to the initiation of interactions and programs:

1. Why should we engage in this activity?
2. Is this activity necessary to prepare students to ultimately function in complex heterogeneous community settings?
3. Could students function as adults if they did not acquire the skill?
4. Is there a different activity that will allow students to approximate realization of the criterion of ultimate functioning more quickly and more efficiently?
5. Will this activity impede, restrict, or reduce the probability that students will ultimately function in community settings?
6. Are the skills, materials, tasks, and criteria of concern similar to those encountered in adult life? (p. 9).

If we follow the above suggestions, the inclusion of parents in our planning becomes a necessity for it is the parents who will assist the schools in planning for community placement, and more importantly, they are the ones who will remain consistently available to the disabled person to assist in transitions between school and community opportunities and later adult opportunities. In chapter 8 the Fergusons offer compelling reasons for teachers and parents to work together. Before such cooperation can be put into practice, many professionals may need to develop more positive attitudes about parents. The following list of assumptions is offered as a way for you to explore your beliefs about parents of disabled students. It was originally developed to reflect more positive attitudes about parents of autistic individuals, but it is applicable to families of other severely disabled persons:

1. The emotional reactions of families of individuals with autism or other severe handicaps are normal, necessary, and potentially productive reactions.
2. Though the family may need professional assistance in managing and educating the child who is handicapped, they are as capa-

ble as the general population of solving other problems without professional input. Their solutions may not be our solutions, and that should be acceptable.

3. Professionals must learn to work within the family's system, the system does not have to change to accommodate professional input.

4. Having an autistic or severely handicapped child may not be the most important problem the family has at a given point in time. It is legitimate for other issues to be given priority, as family needs dictate.

5. The family can be the child's best, most committed, long-term advocate.

6. Parents and professionals share the concern for the long-term functioning of the individual who is handicapped.

7. The family wants to do what is best for the child.

8. Families want to be and should be actively and productively involved in the educational process (Donnellan & Mirenda, 1984, p. 21).

Preparing students with disabilities for living and working in communities is the next challenge we face. Successful placements can reflect years of hard work and dedicated service by teachers and parents. Planning must begin when we set learning objectives and goals for young disabled children. It is never too early to ask what purpose a particular task is aimed at. Merely keeping students occupied is not sufficient. Thinking about what a student will need to be a contributing member of society can help us determine the appropriateness of early interventions and curricula materials.

Chapter 8

Philip M. Ferguson

Dianne L. Ferguson

Philip M. Ferguson is a research assistant in the Specialized Training Program at the University of Oregon. He has taught children with severe, multiple disabilities and worked with numerous parent advocacy organizations. Currently he is working closely with a statewide parent group that focuses on improving their children's transition from school to work and adult life. In addition to a continuing interest in families, his research interests focus on the history of social policy for mental retardation, and the sociology of disability.

Dianne L. Ferguson is an assistant professor of Special Education and Rehabilitation at the University of Oregon. She has been both a teacher and an administrator in educational programs for children labeled severely mentally retarded and has been actively involved with parent advocacy groups on the local and state levels as both the parent of a son who is retarded and physically handicapped and as a trainer for parents and other advocates. Part of her current position involves the preparation of future teachers of children with severe disabilities. Strategies for effective involvement with the families of these students is a major aspect of this preparation. Research interests revolve around the qualitative investigation of parent-professional relationships and curriculum theory in the instruction of students who are severely disabled.

Parents and Professionals

After reading this chapter, you should be able to:

1
Critique the use of the psychodynamic orientation to understand the nature and source of parental reactions to their disabled children.

2
Describe this country's present approach to families and compare it to treatment in the eighteenth and nineteenth centuries.

3
List strategies for fostering parents' involvement in their children's school and community programs.

4
Discuss the advantages of parent support groups.

Parents are popular in special education today. In the past ten years or so, it has become commonplace for textbooks and teachers to talk about the importance of involving parents in their children's educational programs, and the Education for All Handicapped Children Act (Public Law 94-142) requires certain types of parental consultation and consent about programming decisions. It would be difficult today to find an educator who did not claim parents and teachers had to be in close alliance for the optimal development of disabled children.

All too often, however, this discovery of parental importance has been in name only. It is one thing to nod vigorously in assent to the assertion that "parents are crucial to successful special education programs." To create and maintain a program significantly influenced by parental participation, however, is much more complicated. The situation is similar to the "Peanuts" cartoon strip where the ever-superior Lucy explains, "I love mankind; it's people that I can't stand." Special education professionals, in too many cases, reveal their opinions of parents only when pressed in the privacy of the teachers' lounge: "I love parents; it's all these mothers and fathers who cause all the problems."

This chapter will discuss how parent involvement in special education (as well as other areas) needs to be more than a popular slogan. Following the letter of the law for parent involvement is not enough. There must also be a true recognition of the spirit of that law. Indeed, perhaps a better way to think of this whole topic is not as "parent involvement" with professionals, but rather as "professional involvement" with parents. This may seem a small point. In reality, it signifies taking families seriously, instead of as an afterthought whenever parents' signatures are needed.

Real involvement with parents cannot be legislated. Real involvement begins with a simple belief: the most important thing that happens when a couple become parents of a handicapped child is that a couple become parents. Whether that handicap is discovered at birth or later in life; whether it is cognitive, sensory, or behavioral in nature; or whether it is severe or mild—none of these is more important than the family structure itself. Just as teachers are told they must see the diagnostic labels to know their students as individuals, so must teachers also view the parents of those same students as more than mere appendages to the child. Parents are uniquely valuable individuals to anyone involved with children. Parents have more information than anyone else about their children. Teachers must involve themselves with parents and families in ways that truly recognize the individual strengths and needs that go beyond any specific handicap.

Whatever involvement with parents there is today did not spring up overnight. Our country has a long history of parent-professional interaction. First then, we will describe the evolution of professional attitudes toward parents of disabled children. Second, we will present a typology of the various ways professionals have described parents over the last twenty years or so. The third topic will examine specific types of parent-professional involvement currently in use. Finally, we will discuss some specific issues and strategies for improving professional involvement in the future.

History

The history of disability in America, as elsewhere, is closely tied to the history of poverty and society's responses to it. This includes the history of families with disabled children. There have been, of course, affluent families with handicapped sons and daughters. At least through World War II, however, disabled children have captured the sometimes benign, sometimes self-serving attention of society only when the inadequacy of family resources forced society to assist in those children's support. Even today, it is the economic issues surrounding educational, medical, and vocational programs for parents of disabled children that most often govern the services provided.

Colonial Times

In colonial times this connection between economics and the family was overt and unquestioned. The handicap was an economic category that applied more to the whole family than to a specific child. As a result, it mattered little whether the specifics involved orphans, widowed mothers, alcoholic parents, or disabled children. If the functional result was an inability to support its members, then the family was disabled (Rothman, 1971). The matter of community concern was the family's need for economic assistance. Obviously, only those conditions that would keep a child (or the parents) from working were viewed as handicapping.

If the whole family was seen as disabled, the colonists found it only natural to try, when feasible, to maintain the family as a unit. This was done either through direct provision by city fathers of food and other necessities or through a pension of straight cash. Uncles, aunts, cousins, and other relatives were usually expected to help. No particular attempts at remediation were made. There were no separate fields of medicine or psychology to make differential diagnoses. Schooling was mainly by private tutors and available only to the very rich. Instruction in basic skills occurred in the home or by apprenticeship for specific skills. Poverty was seen as ordained by God and, thus, an unavoidable part of society. "The poor are always with us," was a creed of most Puritan communities. Disability was a subcategory of poverty. The disabling condition that caused the poverty was more or less an inevitable instance of God's will. It was the burden of community charity to support those families unable to make their own way (Demos, 1970).

The primacy given to maintaining natural families, and the relative absence of institutional placements of handicapped children, did not make the colonial period a comfortable one for parents. Even wealthy families who had handicapped members were left to their own devices. Provisions for poor families were often cruelly inadequate and stigmatizing (Grob, 1973). Families were sometimes driven from town to avoid community responsibility. Finally, many cities and towns used almshouses as placements for entire families. Such confinement increasingly came to distinguish the fate of disabled and able-bodied poor alike.

Spreading through the colonies throughout the eighteenth century, almshouses came to be used as ramshackle warehouses for physically and mentally disabled children of the poor. The desire to keep the family intact gave way to the familiar cry of cost efficiency. Families either went their way without the child or joined the child in the almshouse.

The Nineteenth Century

In the nineteenth century many changes occurred in our country's approach to families. The newly formed nation began to assume responsibility for problems previously left to individuals. The states especially began to intrude more and more actively into the life of the family. Whole fields of expertise and professionalism arose where none had been before, and most of these new experts had similar ideas about parental authority. Educators, psychologists (called alienists then), criminologists, and social reformers all claimed more and more public responsibility for raising children, especially if disabled. The inevitability with which Puritans had viewed such matters was now scorned by these men (and a very few women) of the new sciences. They proclaimed that with "proper" methods of modern science and religious background, the cycle of poverty and disability could be broken. In a sense, parenting children became much too important to be left to parents. Parents, after all, were the amateurs. At the same time, parents quickly heard the new social message demanding "perfect" children. No longer, said the experts, could failure be condoned in raising productive offspring. Parents, therefore, became increasingly dependent on the new professions for instruction on how to raise their children.

Two opinions from about the same time illustrate the new attitude of educators. Families were now blamed as the cause of their children's handicaps. Where the colonial goal had been to keep the family together, the reformist goal by the middle of the nineteenth century was to take the children away from the parents as soon as possible.

Henry Barnard, one of America's most respected advocates of public education, argued for universal schooling, however, as a way to correct the unfortunate influence of home and family on the children. In the 1850s most children still received little formal schooling unless they came from wealthy families. Barnard and others felt this was dangerous. The corrupting influence of parents had to be overcome by new social institutions. The parents Barnard most disapproved of were those both poor and immigrant who were concentrated in the country's major cities. In 1851 Barnard listed his reasons for wanting early schooling for children of these classes.

No one at all familiar with the deficient household arrangements and deranged machinery of domestic life, of the extreme poor and ignorant, to say nothing of the intemperate—of the examples of rude manners, impure and profane language, and all the vicious habits of low-bred idleness, which abound in certain sections of all populous districts, can doubt that it is better for children to be removed as early and as long as possible from such examples and placed in an infant or primary school, under the care and instruction of a kind, affectionate, and skillful female teacher (Barnard, 1865, p. 294).

A parent both poor and with a disabled child was even more at a risk of professional accusation. Society demanded "perfect" children, yet that, by definition, was what a handicapped child could never be. If parents of typical children were, in general, not to be trusted to raise their children, even less adequate were parents of disabled youngsters. Worse than that, such parents were likely to be blamed for causing the disability in the first place.

Samuel G. Howe, a contemporary of Barnard, also advocated social reform. Howe specialized in issues affecting disabled people. In a report for the state legislature of Massachusetts, Howe gave his opinion on the causes of idiocy (as mental retardation was called then). It was a characteristic combination of morality and biology that led Howe to the door of the poor household.

The moral to be drawn from the prevalent existence of idiocy in society is, that a very large class of persons ignore the conditions upon which alone health and reason are given to men, and consequently they sin in various ways; they disregard the conditions which should be observed in intermarriage; they overlook the hereditary transmission of certain morbid tendencies; they pervert the natural appetites of the body into lusts of divers kinds,—the natural emotions of the mind into fearful passions,—and thus bring down the awful consequences of their own ignorance and sin upon the heads of their unoffending children (Howe, 1976/1846, p. 34).

Reform schools, asylums, residential schools for increasingly specific handicaps (deafness, blindness, mental retardation) all began to appear in the nineteenth century as ways to get disabled children away from their parents. The colonial period operated under the assumption that disability led to inevitable poverty. The nineteenth century reversed that and said poverty almost always led to disability, maladjustment, or mistreatment. An institutional service system staffed by new generations of experts seemed more than willing to assume the parental role.

The Twentieth Century

This tradition of professionals displacing parents as proper nurturers of disabled children has continued to some degree to this very day. At least in the twentieth century, special education began by repeating the formula with only minor variations. After the turn of the century, a new wave of immigration renewed the fears and genuine concern by the members of the helping professions over the state of the family. One solution was to sort out of the regular grades those who could not make it. Some of these children were called retarded, some incorrigible, some disturbed. Whatever they were called, the children in these new ungraded classes were almost always poor, usually Italian (or from some other area of southern Europe), and judged to have a "defective" home life (Hoffman, 1975).

Increasingly in the years up to World War II, educators, psychiatrists, and social workers all borrowed a medical model by which to justify their takeover of parental functions. These experts were the "doctors" to a "sick society." One historian of the family has described the process as one whereby the "helping professions" invaded the family, convinced parents to rely on new scientific techniques and outside advice, and thereby dissipated the family's ability to overcome any special circumstances (Lasch, 1977). Parent education programs, in reality, just reinforced this dependency on experts as the source of "correct" procedure.

Lasch summarized the vicious circle in which families found themselves spinning.

> Having first declared parents incompetent to raise their offspring without professional help, social pathologists "gave back" the knowledge they had appropriated—gave it back in a mystifying fashion that rendered parents more helpless than ever, more abject in their dependence on expert opinion (Lasch, 1977, p. 18).

One rather crude measure of this notion of human services as a growth industry is the rapidly rising number of research articles on families published in professional journals. Table 1 shows that just counting articles on families with special needs (a large proportion of such articles dealing with handicapped children in their homes), the increase immediately after the war was striking. In the eight-year period from 1945 to 1953, almost as many research studies were cited (232) as in the preceding forty-five years combined (280). The table shows the trend continuing down to the 1970s. Even as time spans decrease, the absolute total rises. Clearly, professionals felt as though they had more and more to say about and to families with handicapped children.

Table 1
Articles on Families with Special Needs

	Total	Average per year
1900–1944	280	6.2
1945–1953	232	25.8
1954–1959	353	58.8
1960–1964	543	108.6
1965–1968	602	150.5
1969–1972	728	182.0

Note: From Dempsey, 1981, p. 7.

Box 1
A Sampling of Past Parental Contributions

It is easy to overlook how much parents have done for themselves and their children throughout history. Many innovations in services, support, and public legislation were first created or instigated by parents concerned about their children's welfare. Despite a history of blame from professionals, parents have long been active in educational, medical, legal, residential, vocational, and recreational reform efforts. The following list is just a sample of these parental efforts through the years.

1812   Benjamin Rush, one of the signers of the Declaration of Independence and a noted Philadelphia physician, published his best known work: *Medical Inquiries and Observations upon the Diseases of the Mind.* This was the first text on mental illness published in America. Rush pushed himself to complete the book after his son, John, became severely emotionally disturbed. John was placed under his father's care in the Pennsylvania Hospital in 1810. Although Rush himself died in 1813, his son remained locked in a hospital cell until his death in 1837.

1817   Mason Cogswell, Hartford surgeon and father of a deaf daughter, helped found the American School for the Deaf in Connecticut. This was the first such school in the country and began the noted work of Thomas Gallaudet and Laurent Clerc in America.

1820   Lady Elizabeth Lowther had the first book in English printed specifically for blind readers. The book, the *Gospel of Matthew,* was printed in raised line type (used in France before Braille) and was meant for her blind son.

1823   General Elias Barbee, a state senator and father of a nineteen-year-old deaf daughter, introduced the bill into the Kentucky legislature establishing a school for the deaf in Danville, Kentucky. It was the first state-supported school for deaf children.

1838   John Ball Brown, one of the first orthopedic surgeons in America, opened the country's first orthopedic hospital in Boston. Brown initially turned to orthopedics as a specialty because two of his sons suffered from physical impairments. One son died in youth, and the other followed his father into orthopedics and established the first children's orthopedic ward in 1861.

(continued)

Box 1
(continued)

1866   Theodore Roosevelt, the father of the president, helped establish the New York Orthopedic Dispensary and Hospital. Many innovations in nonsurgical treatment of physical disabilities were first tried there under the direction of Dr. Charles Fayette Taylor. Taylor, in 1859, had successfully treated Roosevelt's daughter Anna for spinal tuberculosis.

1887   Stephen Olin Garrison, a Methodist minister and father of a retarded child, started the Vineland Training School in New Jersey. It was the first such training school in the state and was later to become both a national research center for psychological measurement and the first to offer training programs for teachers.

1930s   Hundreds of parents of retarded children around the country independently started local parent organizations for support and advocacy. Cleveland, Ohio, and Spokane, Washington, had two of the earliest forerunners of the Association for Retarded Citizens.

1940–50   The National Association for Retarded Children (now Citizens) was formed. The United Cerebral Palsy Association was formed from several local chapters in New York. The Muscular Dystrophy Association of America was started by six mothers.

1956   John Holter, a hydraulics engineer whose son was born with spina bifida, developed (along with Dr. Eugene Spitz) the first successful valve for surgically implanted shunts. These shunts are still used to relieve skull pressure by drawing fluid from the child's head, thus reducing the brain damage resulting from hydrocephalus.

1975   Public Law 94-142 was passed. A coalition of parent groups were given much of the credit for the lobbying effort in Congress that finally passed this landmark legislation.

This list barely scratches the surface of parent contributions. What about your own community? One way of understanding parents of disabled children is to know the story of their past and current struggles. Who started the first parent group in your town? What programs or services did parents begin or support locally? What are their current efforts for change?

In summary, then, the history of professional involvement with families of disabled children is characterized by at least two main trends. First, there was a fairly steady tendency to blame parents as either causing or worsening their children's problems. At first, this was done in moralistic terms and ethnic stereotypes. Later, it was done in supposedly "objective" medical/scientific analysis. Second, with increasing specialization experts have claimed more and more functions from traditional parent responsibilities.

The Nature and Source of Parental Reactions

In the last twenty-five years or so, professional approaches to parents have become less and less uniform. Certainly many themes from the past can still be identified today in what is said and written about parents. But now, there are more and more dissenting voices to be heard. Assessment of parental reactions has diversified in approach, and reports of parental involvement programs show a much broader range of services than before.

In this section we will outline the directions taken by educators and other professionals in how they perceive parents. There are major differences in how one perceives parents of disabled children. There are also significant variations in how professionals have tried to become involved with parents. Unfortunately, little attention has been given to possible connections between the two. Is there a link between how professionals perceive the needs and functions of parents and what kinds of parent involvement those professionals offer? To use some human services jargon, is there a logical progression when moving from parental needs assessment to program design and service delivery?

The floodtide of literature pertaining to parental adjustment to a handicapped child has already been noted. To make sense of it all, it is helpful to have an organizational model. There are two important questions that most research on parental attitudes and behavior attempts to answer, at least implicitly.

1. What is the *nature* of parental reaction to having a handicapped child?
2. What is the *source* of parental reaction to having a handicapped child?

Each major perspective on parents can be located according to its answers to these basic questions. Before looking at specific research, the options available for answering the nature and source questions need some brief elaboration.

Most professionals tend to answer the first (or nature) question in one of two ways. The *nature* of parental reaction is perceived in predominantly *attitudinal* or *behavioral* terms. It is true, of course, that this is not always as pure a split as portrayed here. Some professionals use both attitudinal and behavioral categories to interpret parental reaction. Nonetheless, it is fair to divide the research along these lines as the two major orientations that researchers have chosen.

*Teachers can profit by obtaining a parent's perspective on her child.
(Photograph by Mima Cataldo.)*

One way to think of this is as a continuum. Starting with a pure attitudinal approach on one end and a pure behavioral approach on the other end, one can envision all sorts of possible combinations of emphasis along the continuum. Make an imaginary division in the middle of the line. This produces our two main answers to the nature of parental response to having a child with disabilities.

$$\longleftarrow \quad\bullet\quad \longrightarrow$$

Attitudinal   Behavioral

Most research on the nature of parental response has assumed an attitudinal orientation. The categories used in such research usually refer to various emotions or feelings that the parents are said to have in connection with their disabled child. This research tends to talk about what parents feel rather than what they do. The point is that research with this focus makes the claim—either explicitly or implicitly—that the most important factors in understanding parents' reactions are emotional in nature. This does not mean that professionals who use this perspective never talk about what parents actually do. However, what parents do is usually interpreted as arising out of some more basic emotional dynamic. The *nature* of parents' reactions to their disabled child is intrinsically attitudinal.

The behavioral approach tends to focus on what parents *do* instead of how they *feel*. The essence of parental response to a disabled child is in how they behave differently, not how they feel differently. Again, these divisions are seldom rigidly observed in practice. Many behavioral researchers will also discuss how parents' attitudes have developed. The difference in some cases is merely verbal. Whether you study the psychological occurrence of depression in parents or the behavioral pattern of social withdrawal might make little practical difference in some cases. Nonetheless, labels are important; they influence our perceptions. The conceptual gap between the attitudinal and behavioral answers to the basic nature of parental response can be very wide.

Another difference, besides the conceptual categories used, is the research methods of the two approaches. Behavioral studies are much more likely to be large quantitative surveys. Attitudinal approaches are more likely to be small, qualitative, and anecdotal. The reasons for this may be fairly simple. Behaviors are easier to count than emotions. Attitudinal studies in the past have often been clinically based, in-depth interviews. Behavioral studies in the past have often been community-based, survey questionnaires. Finally, although this difference is vanishing, behavioral approaches have done more with fathers and whole family units. The attitudinal approach has tended to emphasize the mother-child pair as most important.

What about the second (or source) question? What is the *source* of parental reaction to a disabled child? Here again there are two broad alternative answers, which also cut cross the attitudinal-behavioral continuum. The two alternative sources are normative and situational. Imagine another line or continuum with the normative perspective at one end and the situational perspective at the other. Because these alternative perspectives may be used by either attitudinal or behavioral approaches, make the new line intersect the first one. Now we have a diagram of possible research orientations that looks like this:

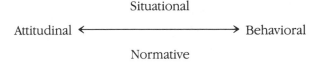

The normative answer to the source question is by far the most common one among professionals. This approach sees the parent-child relationship as the all-important fulcrum upon which the balance of family harmony depends. The disability of the child almost inevitably upsets that balance. The source of problems in parental adjustment is seen as inherent to the disrupted parent-child relationship. As a *rule* or *norm,* the disabled child will be the source of impaired parental behavior or emotion. The disabled child is the *root* of the parents' inevitable problems.

The situational approach to the source question finds much less that is unavoidable or inherent in parental responses. The source of those responses is socially determined and thus varies from situation to situation. This approach has been adopted by professionals only recently and still is a minority position. Rather than a set of abstract norms that the parent inevitably follows, the reaction is said to be concrete and variable. How disruptive the disability is to the family is said to have less to do with the specific handicap and much more to do with social, economic, educational, and historical factors. The parent-child relationship is important but not rule-bound, and no more important than these other determinants of how well a parent's needs are met. How handicapping the child's disability is for both the child and the family is really the *fruit* of a social system that presents more or fewer obstacles to the family's adjustment.

Beginning with the two basic questions of nature and source, we now have four possible professional orientations toward parental response to a disabled child: one for each quadrant of the diagram (Figure 1). Each of these orientations has made important contributions to the understanding of parents. By examining some illustrations of research from each of the four cells, we can better examine the strengths and deficiencies of each position. The four positions are:

1. Psychodynamic
2. Psychosocial
3. Functionalist
4. Interactionist

Psychodynamic Orientation

The single largest body of professional literature on parents uses a psychodynamic frame of reference for parental response. This perspective is attitudinal and normative. The broad purpose of such research is to locate the parents somewhere within the boundaries of the psychoanalytic tradition begun by Freud. It is in the language of this psychological culture that the most common descriptions of the "typical" parent of a disabled child are

		Source of parental adjustment to handicapped child	
		Normative disruption	Situational disruption
Nature of parental adjustment to handicapped child	Attitudes	Psychodynamic	Psychosocial
	Behaviors	Functionalist	Interactionist

Figure 1. *Professionals' reactions to parents.*

stated. Hostility, denial, grief, guilt, defense mechanisms, and a positive goal of acceptance are all prominent terms in this traditional profile of parents. There has been a tendency in the psychodynamic orientation to interpret parents of disabled children as inevitably beset by neurotic tendencies. Many parental behaviors can be explained by this approach as symptomatic of some internalized guilt or anger.

The majority of research of this type reports the personal impressions of social workers or psychologists in the field. A smaller but significant number is more extensive research using various attitude assessment instruments, scales, and interviews. Even in the more quantified studies, though, the interpretation of the data collected is still often very flexible. The author of one of these studies admitted that judging, for example, how "accepting" a parent was of his or her disabled child "must be based on a highly subjective impression" (Zuk, 1959, p. 140).

Now, of course, many professionals would respond that either this subjectivity was not a disadvantage or that there were methods to reduce it. There is, at least, the danger present in most research that people tend to see what they look for, regardless of what is found. The psychological criteria are particularly susceptible to this since no one really sees an emotion at all. The criteria employed to class parents under any of the usual psychodynamic headings are largely left up to the desires and judgments of the professional. And, as one candid researcher has noted, the "parents are rarely acquainted with the criteria in advance" (Barsch, 1968, p. 8). Research on parents often tells us as much or more about the professionals doing the research as it does about the parents.

None of this gainsays the argument that the psychodynamic approach has produced many useful insights. The categories developed by this perspective are certainly applicable to some parents, some times, or in some settings. The psychodynamic focus on neurotic tendencies has produced at least four attitudes commonly applied to parents of disabled children: guilt, anger, denial, and grief or depression.

Guilt.   This is by far the most often mentioned attitude of parents. Perhaps this is so because of the myriad *sources* put forth as causes of the emotion. Indeed, guilt is often interpreted as causative of many of the other attitudes discussed later. Others will argue that guilt is a derivative from other emotions such as anger and denial. The symptoms of guilt illustrate the subjective nature of this approach. Some writers (Solnit & Stark, 1961) see guilt feelings as one extreme reaction to overwhelming grief experienced upon the child's diagnosis. Those writers attribute active parent involvement and dedication to the welfare of the handicapped child to a deep-seated need to compensate for an underlying guilt complex. On the other hand, some professionals have said just the opposite: parental guilt leads to apathetic behavior and depression (McKeith, 1973). This is an example of two completely opposite *behaviors* being assigned to the same emotion by different professionals.

A psychologist from a local university once visited a preschool where we taught. She worked closely with parents of disabled children in her clinic on campus. She came to the school to observe how parents interacted with their disabled children in the classroom (the parents usually stayed to work in the classroom). The day of her visit was also the first day in class for one mother and her two-year-old severely handicapped son. The mother struck us as understandably nervous and eager to please. She had had essentially no help with her child for two years. At one point the mother spilled some milk on her child as she tried to use some special techniques to encourage his swallowing. The mother became upset and began to cry softly. We proceeded with the lesson and the tears stopped shortly. After class, the visiting psychologist said "My, that one mother is certainly struggling with her guilt complex over not getting help sooner for her child." It seemed to us then that although the psychologist had seen exactly the same behavior as we had all morning, we "perceived" a very different account of what took place. What the psychologist called guilt seemed to us a nervous mother very eager to get some assistance with her son. We thought the mother was afraid we might reject her child as a student (as had the other programs she had tried). Surely we and the psychologist should have been the ones to feel guilty at the inadequacies of our professions in helping this woman.

Other examples of parental behavior described as guilt laden are common parent questions such as "What did I do to cause this?" "Why did it happen to me?" Some research has examined religious and social variables as more or less productive of guilt. The problem is keeping all the possible factors from overlapping in such studies. Thus, several writers have found Catholic parents to be much less guilt laden than Protestant or Jewish parents (Zuk, 1962; Hoffman, 1965). However, variables other than religion might also lead to such results. Categories such as income level, family size, ethnic membership, and other possibilities might explain the differences (Wolfensberger, 1983). One might be wary of attempts to capture the effects of religion on a person's life and emotions through questionnaires and brief interviews.

The basic question is whether the behavior cited is accurately described as guilty. One parent writes about the case of a frustrated mother who felt no matter what her action, it would be described as guilty by some professional. The writer then complained: "Is not what appears to be 'guilt feelings' to professionals, merely concern with the child's welfare, mingled with grief over his handicap?" (Patterson, 1956, p. 16). She goes on to suggest the term *regret* as more explanatory of the types of feelings that the psychodynamic orientation calls guilt.

Finally, the behavior of parents being interpreted as guilt laden might be situational in character. When being interviewed in a clinic or a classroom by a doctor or teacher, some parents may respond to accusations whether intended by the professional or not. Outside of that setting—away from the "professional's turf"—perhaps no such feelings occur. The mother in our preschool class would be an example of a parent who behaved very differently at home (and later on in class, too). A friend of ours does the PTA newsletter for her child's school. Every month when she turns in her handwritten copy to the principal to be typed, she practically breaks into a cold sweat worrying that it will be given back with a "C minus" on it with all the spelling errors underlined. Another friend tells of his own guilty response to the doctor giving him his annual physical. "Yes, I still eat too much. No, I still don't exercise regularly. I know my pulse rate should be slower. I am a terrible person. Please forgive me, doctor." Once outside the doctor's office he usually reflects (over a bowl of ice cream) that he is not really that bad a person. Anytime parents talk to the "authorities" about their children, a similar reaction may occur. As the history of professional intervention into child rearing shows, the reaction is not accidental.

Overall, guilt seems to have been overemphasized in the research. The point is not that parents never feel guilty; rather, it is that the psychodynamic orientation has overstated guilt's prevalence as an almost unavoidable normative response to having a handicapped child. This tendency arises again and again within the psychodynamic perspective.

Anger.   Anger (hostility, aggression) is another emotion that the psychodynamic orientation presents as almost inevitable for parents. Usually the anger is described as originally directed toward the disabled child (Zuk, 1962; Pinkerton, 1970). Such feelings are not socially acceptable or appropriate, of course. So the parent redirects this anger toward the teacher, doctor, or another professional involved with the child. The *source* of this emotion is seen as rooted in the parent's displeasure at having an "imperfect" child. Because the parent cannot blame the child for having cerebral palsy, for example, the focus is shifted to the nearest available professional.

Once again, notice some alternative explanations that question the normative perspective. By automatically interpreting displays of parental hostility as based in the parent's own neurotic reaction to the child, the professional avoids examining his or her own performance as possibly inadequate. Seemingly irrational displays of hostility may well be attributable to factors that go far beyond the parent-child relationship to include the insensitivity or simple ignorance of physicians and educators. Rather than a pathological condition, the anger in many cases may be an understandable reaction to professional incompetence or insensitivity in dealing with parents. One parent presents this perspective succinctly: "We *are* angry. We have gone to the helping professions and have received too little help" (Gorham, 1975, p. 522).

Denial.   A third common emotional reaction listed by the psychodynamic orientation is denial (Stanhope & Bell, 1981; Wetter, 1972). Such studies are usually restricted to specific disability labels such as mental retardation, learning disability, autism, or emotional disability. The argument is that the often vague nature of diagnosing and labeling such disabilities is lost on parents

---

Box 2
One Parent's Encounter with the Psychodynamic Model

Mary S. Akerley (1978) has described the service system that breeds anger (justifiably so) in parents.

> It's hot and sunny, a magnificent day. We're on our way south on I-95, heading for the National Society for Autistic Children conference in Orlando. It's a perfect setting for thinking back because if it weren't for Eddie, none of us would be here enjoying this particular drive, in this particular place, on our way to a delightful vacation.
>
> The four kids are, of course, all wearing tee shirts expressing their individual allegiances to some cause, place, or rock group. But so are Mom and Dad. . . .
>
> My tee shirt has two very nasty-looking vultures on it. One is saying to the other: "Patience My Ass . . . I'm Going to Kill Something!" The shirt was a gift from a NSAC friend, another member of the battered parent club. Most of us, like the hungry vulture, have run out of patience and have struck out for ourselves . . . and for our children.
>
> We don't begin in anger. We start out the way all parents of all children do: with respect, reverence really, for the professional and his skills. The pediatrician, the teacher, the writer of books and articles on child development, they are all the sources of wisdom from which we must draw in order to be good parents. We believe, we consult, we do as we are told, and all goes well unless . . . one of our kids has a handicap. [She proceeds to cite an example of professional insensitivity.]
>
> So our poor therapist would not feel entirely useless, we made up interesting problems for him to work on. We specialized in religious crises, taking our cue from an early session (the second one, if I remember correctly) which he filled with the telling of his own life story. He was an ex-priest married to an ex-nun, and they had not waited for Rome to dispense them from their vows before beginning their life together. I'm still not sure of the reason for this astonishing confession—perhaps to set us at ease, perhaps to challenge us to play "Can You Top This?" We tried. And, since we were not allowed to talk about Eddie, we spent a lot of time on the therapist's children, two boys aged three and five, whom their daddy seemed to have a great deal of difficulty managing.
>
> One day he advised us that the entire staff had observed that we acted like strangers in the waiting room before our appointment (it was 8:00 A.M., for God's sake!), whereupon we graciously offered to make love the very next week if the school would provide a comfortable couch. They didn't, but we were finally excused from therapy with the inspiring words, "Well, you've won! You don't have

(continued)

Box 2
(continued)

to come in any more!" Cured, were we? Not really, just vocal. I had been on a fairly well-publicized TV talk show the week before (I was then president of the state chapter of NSAC) and had used the opportunity to blast the inflated costs of private special schools, citing enforced, useless psychotherapy as a prime factor.

Eddie is now in our public school's SLD (specific learning disabilities) program. To be sure, he is still very much on the periphery of life, and that is hard for all of us . . . so near and yet so far. But it is more progress than any of the many people who have worked with him over the years ever dared hope for. We are elated and grateful but I, at least, have not—cannot—forgive those who, instead of helping, added to our pain. I believe there can be no greater sin (pp. 39–40, 47).

---

who just deny the reality that something is wrong with the child. Vain hopes for impossible cures, constant shopping for the latest program or technique, and explaining away inappropriate behavior are all examples of types of parental actions cited as evidence of denial of the basic disability. The more severe the disability, supposedly the less likely is such denial to surface.

Studies usually attempt to demonstrate denial in parents by comparing the parents' estimations of their children's abilities, with professional assessments of the same children. Another parental behavior attributed to denial is sometimes called "doctor shopping," or "teacher shopping." Parents are said to go shopping from doctor to doctor or teacher to teacher until they hear a prognosis optimistic enough for them to "buy" (Baum, 1962).

In this case the professional literature seems to support overwhelmingly the rejection of denial as a *frequent,* much less inevitable, stage of parental reaction (Wolfensberger, 1983). Many parents will reject the use of certain labels (e.g., mentally retarded) as repugnant, yet will be very accurate describing specific behaviors of the child (Heifetz, 1980). The point is, again, that while certainly some parents have trouble "accepting" a limitation on their child's development, the mitigating factors in such a reaction make the attribution of denial a risky one.

The practice of "doctor shopping," for example, has been explained by many parents as something they were forced to do, not something they chose. If a parent goes to five separate professionals and gets five various diagnoses as to what is "wrong," if anything, with a child, which "reality" is it that the parent is denying? If one teacher says a child belongs in a separate class, and another says no, the child just needs a little resource help, how does the parent choose the correct assessment and deny the false one? No one demands that professionals always speak with one voice. Why then do we label neurotic the parents who listen to someone else's words?

Grief. A final area of parental emotion that has received a lot of attention in the psychodynamic orientation is the pattern of grief. Grief itself is, of course, a normal reaction upon learning one's child is disabled. The argument is made, however, that this grief becomes neurotic because the situation is chronic. One famous study, mentioned earlier (Solnit & Stark, 1961), epitomizes this approach. Solnit and Stark (1961) have argued that grief in parents is a two-fold psychological process in reaction to the birth of a severely retarded child. There is bereavement over the loss of the socially demanded and personally anticipated perfect infant. This is coupled with shock and repulsion from the "defective" child actually born.

> In child bearing, the simultaneous loss of one child—the expected and narcissistically invested one—and adaptation to the deviant or defective child makes [*sic*] a demand that is very likely to be overwhelming. There is no time for working through the loss of the desired child before there is a demand to invest the new and handicapped child as a love object (Solnit & Stark, 1961, p. 526).

This passage illustrates the classic language of a psychodynamic orientation. It finds the emotional reaction "overwhelming." It tends easily to become pathological in terms of withdrawal and depression.

Several points need to be made about this description of grief. No one—including Solnit and Stark—would deny that a certain amount of grief upon discovery that one's child is handicapped is normal. What some critics would deny is the association of disability with an inherent tendency for that grief to become excessive and overwhelming. In such cases, argue the psychodynamic adherents, the grief leads to any of a variety of neurotic actions. Either excessive involvement with the child or excessive withdrawal can result. Solnit and Stark have compared this situation with the death of a child. What makes the birth of a handicapped child more emotionally devastating is that the mourning period is commingled with the adjustment to the handicap. The normal grief process is interrupted and this makes it develop neurotically, if not pathologically.

The account given by Solnit and Stark is certainly debatable. Most of the criticisms are made by advocates of the psychosocial approach and will be discussed in that section. However, the limited application of this description of grief must be noted. Solnit and Stark have described a situation in which the child's disability, such as spina bifida or Down's syndrome, is discovered immediately at birth. It is not clear how this situation might differ from one in which the realization of a child's problems is gradual and often uncertain (say with learning disabilities). What is the nature of grief for parents in such cases? Is "grief" even the appropriate term? Is there, perhaps, a certain cathartic value to an intense period of grief as opposed to the extended uncertainty associated with disabilities "discovered" only as the child develops? Little investigation has been made into this comparison.

How might we summarize the psychodynamic approach? Positively, the approach claims to discover deep-seated emotional explanations for those types of parental behavior that most bother professionals. No professional likes to be the object of a parent's hostility, for example. The psychodynamic perspective at least allows the professional to "excuse" the parent's anger as a neurotic symptom caused by the trauma of raising a disabled child.

Negatively, the approach tends to "put the parent on the couch." That is, the perspective creates a laundry list of neuroses from which almost every parent will exhibit an item or two at one time or another. There is a strong tendency to view parents as sick and in need of therapy. The problem is that the angry parent might be justifiably angry at the professional. This perspective encourages the professional to ignore such possible explanations. Anything the parent does is merely further evidence of emotional maladjustment.

It is vital to notice that these neuroses do not just happen to coincide with the disability. The archetype of this perspective portrays the parent as unavoidably emotionally damaged *as the result of* the handicapped child. The handicapped child causes handicapped parents. Some speak of the "imperfect" child causing "overwhelming" grief and despair. Others cite guilt and anger as inevitable feelings attached, as it were, to the diagnosis of impairment.

The extent to which this tendency can be taken is seen in the title of an article called "Parentalplegia" (Murray & Cornell, 1981). The authors' own description of what they mean by this term speaks volumes about the psychodynamic tendency to view parents as "mentally ill."

> Children having conditions of mental retardation or other handicaps involving physical deficiencies are likely to be *causes* of a secondary handicapping condition involving the parents. . . . The authors have chosen the term parentalplegia to describe a secondary psycho-physiological (stress induced) condition that evolves among parents of handicapped children. Parentalplegia seems to be caused by an inability on the part of parents to adjust to the handicap of their children (Murray & Cornell, 1981, p. 201).

Historically, the psychodynamic approach illustrates the major shift in professional attitudes toward parents. Recall that the dominant theme in professional concerns for the family up until World War II was that parents cause or worsen their children's handicaps. This theme reached its height in clinical sophistication and subtlety in the work of Bruno Bettelheim, who specialized in the area of autism. What most parents remember of Bettelheim's message is that the emotional frigidity of the mother caused the withdrawal and autistic behavior of the child. Bettelheim's work is much less fashionable today than when it first appeared. Instead, we have just the reverse in psychodynamic circles. The child handicaps the parents, causing a "secondary psycho-physiological condition." Unfortunately, neither the earlier nor the more recent orientation goes beyond the parent-child relationship to examine the context in which that relationship occurs. The psychosocial approach attempts to correct this.

Psychosocial Orientation

The psychosocial approach also focuses on parents' attitudinal reactions to having a disabled child. However, this approach is situational rather than normative. The emotional categories seen as important tend to be very different from those relied on in the psychodynamic group. Guilt, anger, depression, and denial are replaced by terms such as *stress, chronic sorrow,* and *loneliness.* This perspective has been growing in recent years, but still is used much less often than the psychodynamic approach.

The main difference in the psychosocial categories is implied by its name. Instead of focusing exclusively on the parent(usually the mother)-to-child relationship as with the psychodynamic approach, this approach expands its attention. The social context within which that parent-child relationship occurs becomes much more important. The *nature* of parental reactions remains attitudinal. The *source* of those emotions, though, is seen as largely determined by the social context rather than the handicap itself. As the social context varies, the reaction of parents will also change. In a sense this approach says there is no single, *essential* emotional reaction involved in raising a child with disabilities. Rather, there are numerous possibilities or attitudinal directions that social settings may encourage or allow parents to follow. We will look at three: chronic sorrow, novelty shock, and stress.

Chronic Sorrow.   One of the most influential examples of the psychosocial perspective describes a parental reaction of chronic sorrow (Olshansky, 1961; Wikler, Wasow, & Hatfield, 1981). One can contrast this chronic sorrow to the grief decribed by Solnit and Stark (1961). Olshansky agrees that parents may very well feel profound sorrow and grief upon the discovery of their child's disability. He goes on to admit that for some parents that sadness remains at a certain level. Most parents never reach a point at which they jump out of bed one morning and say, "Oh boy, I'm so glad Johnny is still retarded!" Olshansky's point is that such behavior would be very odd. The sadness persists, but—contrary to Solnit and Stark—there is nothing pathological or overwhelming about it unless made so by factors outside the parent and child. The grief normally experienced by parents is a "natural and understandable response to a tragic fact" (Olshansky, 1962, p. 4). The abnormal aspect of such grief is more often in the professional's assumptions than in the parents' emotions. Sometimes, Olshansky has argued, parents will even perceive the neurosis they are expected to exhibit and obligingly develop the symptoms demanded. The perspective toward parents assumed by a professional can strongly influence how some parents will behave in the presence of that professional (e.g., Box 2).

Novelty Shock.   A second example of the psychosocial approach provides an alternative explanation to the psychodynamic attributions of denial and guilt. This pattern of reaction is novelty shock (Wolfensberger, 1983), which has a superficial similarity to the psychodynamic analysis of Solnit and Stark. Upon the discovery of a child's disability, a parent's expectations will be altered or destroyed. This approach, however, differs from the earlier one in that the specific handicap itself has little to do with the process. The point of novelty shock is that something different from the anticipated occurs. The novelty of the situation produces reactions ranging from bewilderment and confusion to utter dismay. In this analysis the problem is less one of grief induced by a tragic occurrence than one of utter confusion over what has occurred. The crucial factor is not the handicap but the perceived social evaluations and interpretations of the event. Wolfensberger (1967) used the diagnosis of a child as retarded as an example of the process:

> The parents realize that the event is rare and that their expectancies have to be radically revised, but they know virtually nothing about what the realistic expectancies now are. The crucial element is not retardation at all; it is the demolition of expectancies (Wolfensberger, 1967, p. 336).

Stress. A final category of psychosocial orientation comes from a professional who also happens to be the parent of a disabled son (Featherstone, 1980). Stress becomes a category that might manifest itself in any number of ways. The stress is seen as produced primarily by the setting, however, rather than anything inherent to the handicap. For example, a lack of support services may leave a parent with little assistance or respite in coping with the unavoidable needs of the disabled child. Such a parent may begin to feel tense, frustrated, angry, guilty over irrepressible impatience, and just plain burned out. That same parent, when given adequate social support and respite, may experience fewer or none of those reactions. The stress experienced by parents then is reality based and not due to any neurotic distortions. Such "reality stress" is the product of an inadequate service system rather than the emotional turmoil inherent to the psychodynamic hypothesis (Wolfensberger, 1983). As one sensitive professional has mentioned (Menolascino, 1974), it is of little value to inquire of the parent about possible displays of anal fixation when the essential problem is changing twelve diapers a day while wondering how to go about toilet training a multiply handicapped child.

To summarize the psychosocial approach positively, it provides a healthy corrective to the excessive medicalization of parents found in the psychodynamic orientation. Emotions arise in various shapes and forms; what parents feel is the product of myriad influences, not any single factor. Parental reaction to a disabled child is more or less adaptive depending on the social context. There is *no one* natural way or sequence of ways for parents to respond. This makes the job of helping much tougher on professionals. It assumes that services should be based on actual parental need rather than preconceived categories of analysis.

The negative side of the psychosocial perspective is one it shares with

---

Box 3
Stage Theories of Parent Responses

Stage theories are currently popular among many professionals. The common element in these theories is a sequence of phases or stages that parents are said to pass through in a more or less orderly fashion. Often the first stage is shock and the last stage is acceptance or adjustment. What comes in between these two varies tremendously and can be either psychodynamic or behavioral in orientation. Stage theories tend to be normative rather than situational, however, because they hold that a certain order of responses is almost inevitable for parents regardless of the situation.

Many parents we know do not like stage theories. One in particular wrote out his objections for us.

> Stage theories tie me and my feelings up in a neat little box. But I don't feel that clean and tidy. I think any accurate account of my reactions to having a handicapped son must retain a certain ambiguity and a lot of variation. A certain amount of messiness belongs in my world.
>
> I appreciate how having a set of stages all ready for me to pass through helps professionals organize their own responses. Unfortunately, I just never seem to follow their script. Sometimes I feel like I'm the only one acting without a script. No matter what I say, they respond with some well-rehearsed lines that don't relate to me at all. I feel like I'm always missing my cues.
>
> Then there's this "acceptance" stage at the end that I am supposed to reach. The trouble is, I hope I never accept the limitations placed on my child. Some of these limits are unavoidable and some are the needless results of society's neglect. Either way, I don't like them. I can't understand why professionals want me to.
>
> What I have done with my son is not so much go through stages as bridge some gaps. Gaps in information. Gaps in power. Gaps in services. Gaps in trust and cooperation. Until those gaps are bridged completely, I feel that I'll be partially separated from any professional no matter what stage I'm supposed to be in.

---

the psychodynamic outlook. If allowed to become rigid, both views artificially restrict their attention to the attitudinal side of parental response. For far too long the emotional makeup of parents was almost all that professionals examined when seeking to help families. It is not that this attitudinal aspect is unimportant, but by itself the emotional focus has historically proven too narrow a framework to support a solid understanding for helping families with disabled children. The real impetus to do more with parents than counsel them has come mainly from the behavioral views to which we now turn.

Functionalist Orientation

The presence of a disabled child disrupts the family's function according to this approach. That is, the family's behavior becomes dysfunctional because of the disabled child. The behavioral *nature* of the parent's response is seen as inherently maladaptive because of its basis in altered family roles. The dysfunction may surface, according to this view, in any of several areas of family life. Two examples of functional analysis of familial disruption are role model disruption and marital or family integration.

Role Model Disruption.   This example draws its categories from the writings of Talcott Parsons, who is usually identified as the main proponent of functionalism as a branch of sociological theory. Parsons and others "discovered" two main parental roles necessary for smooth family function. These two roles (also called *pattern variables*) are the expressive and the instrumental. In the expressive role, the parent performs those more emotional, affective functions that promote harmony within the family. As usually elaborated (Tallman, 1965), this role falls mainly on the mother. The instrumental role supplies the technical, task-oriented functions that keep the family operating. Predictably, the father is said to serve in the instrumental role.

Using this analysis, several professionals have argued that disabled children prevent parents from adequately filling these roles. The more severe the disability, the more disruption of parental roles. In one case the most disruption is found to occur with the father's function (Tallman, 1965). Usually, the disruption is also said to be worse if the child is male. In such a case, the functionalist analysis describes the father's training for the instrumental role as superfluous, unnecessary. The father is never going to take his son out and teach him how to catch a baseball. The son's skill level will rather remain within fairly low demands of tasks and the expressive functions will continue to dominate well beyond the normal period of infancy. Thus this analysis sees mothers as perhaps feeling comfortable as contributors to the children's well-being. Others feel left out and aimless. The sense of purpose "is less likely for fathers, who have been deprived of the opportunity to function as socializing agents and models for their children" (Tallman, 1965, p. 42).

Other professionals writing from the functionalist perspective (Meadow & Meadow, 1971), however, disagree that the instrumental role cannot be fulfilled. The normal components of the role are unavoidably altered, though. Thus, learning ways to exercise a child with cerebral palsy can become a technical or instrumental function. The pressure also increases for the parents to share both roles. Both parents need to perform both roles at different times. The struggle in that case becomes the social one of having the information needed to perform the new tasks, as well as making adjustments in the balance and composition of the traditional roles.

A final example of role model disruption comes from one of the largest studies of families with disabled children (Farber, 1962). This major study of over 600 families does not depend as much on the specific breakdown of roles into instrumental and expressive categories. More general family roles are seen as crucial instead.

This study identifies two types of role *crisis*. But again, the parents face the crisis because the disability factor is entered into the parent-child equation. The normal role of parenting is itself thought to be disabled because of the disabled child. As before, the role parents are expected to play in their family cycle is arrested by the presence of the handicap. The resulting disruption may pertain to the disappearance of future roles the parent hoped to play, roles formed by goals for family success and achievement (e.g., sending your child to college). The disruption also may relate to the lack of normal, daily roles of family life. Farber has called the first disruption a "tragic crisis," and the latter a "role-organization crisis." The difference between the two is one of ends and means. The tragic crisis involves the *ends* of family life as defined by the parents. The role-organization crisis involves the *means* of daily survival (Farber, 1968).

The tragic crisis can be seen as the behavioral counterpart to the psychodynamic grief over the loss of the "perfect" child. Both have to do with destroyed expectations. In the one case this leads to the attitudinal pathology previously outlined. Here it leads to a kind of behavioral confusion in which parental activity becomes pointless. Upper-class families are usually said to be more susceptible to this tragic crisis because they place more stress on long-range goals. The initial impact at the point of diagnosis is greater in these cases.

The role-organization crisis seems similar at first to the reality stress category attributed to Featherstone (1980) and Wolfensberger (1967). The emphasis in both cases is on the mundane but essential, day-to-day management strategies. However, the functionalist orientation is crucially different in its analysis of cause or source. The role organization crisis conceives itself as wholly intrafamilial in nature and source. The reality stress perspective, on the other hand, goes far beyond the family in identifying the disruptive forces. The difference can be seen in the following quotations:

> [T]he role-organization crisis is concerned with the inability to organize a system of workable roles or means. The presence of a system of workable roles implies an ability to control activities of the individual members. Hence . . . role-reorganization crisis occurs in the realm of what is regarded *as controllable by the family members* [emphasis added] (Farber, 1962, p. 232).

whereas in reality-stress:

> *Forces external to and only partially controllable by the parents* result in situations that make it impossible, exceedingly difficult, or inadvisable for the retardate to remain integrated into the family or the community [emphasis added] (Wolfensberger, 1967, p. 337).

The problem with the functionalist analysis in general is identified here. It is the broader problem of the normative perspective shared by the psychodynamic approach. Functionalism sees the roles as intrinsic to the family, not just social tradition and setting. The disruption, by introducing the disabled child into the family, becomes equally inevitable to the family function. One can remain within the functionalist perspective and argue that roles are not disrupted as much as some claim (Meadow & Meadow, 1971) by the different demands placed on parents of a disabled child. Disruption in role adjustment then occurs "only" as families fail to adjust their own roles to fit the new needs. The roles themselves remain normative.

One can also deny the functionalist orientation itself and argue that family structure is not set and immutable. It is influenced by social setting, social services, and social demands. The entry of women into the work force might be used as an example of how family functions change over time.

Marital or Family Cohesiveness.   This is a second category employed by the functionalist perspective. The assumption is that a disabled child has a largely negative influence on the harmony within the family. Usually this marital harmony is measured by (1) the extent of spousal agreement over domestic priorities for family success and (2) the amount of tension within the family structure (Farber, 1962).

The results of studies of marital harmony have been unclear. Earlier research seemed to indicate gross disruptions in families when a disabled child lived at home (Farber, 1962; Stanhope & Bell, 1981). Parents disagreed on goals for family life. Siblings of disabled children were said to be resentful of their status in the family. Families were seen to withdraw from social interaction in general. One way of showing this supposedly normative disruption was by comparing families of institutionalized disabled children with families in which the disabled child remained at home. Thus, the early studies by Farber and his colleagues claimed the families with institutionalized children were much more relaxed, harmonious, and integrated. They participated more in activities outside the house. However, subsequent studies have shown the danger of professional assumptions concerning what is normative and what is not. In the late 1950s there were relatively few community-based programs for disabled children. Support services for families were erratic or nonexistent. The question unasked by the functionalist researchers was whether this purely *social* factor of a lack of services had more to do with marital harmony levels than did any inherently disruptive influence of the disabled child living at home. Several years later a study revealed that when disabled children living at home were in day programs or schools, marital integration was much higher than in families without such services (Fowle, 1965). What was earlier perceived as normative and unavoidable is now seen as largely dependent on the quality of social support available.

Other studies have mentioned factors apart from the disability as having much more influence on family stability. Income, for example, can affect family tranquility (Barsch, 1968; Breslau, Salkever, & Staruch, 1982). A study of divorce rates of families with genetically disabled children found those rates, on the whole, not significantly different from general rates of divorce (Roesel & Lawlis, 1983).

The point again seems to be that social factors such as community support, educational programming, and financial security have as much to do with family harmony and behavior as does the disabled child. It is surely *not* inherent to family structure that a disabled child drive parents and children apart from each other.

Interactionist Orientation

The interactionist orientation is the last of the four major alternative views of parental response to a disabled child. It is behavioral and situational in terms of our diagram. You can probably predict how it differs from the functionalist outlook. Instead of set functions that families have to fulfill if they are to endure, there are said to be areas of interaction between the family and society. These interactions are not immutable. Specific circumstances continually alter the functions actually served.

One purpose of interactionist research, which is still very limited when compared to other approaches, is to refute the normative assumptions of functionalist research. This has been done just by duplicating functionalist studies, except for improving the services, setting, or support systems.

A second example of interactionism, however, uses different categories from mainstream functionalism. This is the study of stigma. Society brands people with disabilities as undesirable. The result of this stigmatization is discrimination. The various forms of discrimination are often similar to that experienced by many other minorities in our culture. This discrimination process affects parents indirectly through something called courtesy stigma (Goffman, 1963). Just by being parents of a disabled child, parents, too, are excluded from activities, denied services, or just made socially unwelcome (see Figure 2). Parents describe how friends drop away after the birth of a disabled child (Featherstone, 1980). Suddenly parents feel unwelcome when they bring their family to church (Ferguson & Heifetz, 1983).

Socially inflicted problems have also been identified in economic terms. Poor families with disabled children get less attention and lower quality services than well-to-do families. Middle-class families are sometimes impoverished due to financial needs associated with certain disabilities. Other behaviors just beginning to be understood from an interactionist perspective include fatigue (Featherstone, 1980) and powerlessness (Massie & Massie, 1975). All of these categories vary in terms of how much a society has helped meet the needs of families with disabled children. What range of physical, social, and familial resources is available? Finally, the family itself is a changing, evolving unit. It has a unique history preceding the disabled child. It has its own unique future life molded by an array of intangible resources (Kelman, 1964).

The interactionist perspective focuses on three basic factors that need to

Source of parental adjustment to handicapped child

	Normative disruption	Situational disruption

Attitudes	Psychodynamic
	
	Parental neuroses
	    guilt
	    anger
	    denial
	    grief
		Psychosocial
		
		Chronic sorrow
		Novelty shock
		Stress

Behaviors	Functionalist Role disruption Marital disruption Social withdrawal	Interactionist Poor services Stigma Impoverishment Powerlessness Fatigue

Nature of parental adjustment to handicapped child

Figure 2. *Professionals' reactions to parents (completed).*

be seen as equally influential on parental adjustment. First, there are usually some special needs of the child that do, in fact, have behavioral consequences for the parents. Second, there are specific societal contexts within which the family-child interaction occurs. For example, what is and is not treated as deviant? How much stigma is attached to that deviancy? (Perhaps mental retardation is more stigmatized than deafness, for instance.) What is the accepted family and social responsibility to the child? Finally, what is the history of the specific situation? Every family is an evolving unit, but evolving within certain socially defined boundaries (Kelman, 1964).

The Type and Extent of Parental Involvement

The question now shifts. Given our diagram mapping the alternative professional responses to parents, how does this concern specific programs for parent involvement in the schools? We have found that most of the research has been normative in its assumptions about the source of parental response. Thus whatever connection there is should reflect this distribution. The whole point of constructing the diagram is to help clarify how these professional orientations are more than just "so much theory." There are clear implications for parental involvement programs entailed by each of the four perspectives. Practicing teachers and other professionals rarely notice these implications because they have never been asked to examine their basic expectations of parents. These basic expectations are often molded by the underlying responses to parents that have just been outlined (see Figure 2).

This does not mean that the connections between perception and programming are always straight and complete. In fact, what happens, all too often, is that the professional orientation is dramatically out of kilter with the

Box 4
Selected Parent Narratives

One of the best ways to explore the variety of problems and triumphs experienced by parents of handicapped children is to read some accounts written by parents themselves. Other parents also often respond well to reading such stories. A few of the many such parent narratives are briefly described below.

1. Clarke, L. (1973). *Can't read, can't write, can't talk too good either: How to recognize and overcome dyslexia in your child.* New York: Penguin Books. The author gives an account of her experience as the mother of a son with a learning disability, and she provides practical and educational suggestions for others.
2. Featherstone, H. (1980). *A difference in the family: Life with a disabled child.* New York: Basic Books. Written by the parent of a severely multiply handicapped child, this book makes its points through a skillful combination of personal narrative and professional study.
3. Greenfeld, J. (1972). *A child called Noah.* New York: Holt, Rinehart & Winston. This powerful book is the daily journal that was kept by the father of a boy labeled autistic.
4. Greenfeld, J. (1978). *A place for Noah.* New York: Holt, Rinehart & Winston. This book is a sequel to the daily journal published by Greenfeld in 1972.
5. Massie, R., & Massie, S. (1975). *Journey.* New York: Knopf. In alternating chapters, the parents of a son with hemophilia recount their struggles with an ill-equipped system: medical, educational, and social.
6. Park, C. C. (1967). *The siege.* Boston: Little, Brown. This book is a reflective, well-written history of the many trials and triumphs of the mother of an autistic daughter.
7. Schaefer, N. (1982). *Does she know she's there?* Toronto: Fitzhenry & Whiteside. This is a marvelous story of one mother's development into an advocate for her severely retarded daughter as well as others with similar disabilities.
8. Spradley, T. S., & Spradley, J. R. (1978). *Deaf like me.* New York: Random House. In this account of life with a child whose deafness is part of her rubella syndrome characteristics, the parents' efforts at communicating with their daughter culminate with the learning of sign language.
9. Turnbull, A. P., & Turnbull, H. R. III (Eds.). (1978). *Parents speak out: Views from the other side of the two-way mirror.* Columbus, OH: Charles E. Merrill. This unusual and extremely valuable collection of articles was written by professionals in the human services whose own children are disabled.
10. Ulrich, S. (1972). *Elizabeth.* Ann Arbor: University of Michigan Press. The mother of a young blind child writes of the cooperation and success between home and center.

type or extent of parent involvement attempted. When that involvement effort fails the blame is usually laid at the doorstep of "uncooperative" or "apathetic" parents. We suggest that just as often the difficulty may originate in a professional perspective that lags behind the parent programming.

Once again, we will organize our analysis of involvement efforts around two basic questions. What *type* of parent involvement is sought? How *extensive* is that involvement meant to be? The major options of how to involve parents can be located according to the answers given to these questions. As with the research on parental responses, there are two main answers to each of the questions. We end up with a diagram similar to our earlier model. That is, for each of the four basic professional orientations, a corresponding model of parent involvement is implied.

Most professionals have tended to answer the first (or "type") question in one of two ways. The type of parent involvement sought is either *passive* or *active*. Again, these are generalizations that are not always cleanly separated in practice. Nonetheless, most types of parent involvement can be divided according to whether the parent is expected to be essentially a passive recipient or an active contributor. As before, we will place these two alternatives at opposite ends of one continuum.

Type of Parent Involvement

Passive   •   Active

What about the second (or "extent") question? Just how much involvement does a particular program really seek? You can probably guess what the two basic answers are. The extent of parent involvement sought may be either *narrow* or *broad*. As we mentioned at the beginning of this chapter, it is more productive to think in terms of professional involvement with families. The question then becomes how broadly or narrowly the school or center wants to be involved with parents.

By intersecting the broad/narrow option with the active/passive one, we produce our four basic alternatives for parent involvement (Figure 3). We can best explain our four quadrants and how they relate to the earlier diagram by examining each one separately.

1. Narrow-Passive: Parent counseling

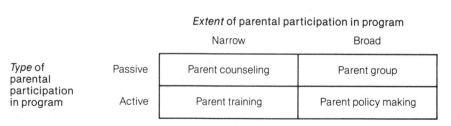

		Extent of parental participation in program	
		Narrow	Broad
Type of parental participation in program	Passive	Parent counseling	Parent group
	Active	Parent training	Parent policy making

Figure 3. *Professionals' models for parental involvement.*

2. Broad-Passive: Parent support groups
3. Narrow-Active: Parent training
4. Broad-Active: Parent empowerment

Keep in mind that these characterizations of the style of parent involvement programs implied by the various professional perspectives do not necessarily describe parents' experiences. Thus, throughout their career, a parent might become involved in all or several of these program types—sometimes at the same time.

Parent Counseling

The psychodynamic orientation logically leads to programming for parents that focuses on individual emotional support to relieve the neuroses inevitably suffered by parents. Sometimes this is done informally by a teacher. Usually, however, a series of counseling sessions led by a social worker or psychologist attempts to help the parent(s) work through their problems (all too often, though, the sessions are organized only for mothers). The parent is the passive recipient of emotional therapy (Briard, 1976). The counseling approach is narrow in that it focuses exclusively on the parents' reactions to the handicapped child. Remember the normative assumption that the parent-child relationship is inevitably disturbed by the presence of a handicapping condition. The parent involvement is then restricted to "repairing" that relationship, which is seen as essentially attitudinal in nature.

Another aspect of the passivity is in the IEP process usually practiced in this model. The parents are expected to *ratify*, or agree to, the educational decisions made for their children. Although Public Law 94-142 specifies their involvement, they are not really expected to contribute to the design of educational plans except to "sign off" on the form that they approve the plan.

Of course, all parents benefit from emotional support, and some parents may benefit from individual counseling. Such parents should have this option available to them (Doernberg, Bernard, & Lenz, 1976). When such counseling becomes the focus of the professional response to parents, however, the almost irresistible tendency is to deflect any more active forms of participation. The question here is whether the individual counseling is the centerpiece or merely an adjunct to the involvement model.

Parent Support Groups

The psychosocial orientation encourages a broader approach to parental involvement corresponding to the breadth of situational factors deemed relevant to parental attitudes. The attitudinal emphasis tends to retain a passive *type* of involvement. Here the group meeting takes preeminence over individual therapy. The focus of the group tends to include more informational services. There might be sessions in which presentations are made on a range of topics from child development to tax breaks to appropriate toys to coping with stress. Group problem solving often occurs in such meetings. At its most passive level these groups are little more than traditional PTA models for special education classes. Not surprisingly, then, schools seem to be most comfortable with this kind of parent programming (Becker, Bender, & Kawabe, 1980). The parents remain primarily passive receivers of help or information. At most they are used as sources of information, which is, of course, properly applied by the experts.

None of this denies a proper role for such group sessions. Several significant functions can be served by broadly based parent information and support groups:

- They can efficiently convey certain basic information, which we sometimes assume everyone knows. These include basics of child development, specific parenting strategies, and the nature and availability of community services.
- By holding meetings at the school, such groups can be an effective way of making parents feel welcome in that setting.
- Parents get to meet each other. This is often the most valuable service of such groups.

The problem with this approach arises if there are no *active* components of real parental participation. Specifically, low-income minority parents mistreated for years by institutional racism and the daily blows of unrelenting poverty cannot be expected to drop everything to come and sit through one more meeting with no real promise of empowering them to control their children's education. Such sessions can easily seem to focus on supposed inadequacies of the parents rather than the system, if only because true parent control continues to seem out of reach (Comer & Schraft, 1980). Whether the parents are being informed or being counseled, it is something done *to* them—not *by* them.

Parent Training

The functionalist orientation has led, over the last ten to fifteen years, to parent involvement programs that stress behavioral training. Here parents are expected to *do* things. However, since the normative focus implies that the parent-child relationship is inevitably impaired and traditional roles disrupted, the parents must be trained to develop new behaviors for their new roles as parents of a disabled child (Bernal & North, 1978). The parent is taught handling, stimulation, feeding, language, discipline, and socializing skills. The training might be either classroom based or home based. A typical model would include home plans or programs written out by the teacher or therapist. There might be manuals guiding the parent through sequenced steps of instruction—some excellent ones are available commercially (Baker,

Some programs encourage the use of parents as classroom helpers. This parent is teaching young children the letters of the alphabet. (Photograph by Mima Cataldo.)

Brightman, Heifetz, & Murphy, 1976). Fathers may even be expected to participate in some phases of programming. The focus is to structure the parents' behavior so they become effective teachers of their children. The implication is that the parents can better serve the child by carrying the professionals' goals over to the home. This model of parent programming allows a more varied involvement of the parents, who are expected to become active teachers of their children. Such programs can effectively address some basic, practical needs of parents.

The problems with this approach again arise when it becomes the only or even the major form of parental involvement. The tendency of this parent training is for the interaction between parent and professional to remain one-sided. The power remains with the professional as the dispenser of knowledge and grader of performance. It is the professional who observes and identifies the parental behavior that needs changing in order to further school objectives. The parent carries over from school; school does not usually carry over from home. The professional provides the training and schedules. The parent must take what is offered or run the risk of being considered uncooperative or inconsistent. Finally, the narrowness of focus seldom allows a questioning of larger social questions that may be causing the problem. It may be institutional behavior that needs changing, but this model by itself seldom deals with that.

Parent Empowerment

The interactionist orientation leads logically to a type and extent of parental involvement that offers the most equal type of interaction between parents and teachers. As a model for professional involvement with parents it also offers the possibility of including the positive aspects of other models from counseling to training. What training there is tends to be broader than before. Parents may be taught an entire methodology, complete with the theoretical framework, so that they can observe, analyze, plan, teach, and evaluate their own programs. Parents in this model are able to acquire true power in administration and policy for their children's education. Sometimes this is quite literally true. In one private early childhood program that integrates severely handicapped and typical children in the same classrooms, the parents actively run the program alongside professionals. They interview, supervise, and evaluate staff; monitor programs; develop new materials and strategies; assist in administration; and help in classrooms (Knoblock, 1982). The parent support group becomes the parent board whose decisions are more than advisory on issues from the budget to curriculum. Even in public school systems such extensive parental control can be initiated. In part, such influence is simply a result of thorough parental participation both in daily classroom function and all aspects of the educational process. "As parents participate in many varied ways, they become increasingly effective decision makers. Thus, while only a few parents at any one time are able to make the investment of time and energy required for participation in decision making, those that do so operate from a sound knowledge base" (Comer & Schraft, 1980, p. 338).

The broader extent of this focus recognizes the range of valid concerns and acts upon them. Respite services; locating dentists, pediatricians, and optometrists willing to work with disabled children; income assistance; protesting budget cuts; campaigning in the media against discrimination; working to improve the neighborhood—all are legitimate concerns of the school because they are unavoidable concerns of the parents. The point of this approach is that the parent is empowered and supported to decide what is or is not needed. Professionals are not excluded from this process, but are a valuable part of it. In fact, the approach affords professionals opportunities to develop many different kinds of relationships with parents.

Finally, the point needs to be made that the breadth of this model allows parents the legitimate choice of *not* being actively involved with *school*. Parents can remain involved with their children without spending time at their children's schools. For some parents the undeniable respite provided by the school day is the most important support provided by the teacher. Such a parent should be allowed that freedom without automatically being labeled "apathetic" and uninvolved. Parents' lives do not begin and end at the classroom door. This is not, of course, an excuse for a "benign neglect" of those parents. Every effort should be made to make sure those parents not previously involved know they are truly welcome and respected.

We now have described all four major alternatives for parent involvement. We have made the conceptual connections with professional perspectives. Figure 4 shows the completed diagram.

Let us summarize what we think are the twelve key assumptions about parents with an inclusive empowering parent involvement program. Some of these are shared with the other three alternatives. However, we argue that only this model fully recognizes all twelve.

1. Parents are the child's primary and most consistent teachers in a very real and active sense.
2. Parents possess a great deal of expertise about their own child—often more than the child's teacher can ever have.
3. Parents know (or can discover) and use a wide variety of methods and techniques with their child that can be successfully emulated by the classroom teacher.
4. Parents can learn.
5. Parents, as a group, possess a wide variety of skills relevant to educational settings.
6. Parents can be a source of labor and support to an educational program.
7. Parents are your peers. They have a need for information and skills that professionals should provide. They also have information and skills to offer in exchange.
8. Parents are people. They have first names, hobbies, and interests. You can talk about cooking, sports, housekeeping, finances, books, or weather. You can develop a personal relationship.
9. Parents are sometimes wrong. Their opinions, beliefs, methods, and concerns must always be respected even if, in your opinion, they are

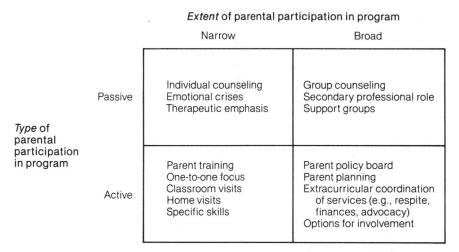

Extent of parental participation in program

	Narrow	Broad
Passive	Individual counseling Emotional crises Therapeutic emphasis	Group counseling Secondary professional role Support groups

Active	Parent training
	One-to-one focus
	Classroom visits
	Home visits
	Specific skills
		Parent policy board
		Parent planning
		Extracurricular coordination
		  of services (e.g., respite,
		  finances, advocacy)
		Options for involvement

Type of parental participation in program

Figure 4. *Professionals' models for parental involvement (completed).*

clearly wrong and inappropriate. Anyone can change with new information or alternatives to choose from. You may be able to provide another perspective or alternative not previously offered.

10. Parents live in the world, not just the world of their disabled child, but the same one you do. Their needs and concerns must be considered in *all* situations. If dad has just been laid off, it may not be the best time to suggest a new piece of adaptive equipment. If another child is just learning to walk, it may not be a good time to ask mom to spend extra time in the evening on math homework.

11. Parents have pride. Your involvement with them should take place not *just* on your turf or at your request. They should be able to meet with you in their home, a nearby restaurant, or wherever they feel comfortable. You should always assume *every* parent is doing the best he or she can.

12. Parents have needs even if you cannot meet them. You have a responsibility not just to recognize these needs but at least to refer parents to someone who can meet them. Develop and maintain a community resources guide so that you know where parents can get family counseling, babysitters, barbers, and doctors. Be willing to help search if you do not know.

The last six points, especially, require a level of personal interest and commitment that few professionals have been prepared to give. The truth is, however, that most parents become very sensitive to professionals' sincerity and genuineness, or the lack of it. Parent involvement programs, regardless of the model, tend to work when people care, not when people just know. Knowing alone is never enough.

Strategies for Parent Involvement

In the Beginning

There is a process to positive, productive, substantive parent involvement. It is neither easy nor short and it does not solve every problem, but it does work.

The process begins with the professional perspective designated interactionist and described earlier. The process is more or less sequential but, as with any process, can respond flexibly to the needs and characteristics of any particular parent or group of parents.

Step 1. Parents and teachers communicate on a regular, consistent basis. This can occur through phone calls, conversations, notebooks/logs, in which both parties write daily, or notes in both directions. The method should be tailored to the individual parent and need not be the same for every parent in the classroom. Some people talk more comfortably than they write and vice versa. It is through this conversation (written or oral) that teachers and parents begin to develop personal relationships. It is a time for teachers to

Ideally, skills learned in school can be generalized to home and community. This child is learning to feed himself. (Photograph by Mima Cataldo.)

emphasize the disabled child's strengths and be positive and optimistic about the child's weaknesses. It is also a time to ask questions and explore the interests and concerns of the parents, both in regard to their child and in general.

Step 2. Parents are frequent visitors in the classroom, and teachers visit homes on a regular (if not as frequent) basis. This is a critical time. Parents will not come to the classroom consistently if there is no incentive. This incentive may be one of learning specific and useful information about working with and handling the child. The teacher should be prepared to involve the parent in the activity of the classroom. The information gained by the teacher during step one will allow an individual approach to each parent's education and involvement. Parents should first be given the information and skills they most want even if they do not match those skills the teacher feels the parents most need. This is the incentive. Parents will try harder to spend time in the classroom if their individual needs—as *they* perceive them—are being addressed.

Step 3. Parents participate in a wider variety of classroom activities. As parents acquire the information and skills they need to manage their own child more comfortably, the classroom becomes an excelllent setting for broadening the parents' perspective beyond their own child. It is a time for helping the parents develop a more global understanding of disabled children, special education, and the school system. The classroom experience assists this growing perspective by giving the parents opportunities to work with other children besides their own, meet other parents, and apply or alter the skills they are developing as they encounter new children. The teacher's role at this time is to involve the parents with children and activities that match each individual parent's interests and skills, remembering always that not all people—parents included—enjoy the same things. Thus, while one parent is joyfully engaged in an arts and crafts project, another is individually tutoring a child in reading, while still another is taking data or making phone calls. Parents, like any volunteer, will only donate their time to your program if they enjoy what they are doing and receive some measure of satisfaction.

Step 4. Parents meet and converse with other parents who are in the classroom at the same time. A growing relationship among parents is critical to this process. Parent-to-parent support is frequently more successful than any amount of professional-to-parent support and should be encouraged for this reason alone. However, it also helps parents broaden their perspective beyond their own concerns and needs as they hear that other parents share them. This time is the embryonic stage of parent groups. As teachers observe the developing relationships among parents they can gather important information. Which parents seem to be the leaders? What are the most commonly discussed problems or concerns? How are parents reacting to their involvement? Is it a good time to expand the involvement beyond the classroom?

In addition to gathering information, the teacher has an important role in facilitating this step. Schedules may need frequent juggling to ensure that more than one parent is visiting class on a particular day. (Frequently, a parent can handle this scheduling.) Teachers must also balance their desire to encourage parent conversations, which can sometimes be disruptive, with those of working individually with a child and maintaining an orderly classroom. This can often be handled by identifying some time during the class when parents can take a coffee break—maybe during the class free time, rest, or snack. If the parent breaks always occur during lessons, this might indicate to parents that their involvement is limited to the less intensive parts of the day.

Step 5. Parents combine as a group. This may occur in a number of ways. Sometimes, a few parents will begin meeting outside class for social reasons, for support, and to discuss problems and concerns. Occasionally, a few of the parents will initiate outside meetings of all the parents to do some or all of these things. Often teachers provide the catalyst for bringing parents together outside the class by suggesting this to the parents (or parent) that seem to be the leaders. Regardless of how the grouping occurs initially, it is the teacher's responsibility to support and assist in a practical way while allowing the parents to take the lead. This might mean helping to find time, facilities, and/or materials for meetings; allowing parents to bring children early or pick them up late from class; and assisting with transportation or child-care arrangements. If the parents fail to invite you, refrain from feeling left out or defensive; parent groups should never be dominated by professionals or professional concerns. Those groups that begin by not even including professionals may develop into the most successful partnerships.

Box 5

Helping Parents Prepare for Professionals' Meetings

Too often parents' only role in IEP meetings, evaluation meetings, or staffings is that of passive participant. Usually, parents enter a room of busy (sometimes even harried) professionals, each armed with file folders, forms, lists, and their own information to contribute to the program planning process. Too frequently, parents feel outnumbered and intimidated—eager and willing to participate, but unsure how. For their part, the professionals typically discharge their legal responsibility with the question, "Do you have any questions or anything to add, Mrs. (Mr.) Jones?"

Instead, teachers can prepare parents to participate actively with a few simple strategies.

1. Let parents know what the meetings will be like—who will be present, who will speak and in what order, and what decisions will be made.
2. Encourage parents to stop the proceedings and ask questions at any time.
3. Advise parents to bring a friend or two. In addition to general support, a friend can take notes, remind parents of things they wanted to ask or question, and discuss the meeting afterward.
4. Help parents prepare and practice a parent narrative—an organized presentation that helps parents have a more formal role in meetings.

Parent Narrative Outline

I. *Description of child.* Often some members of the meeting have never seen or met the child they are discussing. If this might be the case, have parents consider bringing their child and planning their participation. If the presence of the child seems inappropriate, have parents begin their narrative with a general physical and personality description. Some parents we know have even brought along a photograph.

II. *Description of abilities and needs.* Help parents describe "what my child can do and what I think he/she needs to work on." Encourage them to talk only about *abilities.* They can probably rely on others at the meeting to describe what their child cannot do. Instead, help the parents describe what their child needs to work on with specific examples (e.g., getting lunch in the cafeteria, reading the evening newspaper, helping prepare supper, talking more about what they did at school). Help the parent organize this information into the following (or similar) categories:

   1. How my child gets around.

(continued)

Box 5
(continued)

2. How my child communicates.
3. How my child gets along with other children and adults.
4. How my child learns the things we teach him/her.
5. How my child manages on his/her own around home and the neighborhood.

III. *Summary.* Help parents summarize the three or four (or so) most important things they believe their child should accomplish during the next school year or planning period.

IV. *Specific requests.* Help the parent prepare a series of specific requests that describe "the kind of program/services I think would help my child accomplish these important priorities." Encourage parents to describe the features or components of the program they think will meet their child's need rather than requesting a specific program or teacher.

Once the group is formed—however it happens—the teacher is presented with the unique opportunity of sharing information with many parents at the same time. If the teacher is eager to explain the reading program to the parents, it is more efficient to make a group presentation than to repeat the information endlessly as each parent is available. But the limits posed by interactional relationships require that teachers first listen to what the parents want and then negotiate, persuade, and compromise until the meeting agendas can be *jointly* written. Sending out your questionnaire, which asks parents to check or circle those topics on a list that they would like to have presented in a parent group meeting, is not listening and interacting with parents. A committee meeting with balanced numbers of parents and professionals sitting down to generate the list comes closer to the mark.

Once topics are agreed upon and agendas set, the work of the professional really begins. If parents want to learn about management strategies, it is not enough to give an hour lecture from your first week's notes of "Introduction to Behavior Mod." Parents can learn, should be offered, and frequently want an entire course, complete with theory and research. It is important to determine exactly what and how much information parents want and to secure the services of those individuals who can *best* provide such information. Parent group meetings should be viewed as an opportunity to provide information that will allow parents to become *less* dependent upon professionals. We have been involved in a range of meeting topics: a short course in neurology, a course in behavioral methodology and techniques, and income tax breaks. A course in making adapted clothing was taught for several weeks by one of the parents. How to purchase toys and what to do when people are rude in the grocery store are also important topics for such meetings. Sometimes meetings become projects. How can we introduce our children to the regular teachers and nonhandicapped students in the school? Let's work on getting the district to develop a summer school program. The possibilities are endless, and all are valuable if they are meeting parent and professional needs.

Step 6. Parents participate in policy making and program development. Once parents begin to learn the system and its language, they become a powerful force for change. This power multiplies when parents organize into groups. They voice their questions, demands, and criticisms with more force and volume. Too often the professional response to organized, forceful parents is to react defensively—close ranks—and transform a collaborative interaction into an adversarial one. Parents are forced to effect change from outside, to set up alternatives or competitive programs, work through legislatures, courts, and public media, to *fight* for their right to participate in the policy and program decisions affecting their children individually and collectively. That parents have accomplished anything at all in this antagonistic atmosphere impressively testifies to their commitment and skill—to their expertise. That parents as a power group have been able to accomplish sweeping change in the educational system demands that professionals take a second look at their defensive stance toward "militant" parents and parent groups. It is long past time for professionals to recognize and cooperate with parents as a power base. This does not mean forming parent advisory councils, or creating ex officio board positions. Rather, it means giving not just one, but a lot of parents an equal vote. Not just participating in initial interviews for a new teacher, but an equal vote in the final choice. Not just reacting to the newly purchased math curriculum, but participating in the screening and selection process. Not just getting a copy of next year's budget, but helping to create it.

Bugs in the Program

The process just described might be easily dismissed as being too unrealistic, idealistic, impossible, or not talking about "the kind of parents I know." "It could never happen here." We would agree in part—you cannot follow the steps like a recipe. We have tried only to suggest a different professional progression of involvement that grows out of such a perspective. Few programs of parent involvement evolve the same way at the same rate, nor should they. We are talking about interactions and relationships between people that cannot be forced into models or timelines. This perspective and this process allow professionals to approach parents with the belief that there is information and experience to be *shared* as well as needs to be met on both sides. The potential for positive involvement with parents ultimately resides in this belief.

One of the most frequently raised barriers to parent involvement is working parents. When both parents are working the possibility of regular participation in the classroom decreases, but it is not excluded. Parents can be met before or after work, some programs can hold classes on Saturday mornings—say twice a month; early evening conferences or short classes with one or several families are also possible solutions. Of course, this amount of flexibility is almost impossible for teachers to accomplish without the necessary administrative support, but it can and has been done in some programs. Many employers are able and willing to alter work schedules on a regular basis to allow parents to attend class with their child when the parents request it. Several parents we have worked with successfully negotiated such arrangements and were able to attend class one or two times per month (on a consistent schedule of, say, every other Tuesday). Much can be accomplished with infrequent visits provided efforts are made to make maximum use of time, and visits are supplemented with other types of communication (e.g., phone calls, notes, reading materials). In some families of working parents, a relative or employee may be a primary caregiver and available to attend class more frequently than the parent. Involving this person (or persons) provides an additional link with the family.

Another barrier to the kinds of parent involvement we have described involves the additional needs of many low-income, culturally different, very young, or single parents. Often the daily needs and concerns of such families are so overwhelming and so far removed from the classroom that the educational needs of their handicapped children assume relatively low priority. The teacher, for whom the educational needs of the handicapped child are paramount, can easily assume that such parents simply do not care. We would suggest that one must begin with the assumption that all these parents care and demonstrate their caring by meeting the needs of their children as they perceive them. It becomes the professional's burden—and one that needs much more thought and study—to create alternatives for communication and involvement that will more successfully bridge the socioeconomic or cultural gap. If parents seem to respond unfavorably to you, then work through another parent from the same neighborhood if possible.

Once parents combine into groups, sometimes the more educated, articulate parents will begin to dominate to the exclusion of some other parents who are less educated, less articulate, or less aggressive. These less assertive parents will frequently fade away from the group. But in a situation where the opinions and needs of every member need to be addressed, this progression can weaken the effectiveness of the group's purpose and often hastens its demise. One way to encourage broader participation is through subcommittees with different responsibilities.

As Time Goes By

Once parents begin to receive the information, support, and services they have sought since learning about their child's disability, their involvement changes (Darling & Darling, 1982). Some parents find what they seek and begin to establish a balanced, though different, family lifestyle. No longer does the handicapped child dominate family attention and resources. Instead, other family members begin to pursue their own interests and needs. Mothers (or fathers) return to work. Siblings (and spouses) begin to receive some of the attention previously captured by the handicapped child. One result of this shift in family priorities—this newfound equilibrium—may be that parents "fall away" from their previous involvement in special education programs. Ironically, professionals frequently criticize such diminishing involvement of parents when in some cases it actually reflects the success of the professionals' efforts to meet the family's needs.

Rather than decreasing their involvement in special programs, some parents become more extensively involved. Usually this involvement takes the form of active participation in parent advocacy or disability rights groups. Some of these "activist" parents pursue a more extensive involvement because they do not receive the information, services, and support they need. Perhaps there are no, or too few, programs. Perhaps their children's particular constellations of needs are too unique to be easily met by a service network governed by jurisdictional, geographic, financial, and technological constraints. Regardless of the cause, some parents find they must actively create, or cause to be created, the programs and services they need. They assert the power the schools seem to have denied them. Other parents, who have largely found the services they need, actively support these efforts by working with parent advocacy and disability rights groups. Together, such parents empower each other and often succeed in creating a wide variety of social and programmatic changes on behalf of handicapped children.

Whether parents become more or less involved as a consequence of the initial services they encounter for their handicapped child, things rarely stay the same. Whatever the balance a family achieves, it is likely to be a delicate one. Throughout the handicapped child's life, problems and needs arise anew. As children grow and develop, their and their family's needs for information, support, and services continue. But the availability of such assistance usually changes. Thus a parent who finds adequate early childhood services may be dismayed to discover few public school or postschool options. Families who struggle through early years of complicated and frequent medical procedures may find the need for medical support wanes as their child approaches adulthood. Family relocations, changing public attitudes, and vacillating federal and state resources all may suddenly destroy a family's tenuously balanced lifestyle, forcing them to search, once again, for needed assistance.

The experience of raising a handicapped child might best be characterized as including periods of calm, balanced family life punctuated by times when parents must renew negotiation with a society and service system that largely fails to provide continuing and consistent services. It is not so much that new problems and needs arise as that old ones return in new guise. This wearying repetition can breed increasing fatigue, and even bitterness, in some parents.

Many of the strategies previously described in this chapter can help professionals get involved with parents regardless of their children's age.

One important continuing role for professionals is to help parents acquire needed information and form groups to assist other parents through similar situations. For example, most parents need support and assistance as their children move from the ranks of public education to adult service systems.

Some of the strategies discussed earlier may not translate as successfully as time goes by. For example, it is much less appropriate for parents of teenagers to visit and spend time working in their children's classrooms. After all, few parents of nonhandicapped students, if any, are so physically present in their children's education. Yet the needs of handicapped students, as well as the requirements of Public Law 94-142, require that parents and teachers remain in close communication. In fact, as handicapped students approach adulthood the participation of parents in program planning becomes even more vital. Many handicapped students approach their last few years in school with many skills left to learn. Yet the decision to teach one over another increasingly becomes less a matter of preferred educational practice and more a matter of individual and family preference and values (Wilcox & Bellamy, 1982).

We believe that there is much to be learned about parent-professional relationships in secondary and postschool programs. Yet, clearly, one important component of any parent-professional interaction is consistent communication. One practice we have found particularly helpful is "phone hours." Analogous to office hours, phone hours identify a specific weekly time—say 7:00 to 9:00, Tuesday evenings—when parents and teachers can call each other at home without feeling they are violating each others' privacy.

Whatever their specific strategies, professionals must build structures for continued involvement with parents. Those structures must be built on a foundation of trust and communication. From the parent's perspective, such a firm foundation can be many years in the making and involve dozens of professionals from several different fields—all of whom have some form of contact with that family. Thus, it is not enough for a teacher to improve his or her techniques for parent involvement. Teachers, doctors, social workers, and therapists must work together to create better methods of empowering parents. Only then will a system of services be able to respond effectively to differing needs and wants of families as time goes by.

Summary

No parent involvement program is without problems and no analysis without weaknesses. As professionals we have approached parents from too great a distance and too analytical a stance. If we are to succeed at all, the focus of our analysis must shift to ourselves, the professionals. We need to examine our own opinions about parental adjustment and the assumptions our parent involvement programs make about parental needs and abilities. We need to describe explicitly the expectations our program places on parents as well

Box 6
Parent and Advocacy Organizations

Alexander Graham Bell Association for the Deaf
3417 Volta Place, N.W.
Washington, D.C. 20007

American Coalition for Citizens with Disabilities
1346 Connecticut Avenue, N.W.
Washington, D.C. 20036

American Foundation for the Blind
15 West Sixteenth Street
New York, NY 10011

Arthritis Foundation
3400 Peachtree Road, N.E.
Suite 1101
Atlanta, GA 30026

Association for Children with Down's Syndrome
589 Patterson Street
East Meadow, NY 11554

Association for Children with Learning Disabilities
4156 Library Road
Pittsburgh, PA 15234

Association for the Education of the Visually Handicapped
919 Walnut Street
Philadelphia, PA 19107

Canadian Association for the Mentally Retarded
Kinsman NIMR Building
York University Campus
4700 Keele Street, Downsview
Toronto, Ontario, Canada M5R 2K2

Candlelighters
(Parents of children with potentially fatal diseases)
123 C Street, S.E.
Washington, D.C. 20003

Children's Defense Fund
1520 New Hampshire Avenue, N.W.
Washington, D.C. 20036

Cystic Fibrosis Foundation
Suite 309
6000 Executive Boulevard
Rockville, MD 20852

(continued)

Box 6
(continued)

Down's Syndrome Congress
Room 1562
1640 W. Roosevelt Road
Chicago, IL 60608

Epilepsy Foundation of America
Suite 406
1828 L Street, N.W.
Washington, D.C. 20036

International Association of Parents of the Deaf
814 Thayer Avenue
Silver Springs, MD 20910

Juvenile Diabetes Association
23 East Twenty-sixth Street
New York, NY 10010

National Association of the Deaf-Blind
2703 Forest Oak Circle
Norman, OK 73071

National Association for Retarded Citizens
2709 Avenue E, East
Arlington, TX 76011

National Easter Seal Society
2023 W. Ogden Avenue
Chicago, IL 60612

National Federation of the Blind
Suite 212, Dupont Circle Building
1346 Connecticut Avenue, N.W.
Washington, D.C. 20036

National Hemophilia Foundation
Room 1204
19 W. Thirty-fourth Street
New York, NY 10001

National Mental Health Association
1800 N. Kent Street
Rosslyn, VA 22209

National Society for Autistic Children and Adults
1234 Massachusetts Avenue, N.W.
Suite 1017
Washington, D.C. 20005

(continued)

Box 6
(continued)

National Tay-Sachs and Allied Diseases Association
122 E. Forty-second Street
New York, NY 10017

Parents Campaign for Handicapped Children and Youth
1201 Sixteenth Street, N.W.
Washington, D.C. 20036

Spina Bifida Association
343 S. Dearborn Street
Chicago, IL 60604

United Cerebral Palsy Association
66 E. Thirty-fourth Street
New York, NY 10016

as the expectations we are willing to meet for the parents. It is not enough to say, "Parents need to be involved; here is our involvement program."

Parents of handicapped children are not preselected on the basis of their qualifications and knowledge. Nor is there a reverse selection in which only the worst couples are chosen. Rather, allowing for socioeconomic factors relating to the incidence of handicapping conditions in children, the parents represent a cross section of society. They are no better or worse than parents as a whole. Yet the difficult role of raising and caring for a typical child is multiplied many times over for these parents while the services provided simultaneously decrease in adequacy and continuity. How ironic it becomes, then, that the most frequent professional response to such parents has been that they exude guilt, shame, and anger, while wandering about in conflict with their spouses, looking for a proper familial role to assume. One might modestly suggest that the anger would seem justified, if sometimes misdirected—and that the guilt and shame are, perhaps, projected by professionals whose behavior offers these parents too little, too late, too seldom. This is, of course, an unfair generalization. But it is no more unfair than what parents of handicapped children often suffer when facing professionals who see a paragraph from a textbook in front of them instead of a couple just trying to cope.

Chapter 9

Stephen T. Murphy

Jan Nisbet

Stephen T. Murphy is an associate professor of Rehabilitation Services at Syracuse University. Prior to his career as an educator, Dr. Murphy worked as a counseling psychologist developing social and vocational programs for young adults with mental retardation and for older adults with severe psychiatric problems. As an educator, Dr. Murphy has been involved in establishing local community-based, continuing-education and vocational-training, and placement programs for persons with disabilities. Dr. Murphy is the author of numerous book chapters and articles on client-professional issues, vocational assessment centers, and qualitative research methods in rehabilitation. Presently, he is writing a book on the perceptions and experiences of young adults designated learning disabled.

Jan Nisbet is an assistant professor of Rehabilitation Services at Syracuse University. Her project and programmatic efforts are devoted to demonstrating that adolescents and adults with severe disabilities can make a successful transition from school to integrated work in their communities. Currently, she is exploring how to have typical co-workers and employers maximally involved in the placement, training, and employment process. Dr. Nisbet's other interests include desegregation and deinstitutionalization, professional training programs in rehabilitation, developing adaptive devices for persons with physical disabilities, and community/vocational education for students with disabilities.

Disabled Adolescents in the Community

After reading this chapter, you should be able to:

1
Define community living.

2
Discuss adolescent socialization and describe how the experiences of disabled and nondisabled adolescents may differ.

3
Recall the sexual myths that are applied to persons with disability and critique each.

4
List the principles of normalization and apply them to community living options for disabled adolescents.

For most of us, community living means simultaneously being part of a neighborhood, a school, a family and a work situation. It connotes being a member of a group that has common ties or interests and living in close physical and social proximity to each other.

Most citizens will enter the life of their community physically, socially, culturally, educationally, recreationally, and vocationally. They are prepared for such entry early in life. Through the influences of socializing institutions such as the family, school, and peer group, most youngsters are taught the characteristics, requirements, and nuances of their society and of their associated roles and responsibilities.

Historically, individuals with physical, intellectual, behavioral, and emotional disabilities have lived on the fringe of society and on the outskirts of their communities. Depending upon the prevailing sociocultural attitudes toward the disabled, the economic circumstances of the society, the political power of the disabled citizens, and the fear, threat, and animosity the disabled have aroused in other citizens, persons with disabilities have been banished, jailed, isolated, indentured, and sterilized (Foucault, 1965; Kittrie, 1971; Rothman, 1971; Wolfensberger, 1975). Conversely, during some historical periods they have been allowed to participate partially, if not fully, in some of the valued activities of their communities. Today, although persons with disabilities are afforded more rights and opportunities than at any time in history, their successful transition into all phases of societal life cannot be taken for granted. Negative public attitudes, physical and social isolation, impoverished economic opportunities, and low professional expectations still persist. Consequently, full-fledged membership in one's community is troublesome to achieve, frequently granted only equivocally, and in all too many cases denied almost completely. This is especially true for severely, profoundly, and/or multiply handicapped citizens who typically have minimal opportunities to interact in valued ways with nondisabled members of the community or to engage in any community wide activities.

The purposes of this chapter are (1) to describe the socializing experiences faced by adolescents with disabilities within their families, schools, and communities and (2) to introduce the concept of normalization as a set of guiding principles for understanding and addressing the community living problems faced by young persons with disabilities. Several case studies will be used to illustrate the kinds of real life circumstances in which disabled, young persons typically find themselves, and how these situations may be analyzed and addressed within the framework of social integration.

The Socialization Process: An Overview

Ordinarily, youngsters in our society undergo a developmental process called socialization in which they are gradually prepared for community membership by finding out what kind of people they are and what roles they should play within society (Brim, 1966; Scott, 1969). Within the structure and activities of their family, school, and peers, individuals are inculcated with the knowledge, skills, dispositions, and attitudes that are perceived by members of a society as critical for successful social, educational, vocational, recreation/leisure, and sexual functioning within the community. As Scott (1969, p. 17) has noted: "To the extent that an individual correctly perceives (other's) evaluations of him and internalizes them as part of his self-concept, this putative social identity becomes a personal identity in fact." The process of socialization affects not only how individuals think about themselves, but also how they are perceived by others in light of their age, race, sex, occupation, or disability categories. Based on these categories, identities are formed and become essential elements in how the family, school, and peer group treat identified individuals. Adolescents identified as rebellious, disabled persons labeled dependent, and elderly adults considered unproductive are perceived and treated in ways consistent with these labels. All too often individuals come to think of themselves as being what they have been labeled, and thus act accordingly. Wolfensberger (1980) has identified five media through which role expectations are transmitted to persons.

1. The way in which their physical and social environments are structured.
2. The activities that are offered to, provided for, or demanded of individuals.
3. The language that is used with or without them.
4. The way people are congregated and/or juxtaposed to each other.
5. The images and symbols that are associated with such persons.

For the purposes of this chapter we will focus on the socializing influences of the family, schools, and peer groups. It should not be inferred, however, that these are the only socializing forces. The mass media have also been mentioned as an important socializing influence. Neither should it be concluded that there exist unanimous societal opinions about what a disabled person is like, or that such opinions invariably determine individual behavior. Individual responses to surroundings can be very idiosyncratic. Many persons have overcome negative roles foisted on them by socializing institutions; have developed positive self-images; and have achieved important life goals. Nevertheless, reflected in our social institutions are powerful conceptions of what certain kinds of people are like, what kinds of roles they should play, and how they should act. When such conceptions are transmitted by valued, significant others they can become awesome, taken-for-granted behavioral and expectancy guides that affect the ways in which parents raise their children, teachers educate, counselors advise, other children react, and, ultimately, the way disabled persons view themselves.

Adolescent Socialization

During adolescence, socialization for community living intensifies. This period has been characterized as a culturally imposed, change oriented, and sometimes extremely distressing period for adolescents and those with whom they interact. The stress associated with adolescence has been tied to the variety of socially complex and emotionally demanding tasks that are expected of young adults, the ambivalence with which adolescents often confront such tasks, the often contradictory values that must be mediated, and the ambiguous status of the adolescent in contemporary society. Campbell (1969, p. 823) has indicated that during a relatively short developmental period:

> Adolescents are expected to simultaneously broaden their range of social contacts, increase the number of persons who are important to them emotionally and normatively, and become less reliant on parents and the home, and more oriented toward the extra familial, adult community. Also, adolescents are supposed to exercise new behaviors, develop future goals, adopt a sexual identity, select internal standards of judgement and conduct, and acquire the interpersonal, technical, vocational and participatory skills of adulthood.

Family, school, and peer group are as instrumental during adolescence as they were during childhood. As individuals make the transition to adulthood, however, these socializing institutions appear to assume a more focused, directive function, sorting out particular individuals and pointing out what are their most promising social, educational, residential, vocational, and recreation/leisure options. The direction these socializing forces take can often be a problem for disabled young adults as they attempt to assume adult roles in their communities.

Family Responses to Disability during Adolescence

In this section the important, socializing role of the family will be discussed in regard to both typical and disabled adolescents. An attempt will be made to emphasize that families of both disabled and nondisabled youngsters share the same dreams, hopes, and goals toward community living and that any differences between these groups are due more to the physical, social, financial, political and professional contexts with which parents of disabled adolescents must contend than to any inherent psychological anomalies related to being the parent of a disabled person. The importance of parental involvement in preparatory programs also will be discussed.

Inkeles (1969) has stated that the family probably deserves its place as the major socializing force because of its effects on the child's earliest dispositions, attitudes, and behaviors. According to Moore (1969) the family provides instruction, support, admonition, and a setting for learning adult and sex role models, all activities and models that reflect anticipated societal demands. Thomas (1980, p. 63) has written that the family is a peculiar type of social system in which is contained a paradox: "the young child can invest all of his emotional resources in it, yet eventually he must become emancipated from it." Such separation, and the dependent-independent struggle that intensifies during adolescence, is often the most difficult task confronting the individual and the family system. Although parents are frequently seen as major obstacles to such a transition, few parents are blind to the importance of preparing their children for community living.

Currently, the process of socialization within the family remains rather enigmatic. As Inkeles (1969) has observed, we know very little about how parents formulate images of what their child needs to succeed in life and the world, what these images are, where they get such images, and how successfully they are translated into action. It is evident, however, that the majority of parents view their adolescent's entrance into the community as something to be taken for granted and are guided in their decisions and actions by some image of what he or she needs to achieve this end. Thus, although parents may reject their sons' and daughters' rebellious behavior, respond impatiently or harshly to their emerging independence, or chafe at the gradual, incessant, socializing influences of the school and other community sources, they accept such changes because they are anticipated, normative steps toward full community membership. In short, there appears to be a general compatibility of values between parents and representatives of other societal institutions regarding adolescent preparation and transition to community life.

Such compatibility cannot be assumed between professionals and parents of disabled youngsters. Parental values and aspirations often conflict with those around them and make it necessary for parents to forge their own values for their children. For example, contacts with physicians, clergy, counselors, and teachers frequently cause parents to report a conflict of values that results in a pervasive tendency of professionals to discredit them, and thereby reduce their ability to influence their children's services. One parent summed up her experience:

> Professionals apparently thrived on "playing God" or on branding parents as rejecting or overprotective; as hostile or apathetic; as too involved or not involved enough; as having unrealistically high expectations or having none at all. It was a no-win situation for many. Pressures conspired to make them fit the stereotype of burdened parents of tragic errors, even if they felt otherwise (Morton, 1983, p. 81).

Unfortunately, some of the ways professionals perceive and treat parents emanate from their professional training, in which family influences have been characterized as particularly unhelpful to healthy growth and development. For example, Gleidman and Roth (1980), Goldberg (1981), Goldin, Perry, Margolin, Stotsky, and Foster (1971), McDaniel (1976), Sussman (1969), and others have pointed to a lack of parental experience with disabled children, a tendency to overprotect, a failure to acknowledge emerging sexual behavior, and other pathogenic familial tendencies to account for the disabled adolescent's difficulties. In synthesizing this research, McDaniel (1976) has concluded that it is surprising that any disabled adolescents became fully functioning, autonomous members of the community because the overwhelming pattern of familial and sibling interaction with the disabled member is contrary to that which would lead to successful psychological adjustment in an adult" (p. 24).

Recently, a different perspective on the family's responses to a disabled youngster has been communicated. The proliferation of parent groups and parent-authored literature, the legislated emphasis upon heightened parental involvement in service planning and implementation, and the increased attention in the professional literature to parental functioning have stimulated a stinging critique of the pathology model of parental dynamics. No longer is it prevalent to see family interactions uncritically termed psychologically maladaptive, or pathogenic. Rather, the behavior of parents is increasingly being characterized as the normative, predictable responses of any parents who are confronted with a multitude of physical, social, political, financial, and professional obstacles when raising their child (Featherstone, 1981; Gleidman & Roth, 1980; Jones, 1983; Knoblock, 1982; Turnbull & Turnbull, 1980).

Not only are parents of disabled youngsters being viewed differently by others, but also they are viewing themselves and the world differently. As exemplified in the following excerpt, their concerns about transition to community living for their sons and daughters sound very much like concerns of all parents.

> Most of the new generation of parents are determinedly mainstreaming their children into the ordinary pattern of their daily activities. Great gaps still loom for a disabled child. One is social life. . . . Learning leisure time skills, how to have fun with friends, how to get around to meet people and relate to them comfortably are vital skills. Another is the absence of job or vocational opportunities. We can make sure that vocational education is part of the IEP early enough. We should tie into vocational rehabilitation services . . . and aim for as much self-sufficiency as possible.
>
> There is a serious shortage of supervised living arrangements. . . . It is not part of the normalization plan for children to live with parents on and on into old age (Morton, 1983, pp. 87–88).

Parents are no longer uncritically accepting professionals' opinions about raising their children. In fact, a healthy and merited skepticism has grown toward professionals, along with a growing confidence in their parental instincts to do what is best for their child.

It should not be concluded from this discussion that all professionals are insensitive, uncaring, uninformed, and dictatorial—or that they are always, or are the only, culprits in the professional-family malaise. Many parents have reported sensitive, respectful, and knowledgeable treatment by the professionals with whom they have worked. But as a result of mutual distrust and mishandling by both parties, an interaction pattern has developed and precipitated a cycle of behaviors in which stereotypes are firmly established and mutual animosity has prevailed.

There remains a great need for educators and practitioners to acknowledge the family as a strong and valuable socialization and teaching force for community entry. There is almost universal agreement that professionals and parents need to forge a far more effective working relationship based upon mutual respect. Authors (e.g., Featherstone, 1981; Jones, 1983; Turnbull & Turnbull, 1980) have provided specific recommendations on how to accomplish this through policy and clinical changes that emphasize that the socializing instincts of parents of disabled children are as good as those of any parents and should not be excluded from community preparation efforts. Professionals must listen to, interact with, and respect parents' intimate understanding of their sons and daughters and become aware of the forces that may undermine parental effectiveness in influencing the preparatory programs of community living.

The role of the family in secondary and postsecondary programs is different from, but equally important as, their role in elementary school programs. Wilcox and Bellamy (1982) have noted that parental assistance is especially needed during adolescence because hard decisions must be made regarding what is taught, when, and for how long. Such choices are difficult because there is limited training time and a multitude of training needs that must be organized. Further, there are no empirical laws governing the relationship between learning community living skills such as mobility, employment, social, and/or recreation skills and eventual community adjustment. Whether the preceding skills should take precedence over traditional academic skills, in what order they should be taught, and for how long are all value-laden decisions with which parents, professionals, and adolescents should be involved. Because coeducation between school and home enhances learning and reinforces program goals, family involvement can maximize the chances for program success. Obtaining family support, time, and resources toward skill acquisition results in a more intensive program than would be possible using *only* school or agency resources.

Disabled Adolescents in School

The following section describes the socializing influence of the school as it affects disabled and nondisabled students. It also presents the ways in which school policies and practices lead to the delivery of particular socializing messages and experiences for disabled adolescents. Suggestions are made for more fully integrating disabled adolescents into the regular academic and extracurricular settings of the school.

In addition to the family, an important source of socialization is the school, the organization responsible for selecting, organizing, and teaching the knowledge and skills deemed important by contemporary society. The school also decides which students are exposed to which curricula and courses, and at what degrees of difficulty. Implicit in the school's operations, therefore, are a socializing power and a responsibility that extend beyond simply the dissemination of preselected topics.

The school influences adolescent social roles and peer group expectations by recognizing and emphasizing particular academic, athletic, musical, and social skills. Students selected for such honors are often accorded special recognition, assignments, and placements, all of which affect their status with their peers and reinforce desired ways of behaving.

Depending upon the type and severity of disability, parental attitudes and activism, school district orientation toward disabled students, and other social, political, and economic factors, the school experiences afforded disabled and nondisabled students may vary significantly. Some mildly handicapped students, especially those with above average intelligence who require fewer accommodations, may undergo school experiences nearly identical to those of their nondisabled peers. For others who may require more environmental modification, the educational system may represent a dramatic departure from the typical school socialization process.

Assessment and Labeling. Academically, disabled students are frequently hampered by diagnostic evaluations that ironically were devised to discover strengths and weaknesses, uncover learning styles, develop individualized instruction strategies, and alleviate academic and psychological problems. Ordinarily, the performances of disabled children on conventional intelligence scales are compared with normative data derived from nondisabled children. It is therefore presumed that the disabled can legitimately be compared with this population. This presumption, however, may be questionable in light of the social, psychological, physical, familial, and environmental differences that have been found to pervade the lives of disabled children. For example, to what extent are disabled children excluded from the normal range of everyday life experiences? To what extent are disabled children socially isolated and impoverished and not readily involved in traveling, reading, and writing either because of sensory impairments and/or cognitive difficulties? Certainly these social/environmental factors would lead to depressed general information and vocabulary scores, both important elements of intelligence scales (Gleidman & Roth, 1980).

Disabled children may be handicapped during assessment because of their lack of speed, short-term memory, sensory abilities, and motor coordination (Gleidman & Roth, 1980, p. 205). In many cases, the format of the testing must be modified to exclude certain scales and certain requirements of the subtests, or to interpolate the results according to preexisting norms. Thus, the standardized foundations of the instrument are often violated and the results left in the intuitive hands of professionals, many of whom lack experience with or have varied perceptions and lowered expectations of disabled students. Regardless of their intellect, disabled children often score much lower on conventional intelligence scales, and such outcomes are taken for granted as valid indices of abilities. In most instances the tests are not good indicators of potential to learn. Disabled students thus progress through their school careers with overestimated disabilities and underestimated abilities that influence instructors' perceptions and expectations, profoundly affect the manner in which students are treated, and can influence the way the student perceives himself or herself. Low test scores and indices of abilities may also influence where, and with whom, students with disabilities attend school. In some states, for example, if students score below 50 on standardized intelligence measures, they may not be enrolled in regular public schools, but will likely attend large segregated schools without the benefits of interactions with nonhandicapped peers.

Implicit Messages of School and the Educational Process.

Schools are places where activities are designed to define the person's position in the community (Thomas, 1980). This is accomplished through the image the student acquires about himself or herself and projects to others, and through his or her scholastic and extracurricular achievements. In many cases, success in one or both of the latter activities determines the former. For most disabled students paths to involvement in typical and valued academic, athletic, and extracurricular functions are obstructed. Thus, their chances for acquiring and projecting a positive image are significantly reduced. Because of Public Law 94-142, and changes in public perceptions, many more disabled students are being educated in closer proximity to their nondisabled peers. Sometimes this means that some classes are taken along with nondisabled students. Often, however, students with disabilities either are educated in separate sections of regular schools, where they maintain a distinct and isolated schedule, or are taught in completely separate "accessible" facilities for those labeled handicapped.

Even where school officials make significant efforts to educate disabled and nondisabled students together and maximize their contact, there are few instances of well-planned, guided interactions in which disabled students can participate in cooperative activities and productively contribute to a project's success.

Well-meaning school officials can sometimes negate their own efforts by inadvertently failing to grasp the most fundamental aspects of a school's social milieu. Such a situation was described by Joe Biskamp of the Center for Independent Living in Berkeley, California:

> A bunch of us from CIL recently visited a mainstreamed high school. . . . Well, the school seemed very nice and all that, but . . . we didn't see any disabled students using the school's elevators. When we commented on this we were told that the elevators were off limits for all the students. Only the staff could use the elevators . . . the elevators were too dangerous, always breaking down. . . .
>
> Of course the result of this overprotectiveness was that . . . for all practical purposes (the disabled students) were imprisoned on one floor. Now, remember, this was a school in which the staff . . . believed in the value of mainstreaming because it encouraged healthy interactions between able-bodied and disabled kids. Can you imagine what a monkey wrench such a dramatic and all pervasive lack of mobility throws into a disabled adolescent's ability to interact as an equal? (Gleidman & Roth, 1980, p. 229).

School personnel may view segregative and protective procedures as sparing individuals needless frustration and failure and preparing them for realistic community activities. In actuality, by denying such children supportive opportunities to relate cooperatively with nondisabled peers, to display their abilities, and to risk failure, they are minimizing the chances for success and withholding the critical experiences and skills necessary to break the self-fulfilling prophecy of inferiority that accompanies disability. In short, through such practices, the school socializes disabled students and the general public to expect less. Brown et al. (1983) have stated:

> Increasingly, severely handicapped students will function in the wide variety of nonschool environments frequented by nonhandicapped persons who must now learn to interact with and to operate in their presence. Perhaps the reader has had the opportunity of taking a severely handicapped student to an environment that contained inexperienced nonhandicapped persons. The stares, fears, negative comments, and interruptions in routine would be minimized if opportunities to grow up and attend school with severely handicapped students had been provided. Additionally, if one examines some of the many roles and responsibilities assumed by nonhandicapped adults, the benefits of longitudinal and comprehensive interactions with severely handicapped persons can readily be discerned. Consider just three: future service providers, future parents, and prospective employers.

The school must be one of the major sources of assistance for disabled adolescents entering the community. As Brown et al. (1983), Wilcox and Bellamy (1982), and Brolin and Kokaska (1979) have noted, transitional and school programs—that is, preparing students for adulthood—must teach the skills and knowledge necessary to master nonschool environments such as work, domestic, and leisure settings and must work to prevent segregated or institutional placements. Wilcox and Bellamy have described transitional programs for disabled adolescents as serving a dual purpose: (1) preparation for functioning in future work and living environments and (2) effective transition to those environments (p. 6). They have summarized their concerns with the following statement: "While education for nonhandicapped and mildly handicapped students typically focuses on the preparation component, several factors (for example, lack of post secondary options such as community college vocational training and adult education programs) force programs for severely handicapped students into this dual role of preparation and transition" (p. 6).

Social Interactions in the Community during Adolescence

The socializing influences of community social interactions, especially peer group interactions upon the adolescent socialization process, are examined in the following section. It also addresses some of the issues confronting many disabled young adults who must develop interpersonal skills and interact appropriately with nondisabled peers. An attempt has been made to analyze why valued social interactions are difficult to achieve for many adolescents with disabilities, to point to ways in which socializing institutions

Learning to shop for groceries is an example of a functional skill that can lead to independence in community living. (Photograph by Mima Cataldo.)

contribute to those problems, and to describe briefly how to improve the social interactions between disabled and nondisabled students through institutional and programmatic reform.

Early social relationships between maturing young adults are second in importance only to the family as socializing influences (McCandless, 1969). Acquisition of peer group support and values are often viewed as primary areas of emphasis and change during adolescence. The peer group, which is most often formed through high school associations, serves to bridge the gap between childhood and adulthood, providing the young adult with the psychological security of commonly situated peers as he or she moves outward from the family (Goldberg, 1981; Thomas, 1980). Such security is important since the adolescent is expected to learn sensitive, complex social behaviors. Such experiences are not ordinarily provided within the family, the school, or by other adult figures. For example, the development of equal and mutually reciprocal peer relationships, with their fluctuations of shifting intensity and frequency, can be both painful and rewarding. However, adolescents learning the subtleties, pleasures, and pain of social esteem, competency, and intimacy—and a sense of belonging with some group—need such experiences. Whether or not peer associations actually lead to a sense of belonging, ambiguity, or rejection, they are powerful learning activities whose importance is long remembered and whose impact is carried into adult life.

Sexual exploration is another adolescent preoccupation that is shared, encouraged, and supported by peers. Adolescents seek and share sexual information with each other that they do not share with adults. Campbell (1969) has argued further that although close peer associations and sexual exploration and their concomitant behaviors (such as staying out late, experimenting with drugs and alcohol, dressing unconventionally, deceiving authorities) appear to disregard the beliefs and regulations valued by parents and the school, such behavior is expected, tolerated, and even encouraged by most adults. Parents and school officials are believed to view such behavior as a necessary precondition for entry into the community as responsible adults. In fact, such behavior has been viewed as a good diversion and alternative to more serious unlawful behavior.

Sexuality Issues

An integral part of the general adolescent experience is the management of one's rapidly accelerating sexuality, a process that includes the development of sexual feelings and behaviors and the recognition of others, especially peers, as sexual beings (Simon & Gagnon, 1969, p. 741). Daniels, Chipouras, Cornelius, and Makas (1979) have defined sexuality as the integration of physical, emotional, intellectual and social aspects of an individual's personality into ways of thinking, feeling, and behaving that express maleness or femaleness (p. 1). Typically, such integration begins early in the person's life and is assisted primarily and initially through parental modeling, instruction, and guidance. In addition to family influences, the school and peer group also shape sexual development. Taken together, these three socializing institutions provide the adolescent with sexual roles and activities in which to try out, express, and modify his or her development. Young disabled adults experience significant obstacles in managing their emerging sexuality due as much to attitudinal and environmental issues as to factors related to their impairment. American society is bombarded with sexual messages from virtually every major print and electronic medium. Through such mediums sexual images, definitions, ideals, and behaviors are transmitted, highlighting who is, and what attributes are, truly sexual and what is valued sexual behavior. Persons with disabilities, however, are not included in those messages because "an unspoken but nevertheless apparent cultural belief in America is that the right to be a sexual person is reserved for young, physically flawless people; only such mythical models are thought to be capable of, or entitled to sexual feelings" (Thorn-Gray & Kern, 1983, p. 139). Also, as the preceding authors have noted, within our society the most desirable sexual behavior is ordinarily portrayed as meaning "an erect penis, a lubricated vagina, and an orgasmic response" (p. 139). Defined in this way, sexuality loses a vast number of its meaningful manifestations, and the diversity of people who are not able to function according to this standard are devalued (Thorn-Gray & Kern, 1983).

An individual's ability to perform sexual intercourse and achieve orgasm is not the exclusive criterion for assessing one's sexuality. Perceived sociability, physical attractiveness, intelligence, and vocational achievement represent some of the other factors that are used by individuals to size up their own sexuality and that of others. Some of the latter indices may also pose problems for persons with disabilities who frequently lack the prerequisite social skills, physical attributes, mobility, options, personal contacts, and economic circumstances to function in typical dating milieus, thus severely limiting their sexual options.

Sexual Myths

Given the present emphasis upon deinstitutionalization, mainstreaming, and civil rights for citizens with disabilities, the heightened attention directed toward their sexual rights by professionals (Daniels et al., 1979; Gordon, 1974), the apparent relationship between successful social and community adjustment (Haavik & Menninger, 1981), and the seeming openness with which society approaches the subject of sex, it would seem logical that the sexual development and education of handicapped persons would be attended to directly, candidly, and comprehensively. In fact, the opposite is true. With disabled individuals discussions are often complicated by the presence of well-entrenched societal myths. Some of the more prevalent myths include the following (Daniels et al., 1979).

1. *Persons with disabilities are asexual.* This myth stems from the belief that specific disabilities impair people globally, rendering them uninterested or incapable of sexual expression or functioning. In part this myth also results from the narrow conception of sexuality that pervades our culture.
2. *Persons with disabilities are oversexed.* In contrast to the preceding myth, this one refers mostly to persons with intellectual and emotional difficulties. This belief is often elicited as a defense for avoiding sex education programs, which are portrayed as stimulating the latent, uncontrollable sexual urges of such people, which may lead to widespread sexual promiscuousness, assaults. abuse, and deviations.
3. *Disabled people are childlike and need protection, not education.* This myth stems from the perception of some disabled individuals as children who must be protected from sexual corruption. Often these individuals are referred to as "kids" despite their adulthood and/or treated as youngsters through the use of educational materials that are designed for young children and deal only with the most elemental aspects of sexuality. This myth also may be manifested by parents and professionals who fear that knowledge is dangerous and may lead to unchecked sexual activity, promiscuity, pregnancy, and/or marriage, none of which "the child" will be ready for. Sex education is, therefore, viewed as frustrating for the adolescent and troublesome for his or her parents.

4. *Disability is inheritable.* This myth refers both to genetic and social inheritance. Some disabilities are genetically transmitted, most are not. The probabilities of inheriting a disability can be discovered through genetic counseling. However, the myth that disability is socially inherited is also a pervasive, yet unsubtantiated belief that disabled people, because of their limited sensory physical abilities and social skills, will provide impoverished developmental environments for their children.

This myth has led to the segregationist view that people with disabilities should associate and marry only other people with disabilities. The latter belief is often defended on the grounds that most disabled people associate primarily with each other anyway, and that the commonality of having a disability is a sufficient reason for people to be thought of as different from everyone else and upon which to build a relationship.

Although neither of the preceding conclusions is true, they do lead to self-fulfilling conceptions and further faulty assumptions. For example, segregation is often justified on the basis of the fact that disabled persons often associate with each other and that only "socially inadequate" nondisabled persons are attracted to persons with disabilities. This may lead to the perpetuation of further segregated programs, which force individuals with disabilities into closer contact, maximize the chances that they will develop social and sexual relations, and reinforce the belief that such segregation is natural and preferred by disabled individuals. Segregated programs not only separate disabled and nondisabled persons, but also frequently segregate males from females, obstructing the natural emergence of one's own sexual preference.

5. *Parents of handicapped children are opposed to sex education.* This myth refers to the belief that parents of handicapped children object to sexual education. They, like all parents, are very concerned about the sexual development of their children—an interest that may be even more pronounced than that of parents of nondisabled adolescents (Haavik & Menninger, 1981). In addition, parents of young adults with disabilities often have concerns about the physiological growth of their young adults, and the attitudes of others toward their sexual behaviors. However, it has not been demonstrated that they have more objections to sex education programs for their children than other parents. In fact, most parents, including those of disabled children, are looking for assistance in dealing with this issue, and research indicated that such assistance is frequently warranted.

Many times parents (and professionals) provide sex education only when it can no longer be avoided. Hammer, Wright, & Jensen (1967), for example, revealed that parents provided more sex information earlier to their disabled daughters because the onset of menstruation precluded further delays in education. Apparently, however, sexual instruction of adolescent boys could be prolonged. Duffy

(1981), after interviewing severely physically disabled women, found that although parents were the major source of sexual information, many parents did not tell them about menstruation until it actually occurred. These parents expressed surprise that there would be a menstrual period because of the disability.

Conclusions should not be made that parents do not want to address the issue of sexuality with their disabled adolescents or that they will inevitably refuse to do so, except under the most pressing circumstances. As Haavik and Menninger (1981) revealed, parents have expressed an intense concern about the sexual development and behaviors of their handicapped adolescents, particularly issues such as masturbation, birth control, and marriage. Further, when parents seek professional assistance for their disabled adolescent it most often centers around the issue of sexuality (Haavik & Menninger, 1981). Most often, however, parents were immobilized by a lack of knowledge, guidance, and support. Like many parents, they reported feeling unqualified and ill-prepared, and preferred that sexual instruction be provided outside the home (Goodman, Budner, & Lesh, 1971).

6. *If a disabled person has a sexual problem it is most often the result of the disability.* Some disabilities can affect typical sexual activities such as a spinal cord injury or severe cerebral palsy. However, in many cases societal attitudes, treatment environments and procedures, educational deficiencies, and inadequate opportunities are the major causes of sexual difficulties.

In many cases, this myth stems from narrowly equating sexuality with the ability to have an orgasm. Thus, the major problem is not necessarily being sexual or even achieving sexual satisfaction, but of the uninformed perceptions of people regarding the broad character of one's sexual potential.

Implications

The preceding myths have implications for the way in which sexual instruction and programs are conceived, constructed, and operated by parents, professionals, and other community persons (Daniels et al., 1979). In some instances this may mean active suppression, avoidance, or marginal assistance. In more positive circumstances, it may result in actively reaching out to disabled adolescents through intensive purposeful education or counseling, beginning at an early age and continuing through adulthood.

Within the preceding sections, emphasis was given to the fact that disabled adolescents may experience considerable institutional and social isolation from nondisabled peers. Through separate physical arrangements, segregated residential circumstances, and divergent classroom assignments, handicapped adolescents are increasingly assembled for academic and vocational purposes only with other disabled individuals. Because of transportation problems and lack of preparation and encouragement, disabled youngsters often do not participate in extracurricular activities that provide opportunities for extensive interactions. Therefore, they can become very limited in the number of contemporaries to whom they can turn for typical peer interactions.

McDaniel (1976) concluded that the social isolation that frequently accompanies disability is especially acute during adolescence when intimate social relations are so important. This apparent social void seems to create a vicious, self-propelling cycle of deprivation for young, disabled adults. They desire close peer relations that are difficult to achieve because of the negative attitudes, feelings of ambiguity and discomfort, and physical and social separateness on the part of nondisabled adolescents. To increase and improve such contact and to bring about positive changes in attitudes will not be easy for several reasons. First, more than casual contact between disabled and nondisabled adolescents is needed. Weinberg (1978) found that the level and quality of social contact necessary to change the negative attitudes of nondisabled young adults toward disabled peers has to be as frequent and great as that between college roommates. Second, though it has not been proven that nondisabled adolescents hold more devaluing attitudes toward persons with disabilities than other age groups of nondisabled individuals, it has been demonstrated (McDaniel, 1976) that negative peer group attitudes toward the disabled adolescent are pervasive. Third, such attitudes are difficult to change because of the developmental emphasis on physique, social role demands, and peer group standards of appearance and behavior (McDaniel, 1976, pp. 22–23).

The virtual absence of integrated, culturally valuing settings and experiences seriously obstructs the formation of personal acquaintanceships, let alone friendships, between disabled and nondisabled adolescents. For those handicapped young adults who wish to form intimate social and sexual relationships, the obstacles become additive, for as Vash (1981) has stated, personal intimacy often emanates from casual friendships.

> Many [disabled persons] report that most of their romances begin as friendships, contrary to pre-disability patterns. [Persons with disabilities] may, in fact, be seen by the nondisabled majority as sexless. . . . Once the individuals get to know each other, and the strangeness of the disability wears off, the "sexless" image is recognized as inaccurate and the spark of romance may ignite (p. 116).

Transcending one's disability in a society that idolizes physical attractiveness, verbal glibness, physical and behavioral conformity, and athletic prowess is not easy. It requires a pronounced social proficiency and a multitude of environmental opportunities in which to exhibit such proficiencies. Currently, there is a scarcity of the kind of intellectual, social, recreational/leisure, vocational, and residential arenas necessary to stimulate even preemptory recognition of the deep human qualities of persons with disabilities. Such recognition requires early, intense, sustained, and consistent integration of disabled individuals into society's valued settings and activities in appropriate roles in which they can be supported, taught, and supervised to function sucessfully. Such involvement can lead to more fruitful peer relationships during adolescence if contacts are initiated far in advance of adolescence. By the time adolescence occurs the educational, social, residential, vocational, and sexual expectations for the disabled and the nondisabled are firmly, and perhaps irrevocably, divergent.

Principle of Normalization and Community Living

Given that the existing social institutions are not addressing adequately or consistently the community preparation needs of most young adults with disabilities one must ask what can be done. In the remainder of the chapter, a brief outline of the principles of normalization is presented as a guide for social, educational, and rehabilitative interventions. Case studies are used to describe and analyze the numerous community living difficulties facing disabled adolescents in relation to normalization issues.

The concept of living in the community, as used in this chapter, is derived from the principle of normalization, a philosophy and set of practices for the treatment of devalued persons and the conduct of human services. There are three major definitions of normalization, each of which is slightly different. For clarity, the Wolfensberger definitions, which are the most specific and widely circulated in this country, have been used. Recently, Wolfensberger has changed the name of his formulations from "normalization" to "social role valorization," although the material remains essentially unchanged.

Wolfensberger's (1972) statements describe normalization as implying "as much as possible the use of culturally valued means in order to enable, establish, and/or maintain valued social roles for people" (p. 131). It is well beyond the scope of this chapter to explicate all the implications normalization has for community living (Wolfensberger, 1972; 1980; Wolfensberger & Glenn, 1978a, 1978b). However, some of the basic tenets of the principle and their application to the idea of community living and the preparation of adolescents for community living will be discussed briefly.

Underlying the principle of normalization is the concept of deviancy, a status socially imposed on an individual who is perceived as different because he or she possesses a significant and negatively valued characteristic (Goffman, 1963; Wolfensberger & Tullman, 1982). Individuals who have physical, emotional, and cognitive disabilities are generally considered deviant and unjustly devalued and discriminated against by members of society. This treatment not only is reflected in day-to-day social interactions but also is underscored by the segregated, residential, educational, employment, social, and "special" services offered to disabled persons in contemporary American society.

To eliminate or minimize the devaluation of persons with disabilities, normalization adherents have called for the scrutiny of all factors that might cause such discrimination: the perceiver of deviancy, the perceived, and the

Severity of disability should not prevent an individual from fully participating in recreational opportunities. These individuals with physical disabilities are learning to ski. (Photograph by Mima Cataldo.)

social and physical contexts in which the perceptions flourish. Thus, normalization is concerned with the change at the person (disabled and nondisabled), service system, and societal levels.

Cultural Normativeness

Proponents of normalization have called for an emphasis on interactions with and interpretations of disabled persons, which are valuing and culturally normative. But what does culturally normative mean? Action, behavior, appearance, and programs to be labeled culturally normalizing must reflect a cultural typicalness or statistical commonality within a particular community. More than that, however, normalization emphasizes the use of standards that reflect idealized values, or moral imperatives, which, though not necessarily common, are expected and highly regarded within the general community. Wolfensberger and Tullman (1982) have indicated that the goals of normalization have been achieved only if an individual:

1. Has achieved that culturally normative degree of personal autonomy and choice that is enjoyed by most members of society.
2. Has access to the valued experiences and resources of open society as would be typical.

3. Has the freedom and capability to choose and lead a lifestyle that is accessible to at least the majority of people of the same chronological age.

Wolfensberger is careful to point out that the preceding goals are not achievable by everyone and that the qualifying phrase in the normalization definition "as much as possible" should reflect the particular characteristics of the person, the limits of current knowledge, and the individual's own goals, means, and preferences (p. 144).

Heal (1980, p. 39) has listed some of the major corollaries of normalization including cultural normativeness, developmental expectations, integration of activities and services, continuity of services, separation of individuals and their services, and smallness of congregated populations. Combining the definitions of Heal (1980) and Wolfensberger and Tullman (1982), we have briefly described each of the preceding elements, all of which have been quantified for the purpose of evaluating human services programs (Wolfensberger & Glenn, 1978a, 1978b).

> *Cultural Normativeness* refers to the fact that any of the client's roles, labels, behaviors, environments, services, schedules of daily, weekly, or lifetime activities, or any of the expectations and language or forms of address used by those who relate to him or her, should reflect the valued standards of the surrounding culture.

In striving for cultural normativeness in interactions with clients and in the imagery that surrounds education and human services programs, professionals must attend to how clients are addressed (in adult manner rather than childish nicknames), what kinds of skills they are taught (complex, relevant skills rather than simple skills), whether the materials they use are appropriate for the client's chronological age (adult rather than children's supplies), and the name and location of a program (the High Hopes House located in a run-down neighborhood is far less desirable than a typical house in a valued neighborhood that is designated by its street number and blends in with the other houses).

> *Developmental (as Opposed to Medical) Expectations.* Persons with disabilities are viewed as developing individuals with the same needs for physical, social, educational, psychological, vocational growth as other persons, rather than as less than competent or less human individuals with incurable impairments.

Human service professionals must be cognizant of the strengths of disabled persons and do everything possible to break the negative role expectations with which they must deal. Negative expectations are often unconscious and inadvertent, but insidious, and can lead to restrictions in physical and social environments; limited goals and activities provided, offered, or demanded; and a consistent juxtaposition of disabled and devalued groups of people and associations with negative language, images, and symbols.

Societal Integration. Persons with disabilities must have opportunities to interact into the valued social life of his or her community physically, personally, and socially. Integration goes beyond merely being physically present in the environment, which represents only a facilitating step toward individual, valued, social participation.

Professionals working with disabled persons must go beyond mainstreaming and deinstitutionalization, neither of which may be truly integrative, and be sure that their clients are enabled to live in normative housing, be educated and employed, and be involved in recreation, shopping, religious activities, within a valued community, at a meaningful level and with nonhandicapped people.

Continuity of Services. Educational, vocational, residential, recreational, and social services should be available and should include intensive instructions in culturally relevant skills using valued methods of instruction and normative physical settings. Such services should enable individuals to move along a continuum of services from supervision to independence without segregation, and to provide training and support for them in the most stimulating and integrated environments.

Professionals must carefully examine the individualized nature of their services to be sure that each individual is participating in challenging, stimulating, and positive environments. Often, education and adult service programs talk of individualized programs but operate stereotypic, predetermined programs into which disabled persons must fit. Individuals should have the opportunities to participate more autonomously in a variety of more complex settings. Teachers and human services professionals should provide the emotional support and physical resources necessary to facilitate client progress to maximally independent vocational, residential, social, and recreation/leisure settings.

Separation of Programs and Activities. Program activities, such as domiciliary, work, recreation, and counseling should be separate from each other. Also, the activities and programs of people with disabilities should be dispersed throughout a community and not located in one neighborhood or section of town.

Often, education and adult service programs mix program functions so that counseling and/or recreation times overlap with work or training periods. Such an approach is not consistent with the way in which most companies or businesses in our society operate. Therefore, these programs may teach persons culturally inappropriate behaviors that may impair their performance and image in more normalizing environments. Also, such an approach can reduce the effectiveness of the instruction by removing individuals from specified tasks during training periods. Persons with disabling conditions should not be socially, residentially, and vocationally relegated to a particular area of a community. This practice, which is widespread, can be as segregating and stigmatizing as a separate school or place of employment.

Smallness. The numbers of people being served by a particular program should be small enough to maximize any instruction, to enhance the image of the program, and to avoid segregation and cultural deviancy.

The use of small residences and instructional groups enhances the staff's ability to provide individualized and intensive instruction to their clients. Also, such small groups do not draw the negative attention of the nondisabled who then tend to isolate such groups and heighten the segregation and the cultural differentness associated with disabled individuals.

According to the principle of normalization, the transition of the young, disabled adult into the community should occur in ways that closely approximate the integrative processes of the nondisabled. The nondisabled are socialized into the community in a cumulative, gradual, and sequential manner beginning early in their development and intensifying with the onset of adolescence. Thus, it may be argued that the most effective and culturally normative way of achieving full community integration would be to initiate within the family, school, and community, early intensive socializing experiences, to provide the supports necessary for disabled youngsters to remain socially integrated from childhood on, and to teach children with disabilities the prerequisite behaviors of the society. If such early interventions were successful, the ensuing developmental and socializing experiences of disabled adolescents and young adults would likely conform more closely to, and occur together with, the nondisabled.

Case Studies

In the preceding sections of this chapter, some gobal issues that confront disabled, young adults entering the community were outlined. In this section, brief case descriptions are used to illustrate how these generic issues affect individuals in specific circumstances. All the case examples have been derived from real life situations though names, specific details, and some circumstances have been altered or combined to obscure people's identities and to maximize the instructional value of each example.

After the case studies have been presented, we will summarize the community living issues that emerged, highlight their generic character, and discuss them in relation to normalization.

Jeri S.

Jeri S. is a twenty-one-year-old physically handicapped individual with spina bifida who requires the use of an electric wheelchair for mobility. During her eighteen years of public education she received traditional academic curricula, including reading, math, and spelling, in a self-contained elementary classroom with other students who had severe physical handicaps. Beginning in middle school and into her high school years, Jeri was integrated into regular classes with nonhandicapped students. She graduated from high school with a low B average and was accepted as a computer technology major in the local community college. Her college tuition and books were paid for by the Office of Vocational Rehabilitation (OVR), a state agency that serves the vocational training and placement needs of disabled adults.

While in college Jeri lived at home with her parents and was driven each day to campus either by a parent or one of her siblings. Upon successfully graduating from college, she was hired as a computer programmer at a local insurance company that was too far away for her parents to continue driving her. To get to work she had to take public transportation, which was not wheelchair accessible, or use a special dial-a-bus service. The latter service was often unreliable, either arriving too early or late, and was not responsive to sudden changes in work schedules.

Jeri was assisted in joining a car pool with two other individuals. However, she was unable to transfer from the car to the wheelchair and back without assistance, even though she was provided a new wheelchair for just this purpose. She stated that her new chair was uncomfortable, lighter, and designed differently from her old one. Initially, other members of the car pool assisted in transferring her in and out of the car, but they complained to the personnel office that the entire procedure was quite time consuming and potentially injurious to them. Jeri was asked to withdraw from the car pool, and she began taking the special bus. She also experienced some problems transferring from her wheelchair to the toilet and back and requested that she be able to use the company's nursing clinic to obtain necessary assistance. During school and college she always received such assistance from either one of her siblings or a neighborhood friend. The clinic was not very close to her work area, and traveling there required more time away from work than a trip to the women's room. Also, using the clinic required that the nurse and her assistant arrange their schedules so that they were at the clinic during Jeri's breaks to unlock the door or be present to assist her in the bathroom.

Although the company granted Jeri's request to use the clinic, Jeri's supervisor was unhappy with the arrangement because it required extra time and created some complaints among her co-workers. Jeri's inconsistent transportation arrangements to and from work created additional tension between her, her supervisor, and co-workers. After being late several days and unable to remain after hours to complete an important project, Jeri was given a warning by her supervisor that although the quality of her work was excellent, her lack of personal independence and inadequate transportation arrangements were impairing her effectiveness. She was told that unless she solved these problems she would be fired. Upon hearing this, Jeri's parents began driving her to and from work. This constituted a great hardship for them, both of whom worked.

Jeri enjoyed her job and was upset with the problems she was experiencing there. Also, she was unhappy with other aspects of her life. Her social life was limited to occasionally going out to eat or to watching a movie with members of her family. She had no friends her own age, did not date, and belonged to no church or community groups. Jeri's leisure-time activities were also rather circumscribed and consisted mostly of watching TV, reading, or using her personal computer.

On the surface, Jeri appeared to be enjoying a satisfying life. She had an excellent job, a comfortable place to live, and a supportive family. However, she was anxious and unhappy because despite her financial independence she felt isolated from her community and limited in her activities and options. Also, she was experiencing significant difficulty attaining the level of personal independence required to keep her job. Jeri is presently worried about the future. She is plagued with questions. What will happen to her as her parents grow older and her siblings move away with families of their own? How will she get to work and keep her job? Where will she live? With whom will she socialize?

To some degree these questions reflect the anxieties and ambiguities that most young adults experience in their transition from home and school to the community. However, for Jeri the stakes seem higher because the psychological dependence on family and school is combined with real physical dependence that affects not only her emotional well-being, but also her life chances in critical situations.

Tom K.

Tom K. is a twenty-two-year-old severely mentally retarded individual who lives at a large residential facility with approximately one hundred other persons and works in a sheltered workshop. Tom lived at home until about a year ago, when his elderly parents decided they could no longer adequately care for him. Although more physically integrated environments were preferred by Tom and his parents, there existed few openings and inadequate supervision at any of the area's group homes and apartments.

Tom received twelve years of public school education. During this time the school district made many changes, which included the closing of a segregated school, assignment of all students to regular elementary schools, and then assignment to chronological age-appropriate schools. For Tom, these district-wide changes meant that his first eight years were spent in an elementary school, followed by a direct move to high school. There was little or no coordination or continuity between schools; therefore, Tom's high school instruction had little if any relation to his previous instruction.

In high school Tom received mostly academic instruction. He did receive some instruction in independent living skills, but at age twenty-one was only able to function in a small group home or apartment setting with considerable supervision. Consequently, the only residential option available was an overly restrictive, one-hundred-person facility.

From the time Tom turned eighteen, he received three years of vocational training at an accessible medical laboratory where he cleaned hardware and other technical equipment. Tom liked the job, and the director of the lab was willing to hire him part-time, which meant that he could retain his SSI benefits and still work. However, when his parents decided that Tom could no longer live at home, and he had to move outside the city to the only residential facility available, he was unable to continue working at the lab. He had no access to public transportation and there were no other available living arrangements or jobs that could be secured.

After moving to the large residential facility, Tom was referred to a local sheltered workshop that was located about ten miles from the residence. Specialized transportation was provided by the workshop to all the residents of the institution who qualified, and any other clients in nearby communities. Neither Tom, his parents, nor the school personnel with whom he had worked were satisfied with his vocational and residential arrangements. They were anxious to find him less restrictive postschool placements but did not know of any agency that would or could assist them. Through the efforts of Tom's former employer, a part-time job similar to the one he had held was found near the sheltered workshop. Tom would require intensive on-site training and several months of on-site instruction and support. The workshop people agreed to let him take their bus to town, but no one could be found to provide him the on-site services he needed if he was to succeed.

Although Tom received twelve years of education in public schools and other nonsegregated environments and had learned to use city buses and community facilities, the transition from high school to postschool environments resulted in domestic and work placements that were below the expectations of himself, his parents, and school personnel and did not stimulate opportunities to practice and develop community functioning and recreation/leisure skills. This led to enrollment in programs that included only handicapped persons and represented a step backward for Tom, his parents, and school people, all of whom had developed school and job placements for Tom in integrated environments involving mostly nonhandicapped peers and co-workers.

Susan M.

Susan M. is a twenty-one-year-old woman diagnosed as schizophrenic. During her sophomore year of high school, Susan gave the first indications of serious emotional problems. After failing to make a school sports team she became withdrawn, stopped attending school functions with which she had been actively involved, and did not socialize with friends. As Susan became more withdrawn, family tension increased to a point at which a family therapist was seen, but there was no improvement; finally, a psychiatrist was consulted after Susan refused to attend school. Susan was put on medication and soon after was able to return to school, and with counseling she was able to graduate and gain admission to a nursing school.

Susan's first hospitalization occurred during her first semester at nursing school, where she had not been able to form significant relationships, had not participated in school activities beyond class, had stopped taking her medication and going to counseling, and had become easily upset and distracted. A week after voluntarily admitting herself to the psychiatric unit of the local general hospital, she was withdrawn from school and brought home by her parents. After two weeks she was again hospitalized when she reported hearing voices. About three months later she was discharged and started attending a day treatment program where she became bored and self-conscious, feeling that she was not learning anything and did not belong with people whom she perceived as older and more severely handicapped than herself. She finally left the day treatment program.

Over the next year and a half Susan had several short hospitalizations. When not hospitalized, she remained at home watching TV, sleeping, and reading. Her relationship with her parents had deteriorated to the point where she wanted to leave home but there were no domestic placements available to receive the support she needed and wanted. She did not want to live alone. She did volunteer work at a local nursing home, became interested in licensed practical nursing, and applied to the local Office of Vocational Rehabilitation for vocational training as an LPN. Because Susan had stopped taking her medication and attending any agency program, she had been involved in frequent arguments with her parents and area professionals and had missed several OVR appointments. Her counselor did not feel she was ready for LPN training and recommended that she seek additional mental health services and reinvolvement with the day treatment program to more adequately demonstrate her readiness for vocational training. She continued to volunteer at the local nursing home, where she was reported to be well liked by the staff and residents and was a good and consistent worker.

Both Susan and her parents were concerned about her ability to consistently and independently function in the community without support. While she is obviously a capable individual, the episodic nature of her disability often interferes with her activities and relationships in a severe and sustained manner such that employment, housing, and social relations become difficult to sustain.

Robert H.

Robert H. is a twenty-five-year-old man with a diagnosed learning disability who has demonstrated serious reading, spelling, and retention problems and disruptive behavior in school since early childhood. He attended elementary school but his restless behavior and failure to learn resulted in his being tested and diagnosed as mildly mentally retarded. Thus, he was placed in a special class in which he became physically and verbally active and as a result was given an additional diagnosis of emotional disturbance.

Robert's parents did not want him placed in special classes and requested that he be returned to the regular classroom for part of the day. The school did allow Robert to participate in some regular class activities, such as arithmetic, at which he could succeed with minimal help. However, he returned to the special classes for those subjects that required reading, speaking, and writing.

Robert's educational and social problems continued into junior high school, where he functioned much of the day in a small, self-contained class for students with adjustment problems. There his academic performance improved, but his reading and spelling skills were at a third grade level and his behavior continued to be regarded as disruptive by his teachers.

Socially, Robert was very isolated. He did not like the other students in his self-contained class whom he regarded as "dummies," and he was not accepted by students who were attending regular classes. He also had no close neighborhood friends and spent most of his time watching TV at home and building model cars and planes alone. In his last semester of junior high school, Robert was again tested and found to be above average on measured intelligence and to have a learning disability that interfered with his short-term memory and his ability to spell, read, and easily retain what he read. This discovery led to Robert's being placed in a classroom for learning disabled students where he received special education in reading and language instruction designed to improve his ability to retain and organize information.

During high school Robert's academic performance improved somewhat, and with the active encouragement of his parents but in the face of school personnel disapproval, he applied to college. Robert was accepted at a four-year college where he majored in accounting. It was understood by the admissions office that he had a learning disability and would need special accomodations, such as being able to tape lectures, to use computer terminals located in isolated areas, and to receive additional time to complete exams and papers.

Robert completed college in six and a half years, making up courses he failed and completing unfinished class requirements during the summers and semester breaks. He graduated with a low C average and experienced great difficulty with several courses, which he failed and had to retake several times.

Because of his low average, Robert had considerable trouble finding employment. Employers did not understand the term learning disability and wondered how Robert would handle the requirements of their positions, which in many ways were similar to the tasks required of him in school. Two years after graduation Robert was finally hired as an accountant and fired three months later. He was told that he did not follow directions well, was not a fast enough worker, and did not work independently. After a year of searching, Robert has still not found another position. He was married soon after graduation and is supported by his wife and by part-time manual jobs he finds.

A few months ago he discovered that as an individual with a learning disability he qualified for OVR services. He applied to that agency for assistance, noting that his disability required services above and beyond the entry level training provided by OVR if he was to be a competent accountant and to be seriously considered by prospective employers. He requested that he be assisted to enroll in the MBA program, be provided the technically sophisticated tape recording equipment for classroom use, and be given a personal computer. He asked for the computer so that he could do class work at home and in a quiet place without distractions. Also, he felt that the computer would enhance his writing and spelling proficiency and also heighten his marketability with employers, who would see his commitment to his work and would recognize that he could complete unfinished work in the evenings or at home.

Thus far, OVR has balked at these suggestions, noting that Robert has not proven himself competent to enter the accounting field, has performed only marginally well in college even with accommodations, has failed unequivocally in the job market, and is requesting expensive services well beyond the entry level provided to most recipients of OVR. OVR recommended that Robert abandon his aspirations to become an accountant and consider entering another vocational area, possibly carpentry, in which he has an expressed and measured interest and his reading, spelling, and writing deficiencies would be minimally inhibiting.

Robert wants very much to be an accountant and feels that with accommodations and additional training he can succeed in that field. He realizes that he has not performed well in either the academic or vocational spheres, but believes that until recently he knew very little about the accounting field, the nature of his disability (specifically how it affected his performance in school and work), and what sort of services would be required to overcome it and succeed as an accountant. He also feels that most professionals know very little about the nature and consequences of learning disabilities and are often reluctant to rely for advice on "experts" or the people who have such problems. Robert is worried that the decisions affecting his future will be based on financial and clinical considerations that are narrowly defined, predetermined, and based upon faulty conclusions about the nature of his disability.

Community Living Issues

Segregated school and adult service programs frequently deny individuals critical socializing experiences and skill acquisition opportunities.   In three of the case situations the disabled adolescents were segregated in separate programs for the handicapped for at least part of their education. In all cases they were recommended for segregated adult services in which only handicapped individuals participated. Such segregated programs reduced opportunities to participate in the typical socializing experiences with their peers, lessened chances to model age-appropriate behaviors of nondisabled youngsters, and denied the benefits of the same high expectations and positive outlook for achievement and community living as their contemporaries.

Illustrations of this problem may be found in the cases of Jeri and Robert, both of whom were segregated early in their educational careers and both of whom experienced serious difficulties developing the adaptive behaviors

Adaptations can be made to facilitate learning a new skill. The middle skier is blind and is guided down the hill by holding onto a bar. (Photograph by Mima Cataldo.)

they needed to adjust to community living as young adults. Jeri's employment was jeopardized because she had not learned how to transfer properly a skill that should have been an integral part of her educational experiences. Robert never learned how to adapt to his learning disability through accommodations such as additional time, assistive devices, and adaptive learning and retention methods and through social strategies for explaining his disability and coping techniques to others.

Both Jeri and Robert also experienced serious social impoverishments for their segregation. They had made no close friends and either could not readily identify with those handicapped persons with whom they had been grouped or were rejected by their nonhandicapped peers. Rejection by their nondisabled contemporaries stemmed partly from the asocial behavior of Robert and Jeri and partly from the negative attitudes of nondisabled persons. The problem behaviors and attitudes on both sides might have been more positive if they had been targeted for change early in the educational process.

The tendency to continue this pattern of social segregation does not end with the school and early adult years. The self-perpetuating cycle of isolation continues because adaptive social and vocational skills are rarely acquired, perpetuating the rejection by nondisabled peers. Also, once having graduated from high school, disabled young adults are confronted with the hard reality that almost all available community recreation/leisure activities occur in "handicapped only" environments, even reducing the opportunities to meet and interact with nondisabled persons who may share some common interests and skills.

Intervention programs designed to teach disabled students how to live in the community often were not initiated early enough in their educational careers. Many educational programs not only operate in segregated schools, but also often begin too late to affect adaptive behavior change on the part of disabled youngsters and positive attitude change on the part of their nondisabled peers. The lack of early intervention refers to the inattention of the school and the home to early socializing experiences that are critical building blocks for learning community living skills. Segregated services and the absence of early family and school involvement in teaching social and independent living behaviors create cumulative social, vocational, and educational deficits and impoverished community living skills.

In the cases of Jeri, Robert, and Tom, the school continued to stress academic subjects even though there was evidence that these individuals were in desperate need of social, vocational, and independent living skills. While each had seemingly lost interest and had demonstrated little or no progress in academic courses, it is important to avoid prematurely closing any viable educational or vocational doors without careful scrutiny. On the other hand, special educators and other professionals must look beyond the age of twenty-one to determine whether the curricula designed for students is actually preparing them for "successful" life experiences. If the chances for integrated community living are to be enhanced, professionals must be willing to replace traditional academic classes with community-based, meaningful vocational, residential, recreation/leisure, and community experiences.

Community living skills learned during school years were frequently not required in adult environments. The lack of coordination and continuity between school and adult service programs can result in the two systems operating on different training and placement principles. Tom, for example, was more adequately prepared for integrated vocational and domestic environments than was reflected in the restricted, segregated residential vocational settings he eventually inhabited. This resulted from a lack of communication between parents and professionals and from the failure of adult services to have a more extensive array of domestic and vocational options.

The same problem arose in Susan's case when she was denied a vocational training opportunity even though she had developed an excellent record of volunteer work in nearly the same vocational area in which she sought training. The problem in Susan's case appeared to be an exclusive reliance upon a readiness model of vocational services. When she did not demonstrate a level of vocational preparedness according to the prerequisites established by the agency, she was not deemed eligible for services. However, while she did not conform to the agency's definition of readiness, she did perform suitably in her volunteer nursing home position, which closely approximated the work she wanted to do. Rather than recommending that Susan return to a segregated mental health program in which she had done poorly and toward which she expressed dissatisfaction, the adult service providers might have attempted to address some of her deficiencies through on-site supervision while also providing her the opportunities to enlarge her adaptive skills, which had been developed in her integrated school program and successful volunteer position.

Parents were not sufficiently involved in services planning and implementation. Despite the individualized education plan, parents are often not consulted early or regularly enough in the development of long- and short-term services plans. With all the individuals in the case studies, the families were intimately involved in their lives, assisting, supporting, and advocating for them throughout their school and early adult years. However, these families received little help early in their children's lives when some advice on independent living and adaptive skills could have been very helpful. Perhaps Jeri's parents would have worked harder to teach her transfer and mobility skills had they received more encouragement and technical advice from school personnel. Similarly, through more intensive parental and teacher assistance Robert might have learned school and job accommodations and achieved more success in those settings. In Tom's situation, his parents' rather sudden decision that they could no longer properly supervise him could have been anticipated if the parents, school personnel, and adult service providers had established better communication.

In Susan's situation, when her episodic symptoms began early in high school little work was done with her parents or adult service providers to arrange for adequate domestic interventions. Strong supportive services such as parental instruction, counseling, respite, and crisis services might have eased the pressure of the family and perhaps retained stronger family bonds.

There were no individualized programs for adolescents and young adults. In all the case studies, the young, disabled adults manifested characteristics that required individualized attention. The response of the school and/or adult service professional was a reliance upon traditional service delivery methods that are used with the majority of clients.

Jeri, Robert, Tom, and Susan all required on-site supportive services of varying intensity and length. The schools did not know much about such interventions, and adult services were reluctant to provide atypical services. Unfortunately, therefore, persons with disabilities, especially those considered severe, are often not given the necessary support services during and after school years to achieve meaningful community participation. To avoid unnecessary difficulties during and after the transition from school to work, systematic efforts must be made (1) to determine and extend the number of options available to disabled graduates, (2) to ensure that the curricula offered are preparatory for functioning in heterogeneous postschool environments,

(3) to involve parents in the educational and transition planning process, and (4) to desegregate schools and programs to ensure ongoing opportunities to interact with nonhandicapped peers and others.

Summary

The purpose of this chapter was to describe the socializing experiences faced by disabled adolescents within their families, schools, and communities, and to point out that eventual community entrance does not occur automatically or easily for this group. Normalization was offered as a guide for addressing the community living problems of disabled adolescents. A variety of case studies was presented to specifically illustrate the kinds of obstacles disabled young adults must confront and to offer some general suggestions for overcoming such difficulties. A consistent theme throughout the chapter was an emphasis upon system-based obstacles. In addressing the problems disabled adolescents face in becoming fully functioning members of the community, professionals must be willing to intensively address not only the skill deficits of many disabled adolescents but also the shortcomings of the surrounding social institutions and human service programs. It is these services, though designed to prepare and assist adolescents with disabilities for community entrance, that often heighten their problems by exacerbating tensions within their families, separating them from their peers and the normative activities of their society, and providing inadequate community living instruction.

Through new and innovative programs that are occurring throughout the country, it is becoming clear that all disabled adolescents and young adults can learn the complex behaviors and skills to become productive and contributing members of their communities. The real challenge facing parents, educators, and adult service providers is to go beyond the belief that merely obtaining or providing services for disabled adolescents is adequate. To actualize the right of disabled persons to live and function in their communities, human service programs must pursue and develop activities and environments that include disabled, young adults in all valued social institutions and community activities. In addition, adolescents must be taught skills that enable them to see themselves, and to be viewed by others, as not merely being in the community, but belonging there.

Chapter 10

Stephen T. Murphy

Jan Nisbet

Stephen T. Murphy is an associate professor of Rehabilitation Services at Syracuse University. Prior to his career as an educator, Dr. Murphy worked as a counseling psychologist developing social and vocational programs for young adults with mental retardation and for older adults with severe psychiatric problems. As an educator, Dr. Murphy has been involved in establishing local community-based, continuing-education and vocational-training, and placement programs for persons with disabilities. Dr. Murphy is the author of numerous book chapters and articles on client-professional issues, vocational assessment centers, and qualitative research methods in rehabilitation. Presently, he is writing a book on the perceptions and experiences of young adults designated learning disabled.

Jan Nisbet is an assistant professor of Rehabilitation Services at Syracuse University. Her project and programmatic efforts are devoted to demonstrating that adolescents and adults with severe disabilities can make a successful transition from school to integrated work in their communities. Currently, she is exploring how to have typical co-workers and employers maximally involved in the placement, training, and employment process. Dr. Nisbet's other interests include desegregation and deinstitutionalization, professional training programs in rehabilitation, developing adaptive devices for persons with physical disabilities, and community/vocational education for students with disabilities.

Model Education and Adult Services Programs for Young Adults with Disabilities

After reading this chapter, you should be able to:

1
Distinguish between independent living programs and institutional programs.

2
Define recreation and leisure and discuss their importance for young adults with disabilities.

3
Recall examples of model vocational education programs and discuss their similarities and differences.

4
Describe curricula approaches to prepare disabled adolescents for community living.

Normalizing environmental forces affecting the identities of persons with disabilities may not be enough to prepare people for community living. As Schutz, Vogelsberg, and Rusch (1980) have argued:

> Simple exposure to the "patterns and conditions of everyday life which are as close as possible to the norms and patterns of mainstream society" (Nirge, 1969, p. 181) will not guarantee acquisition of the vast array of competencies associated with successful community living (p. 107).

Programs for disabled adolescents and young adults should focus on the systematic instruction of specific community skills. Systematic methods that are part of intervention programs have been employed successfully in a wide variety of settings such as schools, community sites, and human service agencies. Such methods also have been used to develop diverse individual, social, educational, and sexual skills. Some of these skills include community mobility by means such as walking and riding buses; domestic skills (e.g., cooking, housekeeping, laundry skills, and home management); self-care skills (e.g., grooming, dressing, and self-medication); money management (e.g., coin recognition, making change, and budgeting); telephone skills; leisure and social activities (e.g., swimming, bowling, cross-country skiing, and interpersonal skills); vocational skills (e.g., job-seeking behaviors, work behaviors, and specific work skills). Within each of the preceding categories are other skills that were not listed, but have been deemed important for functioning in the community and have been successfully taught to disabled young adults.

Schutz et al. (1980) have also reported that some programs, besides focusing on single skills, have initiated "community living preparation programs." Such programs have been initiated in residential programs and consist of "highly structured skill training components with progressively more normalized routines engineered to ease the transition to greater autonomy and increased responsibility" (p. 116). Anthony (1980) has also advocated a skills approach to learning independent community living behaviors. His techniques, though ostensibly directed toward those classified as "psychiatrically disabled," closely resemble the community living preparation program described by Schutz et al. (1980) and have been used with individuals with other types of disabilities and/or behavioral deficits.

Community Involvement in Planning and Implementing Services

Anthony (1980) has attempted to go beyond the exclusive person-change orientation that has characterized most behavioral approaches within the human service field and has included community interventions.

> There are primarily two types of interventions that rehabilitation practitioners can use to assist the client in changing his or her behavior or to alter the demands of the community so that they are more congruous

with the abilities of the client (p. 15). . . . In addition to rehabilitation treatment programs designed to increase the client's skill level, the rehabilitation treatment process typically involves modifying . . . the client's environment to better accommodate or strengthen the client's present abilities; . . . each client's specific community must be diagnosed as if it too, were a client. That is, the community's strengths and deficits must be assessed with respect to how they might aid or hamper the psychiatrically disabled client's skill performance (pp. 16–17).

Anthony (1980, p. 17) has listed specific examples of community/environmental elements that might need to be changed to enhance an individual's functioning: quality of school programs, parental attitudes and perceptions of neighbors, availability of transportation, willingness of employers to hire, and so forth.

Involving Disabled Young Adults

In the community preparation programs noted previously, there is a prearranged format of instruction. There is, however, little articulation of the disabled person's viewpoint and participation. To what extent do persons labeled "clients" have any influence over which skills are taught, both to the individual or designated community targets? Will individual or community targets be the priority? In what settings and under what conditions will such instruction occur? Whether people have choices and when, how, and where they exert them are often not left to those persons called "clients" or their representatives (Murphy & Salomone, 1983; Murphy & Ursprung, 1983). Chamberlin (1978) has addressed this problem as it pertains specifically to treatment of people labeled mentally ill. However, the points she has made apply to human services in general. "People labeled mentally ill are usually presumed to be incapable of exercising decision-making power in their own best interests (p. 3). . . . [They] become part of a system that deprives them of control over their own life as part of their treatment" (p. 6).

Alternative community programs exist, but here it becomes important to define them. Often there is a veneer of democracy, which permits residents to vote on what to have for dinner or what movie to see, but places real decisions, such as who gets to live in the facility or what the rules are, in professional hands. Although some other alternatives are more truly individualized, the staff dichotomy exists in most. A true alternative is one in which all basic decision-making power is in the hands of those the program serves—a condition that is rare. Where it does exist, it shows how well people can help one another to maximize the strengths and abilities of each other (Chamberlin, 1978, pp. 15–16).

In summary, community services and programs should be designed to teach young adults to live, work, and play in integrated environments. Unfortunately, services have often functioned from a readiness orientation, which requires that persons with disabilities progress through day treatment and sheltered work before getting a job in a local business or industry. Likewise, in residential services, persons may have to live in a group home before moving to a supervised apartment. When this prerequisite is applied to young adults, they may spend their life preparing to live in the community. Many agencies and individuals are developing programs that immediately integrate disabled students and adults into environments required for ultimate functioning (Brown et al., 1981; Ford et al., 1984). Programs are constantly changing to meet individual needs and maximize integration. Therefore, the descriptions of the following school and adult residential, vocational, and recreation/leisure programs should change with time.

Residential and Independent Living Programs

Residential/independent living skills are broad, amorphous entities that may include eating, going to the bathroom, dressing, repairing a wheelchair, housekeeping, and so forth. As wide range as independent living skills may appear, they are no more diffuse and amorphous than the variety of ways, methods, and emphases that have been proposed to ensure their acquisition. The thrust to teach and learn independent living skills has developed somewhat differently for particular groups of disabled individuals. In the following sections, how and why the notion of independent living evolved in the mental health, mental retardation, and physical disability areas will be discussed.

Developing Programs

The deinstitutionalization movements of the 1960s and 1970s in mental disabilities comprised the major impetus for alternative residential and independent living programs. These movements were generated by the civil rights movements for blacks and women, litigation against involuntary commitments and institutionalization as a nonhabilitative treatment, increasing public awareness of the realities of institutional life and federal task reports, and legislation advocating noninstitutional modes of treatment. As Crawford, Thompson, and Aiello (1979) have noted, deinstitutionalization includes several conditions, specifically:

1. The placement of residents outside the institution in community residences.
2. The development of programs to teach residents the necessary skills to remain in the community.
3. The development of community-based residential environments.
4. The provision of services in the community.
5. The education of the community in order to combat resistance to residential placements.
6. The specification of criteria for inpatient admission to avoid inappropriate institutional admission.
7. The generation of methods and procedures for placing residents in

the most sociably, physically, and psychologically appropriate residence.

8. The upgrading of institutions through physical improvements, staff training, improving hiring practices, and enhanced programming.

These conditions—particularly numbers six and eight, which imply that admission to institutions is acceptable under certain circumstances and institutions can be improved—have been questioned by advocates (Taylor, 1982). Deinstitutionalization as a movement did not seriously question the necessity or appropriateness of having large residential facilities for persons with disabilities. Not until the *Pennhurst* lawsuit (i.e., *Halderman v. Pennhurst*) were the issues of the nonhabilation nature of institutions and anti-institutionalization legally raised (Ferleger & Boyd, 1979). Community-based residential programs began to proliferate as a result of increasing documentation of the deleterious effects of institutionalization and the heightened impatience of the courts with the institutional practices. Conroy (1977) found that between 1955 and 1975 there was a 65 percent decline in persons residing in the nation's hospitals for persons labeled mentally disabled. Bruininks, Hauber, and Kudla (1980) reported that about 4,300 community residences existed in 1977, of which 76 percent were less than ten years old. Using data from several studies, Willer, Scheerenberger, and Intaglia (1980) concluded that about 87 percent of persons with mental retardation reside in one of three types of community placements: family care (40 percent), group homes/supervised apartments (30 percent), and natural homes (17 percent).

The results of a study conducted by Scheerenberger and Felsenthal (1977) indicated that developmentally disabled residents living in the community rarely interacted with nondisabled neighbors and had few friends outside their homes. Birenbaum and Seiffer (1976) noted that frequently this lack of social contact was perpetuated, perhaps inadvertently, by staff members, who, in their efforts to reduce negative neighborhood attitudes, tended to isolate residents and restrict them from leaving the premises. The dangers of such circumstances are that residents will never know their neighbors and never be appreciated as individuals. As Wolfensberger (1972) has argued, any individual only has room for a limited number of relationships and will first turn for friendship to immediate peer groups. If the people around him or her are also predominantly disabled, the chances of forming close relationships with nondisabled people and becoming an integral number of the larger community are sharply reduced.

This sort of isolation exists not only for individuals with mental disabilities, but also for severely physically disabled persons involved in independent living programs. In efforts to combat such segregation, members and advocates of the independent living movement have continually expressed their suspicions of long-term adaptive housing arrangements and have encouraged support for fully integrated long-term housing situations. For persons labeled mentally disabled, a number of community placement options have been proposed (Haywood & Newbrough, 1981; Heal, Novak, Sigelman,

The importance of teaching continues into adolescence. Here a teacher assists a student in his reading, a skill that he uses at his community work site. (Photograph by Mima Cataldo.)

& Switzky, 1980); those options attempt to address social integration. Many individuals affiliated with residential programs cannot become unobtrusive easily because their major associations give them away. It has been found that while initial neighborhood resistance to group homes may be high, such opposition appears to subside and becomes indifference with the passage of time (Haywood & Newbrough, 1981). Time alone will not solve the problem of neighborhood acceptance and inclusion of disabled individuals. The reduction in size of group homes and the development of supported apartment arrangements will positively affect community attitudes.

A wide variety of facilities classified as community-based residences exist for disabled persons (Heal, Novak, Sigelman, & Switzky, 1978). Some offer little physical, pedagogical, or psychological advantages over large residential institutions they were meant to replace. In many instances, however, the principle of normalization has pervaded their planning and considerable attention has been given to combating the devaluing and non-normalizing atmosphere indigenous to large residential facilities (Sigelman, Bell, Schoenrock, Elias, & Dauber-Braun, 1978). In most instances, the environment emphasized has been internal, especially rooms and areas within the residence. In fact, the internal environment is often described as an indispensable part of independent living instruction because of its relationship to the acquisition of adaptive skills and, therefore, the probability for community success (Haywood & Newbrough, 1981; Sigelman et al., 1978).

The importance of providing an enriching environment to facilitate the development of meaningful skills is illustrated in Janichi's (1981) comprehensive definition of community residence as a twenty-four-hour, community-based facility designed to provide services to a small number of disabled persons. The major purpose of the residence is to provide a setting within which the domiciliary functions are separated from work, recreation, and educational activities (Wolfensberger, 1972), and the philosophy exists that persons with disabilities can and should live among people who are non-disabled—and should be treated as such.

> A community residence . . . likely any other home must be an environment oriented toward personal growth. It not only should provide the ingredients for learning basic self-care and independent/support skills, but also should provide a diversity of activities . . . a home must supply affection and interpersonal interest; a positive regard and understanding of the disability and its effects on the individual; a sense of stability and feeling of welcomeness for the individual until he/she decides to or can leave the home for a more independent living pattern; a range of opportunities for making the best of abilities and aptitudes, and a share in the common life of a small familylike group of people. . . . Within this context individuals reside in a cooperative situation, sharing work, responsibilities and friendships. Nurturance is provided both by the interpersonal milieu created by the interactions among those who live in the home and by the ambience of the home environment.
>
> Within this context a home must be designed to promote a normal life and the development of individual skills (Janichi, 1981, pp. 60–61).

The following section presents residential and independent living programs that include the involvement of consumers, parents/guardians, and the educational and adult service systems.

Adult Service Residential Agency: United Cerebral Palsy

The residential program of the United Cerebral Palsy Center (UCP) of Syracuse, New York, operates two apartments where eight disabled individuals live. During the planning and implementation of these programs, numerous battles were waged with state administrators regarding funding sources, agency regulations, safety and services, and resident autonomy and environmental normativeness. These battles were fought to ensure homelike living situations for adults with disabilities.

The UCP program consists of two apartments located on different floors of a large apartment building. All the individuals living in the apartment have severe or moderate disabilities including cerebral palsy, hearing and visual impairments, mental retardation, and muscular dystrophy. Some individuals have speech and mobility problems and require considerable assistance in self-care and community functioning.

The UCP program is staffed by a full-time director, bookkeeper/secretary, and apartment coordinator/recreation specialist. Also associated with the program are a part-time psychologist, social worker, occupational therapist, speech therapist, nurse, and physician. All residents have their own personal physician, and professionals meet regularly to develop service plans. Required services are carried out as much as possible by generic community agencies.

The apartments are staffed using a "modified live-in" model. Two staff members are assigned to each apartment, but only one individual is on duty at a time. Each works for several twenty-four-hour periods and is then replaced by the other person, who works the same schedule. During designated periods of the day and evening, additional staff members are brought in to assist with activities such as dressing, eating, and community activities.

The modified live-in model represents an attempt to provide a homelike atmosphere; to avoid the house-parent framework, which is more appropriate for young children; to address the high turnover rate, which seems to plague live-in staff arrangements; and to eliminate the shift routine and night staff, which typify institutional life. The model allows the needed staff privacy and life away from work while also providing prolonged staff-resident contact, continuity, and mutual residency—which is more consistent with typical homes than a frequently changing staff who have morning, afternoon, and evening shifts.

From the very inception of the program, the UCP staff had to fight tenaciously to maintain a homelike environment. The agencies designated to regulate them often were perceived by the staff as intent on overprotecting the residents and on stigmatizing the apartments and residents; their bureaucratic mechanisms resulted in less relevant, individualized, and culturally appropriate programs and more negative images of the residents.

During the planning period, after small apartments had been selected as the units of choice, a commission appointed by the governor of New York concluded that apartment living for individuals with severe disabilities was both fiscally and programmatically unsound and, therefore, deleterious to the residents of such facilities. The commission reported that these apartments were overly expensive to develop, adapt, and administer and that they failed to provide sufficient professional services such as occupational, physical, and speech therapy. The size of the apartments was also a major source of disagreement. The state would not fund anything less than four-person apartments while UCP wanted a maximum of three persons in each apartment. During these initial battles and in subsequent struggles, the UCP staff made maximum use of their supporters in the community and emphasized the importance of teaching human service professionals not only clinical, supervisory, and pedagogical skills, but also political and community organization.

The UCP staff also experienced difficulty maintaining a homelike atmosphere in the face of state safety requirements. Because a disabled person was fatally burned in a state-operated, Medicaid-funded facility, it was required that all water entry points be equipped with a safety mixing valve to ensure that the water not exceed a particular temperature. One of the UCP apartment tenants who had been a long-time nursing home resident enjoyed extremely hot baths, a pleasure he had been denied at his previous residence. The staff felt it important and therapeutic for him and all the other residents to be able to regulate their own hot water. While the safety of the residents was of great concern to them, the staff also felt that regulating water temperatures was an important skill to master and that having a mixing valve was both uninstructive and overly institutional. To date, the staff has not been required to install the valves but has had to demonstrate that the residents are capable of learning and carrying out the skill. A "qualified" psychologist verifies residents' capabilities and attests to the feasibility of the service plan. In addition, staff members must take weekly readings of the water temperature to ensure that it does not exceed 120 degrees F. If it does exceed this temperature it must be reported.

Although the residents live in small apartments in a homelike atmosphere, there are obstacles that interfere with normalized lifestyles:

1. Because the apartments are funded by Medicaid, the noncompetitively employed residents must have eight hours of day programming. This requires that they be involved in an outside program or learn skills within the apartment setting. If the former is chosen, then residents, because of severe physical handicaps, typically qualify only for services in medically oriented day treatment programs that mandate no more than 20 percent of each day be spent in prevocational training activities. If the latter is chosen, then residents learn independent living skills but have very little community contact or opportunities for any type of vocational training.
2. Residents live with two or three other severely disabled persons. This, in itself, interferes with opportunities to live and interact with nonhandicapped persons.

These two barriers must be analyzed, and, federal, state, and local policy changes must be instituted if disabled persons are to *live* and *work* similarly to their nondisabled peers.

Residential Curricula for School-Aged Youth: DeKalb, Illinois

Residential and domestic training programs designed to prepare disabled adolescents to live in the community after graduation from high school have

been developed across the country. Ignoring the need for instrution in domestic or residential environments frequently results in placement in more
restrictive environments. If public schools can work jointly with parents and
adult service providers to develop and provide appropriate levels of instruction in optimal and preferred domestic environments, disabled adolescents
will live more independently in their communities after graduation.

The DeKalb Public School System, under the direction of Dr. Sharon
Freagon of Northern Illinois University, has developed a domestic training
program for disabled students between the ages of twelve and twenty-one.

> The domestic training site used is a five room house rented by the De-
> Kalb County Special Education Agency (DCSEA) which is utilized for day-
> time as well as overnight training for various domestic and independent
> living activities. At present, one resident counselor is available for training
> and supervision in conjunction with the program teachers. A maximum of
> three students can participate in overnight stays at one time. Entrance to
> the house, the bathroom facilities and the basement recreation area is lim-
> ited in independent accessibility to students in wheelchairs (Freagon et al.,
> 1981, p. 55).

The curriculum utilized and the amount of instructional time are dependent upon the chronological age and functional needs of the student.
Priorities of skills to be taught must be based upon a number of critical
dimensions. No two students should receive exactly the same amount, type,
and frequency of domestic instruction. Brown et al. (1979) have suggested
that at least the following dimensions be considered when setting priorities
for curricular conduct: unique student characteristics, parent or guardian
preferences, age appropriateness, functional nature of the skill, social significance, minimization of physical harm and future environments, and relevance to future environments. If these dimensions are considered for every
student, then there are enhanced chances of a successful transition to a least
restrictive adult environment. The students in DeKalb spend more time in
the domestic training site as their age increases. For students between the
ages of twelve and fifteen, this might include five hours per week. When
students are in high school, overnight experiences are available. This not
only prepares the student to be away from his or her family, but also provides
the educational team with opportunities to assess performance beyond school
hours.

Vogelsberg, Williams, and Bellamy (1982) have listed some domestic
skills typically required in the home.

Communication in the Home

Labels items	Gives simple directions
Verbalizes personal information	Carries on conversations
Identifies body parts	Uses the telephone
Identifies physical environment	Answers the door
information	Communicates at mealtimes
Follows directions	Writes letters/notes/lists

Housekeeping
Cleans kitchen
Cleans living room
Cleans bedroom
Cleans bathroom
Stores and replenishes supplies

Food Management
Prepares meal
Eats meal
Cleans up after meals
Replenishes used items

Clothing/Linen Care
Cleans clothes
Dries clothes
Irons clothes
Stores clothes
Cares for shoes
Mends clothes

Money Management
Purchases items
Uses checking account

Personal Financial Management
Balances monthly bank statement
Applies for SSI
Budgets money
Solves financial problems

Household Maintenance
Maintains windows
Maintains plumbing

Maintains walls
Replenishes household items
Makes minor repairs

Outdoor Maintenance
Disposes of trash
Maintains lawn
Maintains walkways and steps

Health and Safety in the Home
Follows proper nutrition
Uses health services
Uses medication properly
Responds to injury
Responds to illness
Responds to emergencies
Responds to fire
Secures home from elements/
  intruders

Telling Time
Tells time
Prepares weekly, monthly, yearly
  schedules
Follows Monday to Friday
  schedule
Follows Saturday and Sunday
  schedule
Follows weekly schedule
Follows monthly schedule
Follows yearly schedule
Adapts to schedule changes

Providing instruction to disabled students in their current homes or proposed future residences must be an option. Many of the skills required in a student's home cannot be determined in a domestic training site. However, Livi and Ford (1984) have suggested that transfer to the home is enhanced by determining the skills necessary to function in the home and then targeting those skills for instruction in a domestic training site. Domestic instruction should teach the skills and activities required to function in either the current or future residence.

Vocational Training Programs

Vocational programs for disabled adolescents and young adults range from sheltered workshops to supported work models in the community. Because work is both respected and necessary for monetary support, it should be a major focus of any school or adult service program. Some vocational programs, however, such as sheltered workshops, hinder rather than facilitate work in integrated environments.

Durand and Neufeldt (1980) have espoused a strong emphasis on individual needs and environmental change in the provision of vocational services. According to them, school- and agency-based services too often emphasize fitting people with disabilities into narrowly defined and limited sheltered vocational training and employment settings, or into inadequately supervised competitive situations for which an individual is insufficiently prepared. Further, they have outlined the vocational service system and a range of employment opportunities that are, or should be, available to a community's disabled members.

1. *Sheltered employment:* A service with a controlled environment is subsidized or requires subsidy from the state, federal, and regional governments. Pay for work should be performance based but will likely require subsidy. Work is meaningful and provided in a work environment that is as close as possible to that found in nonsheltered settings. Equipment should be appropriate and updated. Normally, the work force is comprised only of disabled persons.

2. *Sheltered industry:* This is an industry that employs a work force of largely disabled persons, though there may be some, or even many, nondisabled workers. Industry may be subsidized, but to a lesser extent than a sheltered workshop, and is operated to be cost efficient and production oriented because it is a real business operation that depends upon profit and performance. Workers are paid at least the minimum wage and can earn more if their performance so warrants.

3. *Semi-sheltered employment* (work stations in industry): This is a small or large group of disabled persons working in a regular industry and paid on a performance-based scale. The force of the industry is mostly nonhandicapped. Individuals may be paid minimum wage, depending upon the contribution they make to the group. However, community special wage certificates are available.

4. *Work with support:* This is a regular work setting in a typical business/industry in which an individual is expected to do a job and be paid a typical wage. A training and placement specialist maintains regular contact to see that job stabilization occurs. On-the-job training and other programs in which regular, intensive support and instruction are provided could fit this model.

5. *Individual competitive employment and self-employment:* This exists when an individual works in a regular job but receives no more continuing support than any other worker. It also exists when an individual who is self-employed provides a service that may be purchased on an individual contract basis.

There are 3,000 sheltered workshop programs in the county that serve over 145,000 persons with a variety of disabilities (U.S. Department of Labor, 1977). These workshops have been criticized by a number of writers for a variety of reasons. For example, because of their financial needs, workshops have exploited the clients through extended retentions in the workshop longer than necessary so that the agency can receive funding from contracts that must be completed (Gersuny & Lefton, 1970; Scott, 1967; Ten Broek, 1966). A series of articles from the *Wall Street Journal* (Kwitney & Landauer, 1979a, (1979b) detailed some examples of direct financial exploitation of workshop employees. One workshop, which primarily served persons with intellectual and emotional disabilities, paid starting wages of $.10 per hour, was purported to have a net worth of $1.3 million, and was found to pay half its regular workers only $.40 per hour. The *Wall Street Journal* study also focused on two workshops for the visually impaired. One workshop was found to pay its clients about $2,000 per year while paying its administrative staff and sighted workers an average of $19,600 annually. The other workshop, which totaled about $3.5 million in sales and contract receipts, paid its disabled workers only 11 percent of its total income.

Whitehead (1979) also collected national figures on clients in sheltered employment and concluded that the hourly wage for these workers averaged only 35 percent of minimum wage. The annual earnings for disabled workers

Finding work sites and assisting students in learning the necessary skills is an important function for teachers. (Photograph by Mima Cataldo.)

in sheltered situations averaged a paltry $666. For people with mental re-
tardation, who comprise the largest group attending sheltered workshops,
the average annual salary equals $417. The poverty level—as established in
1976 by the Social Security Administration and which was in effect at that
time—was $2,870; the figure has fluctuated well above that level over the
last eight years.

Independence aside, the demeaning nature of earning such low wages
for a full day's work serves a damaging socializing function regarding how
the disabled individual views himself or herself and is viewed by nondisabled
peers. As Wehman (1981) has argued:

> Working all day for four to five dollars is not a particularly dignified re-
> muneration for one's daily vocational pursuits. It is only natural that the
> individual comes to look upon himself or herself as an inferior per-
> son. . . . Furthermore, nonhandicapped persons who visit sheltered cen-
> ters may leave with a perception that the handicapped worker's value is
> only worth four to five dollars a day. This is an insidious and unfair con-
> clusion (p. 5).

Lack of Competitive Placements by Sheltered Workshops

Two government-sponsored research projects focused on the characteristics
and effectiveness of sheltered workshops. Both studies, conducted by Greenleigh Associates, Inc. (1975) and the U.S. Department of Labor (1977, 1979)
and also referred to as the Whitehead studies (1978, 1979), concluded that
sheltered workshops do not lead to competitive employment for the majority
of workers.

Greenleigh Associates, Inc. (1975) found that between 7 and 13 percent
of workshop employees were placed in community employment. The lower
figure represented the work activities and workshops for the blind while the
higher figure reflected placement of those individuals attending regular workshops. In the workshops studied by the Department of Labor, it was found
that approximately 12 percent of clients are placed in community jobs per
year.

One of the major reasons given for the lack of competitive placement
success is the lack of meaningful skill training and relevant work. Greenleigh
(1975) found that most workshops rely on general production and adjustment
training and employ ambiguous curricula to teach ill-defined work skills and
personal behaviors with the hope that they will lead to placement. From the
available data, it is apparent that this outcome has not been realized.

Greenleigh also found that within the workshop the greatest amount of
client time is spent on supervised production. Greenleigh concluded that
such activity normally consisted of contract work "which was seldom comparable to that in the competitive sector" (p. 14). The authors further noted,
"Jobs allocated to workshops are generally so low skilled, tedious, unre-
warding, and unremunerative that they are seldom found in the competitive
sector" (p. 14). Most workshops, because they lack good production designs

and updated, modern equipment, are not able to compete for contracts that are performed in private industry. Even when some contracts demand complex, difficult operations, tasks that demand the most skill and are most valued are performed by staff or those clients who are classified as high functioning (Pomerantz & Marholin, 1980).

For all the preceding reasons, financial exploitation, poor placement records, tedious and low-skilled work, the majority of disabled workshop employees spend most of their time on supervised production involving boring, low-demand contract work on outmoded equipment. The training they receive is minimal because of continuous production assignments/requirements that are often too general and ill defined. To modify these poor vocational outcomes, adult vocational services must change, and school programs must better prepare disabled adolescents and young adults for community-based work.

Depending upon the individual, the job, the human service agency, and the employer, work settings can be modified to accommodate qualified persons with disabilities to perform certain jobs. Perhaps the jobs will not be done in exactly the same manner or by the same number of persons. Lower employee turnover in certain jobs, tax benefits, and affirmative action regulations are a few of the direct benefits of hiring a disabled worker. To accommodate the training and employment needs of both persons with disabilities and community employers, a multidimensional system of vocational services must be developed. In this way, the employer and the employee have integrated vocational options rather than having only segregated environments in which to function.

Adult Service Vocational Model: Project Employability, Richmond, Virginia

Project Employability began as a model to demonstrate that severely disabled persons could work outside sheltered workshops. Under the supervision of Dr. Paul Wehman, persons previously excluded from vocational rehabilitation services, because of their lack of demonstrated employment potential, are helped to obtain paid work.

> The project uses an on-the-job training model by which a trainee is placed from a local adult activity center into a job opening in the community and supervised on a continual but gradually decreasing basis by project staff. The project staff member helps assure the employer that the job will be completed even during the initial stages of training and assures the trainee and his family that the skills needed for employment will be acquired as the prospective employees performance reaches appropriate standards; the employer may then exercise his option to officially hire the trainee (Wehman, Hill, & Koehler, 1979, p. 276).

The development of a job for the disabled person is based on several factors. These include previous work history; functioning level and physical characteristics (e.g., frequency of on-task behavior, degree of independent mobility, communication skills, self-initiated work behavior, appropriateness of social skills, and presence of additional handicaps in vision, hearing, mobility, etc.); Supplemental Security Income (SSI); living situation and transportation needs; and worker and parent/guardian attitudes and perceptions. Each factor can positively or negatively influence job development. If a client is unable to drive to work, for example, the following options must be thoroughly examined:

1. Consider whether a placement is close enough for client to walk.
2. Complete bus training if public transportation is available and feasible.
3. Investigate whether the area has a bus or van.
4. Take advantage of or develop a car pool.
5. Have a co-worker give trainee a ride.
6. Have parents take the individual to work. (Wehman, Hill, & Koehler, 1979, p. 279)

If none of these can be developed or utilized, then the potential job placement may not be acceptable.

Consider the effect of worker and parent attitudes on job development. As mentioned previously, parents typically have been excluded from program planning and development. Their inclusion early in the process can only facilitate the worker's success. Wehman, Hill, and Koehler (1979) have reported:

> After the parents and client consent to job placement, they should be involved in the initial planning, including discussing the location of the job, type of work required, and any special employer requirements. The location of the job may be a particular source of fear for families of women. For example, we have found that parents of several women did not want their daughters to be placed in a job downtown. If a job coordinator cannot give definite assurances regarding the long-term safety of the client, then certainly the parent's wishes must be viewed as realistic concerns (p. 281).

Once the job selection process has been undertaken, the next step is identifying an appropriate employer. The process by which an employer is identified is as follows: conduct a community job assessment, approach the employer, establish a training period, set up a job interview, and provide supervision and advocacy. Each step requires a systematic approach. To conduct a community job assessment, for example, the placement counselor or trainer must be familiar with available jobs, employment trends, and other community contacts. Approaching an employer without knowledge of his or her business and its place within the community is likely to have a negative result.

Finally, Project Employability and subsequent efforts by Wehman and his colleagues emphasize the need for follow-up and job retention activities by a job advocate. This individual is responsible for providing appropriate levels of supervision and contact after the client is placed and preventing job loss because of poor attendance, co-worker dissonance, worker skill deficits, lack of job satisfaction, family and transportation problems, and other interfering behaviors (Hill et al., 1985).

Project Employability has proven to be an effective model in placing disabled individuals in jobs and avoiding sheltered work and day activity programs. Through the use of a systematic approach of selecting an appropriate job, identification of an appropriate employer, establishing a training period, interviewing for the job, and establishing the follow-up and retention activities, nonsheltered employment can be attained and retained.

Vocational Training and Curricula for School-Aged Youth: Madison Metropolitan School District

The University of Wisconsin-Madison and the Madison Metropolitan School District have collaborated on a longitudinal vocational training program for severely disabled students. The assumptions and procedures of the program have been described by Brown, Branston-McClean, Baumgart, Vincent, Falvey, and Schroeder (1979). Underlying the Madison program is the unerring belief in the physical and social integration of disabled persons. This belief has been spelled out by Brown, Wilcox, Sontag, Vincent, Dodd, and Gruenewald (1979), who have stated that "not only do severely handicapped citizens have the right to be participating members of heterogeneous communities, but that such participation is inherently good" (p. 178). Integration is essential to the education of severely disabled persons if societal integration is to be achieved. The authors have stated:

> The only way that severely handicapped and nonhandicapped citizens will learn to live with, and learn from, each other as fully participating members of complex, adult, heterogeneous, communities is through long-term interaction during the educational years.
> Severely handicapped persons have the right to integrated, nonsheltered, vocational preparation programs since segregated programs are by definition nearly always inferior programs.
> Social integration with nonhandicapped persons in a valued context should comprise the basis for educational/vocational services.
> Architectural modifications, accessible transportation and functional curricula should be employed to further the valuation, integration and instruction of severely disabled students.

Vocational training is a means of achieving societal integration and a developmental process which typically begins in early childhood. This conclusion has resulted in the development of a longitudinal framework for vocational training. Such training is implemented at all school levels from early childhood through high school (Sweet et al., 1982).

Early Childhood and Elementary Training. The early childhood training is viewed as preparatory for later vocational functioning and consists of skills such as assuming responsibility for one's belongings, sharing materials with friends, associating specific places with particular activities, becoming socialized to daily routines and regular tasks, following directions, and communicating requests, comments, and questions at appropriate times.

At the elementary school level, students have specific in-school responsibilities. Disabled children should be expected to work at an activity for at least thirty minutes as preparation for middle school vocational training (Ford, Johnson, Pumpian, Stengert, & Wheeler, 1980). Some of the jobs that teachers select for the children include sweeping, message delivery, table washing, and so forth. Although instruction is provided and performance is evaluated, the primary emphasis is on developing positive work attitudes and behaviors that are rewarded through special attention for jobs completed successfully, undertaken during recreation periods, attempted and/or completed independently, and completed after having sought assistance.

Middle School Training.   During middle school, children from eleven to fifteen are provided vocational training in nonschool or community environments for the first time. Such training is given for at least one half day per week. Vocationally related skills are emphasized as they apply to work environments. The skills could pertain to reading, time, and money; use of public transportation; interpersonal communication; or community orientation. The vocational training program is provided by both classroom and community vocational teachers. These people typically have been trained as special education teachers with an emphasis on providing vocationally oriented curriculum for severely handicapped students. A community vocational teacher's typical day has been described by Brown et al. (1983):

> For example, if two severely handicapped students are to be the instructional responsibility of a Vocational Community teacher on Monday morning, she might meet them in school and then take a public bus with them to a hospital where she would teach vocational skills in the pharmacy until approximately 11:00 a.m. At 11.00 a.m. they might take another public bus to a restaurant where she would teach restaurant skills before returning to school at 12:30 p.m. Thus, she will have directly taught community functioning in the form of restaurant use and public transportation skills and vocational skills in a nonsheltered vocational environment.

Sweet et al. (1982) have noted that the idea of vocational preparation in the middle school is not to match a student with a specific job. Rather, the intent is to familiarize disabled students with a variety of vocational options. Typically, during four years of middle school, students will receive training in at least four different community vocational environments. During their final years of middle school, students receive approximately two half days of vocational training in preparation for the demands of high school training.

High School Training.   Severely disabled high school students ranging in age from fifteen to twenty-one, are initially provided community vocational training for two half days per week with continued emphasis upon vocationally related skills. As the student progresses through high school, 75 percent of his or her schedule is devoted to direct, nonsheltered vocational instruction. Sweet et al. (1982) have reported that during the six or seven years a severely handicapped student may attend high school, he or she will have "received training in as many as ten different non-school vocational environments and at least five different types of work, such as clerical, motel/housekeeping, dishwashing, food preparation and custodial" (p. 3).

Transition Training. Toward the end of high school a transition plan is developed for every student. The plan, described in more detail by Nisbet et al. (1982), is developed by bringing together teachers, parents, community professionals, and other involved parties to identify possible postschool work possibilities. It is based upon the results of this meeting and is individualized, longitudinal, and comprehensive. It includes the involvement of sending and receiving agencies, the participation of parents/guardians, and the expertise of related service personnel. When work possibilities have been indentified, an appropriate job is selected; then the required training, supervision, follow-up, and support are provided.

The last two years of high school have been designated as the transitional period during which some concrete vocational decisions are made, more specific vocational training is provided, more intensive instruction is given, and more active parental and professional participation is solicited. During this time, reviews of the student's training experiences are conducted by the teacher. With the collaboration of other teachers, parents/guardians, related professionals, and staff, reasonable work possibilities are identified and a proposed vocational site is secured. The teacher then provides the necessary training and supervision that the student needs to succeed in the site.

The percentage of time spent by the student in high school decreases dramatically until more time is spent out of school than in school. In part, this is due to the nature and emphasis of the student's preparation for community living. Every attempt is made to structure the student's day according to the requirements of work rather than school, such as traveling from home to work four or five days per week and gradually increasing the number of hours on the job.

Brown et al. (1983) have argued that it is unacceptable to spend twenty-one years of public education preparing a severely handicapped person to function in nonsheltered, heterogeneous, vocational, community environments without working exceedingly hard to prevent graduating students from working in traditional segregated sheltered environments. Too frequently, postgraduation plans are left in the hands of human service personnel who have had little contact with the graduating students, are not familiar with their vocational experiences, and are often associated with sheltered and segregated vocational programs.

Also, parents often do not know about postschool, adult vocational services; are not assertive in the face of professional authority; or lack the time to advocate effectively for their graduating children. Thus, much of the non-sheltered preparation afforded by the nonschool model of training may be negated. The transition period represents a focused attempt to ensure that the last job site selected for the student will be a permanent work site or will lead to a permanent work site in the community.

Outcomes of the Madison Program.   The results of the nonsheltered, nonschool vocational training program at Madison have been reported by Brown et al. (1983). The program was initiated in the mid-1970s and began to result in outcome changes by 1979. Between 1979 and 1982, thirty-eight severely handicapped students graduated from the Madison system. Of that total, twenty-seven, or about 71 percent, entered nonsheltered environments. Twenty-four percent entered sheltered settings and about 5 percent remained at home. These figures were contrasted by Brown et al. with comparable figures compiled by VanDeventer et al. (1981), who reported that between 1971 and 1978, prior to the development of the previously described vocational training program, fifty-three severely handicapped students were graduated from the Madison school system and only one was placed in nonsheltered vocational settings. Except for three students who remained at home, the rest of the graduates were enrolled in sheltered environments.

It may be seen that the preceding program has attended not only to helping persons fit into the existing vocational system, but also to modifying the system and aspects of the surrounding environment to enhance the chances of success with persons for whom vocational services have been largely unsuccessful. The Madison program attempts to address change at both the individual and systemic levels, deals with interactive and interpretive issues, and espouses basic principles that are applicable to any disabled individual.

Recreation/Leisure Training Programs

Leisure and recreational activities are an integral part of daily life in American society. Compton (1981) has noted that in an average lifetime an employed, nonhandicapped person can expect to have about 225,000 hours available for leisure activity or the equivalent of twenty-five years. This amount of time coupled with an increasing preoccupation with exercise and stress reduction, and a willingness to spend large sums of money for leisure, has led to a proliferation of leisure time and recreational clubs, groups, events, materials, and equipment.

Within the past twenty years over four hundred public recreation departments have offered recreation programs to people with disabilities and over two hundred federal recreation areas have made physical accommodations (Nesbitt, 1979a). Further, the visibility of recreation/leisure participants with disabilities has increased dramatically as we see more competitors involved in community activities such as running, swimming, and basketball competitions, some of which are integrated events.

There remains, however, a shortage of truly integrated recreation/leisure programs. Although Nesbitt (1979b) has reported that about 2.5 million persons with disabilities participated in community recreation programs in 1979, this represents only about one in every ten disabled citizens. While these figures represent only rough estimates of the difficulty, they point to the fact that accessibility of public parks and recreational facilities is a serious barrier for physically disabled persons who wish to participate in community programs.

The problem of accessibility, however, goes beyond just physical accessibility. For many young, disabled adults community leisure opportunities are inaccessible because of the lack of adequate skills, participatory opportunities, and support. In enumerating the difficulties faced by disabled participants of the cultural arts, MacNeil (1977) cited not only architectural barriers but also the lack of trained persons to serve disabled individuals and attitudinal obstacles. The responsibility for these obstacles falls on the entire community, but particularly on parents, teachers, and adult service providers who have failed to see the importance of leisure/recreation activities for severely handicapped individuals, who have viewed these activities as something to do rather than something to learn, and who have failed to adequately publicize the problem and develop practical solutions. Occasionally taking disabled persons to baseball games, parks, dances, movies, and shopping malls neither teaches them the skills they need to participate independently and meaningfully in such contexts, nor maximizes their social integration. Accessibility must be viewed as a far broader concept if recreation/leisure is to become a meaningful vehicle for valued community participation for young adults with disabilities. It must connote not only getting into and around leisure facilities but also being able to initiate and become immersed in such activities. This is an important distinction, especially when referring to young, disabled adults, whose manner of introduction to recreation/leisure activities may serve as a model regarding time, degree, and level of participation for a lifetime.

If an individual is to participate fully in his or her community and be viewed as a fully functioning member, he or she must have some leisure and recreational interests and skills. Such expectations have evident implications for the socialization and education of young persons with disabilities. Leisure and recreation skills may no longer be considered peripheral activities to be taught sporadically, delayed, ignored, or exclusively left to professionals and/or family members who may be unfamiliar with instructional techniques, community opportunities, or even the importance of leisure to a person's general development. Instead, recreation/leisure objectives must be integral components of the individual education plan and the individual service plan. The importance of leisure and recreation preparation for individuals with severe disabilities has been emphasized by a number of writers who have noted that the acquisition of such skills (1) positively affects a variety of other skill areas essential for handicapped and nonhandicapped children (Newcomer & Morrison, 1974; Schleien, Kiernan, & Wehman, 1981; Strain, Cook, & Appolloni, 1976); (2) reduces a possible reliance upon aggressive self-

Opportunities for learning recreational skills are important if we expect young adults to use their leisure time profitably. (Photograph by Mima Cataldo.)

stimulation and self-injurious behavior to fill unstructured time periods (Flavell, 1973; Schleien et al., 1981; Voeltz & Wuerch, 1981); (3) increases opportunities to achieve life satisaction that may not be available through other activities (Voeltz, Wuerch, & Wilcox, 1982); (4) allows a break from performing strictly structured tasks in the work and domestic spheres and, perhaps, opportunities to learn and elicit social behaviors at the same time (Murphy, 1981; Neulinger, 1981; Voeltz et al., 1982); and (5) enhances the chances for successful adjustment to community living (Chaseldine & Jeffree, 1981; Gollay, 1981; Intaglia, Willer, & Wicks, 1981).

The question is not whether the acquisition of leisure skills is important for the general development and community adjustment of young, disabled adults, but what skills should be taught, how, and for what reason.

Definition of Recreation and Leisure

Recreation and leisure are used synonomously in the literature despite some attempts to make a distinction between the terms (Pomeroy, 1983). Both concepts refer to a variety of activities including creative, expressive, and receptive experiences in the spheres of art, music and drama; educational and developmental activities in their broadest context; outdoor recreation; social activities; special interests such as hobbies, games, and entertainment; and participatory and spectator sports. Voeltz et al. (1982) have stated that leisure activities should be distinguished from vocational and independent living skills by using the following dimensions: (1) discretionary time, (2) personal preference and choice, and (3) subtlety in time and activity discrimination.

Leisure activities are performed after required tasks have been completed. The options available to an individual are almost limitless and are bound only by the person's abilities, interests, resources, and creativity. Leisure and recreational activities provide the opportunity for individuals to choose how their time will be spent. Voeltz et al. (1982) have emphasized, however, that the right to exercise one's options is restricted when no options are available and few skills have been mastered. Thus, a major emphasis of leisure education should be to develop options by teaching appropriate skills, by making leisure opportunities available, and by allowing people to make choices according to their interests. The questions of what constitutes appropriate leisure activities and how one decides the appropriateness of a specific activity, given the available amount of time and the setting involved, have also been raised as cultural issues in planning leisure curriculum (Putnam, Weider, & Schleien, 1985).

Individuals may choose leisure activities that might be considered work on independent living. For example, one may spend his or her weekends cleaning the house or gardening. Discretion must be used in superimposing our definition of leisure upon others and failing to respect their right to define leisure activities for themselves. "Leisure educators must achieve a delicate balance between teaching skills and behaviors that are characterized as 'leisure activities' and making available to the severely handicapped adolescent the right to engage in preferred activities during leisure time" (Voeltz et al., 1982, p. 78).

Leisure opportunities may be sporadic and may require an ability to select behaviors that are appropriate for the available time, environment, and associated activities. Time spent waiting for transportation or taking trips and time between weekday tasks can often be used as leisure/recreational time if the requisite behaviors exist and appropriate options are available given the physical and social circumstances. These elements may need to be taught to disabled young adults so that they can enjoy such periods and not be devalued in the process. In illustrating this point, Voeltz et al. (1982) have used the example of a doctor's waiting room, in which reading a magazine or engaging in quiet conversation is appropriate behavior, but physical exercise is not (p. 178).

Recreation/leisure education must be initiated early in life and implemented within society's predominant socializing contexts. These contexts include the family, the school, and the general community. In addition, recreation/leisure activities should be implemented in and directed toward integrated environments; should be age appropriate and carried out with valued, intensive instructional materials; and should develop self-initiated skills and include the participation of a variety of socializing agents, such as parents, teachers, and specialized recreation personnel as well as the disabled individual (Putnam et al., 1985).

Adult Recreation/Leisure Services: The College for Living

One example of a program that provides leisure/recreation education is the College for Living (CFL) of Onondaga County, New York. CFL, a comprehensive program of continuing education for severely handicapped adolescents and adults, has three primary objectives: (1) to teach skills of independent living in normalized settings, (2) to facilitate socialization and integration of disabled persons within a college environment, and (3) to help develop positive, responsive attitudes on the part of college students, faculty, staff, and community toward the developmentally disabled adult.

The idea for the program originated with parents whose disabled sons and daughters were not enrolled in any rehabilitation program, or were enrolled in programs judged to be inadequate. Most of these persons were severely disabled and were between the ages of eighteen and thirty. Many parents were concerned that their disabled sons or daughters were not sufficiently involved with nondisabled peers. Community services and programs were nearly always segregated so that, even though disabled, young adults were receiving appropriate training such as vocational preparation or interpersonal skills, there were no nondisabled persons (except the instructor) in either their classes or the community to closely observe, model, or interact with. A major feature of CFL is that programs are conducted on a college campus and in the community, not in separate, segregated facilities. College students of the same age are available and therefore serve as social models for them.

Swimming: One Example of a Recreation/Leisure Program

Onondaga Community College established a program of swimming and water safety instruction for nonswimmers with severe handicaps. Instruction was held during community swimming hours for forty-five minutes to an hour, and participants were encouraged to swim with other pool users after the instruction period. Initially, very few participants remained in the water. Most of them left the pool area after the instruction, got dressed, and waited for their rides. None of the participants expressed any desire to use the OCC pool, or any other community pool, for free swimming during the week or on weekends, although all the participants expressed a liking for the class and for swimming. The pool, however, was located far away from where most class members lived; they could not persuade their parents or group home supervisors to drive them, nor could they generate enough enthusiasm for swimming to take a bus that distance.

The program was transferred to a downtown community pool, where the same instruction was provided by the local YMCA staff at a time when community people were also receiving instruction and swimming. As a result of the change, two members of the class signed up to join the "Y" and began using the pool during their leisure time.

The CFL represents just one type of program addressing the leisure/recreation needs of young adults with severe handicaps. Such programming should have been initiated much earlier in the schools, making the CFL's achievements even more impressive. CFL has yielded promising results thus far with young people whose recreation/leisure needs and skills, all but ignored just a few years ago, have been translated into activities that have reflected competence and have precipitated valued experiences with non-handicapped persons.

CFL offers a small number of leisure classes and depends upon community instructors, with the assistance of CFL volunteers, to provide necessary instruction to individuals. Classes are small, consisting of between five and ten persons, so that individualized instruction can be arranged. Within CFL, integration between disabled students and nondisabled persons is emphasized. Much effort is made to maximize the integrative value of both the instructional process and the learned leisure/recreation skill. Every attempt is made to ensure that during the instruction students are involved in valued social interactions with nondisabled contemporaries. Also emphasized is the relevance of the acquired activity to enhance integration experiences for the student in the future.

Recreation/Leisure Curricula

In many cases compensatory programs such as CFL have been developed for young, disabled adults because recreation/leisure education has been neglected in the public schools. Despite the inclusion of leisure as a related service in Public Law 94-142, such programs are often given a secondary position in curricular considerations (Putnam et al., 1985).

Several authors have recommended that the IEP should be the medium through which a comprehensive program of recreation/leisure activities be planned and taught.

No IEP should be considered even minimally acceptable unless it contains an IEP component that addresses both immediate and longitudinal, comprehensive recreational and leisure needs in representative proportions. [The plan should include] individualized leisure skills for use in school and nonschool environments and . . . facilitate normalized interactions with nonhandicapped individuals (Ford et al., 1984, p. 247).

While Ford et al. (1984) view special education teachers as the primary instructional personnel in developing an individualized recreation/leisure plan, Voeltz et al. (1982) advocate an approach that includes not only teachers and the involvement of nonhandicapped persons in natural settings, but also the participation of both recreation professionals, who specialize in working with the handicapped, and nonhandicapped persons. These authors have stated:

> Perhaps the most important role the special education teacher must play involves altering the existing assumptions of other professionals and the community concerning whether or not youths with severe handicaps can . . . use genuine facilities and activities. . . . Special educators may now need to . . . resist the temptation to overly emphasize the severely handicapped student's need for special designs and special programs. . . . Before implementing a parallel . . . leisure education program, the teacher should survey existing school and nonschool programs to determine if access . . . after needed modifications . . . can be achieved for the students (p. 197).

Parental involvement is also a critical component in leisure/recreation education. Parent-professional collaboration often has been missing from such programming, though family attitudes have been found to be a critical factor in a disabled person's level and type of leisure participation (Wehman & Schleien, 1981). In many instances, school personnel have ignored parental attitudes and concerns regarding their youngster's leisure skills. In some situations the leisure/recreation skills that have been taught have been convenient to the school situation and staff but have not reflected the leisure materials, preferences, or patterns of the family. In instances in which parental attitudes toward leisure skills have been overly restrictive, few attempts have been made to change such views and offer expanded views and viable alternatives.

> Since parents and guardians are the persons most likely to arrange for and monitor the performance of school taught skills in non-school environments, making educational decisions without their systematic input will often drastically diminish the overall value of the educational curriculum (Ford et al., 1984).

Voeltz et al. (1982) have outlined a number of issues that should be considered when teachers, parents, and recreation therapists conduct planning for a recreation/leisure education program. These include (1) family materials and activity resources available in the home, (2) information on the student's current repertoire of leisure behaviors and preferences within the home and neighborhood, and (3) family or neighborhood people resources available for recreation/leisure activities.

Another participant in the planning of leisure/recreation activities should be the young disabled adult. Although Public Law 94-142 and the 1973 Rehabilitation Act have mandated client involvement in their education and rehabilitation planning and service provision, consumers have continued to report difficulties in being meaningfully informed and involved with their program planning (Chamberlin, 1978; Gleidman & Roth, 1980; Murphy & Salomone, 1983; Murphy & Ursprung, 1983; Roth, 1982). For those labeled severely handicapped this problem is greatly magnified because of the aura of incompetence that surrounds them. In the leisure sphere, consumer involvement seems no less critical:

> If the preparation for the leisure domain is to be faithful to the nature of leisure time, severely handicapped learners must not simply acquire skills for a set of activities selected for them by others, but must acquire skills for activities and with materials that they themselves enjoy, prefer, and thus will engage in during free time (Voeltz et al., 1982, p. 189).

To underscore these arguments the preceding authors have pointed to research studies that have found persons with severe handicaps to exhibit strong preferences (Reid, Willis, Jarman, & Brown, 1978) that affect their behavior (Flavell & Cannon, 1976) and that leisure choices could be fostered through training (Voeltz & Wuerch, 1981; Voeltz, Wuerch, & Bockhaut, 1981). Flavell and Cannon (1976) found that the preferences of severely disabled adolescents for specific materials were so closely related to free-time behavior that during periods when only nonpreferred activities were available these individuals were idle 65 percent of the time. On the other hand, when preferred activities were available the disabled young adults were idle only 25 percent of the available time. Voeltz et al. (1982) have outlined specific methods for assessing the interests, preferences, and skill performance levels of severely handicapped persons, noting that even low performance levels should not exclude severely disabled individuals from participating, at least partially, in preferred activities. The authors have added that despite the application of the partial participation strategy (Ford et al., 1984), every effort should also be made to fund leisure/recreation activities that students can perform completely and autonomously whenever they wish.

Strategies for Teaching Recreation/Leisure Activities

Voeltz et al. (1982) have categorized the various ways in which leisure/recreation activities have been addressed.

> 1. *Informal event participation* which consists of relatively unplanned, episodic participation in leisure events such as field trips, school picnics and dances, and trips to the movies and thus may not include formal or systematic instruction.

If informal events include nonhandicapped peers, they can provide valuable social and community experiences; however, most frequently they are carried out in fairly large groups where the opportunities for meaningful instruction and integrative interactions are minimized. As a number of writers on the subject have suggested, this strategy of teaching leisure skills has some value but should not be retained as the only, or a major, approach toward recreation/leisure education.

2. *Formal event participation* focuses on preparing persons for planned events as a culmination of training. Once the training for a particular event is completed, training begins for a new activity. Examples of this approach include: a school concert, class play, special athletic events such as the Special Olympics, and a funeral or anniversary party.

These events often are segregated, involve only nonhandicapped participants, and emphasize mere completion of the task instead of excellence of performance. While such an event has some important advantages (Orelove, Wehman, & Wood, 1982), it can reinforce the notion of separateness to both the participants and the nonhandicapped audience. However, as Voeltz et al. (1982) have related, some of the preparation for formal events may teach skills that are necessary to other settings, such as an integrated school play in which interacting and responsibility are emphasized.

In other instances, participation in certain events may be valuable because the events occur regularly throughout life and members of the community are expected to participate in them. Examples include weddings, birthdays and anniversary parties, and funerals. Participation in these events, however, should include the acquisition of new skills that are likely to be useful to the individual now and in the future.

3. *Individualized play training* emphasizes teaching an individual a single, specific play skill such as electronic pinball playing, dart throwing, frisbee throwing, operating a cassette tape recorder, etc.

This approach is helpful for teaching an individual an activity he or she really wants to learn or has opportunities to use. The skills would also appear to hold some degree of generalizability, assuming that the equipment and opportunities were available. Often these activities represent single skills that may not be applicable in a variety of settings or substitutes for a longitudinal recreation/leisure program that is reflective of changing student age, needs, interests, and circumstances.

4. *Taxonomies of leisure time activities* are exhaustive lists compiled by professionals of all the possible leisure and recreational activities (organized by age and activity types such as play and games, sports and physical development, camping and outdoor activities, crafts, etc.) available to nonhandicapped persons. The taxonomies include a breakdown of the tasks required of individuals performing the activity.

A major problem pointed out by Voeltz et al. (1982) is that taxonomies are geared for nonhandicapped persons. Thus, a teacher or professional searching for a recreation/leisure activity to teach a disabled adolescent—which is consistent with the young adult's skill level—will often arrive at an activity that is more appropriate for a younger child. Those age appropriate activities listed for adolescents are often too complex for young adults with handicaps to master. Also, the task analyses for teaching these activities often presume a level of knowledge and proficiency that has not yet been mastered by adolescents with disabilities. For example, in a camping taxonomy for adolescents there may be instructions on building a fire that include gathering and stacking dry wood, or on cooking by boiling and salting water. While those taxonomies do provide a rich and complete listing of leisure activities, they may exclude those persons with severe handicaps by requiring sophisticated prerequisites.

5. *Leisure curricular strategies* provide a structure which professionals can use to generate individualized leisure and recreation programs. These approaches focus on introducing a model and sample procedures which professionals may follow in teaching disabled persons leisure skills.

Such a framework, while providing an outline and evaluative criteria for professionals, may lack a degree of comprehensiveness and utility for professionals unfamiliar with the entire area of leisure education. They may have difficulty generating what content to include in their program and how to arrange activity skill sequences for instruction.

6. *Leisure curricula and curricular components* focus on providing a comprehensive educational and recreational package which addresses specified leisure education needs.

Basically, these curricula provide professionals with concrete steps for planning and teaching leisure activities to persons with disabilities who may have a full spectrum of needs, or needs in a particular leisure area. The packages include how to conduct environmental analyses, student assessments, classroom organization and instruction strategies, evaluation procedures, and task-analyzed instructional sequences. Voeltz et al. (1982) have noted that while these procedures are extremely detailed and comprehensive, they are not always directed toward disabled young adults, especially those with severe handicaps. Also, because such packages are so detailed, they can lack some breadth (see Voeltz, Apffel, & Wuerch, 1981).

Clearly, no one curricular approach can serve the needs of all students with a variety of disabilities. However, careful consideration of the individual and his or her unique recreation/leisure needs, in combination with curricular strategies, can enhance functioning in the home, in the community, and in the workplace.

Summary

The purpose of this chapter was to describe adult and school-related residential, vocational, and recreation/leisure programs and curricula. These represent current programs that focus on the achievement of maximum integration in community environments. Although each program is successful, coordination of school and adult programs is essential. Without planned and systematic coordination, persons with disabilities may have fewer choices and opportunities than their nondisabled peers. Programs and practices will continue to change and develop and make current practices appear outdated. This is positive. Changes will result in better quality of life for disabled adolescents and young adults.

Postscript

Peter Knoblock

Envisioning the Future for Children

Teaching is an everyday activity and a difficult one at that. Can you find the time and energy to envision what the future could look like for disabled children and their families? Can we help children become as fully functional and skilled as possible while we work with schools, communities, and the general public to become inclusionary rather than exclusionary? In other words, can we create a society in which all persons are valued and included, including disabled persons, and have them seen as contributing and productive? As teachers we can facilitate such a goal by maintaining expectations for our students, developing goals and objectives that will prepare them for the worlds of work, social relationships, and leisure and recreation. We need help from others in the community and in society. At the community level we need to seek the participation of parents and community agencies. At the broader societal level we can advocate social policies and legislation that respond to the needs and futures of disabled persons and their families.

The authors of this text hope that the material they included in their chapters provides you with information, ideas, and encouragement for envisioning a society that includes all persons. One's vision may differ, but what are some general aspects that could be included in future building?

Prevention of Disabilities.   It is reasonable to assume that in a technologically advanced society like ours we can eradicate certain conditions causing disability, or at least modify them. For example, a growing awareness of environmental hazards as potential causes of disability has turned our attention to reducing automobile accidents by enacting legislation requiring the use of seat belts for children, thus reducing the risks of brain injury and other crippling conditions. New York State, for one, has a new law requiring the use of seat belts for children under seven years of age. As this was being written, legislation was proposed to provide more explicit statements on cigarette packages warning of the variety of potential health hazards, and there are those who recommend providing warnings of the dangers of tobacco to pregnant women. The focus on maternal health is increasing as research is showing the devastating effects on infants of fetal alcohol syndrome, the potential ill effects of drug use by mothers, and the importance or proper nutrition during pregnancy.

A prevention focus need not be applied exclusively to infants and young children, but can be an ongoing responsibility of a society to guarantee a quality of life that nurtures children and provides opportunities for maximizing their functioning throughout their development. Malnutrition and hunger in children is inexcusable given the resources we have in America. Nevertheless, there is an alarming number of children whose ability to function intellectually and emotionally is impaired because of lack of food and inadequate diets. Despite the current controversy as to whether a hunger problem exists in our society, no one is refuting the fact that large numbers of families live below the poverty line. The numbers remain large regardless of the income figure used to distinguish those above and below poverty. With poverty come children in families living under increasing stress to feed, clothe, and educate their children. It is a cycle that needs to be broken.

Strengthening the Family.   Despite the rhetoric that exists in this country about the importance of the family, there is much that needs to be done to guarantee the health of the family structure. Examples abound that have relevance for child workers. For example, growing numbers of working parents have increased the need for childcare placements for children of working and single women and men. At the same time, available funds to support day care have been reduced, thus diminishing this opportunity to respond to the needs of parents to work and the concurrent needs of children to have safe, supportive, and developmentally appropriate day-care settings. For disabled children such early placements could ease their transition into preschool learning environments by exposing them to guided opportunities for interaction with nondisabled children. On the more positive side is the growing recognition that school-age children are in need of child care after school hours. So-called latchkey children were previously thought of as poorly socialized children with juvenile delinquency tendencies and behaviors. Now that the issue of supervision has surfaced due to increasing numbers of working parents, it is seen as a potential problem for middle-class families as well. Hence, the stigma of children in this circumstance is somewhat reduced. For example, the New York State Council on Children and Families (1983) submitted a report on school-age child care to the governor and state legislature.

> The urgency of this issue lies in the evidence that, at present, due to a general dearth of child care services that are a) tailored to the needs of the school-age child (5-to-13-year-olds) and b) that families can afford, large numbers of children routinely have no adult supervision every day. Often referred to as "latchkey" children, these youngsters are known to be highly vulnerable to loneliness and fear, household accidents and fire, delinquency, vandalism, truancy, exploitation by older youth or adults, and even teenage pregnancy (p. 1).

Supporting Legislation.   As involved citizens we can keep abreast of legislative efforts to set public policy. For example, in 1983 the Children's Survival Bill was introduced in Congress at the request of the Children's Defense Fund. The bill, though not acted upon at the time, represented a positive agenda for children and families. It included requests for funding for preventive programs for children (child welfare, runaway youth, juvenile justice, and adoption); health care for mothers and children (family planning, immunization, Medicaid continuation in child support, supplemental food); child nutrition and food stamps (school food and other child nutrition programs, raising benefit levels of food stamps); and family support (social services, tax relief for working families). The Children's Defense Fund, a child advocacy organization, has again included the above provisions and others in its "Children's Defense Budget—An Analysis of the President's Funding Year 1986 Budget and Children." It is unlikely that this comprehensive report will be adopted in its entirety, but it is available to members of Congress and concerned citizens and policy makers; it is hoped that major provisions will eventually find their way into our laws and our consciousness.

Community Living Options.   The future we envision includes opportunities for disabled persons to lead independent lives in their communities. For this to happen it is necessary to have school programs that prepare disabled students for independence and to have a range of living options available to them. This range can include respite living opportunities away from families, community residences or group homes, intermediate care facilities (smaller residences), supervised apartment living, boarding with others (sharing space with others), and living in one's own house or apartment. Again, prior preparation for independent living and the availability of community options will only become a reality if public attitudes reflect acceptance and valuing of persons with disability. Professional organizations are taking an important step to foster more positive perceptions of the disabled. For example, several groups have changed their names to include adults: The National Society for Autistic Children has been renamed The National Society for Children and Adults with Autism; The National Association for Retarded Children is now the National Association for Retarded Citizens. These name changes are more than cosmetic: they draw the public's attention to the fact that children grow up and that as adults we will be seeking jobs and community living arrangements for them. The Association for Persons with Severe Handicaps' 11th Annual Conference in Chicago in 1984 was titled "New Life in the Community." That organization has also pursued an aggressive policy urging its members to desist using language and terms that stigmatize or demean handicapped individuals. Its declaration on the use of language states: "TASH supports the use of language that emphasizes the humanity of people with handicaps. Terms such as the autistic, the retarded, the severely handicapped refer to characteristics not full individuals."

Name changes and positive descriptions of persons with handicaps are just two approaches to building positive images of disability. Concerned citizens and professionals are encouraging us to communicate our displeasure to various media when they portray disabled persons as helpless or as freaks. Handicapist orientations in children's books, films, and in magazines and television commercials, to cite just a few of the major offenders, should be discouraged by feedback from those of us seeking to convey positive images of persons with disabilities. If the general public can be helped to develop positive attitudes and to support policies that include all citizens, disabled and nondisabled, then there is more of a likelihood that community living options will become available.

Creative Instructional Practices.   The lack of data supporting the use of particular instructional practices and material has created a dilemma for teachers who seek to use the "correct" approach. Creative instructional programs for students with disabilities may be the ones that evolve from our challenging conventional wisdom and practices. Donnellan (1984) speaks to this issue when she states: "In the absence of conclusive data educational decisions should be based on assumptions which, if incorrect, will have the least dangerous effect on the student" (p. 142). We can respond to this challenge to examine critically our assumptions and programs if we are clear about our long-term goals for students and on that basis create program ingredients that lead to those goals. For those believing in the criterion of ultimate functioning, Donnellan recommends instructional goals leading to "maximal participation, productivity and independence in a wide variety of heterogenous community environments" (p. 142).

Broadening one's role, in addition to challenging one's assumptions, is another creative endeavor. There are teachers striving to become skilled instructional specialists so they can respond effectively to children on a case-by-case basis. In addition, they see themselves as advocates for children and their families. This may involve a variety of teacher behaviors including providing parents with information about their children's rights to receive an appropriate education, assisting families to find community services, and challenging existing practices in their schools. Such behavior involves a broader conceptualization of one's teaching behavior and involves some risk taking for teachers. Increasingly, teachers recognize the need to find a balance between changing the child and changing or improving the schools.

Current Practices: Enhancing Our Vision for Children

As a teacher you can make a contribution in each of the areas previously described. To support legislation you can function as an informed citizen: becoming familiar with federal and local budget plans and how they may affect children with disabilities and their families; writing letters to legislators encouraging continuing support for community-based programs; joining local or national advocacy groups or supporting them with financial assistance; or even running for your local board of education. In the area of prevention, you can utilize your position as an educator to implement programs and roles that contribute to a reduction in the numbers of children with disabilities and to help guarantee equal access to opportunities in education, employment, and community living to persons with disabilities. These contributions, and others, are described in the following sections.

Teachers and Preventive Approaches

There are three levels of prevention work—primary, secondary, and tertiary—and you can assist with each. The goals of primary prevention involve the reduction of new cases of a disability and increasing students' competencies to reduce their vulnerability and dysfunctional behavior, thus increasing wellness. Thinking in preventive terms is sensible considering the extraordinarily high numbers of children identified with disabilities.

Table 1 shows that over four million children received special education

Table 1
Children Receiving Special Education, by Disability for 1984–85 School Year

State	All conditions	Learning disabled	Speech impaired	Mentally retarded	Emotionally disturbed	Hard of hearing & deaf	Multi-handicapped	Ortho-pedically impaired	Other health impaired	Visually handi-capped	Deaf-blind
Alabama	88,015	26,043	19,420	34,186	5,276	727	962	471	595	309	26
Alaska	8,574	5,132	2,347	290	266	129	165	169	34	30	12
Arizona	50,523	26,025	11,385	5,478	5,141	603	698	463	447	283	0
Arkansas	44,670	21,422	9,637	12,169	446	342	337	87	148	80	2
California	370,336	207,661	92,477	27,343	8,814	6,646	5,388	6,928	12,671	2,246	162
Colorado	42,692	20,534	7,695	3,427	7,954	755	1,427	629	0	271	0
Connecticut	62,266	28,870	12,990	4,782	13,083	612	620	323	940	43	3
Delaware	11,355	6,323	1,695	949	2,231	62	23	34	26	11	1
District of Columbia	3,400	1,372	1,632	189	114	49	8	11	22	1	2
Florida	155,854	61,082	50,877	21,443	16,610	1,414	0	1,925	1,885	590	28
Georgia	99,444	31,798	24,363	24,192	16,620	918	0	756	340	452	5
Guam	1,605	652	196	677	24	4	16	21	3	12	0
Hawaii	11,801	7,351	2,307	1,064	379	237	154	238	4	67	0
Idaho	17,776	8,416	4,507	2,731	538	284	328	388	511	72	1
Illinois	212,826	92,091	73,172	23,469	19,521	1,255	0	1,262	1,578	478	0
Indiana	96,273	31,899	40,333	19,173	2,928	678	570	344	29	316	3
Iowa	56,907	22,045	14,227	12,105	5,835	775	688	1,038	0	180	14
Kansas	39,568	16,443	11,663	5,869	3,910	410	295	413	348	193	24
Kentucky	71,791	21,865	25,680	19,026	2,388	519	925	409	567	374	38
Louisiana	76,589	36,933	21,701	10,408	3,598	1,037	622	636	1,268	372	14
Maine	26,056	9,715	6,584	4,152	3,709	369	556	397	412	161	1
Maryland	89,186	47,044	25,684	6,618	3,876	1,030	2,752	783	818	563	18
Massachusetts	125,971	44,196	29,012	26,909	17,348	1,724	2,757	1,341	1,840	787	57
Michigan	150,708	62,029	43,169	14,643	21,085	2,804	1,477	4,613	0	888	0
Minnesota	80,142	36,652	19,091	12,777	7,663	1,336	0	1,378	820	383	42
Mississippi	50,879	20,512	17,088	11,951	399	319	191	315	0	103	1
Missouri	100,203	41,376	31,266	16,838	7,421	730	755	833	677	223	84
Montana	15,302	7,642	4,875	1,338	665	128	340	101	145	49	19
Nebraska	29,959	12,094	9,051	5,031	2,273	391	373	612	0	134	0
Nevada	13,469	7,819	3,062	891	806	131	370	225	109	56	0
New Hampshire	14,136	8,862	2,866	782	1,135	9	136	105	239	1	1

(continued)

Table 1
(continued)

State	All conditions	Learning disabled	Speech impaired	Mentally retarded	Emotionally disturbed	Hard of hearing & deaf	Multi-handicapped	Ortho-pedically impaired	Other health impaired	Visually handi-capped	Deaf-blind
New Jersey	161,763	68,538	60,483	7,895	14,276	1,239	7,497	779	824	217	15
New Mexico	27,786	11,094	8,544	2,676	2,720	282	783	358	1,245	78	6
New York	251,113	129,031	29,788	26,184	36,493	2,849	4,654	1,418	19,233	1,414	49
North Carolina	116,001	52,464	27,246	25,030	6,408	1,271	997	904	1,194	483	4
North Dakota	11,357	5,130	3,905	1,609	388	126	0	124	37	37	1
Ohio	192,087	73,056	56,483	45,512	6,698	2,367	3,463	3,645	0	844	18
Oklahoma	63,537	27,908	20,605	11,485	1,021	596	1,084	385	223	194	36
Oregon	42,397	24,968	11,900	1,903	2,163	270	0	631	449	113	0
Pennsylvania	179,117	67,394	59,591	34,914	12,344	2,610	0	1,110	0	1,143	11
Puerto Rico	39,197	3,973	1,764	21,299	1,230	2,416	2,881	2,220	1,101	2,226	87
Rhode Island	18,159	12,093	3,084	1,196	1,159	174	33	187	159	66	8
South Carolina	71,531	23,183	20,508	19,140	6,049	947	277	784	181	457	5
South Dakota	12,453	4,031	5,482	1,515	440	170	541	159	39	60	16
Tennessee	97,556	43,240	28,891	16,544	2,517	1,420	1,642	1,058	1,629	597	18
Texas	282,762	154,132	67,274	25,373	19,372	963	3,480	3,782	6,685	1,631	70
Utah	40,115	14,426	8,533	3,249	11,756	297	1,230	274	208	109	33
Vermont	7,979	3,708	2,631	1,049	314	93	11	59	87	26	1
Virginia	100,605	43,874	30,049	14,630	7,258	1,240	2,140	583	279	526	26
Virgin Islands*	—	—	—	—	—	—	—	—	—	—	—
Washington	64,109	33,925	14,144	7,662	3,451	1,076	1,110	827	1,658	249	7
West Virginia	42,520	17,158	13,061	9,568	1,821	324	0	273	112	197	6
Wisconsin	72,438	29,573	17,605	11,738	10,694	876	624	642	389	283	14
Wyoming	9,671	5,056	2,535	739	908	96	0	119	183	33	2
American Samoa	116	0	0	116	0	0	0	0	0	0	0
Bur. of Indian Affairs	5,364	3,057	1,250	502	257	31	195	31	28	13	0
Trust Territories*	—	—	—	—	—	—	—	—	—	—	—
Northern Marianas*	—	—	—	—	—	—	—	—	—	—	—
U.S. and Territories	4,128,009	1,822,910	1,115,408	622,428	331,794	48,160	55,575	47,600	62,419	20,724	991

* Not funded on the basis of child count
Note: From U.S. Department of Education.

services and related services under the Education for All Handicapped Children Act, Public Law 94-142. That figure represents an increase of approximately 22,000 from the 1983–84 incidence figures. The largest increase is in learning disabilities—an increase of 34,044 over the previous year, while a drop in the numbers of children identified as mentally retarded was reported. It is likely that many children identified as mentally retarded are reclassified as learning disabled, thus accounting for the shift in numbers reported above.

Primary prevention strategies include system level approaches and person-centered approaches, and each contributes to the well-being of children by helping to avoid maladjustment and by reducing the risk of disability (Cowen, 1985). As a teacher you can encourage your school to adopt an ecological perspective by thinking in terms of troubled systems. Apter (1982) and Apter and Conoley (1984) have argued convincingly for this view by articulating the major points of a systems or ecological approach:

1. Each child is an inseparable part of a small social system.
2. Disturbance is not viewed as a disease located within the body of the child, but rather as discordants (a lack of balance) in the system.
3. Disparity may be defined as a disparity between an individual's abilities and the demands or expectations of the environment—"failure to match" between child and system.
4. The goal of any intervention is to make the system work, and to make it work ultimately without the intervention.
5. Improvement in any part of the system can benefit the entire system.
6. This broader view of disturbance gives rise to the three major areas for intervention: changing the child, changing the environment, and changing attitudes and expectations (Apter, 1982, p. 69).

Adopting a system level approach in which we hold the environment accountable to some extent for "causing" the problem may restrain us from continuing to label and overlabel students, many of whom could be responded to in regular classrooms without further stigmatizing them as deviant. To implement this perspective we need to develop person-centered approaches using education interventions that enhance coping skills. By increasing our efforts to provide teenagers with sex education, for example, we could reduce the staggering incidence of teenage pregnancy. This, in turn, responds to the primary prevention concern of reducing birth defects. Many low birth weight infants are born to young mothers, with both infant and mother at risk. Educational efforts can thus enhance feelings of competency and skill so that young women can make intelligent decisions for themselves and young men can assume responsibility for their sexual behavior.

Secondary prevention involves early identification and intervention with children who have shown signs of difficulty. With judicious use of our resources it is possible to respond helpfully to keep a child in the mainstream. For example, interest in developing prereferral intervention models has that purpose in mind: "The prereferral intervention model is based on an indirect, consultative model of service delivery in which resources are directed at providing intervention assistance at the point of initial referral" (Graden, Casey, & Christenson, 1985, p. 379). This approach is also based on the ecological model in which many environmental factors are considered along with each child's characteristics. It is hoped that problems will be detected earlier and responded to before they seriously interfere with a child's functioning.

There are students, however, whose problems have not been prevented. For them, tertiary prevention is called for, that is, those interventions designed to rehabilitate the individual to allow for positive functioning in schools. This process can begin with the referral system. The Syracuse City School District is one of many school systems implementing a referral process designed to assess and place a student in the most appropriate program. Using the federal guidelines under Public Law 94-142, their referral process is shown in Figure 1. A sound referral process has a child's long-term needs and interests in mind. If one important goal is to prepare a child to function in the community, as we believe it should be, then our social policies as well as our educational interventions will have to reflect that priority.

Teachers and Legislation

Very often the programs you advocate can become realities only when society recognizes their value and supports them financially. Today, the quality of education is at the center of a national debate. As a special educator, it is imperative that you understand the issues so you can function as an informed citizen. Many of these critiques place the blame on students for failing to respond to instruction (National Commission on Excellence in Education, 1983). In contrast, the National Coalition of Advocates for Students maintains that barriers to excellence are what prevent students with disabilities from gaining access to appropriate schooling. They believe our children are at risk due to a variety of issues:

- Racial and class discrimination
- Sex and cultural discrimination
- Special education
- Inflexibility of school structure
- Abuses of testing, tracking, and ability grouping
- Narrowness of curriculum
- Limits of vocational education
- Lack of early childhood programs and support services for youth
- Lack of democratic governance

In their 1985 report "Barriers to Excellence: Our Children at Risk," they have stated:

We do not advocate segregating "children at risk" into special programs. Too much of that has already characterized our schools. Instead, we argue

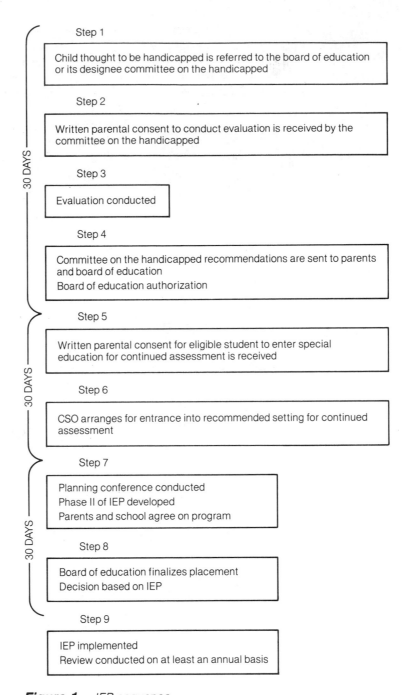

Step 1

Child thought to be handicapped is referred to the board of education or its designee committee on the handicapped

Step 2

Written parental consent to conduct evaluation is received by the committee on the handicapped

Step 3

Evaluation conducted

Step 4

Committee on the handicapped recommendations are sent to parents and board of education

Board of education authorization

Step 5

Written parental consent for eligible student to enter special education for continued assessment is received

Step 6

CSO arranges for entrance into recommended setting for continued assessment

Step 7

Planning conference conducted
Phase II of IEP developed
Parents and school agree on program

Step 8

Board of education finalizes placement
Decision based on IEP

Step 9

IEP implemented
Review conducted on at least an annual basis

30 DAYS (×3, vertical brackets)

Figure 1. *IEP sequence.*

for including the vast majority of these students in the mainstream of teaching and learning and for giving them access to higher standards of academic performance through two major strategies:

· Removing barriers that schools have placed in the way of student learning; and
· Recognizing that many children need extra help to attain the levels of learning of which they are capable (p. v).

The implementation of these two strategies will require the concerted efforts of many persons. As a teacher you will want support from others, and forging partnerships with parents is one way to broaden your support base.

Strengthening Families

As a teacher you can empower families by involving them in their children's education. The Fergusons' chapter, "Parents and Professionals," in this text, includes a model for active parent participation in children's programs that include planning and policy functions.

The Parent Center in Albuquerque, New Mexico, has developed a check list you can use to evaluate the extent to which your program involves parents in various aspects of classroom planning and the specific behaviors you can engage in to include them (see Figure 2).

As we lobby for a national policy to strengthen family economics and health (including mental health), educators and other human service workers can help translate family concerns into policy. Finding ways to respond to latchkey children, those children and adolescents left unsupervised after school, is an example of how schools and communities can pool their resources and expertise. Of course, economics has much to do with this issue and others. Educators and legislators are currently debating who will pay for the rapidly growing numbers of after-school programs for these children.

The hope is that families will feel supported in their efforts to advocate for social policies supportive of their needs and those of their children. One such need, of course, is to feel confident that their children will have opportunities to lead productive lives in the community. The Community and Family Living Amendments Act, a bill introduced in the United States Senate in 1983 by Senator John Chaffee of Rhode Island, is an example of such cooperative advocacy with parents and professionals seeking legislation that provides for a gradual shift of funding from institutions to community settings. At this time the proposed bill has undergone many changes; if passed, it will reflect the input of many interested parties. In the meantime, there is much that you can do to facilitate disabled children's ability to function in the community.

Community Living Options

As a teacher it is important for you to articulate your view of disabled students. Your assessment of their futures will determine the goals and experiences

	OFTEN	SOMETIMES	SELDOM	PRIORITY	PROJECTED START DATE	PERSON(S) RESPONSIBLE
1. Provides written information on consent to test						
2. Provides written information on consent to place						
3. Provides written information on criteria to place						
4. Provides written information on due process procedures						
5. Provides written information on availability of child's records						
6. Has regularly scheduled conferences						
7. Involves parents in planning the IEP						
8. Has a newsletter						
9. Has parent information group meetings						
10. Uses daily/weekly report cards						
11. Makes home visits						
12. Has class handouts						
13. Makes phone calls systematically						
14. Uses "good news" notes						
15. Interprets test results						
16. Arranges skill-training parent workshops (behavior modification, PET [parent effectiveness training], problem solving)						
17. Takes family history						
18. Elicits child strengths from parents						
19. Conducts parental needs and strengths assessment						
20. Has "room" parents						
21. Has parents assist on field trips, parties, etc.						
22. Has parent advisory groups						
23. Has parent volunteers in the classroom						
24. Involves parents in special interest task forces (curriculum, discipline, needs and strengths assessment)						
25. Uses parents as co-partners for other parents						
26. Uses parents as workshop leaders						
27. Other:						

Figure 2. *Parent Involvement Program analysis sheet developed by the Parent Center, Albuquerque, New Mexico.*

you create for them. If independence is a goal, then programs must begin teaching skills that will lead to independent functioning. For example, the following survival competencies for preschool children can prepare them for primary school and ultimately for independent community living.

1. Initiates interactions with adults and peers.
2. Interacts with adults and peers when not the initiator.
3. Demonstrates appropriate isolated play skills.
4. Makes choices from visible and invisible referents.
5. Executes at least one task from start to finish.
6. Listens and attends to a speaker in a large group.
7. Follows at least a one-component direction.
8. Demonstrates turn taking in a small group.
9. Demonstrates mobility from place to place.
10. Manipulates small and large objects.
11. Demonstrates appropriate attention-getting strategies.
12. Adapts to working in more than one room with more than one adult.
13. Demonstrates simple dressing and undressing skills.
14. Attends to task for minimum of fifteen minutes.
15. Adapts to transitions between activities across the day.
16. Expresses ideas to others.
17. Communicates with peers and adults.
18. Toilets independently.
19. Responds to social reinforcement.
20. Asks questions of others (Gaylord-Ross & Holvoet, 1985, pp. 311–312).

The above skills can also be thought of as functional in the sense that the acquisition, maintenance, and generalization of such skills will enable a student to function more competently and more independently. Gaylord-Ross and Holvoet (1985) have considered the following components essential in the development of a functional curriculum:

1. Select functional materials and activities.
2. Teach in functional settings using natural cues whenever possible.
3. Use varied materials and allow students to choose materials whenever feasible.
4. Incorporate communications programs into natural, functional routines.
5. Incorporate motor programs into natural, functional routines.
6. Sequence skills in a logical and normative manner.
7. Incorporate deceleration programs into skill sequences.
8. Teach in groups as well as in one-to-one settings (p. 93).

Ideally, programs will need to be in place each step along the way in a child's school life as preparation for the next level. The development of those programs and utilizing creative teaching approaches and materials is the challenge for teachers.

Table 2

School-Based Integration Markers

Personnel involved	Integration marker	Definition
Administrative and/ or facilities management	· Natural proportion	Percentage of severely handicapped students enrolled at a regular school approximately parallels their percentage in the general population (1%–2%).
	· Age range	Students' age range matches age range of nonhandicapped students (e.g., elementary versus secondary schools).
	· Classroom location	Location of classroom for severely handicapped students is close to similar-age peers and consistent with instructional facility procedures used in assignment of regular education classrooms.
	· Use of general school facilities (restrooms, cafeteria, library, etc.)	Handicapped students share use of general facilities and activities with similar-age nonhandicapped peers and as part of an integrated grouping arrangement reflective of natural proportion.
	· Schedules and groupings	Handicapped students follow general school schedule for similar-age peers (e.g., arrival, departure, lunch, recess periods) and are variously grouped for different activities (including homogeneous and heterogeneous groups).
	· Classroom assignment	Homerooms for all students are integrated (i.e., a severely handicapped student may receive all instruction in a self-contained special education class but begins and ends the day, etc., in a regular fourth grade room if he or she is 9 years old).
	· Administration and resource personnel	Special education staff are supervised by general education personnel (principal, etc.) and access general resource personnel (librarian, physical education teacher, etc.) for instructional consultation and direct programming of their students.
	· Extracurricular activities	Extracurricular activities are integrated, allowing for involvement of handicapped as well as nonhandicapped students.
	· Parent organizations	The Parent-Teacher Association (PTA), etc., is supported as a communication/ involvement vehicle for all parents.

(continued)

Table 2
(continued)

Personnel involved	Integration marker	Definition
Classroom teacher	· Use of general school facilities (restrooms, cafeteria, library, etc.)	See above under "Administrative and/or facilities management."
	· Schedules and groupings in daily instruction	Daily schedule of handicapped students parallels that of nonhandicapped peers (e.g., recess at elementary level, class changes at secondary level) and grouping arrangements reflect both educational and normalization concerns (including use of heterogeneous groups, both small and large groups, etc.).
	· Administration and resource personnel	Special education staff access general education administrative and resource personnel for instructional consultation, including negotiating integration of their students into activities with nonhandicapped peers (e.g., library period integrated with a regular education classroom).
	· Joint class activities with same-age peers	Based upon educational needs and the IEP, special education students are integrated into the regular classroom for selected academic programming (e.g., physical education, story time in first grade, etc.).
	· Extracurricular activities	Handicapped students participate in extracurricular activities of interest to the individual (e.g., an after-school sports activity).
	· Normalized instructional objectives and intervention strategies	Skills being taught to handicapped students are functional and age-appropriate, and the instructional procedures are consistent with criterion conditions as well as with community standards for regular education students (e.g., corporal punishment guidelines are followed).
	· Parent interactions	Parents of severely handicapped students are encouraged to "integrate" themselves into general school parent organizations and events (PTA, etc.).

(continued)

Table 2
(continued)

Personnel involved	Integration marker	Definition
Classroom teacher *(continued)*	· Peer/social interactions	Handicapped and nonhandicapped students are prepared and encouraged to interact with one another in social, play, and other available "natural" contexts during the school day (e.g., recess).
	· Teacher/staff interactions	Faculty meetings are held jointly rather than separately for regular and special education. Special education staff interact socially, etc., with regular education staff rather than segregating themselves along "categorical" lines.

Note: From Meyer & Kishi, 1985.

Teaching Creatively

Our vision of children's futures provides us with a mandate to support social policy changes and to design school and community interventions. However, you may feel that such a comprehensive view is unrealistic. The authors of the chapters in this book encourage you to adopt this broad view of your teaching role. The assumption is that teachers make a difference in the lives of children and their families. To be effective you will have to take risks to learn new approaches that can be utilized with children in your classroom. You will have to be equally cognizant of conditions and relationships in the school at large that also influence child change and your teaching effectiveness.

On the school building level, your ability to develop collaborative relationships with other teachers and administrators can support your classroom efforts. This broader view is helpful, for example, when designing school integration strategies. Meyer and Kishi (1985) have identified a variety of important markers or factors contributing to the integration of disabled and nondisabled students. Table 2 shows these markers, the personnel involved, and the definition of each marker. An analysis of that table shows that many markers are shaped and influenced by other school personnel with whom you have to work out mutually acceptable arrangements; other markers are those for which you, as the teacher, are responsible. Administrators in your school district may determine the proportion of disabled students placed in your school, but you can find ways to include other teachers in your program. For example, many special education teachers ask to join their grade level team, or they may offer to teach a reading group composed of children from other classrooms, thus facilitating the movement of special needs students to other rooms during that time.

On the classroom level you can fine-tune or adjust your instructional approaches to meet the needs of students with a variety of learning problems and learning styles. Bunch (1985) has described a number of adjustments in instruction and materials for secondary students mainstreamed into regular programs. These include adjustments for information gathering and study, adjustments in recording of auditorially presented information, adjustments in instructional presentation, and adjustments in assignment production.

To be a successful teacher requires an openness to new learning and a willingness to accept responsibility for making a difference in children's education. It is hoped that this book will encourage you to pursue working with students who are disabled and who can change and learn when our schools and teachers respond to their needs.

References

Abrahams, R. D. (1973). The advantages of Black English. In J. S. De Stephano (Ed.), *Language, society, and education: A profile of Black English*. Worthington, OH: Charles A. Jones.

Achenbach, T. M. (1975). A longitudinal study of relations between associative responding, IQ changes, and school performance from grades 3 to 12. *Developmental Psychology, 11*, 653–654.

Achenbach, T. M. (1982). *Developmental psychopathology* (2nd ed.). New York: John Wiley & Sons.

Achenbach, T. M., & Edelbrock, C. S. (1978). The classification of child psychopathology: A review and analysis of empirical efforts. *Psychological Bulletin, 85*, 1275–1301.

Achenbach, T. M., & Edelbrock, C. S. (1981). Behavioral problems and competencies reported by parents of normal and disturbed children aged 4 through 16. *Monographs of the Society for Research in Child Development, 46*, (Serial No. 188).

Adelson, E., & Fraiberg, S. (1973). Gross motor developments in infants blind from birth. *Child Development, 45*, 114–126.

Akerley, M. S. (1978). False gods and angry prophets. In A. P. Turnbull & H. R. Turnbull III (Eds.), *Parents speak out: Views from the other side of the two-way mirror* (pp. 39–48). Columbus, OH: Charles E. Merrill.

Albion, F., & Salzberg, C. (1982). The effects of self-instruction on the rate of correct addition problems with mentally retarded children. *Education and Treatment of Children, 5*, 121–131.

Alessi, G. J. (1980). Behavioral observation for the school psychologist: Responsive-discrepancy model. *School Psychology Review, 9*, 31–45.

American Association on Mental Deficiency. (1977). *AAMD Adaptive Behavior Rating Scale-Public School Version*. Washington, DC: Author.

American Psychiatric Association. (1980). *Diagnostic and statistical manual of mental disorders, DSM III* (3rd ed.) (pp. 87–90). Washington, DC: Author.

Amoriell, W. J. (1979). Reading achievement and the ability to manipulate visual and auditory stimuli. *Journal of Learning Disabilities, 12*, 562–564.

Anastasiow, N. J. (1978). Strategies and models for

early childhood intervention programs in integrated settings. In M. J. Guralnick (Ed.), *Early intervention and the integration of handicapped and nonhandicapped children* (pp. 85–111). Baltimore: University Park Press.

Anastasiow, N. J. (1981). Socioemotional development: The state of the art. In N. J. Anastasiow (Ed.), *Socioemotional development* (pp. 1–12). San Francisco: Jossey-Bass.

Andrews, G., Howie, P., Dosza, M., & Guitar, B. (1982). Stuttering: Speech pattern characteristics under fluency inducing conditions. *Journal of Speech and Hearing Research, 25*, 208–216.

Anthony, W. A. (1980). A rehabilitation model for rehabilitating the psychiatrically disabled. *Rehabilitation Counseling Bulletin, 24* (Special Issue), pp. 6–21.

Apter, S. J. (1982). *Troubled children/troubled systems.* New York: Pergamon Press.

Apter, S. J., & Conoley, J. C. (1984). *Childhood behavior disorders and emotional disturbance.* Englewood Cliffs, NJ: Prentice-Hall.

Aronson, M., & Falklstrom, K. (1977). Immediate and long-term effects of developmental training in children with Down's syndrome. *Developmental Medicine and Child Neurology, 19*, 489–494.

Ashcraft, M. H., & Kellas, G. (1974). Organization in normal and retarded children: Temporal aspects of storage and retrieval. *Journal of Experimental Psychology, 103*, 502–508.

Asterita, M. F. (1985). *The physiology of stress.* New York: Human Sciences Press.

Baker, B. L., Brightman, A. J., Heifetz, L. J., & Murphy, D. M. (1976). *Steps to independence.* Champaign, IL: Research Press.

Ballantyne, J. (1977). *Deafness.* London: Churchill Livingston.

Bannatyne, A. (1971). *Language, reading and learning disabilities.* Springfield, IL: Charles C. Thomas.

Bannatyne, A. (1974). Diagnosis: A note on recategorization of the WISC scaled scores. *Journal of Learning Disabilities, 7*, 272–274.

Barnard, H. (1865). Extracts from the sixth annual report of the superintendent of common schools to the General Assembly for 1851. *Journal of American Education, 15*, 293–313.

Barnes, E. (1982). Living together: Teacher behaviors that promote integration. In P. Knoblock (Ed.), *Teaching and mainstreaming autistic children.* Denver, CO: Love.

Barnes, E., Berrigan, C., & Biklen, D. (1978). *What's the difference? Teaching positive attitudes toward people with disabilities.* Syracuse: Human Policy Press.

Barsch, R. H. (1968). *The parent of the handicapped child: The study of child-rearing practices.* Springfield, IL: Charles C. Thomas.

Barton, K., & Cattell, R. (1972). Personality before and after a chronic illness. *Journal of Clinical Psychology, 28*, 464–467.

Bates, E. (1979). *The emergence of symbols.* New York: Academic Press.

Batshaw, M. L., & Perret, Y. M. (1981). *Children with handicaps: A medical primer.* Baltimore: Paul H. Brookes.

Baum, M. (1962). Some dynamic factors affecting family adjustment to the handicapped child. *Exceptional Children, 28*, 387–392.

Bayley, N. (1969). *The Bayley scales of infant development.* New York: Psychological Corporation.

Becker, H. (1963). *Outsiders: Studies in the sociology of deviance.* New York: Free Press.

Becker, H. S. (1967). *The other side.* New York: Free Press.

Becker, L. D., Bender, N. N., & Kawabe, K. K. (1980). Exceptional parents: A survey of programs, services, and needs. *Academic Therapy, 15*, 523–539.

Becker, W., Madsen, C., Arnold, C., & Thomas, D. (1967). The contingent use of teacher attention and praise in reducing classroom behavior problems. *Journal of Special Education, 1*, 287–307.

Beers, C. W. (1908). *A mind that found itself.* New York: Longmans, Green.

Behrmann, M., & Lahm, L. (1984). Critical learning: Multiply handicapped babies get on-line. In M. Behrmann & L. Lahm (Eds.), *Proceedings of the national conference on the use of microcomputers in special education* (pp. 181–193). Reston, VA: Council for Exceptional Children.

Bellamy, G. T., Peterson, L., & Close, D. (1975). Habilitation of the severely and profoundly retarded: Illustration of competence. *Education and Training of the Mentally Retarded, 15*, 174–186.

Bellamy, G. T., Sheehan, M. R., Horner, R. H., &

Boles, S. M. (1980). Community programs for severely handicapped adults: An analysis of vocational opportunities. *Journal of the Association for the Severely Handicapped, 5*(4), 307–324.

Belmont, J. M., & Butterfield, E. C. (1971). Learning strategies as determinants of memory deficiencies. *Cognitive Psychology, 2*, 411–420.

Belmont, J. M., & Butterfield, E. C. (1977). The instructional approach to developmental cognitive research. In R. V. Kail, Jr., & J. W. Hagen (Eds.), *Perspectives on the development of memory and cognition*. Hillsdale, NJ: Lawrence Erlbaum.

Belmont, J. M., Butterfield, E. C., & Borkowski, J. G. (1978). Training retarded people to generalize memorization methods across memory tasks. In P. E. Gruneberg & R. N. Sykes (Eds.), *Practical aspects of memory*. London: Academic Press.

Bemporad, J. R. (1979). Adult recollections of a formerly autistic child. *Journal of Autism and Developmental Disorders, 9*, 179–197.

Bennett, R. (1982). Applications of microcomputer technology to special education. *Exceptional Children, 49*, 106–113.

Benton, A. (1962). Dyslexia in relation to form perception and directional sense. In J. Money (Ed.), *Reading disability progress and research needs in dyslexia*. Baltimore: Johns Hopkins Press.

Benton, A. L., & Pearl, D. (1978). *Dyslexia: An appraisal of current knowledge*. New York: Oxford University Press.

Bercovici, S. (1983). *Barriers to normalization*. Baltimore: Paul H. Brookes.

Bernal, M. E., & North, J. A. (1978). A survey of parent training manuals. *Journal of Applied Behavior Analysis, 11*, 533–544.

Berry, M. (1977). For want of a name. *ASHA, 19*, 943.

Bersoff, D. N. (1982a). Larry P. and PASE: Judicial report cards on the validity of individual intelligence tests. In T. R. Kratochwill (Ed.), *Advances in school psychology: Vol. II*. Hillsdale, NJ: Lawrence Erlbaum.

Bersoff, D. N. (1982b). The legal regulation of school psychology. In C. R. Reynolds & T. B. Gutkin (Eds.), *The handbook of school psychology*. New York: John Wiley & Sons.

Bersoff, D. N., & Grieger, R. (1971). Psychosituational assessment. *American Journal of Orthopsychiatry, 41*, 483–493.

Bettelheim, B. (1967). *The empty fortress*. New York: Free Press.

Bijou, S. W. (1970). What psychology has to offer education—now. *Journal of Applied Behavior Analysis, 3*, 65–71.

Bijou, S. W. (1971). Environment and intelligence: A behavioral analysis. In R. Cancro (Ed.), *Intelligence: Genetic and environmental influences*. New York: Grune & Stratton.

Biklen, D., Bogdan, R., Ferguson, D. L., Searl, S. J., & Taylor, S. J. (1985). *Achieving the complete school: Strategies for effective mainstreaming*. New York: Teachers College Press.

Binet, A., & Simon, T. (1905). Methodes nouvelles pour le diagnostic du niveau intellectuel des anormaux. *L'Annee Psychologique, 11*, 191–244.

Birch, H. G., & Belmont, L. (1964). Auditory-visual integration in normal and retarded readers. *American Journal of Orthopsychiatry, 34*, 852–861.

Birenbaum, A., & Seiffer, S. (1976). *Resettling retarded adults in a managed community*. New York: Praeger.

Blanton, R., & Nunnally, J. (1964). Evaluational language processes in the deaf. *Psychological Reports, 15*, 891–894.

Blatt, B., Biklen, D., & Bogdan, R. (1977). *An alternative textbook in special education*. Denver, CO: Love.

Blatt, B., Bogdan, R., Biklen, D., & Taylor, S. (1977). From institution to community: A conversion model. In E. Sontag (Ed.), *Educational programming for the severely and profoundly handicapped*. Reston, VA: Council for Exceptional Children.

Blatt, B., & Kaplan, F. (1966). *Christmas in purgatory*. Boston: Allyn & Bacon.

Blatt, B., McNally, J., & Ozolins, A. (1979). *The family papers*. New York: Longman.

Bliss, C. (1965). *Semantography*. Sydney, Australia: Semantography Publications.

Block, J. H., & Block, J. (1980). The role of ego-control and ego-resiliency in the organization of behavior. In W. A. Collins (Ed.), *Development of cognition, affect, and social relations*.

The Minnesota symposia on child psychology. Hillsdale, NJ: Lawrence Erlbaum.

Bobath, K., & Bobath, B. (1952). A treatment of cerebral palsy based on the analysis of the patient's motor behavior. *British Journal of Physical Medicine, 15,* 107–117.

Bodenheimer, C. (1982). Sibling support groups. In P. Knoblock (Ed.), *Teaching and mainstreaming autistic children.* Denver, CO: Love.

Bogdan, R., & Biklen, D. (1977). Handicapism. *Social Policy, 8* (March/April), 14–19.

Bogdan, R., & Taylor, S. J. (1982). *Inside out: The social meaning of mental retardation.* Toronto: University of Toronto Press.

Bogen, J. E. (1969). The other side of the brain: Parts I, II, III. *Bulletin of the Los Angeles Neurological Society, 34,* 73–105, 135–162, 191–203.

Bogen, J. E. (1975). Some educational aspects of hemispheric specialization. *UCLA Educator, 17,* 24–32.

Bonvillian, J., Nelson, K., & Rhyne, J. (1982). Sign language and autism. *Journal of Autism and Developmental Disorders, 11,* 125–138.

Bookbinder, S. R. (1978). *Mainstreaming: What every child needs to know about disabilities.* Boston: Exceptional Parent Press.

Bornstein, H., Hamilton, L. B., Saulnier, K. L., & Roy, H. L. (Eds.). (1975). *The signed English Dictionary for preschool and elementary levels.* Washington, DC: Gallaudet College Press.

Bowlby, J. (1969). *Attachment.* New York: Basic Books.

Boyer, E. L. (1983). *High school: A report on secondary education in America.* New York: Harper & Row.

Braginsky, D., & Braginsky, B. (1971). *Hansels and Gretels: Studies of children in institutions for the mentally retarded.* New York: Holt, Rinehart, & Winston.

Breslau, N., Salkever, D., & Staruch, K. (1982). Women's labor force activity and responsibilities for disabled dependents: A study of families with disabled children. *Journal of Health and Social Behavior, 23,* 169–183.

Brewer, G., & Kakalik, J. S. (1979). *Handicapped children: Strategies for improving services.* New York: McGraw-Hill.

Briard, J. K. (1976). Counseling parents of children with learning disabilities. *Social Casework, 57,* 581–585.

Bricker, D., Carlson, L., & Schwarz, R. (1981). A discussion of early intervention for infants with Down's syndrome. *Pediatrics, 67,* 45–46.

Brim, O. G. (1966). Socialization through the life cycle. In O. G. Brim & S. Wheeler (Eds.), *Socialization after childhood* (pp. 1–49). New York: John Wiley & Sons.

Brolin, P., & Kokaska, C. (1980). *Career education for handicapped children and youth.* Columbus, OH: Charles E. Merrill.

Bronfenbrenner, U. (1976). The experimental ecology of education. *Teacher's College Record, 78,* 157–204.

Brown, A. L. (1974). The role of strategic behavior in retardate memory. *International Review of Research in Mental Retardation, 7,* 55–104.

Brown, A. L. (1978). Knowing when, where, and how to remember: A problem of meta cognition. In R. Glaser (Ed.), *Advances in instructional psychology.* Hillsdale, NJ: Lawrence Erlbaum.

Brown, A. L., & Barclay, C. R. (1976). The effects of training specific mnemonics on the metamnemonic efficiency of retarded children. *Child Development, 47,* 71–80.

Brown, A. L., & Campione, J. C. (1977). Training strategic study time apportionment in educable retarded children. *Intelligence, 1,* 94–107.

Brown, A. L., Campione, J. C., & Barclay, C. R. (1979). Training self-checking routines for estimating test readiness: Generalization from list learning to prose recall. *Child Development, 50,* 501–512.

Brown, A. L., Campione, J. C., & Murphy, M. D. (1974). Keeping track of changing variables: Long-term retention of a trained rehearsal strategy by retarded adolescents. *American Journal of Mental Deficiency, 78,* 446–453.

Brown, A. L., Campione, J. C., & Murphy, M. D. (1977). Maintenance and generalization of trained metamnemonic awareness of educable retarded children. *Journal of Experimental Child Psychology, 24,* 191–211.

Brown, A. L., & Hammill, D. D. (1979). *Behavioral rating profile: An ecological approach to behavioral assessments.* Austin, TX: Pro-ed.

Brown, A. L., & Lawton, S. C. (1977). The feeling of

knowing experience in educable retarded children. *Developmental Psychology, 13,* 364–370.

Brown, L., Branston, M. B., Hamre-Nietupski, S., Pumpian, I., Certo, N., & Gruenewald, L. (1978). A strategy for developing chronological age-appropriate and functional curricular content for severely handicapped adolescents and young adults. *The Journal of Special Education, 13,* 81–90.

Brown, L., Branston-McClean, M., Baumgart, D., Vincent, L., Falvey, M., & Schroeder, J. (1979). Using the characteristics of current and subsequent least restrictive environments in the development of content for severely handicapped students. *AAESPH Review, 4,* 3–14.

Brown, L., Falvey, M., Vincent, B., Kaye, N., Johnson, F., Ferrare-Parrish, P., & Gruenewald, L. (1979). Strategies for generating comprehensive, longitudinal and chronological age appropriate individual education plans for adolescent and young adult severely handicapped students. In L. Brown, M. Falvey, D. Baumgart, I. Pumpian, J. Schroeder, & L. Gruenewald (Eds.), *Strategies for teaching chronological age appropriate functional skills to adolescent and young adult severely handicapped students.* Madison, WI: Madison Metropolitan School District.

Brown, L., Ford, A., Nisbet, J., Sweet, M., Donnellan, A., & Gruenewald, L. (1983). Opportunities available when severely handicapped students attend chronological age appropriate regular schools. *Journal of the Association for Persons with Severe Handicaps, 8,* 16–24.

Brown, L., Nietupski, J., & Hamre-Nietupski, S. (1976). The criterion of ultimate functioning and public school services for the severely handicapped. In M. A. Thomas (Ed.), *Hey, don't forget about me: Education's investment in the severely, profoundly, and multiply handicapped* (pp. 2–15). Reston, VA: Council for Exceptional Children.

Brown, L., Pumpian, J., Baumgart, D., VanDeventer, P., Ford, A., Nisbet, J., Schroeder, J., & Gruenewald, L. (1981). Longitudinal transition plans in programs for severely handicapped students. *Exceptional Children, 47,* 625–631.

Brown, L., Shiraga, B., Ford, A., VanDeventer, P., Nisbet, J., Loomis, R., & Sweet, M. (1983). Teaching severely handicapped students to perform meaningful work in nonsheltered vocational environments. In L. Brown, J. Nisbet, A. Ford, M. Sweet, B. Shiraga, R. Loomis, & P. VanDeventer (Eds.), *Educational programs for severely handicapped students* (Vol. 13, pp. 1–100). Madison, WI: Madison Metropolitan School District.

Brown, L., Wilcox, B., Sontag, E., Vincent, B., Dodd, N., & Gruenewald, L. (1979). Toward the realization of the least restrictive educational environments for severely handicapped students. *AAESPH Review, 2,* 195–201.

Bruce, N., & Duchan, J. (1983, May). *The role of intonation in the language of autistic children.* Paper presented at the National Conference on Autism, Toronto.

Bruininks, R. H., Hauber, F. A., & Kudla, M. J. (1979). National survey of community residential facilities: A profile of facilities and residents in 1977. *American Journal on Mental Deficiency, 84,* 470–478.

Bruner, J. (1982). The language of education. *Social Research, 49,* 835–853.

Bryant, N., Drabin, I., & Gettinger, M. (1981). Effects of varying unit size and spelling achievement in learning disabled children. *Journal of Learning Disabilities, 14,* 200–203.

Bryce, M., & Lloyd, L. (1981). *Treating families in the home: An alternative to placement.* Springfield, IL: Charles C. Thomas.

Budin, P. (1907). *The nursling.* London: Laxton.

Budoff, M. (1968). A learning potential assessment procedure: Rationale and supporting data. In B. W. Richards (Ed.), *Proceedings of the first Congress of the International Study of Mental Deficiency.* Reigate (Surrey, England): M. Jackson.

Budoff, M., & Hamilton, J. L. (1976). Optimizing test performance of moderately and severely mentally retarded adolescents and adults. *American Journal of Mental Deficiency, 81,* 49–57.

Budoff, M., & Hutten, L. (1982). Microcomputers in special education: Promises and pitfalls. *Exceptional Children, 49,* 123–128.

Bunch, N. (1985). Adjustments in instruction and materials: Secondary level mainstreaming. *Forum, 11,* 17–19.

Burns, P., & Bozeman, W. (1981). Computer assisted instruction and mathematics achievement: Is there a relationship? *Educational Technology, 21*, 32–39.

Busch-Rossnagel, N. A., & Vance, A. K. (1982). The impact of the schools on social and emotional development. In B. Wolman (Ed.), *Handbook of developmental psychology*. Englewood Cliffs, NJ: Prentice-Hall.

Buss, A. R., & Poley, W. (1976). *Individual differences: Traits and factors*. New York: Gardner.

Butler, K. (1981). Language processing disorders. Factors in diagnosis and remediation. In R. Keith (Ed.), *Central auditory and language disorders in children* (pp. 160–174). Houston: College Hill Press.

Butler, S. R. (1978). Maternal love, an enzyme inducer? *Science, 199*, 445.

Cameron, P., Titus, D., Kostin, J., & Kostin, M. (1973). The life satisfaction of non-normal persons. *Journal of Consulting Clinical Psychology, 41*, 207–212.

Campbell, E. G. (1969). Adolescent socialization. In D. A. Goslin (Ed.), *Handbook of socialization theory and research* (pp. 821–861). Chicago: Rand McNally.

Campione, J. C., & Brown, A. L. (1977). Memory and metamemory development in educable retarded children. In R. V. Kail, Jr., & J. W. Hagan, (Eds.), *Perspectives on the development of memory and cognition*. Hillsdale, NJ: Lawrence Erlbaum.

Carrier, J. (1983). Masking the social and educational knowledge: The case of learning disability theory. *American Journal of Sociology, 88*, 949–974.

Carter, C. (1977). Prospectus on black communications. *School Psychology Digest, 6*, 23–30.

Casey, L. (1978). Development of communication behavior in autistic children: A parent program using manual signs. *Journal of Autism and Childhood Schizophrenia, 8*, 45–49.

Cazden, C. (1979). Peekaboo as an instructional model: Discourse development at home and at school. *Papers and Reports in Child Language Development, 19*, 1–29.

Center for Social Organization of Schools. (1983). *National survey examines how schools use microcomputers*. Baltimore: Johns Hopkins Press.

Center on Human Policy. (1979). *The community imperative*. Syracuse: Center on Human Policy.

Ceretto, M., & Tuma, J. (1977). Distribution of DSM-II categories in a child psychiatric setting. *Journal of Abnormal Child Psychology, 5*, 147–155.

Certo, N., Haring, N., & York, R. (1984). *Public school integration of severely handicapped students*. Baltimore: Paul H. Brookes.

Chaffin, J. D. (1974). Will the real "mainstreaming" program please stand up! *Focus on Exceptional Children, 6*, 1–18.

Chaffin, J., Maxwell, B., & Thompson, B. (1982). ARC-ED curriculum: The application of video game formats to educational software. *Exceptional Children, 49*, 173–178.

Chamberlin, J. (1978). *On our own*. New York: McGraw-Hill.

Chandler, L. A., & Lundahl, W. T. (1983). Empirical classification of emotional adjustment reactions. *American Journal of Orthopsychiatry, 53*, 460–467.

Charlesworth, R., & Hartrup, W. W. (1967). Positive social reinforcement in the nursery school peer group. *Child Development, 38*, 993–1003.

Charlesworth, W. R. (1978). Ethology: Its relevance for observational studies of human adaptation. In G. P. Sackett (Ed.), *Observing behavior, Vol. I: Theory and applications in mental retardation*. Baltimore: University Park Press.

Charlesworth, W. R., & Spiker, D. (1975). An ethological approach to observation in learning settings. In R. A. Weinberg & F. H. Wood (Eds.), *Observation of pupils and teachers in mainstream and special education settings: Alternative strategies*. Reston, VA: Council for Exceptional Children.

Chaseldine, S., & Jeffree, D. (1981). Mentally handicapped adolescents: Their use of leisure. *Journal of Mental Deficiency Research, 25*, 49–59.

Chesterton, G. K. (1922). *Eugenics and other evils*. London: Cassell.

Children's Defense Fund. (1974). *Children out of school in America*. Washington, DC: Author.

Children's Defense Fund. (1984a). *A children's defense budget: An analysis of the President's FY 1985 budget and children*. Washington, DC: Author.

Children's Defense Fund. (1984b). *American children in hunger and poverty*. Washington, DC: Author.

Cicchetti, D., & Pogge-Hesse, P. (1982). Possible

contributions of the study of organically retarded persons to developmental theory. In E. Zigler & D. Balla (Eds.), *Mental retardation: The developmental-difference controversy* (pp. 277–318). Hillsdale, NJ: Lawrence Erlbaum.

Clausen, J. A., & Huffine, C. L. (1975). Sociocultural and social-psychological factors affecting social responses to mental disorder. *Journal of Health and Social Behavior, 16*, 405–420.

Cleary, T. A., Humphreys, L. G., Kendrick, S. A., & Wesman, A. G. (1975). Educational uses of tests with disadvantaged students. *American Psychologist, 30*, 15–41.

Clements, J. E., & Alexander, R. M. (1975). Parent training: Bringing it all back home. *Focus on Exceptional Children, 7*, 1–12.

Cobb, S. (1979). Social support and health through the life course. In M. W. Riley (Ed.), *Aging from birth to death*. Boulder, CO: Westview Press.

Cohen, M., & Nadler, H. L. (1983). The sex chromosomes. In R. E. Behrman & V. C. Vaughan (Eds.), *Textbook of pediatrics*. Philadelphia: W. B. Saunders.

Colarusso, R. P., Martin, H., & Hartung, J. (1975). Specific visual perceptual skills as long-term predictors of academic success. *Journal of Learning Disabilities, 8*, 651–655.

Cole, M., John-Steiner, V., Scribner, S., & Souberman, E. (1978). *L. S. Vygotsky: Mind in Society*. Cambridge, MA: Harvard University Press.

Coleman, M., & Balkany, T. J. (1983). Abnormalities of the ear in Down's syndrome. *Down's Syndrome Papers and Abstracts for Professionals, 6*(1), 1–2.

Coleman, M., & Gillberg, C. (1985). *The biology of the autistic syndromes*. New York: Praeger.

Coleman, Z. (1983). Loss of hearing: Coping with a new reality. In R. L. Jones (Ed.), *Reflections on growing up disabled* (pp. 42–49). Reston, VA: Council for Exceptional Children.

Combs, R., & Harper, J. (1967). Effects of labels on attitudes of educators toward handicapped children. *Exceptional Education, 33*, 399–403.

Comer, J. P., & Schraft, C. M. (1980). Working with black parents. In R. R. Abidin (Ed.), *Parent education and intervention handbook* (pp. 322–348). Springfield, IL: Charles C. Thomas.

Compton, D. (1981). *Therapeutic recreation at the crossroads: Legislate, advocate or abdicate.*

Presentation delivered at the Midwestern Symposium on Therapeutic Recreation, Springfield, IL, April 10.

Condon, W. S. (1975). Multiple response to sound in dysfunctional children. *Journal of Autism and Childhood Schizophrenia, 5*, 37–56.

Condon, W. S., & Sander, L. W. (1974). Neonate movement is synchronized with adult speech: Interactional participation and language acquisition. *Science, 183*, 99–101.

Conference of Executives of American Schools for the Deaf. (1974). *Report of ad hoc committee to define deaf and hard of hearing*. Washington, DC: Author.

Conoley, J. C. (1980). Organizational assessment. *School Psychology Review, 9*, 83–89.

Conroy, J. W. (1977). Trends in deinstitutionalization of the mentally retarded. *Mental Retardation, 15*, 44–46.

Conroy, J. W., & Bradley, V. J. (1985). *The Pennhurst longitudinal study: Combined report of five years of research and analysis*. Philadelphia: Temple University Press.

Coulter, W. A. (1980). Adaptive behavior and professional disfavor: Controversies and trends for school psychologists. *School Psychology Review, 9*, 67–74.

Coulter, W. A., & Morrow, H. W. (Eds.). (1978). *Adaptive behavior: Concepts and measurements*. New York: Grune & Stratton.

Cowen, E. L. (1985). Primary prevention in mental health. *Social Policy, 15*, 11–17.

Crawford, J., Thompson, D., & Aiello, J. (1979). Deinstitutionalization and community placement: Clinical and environmental factors. *Mental Retardation, 17*, 59–63.

Creech, R. (1980). Do you like your larynx? *Communication Outlook, 2*, 1–10.

Crickmay, M. (1966). *Speech therapy and the Bobath approach to cerebral palsy*. Springfield, IL: Charles C. Thomas.

Cromwell, R. L., Blashfield, R. K., & Strauss, J. S. (1975). Criteria for classification systems. In N. Hobbs (Ed.), *Issues in the classification of children, Vol. I*. San Francisco: Jossey-Bass.

Cronbach, L. J. (1975). Five decades of public controversy over mental testing. *American Psychologist, 30*, 1–14.

Cross, T. (1978). Motherese: Its association with the rate of syntactic acquisition in young children.

In N. Waterson and C. Snow (Eds.), *The development of communication*. New York: John Wiley & Sons.

Cruickshank, W., Bentzen, F., Ratzeburg, F., & Tannhauser, M. (1961). *A teaching method for brain-injured and hyperactive children*. Syracuse: Syracuse University Press.

Crystal, D. (1982). *Profiling linguistic disability*. London: Edward Arnold.

Cutler, B. (1981). *Unraveling the special education maze: An action guide for parents*. Champaign, IL: Research Press.

Damon, W. (1983). *Social and personality development*. New York: W. W. Norton.

Daniels, S. M., Chipouras, S., Cornelius, D. A., & Makas, E. (1979). *Who cares: A handbook on sex education and counseling services for disabled people*. Washington, DC: George Washington University Press.

Darley, F. (Ed.). (1979). *Evaluation of appraisal techniques in speech and language pathology*. Menlo Park, CA: Addison-Wesley.

Darley, F., Aronson, A., & Brown, J. (1975). *Motor speech disorders*. Philadelphia: W. B. Saunders.

Darling, R., & Darling, J. (1982). *Children who are different: Meeting challenges of birth defects in society*. St. Louis: C. V. Mosby.

Das, J. P. (1973). Structure of cognitive abilities: Evidence for simultaneous and successive processing. *Journal of Educational Psychology, 35*, 103–108.

Das, J. P. (1983). Aspects of planning. In J. Kirby (Ed.), *Cognitive strategies and educational performance*. New York: Academic Press.

Das, J. P., Kirby, J., & Jarman, R. F. (1975). Simultaneous and successive syntheses: An alternative model for cognitive abilities. *Psychological Bulletin, 82*, 87–103.

Das, J. P., Kirby, J., & Jarman, R. F. (1979). *Simultaneous and successive cognitive processes*. New York: Academic Press.

Das, J. P., Snart, F., & Mulcahy, R. F. (1982). Information integration and its relationship to reading disability. In J. P. Das, R. F. Mulcahy, & A. E. Wall (Eds.), *Theory and research in learning disabilities*. New York: Plenum Press.

Davies, S. P. (1959). *The mentally retarded in society*. New York: Columbia University Press.

Dearborn, W. F., & Rothney, J. W. M. (1963). *Predicting the child's development* (2nd ed.). Cambridge, MA: Sci-Art.

De Hirsch, K. (1952). Specific dyslexia or strephosymbolia. *Folia Phoniatrica, 4*, 231–248.

De Hirsch, K. (1973). Early language development and minimal brain dysfunction. In F. de la Cruz, B. Fox, & H. Roberts (Eds.), *Minimal brain dysfunction: Annuals of the New York Academy of Sciences, 205*, 158–163.

Demos, J. (1970). *A little commonwealth: Family life in Plymouth Colony*. New York: Oxford University Press.

Dempsey, J. J. (1981). *The family and public policy: The issue of the 1980s*. Baltimore: Paul H. Brookes.

Deno, E. (1970). Special education as developmental capital. *Exceptional Children, 37*, 229–237.

Deno, S., Mirkin, P., and Wesson, C. (1984). How to write effective data-based IEP's. *Teaching Exceptional Children, 16*, 96–105.

DesLauriers, A. M., & Carlson, C. F. (1969). *Your child is asleep: Early infantile autism*. Homewood, IL: Dorsey Press.

Detterman, D. K., & Sternberg, R. J. (Eds.). (1982). *How and how much can intelligence be increased?* Norwood, NJ: Ablex.

Dexter, L. A. (1964). On the politics and sociology of stupidity in our society. In H. S. Becker (Ed.), *The other side*. New York: Free Press.

Dickstein, E. (1977). Self and self-esteem: Theoretical foundations and their implications for research. *Human Development, 20*, 129–140.

Dix, D. L. (1970). Memorial to the Legislature of Massachusetts (1843). In B. Blatt, *Exodus from Pandemonium*. Boston: Allyn & Bacon.

Doernberg, N. L., Bernard, M. B., & Lenz, C. F. (1976). Psychoeducational treatment for parents of autistic children. In E. J. Webster (Ed.), *Professional approaches with parents of handicapped children* (pp. 65–93). Springfield, IL: Charles C. Thomas.

Donnellan, A. M. (1984). The criterion of the least dangerous assumption. *Behavioral Disorders, 9*, 141–150.

Donnellan, A. M., & Mirenda, P. (1984). Issues related to professional involvement with families of individuals with autism and other severe handicaps. *The Journal of the Association for Persons with Severe Handicaps, 9*, 16–25.

Drabman, R. S., & Patterson, J. N. (1982). Disruptive behavior and the social standing of exceptional children. In P. S. Strain (Ed.), *Social development of exceptional children*. Rockville, MD: Aspen.

Dreikurs, R., Grunwald, B., & Pepper, F. (1971). *Maintaining sanity in the classroom*. New York: Harper & Row.

Drew, C. J., & Altman, R. (1970). Effects of input organization and material difficulty on free recall. *Psychological Reports, 27*, 335–337.

Duchan, J. (1982). Foreword to communication problems of autistic children: The role of context. *Topics in Language Disorders, 3*, ix–xiv.

Duchan, J. (1983). Autistic children are noninteractive: or as we say. *Seminars in Speech and Language, 4*, 53–61.

Duchan, J., & Katz, J. (1983). Language and auditory processing: Top down plus bottom up. In E. Lasky & J. Katz (Eds.), *Central auditory processing disorders*. Baltimore: University Park Press.

Duchenne, G. B. (1883). *Selection from the clinical work of Dr. Duchenne* (p. 210)). London: New Syndenham Society.

Duff, R. S. (1981). Counseling families and deciding care of severely defective children: A way of coping with "Medical Vietnam." *Pediatrics, 67*(3) (March), 315–320.

Duffy, Y. (1981). *All things are possible*. Ann Arbor: A. J. Garvin.

Dugdale, R. L. (1910)). *The Jukes*. New York: Putnam.

Dunn, J. (1981). The reaction of first-born children to the birth of a sibling: Mothers' reports. *Journal of Child Psychology & Psychiatry, 22*, 1–18.

Dunn, L., & Markwardt, F. (1970). *The Peabody Individual Achievement Test*. Circle Pines, MN: American Guidance Service.

Durand, J., & Neufeldt, A. H. (1980). Comprehensive vocational services. In R. J. Flynn & K. E. Nitsch (Eds.), *Normalization, social integration and community services* (pp. 283–298). Baltimore: University Park Press.

Edgerton, R. (1967). *The cloak of competence*. Berkeley: University of California Press.

Education for All Handicapped Children Act, Public Law 94-142. (1975). *Federal Register*. p. 42478.

Education of the Handicapped. (1984, July 25). ED sets 1984 handicapped child count. *Education of the Handicapped*.

Edwards, D. C. (1968). *General psychology*. New York: Macmillan.

Edwards, M., & Shriberg, L. (1983). *Phonology: Applications in communicative disorders*. San Diego: College Hill Press.

Eells, K., Davis, A., Havighurst, R., Herrick, V., & Tyler, R. (1951). *Intelligence and cultural differences*. Chicago: University of Chicago Press.

Elliott, S. N., & Piersel, W. C. (1982). Direct assessment of reading skills: An approach which links assessment to intervention. *School Psychology Review, 11*, 267–280.

Ellis, A. (1985). Cognition and affect in emotional disturbance. *American Psychologist, 40*, 471–472.

Ellis, N. R., Balla, D., Estes, O., Warren, S. A., Meyers, C. E., Hollis, J., Isaacson, R. L., Palk, B. E., & Siegel, P. S. (1981). Common sense in the habilitation of mentally retarded persons: A reply to Menolascino and McGee. *Mental Retardation, 19*(5) (October), 221–226.

Emde, R. N., Katz, E. L., & Thorpe, J. K. (1978). Emotional expression in infancy: II. Early deviations in Down's syndrome. In M. Lewis & L. A. Rosenblum (Eds.), *The development of affect* (pp. 351–375). New York: Plenum Press.

Engelmann, S., & Bruner, E. (1974). *Teacher presentation book A: DISTAR reading I*. Chicago: Science Research Associates.

Erikson, E. H. (1950). *Childhood and society*. New York: W. W. Norton.

Erikson, E. H. (1982). *The life cycle completed: A review*. New York: W. W. Norton.

Erikson, K. T. (1966). *Wayward Puritans*. New York: John Wiley & Sons.

Escalona, S. (1982). Growing up with the threat of war: Some indirect effects on personality development. *American Journal of Orthopsychiatry, 52*, 600–607.

Evans, I. M., & Meyer, L. H. (1985). *An educative approach to behavior problems*. Baltimore: Paul H. Brookes.

Everard, M. (Ed.). (1976). *An approach to teaching autistic children*. New York: Pergamon Press.

Eyman, R. K., & Call, T. (1977). Maladaptive behavior and community placement of mentally retarded persons. *American Journal of Mental Deficiency, 82*, 137–144.

Fagen, S. A., Long, N. J., & Stevens, D. J. (1975). *Teaching children self-control.* Columbus, OH: Charles E. Merrill.

Farber, B. (1962). Effects of a severely mentally retarded child on the family. In E. P. Trapp & P. Himelstein (Eds.), *Readings on the exceptional child: Research and theory* (pp. 227–246). New York: Appleton-Century-Crofts.

Farber, B. (1968). *Mental retardation: Its social context and social consequences.* Boston: Houghton Mifflin.

Fay, W., & Schuler, A. (1980). *Emerging language in autistic children.* Baltimore: University Park Press.

Featherstone, H. (1981). A difference in the family. New York: Penguin.

Federal Register. (1977, December 29). Washington, DC, 65082–65085.

Ferguson, C., & Snow, C. (Eds.). (1977). *Talking to children.* New York: Cambridge University Press.

Ferguson, P., & Heifetz, L. J. (1983). An absence of offering: Parents of retarded children and their experiences with the clergy. *Pastoral Psychology, 32,* 49–57.

Ferleger, D., & Boyd, P. A. (1979). Anti-institutionalization: The promise of the Pennhurst case. *Stanford Law Review, 4*(31), 717–752.

Fernald, G. (1943). *Remedial techniques in basic school subjects.* New York: McGraw-Hill.

Fernald, W. E. (1912). The burden of feeble-mindedness. *Journal of Psycho-asthenics, 17,* 87–111.

Feuerstein, R. F. (1979). *The dynamic assessment of retarded performers: The learning potential assessment device, theory, instruments, and techniques.* Baltimore: University Park Press.

Feuerstein, R. F. (1980). *Instrumental enrichment: An intervention program for cognitive modifiability.* Baltimore: University Park Press.

Fiedler, M. L. (1975). Bidirectionality of influence in classroom interaction. *Journal of Educational Psychology, 67,* 735–744.

Fisher, A. (1978, August). *Four approaches to classification of mental retardation.* Paper presented at the meeting of the American Psychological Association, Toronto.

Fisher, M. A., & Zeaman, D. (1973). An attention-retention theory of retardate discrimination learning. *International Review of Research in Mental Retardation, 6,* 171–256.

Flavell, J. (1973). Reduction of stereotypes by reinforcement of toy play. *Mental Retardation, 11,* 21–23.

Flavell, J. E., & Cannon, P. R. (1976). Evaluation of entertainment materials for severely retarded persons. *American Journal on Mental Deficiency, 81,* 357–361.

Flavell, J. H. (1976). Metacognitive aspects of problem solving. In L. B. Resnick (Ed.), *The nature of intelligence.* Hillsdale, NJ: Lawrence Erlbaum.

Flavell, J. H. (1978). Metacognitive development. In J. M. Scandura & C. J. Brainerd (Eds.), *Structural/process theories of complex human behavior.* Alphen a.d. Rijn, The Netherlands: Sijthoff & Hoordhoff.

Flavell, J. H. (1981). Cognitive monitoring. In W. Dickson (Ed.), *Children's oral communication skills.* New York: Academic Press.

Flavell, J. H., & Wellman, H. M. (1977). Metamemory. In R. V. Kail, Jr., & J. W. Hagen (Eds.), *Perspectives on the development of memory and cognition.* Hillsdale, NJ: Lawrence Erlbaum.

Fletcher, J. (1972). Indicators of humanhood—A tentative profile of man. *Hastings Center Report, 5*(1).

Flynn, R. J., & Nitsch, K. E. (Eds.). (1980). *Normalization, social integration, and community services.* Baltimore: University Park Press.

Ford, A., Brown, L., Pumpian, I., Baumgart, D., Nisbet, J., Schroeder, J., & Loomis, R. (1984). Strategies for developing individualized recreation and leisure programs for severely handicapped students. In N. Certo, N. Haring, & R. York. *Public school integration of severely handicapped students: Rational issues and progressive alternatives* (pp. 245–276). Baltimore: Paul H. Brookes.

Ford, A., Johnson, F., Pumpian, F., Stengert, J., & Wheeler, J. (Eds.). (1980). *A longitudinal listing of chronological age appropriate and functional activities for school-aged moderately and severely handicapped students.* Madison, WI: Metropolitan School District.

Foucault, M. (1965). *Madness and civilization.* New York: Pantheon.

Fowle, M. (1968). The effect of the severely retarded child on his family. *American Journal of Mental Deficiency, 13,* 468–473.

Fraiberg, S. (1977). *Insights from the blind: Com-*

parative studies of blind and sighted infants. New York: Basic Books.

Francis-Williams, J., & Davies, P. A. (1974). Very low birth-weight and later intelligence. *Developmental Medicine and Child Neurology, 16,* 709–728.

Frankel, R. (1982). Autism for all practical purposes: An interaction view. *Topics in Language Disorders, 3,* 33–42.

Fraser, F. (1971). Etiology of cleft lip and palate. In W. Grabb et al. (Eds.), *Cleft lip and palate.* Boston: Little, Brown.

Fraser, F. (1973). Aspects of etiology and pathogenesis in clinical research in cleft lip and cleft palate. *Cleft Palate Journal, 10,* 110–119.

Freagon, S., Pajor, M., Brankin, G., Galloway, A., Rich, D., Karel, P. J., Wilson, M., Costello, D., Peters, W. M., & Hurd, D. (1982). *Teaching severely handicapped students in the community.* DeKalb: Northern Illinois University.

Fristoe, M., & Lloyd, L. (1978). A survey of the use of nonspeech systems with the severely communication impaired. *Mental Retardation, 16,* 99–103.

Fristoe, M., & Lloyd, L. (1980). Planning an initial expressive sign lexicon for persons with severe communication impairment. *Journal of Speech and Hearing Disorders, 45,* 170–180.

Fulwiler, R., & Fouts, R. (1976). Acquisition of American sign language by a noncommunicating autistic child. *Journal of Autism and Childhood Schizophrenia, 6,* 43–51.

Gagne, R. M. (1977). *Conditions of learning* (3rd ed.). New York: Holt, Rinehart, & Winston.

Gallagher, J. (1972). The special education contract for mildly handicapped children. *Exceptional Children, 38,* 527–535.

Gallagher, J. J., Beckman, P., & Cross, A. H. (1983). Families of handicapped children: Sources of stress and its amelioration. *Exceptional Children, 50,* 10–19.

Gallagher, T. (1981). Contingent query sequences with adult-child discourse. *Journal of Child Language, 8,* 51–62.

Galton, F. (1869). *Hereditary genius.* London: MacMillan.

Gardner, R. A. (1972). The mutual storytelling technique in the treatment of anger inhibition problems. *The International Journal of Child Psychiatry, 1,* 33–64.

Gardner, W. J. (1973). *The dysgraphic states from*

syringomyelia to anencephaly. Amsterdam: Excerpta Medica.

Garmezy, N. (1981). Children under stress: Perspectives on antecedents and correlates of vulnerability and resistance to psychopathology. In A. I. Rubin, J. Aronoff, A. M. Barclay, & R. A. Zucker (Eds.), *Further explorations in personality.* New York: John Wiley & Sons.

Garmezy, N. (1983). Stressors of childhood. In N. Garmezy & M. Rutter (Eds.), *Stress, coping, and development* (pp. 43–84). New York: McGraw-Hill.

Garmezy, N., & Nuechterlein, K. H. (1972). Invulnerable children: The fact and fiction of competence and disadvantage. *American Journal of Orthopsychiatry, 77,* 328–329.

Gartner, A., & Riessman, F. (1983). *The self-help revolution.* New York: Human Sciences Press.

Garvey, C. (1979). Contingent queries and their relations in discourse. In E. Ochs & B. Schieffelin (Eds.), *Developmental pragmatics* (pp. 363–372). New York: Academic Press.

Gast, M., & Nelson, M. (1977). Time-out in the classroom: Implications for special education. *Exceptional Children, 43,* 461–464.

Gaylord-Ross, R. J., & Holvoet, J. F. (1985). *Strategies for educating students with severe handicaps.* Boston: Little, Brown.

Gazzaniga, M. S. (1975). Recent research on hemispheric lateralization of the human brain: Review of the split-brain. *UCLA Educator, 17,* 9–12.

Gerber, P. J. (1977). Awareness of handicapping conditions and sociometric status in an integrated pre-school setting. *Mental Retardation, 15,* 24–25.

Gerken, K. C., Hancock, K. A., & Wade, T. H. (1978). A comparison of the Stanford-Binet Intelligence Scale and the McCarthy Scales of Children's Abilities with preschool children. *Psychology in the Schools, 15,* 468–472.

Gersuny, C., & Lefton, M. (1970). Service and servitude in the sheltered workshop. *Social Work, 15,* 74–81.

Ginsburg, H., & Opper, S. (1979). *Piaget's theory of intellectual development* (2nd ed.). Englewood Cliffs, NJ: Prentice-Hall.

Glass, R., Christiansen, J., & Christiansen, J. (1982). *Teaching exceptional students in the regular classroom.* Boston: Little, Brown.

Gleidman, J., & Roth, W. (1980). *The unexpected*

minority. New York: Harcourt Brace Jovanovich.

Goddard, H. H. (1912). *The Kallikak family: A study in the heredity of feeble-mindedness*. New York: Macmillan.

Goddard, H. H. (1915). The possibilities of research as applied to the prevention of feeble-mindedness. *Proceedings of the National Conference on Charities and Correction* (pp. 307–312).

Goffin, S. G. (1983). A framework for conceptualizing children's services. *American Journal of Orthopsychiatry, 53*, 282–290.

Goffman, E. (1961). *Asylums: Essays on the social situation of mental patients and other inmates*. Garden City, NY: Doubleday, Anchor Books.

Goffman, E. (1963). *Stigma: Notes on the management of a spoiled identity*. Boston: Prentice-Hall.

Gold, M. W. (1972). Stimulus factors in skill training of the retarded on a complex assembly task: Acquisition, transfer, and retention. *American Journal of Mental Deficiency, 76*, 517–526.

Gold, M. W. (1976). Task analysis of a complex assembly task by the retarded blind. *Exceptional Children, 43*, 78–84.

Gold, M. W. (1980). *Did I say that: Articles and commentary on the try another way system*. Champaign, IL: Research Press.

Goldberg, R. T. (1981). Toward an understanding of the rehabilitation of the disabled adolescent. *Rehabilitation Literature, 42*, 66–74.

Goldin, G., Perry, S., Margolin, R., Stotsky, B., & Foster, J. (1971). *The rehabilitation of the young epileptic*. Lexington, MA: D. C. Heath.

Goldman, R., Fristoe, M., & Woodcock, M. (1974). *Perceptual training drills*. Circle Pines, MN: American Guidance Service.

Goldstein, A. (Ed.). (1978). *Prescriptions for child mental health and education*. New York: Pergamon Press.

Goldstein, A. P., Sprafkin, R. P., Gershaw, N. J., & Klein, P. (1979). *Skillstreaming the adolescent: A structured learning approach to teaching prosocial behavior*. Champaign, IL: Research Press.

Goldstein, H., Arkell, C., Ashcroft, S., Hurley, O., & Lilly, M. (1976). Schools. In N. Hobbs (Ed.), *Issues in the classification of children* (Vol. 2). San Francisco: Jossey-Bass.

Gollay, E. (1981). Some conceptual and methodological issues in studying community adjustment of deinstitutionalized mentally retarded people. In R. Bruininks, L. Meyers, B. Sigford, & K. Lakin (Eds.), *Deinstitutionalization and community adjustment of deinstitutionalized mentally retarded people*. Washington, DC: American Association on Mental Deficiency.

Goodman, L., Budner, S., & Lesh, B. (1971). The parent's role in sex education for the retarded. *Mental Retardation, 1*, 43–45.

Gordon, S. (1974). *Sexual rights for the people . . . who happen to be handicapped*. Syracuse: Center on Human Policy.

Gordon, T. (1970). *Parent effectiveness training*. New York: Peter H. Wyden.

Gorham, K. (1975). A lost generation of parents. *Exceptional Children, 41*, 521–525.

Goslin, D. (Ed.). (1969). *Handbook of socialization theory and research*. Chicago: Rand McNally.

Gottlieb, B. H. (Ed.). (1981). *Social networks and social support*. Beverly Hills: Sage Publications.

Gottlieb, J., & Leyser, Y. (1981). Friendship between mentally retarded and nonretarded children. In S. R. Asher & J. M. Gottman (Eds.), *The development of children's friendships*. New York: Cambridge University Press.

Gould, S. J. (1981). *The Mismeasure of man*. New York: W. W. Norton.

Graden, J. L., Casey, A., & Christenson, S. L. (1985). Implementing a prereferral intervention system: Part I. The model. *Exceptional Children, 51*, 377–384.

Greenleigh Associates, Inc. (1975). *The role of sheltered workshops in the rehabilitation of the severely handicapped*. New York: Author.

Grob, G. N. (1973). *Mental institutions in America: Social policy to 1875*. New York: Free Press.

Gross, R. H., Cox, A., Tatyrek, R., Pollay, M., & Barnes, W. A. (1983). Early management and decision making for the treatment of myelomeningocele. *Pediatrics, 12*(4) (October), 450–458.

Grossman, H. J. (Ed.). (1977). *Manual on terminology and classification in mental retardation*. Washington, DC: American Association on Mental Deficiency.

Guidubaldi, J., Cleminshaw, H. K., Perry, J. D., & McLoughlin, C. S. (1983). The impact of parental divorce on children: Report of the nationwide NASP study. *School Psychology Review, 12*, 300–323.

Guilford, J. P. (1967). *The nature of human intelligence.* New York: McGraw-Hill.

Gunnison, J. A., Kaufman, A. S., & Kaufman, N. L. (1983). Interpretation, Part 3: Educational implications of the sequential-simultaneous processing dichotomy. In A. S. Kaufman & N. L. Kaufman, *Kaufman Assessment Battery for Children (K-ABC): Interpretative manual.* Circle Pines, MN: American Guidance Service.

Guthrie, J. T., & Goldberg, H. K. (1972). Visual sequential memory in reading disability. *Journal of Learning Disabilities, 5*, 41–46.

Haavik, S., & Menninger II, K. A. (1981). *Sexuality, law and the developmentally disabled person.* Baltimore: Paul H. Brookes.

Halderman et al. v. Pennhurst State School and Hospital et al. C.A. No. 74-1345 (E.D. Pa. December 23, 1977). *Mental Disability Law Reporter*, September–December, 201–216.

Hammer, S. L., Wright, L. S., & Jensen, D. L. (1967). Sex education for the retarded adolescent: A survey of parental attitudes and methods of management in fifty adolescent retardates. *Clinical Pediatrics, 6*, 621–627.

Hard, M. S. (1890). *Dedicatory address.* Newark, NY: Newark State Custodial Asylum for Feebleminded Women.

Hardy, D. R. (1984). Adoption of children with special needs: A national perspective. *American Psychologist, 39*, 901–904.

Haring, N., & Bateman, B. (1977). *Teaching the learning disabled child.* Englewood Cliffs, NJ: Prentice-Hall.

Hart, V. (1981). *Mainstreaming children with special needs.* New York: Longman.

Hauber, F. A., Bruininks, R. H., Hill, B. K., Lakin, K. C., Scheerenberger, R. C., & White, C. C. (1984). National census of residential facilities: A 1982 profile of facilities and residents. *American Journal of Mental Deficiency, 89*(3), 236–245.

Haywood, H. C., Filler, J. W., Shifman, M. A., & Chatelanat, G. (1975). Behavioral assessment in mental retardation. In P. McReynolds (Ed.), *Advances in psychological assessment* (Vol. 3). San Francisco: Jossey-Bass.

Haywood, H. C., Meyer, C. E., & Switzky, H. N. (1982). Mental retardation. *Annual Review of Psychology, 33*, 309–342.

Haywood, H. C., & Newbrough, J. R. (1981). *Living environments for developmentally disabled persons.* Baltimore: University Park Press.

Heal, L. W. (1980). Ideological responses of society to its handicapped. In A. R. Novak & L. W. Heal (Eds.), *Integration of developmentally disabled individuals into the community* (pp. 35–44). Baltimore: Paul H. Brookes.

Heal, L. W., Novak, A. R., Sigelman, C., & Switzky, H. (1980). Characteristics of community residential facilities. In A. R. Novak & L. W. Heal (Eds.), *Integration of developmentally disabled individuals into the community* (pp. 45–56). Baltimore: Paul H. Brookes.

Heifetz, L. J. (1980). From consumer to middleman: Emerging roles for parents in the network of services for retarded children. In R. R. Abidin (Ed.), *Parent education and intervention handbook* (pp. 349–384). Springfield, IL: Charles C. Thomas.

Heimlich, E. P. (1972). Paraverbal techniques in the therapy of childhood communication disorders. *The International Journal of Child Psychotherapy, 1*, 65–96.

Heisel, J. S., Ream, S., Raitz, R., Rappaport, M., & Coddington, R. D. (1973). The significance of life events as contributing factors in the diseases of children. III. A study of pediatric patients. *Journal of Pediatrics, 83*, 119–125.

Helm, D. (1981). *Conferring membership: Interacting with incompetents.* Unpublished doctoral dissertation, Boston University.

Helm, D. (1982, August 16). *Strategic contextualization: A sensemaking practice.* Paper presented at the International Sociological Association's World Congress of Sociology, Mexico City.

Herr, S. S. (1979). The new clients: Legal services for mentally retarded persons. *Stanford Law Review, 31*(4) (April), 553–611.

Hewett, F. (1968). *The emotionally disturbed child in the classroom.* Boston: Allyn & Bacon.

Hewett, F., & Taylor, F. (1980). *The emotionally disturbed child in the classroom.* Boston: Allyn & Bacon.

Hill, J., Wehman, C., Hill, M., & Goodhall, P. (1985). Differential reasons for job separation of previously employed mentally retarded workers across measured intelligence levels. In C. Wehman & J. Hill (Eds.), *Competitive employment for persons with mental retardation: From research to practice* (Vol. I) (pp. 94–110). Richmond: Rehabilitation Research and Training Center.

Hiltonsmith, R. W., & Keller, H. R. (1983). What happened to the setting in person-setting assessment? *Professional Psychology: Research and Practice, 14*, 419–434.

Hinerman, P. (1983). *Teaching autistic children to communicate*. Rockville, MD: Aspen.

Hobbs, N. (Ed.). (1975). *Issues in the classification of children. Vol II*. San Francisco: Jossey-Bass.

Hobbs, N., & Robinson, S. (1982). Adolescent development and public policy. *American Psychologist, 37*, 212–223.

Hoffman, E. (1975). The American public school and the deviant child: The origins of their involvement. *Journal of Special Education, 9*, 415–423.

Hoffman, J. L. (1965). Mental retardation, religious values and psychiatric universals. *American Journal of Psychiatry, 121*, 885–889.

Hofman, S. (1983). Plunged into the mainstream. In R. L. Jones (Ed.), *Reflections on growing up disabled* (pp. 34–41). Reston, VA: Council for Exceptional Children.

Hofmeister, A. (1982). Microcomputers in perspective. *Exceptional Children, 49*, 115–121.

Holman, A. M. (1983). *Family assessment: Tools for understanding and intervention*. Beverly Hills: Sage Publications.

Holt, J. (1964). *How children fail*. New York: Dell.

Hood-Holzman, L. (1982). The politics of autism: A socio-historical view. *Topics in Language Disorders, 3*, 64–71.

Horner, R. H., & Budd, C. M. (1983). *Teaching manual sign language to a nonverbal student: Generalization and collateral reduction of maladaptive behavior*. Unpublished manuscript, University of Oregon, Eugene.

Howe, S. G. (1976). Remarks on the causes of idiocy. In M. Rosen, G. Clark, & M. Kivitz (Eds.), *The history of mental retardation: Collected papers* (Vol. 1, pp. 31–60). Baltimore: University Park Press. (Original work published 1848).

Howlin, P. (1978). The assessment of social behavior. In M. Rutter & E. Schopler (Eds.), *Autism: A reappraisal of concepts and treatment* (pp. 63–69). New York: Plenum Press.

Hubbell, R. (1981). *Children's language disorders: An integrated approach*. Englewood Cliffs, NJ: Prentice-Hall.

Hudgens, R. W. (1974). Personal catastrophe and depression: A consideration of the subject with respect to medically ill adolescents, and a requiem for retrospective life-event studies. In B. S. Dohrenwend & B. P. Dohrenwend (Eds.), *Stressful life events: Their nature and effects*. New York: John Wiley & Sons.

Hurtig, R., Ensrud, S., & Tomblin, J. (1982). The communicative function of question production in autistic children. *Journal of Autism and Developmental Disabilities, 12*, 57–69.

Imber, S., Imber, R., & Rothstein, C. (1979). Modifying independent work habits: An effective teacher-parent, communication system. *Exceptional Children, 46*, 218–221.

Ingram, D. (1981). *Procedures for the phonological analysis of children's language*. Baltimore: University Park Press.

Inkeles, A. (1969). Social structure and socialization. In D. A. Goslin (Ed.), *Handbook of socialization theory & research* (pp. 615–632). Chicago: Rand McNally.

Intagliata, J., Willer, B., & Wicks, N. (1981). Factors related to the quality of community adjustment in family care homes. In R. H. Bruininks, C. E. Meyers, B. B. Sigford, & K. C. Lakin (Eds.), *Deinstitutionalization and community adjustment of mentally retarded people* (Monograph No. 4). Washington, DC: American Association on Mental Deficiency.

Jackson, N., Jackson, D., & Monroe, C. (1983). *Getting along with others—Teaching social effectiveness to children*. Champaign, IL: Research Press.

Jackson, P. W. (1968). *Life in classrooms*. New York: Holt, Rinehart, & Winston.

Jacob, P. A., Baikie, A. G., Court-Brown, W. M., & Strong, J. A. (1959). The somatic chromosomes in mongolism. *Lancet, 1*, 710.

Janichi, M. (1981). Personal growth and community residence environments. A review. In C. H. Haywood & J. K. Newborough (Eds.), *Living environments for developmentally disabled persons* (pp. 59–102). Baltimore: University Park Press.

Jernberg, A. (1979). *Theraplay*. San Francisco: Jossey-Bass.

Johnson, D., & Johnson, R. (1980). Integrating handicapped students into the mainstream. *Exceptional Children, 42*, 90–98.

Johnson, M. (1984, February–March). The right is the wrong group to plead our rights. *The Disability Rag*.

Johnson, W. (1961). *Stuttering and what to do about it*. Minneapolis: University of Minnesota Press.

Jones, R. (1972). Labels and stigma in special education. *Exceptional Children, 38*, 553–564.

Jones, R. L. (Ed.). (1983). *Reflections on growing up disabled*. Reston, VA: Council on Exceptional Children/ERIC Clearinghouse on Handicapped and Gifted Children.

Junkala, J. (1972). Task analysis and instructional alternatives. *Academic Therapy, 8*, 33–40.

Junkala, J. (1973). Task analysis: The processing dimension. *Academic Therapy, 8*, 401–409.

Kahan, S. E., & Cator, R. S. (1984). Creating a handicap awareness showcase. *Teaching Exceptional Children, 16*, 283–286.

Kanner, L. (1943). Autistic disturbances of affective contact. *Nervous Child, 2*, 217–250.

Kanner, L. (1949). Problems of nosology and psychodynamics of early infantile autism. *American Journal of Orthopsychiatry, 19*, 416–426.

Katz, M. B. (1983). *Poverty and policy in American history*. New York: Academic Press.

Kaufman, A. S. (1979a). *Intelligent testing with the WISC-R*. New York: John Wiley & Sons.

Kaufman, A. S. (1979b). WISC-R research: Implications for interpretation. *School Psychology Digest, 8*, 5–27.

Kaufman, A. S., & Kaufman, N. L. (1977). *Clinical evaluation of young children with the McCarthy Scales*. New York: Grune & Stratton.

Kaufman, A. S., & Kaufman, N. L. (1983). *Kaufman Assessment Battery for Children (K-ABC)*. Circle Pines, MN: American Guidance Service.

Kaufman, N. L., & Kaufman, A. S. (1974). Comparison of normal and minimally brain dysfunctional children on the McCarthy Scales of Children's Abilities. *Journal of Clinical Psychology, 30*, 69–72.

Kavale, K. (1982). Meta-analysis of the relationship between visual perceptual skills and reading achievement. *Journal of Learning Disabilities, 15*, 42–51.

Keating, R. (1979, September 17). The war against the mentally retarded. *New York*.

Kellas, G., Aschcraft, M. H., & Johnson, N. S. (1973). Rehearsal processes in short-term memory performance in mildly retarded adolescents. *American Journal of Mental Deficiency, 77*, 670–679.

Keller, H. R. (Ed.). (1980a). Behavioral assessment. *School Psychology Review, 9*(1) (Special Issue).

Keller, H. R. (1980b). Issues in the use of observational assessment. *School Psychology Review, 9*, 21–30.

Keller, H. R. (1981). Behavioral consultation. In J. C. Conoley (Ed.), *Consultation in schools: Theory, research, technology*. New York: Academic Press.

Keller, H. R. (1983). Assessment. In C. R. Smith, *Learning disabilities: The interaction of learner, task, and setting*. Boston: Little, Brown.

Kelman, H. B. (1964). The effect of a brain-damaged child on the family. In G. H. Birch (Ed.), *Brain damage in children: The biological and social aspects* (pp. 77–99). Baltimore: Williams & Wilkins.

Keogh, B. K. (1969). The Bender-Gestalt with young children: Research implications. *Journal of Special Education, 3*, 15–21.

Keogh, B. K. (1972). Psychological evaluation of exceptional children: Old hangups and new directions. *Journal of School Psychology, 10*, 141–145.

Keogh, B. K., & Hall, R. J. (1974). WISC subtest patterns of educationally handicapped and educable mentally retarded pupils *Psychology in the schools, 11*, 296–300.

Keogh, B. K., & Margolis, J. (1976). Learn to labor and to wait: Attentional problems of children with learning disorders. *Journal of Learning Disabilities, 9*, 276–286.

Keogh, B. K., & Smith, C. E. (1967). Visuo-motor ability for school prediction: A seven-year study. *Perceptual and Motor Skills, 25*, 101–110.

Kephart, N. (1971). *The slow learner in the classroom*. Columbus, OH: Charles E. Merrill.

Kinsbourne, M., & Caplan, P. (1979). *Children's learning and attention problems*. Boston: Little, Brown.

Kirby, J. R., & Das, J. P. (1977). Reading achievement, IQ, and simultaneous successive processing. *Journal of Educational Psychology, 69,* 564–570.

Kirk, S., McCarthy, J., & Kirk, W. (1968). *The Illinois Test of Psycholinguistic Abilities* (rev. ed.). Urbana: University of Illinois Press.

Kittrie, N. (1971). *The right to be different: Deviance and enforced therapy.* Baltimore: Johns Hopkins Press.

Klagsbrun, F. (1977). *Youth and suicide: Too young to die.* New York: Pocket Books.

Knight, C. J., Peterson, R. L., & McGuire, B. (1982). Cooperative learning: A new approach to an old idea. *Teaching Exceptional Children, 14,* 233–238.

Knobloch, H., & Pasamanick, B. (1974). *Gesell and Amatruda's developmental diagnosis: The evaluation and management of normal and abnormal neuropsychological development in infancy and early childhood* (3rd ed.). New York: Harper & Row.

Knoblock, P. (1982). *Teaching and mainstreaming autistic children.* Denver: Love.

Knoblock, P. (1983). *Teaching emotionally disturbed children.* Boston: Houghton Mifflin.

Knoblock, P., & Barnes, E. B. (1979). An environment for everyone: Autistic and nondisabled children learn together. In S. J. Meisels (Ed.), *Special education and development* (pp. 207–228). Baltimore: University Park Press.

Konigsmark, B. W., & Gorlin, R. J. (1976). *Genetic and metabolic deafness.* Philadelphia: W. B. Saunders.

Koppitz, E. (1970). Brain damage, reading disability and the Bender-Gestalt Test. *Journal of Learning Disabilities, 3,* 429–433.

Krasner, L. (1971). Behavior therapy. *Annual Review of Psychology, 22,* 488–532.

Kratochwill, T. R. (1982). Advances in behavioral assessment. In C. R. Reynolds & T. B. Gutkin (Eds.), *The handbook of school psychology.* New York: John Wiley & Sons.

Krug, D., Arick, J., & Almond, P. (1979). *Autism screening instrument for educational planning.* Portland, OR: ASIEP.

Kurland, L. T. (1959). The incidence and prevalence of convulsive disorders in a small urban community. *Epilepsia, 1,* 143.

Kurzweil Computer Products. (1979). Print to speech: The desk top Kurzweil reading machine for the blind. Cambridge, MA: Author.

Kwitney, J., & Landauer, J. (1979a, October 17). How a blind worker gets $1.85 an hour after 20 years on the job. *Wall Street Journal,* p. 1.

Kwitney, J., & Landauer, J. (1979b, January 24). Pay of the blind often trails minimum wage at charity workrooms. *Wall Street Journal,* p. 1.

Labov, W. (1970). The logic of non-standard English. In F. Williams (Ed.), *Language and poverty.* Chicago: Markham.

Lahey, M., & Bloom, L. (1977). Planning a first lexicon: Which words to teach first. *Journal of Speech and Hearing Disorders, 42,* 340–350.

Lakin, K. C., Hill, B. K., Hauber, F. A., & Bruininks, R. H. (1983). A response to the GAO Report, "Disparities still exist in who gets special education." *Exceptional Children, 50*(1) (September), 30–34.

Lakin, K. C. n.d. *Demographic studies of residential facilities for the mentally retarded.* Minneapolis: University of Minnesota, Department of Psychoeducational Studies.

Lambert, N., Hartsough, C., & Bower, E. (1978). *Pupil behavior rating scale.* Monterey, CA: Publishers Test Service, CTB/McGraw-Hill.

Land, S., & Vineberg, S. (1964). Locus of control in blind children. *Exceptional Children, 30,* 257–260.

Landesman-Dwyer, S. (1981). Living in the community. *American Journal of Mental Deficiency, 86*(3) (November), 223–234.

Larry P. et al. v. Wilson Riles et al. Opinion. C-71-2270 RFP (U.S. District Court, Northern District of California, 1979).

Larson, M. (1977). *The rise of professionalism: A sociological analysis.* Berkeley, CA: University of California Press.

Lasch, C. (1977). *Haven in a heartless world: The family besieged.* New York: Basic Books.

LaVigna, G. (1977). Communication training in mute autistic adolescents using the written word. *Journal of Autism and Childhood Schizophrenia, 7,* 135–149.

LaVor, M. L. (1976). Federal legislation for exceptional persons: A history. In F. J. Weintraub, A. Abeson, J. Ballard, & M. L. LaVor (Eds.), *Public policy and the education of exceptional children.* Washington, DC: Council for Exceptional Children.

Lazar, I., & Darlington, R. (1982). Lasting effects of early education: A report from the consortium for longitudinal studies. *Monographs of the Society for Research in Child Development, 47* (2–3, Serial No. 195).

Lee, L., Koenigsknecht, R., & Mulhern, S. (1975). *Interactive language development teaching.* Evanston, IL: Northwestern University Press.

Lefton, L. A., & Valvatne, L. (1983). *Mastering psychology.* Boston: Allyn & Bacon.

Leiderman, P. H. (1983). Social ecology and childbirth: The newborn nursery as environmental stressor. In N. Garmezy & M. Rutter (Eds.), *Stress, coping and development in children.* New York: McGraw-Hill.

Lejeune, J., Gautier, M., & Turpin, R. (1959). Étude des chromosomes somatiques de neuf enfants mongoliens. *Académie de Science, 248,* 1721–22.

Leske, M. (1981). Speech prevalence estimates of communicative disorders in the U.S. *ASHA, 23,* 217–225.

Less, M., Colverd, E. C., Demauro, G. E., & Young, J. (1978). *Evaluating driving potential of persons with physical disabilities.* Albertson, NY: Human Resources Center.

Lewin, K. (1951). *Field theory in social science.* New York: Harper & Row.

Lewis, M., & Brooks-Gunn, J. (1979). Toward a theory of social cognition: The development of the self. In I. Uzgiris (Ed.), *New directions in child development: Social interaction and communication during infancy.* San Francisco: Jossey-Bass.

Livi, J., & Ford, A. (1985). Skill transfer from a domestic training site to the actual homes of three moderately handicapped students. *Education and Training of the Mentally Retarded, 20,* 69–82.

Long, N., & Dufner, B. (1980). The stress cycle or the coping cycle? The impact of home and school stresses on pupils' classroom behavior. In N. Long, W. Morse, & R. Newman (Eds.), *Conflict in the classroom* (4th ed.). Belmont, CA: Wadsworth.

Lovaas, I. (1977). *The autistic child: Language development through behavior modification.* New York: John Wiley & Sons.

Lund, N., & Duchan, J. (1983). *Assessing children's language in naturalistic contexts.* Englewood Cliffs, NJ: Prentice-Hall.

Lund, R. D. (1978). *Development and plasticity of the brain.* New York: Oxford University Press.

Luria, A. R. (1966). *Higher cortical functions in man.* New York: Basic Books.

Luszcz, M. A., & Bacharach, V. P. (1975). List organization and rehearsal instructions in recognition memory of retarded adults. *American Journal of Mental Deficiency, 80,* 57–62.

Lutey, C. (1977). *Individual intelligence testing: A manual and sourcebook* (2nd ed.). Greeley, CO: Author.

MacNeil, R. (1977). Opening minds and entryways at cultural centers. *Parks and Recreation, 12,* 41–44.

Mahler, M., Pine, F., & Bregman, A. (1975). *The psychological birth of the human infant.* New York: Basic Books.

Maier, H. W. (1965). *Three theories of child development.* New York: Harper & Row.

Mandoli, M., Mandoli, P., & McLaughlin, T. (1982). Effects of same age peer tutoring on the spelling performance of a mainstreamed elementary LD student. *Learning Disabilities Quarterly, 5,* 185–189.

Mann, L., & Phillips, W. A. (1967). Fractional practices in special education: A critique. *Exceptional Children, 33,* 311–319.

Marjoribanks, K. (1979). *Families and their learning environments.* London: Routledge & Kegan Paul.

Markman, E. M. (1977). Realizing that you don't understand: A preliminary investigation. *Child Development, 48,* 986–992.

Massie, H. N. (1982). Affective development and the organization of mother-infant behavior from the perspective of psychopathology. In E. Z. Tronick (Ed.), *Social interchange in infancy: Affect, cognition, and communication.* Baltimore: University Park Press.

Massie, R., & Massie, S. (1975). *Journey.* New York: Knopf.

Maybanks, S., & Bryce, M. (1979). *Home-based services for children and families: Policy, practice, and research.* Springfield, IL: Charles C. Thomas.

McAndrew, I. (1976). Children with a handicap and their families. *Child: Care, Health and Development, 2,* 213–237.

McCall, R. B., Appelbaum, M. I., & Hogarty, P. S. (1973). Developmental changes in mental performance. *Monographs of the Society for Re-*

search in Child Development, 38 (3, Serial No. 150).

McCall, R. B., Eichorn, D. H., & Hogarty, P. S. (1977). Transitions in early mental development. *Monographs of the Society for Research in Child Development, 42* (3, Serial No. 171).

McCandless, B. R. (1969). Childhood socialization. In D. A. Goslin (Ed.), *Handbook of socialization theory and research* (pp. 791–820). Chicago: Rand McNally.

McCoy, K. (1982). *Coping with teenage depression: A parent's guide*. New York: New American Library.

McDaniel, J. W. (1976). *Physical disability and human behavior*. New York: Pergamon Press.

McDonald, E., & Schultz, A. (1973). Communication boards for cerebral palsied children. *Journal of Speech and Hearing Disorders, 38*, 73–88.

McKeever, P. (1983). Siblings of chronically ill children: A literature review with implications for research and practice. *American Journal of Orthopsychiatry, 53*, 209–218.

McKeith, R. (1973). Parental reactions and responses to a handicapped child. In F. Richardson (Ed.), *Brain and intelligence* (pp. 131–141). Hyattsville, MD: National Education Consultants.

Meadow, K. P., & Meadow, L. (1971). Changing role perceptions for parents of handicapped children. *Exceptional Children, 38*, 21–27.

Medoff, M. (1980). *Children of a lesser god*. Clifton, NJ: James T. White.

Meeker, M. N. (1969). *The structure of intellect*. Columbus, OH: Charles E. Merrill.

Meeker, M. N. (1975). WISC-R template for SOI analysis. Available from SOI Institute, 214 Main Street, El Segundo, CA.

Mehan, H. (1979). *Learning Lessons*. Boston: Harvard University Press.

Meichenbaum, D. (1977). *Cognitive-behavior modification: An integrative approach*. New York: Plenum Press.

Meichenbaum, D. H. (1975). A self-instructional approach to stress management. In C. Spielberger & I. Sarason (Eds.), *Stress and anxiety* (Vol. 2). New York: John Wiley & Sons.

Menkes, J. H. (1980). *Textbook of child neurology*. Philadelphia: Lea & Febiger.

Menolascino, F. J. (1974). Understanding parents of the retarded—a crisis model for helping them cope more effectively. In F. J. Menolascino & P. H. Pearson (Eds.), *Beyond the limits: Innovations in services for the severely and profoundly retarded* (pp. 172–209). Seattle: Special Child Publications.

Mercer, J. R. (1973). *Labeling the mentally retarded: Clinical and social system perspectives on mental retardation*. Berkeley: University of California Press.

Mercer, J. R. (1979). *Technical manual: System of Multicultural Pluralistic Assessment*. New York: Psychological Corporation.

Mercer, J. R., & Lewis, J. F. (1978). *The System of Multicultural Pluralistic Assessment*. New York: Psychological Corporation.

Mercer, J. R., & Ysseldyke, J. (1977). Designing diagnostic-intervention programs. In T. Oakland (Ed.), *Psychological and educational assessment of minority children*. New York: Brunner/Mazel.

Meyer, L. H., & Kishi, G. S. (1985). School integration strategies. In C. Lakin & R. H. Bruininks (Eds.), *Strategies for achieving community integration of developmentally disabled citizens*. Baltimore: Paul H. Brookes.

Meyers, C. E., MacMillan, D., & Yoshida, R. (1978). Validity of psychologists' identification of EMR students in the perspective of the California decertification experience. *Journal of School Psychology, 16*, 3–15.

Meyers, J., Pfeffer, J., & Erlbaum, V. (1985). Process assessment: A model for broadening assessment. *Journal of Special Education, 19*, 73–89.

Mikkelsen, M. (1982). Parental origin of the extra chromosome in Down's syndrome. *Journal of Mental Deficiency Research, 26*, 143–151.

Miller, J. (1981). *Assessing language production in children*. Baltimore: University Park Press.

Miller, J., & Yoder, D. (1972). On developing the content for a language teaching program. *Mental Retardation, 10*, 9–11.

Milton, G., & Gonzalo, R. (1974). Jaguar cult—Down's syndrome—were—jaguar. *Expedition, 16*, 33–37.

Mischel, W. (1968). *Personality and assessment*. New York: John Wiley & Sons.

Mischel, W. (1969). Continuity and change in personality. *American Psychologist, 24*, 1012–1018.

Mischel, W. (1973). Toward a cognitive social learning reconceptualization of personality. *Psychological Review, 80,* 252–283.

Mischel, W. (1979). On the interface of cognition and personality: Beyond the person-situation debate. *American Psychologist, 34,* 740–754.

Mistretta, C. M., & Bradley, R. M. (1978). Effect of early sensory experience on brain and behavioral development. In G. Gottlieb (Ed.), *Early influences.* New York: Academic Press.

Mitchell, D., Fiewell, E., & Davy, P. (1983). Spina bifida. In J. Umbreit (Ed.), *Physical disabilities and health impairments: An introduction.* Columbus, OH: Charles E. Merrill.

Moll, K. (1968). Speech characteristics of individuals with cleft lip & palate. In D. Spriestersbach & D. Sherman (Eds.), *Cleft palate and communication.* New York: Academic Press.

Molner, G. E. (1978). Analysis of motor disorder in retarded infants and young children. *American Journal of Mental Deficiency, 83,* 213–222.

Montagu, A. (1978). *Learning non-aggression: The experience of non-illiterate societies.* New York: Oxford University Press.

Montagu, A. (1979). *The elephant man.* New York: Dutton.

Mooney, T. O., Cole, T. M., & Chilgren, R. A. (1979). *Sexual options for paraplegics and quadriplegics.* Boston: Little, Brown.

Moore, T. (1975). Stress in normal childhood. In L. Levi (Ed.), *Society, stress and disease: Childhood and adolescence* (Vol. 2). London: Oxford University Press.

Moore, V. E. (1969). Occupational socialization. In D. A. Goslin (Ed.), *Handbook of socialization theory and research* (pp. 861–864). Chicago: Rand McNally.

Morgan, B. L. G., & Winick, M. (1979). A possible relationship between brain N-acetylneuraminic acid content and behavior. *Proceedings of the Society for Experimental Biology and Medicine, 161,* 534–537.

Morris, P. (1969). *Put away.* New York: Atherton.

Morrison, F. J., & Manis, F. R. (1982). Cognitive processes and reading disability: A critique and proposal. In C. J. Brainerd & M. I. Pressley (Eds.), *Progress in cognitive developmental research.* New York: Springer-Verlag.

Morse, W. C., Cutler, R. L., & Fink, A. H. (1964). *Public school classes for the emotionally handicapped: A research analysis.* Washington, DC: Council for Exceptional Children.

Morton, K. A. (1983). Parents, practices and attitudes. In R. L. Jones (Ed.), *Reflections on growing up disabled* (pp. 79–89). Reston, VA: Council on Exceptional Children/ERIC Clearinghouse on Handicapped and Gifted Children.

Mowder, B. A. (1980). A strategy for the assessment of bilingual handicapped children. *Psychology in the Schools, 17,* 7–11.

Murdoch, J. C., Ratcliffe, W., McLarty, D., Rodger, J., & Ratcliffe, J. (1976). Thyroid function in adults with Down's syndrome. *Journal of Clinical Endocrinology & Metabolism, 44,* 453–458.

Murphy, J. (1981). *Concepts of leisure.* Englewood Cliffs, NJ: Prentice-Hall.

Murphy, S. T., & Salomone, P. R. (1983). Client and counselor expectations of rehabilitation services. *Rehabilitation Counseling Bulletin, 27,* 81–94.

Murphy, S. T., & Ursprung, A. (1983). The politics of vocational evaluation. *Rehabilitation Literature, 44,* 2–12.

Murray, J. N., & Cornell, C. J. (1981). Parentalplegia. *Psychology in the Schools, 18,* 201–207.

Mussen, P., & Eisenberg-Berg, N. (1977). *Roots of caring, sharing, and helping: The development of prosocial behavior in children.* San Francisco: Freeman.

Mysak, E. (1968). *Neuroevolutional approach to cerebral palsy and speech.* New York: Teachers College Press.

Naggan, L., & MacMahon, B. (1967). Ethnic differences in prevalence of anencephaly in Boston, MA. *New England Journal of Medicine, 277,* 1119.

Nagle, R. J. (1979). The McCarthy Scales of Children's Abilities: Research implications for the assessment of young children. *School Psychology Digest, 8,* 319–326.

National Association of State Mental Retardation Program Directors, Inc. (1980). *Trends in capital expenditures for mental retardation facilities.* Arlington, VA: Author.

National Coalition of Advocates for Students. (1985). *Barriers to excellence: Our children at risk.* Boston: Author.

National Commission on Excellence in Education

(1983). *A nation at risk: The imperative for educational reform.* Washington, DC: Author.

National Society for the Prevention of Blindness. (1966). *Estimated statistics on blindness and vision problems.* New York: Author.

National Society for the Prevention of Blindness. (1977). *Estimated statistics on blindness and vision problems: Updated statistics for 1976.* New York: Author.

Nealis, J. G. T. (1983). Epilepsy. In J. Umbreit (Ed.), *Physical disabilities and health impairments: An introduction.* Columbus, OH: Charles E. Merrill.

Nebes, R. D. (1974). Hemispheric specialization in commisurotomized man. *Psychological Bulletin, 81,* 1–14.

Neisser, U. (1967). *Cognitive psychology.* New York: Appleton-Century-Crofts.

Nelson, K., & Ellenbert, J. (1977). Neuroepidemiology of chronic diseases: Cerebral Palsy Conference on Neurological Epidemiology. Georgetown University in NINCDS.

Nesbitt, J. A. (1979a). Recreation and concerns in recreation for disabled people. *American Rehabilitation, 5,* 5–9.

Nesbitt, J. A. (1979b). The 1980's: Recreation a reality for all. *Education Unlimited, 1,* 10–17.

Neulinger, J. (1981). *To leisure: An introduction.* New York: Allyn & Bacon.

New York State Council on Children and Families. (1983). *Cooperative strategies for solving the problems of latchkey children.* Albany: Author.

Newark State Custodial Asylum for Feebleminded Women. (1893). *Dedication services.* Newark, NY: Burgess Printers.

Newberger, C. M., & Cook, S. J. (1983). Parental awareness and child abuse: A cognitive-developmental analysis of urban and rural samples. *American Journal of Orthopsychiatry, 53,* 512–524.

Newcomer, B., & Morrison, T. (1974). Play therapy with institutionalized mentally retarded children. *American Journal of Mental Deficiency, 78,* 727–733.

Newhoff, M., Silverman, L., & Millet, A. (1980). Linguistic differences in parent's speech to normal and language disordered children. In *Proceedings of the First Annual Wisconsin Symposium on Research in Child Language Disorders.* Madison: Department of Communicative Disorders.

Newland, T. E. (1971). Psychological assessment of exceptional children and youth. In W. Cruickshank (Ed.), *Psychology of exceptional children and youth.* Englewood Cliffs, NJ: Prentice-Hall.

Nickerson, E. T., & O'Laughlin, K. (1982). *Helping through action: Action-oriented therapies.* Amherst, MA: Human Resource Development Press.

Nirge, B. (1969). The normalization principle. In R. Kugel & A. Shearer (Eds.), *Changing patterns in residential services for the mentally retarded.* Washington, DC: President's Committee on Mental Retardation.

Nisbet, J., Shiraga, B., Ford, A., Sweet, M., Kessler, K., & Loomis, R. (1982). Planning and implementing the transitions of severely handicapped students from school to post school environments. In L. Brown, J. Nisbet, A. Ford, M. Sweet, B. Shiraga, & L. Gruenewald. *Educational programs for severely handicapped students. Vol. XII* (pp. 185–213). Madison, WI: Madison Metropolitan School District.

Northern, J. L. (Ed.). (1980). *Seminars in speech, language, hearing.* New York: Thieme-Stratton.

Novaco, R. (1978). Anger and coping with stress. In J. Foreyt & D. Rathjen (Eds.), *Cognitive behavior therapy, theory, research and procedures.* New York: Plenum Press.

Novak, A., & Heal, L. (Eds.) (1980). *Integration of developmentally disabled individuals into the community.* Baltimore: Paul H. Brookes.

Oakland, T. (Ed.). (1977). *Psychological and educational assessment of minority children.* New York: Brunner & Mazel.

Oakland, T. (1980). An evaluation of the ABIC, pluralistic norms, and estimated learning potential. *Journal of School Psychology, 18,* 3–11.

Oakland, T., & Laosa, L. M. (1977). Professional, legislative, and judicial influences on psychoeducational assessment practices in schools. In T. Oakland (Ed.), *Psychological and educational assessment of minority children.* New York: Brunner & Mazel.

O'Leary, K., & O'Leary, S. (1972). *Classroom management: The successful use of behavior modification.* New York: Pergamon Press.

Olshansky, S. (1961). Chronic sorrow: A response to having a mentally defective child. *Social Casework, 43,* 190–193.

Omizo, M., Radner, S., & McPherson, R. (1983). Modeling: An effective teaching strategy, *Academic Therapy, 13*, 365–368.

Orelove, F., Wehman, P., & Wood, J. (1982). An evaluative review of Special Olympics: Implications for community integration. *Education and Training of the Mentally Retarded, 17,* 325–329.

Ornitz, E., & Ritvo, E. (1968). Perceptual inconstancy in early infantile autism. *Archives of General Psychiatry, 18*, 79–98.

Ornstein, R. (1972). *The psychology of consciousness.* San Francisco: Freeman.

Ornstein, R. (1973). *The nature of human consciousness.* San Francisco: Freeman.

Ornstein, R. (1978, May). The split and the whole brain. *Human Nature, 1*, 76–83.

Orton, S. T. (1937). *Reading, writing and speech problems in children.* New York: W. W. Norton.

Oxman, J., Webster, D. C., & Konstantareas, M. M. (1978). Condon's multiple response phenomenon in severely dysfunctional children: An attempt at replication. *Journal of Autism and Childhood Schizophrenia, 8*, 395–402.

Paivio, A. (1975). Imagery and synchronic thinking. *Canadian Psychological Review, 16*, 147–163.

Paivio, A. (1976). Concerning dual-coding and simultaneous-successive processing. *Canadian Psychological Review, 17*, 69–71.

Pany, D., Jenkins, J., & Schreck, J. (1982). Vocabulary instruction: Effects on word knowledge and reading comprehension. *Learning Disabilities Quarterly, 5*, 202–215.

Paradise, J. L. (1981). Otitis media during early life: How hazardous to development? A critical review of the evidence. *Pediatrics, 68*, 869–873.

Paris, S. G., & Haywood, H. C. (1973). Mental retardation as a learning disorder. *The Pediatric Clinics of North America, 20*, 641–651.

Park, C. C. (1982). *The siege: The first eight years of an autistic child* (2nd ed.). Boston: Atlantic–Little, Brown.

Parkes, C. M., & Stevenson-Hinde, J. (Eds.). (1982). *The place of attachment in human behavior.* New York: Basic Books.

Partlow Review Committee. (1978, October 18). Memorandum. Wyatt v. Hardin.

Patterson, L. L. (1956). Some pointers for professionals. *Children, 3*, 13–17.

Paul, J. L. (1977). Mainstreaming emotionally disturbed children. In A. J. Pappanikou & J. L. Paul (Eds.), *Mainstreaming emotionally disturbed children* (pp. 1–17). Syracuse: Syracuse University Press.

Pear, R. (1984, August 20). Reagan has achieved many goals, but some stir opposition. *The New York Times*, p. A18.

Pennington, B. F., & Smith, S. D. (1983). Genetic influences on learning disabilities and speech and language disorders. *Child Development, 54*, 369–387.

Perlstein, M. (1949). Medical aspects of cerebral palsy. *Nervous Child, 8*, 125–151.

Perrucci, R. (1974). *Circle of madness.* Englewood Cliffs, NJ: Prentice-Hall.

Perske, R. (1979). *Mental retardation: The leading edge, services that work.* Washington, DC: U.S. Government Printing Office.

Perske, R. (1980). *New life in the neighborhood.* Nashville: Abingdon.

Phillips, B. L., Pasework, R. A., & Tindall, R. C. (1978). Relationship among McCarthy Scales of Children's Abilities, WPPSI, and Columbia Mental Maturity Scale. *Psychology in the Schools, 15*, 352–356.

Phillips, J. L. (1969). *The origins of intellect: Piaget's theory.* San Francisco: W. H. Freeman.

Piaget, J., & Inhelder, B. (1969). *The psychology of the child.* New York: Basic Books.

Pieper, E. (n.d.). *Sticks and stones.* Syracuse: Human Policy Press.

Pines, M. (1973). *The brain changers.* New York: Harcourt, Brace & Jovanovich.

Pinkerton, P. (1970). Parental acceptance of a handicapped child. *Developmental Medicine and Child Neurology, 12*, 207–212.

Platt, A. M. (1969). *The child savers.* Chicago: University of Chicago Press.

Pomerantz, D. J., & Margolin, D. (1980). Vocational habilitation: A time for change. In R. J. Flynn & K. E. Nitsch (Eds.), *Normalization, social integration, and community services* (pp. 259–282). Baltimore: University Park Press.

Pomeroy, J. (1983). Community recreation for persons with disabilities. In E. L. Pan, T. E. Backer, & C. L. Vash (Eds.), *Annual review of rehabilitation* (pp. 268–291). New York: Springer.

Poorman, C. (1980). Mainstreaming in reverse with a special friend. *Teaching Exceptional Children, 12*, 136–142.

Prather, E., Hendrick, D., & Kern, L. (1975). Articulation development in children aged 2 to 4 years. *Journal of Speech and Hearing Disorders, 40*, 179–191.

Prechtel, H. (1963). The mother-child interaction in babies with minimal brain damage. In B. M. Fuss (Ed.), *Determinants of infant behavior* (Vol. 2). New York: John Wiley & Sons.

President's Committee on Mental Retardation. (1970). The six hour retarded child. Washington, DC: U.S. Government Printing Office.

Price, M., & Goodman, L. (1980). Individualized education programs: A cost study. *Exceptional Children, 46*, 446–454.

Prizant, B. (1983). Language acquisition and communicative behavior in autism: Toward an understanding of the "whole" of it. *Journal of Speech and Hearing Disorders, 48*, 296–307.

Prizant, B., & Duchan, J. (1981). The functions of immediate echolalia in autistic children. *Journal of Speech and Hearing Disorders, 46*, 241–249.

Public Law 94-142, The Education for All Handicapped Children Act. (1975). 20, U.S.C., 1412.

Pueschel, S. M., & Rynders, J. E. (1982). *Down syndrome: Advances in biomedicine and the behavioral sciences.* Cambridge, MA: Ware Press.

Purvis, J., & Sammet, S. (1976). *Music in developmental therapy.* Baltimore: University Park Press.

Putnam, J., Weider, J., & Schleien, S. (1985). Leisure and recreation services for handicapped persons. In K. Lakin & R. Bruininks (Eds.), *Strategies for achieving community integration of developmentally disabled citizens* (pp. 253–276). Baltimore: Paul H. Brookes.

Quay, H., & Peterson, D. (1967). *Behavior problem checklist.* Urbana: University of Illinois, Children's Research Center.

Rafferty, M. (1981, October 19). Special education carried too far. *Syracuse Post-Standard*, p. A-4.

Rand, Y., Tannenbaum, A. J., & Feuerstein, R. (1979). Effects of instrumental enrichment on the psychoeducational development of low-functioning adolescents. *Journal of Educational Psychology, 71*, 751–763.

Ratner, N., & Bruner, J. (1978). Game social exchange and the acquisition of language. *Journal of Child Language, 5*, 391–402.

Ravitch, D. (1983). *The troubled crusade: American education 1945–1980.* New York: Basic Books.

Redl, F., & Wineman, D. (1951). *Children who hate: The disorganization and breakdown of behavior controls.* New York: Free Press.

Redl, F., & Wineman, D. (1952). *Controls from within: Techniques for treatment of the aggressive child.* New York: Free Press.

Reid, D. H., Willis, B. S., Jarman, P. H. & Brown, R. M. (1978). Increasing leisure activity of physically disabled retarded persons through modifying resource availability. *AAESPH Review, 3,* pp. 79–93.

Report of the Ad Hoc Committee to Define Deaf and Hard of Hearing. (1975). *American Annals of the Deaf, 120*, 209.

Reschly, D. (1978, May). *Comparison of bias in assessment with conventional and pluralistic measures.* Paper presented at meeting of the Council for Exceptional Children. ERIC ED 153–386.

Reschly, D. J. (1979). Nonbiased assessment. In G. D. Phye & D. J. Reschly (Eds.), *School psychology: Perspectives and issues.* New York: Academic Press.

Reschly, D. J. (1982). Assessing mild mental retardation: The influence of adaptive behavior, sociocultural status, and prospects for nonbiased assessment. In C. R. Reynolds & T. B. Gutkin (Eds.), *The handbook of school psychology.* New York: John Wiley & Sons.

Resnick, L. B., Wang, M. C., & Kaplan, J. (1973). Task analysis in curriculum design: A hierarchically sequenced introductory mathematics curriculum. *Journal of Applied Behavior Analysis, 6*, 679–710.

Richer, J., & Richards, B. (1975). Reacting to autistic children: The danger of trying too hard. *British Journal of Psychiatry, 127*, 526–529.

Ringness, T. A. (1975). *The affective domain in education.* Boston: Little, Brown.

Rist, R. C. (1970). Student social class and teacher expectations: The self-fulfilling prophecy in ghetto education. *Harvard Educational Review, 40*, 411–451.

Ritvo, E. R., & Freeman, B. J. (1978). National Society for Autistic Children definition of autism. *Journal of Autism & Developmental Disabilities, 8*, 162–167.

Rivera, G. (1972). *Willowbrook: A report on how it is and why it doesn't have to be that way.* New York: Vintage.

Robinson, H. B., Robinson, N. (1970). Mental retardation. In P. H. Mussen (Ed.), *Carmichael's manual of child psychology* (Vol. 2, 3rd ed.). New York: John Wiley & Sons.

Roesel, R., & Lawlis, G. F. (1983). Divorce in families of genetically handicapped/mentally retarded individuals. *American Journal of Family Therapy, 11*, 45–50.

Rogers, C. (1969). *Freedom to learn*. Columbus, OH: Charles E. Merrill.

Rogers, C. R. (1983). *Freedom to learn for the 80's*. Columbus, OH: Charles E. Merrill.

Rose, M., Cundick, B., & Higbee, K. (1983). Verbal rehearsal and visual imagery: Mnemonic aids for learning disabled children. *Journal of Learning Disabilities, 16*, 352–354.

Rosenblatt, R. (1983). *Children of war*. New York: Doubleday.

Rosenfield, S. (1983). Assessment of the gifted child. In T. R. Kratochwill (Eds.), *Advances in school psychology* (Vol. 3) Hillsdale, NJ: Lawrence Erlbaum.

Rosenhan, D. (1973). On being sane in insane places. *Science 179*, 250–258.

Rosenshine, B. (1983). Teaching functions in instructional programs. *Elementary School Journal, 83*, 335–351.

Rosenshine, B., & Stevens, R. (1986). Teaching functions. In M. Whitrock (Ed.), *Handbook of research on teaching, 3rd edition*. New York: Macmillan.

Rosenthal, R., & Jakobson, L. (1968). *Pygmalian in the classroom*. New York: Holt, Rinehart.

Rosenzweig, M. R., & Bennett, E. L. (1978). Experiential influences on brain anatomy and brain chemistry in rodents. In G. Gottlieb (Ed.), *Early influences*. New York: Academic Press.

Ross, M., & Calvert, D. (1974). The semantics of deafness. In W. Northcott (Ed.), *The learning impaired child in the regular classroom*. Washington, DC: A. G. Bell Association for the Deaf.

Roth, W. (1982). *The handicapped speak*. Jefferson, NC: McFarland.

Rothman, D. J. (1971). *The discovery of the asylum: Social order and disorder in the new republic*. Boston: Little, Brown.

Rothman, D. J. (1980). *Conscience and convenience: The asylum and its alternatives in progressive America*. Boston: Little, Brown.

Rothman, D. J., & Rothman, S. M. (1984). *The Willowbrook wars*. New York: Harper & Row.

Rubin, R. A., & Balow, B. (1977). Perinatal influences on the behavior and learning problems of children. In B. B. Lahey & A. E. Kazdin (Eds.), *Advances in clinical child psychology* (Vol. 1). New York: Plenum Press.

Rugel, R. P. (1974). WISC subtest scores of disabled readers: A review with respect to Bannatyne's recategorization. *Journal of Learning Disabilities, 7*, 48–55.

Rutter, M. (1981). *Maternal deprivation reassessed* (2nd ed.). Harmondsworth, England: Penguin.

Rutter, M., Cox, A., Tupling, C., Berger, M., & Yule, W. (1975). Attainment and adjustment in two geographical areas: I. The prevalence of psychiatric disorder. *British Journal of Psychiatry, 126*, 493–509.

Rutter, M., Maughan, B., Mortimore, P., Ouston, J., & Smith, A. (1979). *Fifteen thousand hours: Secondary schools and their effects on children*. Cambridge, MA: Harvard University Press.

Ryan, W. (1972). *Blaming the victim*. New York: Vintage.

Rynders, J. E., Spiker, D., & Horrobin, J. M. (1978). Underestimating the educability of Down's syndrome children: Examination of methodological problems in recent literature. *American Journal of Mental Deficiency, 82*(5), 440–448.

Sailor, W., Wilcox, B., & Brown, L. (Eds.). (1980). *Methods of instruction for severely handicapped students*. Baltimore: Paul H. Brookes.

Salisbury, C., & Griggs, P. A. (1983). Developing respite care services for families of handicapped persons. *Journal of the Association for the Severely Handicapped, 8*, 50–57.

Salvia, J., & Ysseldyke, J. E. (1978). *Assessment in special and remedial education*. Boston: Houghton Mifflin.

Samuels, S. J., & Anderson, R. H. (1973). Visual recognition memory, paired-associate learning and reading achievement. *Journal of Educational Psychology, 65*, 160–167.

Santiestevan, H. (1979). *Out of their beds and into the streets*. Washington, DC: American Federation of State, County, and Municipal Employees.

Sarason, S. B., & Doris, J. (1959). *Psychological problems in mental deficiency*. New York: Harper & Row.

Sarason, S. B., & Doris, J. (1979). *Educational handicap, public policy and social history*. New York: Free Press.

Sataline, S. (1984, August 15). Beating lead poisoning: Painful cures that may not last. *Syracuse Post-Standard*, p. B1.

Sattler, J. M. (1982). *Assessment of children's intelligence and special abilities* (2nd ed.). Boston: Allyn & Bacon.

Scarr-Salapatek, S. (1975). Genetics and the development of intelligence. In F. D. Horowitz (Ed.), *Review of child development research* (Vol. 4). Chicago: University of Chicago Press.

Scheerenberger, R. C. (1983). *A history of mental retardation*. Baltimore: Paul H. Brookes.

Scheerenberger, R. C., & Felsenthal, D. (1977). Community settings for mentally retarded persons: Satisfaction and activities. *Mental Retardation, 15*, 3–7.

Schleien, S., Kiernan, J., & Wehman, P. (1981). Evaluation of an age appropriate leisure skills program for moderately retarded adults. *Education and Training of the Mentally Retarded, 16*, 13–19.

Schneider, W., & Shiffrin, R. M. (1977). Controlled and automatic human information processing: I. Detection, search, and attention. *Psychological Review, 84*, 1–66.

Schuler, A., & Baldwin, M. (1981). Nonspeech communication and childhood autism. *Language Speech and Hearing Services in the Schools, 12*, 246–257.

Schultz, E. W., & Heuchert, C. M. (1983). *Child stress and the school experience*. New York: Human Sciences Press.

Schutz, R. P., Vogelsberg, R. T., & Rusch, F. R. (1980). A behavioral approach to integrating individuals into the community. In A. R. Novak & L. Heal (Eds.), *Integration of developmentally disabled individuals into the community*. Baltimore: Paul H. Brookes.

Schwartz, M., Duara, R., Haxby, J., Grady, C., White, B. J., Kessler, R. M., Day, A. D., Cutler, N. R., & Rapoport, S. I. (1983). Down's syndrome in adults: Brain metabolism. *Science, 221*, 781–783.

Scott, R. (1967). The factory as a social service organization: Goal displacement in workshops for the blind. *Social Problems, 15*, 160–175.

Scott, R. A. (1969). *The making of blind men*. New York: Russell Sage.

Scull, A. (1981). A new trade in lunacy: The recommodification of the mental patient. *American Behavioral Scientist, 24*(6) (July/August), 741–754.

Seligman, M. E. P. (1975). *Helplessness: On depression, development, and death*. New York: W. H. Freeman.

Selye, H. (1956). *The stress of life*. New York: McGraw-Hill.

Selye, H. (1978). *The stress of life* (rev. ed.). New York: McGraw-Hill.

Senf, G. M. (1981). Issues surrounding diagnosis of learning disabilities: Child handicap versus failure of child-school interaction. In T. R. Kratochwill (Ed.), *Advances in school psychology* (Vol. I). Hillsdale, NJ: Lawrence Erlbaum.

Senf, G. M., & Freundl, P. C. (1971). Memory and attention factors in specific learning disabilities. *Journal of Learning Disabilities, 4*, 94–106.

Sewell, T. E. (1979). Intelligence and learning tasks as predictors of scholastic achievement in black and white first-grade children. *Journal of School Psychology, 17*, 325–332.

Sewell, T. E. (1981). Shaping the future of school psychology: Another perspective. *School Psychology Review, 10*, 232–242.

Shane, H., & Bashir, A. (1980). Election criteria for determining candidacy for an augmentative communication system: Preliminary considerations. *Journal of Speech and Hearing Disorders, 45*, 408–414.

Shatz, M., & Gelman, R. (1973). The development of communication skills: Modifications in the speech of young children as a function of the listener. *Monograph of the Society for Research in Child Development, 38*.

Shepard, W. O. (1970). Intelligence: Development and correlates. In H. W. Reese & L. P. Lipsitt (Eds.), *Experimental child psychology*. New York: Academic Press.

Shiffrin, R. M., & Schnieder, W. (1977). Controlled and automatic human information processing: II. Perceptual learning, automatic attending, and a general theory. *Psychological Bulletin, 84*, 127–190.

Shinn, M. (1978). Father absence and children's cognitive development. *Psychological Bulletin, 85*, 295–324.

Shipe, D., Vandenberg, S., & Williams, R. D. B. (1968). Neonatal Apgar ratings as related to intelligence and behavior in preschool children. *Child Development, 39*, 861–866.

Shotel, J. R., Iano, R. P., & McGettigan, J. F. (1972). Teachers' attitudes associated with integration of handicapped children. *Exceptional Children, 38*, 677–684.

Shprintzen, J., McCall, G., & Skolnick, M. (1975). A new therapeutic technique for the treatment of velopharyngeal incompetence. *Journal of Speech and Hearing Disorders, 40*, 69–83.

Shuell, T. J., & Keppel, G. (1970). Learning ability and retention. *Journal of Educational Psychology, 61*, 59–65.

Siegel, G. (1983). Intervention context and setting: Where? In Miller, J., Yoder, D., & Schiefelbusch, R. (Eds.), *Contemporary issues in language intervention* (pp. 253–258). Rockville, MD: American Speech, Language and Hearing Association.

Sigelman, C., Bell, N., Schoenrock, C., Elias, S., & Dauber-Braun, P. (1978). Alternative community placements and outcomes. Paper presented at the Annual Meeting of the American Association on Mental Deficiency, Denver, CO.

Sigelman, C. K., Novak, A. R., Heal, L. W., & Switzky, H. (1980). Factors that affect the success of community placements. In A. R. Novak & L. W. Heal (Eds.), *Integration of developmentally disabled individuals into the community* (pp. 57–74). Baltimore: Paul H. Brookes.

Silverman, C. (1982). Reaching autistic children: A clinical note. *Topics in Language Disorder, 3*, 58–63.

Simon, W., & Gagnon, J. H. (1969). On psychosexual development. In D. A. Goslin (Ed.), *Handbook of socialization theory and research* (pp. 733–753). Chicago: Rand McNally.

Singer, S. (1978). *Human genetics: An introduction to the principles of heredity*. San Francisco: Freeman.

Sizer, T. R. (1984). *Horace's compromise: The dilemma of the American high school*. Boston: Houghton Mifflin.

Skinner, B. F. (1957). *Verbal behavior*. New York: Appleton-Century-Crofts.

Slavin, R., Madden, N., & Leavey, M. (1984). Effects of cooperative learning and individualized instruction on mainstreamed students. *Exceptional Children, 50*, 434–443.

Sloane, H., & McCauley, B. (Eds.). (1968). *Operant procedures in remedial speech and language training*. Boston: Houghton Mifflin.

Smith, C. R. (1980). Assessment alternatives: Nonstandardized procedures. *School Psychology Review, 9*, 46–57.

Smith, C. R. (1983). *Learning disabilities: The interaction of learner, task, and setting*. Boston: Little, Brown.

Smith, M. B. (1983). Hope and despair: Keys to the socio-psychodynamics of youth. *American Journal of Orthopsychiatry, 53*, 388–399.

Smith, M. D., Coleman, J. M., Dokecki, P. R., & Davis, E. E. (1977a). Intellectual characteristics of school labeled learning disabled children. *Exceptional Children, 43*, 352–357.

Smith, M. D., Coleman, J. M., Dokecki, P. R., & Davis, E. E. (1977b). Recategorized WISC-R scores of learning disabled children. *Journal of Learning Disabilities, 10*, 444–449.

Smithels, R. W., Sheppard, S., Schorah, C. J., Sellar, M. J., Nevin, N. C., Harris, R., Read, A. P., & Fielding, D. W. (1980). Possible prevention of neural tube defects by preconceptual vitamin supplements. *Lancet, 1*, 339–340.

Snow, R. E. (1978). Theory and method for research on aptitude processes. *Intelligence, 2*, 225–278.

Solnit, A. J., & Stark, M. H. (1961). Mourning and the birth of a defective child. *Psychoanalytic Study of the Child, 16*, 523–537.

Sontag, E., Smith, J., & Centor, N. (Eds.). (1977). *Educational programming for the severely and profoundly handicapped*. Reston, VA: Council for Exceptional Children.

Sorce, J. F., Emde, R. N., & Frank, M. (1982). Maternal referencing in normal and Down's syndrome infants. In R. N. Emde & R. J. Harmon (Eds.), *The development of attachment and affiliative systems* (pp. 281–292). New York: Plenum Press.

Sourkes, B. M. (1982). *The deepening shade: Psychological aspects of life-threatening illness*. Pittsburgh: University of Pittsburgh Press.

Spencer, H. (1851). *Social statistics*. London: John Chapman.

Spiro, R., Bruce, B., Brewer, W. (Eds.). (1980). *Theoretical issues in reading comprehension*. Hillsdale, NJ: Lawrence Erlbaum.

Spitz, R. A. (1950). Anxiety in infancy: A study of its manifestations in the first year of life. *International Journal of Psychoanalysis, 31*, 138–143.

Spivack, G., Spotts, J., & Haimes, T. (1967). *Devereaux adolescent behavior rating scale*. Devon, PA: Devereaux Foundation Press.

Sroufe, L. A. (1979). The coherence of individual

development. *American Psychologist, 34,* 834–841.

Stanhope, L., & Bell, R. Q. (1981). Parents and families. In J. M. Kauffman & D. R. Hallahan (Eds.), *Handbook of special education* (pp. 688–713). Englewood Cliffs, NJ: Prentice-Hall.

Stark, J., & Wallach, G. (1982). The path to a concept of language learning disabilities. In K. Butler and G. Wallach (Eds.), *Language disorders and learning disabilities.* Rockville, MD: Aspen Systems.

Starr, R. (1982, January). Wheels of misfortune: Sometimes equality just costs too much. *Harper's,* pp. 7–15.

Sternberg, L., & Adams, G. (1982). *Educating severely and profoundly handicapped students.* Rockville, MD: Aspen Systems.

Sternberg, R. J. (1981). Testing and cognitive psychology. *American Psychologist, 36,* 1181–1189.

Sternberg, R. J., & Detterman, D. K. (Eds.). (1979). *Human intelligence: Perspectives on its theory and measurement.* Norwood, NJ: Ablex.

Stith, C. (1984). Increasing skill transference for the moderately and severely handicapped. *Teaching Exceptional Children, 17,* 63–66.

Stockwell, E. G. (1968). *Population and people.* Chicago: Quadrangle.

Stone, N. W., & Chesney, B. (1979). Attachment behaviors in handicapped infants. *Mental Retardation, 16,* 8–12.

Stout, G. (1979). Some aspects of high performance indoor/outdoor wheelchairs. *Bulletin of Prosthetic Research, 32,* 137–175.

Strain, P., Cook, T., & Appolloni, T. (1976). *Teaching exceptional children: Assessment and modification of social behavior.* New York: Academic Press.

Strain, P. S., Kerr, M. M., & Ragland, E. U. (1979). Effects of peer-mediated social initiations and prompting/reinforcement procedures on the social behavior of autistic children. *Journal of Autism and Developmental Disabilities, 9,* 41–54.

Strauss, A. A., & Lehtinen, L. E. (1947). *Psychopathology and education of the brain-injured child.* New York: Grune & Stratton.

Strickland, C. A. (1954). Two mongols of unusually high mental status. *British Journal of Medical Psychology, 27,* 80.

Sussman, M. (Ed.). (1969). *Sociology and rehabilitation.* Washington, DC: American Sociological Association.

Swart, R. (1979). A secondary-school resource room makes mainstreaming work. *Teaching Exceptional Children, 11,* 77–79.

Sweet, M., Shiraga, B., Ford, A., Nisbet, J., Graff, S., & Loomis, R. (1982). Vocational training: Are ecological strategies applicable for severely multihandicapped students? In L. Brown, J. Nisbet, A. Ford, M. Sweet, B. Shiraga, & L. Gruenewald, *Educational programs for severely handicapped students, Vol. XII* (pp. 99–131). Madison, WI: Madison Metropolitan School District.

Szasz, T. S. (1970). *The manufacture of madness.* New York: Dell.

Takanishi, R., & Spitzer, S. (1980). Children's perceptions of human resources in team-teaching classrooms: A cross-sectional developmental study. *The Elementary School Journal, 80,* 203–212.

Talley, R. C. (1979). Evaluating the effects of implementing the System of Multicultural Pluralistic Assessment: A qualitative perspective. *School Psychology Digest, 8,* 71–78.

Tallman, I. (1965). Spousal role differentiation and the socialization of severely retarded children. *Journal of Marriage and the Family, 27,* 37–42.

Tarnopol, L. (1969). Testing children with learning disabilities. In L. Tarnopol (Ed.), *Learning disabilities: Introduction to educational and medical management.* Springfield, IL: Charles C. Thomas.

Tarver, S. G., & Hallahan, D. P. (1974). Attention deficits in children with learning disabilities: A review. *Journal of Learning Disabilities, 7,* 560–569.

Task Force on Children Out of School. (1970). *The way we go to school: The exclusion of children in Boston.* Boston: Beacon Press.

Taylor, S. J. (1982). From segregation to integration: Strategies for integrating severely handicapped students in normal school and community settings. *The Journal of the Association for the Severely Handicapped, 8*(3) (Fall), 42–49.

Taylor, S., Brown, K., McCord, W., Giambetti, A., Searl, S., Mlinarcik, S., Atkinson, T., & Lichter,

S. (1981). *Title XIX and deinstitutionalization: The issue for the 80's.* Syracuse: Center on Human Policy.

Templin, M. (1957). *Certain language skills in children.* Minneapolis: University of Minnesota Press.

Ten Broek, J. (1966). Sheltered workshops for the physically disabled. *Journal of Urban Law, 45,* 39–70.

Terman, L. M. (1916). *The measurement of intelligence.* Boston: Houghton Mifflin.

Terman, L. M. (1921). A symposium. Intelligence and its measurement. *Journal of Educational Psychology, 12,* 127–133.

Terman, L., & Merrill, M. (1960). *Stanford-Binet Intelligence Scale.* Boston: Houghton Mifflin.

Thomas, A., & Chess, S. (1977). *Temperament and development.* New York: Brunner & Mazel.

Thomas, D. (1978). *The social psychology of childhood disability.* London: Methuen.

Thomas, D. (1980). *The social psychology of childhood disability.* New York: Schocken.

Thomason, J., & Arkell, C. (1980). Educating the severely/profoundly handicapped in the public schools: A side-by-side approach. *Exceptional Children, 47*(2) (October), 114–122.

Thompson, J. S. (1979). *Genetics in medicine.* Philadelphia: W. B. Saunders.

Thompson, R. J., & O'Quinn, A. N. (1979). *Developmental disabilities.* New York: Oxford University Press.

Thorn-Gray, B. E., & Kern, L. H. (1983). Sexual dysfunction associated with physical disability: A treatment guide for the rehabilitation practitioner. *Rehabilitation Literature, 44,* 138–144.

Thorne, J. M. (1979). Deinstitutionalization: Too wide a swath. *Mental Retardation, 17,* 171–175.

Tjossem, T. D., Hansen, T. J., & Ripley, H. S. (1962). An investigation of reading difficulty in young children. *American Journal of Psychiatry, 118,* 1104–1113.

Tomlinson, S. (1982). *A sociology of special education.* Boston: Routledge & Kegan Paul.

Torgesen, J., & Goldman, T. (1977). Verbal rehearsal and short-term memory in reading disabled children. *Child Development, 48,* 56–60.

Tough, J. (1979). *Talk for teaching and learning.* London: Ward Lock Educational Press.

Tucker, J. A. (1977). Operationalizing the diagnostic-intervention process. In T. Oakland (Ed.), *Psychological and educational assessment of minority children.* New York: Brunner & Mazel.

Turnbull, A. P. (1974). Teaching retarded persons to rehearse through cumulative overt labelling. *American Journal of Mental Deficiency, 79,* 331–337.

Turnbull, H. R., & Turnbull, A. (1980). *Parents speak out.* Columbus, OH: Charles E. Merrill.

Turnure, J. E., & Thurlow, J. L. (1975). The effects of structural variations in elaborations on learning by EMR and nonretarded children. *American Journal of Mental Deficiency, 79,* 632–639.

Ulrey, G. (1981). Emotional development of the young handicapped child. In N. J. Anastasiow (Ed.), *New directions for exceptional children: Socioemotional development* (pp. 33–51). San Francisco: Jossey-Bass.

U.S. Comptroller General. (1977, January 7). *Report to Congress: Returning the mentally disabled to the community: Government needs to do more.* Washington, DC: GAO.

U.S. Department of Education, National Center for Education Statistics. (1980). *The condition of education* (Table 2.7). Washington, DC: U.S. Government Printing Office.

U.S. Department of Health, Education, & Welfare. (1975). *Estimated number of handicapped children in the United States, 1974–75.* Washington, DC: U.S. Office of Education.

U.S. Department of Labor. (1977). *Sheltered workshop study, Vol. I: A nationwide report on sheltered workshops and their employment of handicapped individuals.* Washington, DC: Author.

U.S. Department of Labor. (1979). *Sheltered workshop study, Vol. II: Study of handicapped clients in sheltered workshops and recommendations of the secretary.* Washington, DC: Author.

U.S. Government Printing Office. (1982). *Care for the retarded, 1981.* Washington, DC: Author.

U.S. Office of Civil Rights. (1980). *State, regional, and national summaries of data from the 1978 civil rights survey of elementary and secondary schools* (p. 5). Alexandria, VA: Killalea Associates.

U.S. Office of Education. (1977). Education of handicapped children. *Federal Register, 42*, 42478.

Uzgiris, I. C., & Hunt, J. McV. (1975). *Assessment in infancy: Ordinal scales of psychological development*. Urbana: University of Illinois Press.

Uzgiris, I. C., & Lucas, T. C. (1978). Observational and experimental methods in studies of object concept development in infancy. In G. P. Sackett (Ed.), *Observing behavior, Volume I: Theory and application in mental retardation*. Baltimore: University Park Press.

Vacc, N. (1978). Peer tutoring for the mentally retarded. *Education and Training of the Mentally Retarded, 13*, 60–63.

Vail, D. (1966). *Dehumanization and the institutional career*. Springfield, IL: Charles C. Thomas.

Vanderheiden, G. C. (Ed.). (1978). *Non-vocal communication resource book*. Baltimore: University Park Press.

VanDeventer, P., Yelinek, N., Brown, L., Schroeder, J., Loomis, R., & Gruenewald, L. (1981). A follow-up examination of severely handicapped students. In L. Brown, D. Baumgart, I. Pumpian, J. Nisbet, A. Ford, R. Loomis, & J. Schroeder (Eds.), *Curricular strategies that can be used to transition severely handicapped students from school to non-school and post-school environments*. Madison, WI: Madison Metropolitan School District.

Van Riper, C. (1954). *Speech correction: Principles and methods*. Englewood Cliffs, NJ: Prentice-Hall.

Vash, C. (1981). *The psychology of disability*. New York: Springer.

Vellutino, F. (1978). Toward an understanding of dyslexia: Psychological factors in specific reading disability. In A. Benton & D. Pearl (Eds.), *Dyslexia: An appraisal of current knowledge* (pp. 63–111). New York: Oxford University Press.

Vellutino, F. R. (1979). *Dyslexia: Theory and research*. Cambridge: MIT Press.

Vellutino, F. R., Smith, H., Steger, J. A., & Kaman, M. (1975). Reading disability: Age differences and the perceptual deficit hypothesis. *Child Development, 46*, 487–493.

Vellutino, F. R., Steger, J. A., & Kandel, G. (1972). Reading disability: An investigation of the perceptual deficit hypothesis. *Cortex, 8*, 106–118.

Vellutino, F. R., Steger, J. A., & Pruzek, R. M. (1973). Inter- vs. intrasensory deficit in paired associate learning in poor and normal readers. *Canadian Journal of Behavioral Science, 5*, 111–123.

Vernon, M. (1981). Education's "Three Mile Island": PL 94-142. *Peabody Journal of Education*, (October), 214–229.

Voeltz, L. M., Apffel, J. A., & Wuerch, B. B. (Eds.). (1981). *Leisure activities training for severely handicapped students: Instructional and evaluation strategies* (pp. 167–192). Honolulu: University of Hawaii, Department of Special Education.

Voeltz, L. M., Hemphill, N. J., Brown, S., Kishi, G., Klein, R., Fruehling, R., Levy, G., Collie, J., & Kube, C. (1983). *The special friends program: A trainer's manual for integrated school settings* (rev. ed.). Honolulu: University of Hawaii, Department of Special Education.

Voeltz, L. M., & Wuerch, B. B. (1981). A comprehensive approach to leisure education/leisure counseling for the severely handicapped person. *Therapeutic Recreation Journal, 15*, 21–35.

Voeltz, L. M., Wuerch, B. B., & Bockhaut, C. H. (1981). A social validation of leisure training activities with severely handicapped youth. In L. M. Voeltz, J. A. Apffel, & B. B. Wuerch, (Eds.), *Leisure activities training for severely handicapped students*. Honolulu: University of Hawaii, Department of Special Education.

Voeltz, L. M., Wuerch, B. B., & Wilcox, B. (1982). Leisure and recreation. Preparation for independence, integration, and self-fulfillment. In B. Wilcox & G. T. Bellamy (Eds.), *Design of high school programs for severely handicapped students* (pp. 175–209). Baltimore: Paul H. Brookes.

Vogel, E. F., & Bell, N. W. (1968). The emotionally disturbed child as the family scapegoat. In W. G. Bennis, E. H. Schein, F. I. Steele, & D. E. Berlew (Eds.), *Interpersonal dynamics* (rev. ed.). Homewood, IL: Dorsey Press.

Vogelsberg, R. T., Williams, W., & Bellamy, G. T. (1982). Preparation for independent living. In B. Wilcox & G. T. Bellamy (Eds.), *Design of high school programs for severely handicapped students* (pp. 153–175). Baltimore: Paul H. Brookes.

Volpe, J. J. (1981). *Neurology of the newborn.* Philadelphia: W. B. Saunders.

Vygotsky, L. S. (1978). *Mind in society: The development of higher psychological processes.* Cambridge: Harvard University Press.

Waddell, D. D. (1980). The Stanford-Binet: An evaluation of the technical data available since the 1972 restandardization. *Journal of School Psychology, 18*, 203–209.

Wallerstein, J. S. (1983). Children of divorce: The psychological tasks of the child. *American Journal of Orthopsychiatry, 53*, 230–243.

Walls, R. T., Werner, T. J., Bacon, A., & Zane, T. (1977). Behavior checklists. In J. D. Cone & R. P. Hawkins (Eds.), *Behavioral assessment: New directions in clinical psychology.* New York: Brunner & Mazel.

Wanschura, P. B., & Borkowski, J. G. (1974). The development and transfer of mediational strategies by retarded children in paired-associate learning. *American Journal of Mental Deficiency, 78*, 631–639.

Warren, C. A. B. (1981). New forms of social control: The myth of deinstitutionalization. *American Behavioral Scientist, 24*(6) (July/August), 724–740.

Wechsler, D. (1958). *The measurement and appraisal of adult intelligence* (4th ed.). Baltimore: Williams & Wilkins.

Wechsler, D. (1974). *Wechsler Intelligence Scale for Children* (rev. ed.). New York: Psychological Corporation.

Weems, L. (1975, April). *Assessment issues concerning minority children.* Symposium presented at the meeting of the National Association of School Psychologists, Atlanta, GA.

Wehman, P. (1981). *Competitive employment: New horizons for severely disabled individuals.* Baltimore: Paul H. Brookes.

Wehman, P., & Hill, J. W. (Eds.). (1985). *Competitive employment for persons with mental retardation: From research to practice* (Vol. 1), Richmond, VA: Virginia Commonwealth University, Rehabilitation Research and Training Center.

Wehman, P., Hill, J., & Koehler, F. (1979). Placement of developmentally disabled individuals into competitive employment: Three case studies. *Education and Training of the Mentally Retarded, 14*, 269–276.

Wehman, P., & Schleien, S. (1981). *Leisure programs for handicapped persons: Adaptations, techniques and curriculum.* Baltimore: University Park Press.

Weinberg, N. (1978). Modifying social stereotypes of the physically disabled. *Rehabilitation Counseling Bulletin, 21*, 114–123.

Weintraub, F. J., & Ballard, J. (1982). Introduction: Bridging the decades. In J. Ballard, B. A. Ramirez, & F. J. Weintraub (Eds.), *Special education in America.* Washington, DC: Council for Exceptional Children.

Weisz, J. (1979). Perceived control and learned helplessness among mentally retarded and nonretarded children: A developmental analysis. *Developmental Psychology, 15*, 311–319.

Wells, C. (1971). *Cleft palate and its associated speech disorders.* New York: McGraw-Hill.

Werner, E. E., & Smith, R. S. (1982). *Vulnerable but invincible: A study of resilient children.* New York: McGraw-Hill.

Werthman, F. (1978). *The German euthanasia program.* Cincinnati: Hayes.

Wesman, A. G. (1968). Intelligent testing. *American Psychologist, 23*, 267–274.

Wetter, J. (1972). Parent attitudes toward learning disabilities. *Exceptional Children, 39*, 490–491.

Whitehead, C. (1978). A comprehensive action program for sheltered workshops. *Journal of Rehabilitation Administration, 3*, 32–41.

Whitehead, C. (1979). Sheltered workshops—effective accommodation or exploitation. *Amicus, 4*, 273–276.

Whitman, T. L., Hurley, J. D., Johnson, M. R., & Christian, J. G. (1978). Direct and generalized reduction of inappropriate behavior in a severely retarded child through a parent-administered behavior modification program. *AAESPH Review, 3*, 68–77.

Whitman, T. L., Sciback, J. W., & Reid, D. H. (1983). *Behavior modification with the severely and profoundly retarded: Research and application.* New York: Academic Press.

Wiggins, J. (1980). *Personality and prediction: Principles of personality assessment.* Reading, MA: Addison-Wesley.

Wiig, E., & Semel, E. (1980). *Language assessment and intervention.* Columbus, OH: Charles E. Merrill.

Wikler, L., Wasow, M., & Hatfield, E. (1981). Chronic sorrow revisited: Parent vs. professional depiction of the adjustment of parents of mentally retarded children. *American Journal of Orthopsychiatry, 51*, 63–70.

Wilcox, B., & Bellamy, G. T. (1982). *Design of high school programs for severely handicapped students*. Baltimore: Paul H. Brookes.

Wilcox, B., & Sailor, W. (1980). Service delivery issues: Integrated educational systems. In B. Wilcox & R. York (Eds.), *Quality education for the severely handicapped: The federal investment*. Washington, DC: U.S. Department of Education.

Willer, B., Scheerenberger, R. C., & Intaglia, J. (1980). Deinstitutionalization and mentally retarded persons. In A. Novak & L. Heal (Eds.), *Integration of developmentally disabled individuals into the community* (pp. 3–20). Baltimore: Paul H. Brookes.

Wilson, C. C. (1980). Behavioral assessment: Questionnaires. *School Psychology Review, 9*, 58–66.

Windle, C. (1962). Prognosis of mental subnormals. *American Journal of Mental Deficiency, 66*, 1–180.

Wiseman, D., & Hartwell, K. (n.d.). Preface to *Curriculum guide on American government*, Office of Field Services, College of Education, Arizona State University, Tempe, AZ 85287.

Wiseman, F. (1969). *Titticut follies*. [Film] New York: Grove Press.

Wisniewski, H. M., & Kozlowski, P. B. (1982). Evidence for blood-brain barrier changes in senile dementia of the Alzheimer type (SDAT). In F. M. Sinex & C. R. Merril (Eds.), *Annals of the New York Academy of Sciences, 396*, 119–129. New York: New York Academy of Sciences.

Wolfensberger, W. (1967). Counseling the parents of the retarded. In A. A. Baumeister (Ed.), *Mental retardation: Appraisal, education and rehabilitation* (pp. 329–400). Chicago: Aldine.

Wolfensberger, W. (1972). *The principle of normalization in human services*. Toronto: National Institute of Mental Retardation.

Wolfensberger, W. (1975). *The origin and nature of institutional models*. Syracuse: Human Policy Press.

Wolfensberger, W. (1980). The definition of normalization: Update, problems, disagreements, and misunderstandings. In R. J. Flynn & K. E. Nitsch (Eds.), *Normalization, social integra-*

tion, and community services (pp. 71–116). Baltimore: University Park Press.

Wolfensberger, W. (1983a). *Normalization-based guidance, education and supports for families of handicapped people*. Downsview, Ontario: National Institute on Mental Retardation.

Wolfensberger, W. (1983b). Social role valorization: A proposed new term for the principle of normalization. *Mental Retardation, 21*(6), 234–239.

Wolfensberger, W., & Glenn, L. (1978a). *PASS (Program analysis of service systems): A method for the quantitative evaluation of human services*. Handbook Vol. II (3rd ed.) Toronto: National Institute on Mental Retardation.

Wolfensberger, W., & Glenn, L. (1978b). *PASS (Program analysis of service systems): A method for the quantitative evaluation of human services*. Field Manual Vol. II (3rd ed.) Toronto: National Institute on Mental Retardation.

Wolfensberger, W., & Tullman, S. (1982). A brief outline of the principle of normalization. *Rehabilitation Psychology, 27*, 131–145.

Wolpert, J. (1978). *Group homes for the mentally retarded: An investigation of neighborhood property impacts*. Albany: New York State Office of Mental Retardation and Developmental Disabilities.

Wood, F. H. (1982). Affective education and social skills training: A consumer's guide. *Teaching Exceptional Children, 14*, 212–216.

Woodcock, R. (1973). *Woodcock Reading Mastery Tests*. Circle Pines, MN: American Guidance Service.

Woodcock, R., & Johnson, M. (1977). *Woodcock-Johnson Psycho-Educational Battery*. Hingham, MA: Teaching Resources Corporation.

Wooden, K. (1974). *Weeping in the playtime of others*. New York: McGraw-Hill.

Woodward, W. M. (1970). The assessment of cognitive processes: Piaget's approach. In P. Mittler (Ed.), *The psychological assessment of mental and physical handicaps*. London: Methuen.

Wylie, R. C. (1979). *The self-concept: Vol. 2. Theory and research on selected topics*. Lincoln: University of Nebraska Press.

Yacorzynski, G. K., & Tucker, B. E. (1960). What price intelligence? *American Psychologist, 15*, 201–203.

Yard, G., & Thurman, R. I. (1982). Seizure disorders and emotionally disturbed children and youth: An inservice training model. *Behavioral Disorders, 7*, 86–90.

Yoder, D. (Ed.). (1982). Communication interaction strategies for the severely communicatively impaired. *Topics in Language Disorders, 2*(2).

Yoshida, R., MacMillan, D., & Meyers, C. E. (1976). The decertification of minority group EMR students in California: Student achievement and adjustment. In R. Jones (Ed.), *Mainstreaming and the minority child*. Reston, VA: Council for Exceptional Children.

Youngberg, etc., et al., Petitioners, v. Nicholas Romeo, an incompetent, by his mother and next friend, Paula Romeo. (1982). *The United States Law Week, 50*, 4681–4687.

Ysseldyke, J. E. (1973). Diagnostic-prescriptive teaching: The search for aptitude treatment interactions. In L. Mann & D. Sabatino (Eds.), *The first review of special education*. Philadelphia: Journal of Special Education Press.

Ysseldyke, J. E. (1979). Issues in psychoeducational assessment. In G. D. Phye & D. J. Reschly (Eds.), *School psychology: Perspectives and issues*. New York: Academic Press.

Ysseldyke, J., Algozzine, B., Rostollan, D., & Shinn, M. (1981). A content analysis of the data presented at special education placement team meetings. *Journal of Clinical Psychology, 37*, 655–662.

Ysseldyke, J. E., & Salvia, J. (1974). Diagnostic-prescriptive teaching: Two methods. *Exceptional Children, 44*, 613–615.

Zajonc, R. B. (1976). Family configuration and intelligence. *Science, 192*, 227–236.

Zellweger, H., & Simpson, J. (1977). *Chromosomes of man*. Philadelphia: J. B. Lippincott.

Zettel, J. J., & Ballard, J. (1982). The Education for All Handicapped Children Act of 1975 (P.L. 94-142): Its history, origins, and concepts. In J. Ballard, B. A. Ramirez, & F. J. Weintraub (Eds.), *Special education in America*. Washington, DC: Council for Exceptional Children.

Zigler, E., & Valentine, J. (Eds.). (1979). *Project Head Start: A legacy of the war on poverty*. New York: Free Press.

Zinkus, P. W., Gottlieb, M. I., & Schapiro, M. (1978). Developmental and psycho-educational sequelae of chronic otitis media. *American Journal of Disabled Children, 132*, 1100–1104.

Zuk, G. H. (1959). The religious factor and the role of guilt in parental acceptance of the retarded child. *American Journal of Mental Deficiency, 64*, 139–147.

Zuk, G. H. (1962). The cultural dilemma and spiritual crisis of the family with a handicapped child. *Exceptional Children, 28*, 405–408.

pp. 277–278: Excerpt from Pany, D., Jenkins, J., & Schreck, J. (1982). Vocabulary instruction: Effects on word knowledge and reading comprehension. *Learning Disabilities Quarterly, 5*, 202–215. Reprinted by permission.

p. 280, Fig. 2: From Engelmann, S., & Bruner, E. (1974). *Teacher presentation book A: DISTAR reading I.* Reprinted by permission of Science Research Associates.

p. 284: Excerpt from Wiseman, D. E., Hartwell, L. K., Kleiner, J. K., & Van Reusen, A. K. (n.d.). *Curriculum guide on American government.* Office of Field Services, Arizona State University. Reprinted by permission of the authors.

pp. 293–294: Excerpts from Long, N., & Dufner, B. (1980). The stress cycle or the coping cycle? The impact of home and school stresses on pupils' classroom behavior. In N. Long, W. Morse, & R. Newman (Eds.), *Conflict in the classroom.* Belmont, CA: Wadsworth. Reprinted by permission of Indiana University School of Education.

pp. 303–304, Box 7: Reprinted with permission from Jackson, N. F., Jackson, D. A., & Monroe, C. (1983). *Getting along with others: Teaching social effectiveness to children* (Program guide) (pp. 11–12). Champaign, IL: Research Press.

p. 324, Fig. 1: From *The signed English dictionary for preschool and elementary levels* (p. 227) by H. Bornstein, L. B. Hamilton, K. L. Saulnier, & H. L. Roy (Eds.), 1975. Washington, DC: Gallaudet College Press. Copyright 1975 by Gallaudet College. Reprinted by permission.

p. 344: Excerpt from Brown, L., Nietupski, J., & Hamre-Nietupski, S. (1976). The criterion of ultimate functioning and public school services for the severely handicapped. In M. A. Thomas (Ed.), *Hey, don't forget about me: Education's investment in the severely, profoundly, and multiply handicapped.* Reston, VA: Council for Exceptional Children. Reprinted by permission.

pp. 361–362, Box 2: Excerpts from "False Gods and Angry Prophets" by Mary S. Akerley in Ann Turnbull and Rutherford Turnbull, eds., *Parents speak out: Views from the other side of the two-way mirror,* 2nd ed. © 1985. (Original edition 1978.) Reprinted by permission of the publisher, Charles E. Merrill Publishing Company.

p. 394: Excerpt from Wolfensberger, W. (1980). The definition of normalization: Update, problems, disagreements, and misunderstandings. In R. J. Flynn & K. E. Nitsch (Eds.), *Normalization, social integration, and community services.* Baltimore: University Park Press. Reprinted by permission.

pp. 404–406: Excerpts from Daniels, S. M., et al. (1979). *Who cares: A handbook on sex education and counseling services for disabled people.* Washington, DC: George Washington University Press. Reprinted by permission.

pp. 409–410: Excerpt from Wolfensberger, W., & Tullman, S. (1982). A brief outline of the principle of normalization. *Rehabilitation Psychology, 27*, 131–145. Reprinted by permission.

pp. 410–412: Excerpts from Novak, A. R., & Heal, L. W., *Integration of developmentally disabled individuals into the community.* Baltimore: Paul H. Brookes Publishing Co. (P.O. Box 10624, Baltimore, MD 21285-0624), © 1980. Reprinted by permission.

pp. 426–427: Excerpt from "Deinstitutionalization and Community Placement: Clinical and Environmental Factors" by J. L. Crawford, D. E. Thompson, and J. R. Aiello, *Mental Retardation, 17,* pp. 59–63. Copyright 1979 by the American Association on Mental Deficiency. Reprinted by permission.

pp. 432–433: Excerpt from Vogelsberg, R. T., Williams, W., & Bellamy, G. T. (1982). Preparation for independent living. In B. Wilcox & G. T. Bellamy (Eds.), *Design of high school programs for severely handicapped students,* 153–175. Baltimore: Paul H. Brookes. Reprinted by permission.

p. 434: Excerpt from Durand, J., & Neufeldt, A. H. (1980). *Comprehensive vocational services monograph 4.* Reprinted by permission of the G. Allan Roeher Institute, Downsview, Ontario, Canada M3J 1P3.

pp. 437–438: Excerpts from Wehman, P., Hill, J., & Koehler, F. (1979). Placement of developmentally disabled individuals into competitive employment: Three case studies. *Education and Training of the Mentally Retarded, 14,* 269–276. Reprinted by permission.

pp. 448–451: Excerpts from Voeltz, L. M., Wuerch, B. B., & Wilcox, B. (1982). Leisure and recreation: Preparation for independence, integration, and self-fulfillment. In B. Wilcox & G. T. Bellamy (Eds.), *Design of high school programs for severely handicapped students.* Baltimore: Paul H. Brookes. Reprinted by permission.

p. 460: Excerpts reprinted with permission from *Troubled children, troubled systems* by S. J. Apter. Copyright 1982, Pergamon Press, Ltd.

Author Index

Subject Index